*The Grahams of Pennsylvania and Virginia*

Cover Page: Photo of Templar Devotional Items. Photo by Michael Pfeiffer. Reproduced under Creative Commons License BY-SA 4.0

Copyright © 2023 Alicia Graham

All rights reserved.

ISBN: 979-8-218-21428-9

*This book is dedicated to all warriors and patriots of the Graham Clan, including the senior warriors from our branch of the Grayville Grahams:*

*Bobby Gene Graham, Col, USAF*
*Donald Lee Graham, MSgt, US Army*
*Dellas Ray Graham, Capt, USAF*
*Earl William Graham, Lt Col USAF*
*Densil Eugene Graham, Airman, USAF*

# Preface

When I first began researching my husband Barry's genealogy, I never expected the amount of time I would invest. After all, his brother, Jeff, and sister-in-law, Kim, had already traced the Grahams of Grayville, Illinois, to Kentucky and Virginia back to the late eighteenth century, traveling to courthouses and graveyards around the Mid-Western United States. I was simply going to build on their work and locate ancestors in Scotland, with the goal of completing a Graham family history for my grandchildren and extended family.

Little did I realize the job ahead of me. Noted Graham genealogist, Louisa Grace Graeme, wrote in *Or and Sable, a Book of the Graemes and Grahams* that the story of the Border Grahams and the Grahams of Ireland must be told by someone "who can better sing the history of that borderland." I believe she meant that the history was difficult to trace (given the families' habitations in war zones and the resulting loss of records) and would need to be explored by someone else with access to more information than she had in 1903.[1] Now, 120 years later, the digitization of old vital and historical records along with DNA will finally allow us to delve deeper.

Like many of those who researched the ancestry of early "Scots-Irish" (an American term for Scottish people who migrated to Ireland in the 1600s and America in the 1700s) have learned, picking up the trail of these ancestors is easier said than done. Secondary sources such as *Peerage* and published family histories are helpful, but all of them made assumptions, so can't be taken as gospel. Tracing family in Ireland has confounded many due to the loss of Irish vital records when the Public Records Office in Dublin was destroyed in 1922. However, there are Irish property and court records and will indexes that survived. I found my secret weapons in the records of nineteenth-century Irish genealogists who hand-copied thousands of records: Crosslé, Betham, Thrift, and Ffolliott (this is the correct spelling). Their notebooks are in the National Archives of Ireland, on microfilm at the Family History Library in Salt Lake City, Utah, and also in an indexed version that is searchable online via FindMyPast. Much of the material from these greats of Irish genealogy predates the archives' destruction in 1922 and is of immense value to anyone with Irish roots.

Back to my story. With the help of a cousin I found on Ancestry.com, Mike Moser, the first brick wall was overcome. Mike located and synopsized a precious book containing the results of years of research on the Grahams of Lancaster County, Pennsylvania, titled *Our Graham Family History* by John Henry Graham. The book was based on the life's work of Mr. Graham and his sister, Minnie Graham Bulls. After Minnie's death, John Graham continued to research and published the book in 1992. With *Our Graham Family History*, I finally had what I needed to begin the journey to the other side of the Atlantic. Thank you, Minnie, John, and Mike!

---

[1] Louisa Grace Graeme, *Or and Sable : a Book of Graemes and Grahams* (Edinburgh: William Brown, 1903), 643. https://archive.org/details/orsablebookofgra00grae/page/642/mode/2up?q=netherby

At the recommendation of a genealogy buddy, Erica Robertson, my husband took a Y-DNA test with FamilyTreeDNA and subscribed to their Graham Surname DNA Project. Y-DNA, an analysis of the male chromosome, is handy as it can help find ancestors as far back as records have been kept (1,000 or more years ago). The typical and more familiar autosomal DNA data can normally reach back five to six generations. The Graham Surname Project invites prospective members with Graham connections and attempts to unite them with respective DNA matches. In the book I argue that nearly everyone born with the surname "Graham" is a descendant of the first known Graham, a twelfth-century knight named "William de Graham." However most (92%) do not have an unbroken male line; they instead descend through Graham daughters whose husbands and/or sons took the Graham surname.

Through the project, I contacted a "close" match, an eleventh to thirteenth cousin, in Scotland. This Graham cousin had heritage in Northern Ireland as well. He introduced me to Mr. Phil Graham, a noted subject matter expert on Graham history with over 40 years of research on the Grahams in his archives. With Phil's guidance and patience, we slowly progressed, traveling down many paths, some of which we had to abandon. Eventually, we found puzzle pieces on both sides of the Atlantic that began to fit together. One pattern repeated through the generations: the professions of clergymen and military men, leading to the subtitle of this book: "Our Scottish History of Warriors and Saints."

Our starting point was the "often told tradition" in Minnie and John's family: A group of Graham brothers came to America from Northern Ireland, arriving in Philadelphia in 1720. I knew they initially settled in Lancaster County, Pennsylvania, and were devout Presbyterians. And I knew the names and rough ages of two of the brothers and the names of their wives—Christopher Graham and his wife, Margaret Florence Risk, and James Graham "Sr." and his wife, Anne Hanson. Christopher was the eldest. My husband descends from the younger brother, James.

"James Graham" is a common name, which makes it difficult to extricate the specific "James Graham" you are searching for from many others. However, the name "Christopher Graham" is unusual and stands out. Therefore, our strategy was to search for Christopher first, then locate his younger brothers. Knowing the names of the children, grandchildren, and great-grandchildren in the U.S. was also helpful due to the Scottish naming tradition where the eldest son was named after his paternal grandfather, the second eldest son after his maternal grandfather, the eldest daughter after her maternal grandmother, and the second eldest daughter after her paternal grandmother. The Scots adhered to this practice into the twentieth century, so we watched for the repeating pattern of names "Christopher-James-John-William" and "Margaret-Elizabeth-Jane/Janet" in Irish and Scottish records. In parallel, I began learning Irish and Scottish geography and history, including military and church history, family history of neighboring clans, heraldry, archaeology, and DNA—subjects that each contained small clues and opened doors to more Y-DNA cousins, each with their own story and more clues. When combined, these clues wove the story of our branch of the Graham clan and perhaps left behind something that others can use to build their stories.

As the story will always keep growing, I plan to post updates to:
https://grahamsofpaandvaourscottishhistory.blogspot.com/

## Acknowledgments:

I have to start by thanking my awesome husband, Barry. From reading early drafts to helping me debug files in my immense computer library, as I found new ways to break computers and word processing software, to taking and retaking photos I wanted on our trips to Scotland and Israel and giving me quiet time so I could edit, he was as important to this book getting done as I was.

Without my new friend and mentor from Scotland, Phil Graham, there never would be a book. Phil generously shared his treasured research accumulated over a life time, his time, his ideas, and energy to "turn over every stone" in Scotland and Ireland so we could reassemble the lost histories of our Grahams.

Dankeschön to my long-time friend and genealogy buddy, Erica Robertson. Erica, you have always been a source of encouragement as long as I've known you. Because of your "never-give-up" attitude, you have been my role model. You first explained the importance of Y-DNA, which started me down this road. Thank you for your fearlessness, spending hours editing the earliest horrible versions of the book and cheerfully offering ways to make it make sense.

Many thanks to my daughter Elizabeth Graham Everett for her patience and support on this project, spending hours trying to teach me photo editing and even more time remaking the map of Lancaster County, Pennsylvania used in the book. Thank you to my geography expert and son, Bobby, for his help with historical maps of Scotland and granddaughter Violet for her special contribution, a family tree from her perspective.

My deep thanks to my other new friend across the pond, David Noble, for his sage advice and tips on publishing, adjusting the book title to better match the content, and especially on DNA research. I initially resisted digging that deeply into DNA, but thanks to David, I finally jumped in and discovered the missing pieces in the "chain of evidence" behind lost Graham family histories.

A special thank you to the late Bruce Edwin Graham for his enthusiasm, support and patience deciphering old handwritten records and combing through old books to help find the missing pieces of the puzzle. My deep appreciation also goes to Ron Graham, Mike Moser, Tom Field, Dr. Lloyd Graham, Dr. Robin Spencer, Dr. Iain McDonald, and Miranda, my editor at Hale-Phillips Consulting, for their assistance. I am in their debt.

Finally, to everyone who helped me along the way, please accept my gratitude. I apologize that I can't list you all. I hope you find this book worthy.

*Foreword by David Noble*

# Foreword: The Incredible Story of the Grayville Grahams by David Noble

"Where do I come from?" It's a question that we all ask as children. As adults, once we are past the obvious and basic, many of us still ask that same question and genealogy aims to provide the answers.

For many years, flogging through ledgers and then online searching have provided many of those answers but it is only with the advent of genetic genealogy that we have been able to really get to grips with 'where we came from'.

The incredible story of the Grahams of Pennsylvania and Virginia started with that simple, basic question but soon developed into a tale of intrigue, criminal enterprise, politics, emigration, religion and ethnicity spanning millennia.

The author's husband, a Graham, descended from one of four Graham brothers who came to the US in 1720. The brothers set up farms in Pennsylvania. They had come from Northern Ireland (Ulster) seeking a better life. But why were the Graham brothers in Ulster in the first place? Further research revealed that their ancestors joined their famous Armstrong kin and left Scotland eighty years previously, after their laird was allegedly involved in a deadly duel.

The Plantation of Ulster was the organized colonization of Northern Ireland, by James I who intended the plantation to "civilize" the region. Colonists were required to be English-speaking, Protestant and loyal to the king. The fact that the planters were Protestants and the indigenous population was largely Catholic created problems that Ulster still lives with today.

So where in Scotland did the Grahams come from? This is where the story starts to get very complicated. Firstly, you have to understand that surnames didn't come into common usage in the British Isles until the 1400s to help with tax collection and people adopted surnames for a variety of reasons. The surname Graham was adopted by a relatively wide range of people to include husbands and younger sons of Graham daughters. The Grahams in our story were Border Grahams who inhabited the area near the Anglo-Scottish Border.

So where did the Border Grahams come from? This is where the impact of genetic testing enters the story.

All humans have 23 pairs of chromosomes with one of each inherited from the mother and the father. Women have two 'X' Chromosomes and 22 pairs of autosomal chromosomes called "autosomes," while men have one 'Y' Chromosome and one 'X' chromosome together with 22 pairs of autosomes. The Y chromosome is **always** passed from father to son so effectively acts like a watermark in a banknote and it can be traced down the millennia.

The use of autosomal DNA testing which can match males and females is widespread but only a handful of firms offer Y-DNA testing and one such is FTDNA of Houston, Texas.

Autosomal testing is able to reveal matches over 5-6 generations with one generation averaging 30 years, so 150-180 years. However, Y-DNA testing can reveal matches over thousands of years.

*Foreword by David Noble*

All DNA has mutations and the Y-chromosome is no different. Using Polymerase Chain Reaction ("PCR") testing, which most people are familiar with because of COVID-19, geneticists can track the evolution of different mutations called Single Nucleotide Polymorphisms ("SNPs" – pronounced 'Snips') over the millennia.

Geneticists divide men into haplogroups as they are termed and these haplogroups can tell them where the men originated and how they evolved over the millennia. The most common male haplogroup in Europe is R-M269 followed by I-M253 which originated in Scandinavia. So where did the Graham men come from?

Surprisingly, about 30% of male Graham testers with FTDNA are J-M267. It's surprising because the incidence of it is so low in the UK today that it is usually rounded to zero. It actually originated in the Middle East and is the classic Semitic male haplogroup.

According to a 2021 University of Tatu study of J-M267 published in the *Nature* journal [*] the most recent common ancestor (MRCA) of J-M267 lived circa 20,000 years ago and he was probably born in West Asia, i.e. the Levant, Mesopotamia, the Arabian peninsula, Iran, Anatolia, Armenia or the Caucasus.

So why is a Middle Eastern male haplogroup so prevalent amongst Graham testers? The majority of Graham testers have the SNP J-L1253 which occurred in one man born in the British Isles in the 1300s of Middle Eastern descent, so they are all descendants of one man. So what was a man of Middle Eastern descent doing in the British Isles at that time? [**]

You have to look at sub-clades of J-M267, as they are termed, and the British J-M267 men belong to a sub-clade called J-P58. The incidence of J-P58 amongst J-M267 men in the Caucasus, for example, is virtually zero.

So was the Graham ancestor an Arab? The Arabic language has only been around for about 1,500 years, plus the original Middle Eastern ancestor is estimated to have arrived in the British Isles about 3,000 years ago, so Semitic not Arab.

Was he Jewish? The high incidence of J-M267 amongst the Jewish Cohanim suggests that it is possible. However, it is worthy of note that the incidence amongst Ashkenazi Jewish men of the J-P58 subclade is only 14.0%. Studies of Sephardic Jews has shown that the incidence of J-M267 is 15-20%. It has also been discovered that the Jewish Cohanim have a distinctive subclade called the Cohen Modal Haplotype, evidenced by the SNP J-ZS227, which is not shared with British J-M267 descendants. Interestingly, British J-L1253 men have a SNP designated J-L858, which is not shared with the Cohen Modal Haplotype. This SNP occurred in a man born 5,000 years ago and recent testing has shown it is also present in members of the Saudi Arabian and Jordanian royal families, making us all descendants of the same man.

---

[*] Sahakyan, H., Margaryan, A., Saag, L. *et al.* Origin and diffusion of human Y chromosome haplogroup J1-M267. *Sci Rep* 11, 6659 (2021). https://doi.org/10.1038/s41598-021-85883-2

[**] This is where religion, language and ethnicity enter the fray. According to Chiaroni (2009) in the world today the highest incidence of J-M267 occurs in Sudan – 74.3% of Sudanese (Khartoum) men, with other centres of high incidence being Iraq (64.1% amongst Arabs) and Syria (58.8% amongst Damascus Ismailis). Some 46.0% of the Jewish Cohanim are J-M267. Hammer, Michael F., Doron M Behar, et. al. "Extended Y chromosome haplotypes resolve multiple and unique lineages of the Jewish priesthood." *Human Genetics* 126 (2009): 707 - 717.

*Foreword by David Noble*

So who was he? Other scientific research can help narrow down the possibilities. Analysis has shown that 98% of male lines become extinct in 6.4 generations. Men might have no children, only daughters or their sons die before having children themselves.

This sort of Darwinian evolution favours men who have large families of sons, typically wealthy and powerful men. That is not to say that the descendants of poor men don't survive but in all our analysis we are looking at the balance of probabilities. So, in trying to marry up the genetic, documentary and circumstantial evidence it is worth focusing on two strands of research:

- What evidence do we have of the presence of Middle Easterners in the British Isles?
- What do we know about the male lines of wealthy and powerful men with associations to the Graham clan?

With regard to Middle Easterners, there are several candidates:

- **Jewish Diaspora** – although the incidence of J-P58 is quite low amongst non-Cohanim Jewish men, the fact is that Jewish people travelled widely in Europe.
- **Phoenicians** – there is evidence that Phoenician traders visited the UK. Phoenicia is now modern-day Lebanon and existed from 2,500 B.C to 64 B.C.
- **Princess Scota of Egypt** - The 1417 B.C. timeframe for arrival in Britain projected by Y-DNA analysis lines up with the arrival in Ireland in the legends of Princess Scota of Egypt, her husband Gaythelos, and their army. Princess Scota and Gaythelos are key figures in the story of the Foundation of Scotland. Despite inconsistencies in the various story versions, several old chroniclers (e.g., John of Fordun, Manetho) have these story elements in common: the Scots were named after Scota, a daughter of an Egyptian Pharoah; Scota's husband, was a Greek warrior, of "Scythian" ancestry, called "Gaythelos," whom the Gaels are named for; Scota and Gaythelos were driven from Egypt and settled in what is now Galicia in Northern Spain, and then later left Spain and settled in Ireland. Scota's alleged grave site is near Munster in County Kerry, Ireland. The stories tell how Scota and Gaythelos' descendants later migrated to Scotland.
- **Syrian Archers** – a legion of Syrian archers was stationed on Hadrian's Wall in the year 140 A.D. However, this is a long time after the period that analysis has suggested the Graham Middle East ancestor came to the UK.

With regard to the Graham J1 patriarch, we can look at powerful individuals with many sons and Graham clan connections:

The strongest candidate to be the Graham J1 Patriarch is Sir Andrew Moray/Murray of Manuel, armour bearer to King David II, or his biological father. Sir Andrew was likely born between the 1330s and 1340s, as he first married around 1363 and is the suspected spouse of Agnes de Graham, the proposed matriarch of the Border Grahams. The reasons for Sir Andrew's candidature are set out in the book.

We invite you to peruse the wealth of information presented in the book so that you can decide who you think is the Graham J1 patriarch.

# Table of Contents

Chapter 1: Grahams of Lancaster County, Pennsylvania ..................................................... 9

    Early Graham Farms in Southeastern Pennsylvania ............................................... 12

    Early Presbyterian Church History in America ........................................................ 17

Chapter 2: Grahams of Augusta and Buffalo Settlement, Virginia (1738-1782) ............ 20

    Augusta County, Virginia—Christopher Graham's Branch Arrives (1738-1744) ........ 20

    Amelia County (later Prince Edward), Virginia -- James Graham Jr.'s Family Arrive in Buffalo Settlement in 1755 ................................................................................. 23

    Abridged Grayville Graham Pedigree .................................................................... 26

Chapter 3: County Fermanagh, Ireland (1636-1720) ..................................................... 30

    Crosslé "Gold Mine"—Irish Court Records ........................................................... 31

    Military Service: Trooper Christopher Graham and Defending Enniskillen ............ 36

    Other noteworthy members of Brigadier General Wolseley's Horse Regiment: ..... 42

    Another Unusual Name ........................................................................................ 44

    Irish Muster Roll of 1630 ...................................................................................... 44

    Migration Waves from Scotland to Ireland ........................................................... 45

    Border Reivers ..................................................................................................... 46

    Scottish Covenanters and the "Killing Time" ........................................................ 47

    Risk In-Laws ......................................................................................................... 48

    Who Was Lang Will Graham? .............................................................................. 50

    English Graham Origins ....................................................................................... 52

    Tower of Grame ................................................................................................... 56

    Graham-Armstrong History and Key Marriages .................................................... 62

    Back to the Present, and The Grayville Grahams .................................................. 66

Chapter 4: Scotland .......................................................................................................... 68

    Church History ..................................................................................................... 68

    Feudal Superiority Hierarchy ................................................................................ 69

- Knights of Annandale ................................................................................................72
- Origin of the first recorded Graham in Scotland, William de Graham .................72
- Popular theories regarding the origin of William de Graham ...............................74
  - Tancarville Origin Theory .....................................................................................74
  - De Hesdin Origin Theory .....................................................................................75
- A New Origin Theory: The Greystokes of Cumbria ................................................75
- Y-DNA Evidence .........................................................................................................76
- Etymology ....................................................................................................................80
- Could William de Greystoke (Gristock) have become "William de Graham?" .....81
- St. Cuthbert Connection ............................................................................................84
- Comparing the Timeline of Events ...........................................................................86

## Chapter 5: Heraldry .......................................................................................................88
- The Trail of the Scallop Shell ....................................................................................88
- Family Crests ...............................................................................................................91
- Descendants of the Elder Son of William de Graham, Peter ................................94
- The Corries, a Previously Unknown Sept Clan of Clan Graham ..........................94
- "Henry Confusion" ......................................................................................................96
- Sir John "the Last" is a Misnomer ............................................................................98
- Margaret Graham, Another Sister of Sir John "the Last" ....................................102
- Origin of the Border Grahams ................................................................................104
- Black Douglas "Land Grab" .....................................................................................104
- Sir William de Douglas .............................................................................................107
- Sir James Douglas .....................................................................................................109
- The Connection between the Border Grahams and Menteiths ..........................110
- What we know ...........................................................................................................111

## Chapter 6: Y-DNA .........................................................................................................114
- Graham J1 Patriarch .................................................................................................115
- How did the Graham J1s get to Scotland? ............................................................122
- "From Scythia We Descend" ...................................................................................123

- Gaytheolos (Goídel Glas in Gaelic) .................................................................................. 124
- Princess Scota ................................................................................................................. 125
- Other evidence that may support the Princess Scota legend: ....................................... 126
- Three other possible scenarios to explain the arrival of J1 in Ireland and Scotland in the Bronze Age: ..................................................................................................................... 128
  - Phoenician Trader Option: ...................................................................................... 128
  - Picts Option: ............................................................................................................. 129
  - The Syrian Archer Theory: ...................................................................................... 129
- Closest Y-DNA Match ................................................................................................... 132

Chapter 7: Summary .......................................................................................................... 136
- American Immigrant Brothers ...................................................................................... 136
- Irish Military Records .................................................................................................... 136

Table of Figures .................................................................................................................. 136

Endnotes .............................................................................................................................. 143

Appendix A: Irish Geography ............................................................................................ A-1

Appendix B: Scottish Geography ....................................................................................... B-1

Appendix C: Y-DNA ........................................................................................................... C-1

Appendix D: A Primer on the Ancient British and Roman Catholic Churches of Scotland .. D-1

Appendix E: Heraldry ......................................................................................................... E-1

Appendix F: Genealogy of the Border Grahams ............................................................... F-1

Appendix G: Glossary of Relevant Graham Estates and of Their Kin ............................ G-1

Bibliography ........................................................................................................................ 398

# Chapter 1
# Grahams of Lancaster County, Pennsylvania[i]
# 1720-1755

In America's early days, Scots-Irish settlers who first arrived in the late seventeenth century in Puritan Massachusetts reported in letters sent back to Ireland that they were not welcome. The colony of Pennsylvania, however, advertised a novel concept at the time: "freedom of religion." It actively recruited settlers not only from Ireland, Scotland, England, and Wales but also from the Continent of Europe. William Penn's friendly words, recruiting settlers for his Pennsylvania colony, led to Scots-Irish immigrating to Pennsylvania slowly at first and then in major waves, such that entire towns in Ireland were nearly vacated.[2, 3]

As we will learn in Chapter 3, the ancestors of the Grayville, Illinois, Grahams first migrated from Scotland to the Ulster Plantation region of Northern Ireland sometime after 1635. Most Ulster settlers (or *planters*) came from southern Scotland and northern England. While some Border Graham families were banished to Ireland in 1606, these Graham ancestors went to Ireland willingly when land was available for those who wanted to work it. Former Ulster planters came to America for similar reasons, voluntarily arriving in Pennsylvania. [4]

In *The Scotch-Irish: A Social History*, Professor James G. Leyburn explains that William Penn's Provincial Secretary James Logan invited the first group of Scots-Irish to Pennsylvania in 1717/1718 to help settle the borders and be a buffer against certain hostile tribes. Being Scots-Irish himself, Secretary Logan was interested in a particular group of Scots-Irish, famous for key military victories in Enniskillen, Derry, and other battle sites in Ireland in 1689-1691 during the Williamite Wars. Logan wrote in 1720: "At the time, we were apprehensive from the Northern Indians...I therefore thought it might be prudent to plant a settlement of such men as those who formerly had so bravely defended Londonderry and Inniskillen as a frontier in case of any disturbance..." He gave them

---

[2] James G. Leyburn, *The Scotch-Irish, A Social History* (Chapel Hill: University of North Carolina Press, 1962), 184, 190-192, 207. https://archive.org/details/scotchirishsocia0000leyb

[3] Jonathan Bardon, *A History of Ulster, New Updated Edition* (Belfast: The Blackstaff Press, 2001), 124-127.

[4] Lloyd D. Graham, *House Graham, From the Antoine Wall to the Temple of Hymen* (Lulu.com, 2020), 125. https://clangrahamsociety.org/wp-content/uploads/2020/09/House-GRAHAM-eBook.pdf

a large tract of land in what is now Lancaster County, Pennsylvania. The first group named the new settlement Donegal, after their home county in Northern Ireland. We will find in Chapter 3 that the Grayville Graham ancestors played crucial roles during the referenced Williamite Wars.[5]

Per the Philadelphia newspaper, *The Mercury*, a brigantine ship full of Presbyterians or "90 souls" arrived in Philadelphia harbor from Londonderry, Ireland, on 27 October 1720.[6] The Browns, sons of the famous martyr John Brown (1627-1685)[7] and their families and friends were on that ship.

Since the previously referenced "group of Graham brothers" had farms that abutted both Brown farms, they were established simultaneously in the new towns they both helped found (Derry, Hanover, and Paxtang, Pennsylvania), and their families intermarried, author John Henry Graham thus concluded the Grahams arrived on the same ship as the Browns.[8] Per *Scotch Irish Pioneers in Ulster and America*, by Charles Knowles Bolton, the brigantine's arrival in October 1720 was a rare, possibly first, occurrence for a ship entirely of Presbyterians.[9] Furthermore, the brigantine arriving in Philadelphia was a passenger ship not hailing from Germany, which was therefore newsworthy enough to be reported in *The Mercury*. Another family closely tied to the ancestors of the Grayville Grahams was the Armstrong family. The *Chronicles of the Armstrongs* reports a number of "Border Families" from the Brooksboro, County Fermanagh, Ireland area left for Pennsylvania "circa 1721," including some Armstrongs.[10] It is possible these Armstrongs either traveled on the same ship as the Grahams in 1720 or followed soon after hearing good reports from their Graham relatives.

> **John Brown**, the "Christian Carrier," was executed in 1685, by Colonel John Graham of Claverhouse "Bonnie Dundee" (a Montose Graham cousin) in Priesthill, Ayrshire. Brown was a Covenanter—a Presbyterian who refused to acknowledge the king's authority over the Church and swear a loyalty oath to him. Brown's widow, Isabella Brown nee Weir, fled to Ireland with her children soon after his execution. As late as 1929, Appalachian mountaineer descendants of the "Scotch-Irish" still used this threat with their children: "Behave yourself, or Clavers will get you."

Building on the work of past Graham genealogists, there is now sufficient evidence to name three of the four Graham immigrant brothers and to guess the name of the fourth. The eldest brother was Christopher (1670-1746), who married Margaret Florence Risk in Ireland. Other

---

[5] James G. Leyburn, *The Scotch-Irish, A Social History*, 211.

[6] Charles Knowles Bolton, *Scotch Irish Pioneers in Ulster and America* (Boston: Bacon and Brown, 1910), 30. https://electricscotland.com/history/scotsirish/scotchirish00boltrich.pdf

[7] A.L. Brown, *John Brown and Some of His Descendants* (California Genealogical Society, 1948), 1. https://www.familysearch.org/library/books/viewer/121732/?offset=&return=1#page=1&viewer=picture&o=&n=0&q=
[John Brown blurb] Charles Knowles Bolton, *Scotch Irish Pioneers in Ulster and America*, 300.
George Fraser Black, *Scotland's Mark on America* (New York: The Scottish Section of "America's Making," 1921), 12. https://www.google.com/books/edition/Scotland_s_Mark_on_America/dVRwIfh4euQC?hl=en

[8] John Henry Graham, *Our Graham Family History*, 15-16, 51, 121, 125. https://www.familysearch.org/library/books/records/item/598444-our-graham-family-history?offset=1

[9] Charles Knowles Bolton, *Scotch Irish Pioneers in Ulster and America*, 300.

[10] James Lewis Armstrong, M.D., *Chronicles of the Armstrongs* (Queensborough, N.Y: The Marion Press in Jamaica, 1902), 363. https://openlibrary.org/books/OL7027370M/Chronicles_of_the_Armstrongs

brothers were James Sr. (1683-1745), who married Anne Hanson in Ireland, and John (1674-1743).[11] Per the Scottish naming patterns of the time,[12] I surmised that the fourth brother, who died in Pennsylvania after 1729, was named William, since his eldest grandson is named William.[13] Since the four brothers all named their eldest sons "John," it can be further deduced that their father was also named "John." Three of the brothers named their daughters "Margaret," so it is possible that their mother was named Margaret. It appears that brother John did not have any daughters. For clarity, I color-coded the families of each of the four Graham brothers who arrived in Pennsylvania in 1720.

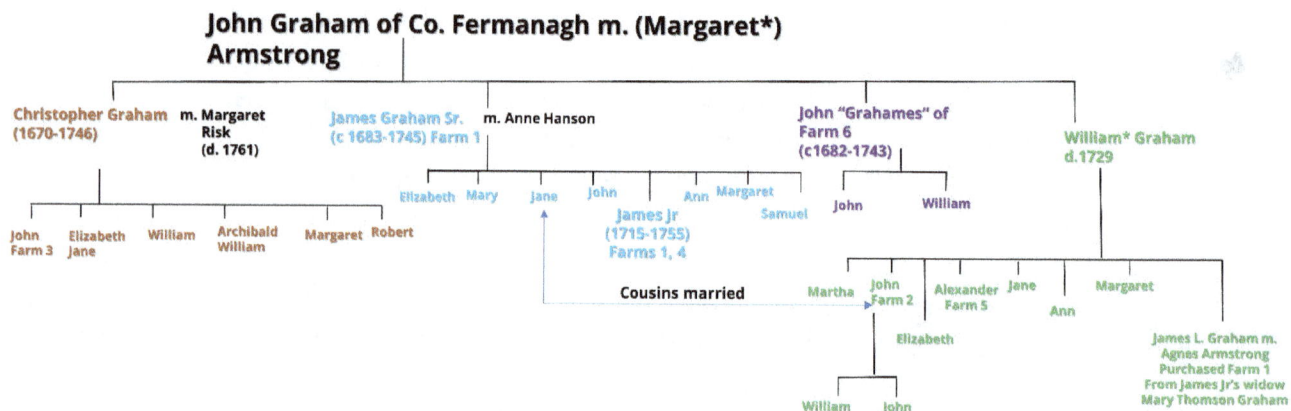

Figure 1: Descendants Chart of the Four Graham Brothers who emigrated to Pennsylvania from Ireland in 1720 along with their wives and children [11]

---

[11] Figure 1: John Henry Graham, *Our Graham Family History*, 11-15.

[12] FamilySearch Wiki contributors, "Scotland Personal Names," FamilySearch Wiki, accessed 28 October 2022. https://www.familysearch.org/en/wiki/index.php?title=Scotland_Personal_Names&oldid=4943222

[13] FamilySearch Wiki contributors, "Scotland Personal Names," FamilySearch Wiki, accessed 28 October 2022. https://www.familysearch.org/en/wiki/index.php?title=Scotland_Personal_Names&oldid=4943222

## Early Graham Farms in Southeastern Pennsylvania

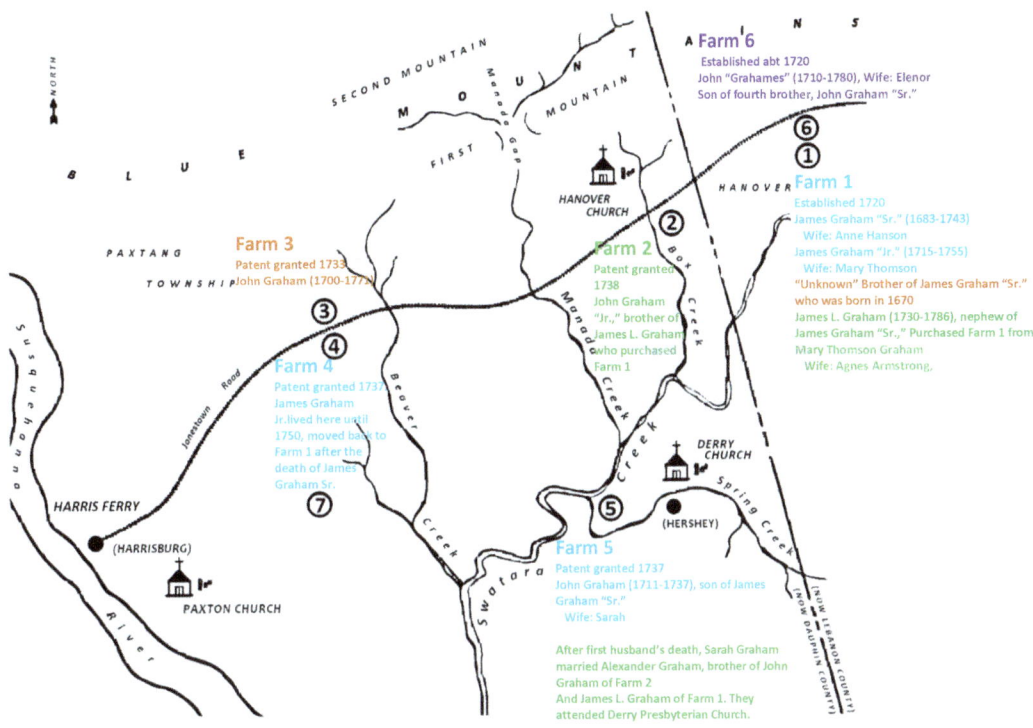

*Figure 2: Original Figure drawn by Leon Spangler in Our Graham Family History depicting the locations of the Graham Farms in the newly established townships of Derry, Hanover and Paxton/Paxtang Pennsylvania. Enhanced by **Elizabeth Graham Everett**.* [14]

Names of Owners have been added and color coded: eldest brother Christopher's family is in rust orange, James Sr.'s family in blue, John's family in purple and the family of William* is in green [15]

---

[14] Figure 2: John Henry Graham, *Our Graham Family History*, 11-14.
[15] John Henry Graham, *Our Graham Family History*, 8, 11-14.

*Our Graham Family History* by John Henry Graham, *Notes and Queries Historical and Genealogical/Chiefly Relating to Interior of Pennsylvania Series 3 Volume III*,[16] and Dr. Herndon's work contain a detailed collection of Graham family records which will allow us to organize the family's whereabouts.[17] The Graham families were initially clustered on the eastern edge of the region, on Farms 1 and 6, and over time, as their families grew, gradually moved west.[18]

## FARM 1:

Per author John Henry Graham, "This is the James Graham farm. Three men named James Graham occupied this farm from circa 1720 to 1786. They were: James Graham (Sr.) (circa 1683-1745); his son, James (Jr.) (circa 1715 - circa 1755); and his nephew, James L. Graham (1730-1786). On 15 October 1744, James Graham (Sr.) obtained a warrant for this 181-acre farm in the east end of Hanover Township, Lancaster." Nephew James L. and his wife Agnes Armstrong had no children and are buried in the Hanover Church cemetery.[19]

Autosomal DNA Triangulation analysis uses the match of two Grayville Graham third cousins (Barry S. Graham and Ron Graham) whose grandfathers were born in Grayville and who were also descendants of James Graham Sr., to compare with the results of a third American who is a confirmed descendant of Christopher Graham. This American does not appear to be related to the Grayville Grahams in another way. The comparison of the three indicates they are distant (possibly seventh) cousins.[20] The overlap is on Chromosome 1. This overlap demonstrates a family relationship between Christopher and James Graham Sr. and, given the historical information, indicates the two were likely brothers.[21]

Genealogist Minnie Bulls deduced that James Graham Jr. married Mary Thomson, daughter of the famous Reverend John Thomson, circa 1733. As stated, Christopher Graham (1670-1746) was the eldest of the four Graham brothers and was about 10-15 years older than James Graham Sr. James Graham Sr. was both the uncle and the father-in-law of John Graham. According to existing land records, these two Graham men lived on separate farms in Hanover Township (then Lancaster County) by about 1730. James (Sr.) and his brother, William*, father of John Graham, settled on these two farms in 1720/1721. The Hanover Presbyterian Church was established in 1737 on land immediately north of John Graham's farm. James Graham Sr. died in 1745, leaving a will that bequeathed his farm to his oldest living son, according to colonial property law. This son was also

---

[16] William Henry Egle, *Notes and Queries Historical and Genealogical /Chiefly Relating to Interior of Pennsylvania Series 3 Volume III* (Harrisburg, Pennsylvania: Harrisburg Publishing Co., 1894-1901), 89-90. https://www.familysearch.org/library/books/viewer/857668/?offset=0#page=5&viewer=picture&o=&n=0&q=

[17] John G. Herndon, "The Reverend John Thomson (Concluded)," *Journal of the Department of History*, Vol. 21, No. 1, The Presbyterian Historical Society of the Presbyterian Church in the U.S.A. (1943): 48. http://www.jstor.org/stable/23324126 .

[18] John Henry Graham, *Our Graham Family History*, 11-14.

[19] John Henry Graham, *Our Graham Family History*, 11-14.

[20] Roberta Estes, "Triangulation for Autosomal DNA," DNAeXplained-Genetic Genealogy, 21 June 2013. https://dna-explained.com/2013/06/21/triangulation-for-autosomal-dna/

[21] MyHeritage, "How to Use the Chromosome Browser for Genealogy," accessed: 28 October 2022. https://education.myheritage.com/article/how-to-use-chromosome-browsers-for-genealogy/?utm_source=help_center&utm_medium=organic_help_center&utm_campaign=FAQ_link

named "James" and was designated "James (Jr.)" by authors John Henry Graham and Minnie Graham Bulls. In his will, James (Sr.) named his sons James Jr. and Samuel and sons-in-law John McClure and Hugh Semple, who were also neighbors. Reverend Richard Sankey and Patrick Watson (a Graham relative) were named as executors of James' (Sr.) will, but they renounced in favor of "James (Jr.) and his mother Anne." On 13 November 1745, an inventory of the personal effects left by James Graham (Sr.) was signed by William Watson (another Graham relative and neighbor in Hanover Township) and by his son-in-law, James Dixon. Dixon, born in Ireland, married Jane Graham—widow of John Graham and daughter of James Graham (Sr.).[22]

## FARM 2:

Per author John H. Graham: "This is the John Graham farm. John, nephew and son-in-law of James (Sr.), was living on this 212-acre farm (Hanover Township on Bow Creek near the Hanover Presbyterian Church) at the time of his death in 1743." John's wife, Jane Graham, was James Sr.'s daughter. This John was also the brother of James L. Graham (1730-1786) from Farm 1 and Alexander Graham from Farm 5. The man John H. Graham, noted as "UNKNOWN (2) Died after 1729 in Pennsylvania," is assumed to be William,* the father of these three brothers: John Graham on Farm 2, as well as James L. (1730-1786) who purchased Farm 1 from the widow of a cousin, James Jr., and Alexander who married Sarah, widow of cousin John Graham.

## FARM 3:

John H. Graham observes, "Another John Graham was the first 'occupant' of Farm 3. He took a warrant for this land in Paxtang Township (aka: Paxton) in 1733.[23] A patent was issued in his name in 1737,[24] but no further record of him in Pennsylvania exists." I believe this is likely because he departed for Virginia a few years later. Farms 3 and 4 (

Figure 2) are seven miles west of the Hanover Presbyterian Church along Jonestown Road. This John is believed to be Christopher Graham's eldest son John (1700-1771). George Cleek's book *Early Western Augusta Pioneers* confirms Christopher Graham's sons departed from Paxtang, Pennsylvania, for Augusta County, Virginia, circa 1738. Christopher joined them after 1740.

---

[22] John Henry Graham, *Our Graham Family History*, 11-15.

[23] William Henry Egle, *Notes and Queries Historical and Genealogical /Chiefly Relating to Interior of Pennsylvania Series 3 Volume III* (Harrisburg, Pennsylvania: Harrisburg Publishing Co., 1894-1901), 89.

[24] Ancestry.com, *Pennsylvania, U.S., Land Warrants and Applications, 1733-1952*, Ancestry.com Operations, Inc., accessed 24 March 2023.
https://www.ancestry.com/search/collections/2350/?name=john_graham&event=1737_lancaster&count=50&event_x=0-0-0_1-0

## FARM 4:

We know from John H. Graham that "an unidentified James Graham took a warrant on this land in Paxtang Township, Lower End, on January 23, 1737,[25] but it was not surveyed or patented until after Graham had left the land." Minnie Graham Bulls "postulated that the James Graham on this farm may have been James (Jr.) of Farm 1, who probably married around 1733 and took his new family to a farm other than his father's. He was on the tax-assessment list for Paxtang Township in 1749 and 1750, but he was back on Farm 1 in 1751." [26]

## FARM 5:

From *Our Graham Family History*: "Sarah Graham, wife of John Graham who died intestate in 1737, is named on the warrant for this farm in Derry Township. The warrant is dated 1737. Sarah's second husband was Alexander Graham, brother of John Graham of Farm 2. Sarah and Alexander were members of the Derry Presbyterian congregation."[27, 28, 29]

---

[25] Ancestry.com, *Pennsylvania, U.S., Land Warrants and Applications, 1733-1952*, Ancestry.com Operations, Inc., accessed 24 March 2023.
https://www.ancestry.com/search/collections/2350/?name=james_graham&event=1737_lancaster&count=50&event_x=0-0-0&name_x=1_s

[26] John Henry Graham, *Our Graham Family History*, 11-15.

[27] John Henry Graham, *Our Graham Family History*, 11-15.

[28] George Washington Cleek, *Early Western Augusta Pioneers*, Part XIII Graham Family (Baltimore: Genealogical Publishing Co., 1992), 361-364.
https://www.google.com/books/edition/Early_Western_Augusta_Pioneers/hk4bAAAAYAAJ?hl=en

[29] John Henry Graham, *Our Graham Family History*, Figure 3, 15.

*Figure 3: Old Derry Presbyterian Church, Hershey Pennsylvania, First Presbyterian Church in America, from Postcard Collection of U.S. Presbyterian Historical Society* [30]

## FARM 6:

"John Grahames," who died in 1743, left his estate to his unnamed wife and sons, William and John Graham Jr. John Graham Jr. also had a son and grandson named John, the latter of whom fought in the American Revolution in 1776 and was taken captive by the British regulars. John Graham Jr. (circa 1710-1780) lived on this 200-acre farm in Hanover Township, East End. His wife was "Elenor." Farm 6 abutted the north side of Farm 1. John Graham Jr.'s wife Elenor is likely the daughter of Michael Graham from Farm 7. [31]

## FARM 7:

Michael Graham (b: circa 1710; d. after 1777 in North Carolina), son of Arthur Graham from Nantmeal, Pennsylvania, took a warrant on this farm in Paxtang Township, Lower End, in 1750, but he was living there before that date. From *Our Graham Family History*: "Michael and his wife [Elizabeth], who bore him ten children, were, at least in the early days, members of the Rev. John Elder's Paxtang Presbyterian Church. His son William, a student of 'New-Sider' Rev. John Roan and a 1773 Princeton graduate, was a founder of Washington and Lee College in Lexington, Virginia." Michael Graham of Farm 7 had a daughter "Eleanor" and a sister "Helinor." The name Eleanor is unique and not found elsewhere in our Graham line, which supports the conclusion that the "Elenor" who married John Graham of Farm 6 was Michael's daughter. Michael Graham is not directly related

---

[30] Figure 3: Wikimedia Commons contributors, "File:Hershey PA Old Derry PHS261.jpg,"Wikimedia Commons, the free media repository, accessed 1 January 2023.
https://commons.wikimedia.org/w/index.php?title=File:Hershey_PA_Old_Derry_PHS261.jpg&oldid=630483875

[31] John Henry Graham, *Our Graham Family History*, 11-15.

to the four Graham brothers, Christopher, James Sr., John, and William, who arrived in Philadelphia in October 1720.³²

*Figure 4: Paxtang Presbyterian Church, Harrisburg, Pennsylvania from Postcard Collection of the U.S. Presbyterian Historical Society* ³³

## Early Presbyterian Church History in America

The first presbytery in America, the Presbytery of Philadelphia, was organized in 1705. The Synod of Philadelphia was constituted in 1717. As the young colony moved westward and the church moved with it, the Presbytery of Donegal was brought into being on 21 September 1732. It consisted of five ministers: James Anderson, John Thomson, Adam Boyd, William Orr, and William Bertram. It had five congregations at that time: Chestnut Level, Donegal, Little Britain, Middle Octorara, and Pequea. The first Derry Church building was erected in 1720. Nearby, the Paxtang congregation formed in 1720 but was later "organized" in 1732.³⁴ In 1732, Paxtang and Derry were served by the same pastor, Reverend William Bertram.³⁵ While James Graham Sr.'s family lived near and attended church at Derry, brother Christopher's family eventually settled in Paxtang and attended church there. As stated, James Sr.'s son, James Graham, Jr., married Mary Thomson, daughter of Reverend John Thomson circa 1733.³⁶

---

³² John Henry Graham, *Our Graham Family History*, 11-15.
³³ Figure 4: Wikimedia Commons contributors, "File:Harrisburg PA Paxtang Presby PHS253.jpg,"Wikimedia Commons, the free media repository, accessed 1 January 2023.
https://commons.wikimedia.org/w/index.php?title=File:Harrisburg_PA_Paxtang_Presby_PHS253.jpg&oldid=630483889
³⁴ "History," Derry Presbyterian Church, U.S A., accessed 1 January 2023. https://www.derrypres.org/about/history/
³⁵ Bobby Dobbins, "History of Hanover Church, Dauphin County, PA," *Genealogy Trails History Group* (Dauphin County Historical Society, 1878), http://genealogytrails.com/penn/dauphin/hanover_church_history.html
³⁶ George Washington Cleek, *Early Western Augusta Pioneers*, Part XIII Graham Family, 361-364.

*Figure 5: Reverend John Thomson Grave Marker, Centre Presbyterian Church Cemetery, Mooresville, N.C. Photo by L. Nelson, 31 May 2020* [37]

**Reverend John Thomson**, Father-in-law to James Graham Jr., was born about 1690[37] and, per his epitaph, written by Rev. E.F. Stockwell of Statesville, North Carolina "on the banks of the River Foyle,"[38] which is somewhere near Londonderry, Ireland. He began his studies to become a Presbyterian minister at the University of Glasgow in 1706 and earned a Master of Arts degree in 1711. His first job was in BallyBay, County Armagh, Ireland, from 1711-1714. He arrived in America in 1715, was ordained in 1717, and was first assigned to the presbytery in Lewes, Delaware, where he served until 1729.[39] He then served Middle Octorara in Lancaster County, Pennsylvania, until 1733 and Chestnut Level, Pennsylvania, from 1733-1744. During his posting to Chestnut Level, he played key roles in the Philadelphia Synod, a council of church representatives from Pennsylvania and neighboring colonies. He was elected clerk to that body in 1736. He is known for his authorship of Presbyterian doctrine, the leadership of the "Old Side" party within the church, which was part of the "New Side/Old Side" controversy, and his proposal to the synod to establish "a public school or seminary of learning" funded by the church. The school first met in Great Valley (New London), Pennsylvania, but in 1767 was moved to Newark, Delaware, and was renamed "Newark Academy." In 1914 it was again renamed "the University of Delaware," one of the oldest public universities in the United States.[40]

In 1737, a committee on which Rev. Thomson was serving was directed to pay a missionary visit to "people of our persuasion" in the "back parts of Virginia," specifically the new settlement of

---

[37] Figure 5: Find a Grave®, "Reverend John Thomson (1690-Sep 1753)", Memorial ID 162130257, Centre Presbyterian Church Cemetery, Mooresville, Iredell County, North Carolina, created by Roanna Dolan Griffin, contributor ID 47928961, photo by L. Nelson, contributor ID 47321592, 31 May 2020, https://www.findagrave.com/memorial/search?firstname=john&middlename=&lastname=thomson&birthyear=1690&birthyearfilter=&deathyear=&deathyearfilter=&location=North+Carolina%2C+United+States+of+America&locationId=state_29&memorialid=&mcid=&linkedToName=&datefilter=&orderby=r&plot=

[38] John G. Herndon, "The Reverend John Thomson (Concluded)," *Journal of the Department of History*, Vol. 21, No. 1, 48.

[39] Harold J. Dudley," John Thomson, 1690-1653," Dictionary of North Carolina Biography and NCPedia, 1996. https://www.ncpedia.org/biography/thomson-john

[40] John G. Herndon, "The Reverend John Thomson," *Journal of the Department of History*, Vol. 20, No. 4, The Presbyterian Historical Society of the Presbyterian Church in the U.S.A. (December, 1942): 116-158. http://www.jstor.org/stable/23323946 .

Beverly Manor, to assess their needs, including winter supplies. In 1738, the synod requested assurances from the Virginia governor that Presbyterians settling in the "back parts of Virginia" would be permitted to practice their faith and be released from having to pay tithes to the Anglican Church.[41] At that time, the Anglican Church was the established church of Virginia. Later that year, the Virginia colonial governor, Sir William Gooch, provided assurances of religious freedom under the Act of Toleration. He pledged that "Ulster Settlers were desired on the frontier and their worship would be respected."[42] In 1739, Rev. Thomson requested release from the Donegal Presbytery to serve in Virginia but was denied. However, Rev. Thomson was able to visit settlements in Augusta County, Virginia, in 1738 and 1739, where former parishioners from Paxtang (Paxton), Pennsylvania, lived, including the family of Christopher Graham and daughter Esther Thomson Crockett, wife of Samuel Crockett, a distant cousin of American frontiersman Davy Crockett. Rev. Thomson again requested release in April 1744 to serve in Virginia and was finally approved. He settled with a contingent of his congregation from Pennsylvania in the Buffalo Settlement of Amelia County, now Prince Edward County, Virginia.

Thomson traveled to Anson County, North Carolina, in 1751 and died there in 1753 on the eve of the French and Indian War when raids on frontier settlements were common. This may account for his burial beneath the floor of his cabin, where his son-in-law, Samuel Baker, was also buried. The site eventually became known as Baker's Grave Yard, and was surrounded by a rough rock wall.[43]

---

[41] John G. Herndon, "The Reverend John Thomson (Concluded)," Journal of the Department of History, Vol. 21, No. 1, 35.

[42] Virginia Legislative Papers, "The Virginia Magazine of History and Biography," Vol 13, No 1 (1905), 40. https://www.jstor.org/stable/4242723

[43] John G. Herndon, "The Reverend John Thomson (Concluded)," Journal of the Department of History, Vol. 21, No. 1, 35, 36, 43-45.

## Chapter 2
## Grahams of Augusta and Buffalo Settlement, Virginia[ii]
## 1738-1782

### Augusta County, Virginia—Christopher Graham's Branch Arrives 1738-1744

Christopher Graham was a former cavalry trooper, a veteran of the Williamite Wars in Ireland, and the eldest of the four Graham brothers who arrived in Philadelphia, Pennsylvania, in October 1720 from Londonderry, Ireland. From Augusta County, Virginia records, we know that Christopher was born in 1670 and he lived in/near Paxtang, Pennsylvania, for 20 years. I deduced that for a portion of that time, the family lived together on **FARM 1** and gradually dispersed. Brother Christopher moved with his eldest son John to **FARM 3** in Paxtang (Paxton),[44] Pennsylvania prior to 1733. Author George Cleek, in his *Early Western Augusta Pioneers,* provides abstracts of Augusta County. These Virginia records confirm that the Christopher Graham and family who settled in Augusta County was the same family from Paxtang, Pennsylvania,[45] and provide evidence that the John Graham of **FARM 3** was Christopher's son. Christopher followed his sons at age 70 to Augusta County, Virginia, in 1740 and died in Augusta County, Virginia, before February 1746, the date his will was probated.[46]

Christopher's sons, John and Robert**,** his son-in-law, William Elliott Jr., plus William Elliott Sr. were granted land patents in the Calfpasture in Augusta County, Virginia (between Staunton, Virginia, and the current border with West Virginia) in 1746, 1760, 1748 and 1745 respectively.[47] The year John and Robert likely arrived in Augusta County, Virginia (Figure 6)—1738, is the year the American Presbyterian Church leadership, the Philadelphia Synod, received assurances from the Virginia colonial governor that settlers on the Virginia frontier would be permitted to practice

---

[44] John Henry Graham, *Our Graham Family History,* 15.

[45] George Washington Cleek, *Early Western Augusta Pioneers,* 361-364.

[46] Lyman Chalkley, *Chronicles of the Scotch-Irish Settlement in Virginia, 1745-1800. Extracted from the Original Court Records of Augusta County,* Vol. III (Rosslyn, Virginia: Mary S. Lockwood, 1912), 6. https://www.familysearch.org/search/catalog/258900?availability=Family%20History%20Library

[47] Meredith Leitch, *Colonial land patents and grantees : Calfpasture Rivers, Augusta County, Virginia (*Staunton, Virginia: Meredith Leitch, 1947), Map. https://www.loc.gov/resource/g3883a.la001212/?r=0.245,0.355,0.322,0.186,0

Presbyterianism without harassment.[48] John Risk, a probable cousin of Christopher's wife Margaret Florence Risk, also acquired 300 acres in nearby Beverley Manor in 1740 (Figure 7).[49, 50] In 1780, Christopher's great-grandchildren, orphans of John Graham's son, Robert Graham, and their guardian and maternal uncle, Major Andrew Lockridge, were awarded 50 acres in Virginia for Robert's service in Captain William Preston's Company of Rangers.[51, 52]

For reference, the families that intermarried with the ancestors of the Grayville Grahams in the 1st generation (in Ireland) were: Armstrong, Hanson, and Risk. The 2nd generation (mainly in America): Armstrong, Brown, Elliott, Feamster, Henderson, Hicklin, Innis, May, McClure, Miller, Semple, and Thomson. The 3rd generation: Armstrong, Beatty, Bell, Carlisle, Clark, Givens, Hamilton, Kincaid, Lockridge, McClenahan, Patton, Walkup, and Wallace.

---

[48] "Virginia Legislative Papers," *The Virginia Magazine of History and Biography*, Vol. 13, No 1 (Richmond, Virginia: Virginia Historical Society, July 1905), 40. https://www.jstor.org/stable/4242723

[49] Ancestry.com, *Virginia Genealogical Society Quarterly and Magazine of Virginia Genealogy*, Vol. 30, Number 4, Virginia Land Patent Book 29, Ancestry.com Operations Inc. (November 1992): 309. https://www.ancestry.com/search/collections/6131/?name=_rusk.

[50] John R. Hildebrand, "The Beverley Patent, 1736," Scale [ca. 1:79,200], FamilySearch, accessed 28 December 2022. https://www.werelate.org/wiki/Image:RiskJohnBeverleyNW300acres.JPG
https://www.familysearch.org/library/books/viewer/429080/?offset=&return=1#page=1&viewer=picture&o=&n=0&q=

[51] John Frederick Dorman, 1961-1971. *Orange County Virginia : Deed Books.*, Book 4 (Washington D.C: J.F. Dorman, 1961-1971), 42, 114-117.

[52] Lyman Chalkley, *Chronicles of the Scotch-Irish Settlement in Virginia*, 1745-1800, 212.

The Grahams of Pennsylvania and Virginia

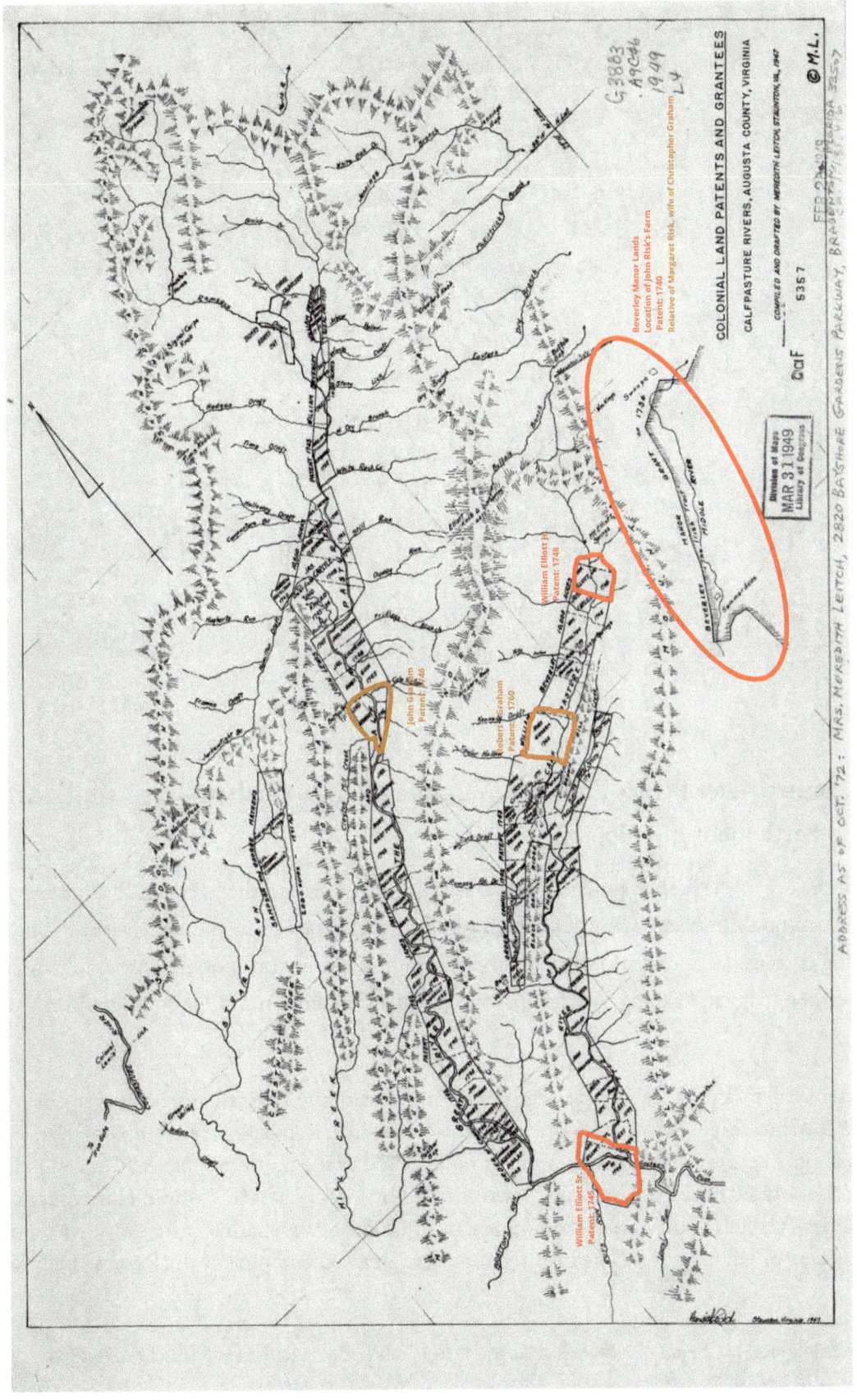

Figure 6: *Calfpasture Map in Augusta County, Virginia showing Family Land Patents as it appeared in the mid-1700s from the U.S. Library of Congress; Patents of Christopher Graham's sons are outlined in orange.* © Copyright Meredith Leitch.

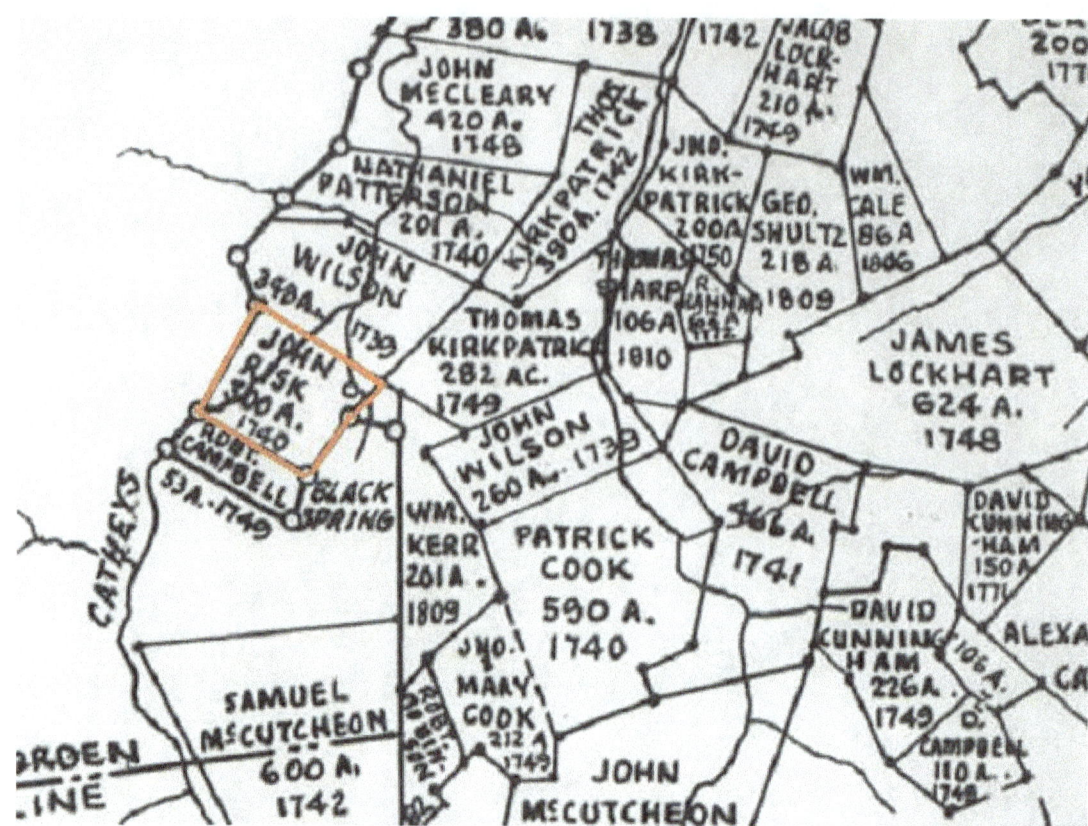

*Figure 7: Clip of the Beverly Manor Land Patent of 1810 showing Family Land Patents From the U.S. Library of Congress* [53] *© Copyright J.R. Hildebrand.*

## Amelia County (later Prince Edward), Virginia -- James Graham Jr.'s Family Arrive in Buffalo Settlement in 1755

On the eve of the French Indian War, various hostile tribes and their French allies raided settled areas on the Pennsylvania frontier, which was just east of the Susquehanna River at the time. In 1747, leading citizens in Lancaster County organized a militia for the common defense, and James Graham Jr., then living in Paxtang Township, was named a Captain. From *Our Graham Family History*:

> After General Braddock's defeat near Fort Duquesne in July 1755, the French urged their allied tribes to attack all settlers along the frontier, and the situation deteriorated rapidly in the Paxtang/Hanover communities, which were exposed to the mountain passes. On 25 October 1755, about 30 men from Paxtang Township, led by John Harris (for whom Harrisburg is named), Captain John McKee, and others, went up the Susquehanna to investigate a reported massacre of white settlers. The investigators were attacked and nine of the Paxtang men were

---

[53] Figure 7: John R. Hildebrand, "The Beverley Patent, 1736," Scale [ca. 1:79,200], FamilySearch, accessed 28 December 2022. https://www.werelate.org/wiki/Image:RiskJohnBeverleyNW300acres.JPG
https://www.familysearch.org/library/books/viewer/429080/?offset=&return=1#page=1&viewer=picture&o=&n=0&q=

later reported killed. Numerous historical records describing the last months of 1755 tell of this and other similar events and of the associated fear experienced in the Paxtang and Hanover communities, as many men were killed and women and children either killed or carried away [by the "marauding Indians," tribes allied with the French.]

Twenty-eight men signed the Hanover petition begging for assistance from the government in Philadelphia. It describes a deserted area near the mountains, which is where the Graham farms were located. After the threat of raids had passed in the Paxtang and Hanover communities in the 1750s, many of the families who fled in 1755-1756 returned to their farms. Apparently, William Graham, son of John, may have remained on **Farm 2** throughout the war.

James Graham Jr., associated with **Farm 1**, is reported in the 1756 tax rolls as having "fled." Since he did not appear on the Pennsylvania casualty lists, author Mary Graham Bulls later deduced that James, along with his wife, Mary Thomson Graham, sons, and others, left Southeastern Pennsylvania in 1755 to join the rest of their friends and family in the Buffalo Settlement in Amelia County, Virginia. However, James Jr. was killed en route. Mary and her sons, Thomas (1736-1810), Samuel (1739-1816), and James [(III) 1750-1809], and daughters Elizabeth (1734-1833), Margaret (1737-1791), Mary (1742-1830) and Ann (1751-1819), then settled in the Buffalo Settlement on 719 acres abutting her father John Thomson's land (Figure 8). However, it appears that Thomas did not join his family in Virginia immediately. From John H. Graham, we learn his whereabouts: Thomas and a John Davies served as scouts to ensure the friendly tribes were given safe passage through Scotch-Irish communities. The friendly tribes were in a state of near panic at the onset of the French and Indian War. In a meeting between Lieutenant Governor Robert Hunter Morris, other officials, and tribal leaders on 17 January 1756, "Thomas Graeme" is recognized. During the meeting, Chief David made a long speech to the Lt. Governor and the people of Pennsylvania. He said that the tribal leaders had "adopted Thomas Graeme who tis now among us a warrior, we now inform you that we have given him the name Kos Showweyha ... to confirm this we give a string of Wampum." [54]

After Mary died in 1758, her eldest son Thomas possessed the land. When middle son Samuel was 21 years old, Thomas sold him half the land for five shillings. Her youngest son James (III) was still a minor. He later acquired a tract of land just west of his brothers in 1783. [55]

---

[54] John Henry Graham, *Our Graham Family History*, 20.
[55] John Henry Graham, *Our Graham Family History*, Figure 4, 17-20, 31, 122.

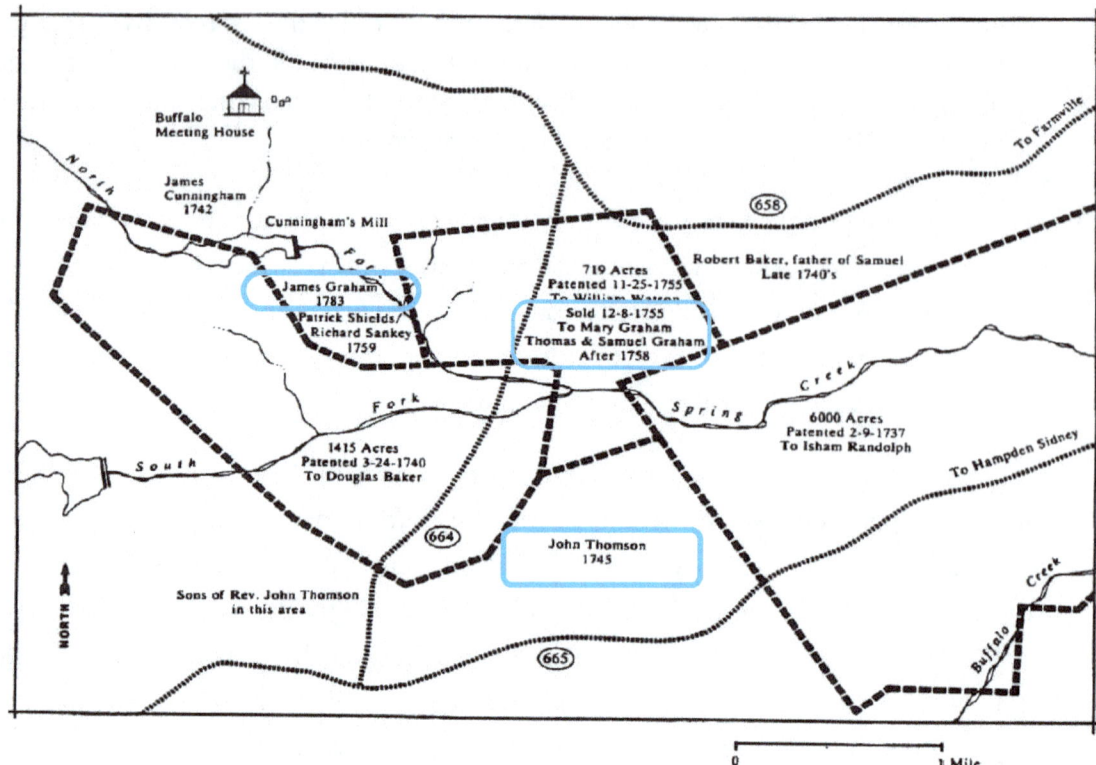

*Figure 8: Original Figure drawn by Leon Spangler featured in Our Graham Family History of Buffalo Settlement in Amelia County, Virginia, showing Family Land Patents as it appeared in the mid-1700s. Lands of James Graham Jr.'s sons are marked in blue.* [56]

Brothers Thomas, Samuel, and James (III) served in the American Revolutionary War and thus received Land Warrants in Kentucky.[57] As a general rule, the Revolutionary War veterans, or their heirs, from Virginia received land warrants in Kentucky,[58] and veterans, or their heirs, from North Carolina received land in either North Carolina (confiscated Loyalist Land or unsettled western North Carolina)[59] or the Tennessee Territory. The Tennessee Territory was initially part of North Carolina, and the Kentucky Territory was initially part of Virginia.

---

[56] Figure 8: John Henry Graham, *Our Graham Family History*, Figure 4, 22.

[57] Ancestry.com, *Abstract of Graves of Revolutionary Patriots*, Vol.:2, E-K, Ancestry.com Operations Inc., accessed 27 December 2022. https://www.ancestry.com/search/collections/4110/?name=samuel+_graham&count=50&name_x=_1

[58] FamilySearch Wiki contributors, "Kentucky Military Records," FamilySearch Wiki, accessed 20 October 2022. https://www.familysearch.org/en/wiki/index.php?title=Kentucky_Military_Records&oldid=4980079.

[59] FamilySearch Wiki contributors, "North Carolina Land and Property," FamilySearch Wiki, accessed 25 December 2022. https://www.familysearch.org/en/wiki/index.php?title=North_Carolina_Land_and_Property&oldid=5091547

**iii** Based on the birth onboard of twins William and Andrew Brown on 30 June 1720,[60] the ship reported in the *Mercury* likely left Londonderry, Ireland around mid-June 1720. In the 1700s, the transatlantic journey for a brigantine, a two-masted sailing vessel, usually took six to twelve weeks. The time to travel was dependent on the wind and the weather.[61] Years later, after he had settled in Virginia, John Graham [eldest son of Christopher] reported that he and his family experienced a great storm during their voyage from Ulster.[62] July-October is the height of the Atlantic hurricane season, so it would explain the extra-long journey of four and a half months and why one of the passengers recalled years later a "great storm" during that voyage. Perhaps they had to divert to Bermuda for repairs.

## Abridged Grayville Graham Pedigree

Throughout the family tree of the Grahams from Grayville, Illinois, we find many who served in the military and as clergymen. The same can be said for the Grahams that lived generations before, hence the subtitle of this book, "Our Scottish History of Warriors and Saints."

The youngest son of militia captain James Graham Jr. and Mary Thomson Graham, daughter of Rev. John Thomson, was James Graham **(III)** (1750-1809), who, like his brothers, served in the Revolutionary War. James (III) married Jane Morrison (1738-1821) and settled in Union County, Kentucky. Their younger son, John Graham (1786-1858), married Mary Peters (1792-1875) and settled in White County in Southern Illinois.[63] John and Mary's eldest son, James Robinson Graham (1810-1884), was born in Union County, Kentucky,[64] and was buried in

> **Did you know?**
> The boundary for White and Edwards County Illinois goes through the center of Grayville, hence the reason why some Graham vital records are from White and some are from Edwards County.

---

[60] A.L. Brown, *John Brown and Some of His Descendants* (California Genealogical Society, 1948), 1. https://www.familysearch.org/library/books/records/item/121732-redirect#page=1&viewer=picture&o=&n=0&q= )

[61] Reference.com Staff Writer, "How Long Did It Take to Get Across the Atlantic in the 1700s?." 26 March 2020. https://www.reference.com/history/long-did-across-atlantic-1700s-aaa802df642b99a3

[62] Oren Frederic Morton, *History of Rockbridge County, Virginia (*Staunton, Virginia: The McClure Company, Inc., 1920), 89. https://archive.org/details/historyofrockbri00mortrich/page/88/mode/2up?q=89

[63] John Henry Graham, *Our Graham Family History*, 148-153, 357.

[64] 1850 United States Federal Census, Year: 1850; Census Place: District 13, White, Illinois; Roll: M432_132; Page: 273B; Image: 21; Page: 323B; Image: 123. https://www.archives.gov/research/census/1850

[Did you know? Blurb] "City: Grayville, IL-zipcode," Zip Code Query, accessed 25 January 2023wikip. https://il.postcodebase.com/city/GRAYVILLE .

White County, Illinois.⁶⁵ He married Susanna Davenport (1822-1860) and then later married Arazena Elliott Cherry a year after Susanna's death in 1860. James Thornton Graham (1844-1889) was the eldest son of James Robinson Graham and Susanna Davenport. James Thornton Graham married Catherine Hallam (1846-1882) in 1871. ⁶⁶Their sons were Earnest Earl Graham (1871-1910) and Everett Graham (1876-1929).

—Earnest Earl Graham married Rachel Marie Short (1882-1972). Their son, Ernest William Graham (1907-1985), served in the Army Air Corps during WW II and the Air Force in the Korean War.

—Everett Graham, the younger son of James Thornton Graham and Susanna Davenport Graham, married Ethel Dell Brown (1883-1918). Their son Clyde Graham (1904-1982) married Edith Pollard (1907-2000) in 1927. Clyde and Edith's children: Ava, Donald (Don), Densil, Dellas, Bobby, and Larry Graham. Don served in the Army in the Korean War, Dellas joined the Air Force

*Figure 9: James Thornton Graham (1846-1889) of Grayville, Illinois (Generation 5). Photo provided courtesy of Ron Graham.*

right after college as an engineer, and Bobby was a command pilot in the Air Force and served for 27 years. Don's son became an evangelical pastor. Densil also had a son who became an evangelical pastor and another son who is a former dean and now senior director for an association of theological colleges.

— Bobby married Shirley Moody in 1959. Their eldest son Jeffery served in the Army as a helicopter pilot for 20 years and their second son, Barry, served as an engineer in the Air Force for 20 years. Their youngest son Kenneth died at age 23 but left a legacy among his family and church friends, encouraging his friends to pursue their musical and pastoral aspirations.

For the detailed Grayville Graham Family tree see link to genealogy on Ancestry.com (requires paid account) go to "The Grahams of Grayville, Illinois": https://www.ancestry.com/family-tree/tree/186073402/recent

---

⁶⁵ Patricia S. Davis, *Index to Harriet Vaught's Cemeteries of White County, Illinois*, Vol. 2 (Marion, Illinois: 1995), 71, 266. Cemeteries of White County, Illinois; v. 02   (Requires Account.)
https://www.familysearch.org/library/books/records/?navigation=&perpage=&page=1&sort=_score&search=Cemeteries+of+White+County%2C+Illinois%2C+Volume+2&fulltext=1&bookmarks=0#title
⁶⁶ White County Historical Society, *History of White County, Illinois* (Chicago, Illinois: Interstate Publishing Company, 1883, reprinted 1966), 774, 931. https://www.familysearch.org/library/books/records/item/535197-history-of-white-county-illinois?offset=358703

An abbreviated version of the tree can be found on Family Search
https://www.familysearch.org/tree/pedigree/landscape/LVV9-4Q8 (Requires free account.)

And also, the "Grahams of Grayville, Illinois" tree on MyHeritage.com
https://www.myheritage.com/site-family-tree-454506211/gierwatowski?familyTreeID=9

Figure 10: Depiction of Our Branch of the Grayville Grahams by Violet P. Graham

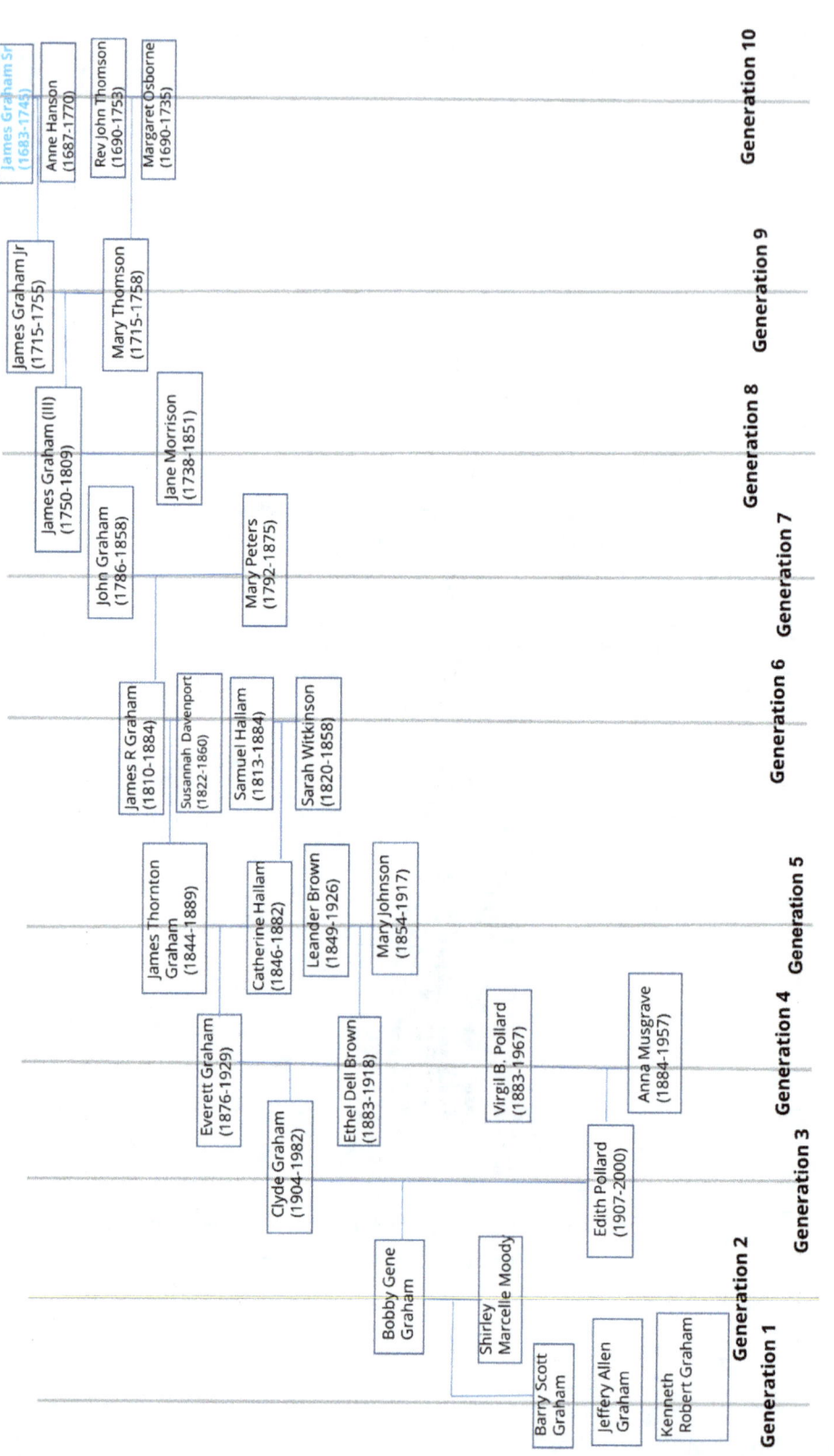

*Figure 11: Paternal Pedigree of Grayville, Illinois Grahams*

# Chapter 3
# County Fermanagh, Ireland[iv]
# 1636-1720

The Plantation of Ulster was the organized colonization of Northern Ireland, a result of the Nine Year's War (1593-1603), which was an organized rebellion in Ireland against English rule. The year 1603 is also significant as the thrones of Scotland and England had been unified in 1603 by James VI of Scotland, who became James I of England. James I intended to use the plantation to "civilize" the region that was the least populated in Ireland and establish key military garrisons in case of further conflicts with the Irish.[67]

The Ulster Plantation comprised an estimated half a million acres in Counties Armagh, Cavan, Fermanagh, Tyrone, Donegal, and Londonderry. While some privately-funded plantations began as early as 1606, the official government-sponsored plantation began in 1609. The colonists (or "British tenants") were required to be English-speaking, Protestant, and loyal to the king. The settlers were also required to maintain arms and attend an annual military "muster." The Scottish settlers were predominantly Presbyterian Lowlanders, and the English were mainly Anglicans. Their culture differed from that of the native Catholic Irish. Although some "loyal" natives were granted land, the native Irish reaction to the plantation was generally hostile, resulting in armed rebellions in 1641, again in 1689-1693, the eighteenth century, the nineteenth century, and into the twentieth century. One casualty of the conflicts that impacts Irish genealogical research today was the destruction of the Public Records Office in Dublin in 1922 and most vital records stored within it.[68]

From the previous section, we know there were four Graham brothers: Christopher (1670-1746), James Sr. (circa 1683-1745), John (circa 1674-1743), and the fourth, possibly named William* (circa 1675-aft. 1729), who arrived in Philadelphia on 27 October 1720 on a brigantine ship that left

---

[67] Jonathan Bardon, *The Plantation of Ulster* (Dublin: Gill & Macmillan, 2011), 214.
https://catalogue.library.ulster.ac.uk/items/1313366?query=ulster&resultsUri=items%3Fquery%3Dulster%26offset%3D80
[68] Jonathan Bardon, *A History of Ulster, New Updated Edition* (Belfast: The Blackstaff Press, 2001), 124-128.

Londonderry, Ireland in June 1720. The first question was: "Were these brothers from the port city of Londonderry, or was that a travel stop?" The destruction of the Public Records Office archives in Dublin in 1922 made the task of finding our Grahams in Ireland daunting. However, not all hope was lost, thanks to the work of nineteenth century genealogists Crosslé, Betham, Thrift, and Ffolliott.

## Crosslé "Gold Mine"—Irish Court Records

The Crosslé genealogical abstracts were created by Dr. Francis Crosslé and his son Philip Crosslé in the late nineteenth century. They hand-copied prerogative court wills, military pay records, and civil court records from 1620 to 1804. William Betham created abstracts of pre-1800 wills and reconstructed family trees and detailed pedigrees. Gertrude Thrift (1872-1951) cultivated a collection of 150,000 abstracts containing transcripts and notes from military commission books, parish registers, exchequer bill books, prerogative grants, chancery bill books, freeman rolls, wills, family trees, and pedigree charts. Rosemary Ffolliott compiled a comprehensive catalog of biographical notices from Irish newspapers from 1756-1850.[69]

Our clues from U.S. records: the eldest Graham brother (the one with the most unique name of the four), Christopher Graham, was born in 1670. He lived in/near Paxtang, Pennsylvania, for 20 years, was a devout Presbyterian, followed his sons to Virginia after 1738, and died in Augusta County, Virginia before February 1746, the date his will was probated.[70] The initial records search in Ireland for Christopher Grahams suggested our Christopher's family was from County Fermanagh [fer-**man**-*uh*].

After reading many pages of Crosslé handwritten abstracts, I found the "breakthrough" record that finally pointed to *our* Christopher Graham (1670-1746). It was a copy of depositions taken on 21 November 1711 from witnesses in a civil lawsuit over land in Tullycarrick, County Fermanagh, Ireland. See Figure 12. My transcription, with abbreviations spelled out, can be read below it.

---

[69] Bobby Forrest, "Crosslé, Groves, Betham and Thrift," *Ulster Genealogy and Local History*, 2017, accessed 13 October 2022. http://www.ulstergenealogyandlocalhistoryblog.com/2017/10/crossle-groves-betham-thrift.html

[70] Lyman Chalkley, *Chronicles of the Scotch-Irish Settlement in Virginia*, 1745-1800, 6.

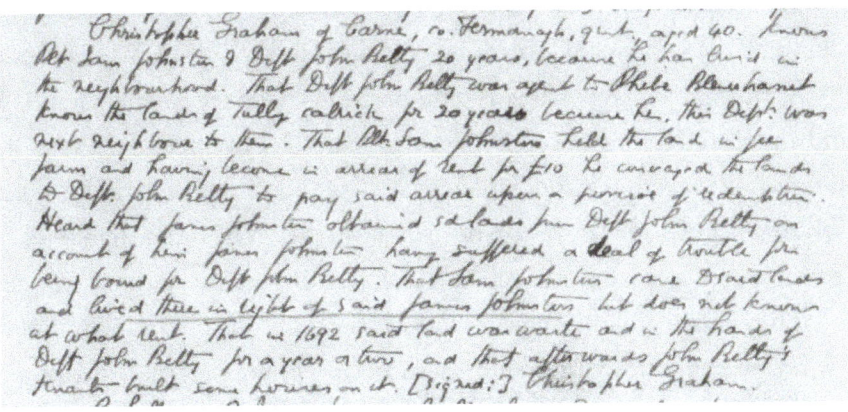

*Figure 12: Co Fermanagh Deposition of Christopher Graham, gentleman, age 40, taken in November 1711 (from Crosslé Genealogical Abstracts). Image Courtesy of the National Archives of Ireland. [71]*

Christopher Graham of Carne, County Fermanagh, gentleman, aged 40, knows Plantiff James Johnston and Defendant John Beatty 20 years, because he has lived in the neighborhood. That Defendant John Beatty was agent to Phebe Bleuerhanet, knows the lands of Tully Cabrick (spelled "Tully Calrick" in the deposition after this one) for 20 years because he, this Defendant, was next neighbors with them. That Plantiff James Johnston held the land in fee farm and having become in arrear of rent for 10 pounds, he conveyed the lands to Defendant. John Beatty to pay said arrear upon a promise of redemption. Heard that James Johnston obtained said lands from Defendant John Beatty on account of him James Johnston having suffered a deal of trouble for being bound for Defendant John Beatty. That James Johnston cared for said lands and lived there in light of said James Johnston that does not know at what rent. That in 1692 said land warranted and in the hands of Defendant John Beatty for a year or two, and that afterwards John Beatty's tenants built some houses on it. [signed:] Christopher Graham

Christopher Graham's title of "Gentleman"[71] indicates he was of the gentry class, of the means to purchase the title "Gentleman." Titles or "Tituladoes" of Gentleman, Knight, Esquire, and certain military ranks were available for purchase at that time. This Christopher Graham was 40 years old in November of 1711, which puts his birth year at 1670, and matches the birth year in the U.S. records of the eldest brother, Christopher. Carne, or Carn, is a townland in the civil parish of Magheraculmoney, in County Fermanagh, and is two miles from the townland of Tullycallrick, the location of the disputed property.

---

[71] Figure 12: FindmyPast.com, "Christopher Graham in 1711," Beatty notebooks, Vol. 11 and 12, *Crosslé Genealogical Abstracts, 1620-1850*, accessed 27 December 2022. (Requires Account.) https://www.findmypast.com/transcript?id=IRE/NAI/GENABS/00596456/1 .

We know from the Beatty notebooks, derived from the Equity Exchequer books, and recorded in the Crosslé abstracts, that Christopher's own post-war land lease also began in 1692 (the agent was Thomas Cochranie), the same year Christopher left the military.[72] It seems that his lease was due to lapse about 1723, which may have influenced his decision to move to America in 1720. That expiring lease in Ireland and the initial invitation by James Logan, the Provincial Secretary of Pennsylvania, offering land rent-free to recruit battle-hardened settlers and soldiers from Northern Ireland to move to the Pennsylvania frontier may have also been an influence. The other item affecting the decision to move was a practice of Ulster landlords called "Rack Renting." The landlords dramatically raised rent when the land lease expired. The average term of a lease in Ulster was 31 years, significantly longer than in Scotland, which was the attraction to Northern Ireland in the first place. Most new leases were issued soon after 1691 at the conclusion of the Williamite Wars. Previous leases issued to Protestants had been voided by the 1689 Act of Attainder. The result was thousands of Ulster leases expiring close to the same time, an average of 31 years later, in the 1720s and 1730s. Land became scarce, and the new leases went to the highest bidder. Farmers were outraged. Many refused to pay the higher rents and either returned to Scotland or crossed to America.[73] Significant waves of emigration from Ulster to America continued throughout the eighteenth century, so by 1776, one in six men in America was an Ulster Scot.[74] Various studies estimate the number of Scots-Irish in the Continental Army from 40 to 70 percent depending on the regiment.[75] George III and his advisors received regular reports on the demographics of the American rebels. More than once the American Revolution was characterized as a "Scots Presbyterian Revolt."[76]

It was a special Catholic Parliament that passed the Act of Attainder in Dublin, called by James II, on 25 March 1689. It revoked the Settlement Acts of Ireland of 1652 (English Parliament) and 1660 (Charles II), and all Settlement and Plantation acts going back to 1583. Families that had been in Ireland for over 100 years, some of whom had intermarried with Catholic families, were required to surrender their lands and possessions and leave. Many chose to stay in Ireland and retreat to the safety of Enniskillen. However, over a thousand persons, heads of households and some wives that remained

---

[72] FindmyPast.com, "Exchequer Judgment Book 1690-1715," *Crosslé Genealogical Abstracts, 1620-1850*, 46, accessed 27 December 2022. (Requires Account.)
https://search.findmypast.com/record?id=S2%2FIRE%2FNAI%2F007634856%2F00644&parentid=IRE%2FNAI%2FGENABS%2F01138765%2F1

[73] James G. Leyburn, *The Scotch-Irish, A Social History,* 181-195, 212.

[74] Fred DeArmond, "Scotch Irish Heritage," *White River Valley Historical Quarterly,* Vol. 4, Number 4 (Summer 1971): 10. https://thelibrary.org/lochist/periodicals/wrv/v4/n4/s71i.htm

[75] Thomas Fleming, "Yankee Doodle with a Brogue," *Irish America Magazine,* accessed 27 December 2022. https://www.irishamerica.com/2020/07/yankee-doodle-with-a-brogue-the-irish-in-the-american-revolution-2/

[76] Jonathon Van Maren, "The American Revolution was a Presbyterian Revolt," The BridgeHead , 6 July 2020. https://thebridgehead.ca/2020/07/06/the-american-revolution-was-a-presbyterian-revolt/

in Ireland, were imprisoned in Dublin while James II considered what to do with them as he prepared to fight the invading forces of William III.[77]

William Trimble states in *The History of Enniskillen, Volume II:* "Those attainted under the Parliament of 1689 Act in the County Fermanagh were as given below, and the names of several local families are recognized: Adam Betty [alternate spelling for Beatty], Gentleman from Carne, John Betty, Gentleman from Adverney, Rowland Betty, Gentleman from Ardverny." These Beattys from Advarney were "next" neighbors of Christopher's, named in the referenced 1711 lawsuit. John Beatty, the defendant in the referenced deposition, would have lived in the household of Adam Beatty near Christopher Graham's Carne estate. "Rowland Beatty of Ardvarney," is mentioned later in Crosslé Abstracts in the same civil case involving his family and the Johnstons.[78] See map in Figure 13.

Conclusion: If Christopher knew his Beatty/Johnston neighbors for 20 years, he could not have arrived in Carne before 1691, which is one reason neither he nor any other Grahams appear on the County Fermanagh 1689 Protestant Attainders List. Another reason is that only landed gentry or freeholders appeared on the Attainders List.[79] Christopher was 19 years old in 1689. In 1689, he likely lived with his family and Armstrong relatives near Brookebrough, County Fermanagh. Families stuck together in those dangerous times.

---

[77] Cecilia L. Fabos-Becker, *The Act of Attainder, March 25, 1689, Dublin, Ireland; List of the Attainted, Introduction,* 1-2, accessed 22 December 2022. https://www.americeltic.net/files/Intro-ExtractsOfWalterHarris1749Book-ListofAttaintedProtestantsandCatholicsinIreland.pdf

[78] William Copeland Trimble, *The History of Enniskillen, Vol. II, With References to Some Manors in County Fermanagh* (Enniskillen: William Trimble, 1920), 610. https://archive.org/details/historyofenniski02trim/page/610/mode/2up

[79] William King, *The State of the Protestants of Ireland under the Late King James's Government in which their carriage towards him is justified, and the absolute necessity of their endeavouring to be freed from his government, and of submitting to their present Majesties is demonstrated* (London: Robert Clavell, 1691; Ann Arbor, Early English Books-Text Creation Partnership, 2011), 242-288. https://quod.lib.umich.edu/e/eebo/A47446.0001.001/1:6.1?rgn=div2;view=fulltext

*Figure 13: Parish Magheraculmoney, Co Fermanagh, Ireland – Placename data from The Northern Ireland Place-Name Project' at Queen's University Belfast and licensed under CC BY 4.0. See Appendix A for more on Irish Geography.* [80]

---

[80] Figure 13: Queen's University, Belfast, "Advanced Place Name Search," Placenamesni.org, Northern Ireland Place-Name Project, accessed 30 December 2022. https://experience.arcgis.com/experience/9b31e0501b744154b4584b1dce1f859b/page/Place-Name-Search/

## Military Service: Trooper Christopher Graham and Defending Enniskillen

By July of 1689, the situation in the northern Irish counties had deteriorated. The local Irish, under the support of James II and the French, were launching attacks on British settlements. British farmers had abandoned their farms throughout the Ulster Plantation region, and many retreated to the safety of Enniskillen, the central city and fortress of County Fermanagh. Enniskillen established a local militia to defend their town and spent the rest of the year preparing for a siege. The town elders of both Enniskillen and the northern port town of Derry wrote and signed the famous letters to King William III and Queen Mary in July 1689 requesting assistance.[81] The subsequent conflict became known as "The Williamite War or Wars." One of the fifteen couriers tasked with delivering the letters to the Scottish Privy Council in Edinburgh was "Kirstie" (nickname for Christopher) Grahame. The Scottish Privy Council records from November 1689 show the council requesting "safe passage" for the return trip: that any available British mariner in the Irish Sea give the group, which included "Kirstie Grahame,"[82] a free ride back to Ireland. From the council letter:

> ... to discharge all masters of warr ships, privateirs or others cruizing upon the west coast of Scotland or Irish coasts belonging to their Majesties to trouble the petitioner or these under his command from passing to Ireland with their armes, and alsoe to recommend to the masters of the severall westerne sea ports of this kingdom and furnish the petitioner with boats and provissiones fitt for their transportationes to Darrie or any other convenient place in that kingdome upon their own expences; the quhich petitione being read in presence of the saids Lords they ordained the petitioner to give in ane condescendance of the number of his men and of their designationes, and accordingly the said petitioner haveing given in ane particular condesendance of the said men as followes, viz. :- George Poack of Killileach and County of Down, Gaven Patersone of the same, John Pattersone of the same, Nicolas Woods of the same, Robert Greir of Ballany, John Dougan of Bellywalter and said countie, John Mullan of Undergee and County Ardmach, Robert Rodgers of the same, Umphra Stivens of the same, Richard Graham of Mullachbreck and said county, Heugh Hamiltone of the same, James Hamiltone of Ords and County Down, Kirstie Grahame of the same, Robert Greir of the same, Gilbert Greir of the same: Ther Majesties High Commissioner and Lords of Privy Councill haveing this day considered the abovewrittin list con- descended one be the petitioner, they allow him a pass for himself and the fyftein men abovewrittin condescended on by him to goe for Ireland.[83]

---

[81] N.F.B., "Ireland's Wars: Enniskilleners," NeverFeltBetter, Paragraph 3, 11 February 2015. https://neverfeltbetter.wordpress.com/2015/02/11/irelands-wars-enniskilliners/

[82] Thomas Witherow, *Derry and Enniskillen in the year 1689: the story of some famous battlefields in Ulster*, Fourth Edition (Belfast: W. Mullan & Son, 1913), 409-416. https://archive.org/details/derryenniskillen00withrich/mode/2up?ref=ol&view=theater&q=graham

[83] J. Hill Burton et al, *The Register of the Privy Council of Scotland*, 3rd ser.: Vol. XIII 1686/1689 (Edinburgh: H.M. General Register House, 1898), 425. The Register of the Privy Council of Scotland, 3rd ser.: volume XIII 1686/1689

Curiously, none of the fifteen are listed as "from" County Fermanagh or Derry. However, since this is a letter written to mariners, it is fitting that most of the locations listed are accessible by boat. There are three other men listed in "Kirstie's" group: James Hamiltone, of "Ords and County Down," Robert Grier, and Gilbert Grier "of the same." "Ords" is likely the Ards Peninsula which includes Bangor Parish and is only about 40 miles from the Scottish coast. "James Hamiltone" is from Bangor and is the same Colonel James Hamilton who commanded the Inniskilling Regiment of Foot.[84] Per Crosslé's Abstracts, we know Robert Grier was actually from Muckamore, County Antrim,[85] and is owed money in 1690 by "Capt Matthew Webster's formerly Capt Martin Armstrong's" Troop of Horse, which was also Christopher Graham's troop.[86] Most of the troop's creditors had some connection with the unit. Christopher's regiment, which had been camped at Dundalk (50 miles south of Belfast), was on winter leave by November 1689[87] for members to go home and shelter. "Kirstie" was likely assigned to Col. Hamilton for the mission to Edinburgh, perhaps as a bodyguard. For security reasons, it is understandable why the council failed to identify the men's titles or military ranks in the referenced letter.

The subsequent discovery "mined" from *Crosslé Genealogical Abstracts* regarding Trooper Christopher Graham were Irish military financial records from 1690-1693[88] regarding "Capt Matthew Webster's troop, formerly Capt Martin Armstrong's." Capt. Martin Armstrong, the first troop commander, was killed on 11 February 1690 at the Battle of Killeshandra, County Cavan, and was replaced by Capt. Matthew Webster of Enniskillen.[89] This troop was part of the Regiment of Horse commanded by Colonel William Wolseley. Colonel Wolseley was promoted to Brigadier General in

---

[84] Harvey George Johnston, *The Heraldry of the Hamiltons: with notes on all the males of the family, description of the arms, plates and pedigrees* (Edinburgh and London: W & A.K. Johnston Limited, 1909), 71. https://archive.org/details/heraldryofhamils00john

[85] "Robert Grier," *Ireland, Diocesan and Prerogative Wills & Administrations Indexes, 1595-1858,* FamilySearch, 19 December 2019. (https://familysearch.org/ark:/61903/1:1:WGC3-CC6Z

[86] FindmyPast.com, "Beatty notebooks, v. 6-12," *Crosslé Genealogical Abstracts, 1620-1850*, 240, accessed 27 December 2022. (Requires Account.)
https://search.findmypast.com/record?id=S2%2FIRE%2FNAI%2F007634818%2F00600&parentid=IRE%2FNAI%2FGENABS%2F00602219%2F1  Also available in non-indexed form at:
https://www.familysearch.org/search/catalog/234637?availability=Family%20History%20Library

[87] Richard Cannon, *Historical Record of the Sixth, or Inniskilling Regiment of Dragoons, Containing an Account of the Formation of the Regiment in 1689, and of Its Subsequent Services to 1846* (London: Parker, Furnivall, & Parker, 1847), 15. https://ia803208.us.archive.org/28/items/cihm_48344/cihm_48344.pdf

[88] FindmyPast.com, "Beatty notebooks, v. 6-12," *Crosslé Genealogical Abstracts*, 240-244, accessed 27 December 2022. (Requires Account.)
https://search.findmypast.com/record?id=S2%2FIRE%2FNAI%2F007634818%2F00600&parentid=IRE%2FNAI%2FGENABS%2F00602219%2F1

[89] W. Copeland Trimble, *The History of Enniskillen with reference to some manors in co. Fermanagh: and other local subjects* Vol. II, 630.

1693.[90] At this time and until 1751, military units were known by the name of their commanding officer.[91]

Crosslé provides us with a comprehensive list of Capt. Webster's Enniskillen Troop of Horse members in December 1693:

Trumpeteers: John Armstrong, Phillip Hegin

Corporals: Richard Young, Matthew Young, John Anderson

Troopers: James Armstrong, Simon Armstrong, John Armstrong Senior, John Armstrong Junior, George Anderson, Francis Blacklaw, Arthur Beatty, John Beatty Senior, John Beatty Junior, Richard Beatty, William Beatty, Archibald Beatty, Thomas Beatty, Robert Buchanan, Henry Ball, John Baxter, William Elliott, Archibald Elliott, William Gilchrist, John Faier, Andrew Ferguson, Christopher Graham, James Harknesse, Josiah Hindman, James Irwin, Francis Little, George Little, Richard Martin, John Martin, John Murrow, William Mairty, James Nixon, William Ormiston, Mungo Ormiston, Edward Pickin, Richard Reynolds, John Read, John Stante, John Wiggins, John White, Robert Armstrong, George Armstrong, John Armstrong.[92]

---

[90] Wikisource contributors. "Dictionary of National Biography, 1885-1900/Wolseley, William (1640?-1691)," Wikisource, accessed 27 December 2022. https://en.wikisource.org/w/index.php?title=Dictionary_of_National_Biography,_1885-1900/Wolseley,_William_(1640%3F-1691)&oldid=11771181

[91] Inniskillings, "The Forgotton Regiment: Enniskillen's Third Regiment," The Inniskillings Museum, 22 October 2018. https://inniskillingsmuseum.com/the-forgotten-regiment-enniskillens-third-regiment/

[92] Figure 14: Philip Crosslé, Beatty notebooks, v. 6-12, "Petitions to Commissioner's for Stabling the Aks of the Army 1689-1699," *Crosslé Genealogical Abstracts*, 240- 244.

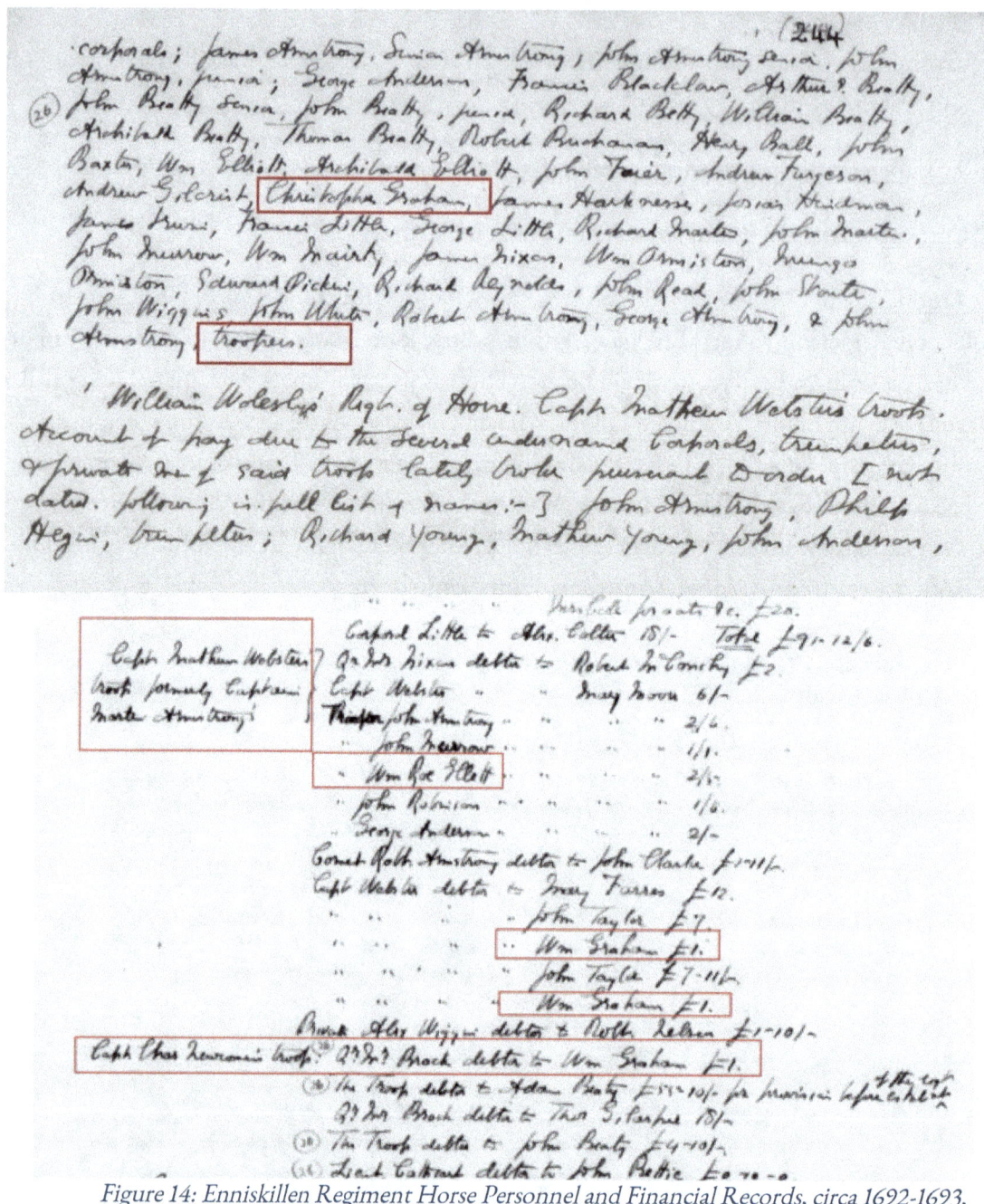

*Figure 14: Enniskillen Regiment Horse Personnel and Financial Records, circa 1692-1693, Crosslé Genealogical Abstracts. Images Courtesy of the National Archives of Ireland* [92]

These records confirm the whereabouts of Christopher Graham (1670-1746) before 1692. He served in Captain Armstrong's and subsequently Captain Webster's Troop of Horse (cavalry unit) based in Enniskillen (Inniskilling), County Fermanagh, from about 1688-1692. This was the time period of the previously mentioned Williamite Wars in Ireland, the conflict between Jacobite supporters of deposed monarch James II and Williamite supporters of his successor, William III,[93] who shared the British throne with his wife, Queen Mary, daughter of James II. The militia based in Enniskillen became known as the "Inniskilleners." It earned a reputation for being fierce on the battlefield, a reputation that would win them that invitation by the Pennsylvania Provincial Secretary years later.

The first recorded battle for the Inniskilling cavalry was as a civilian militia of Williamites based at Enniskillen against a much larger Jacobite military force (2,000 Williamites vs. 5,000 Jacobites). They proved themselves at the Battle of Newtown Butler (also spelled Newtownbutler) in July 1689, inflicting heavy casualties on the Jacobites with few losses of their own. Roughly 500 Jacobites chose to risk drowning in Lough Erne rather than face the "Inniskilleners." [94] Few survived the swim to the other shore.

J. G Simms writes: "Newtownbutler was a shattering defeat for King James."[95] After Newtown Butler, six Williamite regiments of regular army units were formed, commanded by professional soldiers who had arrived on the relief fleet at Londonderry in 1689: three of Foot, (Hamilton's,

*Figure 15: Lough Erne Looking WSW at Muckross, 25 April 2021.*
*Lough Erne CC-BY-SA/2.0 - © Kenneth*
*Allen - geograph.org.uk/p/6818563*

---

[93] William Alexander Macguire, *Kings in conflict: the revolutionary war in Ireland and its aftermath, 1689-1750* (Belfast: Blackstaff, 1990), 2.

[94] W. Copeland Trimble, *The History of Enniskillen with reference to some manors in Co. Fermanagh: and other local subjects*, Vol. II, 572, 643.

[95] J. G. Simms, "The Williamite War in South Ulster." *Clogher Record* 10, no. 1 (1979): 160-161. https://www.jstor.org/stable/27695795

Lloyd's, and Tiffin's), two of Dragoons, (Conynham's and Whynn's) and one of Horse (Wolseley). The "Inniskillener" Troops of Horse were activated into the regular army and placed in a regiment under the command of Colonel William Wolseley as confirmed by the Crosslé Abstracts Beatty Notebooks.[96]

"Gentlemen," cried King William at the Boyne, "I have heard much of your exploits, and now I shall witness them."

*Figure 16: Artist Rendering of King William III and the Inniskilling Regiment of Horse at the Battle of the Boyne, 11 July 1690, Artist: T.A. Mercer* [99]

Historian Richard Cannon writes: "The INNISKILLING troopers had made their name a terror to their opponents, and were highly esteemed in the English army. George Warter Story, the historian of these wars, states, 'I went three miles beyond the camp, where I met the Inniskilling horse and dragoons, whom the Duke (Schomberg) had ordered to be an advance-guard to his army. I wondered much to see their horses and equipage, hearing before what feats had been done by them.'... The INNISKILLING cavalry performed several feats of gallantry, on detached services, during the period the army was at the unhealthy camp at Dundalk [in late 1689]; and subsequently returned to their own country for winter quarters." [97, 98]

At the Battle of the Boyne on 11 July 1690, King James II and King William III entered the battlefield. Per Figure 16 from Trimble's "History of Enniskillen, Volume II," upon meeting the Inniskilleners, King William is quoted as saying: "Gentlemen, I have heard much of your exploits, and

---

[96] Inniskillings, "The Forgotton Regiment: Enniskillen's Third Regiment."

[97] Richard Cannon, *Historical Record of the Sixth, or Inniskilling Regiment of Dragoons, Containing an Account of the Formation of the Regiment in 1689, and of Its Subsequent Services to 1846*, 215. https://www.gutenberg.org/files/55536/55536-h/55536-h.htm

[98] Trimble A. Mercer, artist, *The History of Enniskillen with Reference to some Manors in Co. Fermanagh: and other Local Subjects*, Vol. II (Enniskillen: William Trimble, 1920), 491. https://archive.org/details/historyofenniski02trim/page/642/mode/2up?q=gentlemen+exploits+witness+them&view=theater

now I shall witness them." William chose the Inniskilling Horse Regiment to lead them into battle.[99] Towards the end of the battle, William suffered a "close shave." A Jacobite gunner fired a parting shot which struck his boot, grazing his leg. William gave the bloodstained lace ruffle from the top of his boot to one of the officers who tended to his injury, Lieutenant Claudius Beatty of the Inniskilling Horse. This ruffle is on display at the National Army Museum in London.[100] Lt. Beatty, as well as the other Beattys in the troop, was a relative by marriage to the troop's first commander, Captain Martin Armstrong.[101]

## Other noteworthy members of Brigadier General Wolseley's Regiment of Horse:

—Lt. Robert Johnston, Lt. James Johnston, Quartermaster Gerrard Irvin, Quartermaster Francis Aldridge.

—"H.D." (highly decorated) officers: Lt. James Johnston, Lt. Claud Betty (Beatty), Lt. Francis Aldrich, Cornet Robert Armstrong.

In the list of accompanying debts due to soldiers and officers, Figure 14, a number of Beattys are mentioned as well as Peter and John "Gram" and a William Graham. Another individual of interest mentioned was Samuel Hanson, a supply officer from High Lake, Co. Roscommon. Hanson was an unusual name to find in Ireland at that time. Since James Graham Sr. married his wife, Anne Hanson, in Ireland, this Samuel Hanson would be a good fit to be her father or another relative. One of James Graham Sr. and Anne Hanson's younger sons was named Samuel. The Scottish naming pattern suggests that Samuel Graham may have been named after a maternal grandfather named "Samuel Hanson." The other less likely option could be that Anne Hanson's parents were John and Mary Hanson, Anglicans from Mellick, County Kildare, who had a daughter, Anne. It is a possibility that this John and Mary fled to the safety of Enniskillen after their lands were confiscated in 1689.[102]

Just sixty years previously, per the 1630 Muster Roll, the Ulster Plantation was organized by family. As a result, the civilian militias were locally based and consisted of family members, in-laws, and close neighbors.[103] Crosslé can confirm that all the Beattys from Captain Martin Armstrong's Troop of Horse were related to each other and also to Captain Martin Armstrong via marriage. Per Crosslé's

---

[99] Figure 16: Trimble A. Mercer, artist, *The History of Enniskillen with Reference to some Manors in Co. Fermanagh: and other Local Subjects*, Vol. II (Enniskillen: William Trimble, 1920), 643.

[100] National Army Museum, "Jacobite Retreat, Battle of the Boyne," National Army Museum, Chelsea, London, accessed 27 December 2022. https://www.nam.ac.uk/explore/battle-boyne

[101] FindmyPast.com, "Kilmore Wills, Beatty Notebooks, v6-12," *Crosslé Genealogical Abstracts,* FindmyPast, 289-290, accessed 27 December 2022. (Requires Account.) https://search.findmypast.com/record?id=S2%2FIRE%2FNAI%2F007634818%2F00636&parentid=IRE%2FNAI%2FGENABS%2F00604591%2F1

[102] FindmyPast.com, "Kilmore Wills, Beatty Notebooks, v6-12," *Crosslé Genealogical Abstracts,* FindmyPast, 289-290, accessed 27 December 2022.

[103] Robert John Hunter, "Families and Kinship," Muster Rolls c1630, Introduction, *The R.J. Hunter Collection.*

Beatty Notebooks, we find that Captain Armstrong married John Beatty's daughter, Jennett, and that John Beatty was the brother of Lt. Claud Beatty, who received the blood-stained ruffle from King William III. Martin's brother was Cornet Robert Armstrong of Wattlebridge, County Fermanagh (12 miles south of Macguiresbridge).[104] I believe Robert married a daughter of William Graham, the William Graham listed in Figure 14, who is owed a total of three pounds for provisions to the Regiment of Horse. William Graham's will, recorded on 12 March 1715 in Tullinagoga, in Parish Magheraculmoney (Figure 13, close to Christopher Graham's land in Carne), names a grandson of William: "Robert Armstrong."[105] Since Christopher was the only Graham in Captain Martin Armstrong's militia troop and was 18-19 years old in 1689, he would have been connected to his commander in some way, perhaps as a nephew, or cousin to Robert Armstrong's wife, possible daughter of the previously mentioned William Graham. Based on the Scottish naming pattern, in heavy use at the time, the name "Christopher" is common to Armstrongs but not to Grahams, which suggests that Christopher Graham's mother was an Armstrong. There were few Grahams in County Fermanagh in the 1680s and only two known Christopher Grahams: the second died in Derryinch, in Parish Trory, County Fermanagh, in 1691.[106] The Trory Grahams used the same Christopher-James-John-William naming pattern for generations and are likely cousins of the four brothers who left for America in 1720. The Trory Grahams later moved to Parish Kilmore in County Monaghan as the Devernish Abbeylands they lived on had become overcrowded.[107, 108]

The Williamite Wars that began in 1688 ended with the Treaty of Limerick in October 1691. John Beatty Sr., John Beatty Jr., several other Beattys, James Johnston, and William and Archibald Elliott (whose children later married Christopher Graham's children and settled in Augusta County, Virginia) all served in Captain Martin Armstrong's/Captain Matthew Webster's Troop of Horse. Christopher would have known the Beattys and James Johnston as early as 1688-89 from their time in the military together, which matches his statement from the November 1711 court deposition stating he has known both the plaintiff and defendant for 20 years. Wolseley's Horse Regiment started with

---

[104] FindmyPast.com, "Beatty notebooks, v. 6-12," *Crosslé Genealogical Abstracts*, FindmyPast, 167, accessed 27 December 2022. (Requires Account.)
https://search.findmypast.com/record?id=S2%2FIRE%2FNAI%2F007634818%2F00726&parentid=IRE%2FNAI%2FGENABS%2F00606404%2F1

[105] FindmyPast.com, "Armstrong Envelope, Clogher Grant Book," *Crosslé Genealogical Abstracts*, FindmyPast, accessed 27 December 2022. (Requires Account.)
https://search.findmypast.com/record?id=S2%2FIRE%2FNAI%2F007634816%2F00334&parentid=IRE%2FNAI%2FGENABS%2F00559590%2F1

[106] FindmyPast.com, *Ireland Diocesan And Prerogative Wills & Administrations Indexes 1595-1858*, Clogher Diocese, FindmyPast, accessed 27 December 2022. (Requires Account.)
https://search.findmypast.com/record?id=IRE%2FDIOC%2F007246604%2F00133&parentid=IRE%2FDIOC%2FWILL%2F00100915

[107] William Copeland Trimble, *The History of Enniskillen, Volume II, With References to Some Manors in County Fermanagh*, 292.

[108] Sue Pedersen, "James Graham, 1681-1747," Wikitree, 4 October 2015.
https://www.wikitree.com/wiki/Graham-8665

25 troops, was reduced to 12 troops in 1690, and then disbanded/merged with the dragoons in 1697 (Peace Treaty of Ryswick and Wolseley's death both occurred in 1697).[109]

## Another unusual name

While the first name Christopher is unusual for a Graham, so is the name "Lancelot," the name of two of Christopher Graham's grandsons, one of whom he shared with his fellow troop member, William Elliott Sr. Lancelot Irvine served as a Lieutenant in Wolseley's Inniskilling Regiment of Horse, so he would have been a comrade-in-arms of Christopher Graham, and William and Archibald Elliott. Lt. Lancelot Irvine died unmarried in 1701.[110] Naming children after a war hero was a common way for his former comrades to honor him, which would explain the Lancelots among Christopher Graham's and the Elliott descendants.

## Irish Muster Roll of 1630

The Ulster Plantation was the settlement of land in the northern Irish counties that had been previously confiscated by people loyal to the English Crown. The plantation was organized using "undertakers," persons who received and managed the land and its tenants. They were called "undertakers" because they had to "undertake" certain conditions, including building a house and "bawn"—a fortified barn—and settle the land with a minimum number of people of the Protestant faith who could become militia in times of trouble. The height of the Plantation period was from 1610 to about 1630.[111] The requirement for undertakers to settle 24 men from ten families per thousand acres meant that each family consisted of a father and one or more adult sons. When a family arrived in Ulster around 1615, the father would have been forty and the younger sons at least eighteen. By 1630, the father would have been in his late fifties or early sixties, and the sons in their thirties or forties. A family connection is likely if a surname recurs two or three times in the muster list for the same estate.

The conditions of the plantation in Ulster required English and Scottish undertakers to "have ready in their houses at all times a convenient store of arms, wherewith they may furnish a competent number of men for their defense, which may be viewed and mustered every half year, according to the manner of England." The servitor grantees, who were not obliged to introduce colonists, were also to "have a convenient store of arms in their houses." Not surprisingly, no such requirement was imposed on the native Irish grantees on the plantation.[112] We know from R.J. Hunter, Muster Roll subject matter expert, that the muster roll, useful as a type of census, was conventionally dated as "circa 1630"

---

[109] Richard Cannon, *Historical Record of the Sixth, or Inniskilling Regiment of Dragoons, Containing an Account of the Formation of the Regiment in 1689, and of Its Subsequent Services to 1846*, 7-8.

[110] John Irvine, *A Brief Account of the Irvine Family of Co. Fermanagh* (Dublin: Robert T. White, 1934), 44. https://deriv.nls.uk/dcn23/9547/95472888.23.pdf

[111] Bruce Orr, "Plantation of Ireland: Part Two 1610-1630," Tartans.com, 26 December 2019. http://www.tartans.com/articles/plantscot2.html

[112] R. J. Hunter, *Men and Arms:, The Ulster Settlers, c. 1630*. Kindle Edition, Kindle Locations 119-123, 257-264.

despite being produced by Lt. William Graham between 1628, when he was appointed muster-master, and 1634, when he presented his findings to the lord deputy, Sir Thomas Wentworth. The muster roll for County Fermanagh was recorded in the Spring of 1629. Lt. William Graham was the second son of Sir Richard Graham, who had come to Ireland with his younger brother, Sir George Graham, during the Nine Years' War (1594-1603). Sir Richard and Sir George were sons of Fergus Graham of Mote, second son of Lang Will Graham, chief of the Border Grahams.[113] R.J. Hunter surmised that the order in which the counties appear in the muster roll—Cavan, Armagh, Fermanagh, Tyrone, Londonderry, Antrim, Donegal, Down, and Monaghan—is probably the sequence in which the musters were conducted.[114]

Four Grahams appear on the 1629 Muster Roll of Co. Fermanagh in Parish Aghalurcher, which included the Macguiresbride and Brookeborough areas:[115] Robert Graham and sons James and Robert, who held Aghamore and Durosse, along with Adam Armstrong and the Hendersons. The fourth Graham, a "John Grahame," held Drumcroo which was next to Aghamore, indicating a relationship to Robert Graham and his sons. Also on this same Parish Aghalurcher Muster Roll is a William Elliott,[116] a potential ancestor of the Elliotts who served with Trooper Christopher Graham in 1688-1692, and also Adam Beatty and his sons, whose descendants would serve in the same Enniskillen Regiment of Horse and would later become neighbors of Christopher Graham (1670-1746) in Parish Magheraculmoney. Robert Graham of Aghamore the elder may have been Robert Graham of Mylees, who was a younger son of William Graham of Mylees, son of Richard Graham of Netherby, and his second wife, and therefore a great-grandson of Lang Will. Both Robert Grahams were born circa 1570. Robert Graham of the Mylees disappears from Scottish records after 1600,[117] supporting the belief that Robert Graham of Aghamore, Ireland and Robert Graham of the Mylees are the same person.

Conclusion: Robert Graham of Mylees and possibly Aghamore was not directly related to the patriarch of the Grayville Grahams who did not arrive in Ireland until after 1635.

## Migration Waves from Scotland to Ireland

There were generally four waves of migration from Scotland to Ireland in the seventeenth century. First, in 1606, a group of mercenaries known as "Border Reivers," most of whom were Grahams, were sentenced to transport to Ireland due to problems they caused at the Scottish/English border and/or to permit confiscation of their valuable farm lands. Most of the Reivers had returned to

---

[113] John O'Hart, *Irish Pedigrees Volume II* (Dublin: James Duffy and Co Limited, 1892), 232. https://ia600202.us.archive.org/12/items/irishpedigreesor01ohar/irishpedigreesor01ohar.pdf

[114] Robert John Hunter, "Families and Kinship, Muster Rolls c1630, Introduction," The R.J. Hunter Collection. https://www.therjhuntercollection.com/resources/muster-rolls-c-1630/introduction/

[115] Fermanagh Genealogy Centre, "Map of Fermanagh," Fermanagh Genealogy Centre, 2018, accessed 15 October 2022. https://fermanaghgenealogy.org/map/

[116] R. J. Hunter, *Men and Arms:, The Ulster Settlers, c. 1630*, Kindle Edition, Kindle Locations 2827-2935.

[117] Richard T. Spence, "The Pacification of the Cumberland Borders, 1593-1628," *Northern History*, 13:1 (1977): 84.

Scotland a few years later.[118] Secondly, beginning in 1615, the new arrivals to Ireland were either Scottish or English planters brought there to colonize Northern Ireland for the English. The plantation was called "Ulster."[119] During the third wave, 1679-1688, most immigrants to Ireland were escaping Scottish "Covenanters."[120] The fourth wave of migration was in the 1690s due to a Scottish famine called the "Seven Ill Years."[121]

## Border Reivers

From the fourteenth to the seventeenth centuries, due to the continual Anglo-Scottish wars, the region near the Scottish-English Border transformed into a frontier of sorts--without law and order. Clan loyalty was paramount, above loyalty to sovereign and country. This was the time of the Border Reivers (Robbers). The continuing threat of conflict offered little incentive to farm.[122]

Ben Johnson writes: "The *reiving* (raiding or plundering) of livestock became the principal business of the Border families... Reiving was simply a way of earning a living, and Scottish Reivers were just as likely to raid other Scots as to raid across the English Border...When England and Scotland were at war, it could become very much a border affair, with Reivers providing large numbers of cavalry. The battles of Otterburn (1388), Flodden Field (1513), and Solway Moss (1542) are all linked with the Reivers."[123]

It was only following the Union between England and Scotland in 1603 that a concerted effort was made by James I (VI of Scotland) to rid the border of Reivers. He also wanted their fertile lands for his friend, the earl of Cumberland.[124] James renamed the Borders 'the Middle Shires.' In 1605, he established a commission to bring law and order to the region. In the first year of the commission's existence, it executed 79 individuals; in the following years, scores more were hanged. Other Reivers were encouraged to leave or serve as mercenaries in the armies of continental Europe. The Border Grahams and some Armstrongs were singled out for special treatment and were banished to Ireland in

---

[118] Lloyd D. Graham, *House Graham, From the Antoine Wall to the Temple of Hymen*, 124-126.
[119] Bruce Orr, "Plantation of Ireland: Part Two 1610-1630," Tartans.com.
[120] Mary McKee, FindmyPastUS, "Ulster and the Scottish Killing Times, When Covenanters Were Hunted and Executed," Irish Central, 21 August 2015. https://www.irishcentral.com/roots/ulster-and-the-scottish-killing-time
[121] Karen J. Cullen, *Famine in Scotland - the "Ill Years" of the 1690s* (Edinburgh: Edinburgh University Press, 2010), 1-9. http://www.jstor.org/stable/10.3366/j.ctt1r279x
[122] Ben Johnson, "The History of the Border Reivers," Historic UK, accessed 30 October 2022. https://www.historic-uk.com/HistoryUK/HistoryofScotland/The-Border-Reivers/
[123] Ben Johnson, "The History of the Border Reivers," Historic UK.
[124] Clan Graham Society, "First Graham of Netherby," accessed 30 October 2022. https://clangrahamsociety.org/the-first-graham-of-netherby/

1606[125]; however, most had returned to Scotland by 1618.[126] See Appendix F, Border Graham Genealogy.

## Scottish Covenanters and the "Killing Time"

During the third migration wave of 1679-1688, most immigrants to Ireland were escaping Scottish "Covenanters," Presbyterian dissenters who refused to sign a pledge acknowledging the king's authority over the Church or swear a loyalty oath to him. The Covenanters were involved in civil unrest and battles with government troops. By 1679, Covenanters were rounded up en masse, tried, and executed—hence the designation "Killing Time"[127] and the stories of "Bluidy Clavers" told in American mountaineer households centuries later. Consequently, many devout Presbyterians fled to Ireland.[128] Scottish genealogist Phil Graham remembers similar "Bluidy Clavers" tales told in Scotland and in Ireland. Knowing that the Grayville Graham ancestors were devoted Presbyterians in America and were close friends of known covenanting families, Minnie Graham Bulls theorized that these Grahams were also Covenanters. After an exhaustive search of FindMyPast's Covenanter database, I could find only one Graham who might possibly fit our family: a James Graham of Moffat, Dumfriesshire, who was indicted in 1683 for harboring accused Covenanters.[129] However, I could not find any other evidence or familiar names among his associates to tie this James to the Grayville Grahams. He may have been a relative.

Conclusion: The more likely scenario to explain how the Grahams who settled in Lancaster County, Pennsylvania became "devout Presbyterians" is that they acquired their Presbyterian religion from their wives. The wife of Christopher Graham, Margaret Florence Risk, is a crucial link.

---

[125] George MacDonald Fraser, *The Steel Bonnets, The Story of the Anglo-Scottish Border Reivers* (New York: Skyhorse Publishing, 2008), 362-364.
https://www.google.com/books/edition/The_Steel_Bonnets/yYWqJF6UyAUC?hl=en&gbpv=1&bsq=commission
[126] R. T. Spence, "The Pacification of the Cumberland Borders, 1593-1628," 121.
[127] James G. Leyburn, *The Scotch-Irish, A Social History*, 125-126, 150.
[128] Michael Montgomery, "Clavers From Ulster to America," Ulster Scots Academy ®, accessed 30 October 2022. http://www.ulsterscotsacademy.com/scotch-irish/futa/clavers.php
[129] FindmyPast.com, *Scottish Covenanters, 1679-1688*, FindMyPast, accessed 15 October 2022. (Requires Account.) https://search.findmypast.com/search-world-records/scottish-covenanters-1679-1688.

## Risk In-Laws

Using colonial land records,[130] and the birth years of her father and husband,[131] we can estimate the birth year in Ireland of Margaret Graham Elliott, the eldest child of Christopher Graham and Margaret Florence Risk. We can estimate Margaret's birth year and therefore her parents' marriage year at about 1695. "Risk" is a rare surname, and "rare" is our friend in genealogy. Searching the entire Covenanter Lists for Risks, we find only four records total:

1. **David Risk of Ballachin Rain; Stirlingshire** who died on 22 June 1699 and was buried in Glasgow. Participated in the rebellion of 8 September 1679.
2. **John Risk of Kilearne Parish** who was indicted 28 April 1683 for actively participating at the rebellion at Bothwellbridge in June 1679
3. **John Risk of Galbraith, Stirlingshire** was indicted in June 1683 for participating in the rebellion and was declared a fugitive.
4. **A Maltman surnamed Riske, believed to be William Riske, of Lanarkshire**. He was indicted in May 1683 for participating in several rebellions. He died in Glasgow on 11 July 1699, 20 days after David Risk above.[132]

There is also a burial record for a weaver, John Risk, who died in Glasgow on 13 Sep 1699. The deaths of three Risks so close together in 1699 imply a connection: perhaps due to Covenanter executions or, more likely, the Scottish famine and associated illness (Seven Ill Years) that began in 1695 and greatly impacted Glasgow in 1698-99.[133]

Given the rarity of the surname Risk, the proximity of these four locations to each other, the tie of the Risk family to the whisky business, and the proximity of these four locations to distilleries or related businesses (e.g., maltman), it appears that these four Risks were related to each other.

There are two Rusk (alternate spelling for Risk) men (William and Robert) found living in Donegal Township, Lancaster County, Pennsylvania, near the Grayville Graham ancestors in the

---

[130] Mary Louise Marshall Hutton, *Seventeenth Century Colonial Ancestors of Members of the National Society Colonial Dames XVII Century, 1915-1975*, Vol. I (Baltimore: Genealogical Publishing Company, 1976), 107. https://www.google.com/books/edition/Seventeenth_Century_Colonial_Ancestors_o/P0FlAAAAMAAJ?hl=en&gbpv=1&bsq=graham

[131] Find a Grave®, "William Elliott Sr. (12 Jul 1699–1795)", Memorial ID 148217913, Tinkling Spring Presbyterian Church Cemetery, Virginia, Maintained by L Evans (contributor 47540766), 23 June 2015. https://www.findagrave.com/memorial/148217913/william-elliott:

[132] FindmyPast.com, *Scottish Covenanters, 1679-1688*, accessed 27 December 2022. (Requires Account.) https://search.findmypast.com/search-world-records/scottish-covenanters-1679-1688

[133] FindmyPast.com, *Scotland Parish Death and Burials, 1564-2017*, FindmyPast-©Glasgow & West of Scotland Family History Society, accessed 27 December 2022. (Requires Account.) https://www.findmypast.com/transcript?id=GBPRS%2FGLASGOW%2FBUR%2F222756

1730s.[134] According to Virginia court and property records, the same Rusks/Risks later followed Christopher Graham's clan to Augusta County, Virginia, (Figure 7) and intermarried with Christopher and Margaret Graham's descendants.[135]

There are few Risks or Rusks in Ireland until later in the eighteenth century. The earliest surviving Irish Risk record I could find is a will abstract in Crosslé for "John Rusk Jr" from "Raratery," Parish Kilmore, County Monaghan, February 1732.[136] Since the Risks were concentrated near Glasgow and western Stirlingshire, that limits the possibilities for Margaret Florence Risk's origins. It is quite possible that Margaret was a daughter of John Risk, the fugitive of Galbraith in Stirlingshire or the John Risk of Kilearne. Both John Risks are the right age to be her father and both fled their homes. Most fugitives headed to Ireland just before the start of the Williamite Wars. Since returning to Scotland at the beginning of the wars in 1689 was not an option, these Risks might have taken refuge in Enniskillen, County Fermanagh, which would explain how a young Margaret Florence Risk would have met Trooper Christopher Graham and how he and his brothers later became devout Presbyterians.

Also of note from the County Monaghan Clones Parish burial registers: that particular register only began in 1682, and there was the four-year gap in records from 1688 to 1692 with the following note after a record from 2 March 1688: "The nineteenth day of this month, the last of the protestant inhabitants deserted the town and the parish of Clownie, the Irish possession themselves of that part of the countrie."[137] As a result of the Williamite Wars that began in 1688; that area was occupied by Jacobite armies. As stated, Protestant farmers/villagers either fled Ireland altogether or headed to the fortress town of Enniskillen in County Fermanagh for protection. There are Grahams in the Clones (County Monaghan) parish records after 1692, but it appears that some stayed in the Enniskillen area after the war.[138] More questions arise regarding the origins of these Irish Grahams. When did they leave Scotland? Where did they initially settle in Ireland? To search for the answers, let's start with the most famous branch of Grahams to be resettled in Ireland in the seventeenth century, the sons of Lang Will Graham and their families.

---

[134] Ancestry.com, *Pennsylvania, U.S., Land Warrants and Applications, 1733-1952,* Ancestry.com Operations, Inc., accessed 27 December 2022. (Requires Account.)
https://www.ancestry.com/search/collections/2350/?name=_rusk&count=50

[135] J.R. Hildebrand, "The Beverley Land Patent, Including Original Grantees, Orange and Augusta Co. VA containing 92,100 Acres, SouthWest Section, 6 November 1736," August 2020.
http://www.usgenwebsites.org/vagenweb/augusta/BeverlyPatent.html

[136] FindmyPast.com, *Index of Irish Wills 1484-1858,* FindmyPast, accessed 27 December 2022. (Requires Account.)
https://www.findmypast.com/transcript?id=IRE%2FENEC001%2F58099

[137] FindmyPast.com, "Clones, Baptisms, marriages & burials, 1682-1907," *ffolliott Parish Registers,* FindmyPast, 494, accessed 27 December 2022. (Requires Account.)
https://search.findmypast.com/record/browse?id=s%2Fire%2Fwaterford%2Fffolliott-registers-30%2f00006

[138] N.F.B., "Ireland's Wars: Enniskilleners," Never Felt Better, Paragraph 3.

## Who Was Lang Will Graham?

Lang Will Graham was born about 1468 in the Dryfe Valley in Dumfriesshire, Scotland and was considered the chief of the Border Grahams. He was also known by the title "Laird of Mosskesswra" and as "William Graham of Stuble." [139] Alternate spellings for "Stuble" are "Stubhill," "Stobohill," and "Stobhill." It turns out there are multiple "Stobohills" or similar names. However, the Stobohill that was the home of Lang Will would have been the one in Hutton and Corrie Parish, as shown in the map in Figure 19.[140]

The referenced Hutton and Corrie lands can be documented in the possession of Lang Will's grandfather, the elder William Graham of Mosskesswra. As detailed in the summary of land charters at the end of Appendix F, in July 1456, the Douglases gave the ancestors of the Border Grahams (William, Robert, Richard, and John Graham) twelve days' notice to prove their claims on certain lands in Hutton, lands the Grahams claimed had been in their family's possession for over 100 years. The Grahams were initially unsuccessful in retaining these lands.[141] "William the Grahame" (grandfather of Lang Will and John Graham of Gillesbie) was probably lobbying the court and all his connections to get his lands back. In May 1463, Euphemia Graham, sister of Malise Graham, Earl of Menteith, resigned some of her estates to trade for the lands of Mosskesswra, Nether (Lower) Dryfe, and Bedokholme in Hutton so they could be granted to "William the Grahame," presumably to return them.[142] See Abbreviated Historical Chronology of the Border Grahams in Appendix F, Border Graham Genealogy. See also Figure F-9, Depiction of Mosskesswra Barony-- the Graham Lands of Superior (Upper) Dryfe and Nether (Lower) Dryfe.

In about 1515, Lang Will lost his lands in Scotland due to a series of court actions, fines, and apprisements (land belonging to debtors sold for the debt's payment). He and his large family left Scotland and resettled near Langtown (Longtown) in England, and per Phil Graham, likely the origin of his nickname "Lang Will."[143] A.W. Cornelius writes:

> William Graham of Stuble is supposed to have come to Arthuret in Cumberland from the Eskside of Dryfesdale...William probably had brothers. He certainly had enough of the same name about him to make the Grahams important early in the sixteenth century. A very full

---

[139] Darrin Lythgoe and Andrew J. MacFarlane, "William 'Lang Will' Graham of Stuble," *Clan MacFarlane and Associated Clans Genealogy*, accessed 27 December 2022. https://www.clanmacfarlanegenealogy.info/genealogy/TNGWebsite/getperson.php?personID=I14769&tree=CC

[140] Charles Adrian Kelham, *Bases of Magnatial Power in Later Fifteenth-Century Scotland* (Edinburgh: University of Edinburgh, 1986), 195. https://www.era.lib.ed.ac.uk/bitstream/1842/6867/1/372968.pdf

[141] R.C. Reid, "The Border Grahams and Their Origins," *Transactions of the Dumfries and Galloway Natural History and Archaeological Society (TDGNHAS)* No. 3038 (1961): 89.

[142] Historical Manuscripts Commission, *The Manuscripts of the Duke of Hamilton, Knight, Eleventh Report, Appendix, Part VI* (London: Her Majesty's Stationery Office, 1887), 18. https://archive.org/details/manuscriptsofduk00greauoft/page/18/mode/2up?ref=ol&view=theater&q=moskeswra

[143] R.C. Reid, "The Border Grahams and Their Origins," 91.

account of his immediate descendants is given us in a report made by Thomas Musgrave in 1583 to Cecil, Lord Burghley. Musgrave is careful not to mention... that he had slaid a grandson of William Graham. This made him anxious to present to the powerful minister of Queen Elizabeth a report hostile to the family who were retaliating on him.[144]

Lang Will was again identified as the clan chief of the Grahams residing at the Scottish-English border by Lord Thomas Scrope of Bolton, the English Warden of the Western March, in a 1583 letter to the same William Cecil, first Baron Burghley (sometimes spelled Burleigh), Chancellor for Elizabeth I. Scrope refers to Will as "William Graham, Laird of Mosskesswra, who had a daughter married to David Graham of Netherby."[145] This David Graham of Netherby was already living in Cumberland before 1515, the year Lang Will and his family arrived in Cumberland. Lang Will may have sought help from his daughter and son-in-law living at Netherby when they first arrived in English territory. David Graham may have also been a distant cousin, a descendant of David Graham of Corbridge d. 1278, Northumberland, brother of Sir Nicholas de Graham of Dalkeith.[146] See Figure 38.

---

[144] A. W. Cornelius, "The Grahams of the Border," *The Scottish Antiquary* or *Northern Notes and Queries 9*, no. 36 (1895): 160–166. https://www.google.com/books/edition/The_Scottish_Antiquary/Zdyk2WG8ILQC?hl=en&gbpv=1&bsq=netherby

[145] R.C. Reid, "The Border Grahams and Their Origins," 105.

[146] Amanda Beam, John Bradley, Dauvit Broun, John Reuben Davies, Matthew Hammond, Neil Jakeman, Michele Pasin and Alice Taylor (with others), *People of Medieval Scotland (PoMS) 1093-1371* (Glasgow and London: 2019), PoMS, "No. 944-David Graham of Corebridge," accessed 31 October 2022. https://www.poms.ac.uk/record/person/944/

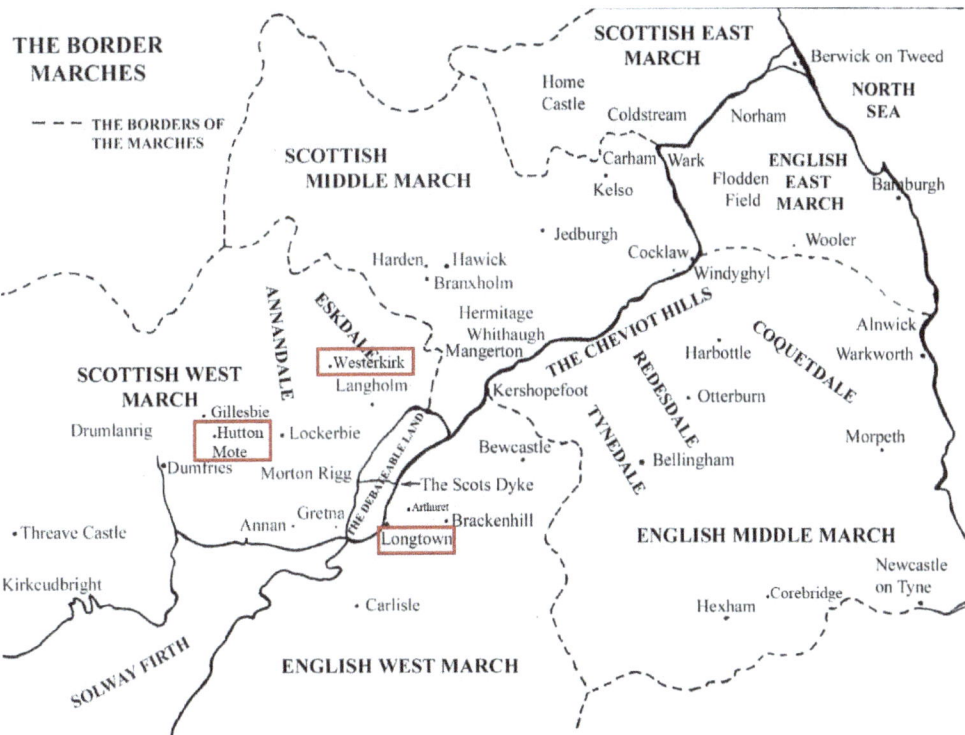

*Figure 17: Map of the Scottish English Border showing divisions into Marches, by Tom Moss. Reproduced here under Creative Commons License BY. With additions.* [147]

## English Graham Origins

It is noteworthy that Sir Nicholas de Graham of Dalkeith and his siblings (Figure 38) all had ties to Northumberland, particularly Tynedale, with the exception of brother Peter, hence the reason there seemed to be Grahams living on the English side of the border assisting Lang Will when he first arrived. The Chronology in Appendix F indicates that Lang Will's family acquired Arthuret in the Debatable Land[148] when Will was still a youth, perhaps from their Northumberland cousins. Apparently, they acquired Netherby via marriage to the previously mentioned David Graham of Netherby.

Lord Burghley writes of the Grahams of Scottish origin in 1596: "William Graham, alias Long Will, banished out of Scotland about 80 yeiris since (circa 1515) came into England and brought with him eight sonnes whom he planted neare the said river of Eske. By this William doe the Earls of Mounteth and Montrose in Scotland claims interest of the service of all Grames as descended out of

---

[147] Figure 17: Tom Moss, "Border-Reivers-March-Wardens-of-the-English-Scottish-Border," *Border Reivers from the 13th to the 17th Centuries*, 26 September 2010. https://wwwborderreiverstories-neblessclem.blogspot.com/2013/01/border-reivers-march-wardens-of-english.html

[148] Tom Moss, "Border-Reivers-March-Wardens-of-the-English-Scottish-Border," *Border Reivers from the 13th to the 17th Centuries*, 26 September 2010. https://wwwborderreiverstories-neblessclem.blogspot.com/2013/01/border-reivers-march-wardens-of-english.html

their houses."¹⁴⁹ In an attempt to make his case against Lang Will's descendants, Lord Thomas Scrope, Warden of the English West March, logged detailed accounts of their crimes from 1595 to 1603. His superior, Lord Burghley exaggerated and used the term "banished" in 1596 to describe the circumstances leading up to Lang Will's departure from Scotland and resettlement in England around 1515, which is inaccurate. His information was based on Scrope's letters and Thomas Musgrave's skewed report. Lord Burghley may have also used the term to help justify the Border Commission's proposal to "banish" Border Grahams in 1605/1606.¹⁵⁰ The records show several successive "apprisements" (foreclosures) of Lang Will's lands to collect fines. Later, in Cumberland, he seems to have held lands from the English Warden free of rent as long as he served English interests.¹⁵¹

In 1537, William was still active enough to act as an assessor for England at an assize in Kirkandrews. He died circa 1540, for in 1537, his son, Arthur Graham, petitioned the English Crown that he and his brothers should have Letters Patent to sit as free (of rent) as their father before them. "Our father, yet alive, has dwelt on Esk for 60 years and till now was never rent demanded of him."¹⁵²

The family's chief seat was Netherby (initially a fortified pele (peel) tower). A. W. Cornelius Hallen wrote in 1895 that by the time he reached old age,

> William Graham, "Lang Willie" as he was usually styled, had eight sons and thirty-three adult grandsons ready to join in the foray. The power of such a family must have been immense. They had, moreover, dependents— illegitimate slips, allies by marriage,— who regarded the Lairds of Netherby and Mote as the chiefs of a band that guarded the west borders from invasion and kept their larders filled with other mens' beeves.¹⁵³

R.C. Reid elaborates: "The Grahams built eight or nine towers impregnable to the power of the Scottish Warden. The present Netherby Hall was built around one of these ancient towers.¹⁵⁴ Their neighbors were forced to take the Graham daughters in marriage without a tocher (dowry),

---

¹⁴⁹ R.C. Reid, "The Border Grahams and Their Origins," 86.

¹⁵⁰ Electric Scotland, "The Great Historic Families of Scotland, The Grahams of Esk, Netherby, and Norton-Conyers," accessed 31 October 2022. https://electricscotland.com/webclans/families/grahams_esk.htm

¹⁵¹ R.C. Reid, "The Border Grahams and Their Origins," 106.

¹⁵² *Letters and Papers, Foreign and Domestic, Henry VIII, Volume 12 Part 1, January-May 1537.* Edited by James Gairdner (London: Her Majesty's Stationery Office 1890), 560, *British History Online*, accessed December 28, 2022. http://www.british-history.ac.uk/letters-papers-hen8/vol12/no1

¹⁵³ A. W. Cornelius Hallen, "The Grahams of the Border," *The Scottish Antiquary, or, Northern Notes and Queries* 9, no. 36 (1895): 166.

¹⁵⁴ Figure 18: William Camden, Christopher Saxton, and William Kip, "Cvmbria sive Cvmberlandia qua olim pars Brigantum," map, [1:234,100 approximately], William Camden's Britain,1637. Retouched and digitized by McMasters University, Hamilton, Ontario, Lloyd Reeds Map Collection. https://dcs1.lib.mcmaster.ca/islandora/object/macrepo%3A24798

which did not increase their popularity. In 1542 the Grahams were not more than 20-30 at most; by 1578, they were 16-18 score (320-360) and well horsed." [155]

*Figure 18: Cumberland Map by Christopher Saxton, 1637, Showing Debatable Lands and Graham Towers Along the River Esk. Provided by Lloyd Reeds Map Collection, McMaster University Library* [154]

The Grahams of Esk and Netherby descend from "Lang Will."[156] According to Lord Burghley's report, by 1516, William Graham the younger ("Lang Will") and his family had initially taken up residence along with six sons and other kinsmen in the "Debatable Land" on the south bank of the Esk River near the Solway Firth. His residences in the Debatable land included the English towns of Arthuret, Netherby, and Longtown.[157] Lang Wills' eight famous sons were: Richard Graham of Netherby, Fergus Graham of Mote, George Graham of the Fauld, Arthur Graham of Canobie, John Graham of Medoppe "the Braid," Thomas Graham of Kirklanders (a.k.a. Kirkandrews-on-Esk), William Graham of Carlisle, and Hutchin Graham of the Guard/Gard. Several of these sons became leaders of the Border Reivers who were accused of cattle and sheep rustling and similar crimes. It was Lang Will Graham's sons, families and tenants who were singled out as the key instigators among

---

[155] R.C. Reid, "The Border Grahams and Their Origins," *Transactions of the Dumfries and Galloway Natural History and Archaeological Society (TDGNHAS)* No. 3038 (1961): 105.

[156] Clan Graham Society, "First Graham of Netherby."

[157] Great Britain, Record Commission, *State papers, published under the authority of His Majesty's Commission: King Henry the Eighth,* Vol. 5 (London: G. Eyre and A. Strahan, printers to the King's Most Excellent Majesty, 1836), 195-196, https://archive.org/details/statepaperspubli05grea/page/194/mode/2up?q=bishop+stewart

Border Reivers and in 1606, as advocated by Lord Burghley, were ordered to be "banished" to Roscommon, Ireland, along with their families. [158]

Dr. Lloyd Graham writes in *House Graham, From the Antoine Wall to the Temple of Hymen*:

> The Grahams were localized on both sides of the Border in the Western March, which was usually more violent than either the Middle or Eastern March. In particular, the families of the eight sons of Long Will Graham (Lang Will of Stuble), were planted in and around the Debatable Land, a region adjacent to the river Esk claimed by both Scotland and England. Seemingly from Dryfesdale in Dumfriesshire, with roots in Mosskesswra or Mosskesso of the same country, he had allegedly dwelt on the Esk since 1477 and his part of the Debatable Land was renewed by Henry VIII in 1538, on the understanding that he and his family would oppose the Scots.[159]

Lang Will's brood was the most famous and best documented of the Border Clans due to the constant trouble they were in with the Scottish Privy Council[160] and the Scottish and English wardens. Lang Will's genealogy is documented in Appendix F. Dr. Graham explains that the Grahams were the largest family on the western border, and played a significant role in a highly organized blackmail industry.[161] One of their best known stunts was the legendary rescue of Kinmont Willie Armstrong. John C. Armstrong describes:[162]

> **Did you know?**
> The Border Grahams were instrumental in the famous prison break of Kinmont Willie Armstrong, immortalized in a ballad called "Kinmont Willie" in the *The Border Minstrelsy* anthology by Sir Walter Scott.

> The perfectly executed prison break on a dark and stormy night has been the source of stories for centuries. Lord Buccleugh, the organizer of the event, candidly admitted in the Border Papers, 1597, that 'I could nought have done that matter

---

[158] J. Bain, *The border papers: Calendar of letters and papers relating to the affairs of the borders of England and Scotland preserved in Her Majesty's Public Record Office*, Vol. I, 1560-1594,Vol. II 1595-1603 (London, Edinburgh: H.M. General Register House, 1894), 123, 124, 135, 136, 142, 176, 177, 270, 751, 778, 779, 807. https://archive.org/details/borderpaperscale02grea/mode/2up?q=burghley

[159] Lloyd D. Graham, *House Graham, From the Antoine Wall to the Temple of Hymen*, USA, 118.

[160] John Hill Burton, David Masson, *The Register of the Privy Council of Scotland.* Edinburgh, First Series (Edinburgh: H.M. General Register House, 1878-1889), Vol. II, 68-69, 538-541; Vol. VII, 726-727; Vol. VIII, 62-63, 138-139, 140-143, 518-519, 704-711; Vol. IX, 808-809. https://catalog.hathitrust.org/Record/100404514

[161] Lloyd D. Graham, *House Graham, From the Antoine Wall to the Temple of Hymen*, 119.

[Did you know? Blurb] Sir Walter Scott, *Minstrelsy of the Scottish Border*, Vol. 1, "Kinmont Willie," (Edinburgh: Longman, Hurst, Bees, Orme and Brown, London: A. Constable and Co. Edinburgh, 1821), 181-211. https://electricscotland.com/history/other/minstrelsyofscot01.pdf

[162] John G. Armstrong, "The Debatable Armstrongs and Their Graham Relations," pdf reprinted by permission of Armstrong Clan Association News (2009), 1-3. https://clangrahamsociety.org/wp-content/uploads/2020/01/TheDebatable-ArmstrongsandtheirGrahamRelations-JohnGArmstrong.pdf

without the great friendship of the Grames of Esk, and specially my guid friend Francie of Canobie, and of his brother, Langton; and of Walter Grame of Netherbye.' [163, 164]

As relations between Scotland and England improved and the countries were joined into the Kingdom of Britain, the need for a buffer zone against the English waned. From Dr. Graham: "The accession of James VI of Scotland as James I of England brought an end to cross-Border rivalries between the two countries... James approved of Lord Burghley's recommendations to pacify a region that was no longer at the fringes of two separate kingdoms but rather at the 'Verie hart of the cuntrey,' took to purging the Borderland of its endemic banditry once and for all." James issued a proclamation in 1605 to expel the troublesome Grames to the Netherlands and then to Ireland in 1606.[165] The "Grames" weren't the only border family being singled out for punishment, a few of their "guid friends," the Armstrongs, were also named in the banishment orders.[166] I believe the Armstrongs, specifically the sons of Colonel William Armstrong, are the key to locating the Scottish patriarch of the Grayville Grahams, who I will argue is John Graham of Gillesbie, brother of Lang Will. My investigation is centered around a famous story about a tower.

> **Did you know?**
> Colonel Will Armstrong, supported Charles II, as did his boss, Lord Traquair, in the English Civil Wars (1642-1646). Colonel Armstrong was assumed killed in battle in Scotland. The name Christopher is common to this Armstrong line, supporting the belief that Trooper Christopher Graham, who arrived in America in 1720, was a descendant of "Christie's Will."

## Tower of Grame

Sir Walter Scott's story of Colonel Armstrong, a.k.a "Christie's Will," and the "deserted Tower of Grame" is an important link between both families. Side note on watch towers: rivers were a way for invading forces to quickly travel, therefore the Mosskesswra (Moskesso, Moskessen) barony would have had a watch tower [167] along the primary river, the Dryfe Water. This was a system inherited from the Romans who built Hadrian's Wall in the Borders Region.[168] The tower's primary purpose would be to provide a high, safe place from which a sentinel could observe the surrounding area.[169]

---

[163] John G. Armstrong, "The Debatable Armstrongs and Their Graham Relations," 3.
[164] J. Bain, *The Border Papers: Calendar of letters and papers relating to the affairs of the borders of England and Scotland preserved in Her Majesty's Public Record Office*, Vol. I, 1560-1594, Vol. II 1595-1603 (Edinburgh: H. M. General Register House, 1894, 1896), 367. https://archive.org/details/borderpaperscale02grea/mode/2up?q=burghley
[Did you know blurb] James Lewis Armstrong, M.D., *Chronicles of the Armstrongs,* 309-320.
[165] Lloyd D. Graham, *House Graham, From the Antoine Wall to the Temple of Hymen,*. 124-125.
[166] J. Bain, *The Border Papers: Calendar of letters and papers relating to the affairs of the borders of England and Scotland preserved in Her Majesty's Public Record Office*, Vol. I, Vol. II 1595-1603 (London, Edinburgh: H.M. General Register House, 1894), 826-827. https://archive.org/details/borderpaperscale02grea/mode/2up?q=burghley
[167] Castle Architecture-Towers, "Watchtowers (Guettes)," Castles and Manor Houses Around the World, accessed 23 January 2023. https://www.castlesandmanorhouses.com/architecture_02_towers.htm
[168] David J. Breeze and Sonja Jilek, *Frontiers of the Roman Empire* (Edinburgh: Historic Scotland, 2008), 68-69. https://limes.univie.ac.at//FRE_DOWNLOADS/FRE_The_European_Dimension.pdf
[169] Castle Architecture-Towers, "Watchtowers (Guettes)," Castles and Manor Houses Around the World, accessed 23 January 2023.

Sometime in the sixteenth century, the Grahams of Gillesbie replaced the Mosskesswra tower with the Gillesbie tower in blue, as shown in Figure 19.

The abandonment of the Gillesbie Graham tower is significant to our timeline,[170] because of the tradition recited by locals centuries later that the departure of the Gillesbie Grahams for Ireland coincided with the desertion of their tower. This can help us estimate the arrival timeframe in Ireland of not only the Gillesbie Grahams but the Armstrongs. We know that soon after Colonel William Armstrong's adult sons left for Ireland, he imprisoned a judge named Lord Durie in the "deserted Tower of Grame." While he never followed his sons to Ireland, "Christie's Will" lived on through his descendants, one of whom may have been Trooper Christopher Graham (1670-1746).

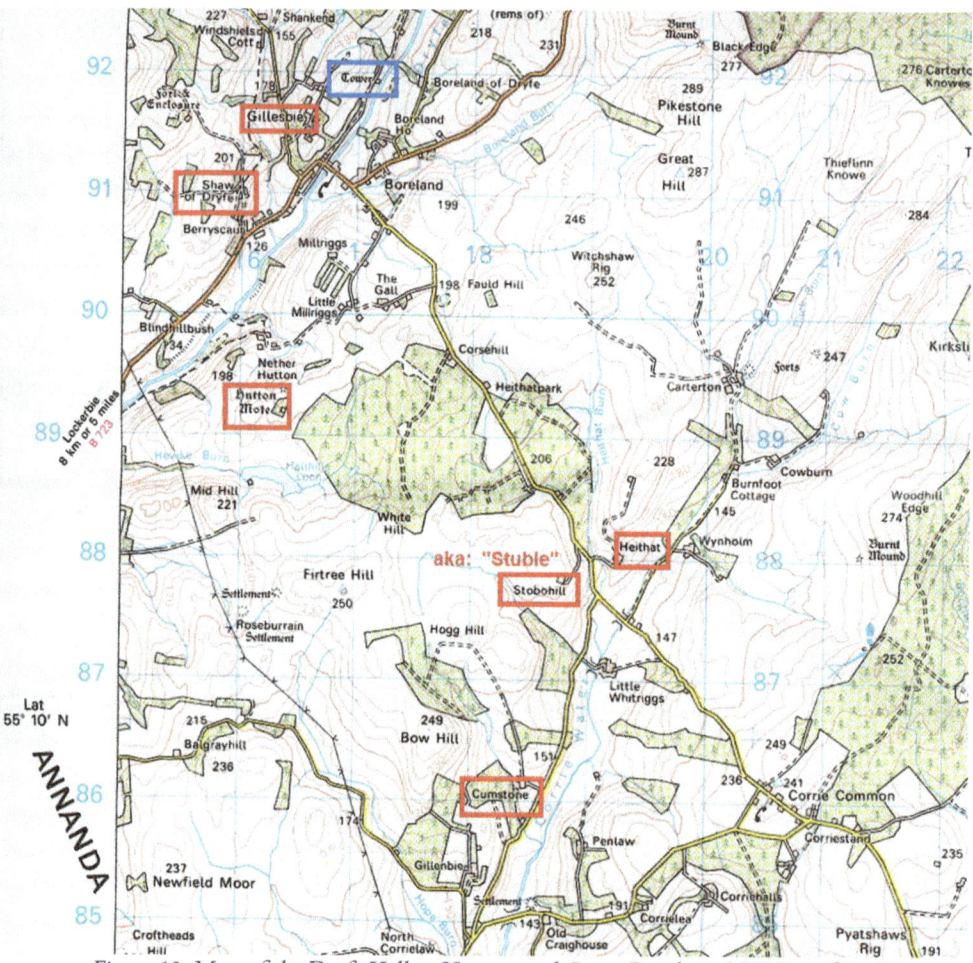

Figure 19: Map of the Dryfe Valley, Hutton and Corry Parish, in NW Dumfriesshire, Scotland; Ordnance Survey (map GB.) Landranger Series SCALE OF 1; 50 000, SHEET NO 79 HAWICK & ESKDALE (LANGHOLM) Ordnance Survey licence number 100066333. All rights reserved. © Copyright and database right 2022.

---

[170] Ancient Monuments, "Gillesbie Tower in Annandale North and Dumfries and Galloway," ID: SM10433.

**The Armstrongs of Macguiresbridge in County Fermanagh, Ireland,** are descendants of the famous Colonel William Armstrong of Langholm, Scotland, as are Captain Martin Armstrong and his brother Cornet Robert Armstrong who served in the same Enniskillen Troop of Horse[171] as Christopher Graham (1670-1746). Given the documented pedigree of this branch of the Armstrongs and their origins in Langholm, Scotland, they are a significant clue to determining our Grahams' origins in Scotland. I believe that the patriarch of the Grayville Grahams, a Gillesbie Graham, moved from Scotland to County Fermanagh, Ireland with the Langholm Armstrongs. This belief is based on military records, naming patterns, geographic proximity, and Y-DNA. Y-DNA, or analysis of the male chromosome, is useful as it can help find ancestors as far back as they have been keeping records (1,000 or more years ago).[172] The closest Y-DNA match to the Grayville Graham test subjects (Barry and Ron Graham), who is from Canada, and whose ancestors trace to Westerkirk and Langholm in the eighteenth century, has several Langholm Armstrongs in his tree. He also has a number of James, John, Robert and William Grahams and one Christopher Graham.

We can initially estimate that Captain Edward Armstrong, son of Colonel William Armstrong, and family settled on estates in Brookeborough, and Macguiresbridge, County Fermanagh, Ireland, sometime after the Irish Muster Roll of 1629 and before 1642.[173] His grave and the graves of his children, grandchildren, brother Alexander and a few Grahams, are clustered together in a churchyard in Agahvea, a mile from Brookeborough.[174] Macguiresbridge and Brookeborough are located in the Townland of Drumgoon.[175] Just south of Macguiresbridge is the Graham estate of Drumgoon. The coat of arms of the Grahams of Drumgoon includes the traditional Graham escallops but also the strong "arm bendy" borrowed from the Armstrong armorials (Figure 20).[176]

*Figure 20: Armorial of the Grahams of Drumgoon, Ireland, By SurnameCoatsofArms.uk* [176]

Colonel William Armstrong was known as "Christy's Will" as he was the son of Christopher Armstrong of Barnegleish the younger and Catherine Graham (granddaughter of Thomas Graham of Kirklanders, great-granddaughter of Lang Will). See Figure 21. Colonel Armstrong's role in the kidnapping of Lord Durie, a judge of the Court

---

[171] James Lewis Armstrong, M.D., *Chronicles of the Armstrongs*, 317.

[172] Family Tree DNA (FTDNA), "Your DNA Guide, Which Y-DNA Test is Best?" accessed 1 November 2022. https://www.yourdnaguide.com/ydna#:~:text=YDNA%20is%20the%20DNA%20inherited,back%20than%20autosomal%20DNA%20tests.

[173] James Lewis Armstrong, M.D., *Chronicles of the Armstrongs*, 317-320, 309-310.

[174] Noel Macguire, "Inscriptions from Aghavea, Co. Fermanagh," Clogher Record, Vol. IV, No. 1 and 2 (1960): 105. https://doi.org/10.2307/27695508 . James Graham, who died in 1717 and was buried in Aghavea.

[175] "Ireland," GENUKI, accessed 31 December 2022. https://www.genuki.org.uk/big/irl

[176] Figure 20: SurnameCoatsofArms.UK, "Graham (Ireland) Coat of Arms (Family Crest)," accessed 25 December 2022. https://surnamecoatsofarms.uk/shop/?s=graham

of Session, who was about to rule against his superior Lord Traquair, in 1642/43,[177] was made famous by Sir Walter Scott in the ballad "Christie's Will" from *The Minstrelsy of the Border* anthology.[178] Colonel Armstrong kept Lord Durie hostage for three months in the "deserted Tower of Grame" on the waters of the Dryfe (Figure 19). Tradition holds that this deserted tower was the Tower of the Gillesbie Grahams.[179] The desertion of this tower along with the incident with the judge, are fairly well documented events for the time and allow us to conclude the Gillesbie Grahams and the colonel's sons departed Scotland before 1642.

**The Gillesbie Grahams** were descendants of John Graham of Gillesbie and Brackenwra, brother to Lang Will, who first appear on record in 1470.[180] The Gillesbie Grahams are later mentioned in legal documents in 1480, 1508, and 1515 where John Graham of Gillesbie was charged, along with his brother, of ingathering and failing to distribute the "teinds" (tithes)[181] to the local vicarage.[182] However, it seems John and his family were not financially ruined by the ruling and subsequent fines like his brother's clan was, for, in 1541, there is a record of a James Graham of Gillesbie AND Mosskesswra, with forty retainers at the Wapenshaw (muster roll gathering and weapons inspection) at Burnswark. In 1567, James' son John Graham of Gillesbie was granted additional lands in that area called Heithat (Figure 19) and Branriggs. In 1579 and 1618, a John Graham of Gillesbie is named among other Border lairds.[183] Robert Graham of Gillesbie acted as a cautioner (cosigned a loan) for a bond for the minister of Hutton in 1624, and James Graham of Gillesbie also acted as a cautioner in December 1635.[184] Then there is a 33-year gap before we can find any evidence of a Gillesbie Graham in Scotland. I believe that is because the laird of Gillesbie, possibly the James Graham who acted as a cautioner in 1635, and his family left Scotland after 1635.

---

[177] John G. Armstrong, "The Debatable Armstrongs and Their Graham Relations," 3.

[178] Sir Walter Scott, *The Poetical Works of Sir Walter Scott* (Philadelphia: E. L. Carey and A. Hart, 1839), 192-194. https://www.google.com/books/edition/The_Poetical_Works_of_Sir_Walter_Scott_C/Ni9DAQAAMAAJ?hl=en&gbpv=1&dq=scott+of+hutton+moffat+scotland&pg=PA192&printsec=frontcover

[179] Col. William Rogerson, *Hutton Under the Muir* (Dumfries, Scotland: Dumfries and Galloway Courier and Herald, 1908), 26-28, 39.
https://www.google.com/books/edition/Hutton_under_the_muir_notes_on_the_past/BiwVAAAAQAAJ?hl=en&gbpv=1&bsq=gillesbie

[180] *Registrum Honoris de Morton, Volume II: Ancient Charters* (Edinburgh: The Bannatyne Club, 1858), 216-217. https://archive.org/details/registrumhonoris02bann/page/n3/mode/2up?ref=ol&view=theater

[181] Scottish Archive Network, "teinds," Research Tools, accessed 7 January 2023. https://www.scan.org.uk/researchrtools/glossary_t.htm

[182] R.C. Reid, "The Border Grahams and Their Origins," 93.

[183] Col. William Rogerson, *Hutton Under the Muir*, 25, 26, 31.

[184] R.C. Reid, "The Border Grahams and Their Origins," 93-94.

The 1908 book, *Hutton Under the Muir* by Colonel William Rogerson of Gillesbie, provides a possible reason for this 33-year "record gap." He writes: "A tradition may be given in the words of an ancient servitor of Shaw: 'the lairds of Gillesbie and Shaw were related; they met on the Winshields bog and quarreled, one had on his armour and killed the other and fled the country.'" Colonel Rogerson further reports from an interview with a local Graham that the Graham tower of Gillesbie[185] ceased to be inhabited "about 1641." [186] Coincidentally, Colonel Armstrong's adult sons, Captain Edward, Alexander and John, also left for County Fermanagh, Ireland, around 1641.[187] The timing of the departure of the Grahams of Gillesbie and Armstrongs of Langholm from Scotland overlapping, and given their close association in Ireland, suggests the two groups departed for Ireland together. The families intermarried in Ireland, but also in Scotland. Why did Colonel Armstrong feel secure in using the abandoned Tower of Grame for such a risky mission unless he knew the owners very well?

It appears the remaining Grahams in the Dryfe area after 1641 clustered further south: in Shaw, Millriggs, Cumstoun, and near the tower at Hewke Burn, Figure 19, implying in the referenced battle between the lairds of Gillesbie and Shaw, that it was the laird of Shaw who was killed and it was the laird of Gillesbie who fled the country with much of his clan. [188]

There was at least one Gillesbie Graham who remained behind in Scotland. In October 1668, John Graham of Gillesbie was the grantor of a bond (mortgage) on his lands,[189] and again in March of 1669, John Graham and his wife Margaret Scott granted another bond and a tack, which allowed a renter to take possession of said lands for a set rent.[190] In October of 1670, John granted a third bond on his lands, suggesting he was heavily in debt.[191] By 1699, the Gillesbie estate was owned by Robert Scott of Coshogle, brother to Francis Scott of

> **Did you know?**
> A bond was equivalent to a second mortgage. A tack was a lease with subleasing privileges. Specifically, it was a contract between a proprietor and a tenant (or 'tacksman') in which the tacksman could enjoy possession of the proprietor's land for a certain time on payment of a set rent. The grantee could transmit his right to a third party, which was done by means of an assignation.

---

[185] Ancient Monuments, "Gillesbie Tower in Annandale North and Dumfries and Galloway," ID: SM10433, accessed 15 October 2022. https://ancientmonuments.uk/123372-gillesbie-tower-annandale-north-ward#.Y0dVzXbMJPa

[186] Col. William Rogerson, *Hutton Under the Muir*, 26.

[187] James Lewis Armstrong, M.D., *Chronicles of the Armstrongs*,. 317-320, 309-310.

[188] Edward Aglionby, "The Aglionby Platt of the Opposite Border of Scotland to Ye West Marches," Dec 1590, Gatehouse Gazetteer, accessed 27 December 2022. http://www.gatehouse-gazetteer.info/APHome.html

[189] Scottish Record Office, *Index to Register of Deeds, 1668,* Vol. VIII (Edinburgh: His Majesty's Stationery Office, 1924), 181. https://www.google.com/books/edition/Indexes/6ISQFt6Y5ekC?hl=en&gbpv=1&bsq=%20gillesbie

[Did you know blurb] "bond," and "tack," Research Tools, *Scottish Archive Network*, accessed 7 January 2023. https://www.scan.org.uk/researchrtools/glossary_t.htm

[190] Scottish Record Office, *Index to Register of Deeds, 1669,* Vol. IX (Edinburgh: His Majesty's Stationery Office, 1926), 177. https://www.google.com/books/edition/Index_to_Register_of_Deeds_Preserved_in/C8wRAAAAIAAJ?hl=en&gbpv=1&bsq=graham

[191] Scottish Record Office, *Index to Register of Deeds, 1670,* Vol. X (Edinburgh: His Majesty's Stationery Office, 1926), 170. https://www.google.com/books/edition/Index_to_Register_of_Deeds_Preserved_in/vsQRAAAAIAAJ?hl=en&gbpv=1

Gilmanschleuch.¹⁹² John's Scott in-laws likely were the ones who held the bonds on the Gillesbie land and apparently took possession of Gillesbie between 1670 and 1699. I suspect this last known Gillesbie Graham in Scotland, John Graham of Gillesbie and his wife Margaret Scott, may have been the ancestors of the Canadian Y-DNA cousin of the Grayville Grahams. Their Canadian cousin's oldest known ancestors lived in Parishes: Hutton and Corrie, Westerkirk and Langholm, Scotland in the mid-late 18th century.

Comparing ages/historical dates and the closeness (genetic distance) of the Canadian match of the Grayville Grahams, as detailed in the Y-DNA chapter, indicate their common ancestor was born approximately between 1550 and 1580 (about thirteen generations ago).¹⁹³ Therefore, it would have been the paternal grandfather (generation 12) of the American immigrant brothers, Christopher, James, John, and William* Graham (generation 10), who left Scotland for Ireland presumably with Captain Edward Armstrong and brothers John and Alexander.¹⁹⁴ The Graham brothers' grandfather would have been born in the early 1600s, and could have joined the other Gillesbie Grahams and Armstrongs headed for Ireland circa 1641. See notional pedigree in Figure 22. Based on Irish records consolidated in FindmyPast, and per the Scottish naming pattern, there are four strong candidate fathers/uncles (generation 11) of the Graham immigrant brothers: Christopher Graham (1670-1746), James Graham Sr. (1683-1745), John Graham (1674-1743), and William* (1683-aft. 1729) in County Fermanagh whose birth years are projected to be 1630-1644:

1. James Graham, d. 1717, buried in Armstrong family crypt in Agahvea, a mile from Brooksboro, County Fermanagh.¹⁹⁵
2. William Graham, d.1715, of Tullingoga, near Ederney and Carn and the Armstrong Terwinney estate all in Parish Magheraculmoney, County Fermanagh. His heir is his grandson, Robert Armstrong.¹⁹⁶
3. Christopher Graham of DerryInch, Parish Trory, County Fermanagh, d. 1691.¹⁹⁷ His descendants use the Christopher-James-John-William naming pattern.

---

¹⁹² R.C. Reid, "The Border Grahams and Their Origins," 94.

¹⁹³ FamilyTreeDNA, "If two men share a surname, how should the genetic distance at 111 Y-chromosome STR markers be interpreted?" 5 Genetic Distance (GD), FTDNA Help Center, accessed 1 November 2022. https://learn.familytreedna.com/y-dna-testing/y-str/two-men-share-surname-genetic-distance-111-y-chromosome-str-markers-interpreted/#:~:text=A%20111%2F111%20match%20indicates,two%20generations%20(1st%20cousins).&text=A%20110%2F111%20match%20indicates,are%202nd%20cousins%20or%20closer

¹⁹⁴ James Lewis Armstrong, M.D., *Chronicles of the Armstrongs*, 362.

¹⁹⁵ Noel Macguire, "Inscriptions from Aghavea, Co. Fermanagh," 105.

¹⁹⁶ FindmyPast.com, "Armstrong envelope, Clogher Gt Book, 1712-1733," *Crosslé Genealogical Abstracts*, FindmyPast, Item 84, accessed 27 December 2022. (Requires Account.) https://search.findmypast.com/record/browse?id=s2%2fire%2fnai%2f007634816%2f00334

¹⁹⁷ FamilySearch, *Ireland, Diocesan and Prerogative Wills & Administrations Indexes, 1595-1858*, images digitized by FamilySearch, National Archives of Ireland, Dublin (19 December 2019): 133. (Requires Account.) https://familysearch.org/ark:/61903/1:1:WGHS-J5T2

4. John Graham, d. 1703, County Fermanagh[198]

There are few Grahams in County Fermanagh in the late 1600s, and, given their similar ages, naming pattern (Christopher-James-John-William), and connections to the Armstrongs, these four candidates could be brothers. They are too young to be the generation who migrated to Ireland circa 1641 (generation 12). They would have been born in Ireland or were young children when their parents left Scotland. Of the four candidates listed above: the John Graham, who died in 1703, is the best fit to be the father (generation 11) of the four brothers who left Ireland for Pennsylvania in 1720, as the other three candidates and families are accounted for after 1720. In addition, the aforementioned American brothers Christopher, James, John, and William (generation 10) all named their eldest sons "John," indicating their father (generation 11) was also named "John." Their grandfather (generation 12) would have been born around 1600-1610 (which lines up with the Y-DNA analysis—a generation after the common ancestor who was born circa 1580) and, therefore, the right age to marry a sister of Colonel William Armstrong. A grandmother who was a sister of Colonel William Armstrong and/or a mother who was also an Armstrong, would explain the familial connection of young Trooper Christopher Graham (b. 1670) to his commanding officer, Captain Martin Armstrong,[199] and Martin's brother, Cornet Robert Armstrong.[200] Martin and Robert were nephews of Captain Edward Armstrong and grandsons of Colonel William Armstrong.[201]

## Graham-Armstrong History and Key Marriages

Previously, in the sixteenth century, several key marriages between the Armstrongs and Grahams were arranged to quell an old (sixteenth century) feud between the Grahams and Armstrongs living on the Scottish-English border. The scheme was successful, as later generations of Border Grahams and Armstrongs were closely allied, such as the previously mentioned Drumgoon Grahams and the Macguiresbridge Armstrongs, in County Fermanagh. From the Armstrong-Graham

---

[198] FindmyPast.com, *Diocesan and Prerogative Wills & Administrations Indexes, 1595-1858*, images digitized by FamilySearch, National Archives of Ireland, accessed 27 December 2022. (Requires Account.) https://search.findmypast.com/record?id=IRE%2FDIOC%2F007246604%2F00133&parentid=IRE%2FDIOC%2FWILL%2F00100924

[199] FindmyPast.com, "Beatty notebooks, v. 6-12," *Crosslé Genealogical Abstracts, 1620-1850*, FindmyPast, 240, accessed 27 December 2022. (Requires Account.) https://search.findmypast.com/record?id=S2%2FIRE%2FNAI%2F007634818%2F00600&parentid=IRE%2FNAI%2FGENABS%2F00602219%2F1

[200] FindmyPast.com, "Beatty notebooks, v. 6-12," *Crosslé Genealogical Abstracts, 1620-1850,* accessed 27 December 2022. (Requires Account.) https://search.findmypast.com/record?id=S2%2FIRE%2FNAI%2F007634818%2F00600&parentid=IRE%2FNAI%2FGENABS%2F00602219%2F1

[201] James Lewis Armstrong, M.D. *Chronicles of the Armstrongs,*. 345, 362.

marriages[202] summarized in "The Debatable Armstrongs and Their Graham Relations" by John C. Armstrong (Figure 21), we can systematically review potential candidates to be ancestors of the Grayville Grahams --or rule them out. We can also deduce a few more key marriages to help in our investigation.

1. Lang Will Graham's wife was named Helen. The discovery in the rare surviving fragments of a Church of Arthuret baptismal book names Helen, mother of Richard Graham of Netherby, as godparent to Sandy Armstrong. William and Helen named one of their older sons "Thomas." That, and being a godmother to Sandy Armstrong implies Helen was a Mangerton Armstrong.[203]
2. Richard of Netherby's wife was named Isabel/Isabella. Isabel served as godmother to Sandy Armstrong's son Herbert, also implying she was an Armstrong. Like his father, Herbert was baptized at Arthuret Church.[204] Some genealogies record that Isabella was buried in "Luss." Phil Graham, who has been studying this family for years, suspects this refers to Luce Church in Hoddom, now a defunct church, not the Luss in Dunbartonshire.
3. Richard's son, William of Mylees, married a daughter of Mangerton. After his first wife died, he married Robin Elliott.[205] I suspect William and Robin's son, Robert of Mylees, is the same Robert Graham who moved to Aghamore, County Fermanagh, Ireland, between 1615-1629. His older half-brothers were named in his father's will.[206] William of Mylees (Millees) had at least thirteen sons by two wives,[207] so not surprising that there weren't enough lands for all of them and the younger sons left to find their fortunes elsewhere. The Ulster Plantation offered a way to get access to fertile farm land.

---

[202] Author's note—When Christopher Armstrong of Barngleisch, a.k.a. "John's Christie," was born in 1526 in Dumfriesshire, Scotland, his father, Sir John Armstrong of Gilknockie, was 46, and his mother, Lady Elizabeth Graham of Montrose, was 31. Christopher married Catherine Graham of Gorthe about 1551 in Langholm, Dumfriesshire, Scotland. They were the parents of at least eight sons. He died on 22 September 1606 in Langholm at the age of 80. Christopher Armstrong (1526-1606)," FamilySearch, accessed 2 January 2023. (Requires Account.)
https://ancestors.familysearch.org/en/M4CK-C8X/sir-john-christopher-armstrong-1526-1606
–A son of George Graham of the Fauld married a daughter of Harelaw Armstrong.
–A grandson of this same George Graham of the Fauld married a daughter of the Armstrong Laird of Whitlaugh.
–Lady Elizabeth Graham of Montrose married John Armstrong of Gilnockie circa 1510 (the same one who was executed along with his entourage by the teenage James V.
–Their grandson, Christopher Armstrong of Barnegleisch, married Gorthes Catherine Graham, daughter of George Graham, granddaughter of Thomas Graham of Kirklanders (a.k.a. Kirkandrews-on-Esk)
–Marie Graham of Netherby married John Armstrong of the Hollows. From the Phils Netherby booklet, there were marriages between Netherbys and Armstrongs of the Hollows.
–Kinmount Willie married a daughter of Hutchin Graham.
–William Graham of Mylees' son, Fergus, married a daughter of Kinmount Willie Armstrong
–A daughter of Fergus of the Mote married an Armstrong of Cafell.
–Arthur Graham of Canobie married an Armstrong of Mangerton
[203] R. T. Spence, "The Pacification of the Cumberland Borders, 1593-1628," 82.
[204] R. T. Spence, "The Pacification of the Cumberland Borders, 1593-1628," 81-84.
[205] A. W. Cornelius Hallen, "The Grahams of the Border," 162.
[206] R. T. Spence, "The Pacification of the Cumberland Borders, 1593-1628," 81-84.
[207] A. W. Cornelius Hallen, "The Grahams of the Border," 162.

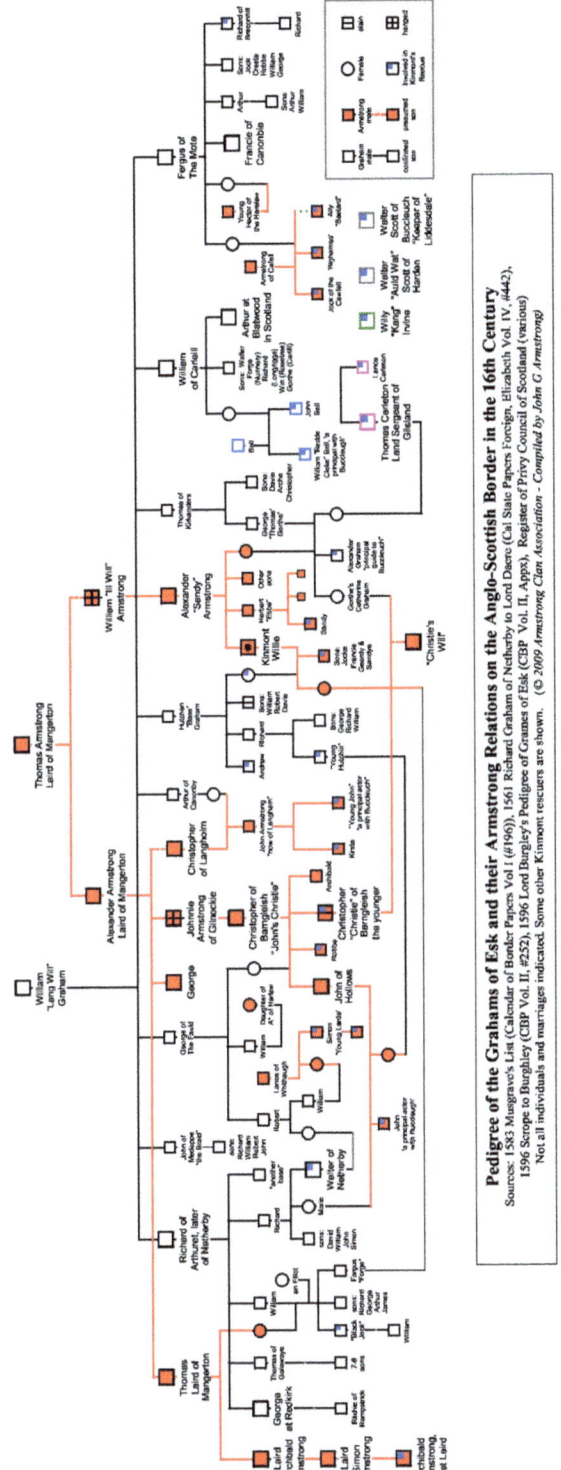

*Figure 21: Pedigree of the Grahams of Esk and Their Armstrong Relations-by John C. Armstrong. John G. Armstrong, "The Debatable Armstrongs and Their Graham Relations," 3.*

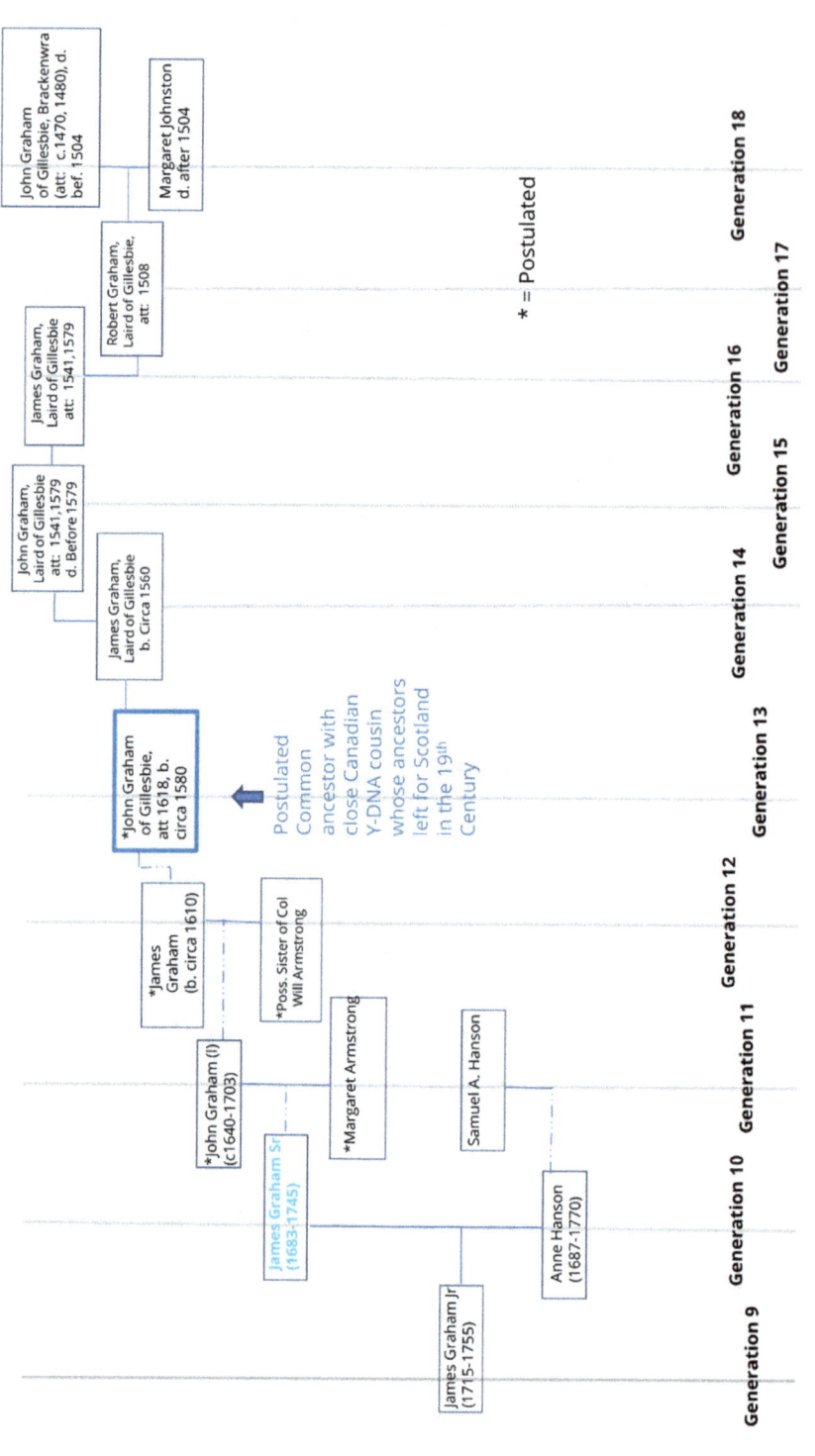

Figure 22: Notional Paternal Pedigree of James Graham Jr. to John Graham of Gillesbie and Brackenwra, Brother of Lang Will Graham of Stuble

## Back to the Present, and The Grayville Grahams

Figure 22 shows a notional pedigree of the Grayville, Illinois Grahams. It starts with James Graham Jr. (generation 9) then to James Graham Sr. (generation 10) to James' postulated father (generation 11), the John Grahame who died in County Fermanagh in 1703, and ultimately to John Graham of Gillesbie, Brackenwra, in Hutton, (generation 18) att (attestation date -the first proof of John's existence): 1470, who was a brother of Lang Will Graham, chief of the Border Grahams. Y-DNA results are consistent with this pedigree. See Appendix C, Table C-1. They indicate that suspected Lang Will Graham descendants are more distant matches to the Grayville Grahams than descendants of John of Gillesbie. As more men participate in Y-DNA testing, new results may require a reassessment of this pedigree.

The unique naming pattern is also explained: Christopher, James, and William are Armstrong names. John, James, and Robert are names of Gillesbie Graham lairds from 1470 to 1635. "James Graham" is found in the seventeenth century records of the Shaw Grahams, a cadet[208] of the Gillesbie Grahams.[209] "Kirstie" (a nickname for Christopher) Grahams are found among the Grahams of Millriggs, descendants of the first John Graham of Gillesbie[210] (see map in Figure 19 and records the Chronology in Appendix F). The Armstrongs of Mangerton were the progenitors of the Armstrongs of Macguirebridge, Ireland, and the Armstrongs of Langholm, Scotland.[211] The closest Y-DNA match to the Grayville Grahams from Canada has ties to Langholm, Scotland, as his oldest ancestors are from Langholm and Westerkirk, Scotland, in the eighteenth century.

---

[208] In heraldry and history, a cadet branch consists of the male-line descendants of a patriarch's younger sons (cadets).
[209] Col. William Rogerson, *Hutton Under the Muir*, 26.
[210] Scotland, *The Register of the Privy Council of Scotland*. (Edinburgh: H.M. General Register House, 1877), First Series, Vol. 9, 712-713, 808-809. https://catalog.hathitrust.org/Record/100404514 [Grahams of Millriggs]
[211] James Lewis Armstrong, M.D. *Chronicles of the Armstrongs*, 317-320, 309-310.

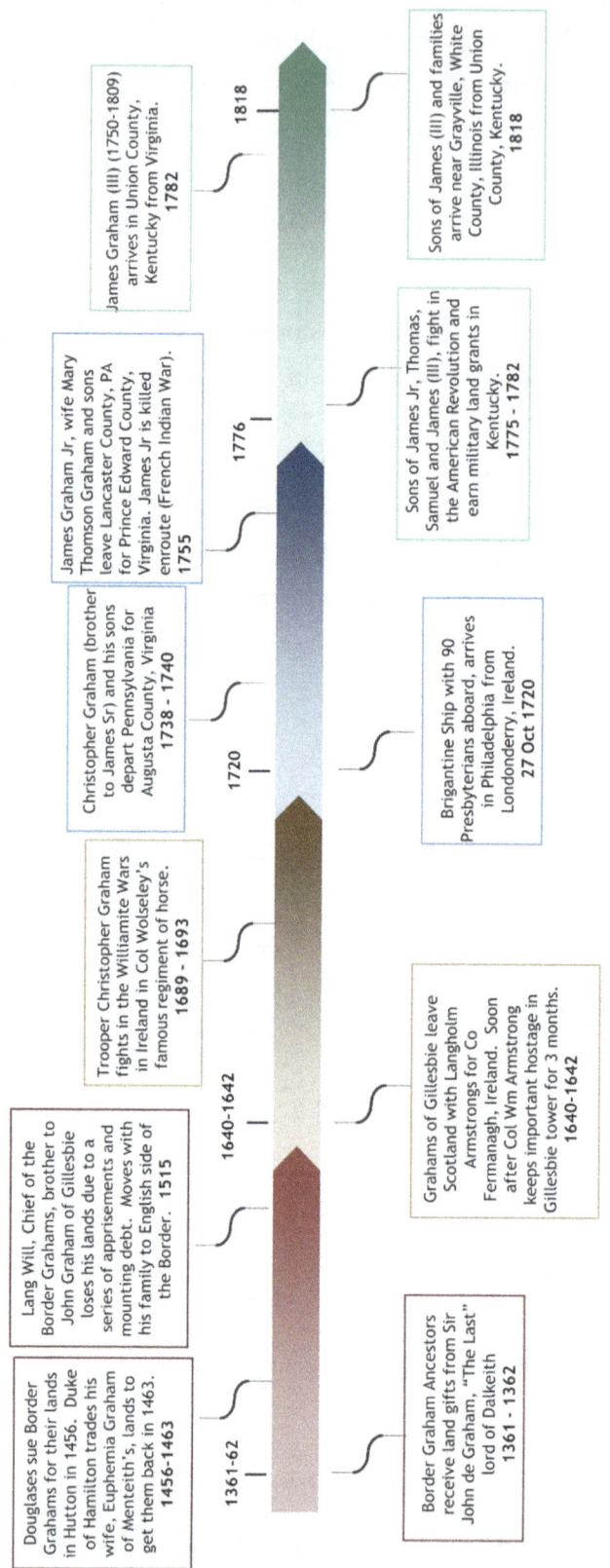

Figure 23: *Timeline from the Beginnings of the Border Grahams to the Arrival of their Descendants in Grayville, Illinois in 1818*

# Chapter 4
# Scotland[v]
# Early Scottish History (Going Way Back and Working our Way Forward)

## Church History

Because the churches played a pivotal role in government and were major landowners in medieval times, it is crucial to understand their history and the saints relevant to Graham family history. Many early Grahams were senior churchmen, Chancellors, and Chamberlains of church properties, beginning with the Christian Culdee churches and then transitioning to the Roman Catholic churches after the Normans arrived in Scotland. Appendix D includes a primer on both Culdee Christian and Roman Catholic saints.

The **Culdees** (Irish: *Céilí Dé*, lit. "Spouses of God") were members of Christian monastic communities of Ireland, Scotland, Wales, and England in the Middle Ages. Church and university scholars suspect their theology was derived from teachings and customs of missionaries of the Coptic Church.[212] These missionaries may have arrived in Ireland as early as 400 A.D. Coptic Church documents state their church was founded in Egypt in the first century A.D. by St. Mark, the gospel writer.[213] Along those lines, one saint important to the Culdees was Saint Catherine of Alexandria, Egypt.[214]

Another major Culdee saint was Saint Patrick, missionary to and patron saint of Ireland.[215] Dumbarton, Scotland, is a claimant as the birthplace of St. Patrick.[216] Church historians note the irony that the patron saint of

---

[212] Geoffrey Saxby, Swinburne University of Technology, "The Celts and Copts and St. Anthony, Notes on pre-Augustine Coptic and Celtic churches," ResearchGate, October 2020, 1-2. https://www.researchgate.net/publication/344691781_The_Celts_and_Copts_and_St_Anthony_-_Notes_on_pre-Augustine_Coptic_and_Celtic_churches

[213] Seraphim Abba, "On the Trail of Seven Coptic Monks in Ireland," The British Orthodox Church, accessed 28 December 2022. https://britishorthodox.org/miscellaneous/on-the-trail-of-seven-coptic-monks-in-ireland/

[214] Geoffrey Saxby, Swinburne University of Technology, "The Celts and Copts and St. Anthony, Notes on pre-Augustine Coptic and Celtic churches," 2.

[215] Thomas McLaughlan, *The Early Scottish Church from the First to the Twelfth Century* (Edinburgh: 1865), 95. https://archive.org/details/earlyscottishchu00macl

[216] Archibald B. Scott, *The Pictish Nation, Its People and Its Church* (Edinburgh and London: T.N Foulis, 1918), 24. https://archive.org/details/pictishnationits00scotrich/page/24/mode/2up

Ireland was a Scotsman (St. Patrick) while the first patron saint of Scotland was an Irishman (St. Kessog).[217] When the Catholic church was established in Rome, the Coptics in Egypt and Culdees in Ireland and Scotland were unaffected until hundreds of years later. In Scotland, Culdees were more numerous than in Ireland: they controlled thirteen monastic establishments, eight in connection with cathedrals.[218] Roman Catholicism arrived in Scotland with the Normans in the early twelfth century. It was not, however, until 1250 A.D. that Scotland officially converted from Culdeeism to Roman Catholicism.[219]

Connections of Graham families to many former Culdee Church lands (e.g., St. Patrick, St. Kessog) indicate that their ancestors had leadership roles in the Culdee church, mainly as caretakers of the pastoral staff called "custodiers." **They made the lands hereditary in their families, and exercised jurisdiction over the ancient sanctuary boundaries.**[220] To play important roles in the Culdee church indicates those families were in Scotland before the arrival of the Normans in 1124. The Normans were devout Roman Catholics, and it would have been out-of-character for them to convert to Culdeeism in large numbers.

## Feudal Superiority Hierarchy

Church lands and the feudal system of Scotland were intertwined, warranting a short explanation of the feudal superiority hierarchy. A person whose property was erected into a lordship ranked above a simple baron. An owner of an earldom would be superior to a person with a single lordship. Someone whose lands were incorporated into a Marquessate was superior to both. A man owning a fief elevated into a Dukedom was exalted above all three. The terms of superiority from greater to lesser are thus: Feudal Duke, Feudal Marquess, Feudal Earl, Feudal Lord, and Feudal Baron.[221]

A regality was a territorial jurisdiction in old Scots law that only the king could create and was a superior jurisdiction to a barony. A lord of a regality had a civil jurisdiction equal to that of the King's sheriff and more extensive criminal jurisdiction, equivalent to that of the High Court of Justiciary (except for treason).[222] By 1387, the former Graham estate of Dalkeith had become a regality. Baronies consolidated under Dalkeith in 1387 included Abercorn, Mosskesswra, Kilbucho and Newlands, and Hutton.[223]

After his coronation in 1124 A.D., King David I of Scotland established bishoprics and cathedrals staffed with Roman Catholic clergy. The native Celtic Church was undermined by internal decay. They were under a tribal system

---

[217] Hamish MacPherson, "The history of Scotland's 'first' patron saint, Saint Kessog," *The National*, 8 March 2020. https://www.thenational.scot/news/18288418.history-scotlands-first-patron-saint-saint-kessog/

[218] Nihil Obstat and Remy Lafort, "Censor. Entry for 'Culdees,'" StudyLight.org-The Catholic Encyclopedia (New York: Robert Appleton Company, 1914). https://www.studylight.org/encyclopedias/eng/tce/c/culdees.html .

[219] Rev.J.A. Wylie, *The History of the Scottish Nation*, Vol. 3 (London: Hamilton, Adams and Co., 1886), 203-204, 298. https://www.originofnations.org/books,%20papers/history%20of%20the%20scots/scothistvol3.pdf

[220] Dugald Butler and Herbert Story, *Scottish Cathedrals and Abbeys* (London: A & C Black, Edinburgh: R & R Clark Limited, 1901), 2-3. https://archive.org/details/scottishcathedra00butl/page/2/mode/2up?ref=ol&view=theater&q=custodiers

[221] George Wallace, *The Nature and Descent of Ancient Peerages*, second edition (Edinburgh: C. Elliott, 1785), 127-130. https://archive.org/details/naturedescentofa00wall/page/n12/mode/1up?ref=ol&view=theater&q=earldom

[222] Dictionaries of the Scots Language Online, "Regality, Scottish National Dictionary," Vol. III (1968), accessed 3 November 2022. https://www.dsl.ac.uk/entry/snd/regality

[223] *Registrum Honoris de Morton, Volume II: Ancient Charters*, 138-139, 148-150, 154-157.

(vs. territorial) where bishops were under the monastic rule, and were subject to the abbot of the nearest monastery. The Culdee recluses were not pledged to celibacy. Many of them were married and were succeeded in office by their sons. They were not dedicated for life to their calling, but were free at any time to change it for another.[224, 225]

## David I, King of Scots (reigned 1124-1153)

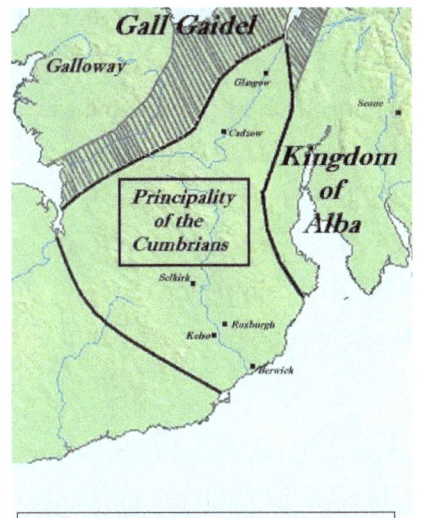

Figure 24: Cumbrian Territory Boundaries Prior to 1124 [227]
CC BY-SA 2.5

As a young boy, Prince David was forced into exile to the English court after his father's death, when his uncle Donald III, known as Donald Bane (Domnall mac Donnchada), seized the Scottish throne. In England, David received a Norman education. He married an Anglo-Norman heiress, Matilda, Countess of Northumberland and Huntingdon, thus acquiring vast estates in Northern England. With the assistance of the English King, his brother-in-law and mentor, Henry I, David became the Prince of Cumbria (1113-1124).[226] When he moved to Cumbria, Figure 24, he established feudal lordships in the west of his Cumbrian principality[227] for the leading members of his military entourage who kept him in power.[228] I believe the first documented Graham, William de Graham, was part of this entourage.[229] David I spent much of his time at his castles in southern Scotland and Cumbria, particularly in Roxburgh and Carlisle. He died in 1153 at Carlisle.[230]

The beginnings of feudalism in Scotland are attributed to David I. This is defined as "castle-building, the regular use of professional cavalry ("knightly" skills that influenced Grahams for centuries), the knight's fee," a unit of measure of land deemed sufficient to support a knight, as well as the practices of "homage and fealty."[231] The feudal system in Britain began in England immediately following the Norman Conquest of 1066. All land in England was claimed by William the Conqueror as his absolute right, the commencement of the royal demesne, also known as "crown land." The king made grants of very large tracts of land under various forms of feudal tenure from his demesne, generally in the form of feudal baronies.[232]

---

[224] Dugald Butler and Herbert Story, *Scottish Cathedrals and Abbeys*, 2-3.
[225] "Culdees," *McClintock and Strong Bible Cyclopedia*, accessed: 3 November 2022. https://www.biblicalcyclopedia.com/C/culdees.html
[226] Richard Oram, *David: The King Who Made Scotland* (Stroud, Gloucestershire, UK: Tempus Publishing Limited, 2004), 41, 63-70.
[227] Figure 24: Wikimedia Commons contributors, "File:DavidianCumbria.JPG," Wikimedia Commons, the free media repository, accessed December 26, 2022. https://commons.wikimedia.org/w/index.php?title=File:DavidianCumbria.JPG&oldid=451116489.
[228] Author's Note—As king, David I set up large-scale marcher lordships in strategic locations for Norman land barons and their knights, such as Annandale for Robert de Brus; Cunningham for Hugh de Morville, whom David made Constable of Scotland; Liddesdale for his cupbearer, Ranulf de Soule; and Strathgryfe for his steward, Walter Fitzalan. Richard Oram, *David: The King Who Made Scotland*, 59-63.
[229] Richard Oram, *David: The King Who Made Scotland*, 59-63.
[230] Ruth M. Blakely, *The Brus Family in England and Scotland, 1100-c1290* (Durham, UK: University of Durham, 2000), 34-36. http://etheses.dur.ac.uk/1594/
[231] USLegal.com, "Knights Fee Law and Legal Definition," accessed 27 December 2022. https://definitions.uslegal.com/k/knights-fee/#:~:text=Knight's%20fee%20means%20the%20amount,describe%20the%20value%20of%20land.
[232] Wikisource contributors, "1911 Encyclopædia Britannica/Demesne," Wikisource, accessed 23 January 2023. https://en.wikisource.org/w/index.php?title=1911_Encyclop%C3%A6dia_Britannica/Demesne&oldid=9042993

Contrary to writings from early historians, [233] not all of David's friends and trusty knights who served him in Cumbria were French-speaking Normans. David's early land charters, like the 1127 charter for St. Cuthbert church in Edinburgh include signatories such as his son, Earl Henry, William de Graham,[vi] Thor de Trauernent (a.k.a. Thor son of Swain), and Mael Bethad de Libertona.[234] The charter of Holyrood Abbey granting the land for the abbey, dated about 1125,[vii] was signed by William de Graham, Peter de Brus, "Norman Sheriff," Edward the Chancellor, Herbert the Chamberlain, Rodbert, Bishop of St. Andrews, John, Bishop of Glasgow, Gospatric, brother of Dolfin, Walter the chaplain, and a number of individuals without surnames believed to be knights.[235] Thor de Trauernent was of Danish heritage, believed to be from an established Yorkshire family, and was made Sheriff of Edinburgh. His first name was "Normanized" in later documents to the more acceptable "Durand."[viii] In addition, the name of Mael Bethad, who was a Gael, was corrupted to "Malbead," "Malbet," and "Macbeth."[236] Mael Bethad de Libertona was a major landowner and a donor of lands in honor of St. Cuthbert. Significantly, the 1127 church charter was dedicated to a native Culdee saint had no signatures from the Norman land barons who were Roman Catholic, implying the signatories followed Culdeeism and were not Norman-born. As stated, Scotland did not officially convert to Roman Catholicism until 1250 A.D.

That raises questions: Was William de Graham raised as a Culdee? Was the surname "Graham" also the result of corruption, possibly due to anglicization and/or multiple translations to/from the abbreviated Latin used in land charters and documents of medieval times?

---

[233] Green, Judith A. "David I and Henry I." *The Scottish Historical Review* 75, no. 199 (1996): 1–19. http://www.jstor.org/stable/25530706

[234] Michael Gervers, *Documents of Early England Data Set (DEEDS),* University of Toronto, 1975-present, Charter Number: 05130072, accessed 27 December 2022. https://deeds.library.utoronto.ca/charters/05130072

[235] The Bannatyne Club, *Liber Cartarum Sancte Crucis, Munimenta Ecclesiae Sancte Crucis de Edwinesburgh,* (Edinburgh: 1840), 6. https://archive.org/details/libercartarumsan00bann/page/6/mode/2up

[236] G.W.S. Barrow, *The Acts of William I King of Scots 1165–1214, Regesta Regum Scottorum,* Vol. II (Edinburgh: 1971), 64, 65, 160. https://archive.org/details/actsofwilliamiki0002barr/page/64/mode/2up

# Knights of Annandale

The knights established in Annandale by the Bruce (Brus) family included the Corries, Kirkpatricks, and Crosbies. They became known as the knights of Annandale.[237] Little is known of them prior to their appearance in Annandale in the early twelfth century. These knights became Scots loyal to the Bruces and integrated quickly into the West Marches by marrying their children into local families.[238] We do know that Robert de Brus, first Lord of Annandale, had twenty knights' fees in Yorkshire and ten in Annandale, meaning his ten household knights would have been assigned individual demesnes around Annandale to provide security.[239] The demesne, in this case, the specific domestic estate belonging to a knight, later became a barony for the Manor or Motte,[240] often called a "bordland" or "boreland."[241] As shown in Appendix F, "Border Graham Genealogy," these were subdivided when the families expanded or intermarried with their neighbors. The ten estates, called knights' fees, plus the lord of Annan's land, soon became eleven Motte and Bailey sites (Figures F-12, F-14), with the Motte of Hutton extending eastwards as far as Bracanwra Mill on the west side of the River Esk, opposite the King's manor of Stablegordon.[242] The Motte of Hutton in Nether Hutton would later become the home of the Border Grahams. The other castle sites formed the basis for the civil parish and barony boundaries seen in Scottish maps hundreds of years later.

It is actually the Motte and Bailey castle sites that are our focus in Annandale. See Appendix F for a detailed report on each Motte/Mote site, who got them, which were destroyed during the Wars of Independence and which were rebuilt. Studying these sites helps trace the knights of Annandale and determine their connection to the Border Grahams.

# Origin of the first recorded Graham in Scotland, William de Graham

William de Graham (b. circa 1080- d. after 1150) is the first Graham found in Scottish records. He attended the coronation of David I in 1124.[243] He was a witness on a number of medieval land charters in the years: 1127, 1139, 1141, circa 1141, circa 1142, circa 1150. Charter witnesses were clergy, knights, nobility/major landowners, or administrators appointed by the monarchy.[244] By process of elimination, we can deduce William de Graham was a knight. The

---

[237] "The Jardine Clan," The Border Reivers, accessed 28 December 2022. http://www.borderreivers.co.uk/Border%20Families/Surnames/Jardine%201.htm

[238] J.E. Corrie, *Records of the Corrie Family, 802-1899 A.D.* (London: Mitchell and Hughes, 1899), 130. https://archive.org/details/recordsofcorrief01corr

[239] Ruth M. Blakely, *The Brus Family in England and Scotland, 1100-c ,1290*,.46, 151.

[240] George Ghidrai, "Motte and Bailey Castle, the original Castle design," The World of Castles, accessed 3 November 2022. https://www.castlesworld.com/tools/motte-and-bailey-castles.php

[241] Angus J. L. Winchhester, "The Distribution and Significance of 'Bordland' in Medieval Britain," *The Agricultural History Review* 34, no. 2 (1986): 129–39. http://www.jstor.org/stable/40274465

[242] "Hutton Mote," Canmore Record of the National Historic Environment, Canmore ID 66755, April 2010. https://canmore.org.uk/site/66755/hutton-mote

[243] Claire Brooks, "Theories on the Origins of the Grahams," *Clan Graham Society Newsletter* (1998). https://clangrahamsociety.org/theories-on-the-origins-of-the-grahams/

[244] Michael Gervers, *Documents of Early England Data Set (DEEDS),* Charter Numbers: 05130072, 05130121, 05130134, 05130135, 05130153, 05130230, accessed 27 December 2022. https://deeds.library.utoronto.ca/deeds-context-search?keywords=graham&alt-spell-on=on&date-start=&date-end=

popular theory advanced by *Peerage*²⁴⁵ has been he was a Norman knight. I believe this is unlikely. As I will discuss, there was a shortage of Normans in Northern England and Scotland, and the majority of Anglo-Norman knights were household knights of the Norman land barons. William de Graham was not a household knight. He was an independent knight. Historian G.W.S Barrow noted that in some charters William de Graham also acted as a justiciar (judge) of Lothian, but in other cases signed below a known sheriff. Perhaps he was the deputy to his neighbor, Thor son of Swain, Sheriff of Edinburgh. David I granted William de Graham the estate of Dalkeith near Edinburgh between 1124-1127 when other knights and supporters of the king were also being granted lands. While the original land charter does not survive, there is a surviving charter transferring Dalkeith to a subsequent heir, Sir James Douglas, knight, in 1369 by David II. This charter makes the grant with the caveats: "in feu and heritage."²⁴⁶ Knights were granted heritable lands or fiefs "for homage and service; in feu [land tenure] and heritage."²⁴⁷ Fiefs were often rewards for previous military service but were also intended to help support the knight and his heirs to provide future military service.²⁴⁸ Dalkeith was a fief.

When he claimed the Scottish throne previously held by his older brothers who all died prematurely, David I brought with him "trusted men" to an unwelcome environment in Edinburgh. William de Graham's presence at the coronation of David I in 1124 implies he would have had some relationship with David prior to that point, and was one of those "trusted men." We can assume he served David I as a knight before 1124, when David was Prince of Cumbria, and then after 1124 in the struggle to subdue David I's nephew, Malcolm.²⁴⁹

Independent knights at the time were expected to finance their own expenses and were usually younger sons from established families. The new landed barons were Normans and they hired household knights, which did not require the same credentials.²⁵⁰ Nevertheless, these barons were not established in Cumbria (what is now Southern Scotland and parts of northern England) until *after* 1124. William de Graham and his descendants were not closely associated with those landed barons until a few generations later,²⁵¹ supporting the belief that William would have been the kind of knight who was from a native, established family, not a loner who traveled to Scotland from parts unknown.

Coincidentally, by 1124, Yorkshire was running low on "enfeoffments" (fiefs or land grants for knights or other public servants) and ran out of them by 1135. This would explain why so many younger sons from Yorkshire would need to go elsewhere (Scotland) to get land. Thor, son of Swain, who is on the same Scottish charters as William de Graham, his neighbor, is the right age to be a younger brother to Adam, son of Swain. Adam and Henry, sons of

---

²⁴⁵ Sir James Balfour Paul, *The Scots Peerage, Founded on Wood's Edition,* Vol. VI (Edinburgh: David Douglas, 1909), 191. https://archive.org/details/scotspeeragefoun06pauluoft/page/n5/mode/2up?q=graham

²⁴⁶ PoMS, "No. 10942, person summary," accessed 6 January 2023. https://www.poms.ac.uk/record/source/10942/

²⁴⁷ Weebly, "What was Feudalism?" Brewminate, 1 March 2021. https://brewminate.com/rights-and-responsibilities-under-the-medieval-system-of-feudalism/

²⁴⁸ The Editors of *Encyclopaedia Britannica,* "Definition of Fief," accessed 18 October 2022. https://www.britannica.com/topic/fief

²⁴⁹ Richard Oram, *David: The King Who Made Scotland,* 77.

²⁵⁰ Christopher Gravett, *English Medieval Knight 1200-1300* (Oxford, UK: Osprey Publishing LTD, 2002), 7-8.

²⁵¹ Rev. William Graham, *Lochmaben Five Hundred Years Ago* (Edinburgh: Trinity, 1865), 56. https://www.google.com/books/edition/Lochmaben_five_hundred_years_ago_or_sele/XlpZAAAAcAAJ?hl=en&kptab=editions&sa=X&ved=2ahUKEwilhM2AlJL7AhUslWoFHTkyAYEQmBZ6BAgQEAg

Swain from Yorkshire, later acquired extensive lands in the Eden Valley in Cumbria/Cumberland[252] close to Carlisle and Greystoke Barony in England.[253]

# Popular theories regarding the origin of William de Graham

The best known are the Tancarville and de Hesdin origin theories. In *House Graham*, Dr. Lloyd Graham analyzes these origin theories in detail and highlights inconsistencies. Phil Graham and I independently studied these theories and arrived at similar conclusions to Dr. Graham.[254]

<u>Tancarville Origin Theory</u>

"The Chamberlain Story" by Dennis D. Chamberlain, published in 2018, and *The Norman People*, published by Henry S. King and Co in 1874, theorize that the Grahams and the Chamberlains were descendants of Norman nobleman William de Tancarville, son of Raoul, Chief Chamberlain of Normandy and Angleterre (England). Their evidence:

1. The escallop(scallop shells), used by subsequent generations of Grahams, are in the Chamberlain coat of arms, and
2. The de Tancarvilles held the office of Chamberlain in the Duke's (William the Conqueror) household in France and then held the office of Seneschal of Grantham in Lincolnshire.[255]

They surmised that the surname "Graham" was derived from "de Grantham" because in medieval times, "Grantham" was pronounced and written in official documents with the middle "nt" dropped. However, the villages named "Greatham" throughout Britain were also spelled "Graham" in medieval documents. Per the Documents of Early England Dataset (DEEDS) database, managed by the University of Toronto Libraries, of the ten places called "Graham" in English documents: "Four misspell 'Greetham, Lincolnshire' [Grantham] as 'Graham.' However, the land charters also misspell 'Greatham' in Sussex, Salisbury and Durham as 'Graham' as well."[256]

The use of escallops in family armorials is not unique to the Grahams. The shells are associated with St. Michael the Archangel (*Saint Michel Archange* in French), patron saint of warriors, and with St. James the Greater, patron saint of Spain, and are especially popular amongst families from Normandy, Brittany, and Poitou in France. At least 115 established families post-Norman conquest used escallops in their coats of arms.[257]

---

[252] Archibald Lawrie, *Early Scottish Charters Prior to A.D. 1153: with Notes and an Index* (Glasgow, 1905), 375.
[253] Paul Dalton, "Feudal Politics in Yorkshire, 1066 x 1054" (Phd Thesis, University of Sheffield, 1990), 95, 157. https://etheses.whiterose.ac.uk/1870/
[254] Lloyd D. Graham, *House Graham, From the Antoine Wall to the Temple of Hymen*, 23-29.
[255] Dennis D. Chamberlain, The Chamberlain Story, 20 July 2018. http://www.thechamberlainstory.com/2018/07/20/chamberlain-dna-tancarville/
[256] Michael Gervers, *Documents of Early England Dataset (DEEDS)*, University of Toronto Libraries, accessed 17 October 2022. https://deeds.library.utoronto.ca/deeds-search?keywords=graham&search_field=all&date-start=&date-end=&q=deeds-search&fq%5B0%5D=issued_country%3A%22England%22
[257] Duane L.C.M. Galles, "Pilgrims and Heraldry," The Heraldry Society, *Coats of Arms* No. 145 (Spring 1989), accessed 27 December 2022. https://www.theheraldrysociety.com/articles/pilgrims-and-heraldry/

"The Chamberlain Story" discusses Y-DNA results: multiple groups of Chamberlains with ties to Normandy and over a dozen diverse DNA groups unrelated to one another. Only one of the groups could be direct male line descendants of William de Tancarville. The authors concluded more study was needed. The Chamberlain Y-DNA Surname Project on FamilyTree DNA is looking for more participants surnamed Chamberlain and Tancarville towards that goal.[258]

De Hesdin Origin Theory

Beryl Platts asserted in volumes 1 and 2 of *The Origin of Heraldry* that William de Graham was the son of Flemish noble Arnulf de Hesdin. The de Hesdin armorials were azure (blue background) with three gold escallops in chief. (See Appendix E on Heraldry for an explanation of heraldic terminology). Arnulf had four or five children: sons Walter, William, and Arnulf, and a daughter, Avelina. Platts asserts that Walter de Hesdin and Walter FitzAlan, progenitor of the Stewarts, are the same man, and that William de Hesdin and William de Graham are one and the same, citing numerous Scottish documents where the Stewarts and Grahams call each other "cousins." Due to generations of intermarrying, nearly all Scottish nobles were third cousins or closer by the thirteenth century, as evidenced by the numerous papal dispensations granted for Scottish nobles marrying who were related in the fourth degree of consanguinity. Platts also cites instances of spelling "Grantham" without the middle "nt" in medieval documents, i.e. "Graham."[259] However, as stated, villages named Greatham throughout Britain were also spelled "Graham" in medieval documents.

## A New Origin Theory: The Greystokes of Cumbria

To be invited to David I's coronation in 1124, the knight William de Graham would have served David before then, when David was the Prince of Cumbria and Earl of Huntingdon in Northumbria. Sir James Balfour Paul's *Peerage* surmised in 1909 that William de Graham was possibly associated with the Earls of Dunbar, descendants of Northumberland governor, Gospatric, and must have descended from a family who lived in Northumbria, given his descendants' connections to Northumbria, specifically Tynedale, for nearly two centuries.[260]

There are two primary options for William de Graham's origins: either he was Anglo-Norman, or he was a native: from Cumbria, Northumberland, or the vicinity. Cumbria was located in what is now

> **Did you know?**
> It wasn't until the Treaty of York signed 25 September 1237 between Alexander II of Scotland and Henry III of England that the border between England and Scotland was officially defined for the first time. Alexander II quitclaimed his hereditary rights to Cumberland, Northumberland and Westmoreland to England, but retained Tynedale, Hexhamshire and Redesdale.

---

[258] "Chamberlain DNA Surname Project," FamilyTree DNA, accessed 28 December 2022. https://www.familytreedna.com/public/Chamberlain?iframe=ycolorized

[259] Claire Brooks, "Theories on the Origins of the Grahams, de Hesdin theory," *Clan Graham Society Newsletter* (1998). https://clangrahamsociety.org/theories-on-the-origins-of-the-grahams/

[ Did you know? Blurb] "On September 25th 1237 The Treaty of York was agreed between the kings Alexander II of Scotland and Henry III of England," ScotiaNostra, accessed 23 January 2023. https://scotianostra.tumblr.com/post/696384512455753728/on-september-25th-1237-the-treaty-of-york-was?is_related_post=1

[260] Sir James Balfour Paul, *The Scots Peerage, Founded on Wood's Edition,* Vol. VI (Edinburgh: David Douglas, 1909), 193. https://archive.org/details/scotspeeragefoun06pauluoft/page/n5/mode/2up?q=graham

Southern Scotland and parts of northern England (Figure 24). The Scottish border stretched further south during the time of David I.²⁶¹ Regarding the second option, the strongest candidate family to be ancestors of William de Graham with connections to Cumbria and Northumberland is the Greystoke family. The Greystokes descended from the Danes who formerly controlled Yorkshire (Figure 25)²⁶² and may have been related to Queen Sybill of Scotland.²⁶³

## Y-DNA Evidence.

We know that the Graham clan grew very powerful, as evidenced by their many sept clans. Sept clans were connected to the Graham clan via marriage to Graham heiresses. In a feudal economy, land was power and marriage was the most common way to acquire more of it. These husbands or a younger son inheriting his mother's lands would typically take the surname of the estate, which belonged to their wife/mother. Another way to create a sept clan was for a son-in-law to swear fealty to his father-in-law's clan if it was more powerful than his own.²⁶⁴ Because Y-DNA is passed down the male line, and hereditary surnames usually are as well,

*Figure 25: Kingdoms of Britain circa 886 A.D.* ²⁶²

comparing the two will allow us to project the origins of the various Graham families. Over 707 men representing over 96 Y-DNA groups in the Graham Y-DNA Surname Project sponsored by Family Tree DNA (FTDNA)²⁶⁵ indicates there were likely more sept clans than are officially documented. With these new sept clans, the Graham DNA was

---

**Septs**
In Scottish clans, septs are families that followed another family's chief. These smaller septs would then comprise, and be part of, the chief's larger clan. A sept might follow another chief if two families were linked through marriage; or, if a family lived on the land of a powerful laird, they would follow him whether they were related or not.

**Cadets**
In heraldry and history, a cadet branch consists of the male-line descendants of a patriarch's younger sons (cadets). Such offspring were not expected (required?) to produce any offspring - though of course may did so. In some cases, the cadet branch would become successful and perhaps own land and be awarded titles: laird or a knighthood or even higher rank. Such significant branches often became associated with a particular geographic location and became acknowledged as (Surname) of "X."

---

²⁶² Figure 25: Wikimedia Commons contributors, "Atlas of the United Kingdom," *Wikimedia Commons,* accessed 16 April 2023. https://commons.wikimedia.org/w/index.php?title=Atlas_of_the_United_Kingdom&oldid=748934236

²⁶³ Paul Dalton, "Feudal Politics in Yorkshire, 1066 x 1054" (PhD Thesis, University of Sheffield, 1990), 168.

²⁶⁴ Ann Belanger, "Cadets and Septs of the Grahams," Clan Graham Society, accessed 18 October 2022. https://clangrahamsociety.org/about/#septs

[Blurb on Septs, Cadets] "Septs, Cadets," The Clan Buchanan, accessed 5 December 2022. https://www.theclanbuchanan.com/what-are-septs

²⁶⁵ FamilyTreeDNA, "Graham Surname DNA Project," accessed 28 December 2022. https://www.familytreedna.com/groups/graham/about/background

passed down the female side. Given so many Y-DNA types, it was difficult to isolate direct male line descendants of William de Graham. In *House Graham*, Dr. Lloyd D. Graham asserted in 2020 that the "Noble Grahams," direct male line descendants of the younger son of William de Graham, were of the I-M253 haplogroup, which is Scandinavian in origin.[266] That evidence was based on two things: first, the fact that the east coast of Scotland had long enjoyed ties with Scandinavian countries; and secondly, the fact that I-M253 kept recurring among the few Y-DNA testers who had credible links to the Grahams of Montrose or at least to the Montrose region, including a confirmed descendant of the Grahams of Glenny and Gartmore. *The Scots Peerage* lists these Graham families as descending from the Earls of Menteith.[267] Thanks to the tenacity of Mr. Rob Sinclair in searching out test subjects, in November 2021, another male with confirmed Montrose heritage, via the Graemes of Inchbrakie,[268] Alex Graeme, was also confirmed as I-M253.[269] Only 8% of the Graham project participants tested as I-M253, indicating the other 92% with differing Y-DNA types were descendants of Graham ancestral daughters (unofficial sept clans). William de Graham descending from the Norse Lords of Greystoke is consistent with the DNA test data, as it well-documented that both the Grahams of Montrose and Menteith descend from the younger son of William de Graham, Alan de Graham.[270,271] Recent Y-DNA results are therefore compatible with the Greystoke origin theory (I-M253 haplogroup, Scandinavian). The other Graham origin theories are based on Norman French or Flemish origins and are less likely to be I-M253. Norman vassals were thinly spread in the northern territories, and the "Normans" that migrated to Britain after the Conquest came from all over France, from Flanders and from Iberia.[272]

The Normans had a policy of disenfranchising the Saxons, who had been in power pre-conquest, from their lands and government positions and replacing them with Normans.[273] The Danes were not popular with the Normans either, especially after the attempted Yorkshire Anglo-Danish rising of 1069.[274] The Danelaw kingdom (Figure 25 [275]), included sixteen shires: Leicester, York, Lincoln, Suffolk, Cambridge, Nottingham, Derby, Essex, Sussex, Norfolk, Northampton, Huntingdon, Bedford, Hertford, Middlesex, and Buckingham. The kingdom was established in the wake of the Danish Conquest in the ninth century and was officially disestablished with the Norman Conquest in 1066.[276]

---

[266] Lloyd D. Graham, *House Graham, From the Antoine Wall to the Temple of Hymen*, 30-32.
[267] Sir James Balfour Paul, *The Scots Peerage, Founded on Wood's Edition*, Vol. VI, 147-148.
[268] "Patrick Graham, First of Inchbrakie," The Peerage, Person Page 10829, 21 December 2018. http://www.thepeerage.com/p10829.htm#i108287
[269] FamilyTreeDNA, "Graham Surname DNA Project."
[270] William Jewell, *The Golden Cabinet of True Treasure* (London: John Crosley, 1612; Ann Arbor: Text Creation Partnership, 2011), 167. http://name.umdl.umich.edu/A04486.0001.001
[271] Lloyd D. Graham, *House Graham, From the Antoine Wall to the Temple of Hymen*, 128.
[272] BBC, "David I and the Impact of the Norman Conquest," accessed 18 October 2022. https://www.bbc.co.uk/legacies/immig_emig/scotland/borders/
[273] Regina Jeffers, "The Norman Invasion Begins with William I," Every Woman Dreams, 5 March 2012. https://reginajeffers.blog/2012/03/05/the-norman-invasion-begins-with-william-i/
[274] D.C. Douglas, *William the Conqueror, The Norman Impact upon England* (Berkeley and Los Angeles: University of California Press, March 1964), 218-220. https://erenow.net/biographies/william-the-conqueror-the-norman-impact-upon-england/
[275] Wikimedia Commons contributors, "File:Britain 886.jpg," Wikimedia Commons, the free media repository, accessed 6 December 2022. https://commons.wikimedia.org/w/index.php?title=File:Britain_886.jpg&oldid=661043086
[276] "When Vikings Ruled in Britain, The History of Danelaw," Sky History, accessed 11 November 2022. https://www.history.co.uk/articles/when-the-vikings-ruled-in-britain-a-brief-history-of-danelaw

Therefore, many of Saxon, Norse, Gaelic, and other heritage, particularly those with estates they wished to retain, or government jobs they wanted to keep, changed their names to Norman-acceptable names and did their best to "blend in." They were also influenced by stories of the St. Bryce's Day Massacre, a mass killing of Danes in the Kingdom of England on 13 November 1002 A.D., ordered by King Æthelred the Unready.[277] Despite a substantial Danish population in the Danelaw region of Britain pre-Norman Conquest,[278] it seems Danish names had nearly "disappeared" from record books a few generations later. One such case was the thane (high ranking vassal) of King Henry I, Forne Sigulfson. Forne owned estates in Yorkshire, Northumberland, and Cumberland. We know the most about his Yorkshire and Cumberland estates because they were listed in the Domesday Book of 1086, a detailed accounting of estates throughout England for the purposes of assessing taxes.[279] Forne had other lands not included in Domesday, such as Coquetdale in Northumberland, Coniscliffe in County Durham, and probably estates in Upper Teesdale. Not surprising that he held lands in Northumberland given his father's long-time service as deputy to the earl of Northumbria.[280] In *Forne Sigulfson-The "First" Lord of Greystoke in Cumbria,* Dr. Stephen M. Lewis of Université de Caen Normandie explains that the first Norman-recognized Lord of Greystoke was Forne Sigulfson of Yorkshire. "Sigulf" is sometimes recorded as "Ligulf" since the letters "S" and "L" have often been conflated or confused.[281] This Sigulf should not be confused with "Ligulf of Lumley," a relative of the earls of Scarborough.[282] Forne's estate name in Cumbria was recorded by several spelling variants: Greystock, Graystock, Greystoke, Graystone, Graistock, Craystock, and Gristock.[283]

Twenty years after the Norman Conquest (1086), William II (William Rufus) recognized that he was running low on "trusted men" in Yorkshire and other frontier areas. There was also pressure on his overcommitted Norman vassals to return to France, so they were largely absent from their northern estates. It made sense to allow native tenants to remain on the lands,[284] which accounts for the much higher percentages of non-Norman Y-DNA analyzed in Appendix C. However, it wasn't until the reign of William II's younger brother, Henry I, that the governance of the northern territories became better organized. Henry's thirty or so "new men" were considered a northern extension of the royal court of his government.[285]

---

[277] Matthew Firth, "The St. Brice's Day Massacre: History, Archaeology and Myth," The PostGrad Chronicles, accessed 27 December 2022. https://thepostgradchronicles.org/2019/11/13/the-st-brices-day-massacre-history-archaeology-and-myth/

[278] Lise Brix, "Why Danish Vikings Moved to England," Science Nordic, updated 23 February 2017. https://sciencenordic.com/denmark-society--culture-videnskabdk/why-danish-vikings-moved-to-england/1442885

[279] Anna Powell Smith, "Forne, Son of Sigulf," *Open Domesday*, accessed 27 December 2022. https://opendomesday.org/name/forne-son-of-sigulf/

[280] Paul Dalton, *Feudal Politics in Yorkshire, 1066 x 1054*, 68.

[281] Stephen M. Lewis, Université de Caen Normandie, "Forne Sigulfson-The 'First' Lord of Greystoke in Cumbria," The Wild Peak (blog), 2013. https://thewildpeak.wordpress.com/2013/03/30/forne-sigulfson-the-first-lord-of-greystoke-in-cumbria/

[282] Clarence E. Pearsall, Hettie May Pearsall, and Harry L. Nealle, *The History and Genealogy of the Pearsall Family in England and America*, Vol. 1, Chapter 11 (San Francisco: H.S. Crocker Co. Inc., 1928), 312. http://www.pearsall-family.org/HGPearsallFamily_PDF.htm

[283] The Internet Surname Database, "Last Name: Greystoke," SurnameDB, accessed 28 December 2022. https://www.surnamedb.com/Surname/Greystoke#ixzz76sQWNFRw

[284] Paul Dalton, *Feudal Politics in Yorkshire, 1066 x 1054*, 11, 47, 50.

[285] Stephen M. Lewis, "Forne Sigulfson-The 'First' Lord of Greystoke in Cumbria."

Forne Sigulfson (de Greystoke), whose father served Gospatric, Earl of Northumbria, before the Norman Conquest,[286] was one of King Henry I's trusted officers ("new men") in the northern territories in the 1120s. He witnessed a number of important charters including the Foundation of Scone Priory in Scotland in 1114 in honor of the late Queen Sybilla, daughter of Henry I.[287] Archibald Lawrie writes in *Early Scottish Charters with Notes* that in the Scone charter "Forn appears as an assenter, 'assensum prebeo,' he poses as a man of rank and influence."[288] As Henry I's delegate in the Northern Territories, it would fit that Forn would be sent to the ceremony that honored the late queen who was a daughter of Henry I. Forn's co-signatories on English charters included others of "Henry's men," such as Robert de Brus, of Yorkshire and Lord of Annandale, and David, Prince of Cumbria (later David I of Scotland). Between approximately 1106 and 1112, Forne was a witness to the foundation charter of Wetheral Priory in Cumbria. Between 1115 and 1122, "Forne son of Sigulf" was himself granted land in Thornton-le-Moor in Yorkshire.[289] [290]Forne acquired other lands in Yorkshire by 1086, including Nunburnholme, Millington, and Biebly, which were later added to Greystoke barony.[291] Per Dr. Lewis:

> All of this establishes without too much doubt that Forne was already a significant force in the North before King Henry visited Carlisle in 1122 [and met Forne's daughter, Edith.] This is confirmed by the fact that Forne appeared at the gathering in 1121 of the "principales vires" or "chief men," such as Robert de Brus, Alan de Percy, Walter Espec, Robert de Witeleven, and Odard, sheriff of the Northumbrians who heard the claim of the community of St. Cuthbert to Tynemouth Priory.[292]

Dr. Lewis argues that in an effort to garner favor with the Normans, Forne named his first son "Ivo" after the first Norman "strongman" Ivo de Taillebois, sent by William Rufus to try to subjugate Cumbria. Other nobles not in favor with the Normans lost their estates.[293] Forne's daughter Edith became a concubine of Henry I and bore Henry a son, Robert Fitz Roy, and a daughter, Adeliza Fitz Edith.[294] After Forne's death about 1129/30, Ivo was confirmed by Henry I in Forne's northern estates—including the barony of Greystoke.[295] David I and Robert de Brus witnessed the

---

[286] Stephen M. Lewis, Université de Caen Normandie, "Forne Sigulfson-The Normans Come to Cumbria," The Wild Peak (blog), 2013. https://thewildpeak.wordpress.com/tag/ivo-taillebois/

[287] Archibald Lawrie, *Early Scottish Charters Prior to A.D. 1153* (Glasgow, 1905), 28-30. https://archive.org/details/earlyscottishch01lawrgoog/page/28/mode/2up?q=scone

[288] Archibald Lawrie, *Early Scottish Charters Prior to A.D. 1153: with Notes and an Index* (Glasgow, 1905), 286. https://archive.org/details/earlyscottishcha00lawruoft/page/286/mode/2up

[289] William Farrer, *Early Yorkshire Charters: Being a Collection of Documents Anterior to the Thirteenth Century Made from the Public Records, Monastic Chartularies, Roger Dodsworth's Manuscripts and Other Available Sources*, Vol. II (Edinburgh: Ballantyne, Hanson and Co., 1915), 511. https://archive.org/details/earlyyorkshirech02farruoft/page/510/mode/2up?q=thornton

[290] Paul Dalton, "Feudal Politics in Yorkshire, 1066 x 1054," 68, Table 11 after p. 73.

[291] Anna Powell Smith, "Forne, Son of Sigulf," *Open Domesday*, accessed 27 December 2022. https://opendomesday.org/name/forne-son-of-sigulf/

[292] Stephen M. Lewis, "Forne Sigulfson-The 'First' Lord of Greystoke in Cumbria."

[293] Stephen M. Lewis, "Forne Sigulfson-The Normans Come to Cumbria."

[294] Stephen M. Lewis, Université de Caen Normandie, "Edith Forne Sigulfson—King Henry's Mistress," The Wild Peak (blog), 2013. https://historyofcumbria.wordpress.com/2013/03/26/edith-forne-sigulfson-king-henrys-mistress/

[295] William Farrer, *Early Yorkshire Charters: Being a Collection of Documents Anterior to the Thirteenth Century Made from the Public Records, Monastic Chartularies, Roger Dodsworth's Manuscripts and Other Available Sources*, Vol. II, 511. https://archive.org/details/earlyyorkshirech02farruoft/page/510/mode/2up?q=thornton

charter confirming the barony of Greystoke under Ivo between 1130 and 1131.[296] Ivo started building Greystoke Castle soon thereafter.[297] The Greystoke (a.k.a. Gristock) family was certainly well-connected and well-established, Norman-recognized, and also located in or near Cumbria during the timeframe that David I was Prince of the Cumbrians (1113-1124). Forne and Prince David worked together in their service to Henry I and were co-signatories on a number of charters. Therefore, the Greystoke family fits the profile for one or more of their younger sons to serve Prince David in Cumbria and Northumberland, and King David I of Scotland as a trusted knight(s).

Like his mentor, Henry I, David I relied heavily on his "trusted men," officers of his royal court. These "trusted men" were the progenitors of the established or titled families in Scotland.[298] The Greystokes,[299] and later the Grahams, were established families and part of David I's inner circle.

## Etymology.

Medieval Britain was a melting pot of ethnicities and languages: Celts, Picts, Britons, Angles, Saxons, Norse, Norman French, and others. As stated, "Gray-ham" or "Graham" could be an anglicization of Greystoke, and/or the result of corruption of the estate name when translated to/from the abbreviated Latin used in medieval documents. "Gristock" is a variant of Greystoke seen in early documents, and is perhaps the original version of the name for the land.[300]

Examining the name "Gristock": "Gris" is Norse for boar or pig.[301] "Stock" is from the Norse *stokkr* and from the Old English *stocc* for "Tree trunk." However, "stock" evolved to be used for house or place.[302] Essentially, "Gristock" is Norse for "home of the boars." For example, per Dr. Lewis, the Greystoke Barony contained the ancient village of Grisdale, which is Norse for "valley of the boars."[303] Furthermore, *gris* is also Latin and French for "gray," so it is understandable how those writing land deeds could have transcribed the unfamiliar name "Gristock" to Latin and then to English and got "Gray-ham" or "Greystoke" or even "Graystone." "Ham" was borrowed from the Old English and meant "home, homestead, estate." Later, the Norman French changed the meaning of ham to "village without a church," hence the word "hamlet."[304] "Stone" was also used to mean lands or estates, as stones were used for boundary

---

[296] Richard Sharpe, *Norman Rule in Cumbria 1092-1136* (Carlisle: Cumberland and Westmoreland Antiquarian and Archaeological Society, 2006), 41, footnote 96. https://www.google.com/books/edition/Norman_Rule_in_Cumbria_1092_1136/YQkXAQAAIAAJ?hl=en

[297] "Greystoke Castle," Visit Cumbria, accessed 28 December 2022. https://www.visitcumbria.com/pen/greystoke-castle/

[298] Paul Dalton, "Feudal Politics in Yorkshire, 1066 x 1054," 166-169.

[299] John William Clay, *The Extinct and Dormant Peerages of the Northern Counties of England* (London: J. Nisbet & Co. Ltd, 1913), 94-98. https://archive.org/details/extinctdormantpe00clay/page/94/mode/2up?q=forne

[300] The Internet Surname Database, "Last Name: Greystock," SurnameDB, accessed 18 October 2022. https://www.surnamedb.com/Surname/Greystock

[301] Wiktionary contributors, "gris," Wiktionary, The Free Dictionary, accessed 4 November 2022. https://en.wiktionary.org/w/index.php?title=gris&oldid=69567367

[302] Wiktionary contributors, "stoc," Wiktionary, The Free Dictionary, accessed 5 December 2022. https://en.wiktionary.org/w/index.php?title=stoc&oldid=68776363

[303] Stephen M. Lewis, Université de Caen Normandie, "Grisdales of Matterdale, Grisdale 1332," The Wild Peak (blog), 2013. https://grisdalefamily.wordpress.com/tag/barons-of-greystoke/

[304] "Hamlet," AlphaDictionary.com, accessed 28 December 2022. https://www.alphadictionary.com/goodword/word/hamlet#:~:text=This%20ham%20was%20borrowed%20from,borrowed%20back%20as%20English%20haunt.

markers.[305] This would explain how "Gris-stock" became Grey-stoke and Gray-stone and later "Gray-ham" when Gristocks traveled far from their homes to Scotland. It would also explain why the boar is a popular symbol in some Graham armorials.

## Could William de Greystoke (Gristock) have become "William de Graham?"

Dr. Lewis believes that it is likely that Forne had other children besides Ivo.[306] The reason daughter Edith was well documented was due to her status as a concubine of the king. There seems to be a significant age difference between Edith and her elder brother, Ivo[307] (see Figure 37). Given Forne's previous efforts to garner favor with the Normans, it would not be unreasonable to speculate that he named one of his younger sons after the Norman king William II. In comparison, his son Ivo had a son and grandson named "William." "William de Gristock" could have been corrupted into "William de Graham" when he followed Prince David to the Scottish court in Edinburgh to attend the latter's coronation in 1124. David was born in circa 1084, and William de Graham's birth year is estimated to be circa 1080, making William and David close in age. In 1124, Greystoke Castle was not yet built, Ivo was the eldest and heir anyhow, fewer new enfeoffments were available, so younger son William's prospects if he stayed in Yorkshire or Cumbria were dim. Paul Dalton writes in *Feudal Politics in Yorkshire* that King David's court was a magnet for sons of important Northumbrian and Cumbrian nobles who were sent there as apprentices to acquire an upbringing, education and a career.[308]

As previously stated, younger sons of landed families would have had the options of serving as a knight, marrying an heiress to acquire land, or serving the church. Ruth Blakely also writes that the officers in King David's court were known to be "younger sons or lesser barons with no substantial land in England."[309] William de Graham's colleague and neighbor in Scotland, Thor, Son of Swain, of Tranent, also meets this description. Thor's final land charter from 1150, recorded in the University of Toronto's DEEDS database, is noteworthy. In it he transfers all lands he had previously donated to the Church of Tranent to Holyrood Abbey. A witness to this charter is another neighbor named "Edmund, son of Forn," another possible son of Forne Sigulfson.[310] The 1178 charter copied below shows that Edmund is not only a neighbor to Thor of Tranent but also to William de Graham of Dalkeith.[311] It would not be surprising for David I to grant brothers lands near each other or for one family member to subdivide land to share with the other. Thor, son of Swain's probable brothers, Adam and Henry, acquired land in the Eden Valley in Cumbria, close to Greystoke, in addition to their Yorkshire estates.[312] Interestingly, it appears that the Fitz Swains became neighbors to the Greystokes in Cumberland, while their younger brother became neighbors to Forne's children in Scotland at a time when Yorkshire was running low on enfeoffments.

---

[305] The Internet Surname Database, "Last Name: Stone," SurnameDB, accessed 18 October 2022. https://www.surnamedb.com/Surname/Stone

[306] Stephen M. Lewis, "Forne Sigulfson-The 'First' Lord of Greystoke in Cumbria."

[307] Stephen M. Lewis, Université de Caen Normandie, "Edith Forne Sigulfson—King Henry's Mistress."

[308] Paul Dalton, "Feudal Politics in Yorkshire, 1066 x 1054," 95, 157, 166.

[309] Ruth M. Blakely, "The Brus Family in England and Scotland, 1100-c. 1290," 36.

[310] Michael Gervers, *Documents of Early England Data Set (DEEDS) database*, University of Toronto, 1975-present, Charter Number: 05130214, accessed 18 October 2022. https://deeds.library.utoronto.ca/charters/05130214/Forn

[311] PoMS, "No. 2199," accessed 18 October 2022. https://www.poms.ac.uk/record/source/2199/

[312] Paul Dalton, "Feudal Politics in Yorkshire, 1066 x 1054," 157, 158, 177, 184.

From a Scottish land charter dated 1178:

> Abbot Archibald and convent of Dunfermline for William, son of Engelram (Ingram), son of, have granted, with assent of congregation, in feu and heritage, land that is called "Pontekin" (probably Pinkie, MLO) which [Edmund, his grandfather, living in reign of David], had obtained, free and quit of all servitude and complaint that pertains to land besides what pertains to crown. Also, to augment his possessions, abbot grants to him 10 jugera which are situated between above-mentioned land and boundaries of Tranent (ELO) next to Wallyford (MLO). And if his man shall forfeit land of Inveresk (MLO), he shall thus have forfeiture and if abbot's man shall forfeit land then abbey shall have forfeiture. The grass of all manors, that is of Inveresk, will be communal between their men, and abbot further grants to him liberty to stay behind from king's armies unless it is a common army [from] which men of Inveresk and of Monkton (ELO) should not be able to remain at home, and then only one man shall come; in regards to mills, however, abbot grants to him that liberty [which] in English is called "runtfre."[313]

Edmund, son of Forn's, estate of "Pontekin" or "Pinkie" is four and a half miles north of Dalkeith near Musselburgh. Some genealogists believe that Edmund is the progenitor of the Edmonstone Clan,[314] which originated in the area of Musselburgh.[315] There are several "I-M253 Scandinavian" groups in the Edmondson Y-DNA Project.[316] It will require future research to determine if any of them descend from the same patriarch as William de Graham. Two younger sons of Forne would fit the description of David I's royal court members: "younger sons or lesser barons with no substantial land in England." There is a third potential brother of William de Graham who remained in Yorkshire. The potential brother, or perhaps his son, was called "Alanus Forn." Alanus witnessed an 1167 Ryedale land charter, which was near Forne Sigulfson's Yorkshire holdings.[317] In addition, Forne is the right age to be the father of both William de Graham and Edmund Forn. Forne's oldest son Ivo was born in circa 1072; William de Graham was born circa 1080. Edmund seems to be a similar age. There may also have been a sister and her husband "William" living in the neighborhood of Dalkeith. Sometime between 1165 and 1214, King William "The Lion" renewed previous land gifts given to Newbattle Abbey in Dalkeith.[318] The land previously donated by "William, son-in-law of Sorn" was thus described: "land within south port of burgh of Edinburgh,"[319] which is also in the area of Musselburgh, where, coincidentally, Edmund Forn's estates were. Therefore, given the timeframe and proximity to Dalkeith, this William,

---

[313] PoMS, "No. 2199," accessed 18 October 2022. https://www.poms.ac.uk/record/source/2199/

[314] Sir Archibald Edmonstone of Duntreath, *The Genealogical Account of the Family of Edmonstone of Duntreath* (Edinburgh: 1875), 16. https://deriv.nls.uk/dcn23/9535/95353466.23.pdf

[315] George F. Black, *The Surnames of Scotland: Their Origin, Meaning and History* (New York : New York Public Library, 1946), 239. https://babel.hathitrust.org/cgi/pt?id=mdp.39015011274175&view=1up&seq=335&q1=edmonstone

[316] "Edmondson and Variants," FamilyTreeDNA, accessed 28 December 2022. https://www.familytreedna.com/groups/edmondson-surname-y-dna-project/about

[317] William Farrer, *Early Yorkshire charters; being a collection of documents anterior to the thirteenth century made from the public records, monastic chartularies, Roger Dodsworth's manuscripts and other available sources*, Vol. I (Edinburgh: Ballantyne, Hanson and Co., 1914), 325. https://archive.org/details/earlyyorkshirech01farruoft/page/324/mode/2up?q=forn

[318] PoMS, "No. 374," accessed 18 October 2022. https://www.poms.ac.uk/record/source/374/
[Did you know? Blurb] Mindy Young, "Medial S: The Old English S That Looks Like an F," Online Writing Jobs, 27 April 2017. https://www.onlinewritingjobs.com/fun-stuff/medial-s-the-old-english-s-that-looks-like-f/#:~:text=It's%20actually%20a%20letter%20called,English%20orthography%20until%20the%201800s

[319] PoMS, "No. 374," accessed 18 October 2022. https://www.poms.ac.uk/record/source/374/

"son-in-law of Sorn," may very well have been a son-in-law to Forne Sigulfson and brother-in-law to William de Graham.

Phil Graham and I initially derived the Greystoke theory by following the trail of the Kirkpatricks. The Grahams and the Kirkpatricks were comrades for centuries. Early Scottish history shows Kirkpatricks closely associated with the Grahams, signifying a familial bond. Both families rushed to the aid of Sir William Wallace in defense of Lochmaben Castle in 1297.[320] In a 16 June 1357 land charter, Roger Kirkpatrick, "Rogero de Kirkpatrik" as written in Latin, is named as a "dear cousin" to John de Graham, Lord of "Maskesswra."[321] Gradually, former St. Patrick church lands that had been in the possession of the Kirkpatricks transferred into the hands of the Grahams. Lands could be transferred via inheritance, marriage, or royal charter. Ivo and Roger Kirkpatrick, the earliest recorded Kirkpatricks, were knights like William de Graham. See the "Knights of Annandale" in Appendix F.

> **Did you know?**
> The "S" and "F" have been interchanged in transcription from the Latin charters so frequently "Forn" is transcribed "Sorn."

Henry I's reign (1100-1135) began fourteen years after Domesday was published. In *The Pipe-rolls, Or Sheriff's Annual Accounts of the Revenues of the Crown for the Counties of Cumberland, Westmoreland and Durham,* which cover the reigns of Kings Henry I, Richard I, and John, the authors note:

> When Henry I resumed possession of Cumberland, he founded five additional Baronies: Coupland, Allerdale,[322] Wigton, "Graystock" and Levington, reserving to the Crown the City of Carlisle, and the Forest of Cumberland. He granted control of these baronies to his "trusted men": Copeland to William de Meschines,[323] Allerdale to Waldieve, son of Gospatric, Wigton to Odard, son of Hildret, Levington to Richard de Bogville (Boyville), knight, and "Graystock" was granted to Forne, son of Lyolph (Sigulf).[324]

---

[320] Rev. William Graham, *Lochmaben Five Hundred Years Ago* (Edinburgh: Trinity, 1865), 56. https://www.google.com/books/edition/Lochmaben_five_hundred_years_ago_or_sele/XlpZAAAAcAAJ?hl=en&kptab=editions&sa=X&ved=2ahUKEwilhM2AlJL7AhUslWoFHTkyAYEQmBZ6BAgQEAg

[321] William Fraser, *The Annandale Family Book of the Johnstones, Earls and Marquises of Annandale,* Vol. I (Edinburgh: 1894), 10-11. https://archive.org/details/annandalefamilv100fras/page/10/mode/2up

[322] Wikimedia Commons, "Map of Cumbria, with Allerdale highlighted, derivative work": Renly from {{created using Ordnance Survey data, 2011. https://commons.wikimedia.org/wiki/File:Allerdale_UK_locator_map.svg

[323] Nev. Ramsden, "The Barony of Copeland," *A Copeland Journal,* November 2012. http://rumbutter.info/gen-cumb-nr-places-copeland-journal/barony

[324] John Hodgson-Hinde and William Dickson, *The Pipe-rolls, Or Sheriff's Annual Accounts of the Revenues of the Crown for the Counties of Cumberland, Westmoreland and Durham* (Newcastle: T. and J. Hodgson, Society of Antiquaries of Newcastle Upon Tyne, 1847), lxii-lxvi. https://archive.org/details/piperollsorsher00dickgoog/page/n77/mode/2up?q=copeland

## St. Cuthbert Connection.

St. Cuthbert was a Christian saint in the Celtic Culdee tradition and the patron saint of Northumbria (Appendix D).[325] Forne Sigulfson, was a benefactor to the Priory of Hexham in Northumberland,[326] like his Grimthorpe cousins, from Lincolnshire.[327] Hexham Priory was a convent known for its connection to St. Cuthbert. This may explain Forne's involvement in mediating the claim of the monks of St. Cuthbert to Tynemouth Priory and why the first charter his theorized son, William de Graham, witnesses is for a church dedicated to St. Cuthbert.[328] Forne had ties to Northumbria as he possessed estates near Coquetdale in Northumberland[329] and his father, Sigulf, served Gospatric, Earl of Northumbria as his deputy. In the eleventh and twelfth centuries, it was uncommon for the patrons of Culdee monasteries and priories to be Normans since Normans were Roman Catholic.[ix] The Canmores, Scottish Royal family, did embrace Culdee saints like St. Cuthbert, St. Columba, and St. Patrick and also Celtic traditions in an effort to avoid a schism between the native Culdee Church and Rome.[330]

*Figure 26: St. Cuthbert Church, Edinburgh Castle in Background. Photo by Barry S. Graham.*

*Figure 27: The Cross Pattée of the Knights Templar* [332]

*Figure 28: St. Cuthbert's pectoral cross, from the 5th century, one of the few items of value to have survived from the shrine. It is made of gold and garnets. © Durham Cathedral and Jarold Printing* [331]

---

[325] "St. Cuthbert," Catholic Online, accessed 29 December 2022. https://www.catholic.org/saints/saint.php?saint_id=491

[326] James Raine, *The Priory of Hexham, Its Chroniclers, Endowments and Annals*, Vol. I (Durham: The Surtees Society, Andrews and Co, 1864), 59. https://archive.org/details/prioryofhexham01rain

[327] David X. Carpenter, Faculty of History, University of Oxford, "William Fitz Ulf, Soke Tenant in Pocklington (Yorks ER), Archive of the Dacre Family," *The Charters of William II and Henry I Project* (20 October 2014): 2,5. https://actswilliam2henry1.files.wordpress.com/2013/04/h1-william-fitz-ulf-2014-1.pdf

[328] Stephen M. Lewis, "Forne Sigulfson-The 'First' Lord of Greystoke in Cumbria."

[329] William Farrer, *Early Yorkshire charters; being a collection of documents anterior to the thirteenth century made from the public records, monastic chartularies, Roger Dodsworth's manuscripts and other available sources*, Vol. I, 325. https://archive.org/details/earlyyorkshirech01farruoft/page/324/mode/2up?q=forn

[330] "Saint November 16: St. Margaret of Scotland," Catholic News World, 15 November 2015. http://www.catholicnewsworld.com/2015/11/saint-november-16-st-margaret-of.html

Three important points regarding St. Cuthbert:

1. The striking resemblance of the Cross of St. Cuthbert[331] to the Templar cross[332] (Figure 27 and 28), also called a "cross pattée")
2. David I brings St. Cuthbert to Scotland in charters dated 1127 and 1128.[333] Concurrently, he established the Scottish Order of the Temple of Solomon or Knights Templar in 1128.[334]
3. Alan, grandson of Gospatric I, and other family members are witnesses on key charters donating land to the monks of St. Cuthbert.[335] There seem to be parallels with the Dundaff Grahams in the thirteenth century.[336] Perhaps this Alan held a similar financial role in the Templars in the twelfth century that the Dundaff Grahams held in the thirteenth? See Appendix D.

Forne's death is estimated to be 1129/1130, when his son Ivo appears in the pipe rolls of Henry I in his stead. Per Dr. Lewis: "Forne's 'Greystoke' family continued as Lords of Greystoke in a direct male line until 1306," when more distant relatives succeeded to the title: first the lords of Grimthorpe (Fitzwilliams), then the Dacres.[337] The Greystoke barony remained in the Grimthorpe/Fitzwilliam family in the male line until 1487, when it passed by the distaff (female) side to Thomas Dacre, second Baron Dacre, and to the Barons Dacre of Gilsland. In 1488, Sir Thomas Dacre eloped with Elizabeth Greystoke, Sixth Baroness Greystoke (10 July 1471 – 14 August 1516), daughter of Sir Robert de Greystoke and Lady Elizabeth Grey. In 1571, Greystoke passed to the Howards—the Dukes of Norfolk.[338] [339] In 1566, Lady Elizabeth Dacre inherited Greystoke Castle on the death of her husband. She then married Thomas Howard, Duke of Norfolk, and his three sons married her three daughters, securing the transfer of

> **Fun Fact**
> When Edgar Rice Burroughs wrote the first of his *Tarzan* novels in 1912, he based it on the lords of Greystoke, having met one of the Howards when both were on assignment in South Africa.

---

[331] Figure 28: "The Keeper of the Shrine," Durham World Heritage Site, St. Cuthbert's Pectoral Cross, accessed 25 December 2022. https://www.durhamworldheritagesite.com/learn/architecture/cathedral/intro/cuthbert-shrine/keeper-of-the-shrine

[332] Figure 27: Wikimedia Commons contributors, "File:Knights Templar Cross.svg," Wikimedia Commons, the free media repository, accessed 6 December 2022. https://commons.wikimedia.org/w/index.php?title=File:Knights_Templar_Cross.svg&oldid=683925021

[333] "Our History," The Parish Church of St. Cuthbert, accessed 28 December 2022. https://stcuthberts-edinburgh.churchdesk.com/page/39/our-history

[334] "The Order of the Temple in Scotland," The Knights Templar, accessed 28 December 2022. https://www.theknightstemplar.org/scottish-templars/

[335] Sir Archibald Lawrie, *Early Scottish Charters, Prior to 1153 AD*, 80, 90, 93, 96, 100, 108, 110, 147, 148, 150, 159, 162, 180, 181, 187, 188, 189, 197.

[336] PoMS, "No. 2005-David Graham (III), Sheriff of Berwick," accessed 12 November 2022. https://www.poms.ac.uk/record/person/2005/

[337] Stephen M. Lewis, "Forne Sigulfson-The Normans Come to Cumbria."

[Fun Fact Blurb] "Tarzan!" Stafford House, accessed 27 December 2022. http://www.stafford-house.co.uk/information-contact-us/things-to-do-and-where-to-go/tarzan/

[338] C. Clay and D.E. Greenway, *Early Yorkshire Families* (United Kingdom: Yorkshire Archaeological Society, 1973), 38-39. https://www.google.com/books/edition/_/dIlnAAAAMAAJ?hl=en&gbpv=1&bsq=greystoke

[339] W. Hylton Dyer Longstaffe, "The Heirs-General to Radclyffe of Derwentwater, and the Heirs-Male to Dacre of Greystock," *Archaeologia Aeliana Series 2*. Vol 2, Society of Antiquaries of Newcastle (1858): 137-158. https://doi.org/10.5284/1059369.

Greystoke to the Howards, who, after 500 years, still own the property today.[340, 341]

## Comparing the Timeline of Events.

Dr. Lewis provides evidence that Forne's father, Sigulf, was "Gospatric's man." In other words, he was second-in-command to Gospatric, Earl of Northumbria, and possibly related to him via marriage.[342] Gospatric recognized "Sygulf" as a major landholder/ruler in Cumbria, one who was to be emulated, in a famous letter written in Old English sometime after 1067. In addition, Nunburnholme in Yorkshire was transferred to Sigulf in 1072, the same year Gospatric was removed as earl for the final time. By 1086, Nunburnholme had transferred again, this time to Sigulf's son, Forne. "Forne, son of Sigulf" is mentioned in Domesday Book of 1086 as holding a manor at Nunburnholme in East Riding of Yorkshire.[343] Domesday omitted Northumbria and Cumbria; as neither had yet come under Norman control.[344] We know about Forne's Northumberland lands through another source.[345] About forty years later, the Greystokes and Gospatric descendants had intermarried (Edgar, son of "Gospatric III," and Alice de Greystoke married circa 1127[346]). See Figure 37. Greystoke Castle is only a few miles from the Allerdale boundary,[347] so the families' properties were near each other.[348]

---

[340] "Thomas Howard, Fourth Duke of Norfolk (1536-1572)," British Armorial Bindings, *University of Toronto Libraries*, 2021. https://armorial.library.utoronto.ca/stamp-owners/HOW010

[341] Rev. Charles Henry Hartshorne, *Feudal and Military Antiquities of Northumberland*, Bell and Daldy (1858), 76. https://openlibrary.org/works/OL7718082W/Feudal_and_military_antiquities_of_Northumberland_and_the_Scottish_borders

[342] Some individual genealogies claim Forne married Gospatric's sister, Wulflead. Géry Vander Goten and Nadine Jacob, "Wulflead of Atholl," Genea.net, accessed 28 December 2022. https://gw.geneanet.org/u649578?lang=en&iz=461&p=wulflead&n=of+atholl

[343] Anna Powell Smith, "Forne, Son of Sigulf."

[344] Stephen M. Lewis, "Forne Sigulfson-The 'First' Lord of Greystoke in Cumbria."

[345] William Farrer, *Early Yorkshire charters; being a collection of documents anterior to the thirteenth century made from the public records, monastic chartularies, Roger Dodsworth's manuscripts and other available sources*, Vol. I, 325.

[346] Montgomery and Rowntree Families and Genealogy, "Alice de Greystoke," Monty's History Notes, accessed 28 December 2022. http://www.montyhistnotes.com/genealogy/getperson.php?personID=I708&tree=MontyHistNotes_II

[347] Figure 29: Wikimedia Commons contributors, "File:Cumbria UK locator map 2010.svg," *Wikimedia Commons*, accessed 16 April 2023. https://commons.wikimedia.org/w/index.php?title=File:Cumbria_UK_locator_map_2010.svg&oldid=488795389

Figure 30: "Welcome Furness and Westmoreland," Simon Fell, Member of Parliament for Barrow and Furness, accessed 15 April 2023. https://www.simonfell.org/news/furnessandwestmorland

[348] Anna Powell Smith, "Forne, Son of Sigulf."

*Figure 29: The Ceremonial County of Cumbria in Northwest England.* [347] *CC BY-SA 3.0*

*Figure 30: Pre-April 2023 District Boundaries for Cumbria: Allerdale (orange), and Copeland (gold) and Carlisle (blue) Districts; Greystoke is located in the district of Eden (lime green), a few miles from the from the boundary with Allerdale.* [347]

# Chapter 5
# Heraldry[x]

## The Trail of the Scallop Shell

Most Graham armorials since the third Sir Henry de Graham, grandson of William de Graham (circa 1230),[349] have one thing in common: escallops or scallop shells ("escallop" is the term used in heraldry). Other families that use the escallop in their armorials have Norman origins, which indicates the use of the symbol arrived in Britain with the Normans. Per Duane Galles of the Heraldry Society, the escallop was associated with St. James, but also St. Michael the Archangel in Normandy, Brittany, and Poitou.[350] He is primarily depicted as a warrior clad in armor and is considered a patron saint of warriors.[351] The escallop appears prominently in the arms of the Norman abbey dedicated to Saint Michael,[352] Mont Saint-Michel, built in the eighth century. (Figure 31).[353] In 1067, the monastery of Mont Saint-Michel gave its support to William the Conqueror in his claim to the throne of England. For that, he

*Figure 31: The Arms of Mont Saint-Michel, Art by Euryel.*[352] *CC-BY-SA 3.0*

---

[349] J. H. S., "The Grahams: The First Line of the Grahams (Continued)," *The Scottish Antiquary, or, Northern Notes and Queries* 17, no. 68 (1903): 178. http://www.jstor.org/stable/25517111.

[350] Duane L.C.M. Galles, "Pilgrims and Heraldry."

[351] Jose Gonzalez, "The Warrior Angel with a Message," Google Arts and Culture, accessed 4 November 2022. https://artsandculture.google.com/usergallery/god-s-warrior-angel-with-a-message-jose-gonzalez/hQKitjyv0Db2IQ

[352] Figure 31: Wikimedia Commons contributors, "File:Arms of Mont-Saint-Michel Abbey.svg," Wikimedia Commons, the free media repository, accessed 21 February 2023. https://commons.wikimedia.org/w/index.php?title=File:Arms_of_Mont-Saint-Michel_Abbey.svg&oldid=702109558

[353] Duane L.C.M. Galles, "Pilgrims and Heraldry."

rewarded them with properties and grounds in England.[354] Families from Northern France with the surname "Michel" also made use of the escallop in *armes parlantes*. For example, the Norman family of Michel de Cambernon "bore Azure, a Cross between four Escallops Or," which means it was blue with a gold cross between four gold scallop shells (Figure 32).[355] See Appendix E for more information on heraldry terminology.[356]

Figure 32: Armorial of Michel de Cambernon. CC BY 4.0 [355]

The Most Distinguished Order of Saint Michael and Saint George is a British order of chivalry founded on 28 April 1818 by George IV while he was acting as Prince Regent. The order is named in honor of two military saints: St. Michael and St. George. The badge of the order shows St. Michael trampling Satan on the front side, while the reverse shows St. George on horseback slaying a dragon. Their current Grand Master is Prince Edward, Duke of Kent.[357]

The iconic scallop shell symbol is most famously connected throughout Europe with the Patron Saint of Spain, St. James the Greater, the Apostle and fisherman. He is also considered the patron saint of pilgrims. James and his brother John left their lives as fishermen when Jesus summoned them as described in all four gospels. Following the crucifixion of Jesus Christ, James made a pilgrimage to the Iberian Peninsula to evangelize, and when he returned to Judea, he was beheaded by King Herod Agrippa I in the year 44 A.D., as detailed in Acts Chapter 12 of the New Testament. The remains, or relics, of St. James the Greater were then transported by his followers to the Iberian Peninsula and are said to be buried in Santiago de Compostela in Galicia, Spain, where scallop shells are common.[358]

**Did You know?**
Today, the French still call scallops "Coquille-Saint Jacques," the Dutch: "sint-jakobschelpen," and the Germans: "Jakobsmuscheln."

Figure 33: Collar of the French Royal Order of Saint Michael the Archangel. CC-BY-SA 3.0 [361]

---

[354] Wikibooks contributors, "Saint Michael: Early Anglo-Saxon Tradition/Saint Michael and the Norman Conquest of England," Wikibooks, The Free Textbook Project, accessed 4 November 2022. https://en.wikibooks.org/w/index.php?title=Saint_Michael:_Early_Anglo-Saxon_Tradition/Saint_Michael_and_the_Norman_Conquest_of_England&oldid=4086057

[355] Figure 32: Wikimedia Commons contributors, "File:Blason famille Michel de Cambernon.svg," Wikimedia Commons, the free media repository, accessed 25 December 2022.
https://commons.wikimedia.org/w/index.php?title=File:Blason_famille_Michel_de_Cambernon.svg&oldid=708359775

[356] Duane L.C.M. Galles, "Pilgrims and Heraldry."

[357] "Order of St. Michael and St. George," Military History Fandom, accessed 4 November 2022.
https://military-history.fandom.com/wiki/Order_of_St_Michael_and_St_George

[358] Gail Delahunt, "Everything you need to know about St. James the Greater," Follow the Camino, 27 December 2019.
https://followthecamino.com/en/blog/history-of-the-apostle-saint-james/

The crusaders of the Order of St. James of Compostela, protectors of pilgrims, pioneered the shell[359] as their own symbol.[360] The shell was later adapted by the families serving in the Crusades and by the French royal Order of Saint Michael the Archangel, founded in 1469 by Louis XI. The collar of the Order was composed of scallop shells linked by gold chains (Figure 33) from which a pendant with an image of the Archangel Michael battling a dragon was depicted.[361] The final piece of evidence to connect the shell to both St. Michael and St. James is the "Camino de Santiago." The "Camino de Santiago," or "Way of St. James," is a network of pilgrimage trails built in the ninth century from Spain to France and Portugal to Italy and is marked with scallop shells.[362] As stated, the shell also appears prominently in the arms of the Norman abbey of Mont Saint-Michel, which, coincidentally, is the first stop on the Camino for pilgrims beginning their journey in Northwest France.[363] The Camino physically connected the two saints in the ninth century through the now famous trails that joined St. Michael's Abbey with St. James' burial site in Galicia, Spain.

*Figure 34: Extracted image of Saint James from the altarpiece in church of Mount San Martino, Italy painted by Carlo Crivelli circa 1480.* [366]

Influenced by the Normans, many British families engaging in the Crusades[364] adopted the scallop shells in their coats of arms. The timing of the popularity of Saint Michael and the use of scallop shells in coats of arms, including the Graham Coats of Arms, can be tied to the arrival of the Normans.[365] In fact, the early use of the shells in heraldry and dedications to St. James[366] and St. Michael the Archangel can be indicators to help identify families with Norman connections or families who were

---

[359] The popularity of the scallop shell and its association with St. Michael the Archangel in Normandy may be due to the legend that St. James of Compostela visited Charlemagne (747-814) in a dream and urged him to liberate his forgotten tomb in Spain from the Saracens. St. Michael the Archangel, as the patron saint of warriors, would have been tied to the campaign to liberate Spain. "History of Charlemagne and Roland, Compostela and the Legend of the Milky Way," Compostela, Joining Heaven and Earth, accessed 7 March 2023. https://compostela.co.uk/mythology/charlemagne-and-the-legend-of-the-milky-way/

[360] Charles Moeller, "Order of Saint James of Compostela," *New Advent- The Catholic Encyclopedia.* Vol. 13. (New York: Robert Appleton Company, 1912), accessed 27 December 2022. http://www.newadvent.org/cathen/13353a.htm

[361] Figure 33: Wikimedia Commons contributors, "File:Keten van de Orde van Sint Michael 1660.jpg," Wikimedia Commons, the free media repository, accessed 25 December 2022. https://commons.wikimedia.org/w/index.php?title=File:Keten_van_de_Orde_van_Sint_Michael_1660.jpg&oldid=704323928

[362] "Routes of Santiago de Compostela in France," Unesco-World Heritage Convention, accessed 28 December 2022. https://whc.unesco.org/en/list/868

[363] "Mont Saint Michel to Jean D'Angely," Camino Pilgrim, The Confraternity of St. James, accessed: 4 November 2022. https://www.csj.org.uk/mont-saint-michel

[Did You Know? Blurb] English to French translation for scallop: https://en.bab.la/dictionary/english-french/scallop; English to Dutch translation for scallop: https://en.bab.la/dictionary/english-dutch/scallop; English to German translation for scallops: https://m.interglot.com/en/de/?q=scallops

[364] University of Exeter, "Norman dominance of Europe inspired first crusades in the Holy Land, new book claims," Phys.org, 7 September 2022. https://phys.org/news/2022-09-norman-dominance-europe-crusades-holy.html

[365] Anthony Foljambe Blog, "Chaptre the 17th, The Scallop Shells Crusades," Anthony Foljambe 1615-1669: An English Normand in America, accessed 27 December 2022. https://anthonyfoljambe.blogspot.com/2017/01/chaptre-17th-scallop-shells-crusades.html

[366] Figure 34: Wikimedia Commons contributors, "File:Carlo Crivelli 064.jpg," Wikimedia Commons, the free media repository, accessed 25 December 2022. https://commons.wikimedia.org/w/index.php?title=File:Carlo_Crivelli_064.jpg&oldid=706789331

involved in the Crusades and supported the knightly orders (Templars, Hospitallers, Trinitarians).[367]

# Family Crests

The family crest of the Grimthorpes, cousins of the Greystokes, includes a boar,[368] and the family armorials for the Grimstons and Grimbys, possible relatives, also have boars.[369] "Grim" is Old Norse for "fierce."[370] The boar is the ancient Pictish, Norse, and Celtic symbol for courage and strength in battle.[371] In Scottish heraldry, the boar is drawn "couped," or erased below the neck[372] and is frequently found in burial places of Celtic chieftains.[373] It can be argued that the Norman equivalent symbol of the boar would be the symbol of the patron saint of warriors, Saint Michael the Archangel. St. Michael is sometimes represented by a dragon but also by the escallop.[374] As locals "Normanized" their names to garner favor with the Norman court,[375] perhaps they also "Normanized" their armorials? As discussed, "Grayham or Graham" could be a variant of the Gristock (Greystoke) surname when translated to/from the abbreviated Latin used in medieval documents. I believe the original spelling for this barony was indeed "Gristock," where "Gris" is Norse for "boar" [376] and "stock" is from the Norse *stokkr* and the Old English *stocc* for "tree trunk" (later used to mean "place").[377] This could explain why tree trunks are found in Graham heraldry and why the alternate symbol on many Graham armorials is the boar. Grimes is believed to be an alternate spelling for "Graham," particularly in Ireland, and the Grimes family uses the tree trunk in their coats of arms.

*Figure 35: Boar's Head Couped (cut off)-Scottish style—A Complete Guide to Heraldry, by Arthur Charles Fox-Davies, published in 1909.*

Lang Will Graham's son, Fergus of Mote, included a tree trunk and a boar's head in his coat of arms[378] (Figure 36). Phil Graham believes Fergus of Mote may have chosen the uprooted tree to symbolize his family being uprooted

---

[367] "The Great, Parliamentary, or Bannerets' Roll, c. 1312," part of the British Museum's manuscript collection, Aspilogia, accessed 27 December 2022. http://www.aspilogia.com/N-Parliamentary_Roll/N-0592-0701.html

[368] "Grimthorpe Family Crests," My Family Silver, accessed 8 November 2022. https://www.myfamilysilver.com/crestfinder-search/grimthorpe-family-crest

[369] "Whitehall, February 16, 1886," *The London Gazette*, 744. https://www.thegazette.co.uk/London/issue/25559/page/744

[370] Ross G. Arthur, *English-Old Norse Dictionary*, Publication Linguistic Series (Cambridge, Ontario: 2002), 53. https://www.yorku.ca/inpar/language/English-Old_Norse.pdf

[371] Symbols.com, "Boar," STANDS4 Network, accessed 4 December 2022. https://www.symbols.com/symbol/boar .

[372] Figure 35: Arthur Charles Fox-Davies, "Beasts," *A Complete Guide to Heraldry* (Edinburgh: T.C. & E.C. Jack, 1909), 199, accessed 17 December 2022 via Wikisource. https://en.wikisource.org/wiki/A_Complete_Guide_to_Heraldry/Chapter_12

[373] Jen Delyth, "Boar," Celtic Art Studio, accessed 27 December 2022. https://www.celticartstudio.com/symbol/f/SYMBOLS/88

[374] Duane L.C.M. Galles, "Pilgrims and Heraldry."

[375] Stephen M. Lewis, "Forne Sigulfson-The Normans Come to Cumbria."

[376] Wiktionary contributors, "gris," Wiktionary, The Free Dictionary, accessed 4 November 2022. https://en.wiktionary.org/w/index.php?title=gris&oldid=69567367

[377] Wiktionary contributors, "stoc," Wiktionary, The Free Dictionary, accessed 5 December 2022. https://en.wiktionary.org/w/index.php?title=stoc&oldid=68776363

[378] Figure 36: Robert Riddle Stodart, *Scottish Arms, Being a Collection of Armorial Bearings A.D. 1370 – 1678* Vol. I, William Patterson (Edinburgh: 1881), n206 (Plate 79A). https://archive.org/details/ScottishArmsV1/page/n205/mode/2up?q=79A

from their home in Hutton Parish in Scotland and transplanted in northern England. Another prominent example of the use of boars' heads in Graham armorials: Sir Nicholas de Graham, of Dalkeith, Abercorn, and Eskdale, used three boars' heads surrounding a shield of three escallops in chief in his seal in 1260.[379] However, in the 1296 Ragman Roll, Sir Nicholas used the three escallops in chief (without the boars), common to the Montrose and Dalkeith Grahams.[380] The shield of his brother, Peter/Pieres de Graham, had three boar's heads and no shells at all.[381] The seal of Sir Nicholas' son, Sir John de Graham of Mosskesswra (d. 1337), was similar to his father's—three boars' heads surrounding a shield of three escallops in chief, but with another boar's head on the shield itself.[382] Sir Patrick Graham of Dundaff and Kincardine used a similar seal (except it was two boars' heads) in 1292.[383] Further, the Grahams of Orchill, a cadet of the house of Montrose, used a boar's head in their armorials.[384]

*Figure 36: Arms of Fergus Graham of Mote* [378]

There is substantial historical evidence, complemented by Y-DNA data from the FTDNA Graham Surname Project, to support the theory that William de Graham, the first recorded Graham, was of the Norse family of the Greystokes of Cumbria and Yorkshire. The Greystokes and Earl Gospatric's families were geographically close, loyal to each other, and possibly cousins.[385] The important conclusion to draw here is if the relationship between the families began *before* the Norman conquest (1066A.D.), then neither family was of Norman origin. In addition, the Greystokes, William de Graham, Gospatric's family, and the Kirkpatricks had ties to the Native Culdee saints (such as St. Cuthbert and St. Patrick),[386] another indication that the families were not Norman.

Furthermore, based on: research into Graham genealogy, familial bonds, sept clans, land ownership through knighthood, heraldry, the locations and proximity of Graham and Greystoke lands on historical maps, land charter records, and Y-DNA, we can say the first recorded Graham, William de Graham, was of Norse (likely Danish) origin. There is a strong case that he descended from the Greystokes of Cumbria. As participation in the FTDNA surname projects grow and project members expand their level of DNA testing, the particular branches of William de Graham's descendants can be further determined.

---

[379] J.H. Stevenson, *Heraldry in Scotland,* Volume I (Glasgow: James Maclehose and Sons, 1914), 20, Plate II-4. https://ia800300.us.archive.org/14/items/heraldryinscotla01stev/heraldryinscotla01stev.pdf

[380] Bruce A. McAndrew, "The Sigillography of the Ragman Roll," *Proceedings of the Society of Antiquaries of Scotland,* (2000); *706*. Retrieved from http://journals.socantscot.org/index.php/psas/article/view/10060

[381] Lloyd D. Graham *House Graham, From the Antoine Wall to the Temple of Hymen*, 1-5.

[382] William Fraser, *The Annandale Family Book of the Johnstones, Earls and Marquises of Annandale,* Vol. I, 10-11.

[383] Bruce A. McAndrew. *Scotland's Historic Heraldry* (United Kingdom: Boydell Press, 2006), 137.

[384] J.H. Steveson, *Heraldry in Scotland,* Vol. II (Glasgow: James Maclehose and Sons, 1914), 290. https://ia600304.us.archive.org/3/items/heraldryinscotla02stev/heraldryinscotla02stev.pdf

[385] Géry Vander Goten and Nadine Jacob, "Wulflead of Atholl."

[386] Josh Mittleman, Steve Roylance, and Pedr Gurteen, "Concerning the Names *Patrick, Pádraig, Patricia,* and the Like," MedievalScotland.org, 30 November 1998. https://medievalscotland.org/problem/names/padraig.shtml

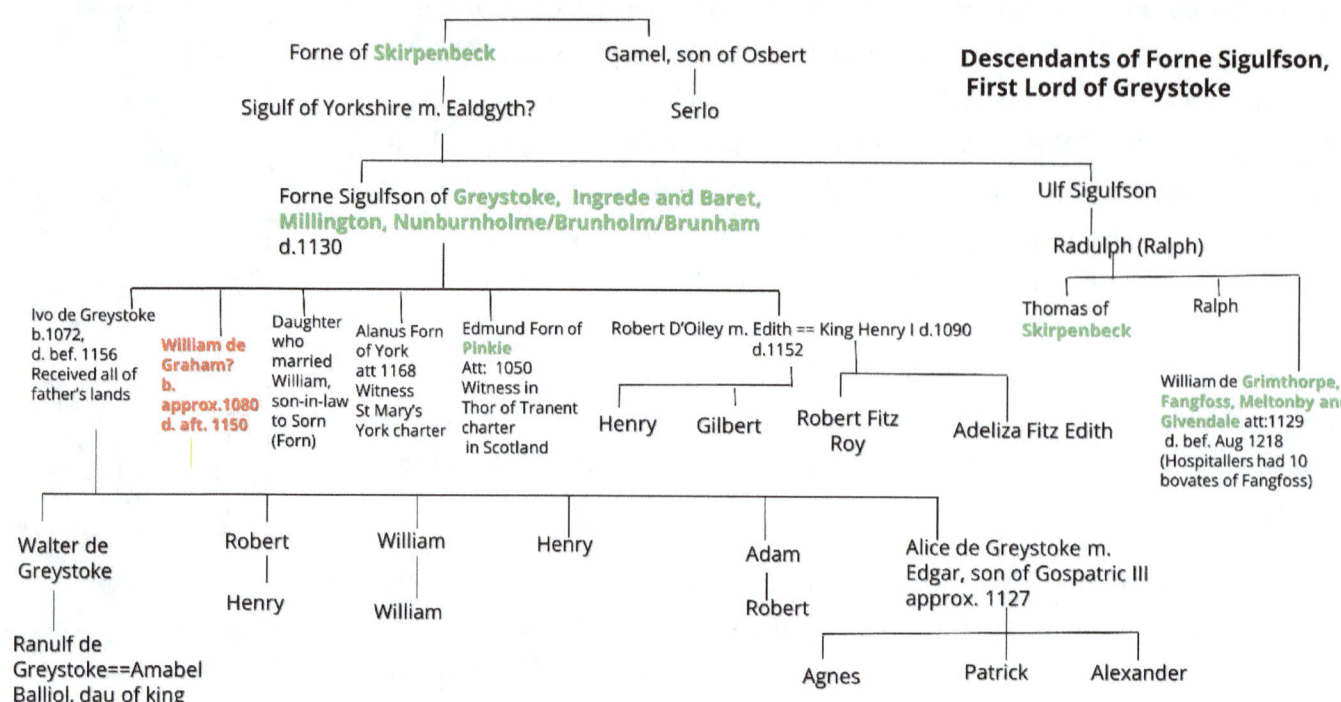

Figure 37: Proposed Ancestry of William de Graham, First Documented Graham in Scotland [387, 388, 389, 390, 391, 392, 393]

---

[387] Paul Dalton, "Feudal Politics in Yorkshire, 1066 x 1054," 68.

[388] William Farrer, *Early Yorkshire Charters: Being a Collection of Documents Anterior to the Thirteenth Century Made from the Public Records, Monastic Chartularies, Roger Dodsworth's Manuscripts and Other Available Sources*, Vol. II, 511. https://archive.org/details/earlyyorkshirech02farruoft/page/510/mode/2up?q=thornton

[389] Paul Dalton, "Feudal Politics in Yorkshire, 1066 x 1054," 157, 158, 177, 184.

[390] PoMS, "no. 374," accessed 18 October 2022. https://www.poms.ac.uk/record/source/374/

[391] Stephen M. Lewis, "Forne Sigulfson-The 'First' Lord of Greystoke in Cumbria."

[392] David X. Carpenter, Faculty of History, University of Oxford, "William Fitz Ulf, Soke Tenant in Pocklington (Yorks ER), Archive of the Dacre Family," *The Charters of William II and Henry I Project* (20 October 2014): 2,5. https://actswilliam2henry1.files.wordpress.com/2013/04/h1-william-fitz-ulf-2014-1.pdf

[393] Anna Powell Smith, "Forne, Son of Sigulf."

## Descendants of the Elder Son of William de Graham, Peter

William de Graham received the lands of Dalkeith circa 1124 from David I, King of Scots. These estates were inherited by William's elder son Peter. The lands passed to Peter's son, Sir Henry, and then his son, the second Sir Henry de Graham, Lord of Dalkeith and Hutton. The second Sir Henry acquired the lands of Hutton, Tarbolton, and Kilbucho via marriage to Christiana, daughter of Idonea Comyn and Adam Fitz Gilbert (see Figure 38).[394, 395] The children of the second Sir Henry and Christiana included: the third Sir Henry, a son Nicholas[396] and possibly two daughters, one of whom married a Corrie.[397]

## The Corries, a Previously Unknown Sept Clan of Clan Graham

What is not widely known is that the Corrie/Corry family became a Sept Clan of the elder line of William de Graham in the thirteenth century. In a charter from circa 1214, Henry Graham, Lord of Hutton, granted a lease of the lands of Over Dryfe to Sir David of Torthorwald and named witnesses Sir Nicholas de Graham and "Henricus de Graham, filius Radulpho de Corry"—or Henry de Graham, son of Ralph Corry.[398] At the time, younger sons did not necessarily inherit their father's property and surname, as that right was reserved for the eldest son. As such, they were at liberty to choose the surname that was most expedient for them. It wasn't until the sixteenth century, with the introduction of parish registers, that hereditary surnames for all became common.[399]

---

[394] Jane Brankstone Thomas, J.C. B. Sharp, and Michael Anne Guido, "A Cumberland Family with Medieval Roots in Scotland and Northern England: A Study Gilbert Fitz Richer and His Descendants," Foundation for Medieval Genealogy, *Foundations* (2008): 360. https://fmg.ac/phocadownload/userupload/foundations2/JN-02-05/358Richer.pdf

[395] PoMS, "No. 5972-Tarbolton," accessed 18 October 2022. https://www.poms.ac.uk/record/source/5972/; PoMS, "no. 4425-Kilbucho," accessed 18 October 2022. https://www.poms.ac.uk/record/source/4425/; PoMS, no. 11964-Hutton, accessed 18 October 2022. https://www.poms.ac.uk/record/person/11964/

[396] Sir James Balfour Paul, *The Scots Peerage, Founded on Wood's Edition,* Vol. VI (Edinburgh: David Douglas, 1909), 197-198. https://archive.org/details/scotspeeragefoun06pauluoft/page/n5/mode/2up?q=graham

[397] J.E. Corrie, *Records of the Corrie Family, 802-1899 A.D.,* 133.

[398] *Registrum Honoris de Morton, Volume II: Ancient Charters,* 2-3.

[399] Ellen Castelow, "Surnames," HistoricUK, accessed 1 January 2023. https://www.historic-uk.com/CultureUK/Surnames/

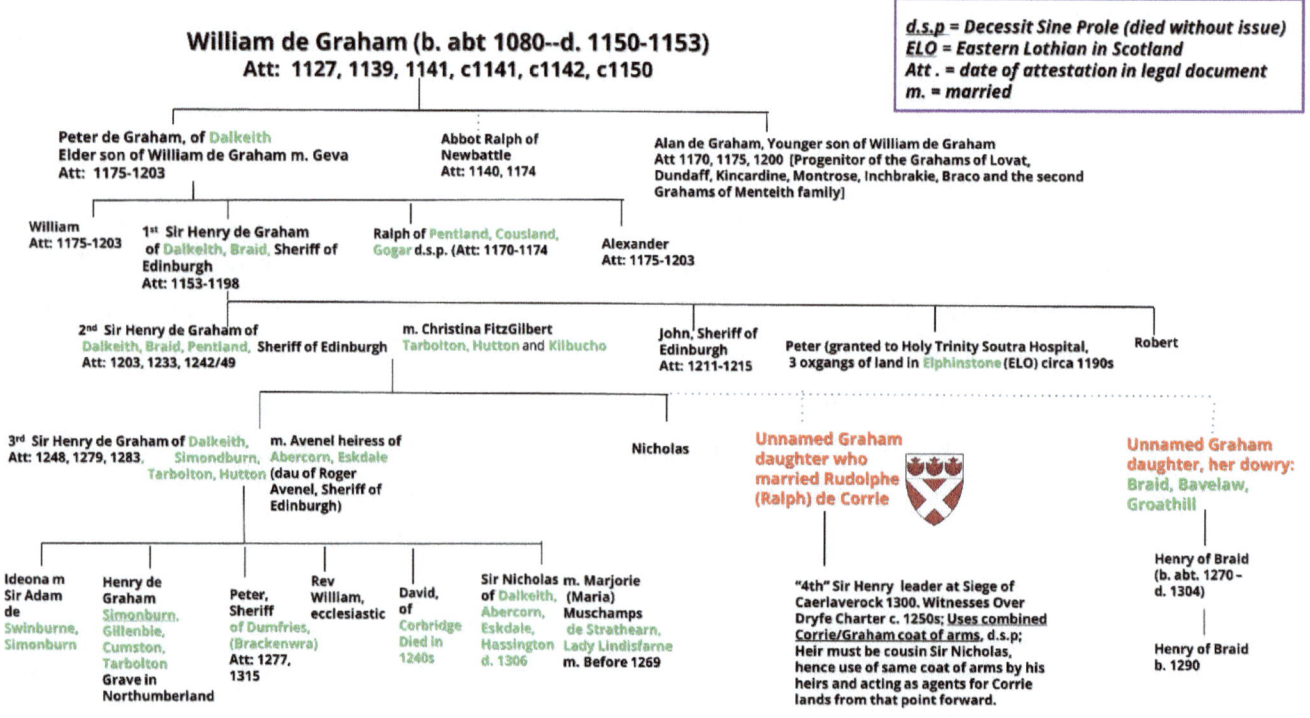

*Figure 38: Amended William de Graham Tree Showing Line of his Elder son, Peter, Lord of Dalkeith*

## "Henry Confusion"

Early genealogists, like *Peerage*, seem to have confused "Henry of Braid," the "third Sir Henry de Graham," and the "fourth Sir Henry de Graham" with each other. All three Henrys lived in the same time period.

Reviewing primary source documents to detangle the "Henry confusion," we find multiple "Henrys of Braid." Braid was a locational surname for a family related to the Dalkeith Grahams. The first Henry of Braid served as Marischal and also Sheriff of Edinburgh circa 1200 [400] and acquired the Braid lands in Pentland.[401] The second Henry of Braid paid teinds (tithes) on Bavelaw lands to Holyrood Abbey between 1235 and 1236. The third Henry of Braid acquired the lands of Braid from his wife.[402] He died in 1304 or 1305 leaving a son, also named Henry, who was fifteen years old in July 1305.[403] In 1338, the fourth Henry of Braid and his daughter and heir Elizabeth Alburgh, made donations of Braids lands to St. Mary's Abbey of Newbattle[404] which was associated with the Dalkeith Grahams[xi] and the Knights Templar.[405]

Because the "first Sir Henry de Graham" was serving as Sheriff of Edinburgh about the same time that the first Henry of Braid[406] served, and the Dalkeith Grahams verified generations later that they had inherited "Braid Wood,"[407] it can be deduced that the first Sir Henry de Graham and the first Henry of Braid were the same person. Sir Henry de Graham's heir, the "second Sir Henry de Graham" was likely also the second Henry of Braid. They lived during the same time period. However, the third Henry of Braid was a son of a Graham daughter, likely nephew of the third Sir Henry de Graham, acquiring the Braids land from his mother,[408] indicating she was the daughter of the second Sir Henry de Graham (Figure 38) and sister to the "third Sir Henry de Graham."

The "third Sir Henry de Graham" of Dalkeith and Hutton was heir to the "second Sir Henry de Graham" and his wife, Christina Fitz Gilbert. Christina was the daughter of Adam Fitz Gilbert and Idonea Comyn.[409] The "third Sir

---

[400] G. W. S. Barrow, *Regesta Regnum Scottorum, Volume II, The Acts of William I (1165-1214)* (Edinburgh: University Press, 1971), 38. https://archive.org/details/actsofwilliamiki0002barr/page/38/mode/1up?view=theater&q=braid

[401] Since we believe the first Henry of Braid was the first Sir Henry de Graham, he inherited Braids lands in Pentlands from his uncle Ralph Graham who died without heirs.

[402] PoMS, "No.9004-Dower of Mother of Henry of Braid," accessed 11 December 2022. https://www.poms.ac.uk/record/source/9004/

[403] PoMS, "No. 18935," accessed 18 October 2022. https://www.poms.ac.uk/record/person/18935/

[404] William Robertson, Esq., *An index, drawn up about the year 1629, of many records of charters, granted by the different sovereigns of Scotland between the years 1309 and 1413, most of which records have been long missing. With an introduction, giving a state, founded on authentic documents still preserved, of the ancient records of Scotland, which were in that kingdom in the year 1292*, No. 180 (Edinburgh: Murry and Cochrane, 1798), 83.
https://www.familysearch.org/library/books/viewer/365596/?offset=&return=1#page=1&viewer=picture&o=&n=0&q=

[405] POMs, "No. 4968-Knights Templar," accessed 11 December 2022. https://www.poms.ac.uk/record/person/4968/; PoMS Transaction Factoid, no. 57051, accessed 11 December 2022. https://www.poms.ac.uk/record/factoid/57051/

[406] G. W. S. Barrow, *Regesta Regnum Scottorum, Volume II, The Acts of William I (1165-1214)* (Edinburgh: University Press, 1971), 38, 40. https://archive.org/details/actsofwilliamiki0002barr/page/40/mode/1up?view=theater&q=graham

[407] PoMS, "No. 7444-Newbattle Registrum," accessed 3 March 2023. https://www.poms.ac.uk/record/source/7444/

[408] PoMS, "No.9004-Dower of Mother of Henry of Braid," accessed 11 December 2022. https://www.poms.ac.uk/record/source/9004/

[409] Idonea was the daughter of Richard Comyn, a justiciar (judge), and Hextilda of Tynedale, granddaughter and heiress of Donald Bane, previous king of Scotland. Thomas, Sharp, and Guido, "A Cumberland Family with Medieval Roots in Scotland and Northern England: A Study Gilbert Fitz Richer and His Descendants," Foundation for Medieval Genealogy, *Foundations* (2008), 360.

Henry" also acquired extensive estates in Eskdale and Abercorn through his marriage to the daughter and heiress of Roger Avenel.[410]

The Henry de Graham who was the son of Ralph Corry (Figure 38) was the "fourth Sir Henry" and likely a grandson to the "second Sir Henry" of Dalkeith and Hutton via an unnamed daughter who was the wife of Ralph Corry. Henry was a first or Christian name associated with the Grahams, not the Corries/Corrys. The "fourth Sir Henry," led a cavalry company at the Siege of Caerlaverock in 1300, and may have died in that battle since the famous observer, a Franciscan Friar named Walter de Exeter, reported that Henry's company sustained heavy casualties. This Henry died without children. It seems his heir was his cousin, Sir Nicholas de Graham, as Nicholas' heirs are later found using the same combined Corrie-Graham coat of arms in Figure 39 in certain land charters for lands connected to the Corrie/Corry family.[411]

*Figure 39: Coat of Arms of the Grahams of Dalkeith, Abercorn, Eskdale, First Used by the "Fourth Sir Henry de Graham," 1300; Newm30, CC BY-SA 4.0* [413]

*Figure 40: Corrie of Newby Coat of Arms granted to Sir Walter de Corrie with the fief of Newby, 1296. This saltire (X-shaped cross) was used by vassals of the Bruces of Annandale. By Brianann MacAmhlaidh, CC BY-SA 4.0* [414]

The banner of the "fourth Sir Henry" was documented in the poem "The Siege of Carlaverock," attributed to Walter of Exeter. The banner was described: "Arms red as blood, with a white Saltier and chief, on which he had three red escallop shells,"[412] as shown in Figure 39.[413] Four years prior, in 1296, Sir Walter de Corrie, a close relative, was granted the fief of Newby and adopted the Bruce armorial with the white saltire (an X-shaped cross) on a gules (red) field (Figure 40), indicating the Corries were in the service of the Bruces.[414] In fact, the Corries were keepers of the

---

[410] J. H. S. "The Grahams: The First Line of the Grahams (Continued)," *The Scottish Antiquary, or, Northern Notes and Queries* 17, no. 68 (1903), 178. http://www.jstor.org/stable/25517111

[411] William Fraser, *The Annandale Family book of the Johnstones, Earls and Marquises of Annandale*, Vol. I, 10-11.

[412] Walter of Exeter, Franciscan Friar and Witness to the Siege, *The Siege of Carlaverock*, 1300, accessed 18 October 2022, https://www.deremilitari.org/RESOURCES/SOURCES/carlaverock.htm

[413] Figure 39: Wikimedia Commons contributors, "File:K-094-Coat of Arms-GRAHAM-Henry de Graham ('Henri de Graham').png," Wikimedia Commons, the free media repository, accessed 28 December 2022. https://commons.wikimedia.org/w/index.php?title=File:K-094-Coat_of_Arms-GRAHAM-Henry_de_Graham_(%22Henri_de_Graham%22).png&oldid=625987333

[414] Figure 40: Wikimedia Commons contributors, "File:Arms of Corrie (or Currie) of Newbie.svg,"Wikimedia Commons, the free media repository, accessed 28 December 2022. https://commons.wikimedia.org/w/index.php?title=File:Arms_of_Corrie_(or_Currie)_of_Newbie.svg&oldid=592588667

Bruce castles while the Carruthers served as hereditary bailie of Lochmaben for the Bruces.[415] The shield in Figure 39 combined the saltire of the Corries/Corrys with the escallops of the Grahams. See Appendix E for more on heraldry.

As shown in Figure 38, other children of the "third Sir Henry" included Peter de Graham, Sheriff of Dumfries; Idonea de Graham (who married Adam Swinburne); and Sir Nicholas de Graham of Dalkeith, Abercorn, and Eskdale (who married Maria, or Marjorie, daughter of the Earl of Strathearn). Sir Nicholas de Graham was one of the nominees of Robert the Bruce when, in 1292, the latter became a competitor for the crown. Sir Nicholas and Maria's son and heir was Sir John de Graham. His son was also known as Sir John de Graham of Dalkeith, Lord of Mosskesswra.[416] The younger Sir John was also recorded with a third title. In 1357, he signed a charter gifting lands to "beloved cousin" Roger de Kirkpatrick with the signature "John de Corry," using the "Laird of Mosskesswra" seal with the combined Corrie-Graham coat of arms.[417] He used the same name again in January 1361 when he resigned the lands of Crunzierton, Mollin Raehills, and Minnygap to James Douglas, new Lord of Dalkeith.[418] By studying the elder line of William de Graham and its scattering circa 1361-1363 with the alleged last Lord of Dalkeith surnamed Graham, many lost Graham connections may be found, such as the origin of the Border Grahams.

## Sir John "the Last" is a Misnomer

As stated, the younger Sir John de Graham (circa 1320-1362), dubbed "the Last" by *Peerage* [419] as he was the last Graham to hold the title "Lord of Dalkeith," was known by a second title: "Laird of Mosskesswra." This sobriquet was derived from the Mosskesswra lands inherited from Ideona Comyn, wife of the second Sir Henry de Graham. See historical chronology in the back of Appendix F for documentary evidence.[420] Sir John's nickname "the Last" is a misnomer, as Sir John did have children: sons named John, Alan, and possibly Nicholas, the "Vicar of Tarbolton."[421] Nicholas was a priest, so he did not marry. However, John and Alan had legitimate claims to Dalkeith, hence the need for the Douglases to get them to resign their rights. There is a 1370 charter copied in Appendix F by "John Graham of Auchincloich," son and heir of Sir John de Graham of Dalkeith, "the Last," resigning the rights of all "his lands of Dalkeith" to Sir James Douglas.[422] In a 1373 charter, son Alan de Graham, Lord of Morton, resigned his rights to Hutton to the Douglas family.[423]

Sir John "the Last" gifted or resigned many of his estates in his lifetime:

---

[415] J.E. Corrie, *Records of the Corrie Family, 802-1899 A.D.*, 136, 139.
[416] Andy King, "War, Politics, and Landed Society in Northumberland, c1296-c1408" (PhD Thesis, Durham University, 2001), 6. http://etheses.dur.ac.uk/1729/
[417] William Fraser, *The Annandale family book of the Johnstones, Earls and Marquises of Annandale*, Vol. I, 10-11.
[418] PoMS, "No. 5121," accessed 18 October 2022. https://www.poms.ac.uk/record/place/5121/
[419] Sir James Balfour Paul, *The Scots Peerage, Founded on Wood's Edition*, Vol. VI, 196.
[420] Thomas, Sharp, and Guido, "A Cumberland Family with Medieval Roots in Scotland and Northern England: A Study Gilbert Fitz Richer and His Descendants," Foundation for Medieval Genealogy, *Foundations* (2008): 360.
[421] William Robertson, Esq., *An index, drawn up about the year 1629, of many records of charters, granted by the different sovereigns of Scotland between the years 1309 and 1413, most of which records have been long missing. With an introduction, giving a state, founded on authentic documents still preserved, of the ancient records of Scotland, which were in that kingdom in the year 1292*, No. 284, 93.
[422] John Reid, "Material for a Place Name Survey of East Stirlingshire," 109. https://spns.org.uk/wp-content/uploads/2019/12/John-Reids-East-Stirlingshire-place-name-data-v2019.pdf
[423] *Registrum Honoris de Morton, Volume II: Ancient Charters*, 88, 115, 117-119.

- Granted Elphinstone[424] and part of Elliston in Roxburghshire to his cousin, John, son of Richard de Grame[425] (1361, see Figure 41).
- Gifted Over Dryfe and Wamphray/Drumcreth to Sir Roger Kirkpatrick, "beloved cousin" (Over Dryfe in 1355, Wamphray/Drumcreth in 1357). Sir Roger was murdered shortly thereafter in June 1357, so there is a question whether Sir Roger ever took possession of Wamphray and if it reverted back to the Grahams after his death.[426]
- Resigned Tarbolton in favor of Sir John Stewart (1357).[427]

Sister Sybilla and her husband, Sir William More/Mure, received lands in the sheriffdom of Edinburgh, to include lands in Ravelston, Dean and Upper Merchiston, possibly as a tocher or dowry, upon their marriage which was probably around the same time her siblings were marrying, in the 1340s. Sometime between her marriage and 1363, she and her husband also received lands in West Binns in the barony of Abercorn.[428] The younger Sir John de Graham granted the lands of Kilbucho in Peeblesshire as a tocher to his sister Elizabeth upon marriage to Sir William Douglas of Lugton in 1341.[429] Puzzlingly, in 1342, "John Graham, Lord of Abercorn" made a second extremely generous grant of the entire Dalkeith barony to the same brother-in-law, Sir William.[430] Elizabeth and William Douglas had a single child, a daughter named Mary, who died childless about 1368.[431] Her mother, Elizabeth de Graham, later married Hugh Dacre on the death of William Douglas in 1353.[432]

> **Did you know?**
> In 2006, the producers of the movie "The Davinci Code" filmed a number of key scenes at Rosslyn Chapel.

### Knightly Orders

The younger Sir John "the Last's" Temple lands included lands surrounding Rosslyn, such as Pentland and Balantrodoch, the center of Templar activity after 1229.[433] These lands had been co-owned nearly a century before by the Grahams, their sponsored Abbey of Newbattle, and also the Sinclairs.[434] "Temple lands" would be lands associated with one of the knightly orders : Templars, Hospitallers, or Trinitarians. A search of the PoMS database shows a long list of approximately 38 land gifts associated with the Knights Templar (such as the town of Cliftoun gifted by Henry

---

[424] PoMS, "No. 10636-Elphinstone," accessed 19 October 2022. https://www.poms.ac.uk/record/source/10636/
[425] T.J. Carlyle, *The Debateable Land* (Dumfries, W.R. McDarmid and Co., 1868), 10. https://ia600206.us.archive.org/0/items/debateablelandr00carlgoog/debateablelandr00carlgoog.pdf
[426] William Fraser, *The Annandale Family book of the Johnstones, Earls and Marquises of Annandale*, Vol. I, 11.
[427] William J. Dillon, "The Trinitarians at Failford," *Ayrshire Archaeological and Natural History Society Vol 4*,(1957): 76, 91-93. https://aanhsorg.files.wordpress.com/2018/08/the-trinitarians-of-failford.pdf
[428] PoMS, "No. 23320-William More," accessed 6 November 2022. https://www.poms.ac.uk/record/person/23320/
[429] PoMS, "No. 4425-Kilbucho," accessed 19 October 2022. https://www.poms.ac.uk/record/source/4425/
[430] PoMS, "No. 10192-Dalkeith," accessed 19 October 2022. https://www.poms.ac.uk/record/source/10192/
[431] PoMS, "No. 23802-Mary Douglas died without heirs circa 1369," accessed 20 October 2022. https://www.poms.ac.uk/record/person/23802/
[432] Sir James Balfour Paul, *The Scots Peerage, Founded on Wood's Edition,* Vol. VI, 342.
[433] PoMS, no. 16175-Sir Henry Sinclair's gift of Pentland, accessed 12 November 2022. https://www.poms.ac.uk/record/person/16175/; PoMS ,no. 4968-Balantrodoch, accessed 12 November 2022. https://www.poms.ac.uk/record/person/4968/; PoMS, no.580-Lands of Pentland, Cousland (Elphinstone) and Gogar in Lothian for Ralph Graham, accessed 12 November 2022. https://www.poms.ac.uk/record/source/580/
[434] Robert Ferguson, *The Knights Templar in Scotland*, The History Press (Stroud, Gloucestershire: 2010), 47-50, 113. https://archive.org/details/knightstemplarsc0000ferg/page/n5/mode/2up?_autoReadAloud=show&view=theater&q=rosslyn .

de Graham) between 1220 and 1272 in the custody of David Graham, Sheriff of Berwick.[435] David was a suspected Templar financier. The elder Sir John Graham of Dalkeith (d. 1337) was a master of the Scottish Trinity Order of Failford.[436] For more on the knightly orders, See Appendix D.

---

[435] PoMS, "No. 2005-David Graham (III), Sheriff of Berwick," accessed 12 November 2022. https://www.poms.ac.uk/record/person/2005/
[436] William J. Dillon, "The Trinitarians at Failford," *Ayrshire Archaeological and Natural History Society* Vol 4, 76, 91-93.
[Rosslyn Chapel blurb ]"The DaVinci Code," Rosslyn Chapel 1446, accessed 12 November 2022. https://www.rosslynchapel.com/about/the-da-vinci-code/

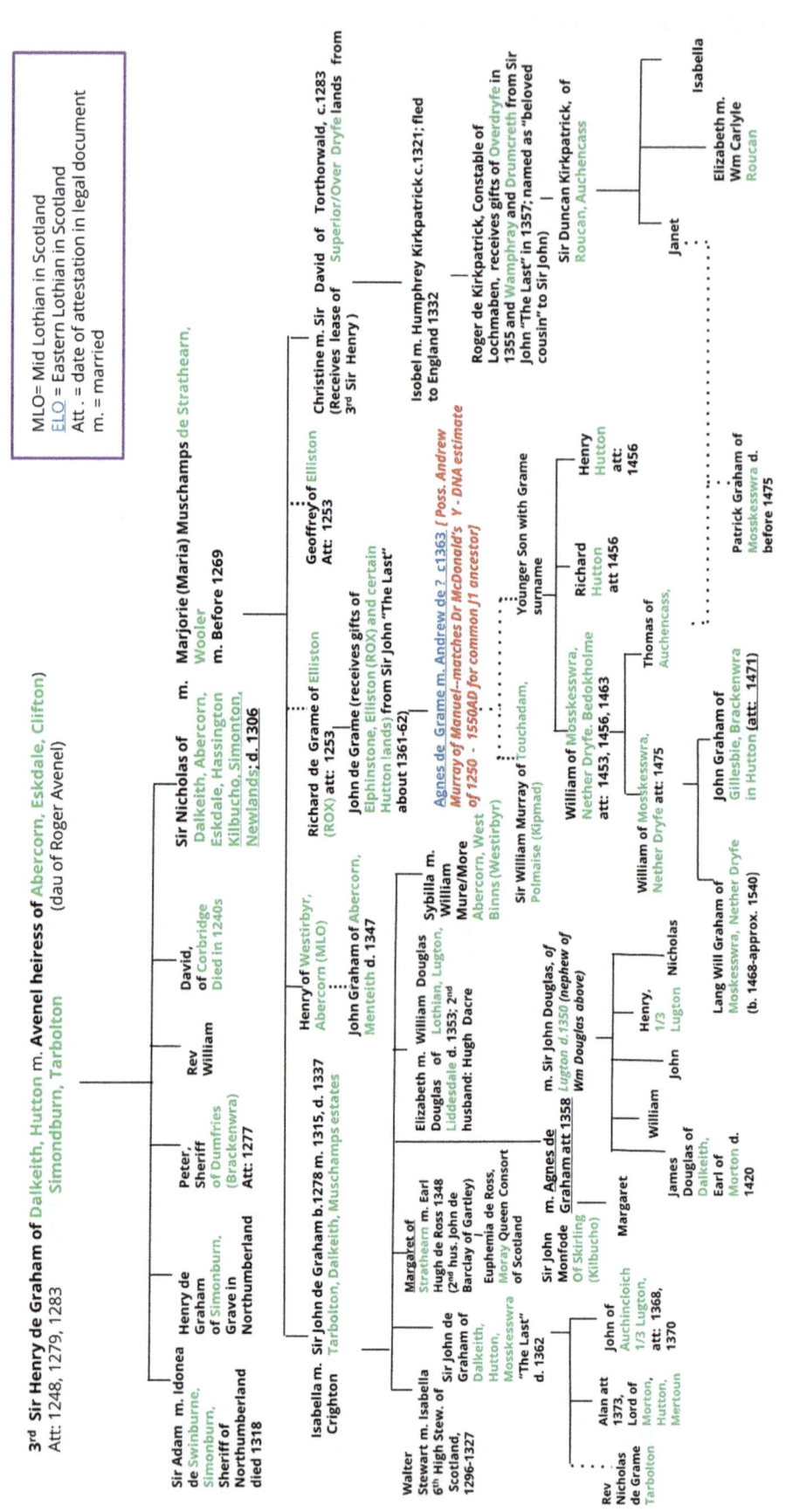

*Figure 41: Descendants of the 3rd Sir Henry de Graham of Dalkeith and Hutton and the Proposed Origin of the J1 Border Grahams*

## Margaret Graham, Another Sister of Sir John "the Last"

To further correct previous family histories, it is also necessary to focus on Margaret Graham, a sister of Sir John "the Last." Upon investigation, it can be determined that Margaret Graham of Strathearn, who died in 1348 and married Hugh, Earl of Ross, is of the elder Graham line, and sister of Sir John de Graham "the Last" (Figure 41). She would have received her grandmother's (Maria/Marjorie) Strathearn lands as her tocher/dowry. Her daughter, Euphemia de Ross, became Queen Consort of Scotland upon her marriage to Robert II.

Genealogist John Ravilious lists evidence to support his conclusion that Margaret Graham descended from the elder line of William de Graham (Dalkeith, Abercorn) and *not* the younger line (Montrose, Menteith), which has been the prevailing theory.[437]

> **Did you know?...**
> After 1215 A.D., the Fourth Lateran Council reduced the forbidden degrees for marrying couples from seven to four. A marriage between persons related in any of these ways was accounted incestuous, and the children illegitimate. The pope could grant a waiver called a "," for a fee. Scottish nobles intermarried frequently, requiring dispensations. Therefore, the ample collection of papal dispensations is a useful resource to determine relationships between established families.

I. The first evidence is found in a 1329 papal mandate indicating that Margaret is from the church diocese of St. Andrews.[438] If Margaret were a daughter of the lord of Montrose, her church-related documents would have listed her diocese as Brechin. The papal dispensation for the second marriage of Margaret's would-be brother, Sir David Graham of Montrose, indicates he is from the diocese of Brechin.[439] However, Abercorn and Dalkeith were located in the diocese of St. Andrews. Agnes de Graham, sister of Sir John "the Last" and mother of Sir James Douglas of Dalkeith, was identified as being of St. Andrews in the dispensation for her marriage to Sir John Douglas.

II. Based on the timeline, Margaret would be a daughter of the elder Sir John Graham of Dalkeith and Abercorn (d. 1337) and sister of the above-named Agnes. It is not surprising that Hugh, Earl of Ross, would have chosen a daughter of Sir John Graham of Dalkeith as his second wife. In the early fourteenth century, they were the senior and wealthiest

---

[437] John P. Ravilious, "Queen Euphemia and Her Ancestry," *The Scottish Genealogist*, The Scottish Genealogy Society (June 2017): 49-50. https://www.academia.edu/35370666/Queen_Euphemia_and_her_ancestry_TSG_LXIV_2_49_52

[By the Way blurb] Richard Burtsell, "Consanguinity (in Canon Law)," *New Advent-The Catholic Encyclopedia*, Vol. 4 (New York: Robert Appleton Company, 1908), accessed 28 December 2022.

[438] John P. Ravilious, "Queen Euphemia and Her Ancestry," *The Scottish Genealogist*, The Scottish Genealogy Society (June 2017): 49.

[439] Cushnie Enterprises, "Map of the Medieval Scottish Dioceses," Early Church in Northern Scotland (ECNS), accessed 28 December 2022. https://www.cushnieent.com/medievalchurch/map_scotland.htm

family of that name, with their holdings including lands in the Lothians, Eskdale, Ayrshire, and Dumfriesshire.

III. As Countess of Strathearn, Margaret's daughter, Euphemia, confirmed her husband Robert's grant of Keillour to James Douglas of Dalkeith at Perth on 28 February 1369/70. Significantly, in the charter, Countess Euphemia describes James Douglas as "our dear cousin lord James de Douglas, knight, lord of Dalkeith." Her mother, Margaret, was a sister of James' mother, Agnes Graham Monfode Douglas. Euphemia first married John Randolph, third earl of Moray. After John's death, she married Robert II and became Queen Consort of Scotland.[440]

How sisters Elizabeth and Margaret, daughters of the elder Sir John de Graham (d. 1337) got confused for each other:

1) First, in 1764, Sir Robert Douglas of Glenbervie published *The peerage of Scotland: containing an historical and genealogical account of the nobility of that kingdom, 1694-1770,* in which he erroneously reported that Sir William de Douglas married Margaret de Graham of Abercorn/Dalkeith.[441]

2) Second, in 1904, *The Scots peerage: founded on Wood's edition of Sir Robert Douglas's Peerage of Scotland; containing an historical and genealogical account of the nobility of that kingdom,* edited by Sir James Balfour Paul (1846-1931), corrects the earlier *Peerage* information, insisting Sir William de Douglas had only one known wife and that was Margaret's sister, Elizabeth de Graham.[442]

3) However, a number of publications derived from the earlier *Peerage* account repeated the erroneous information that Margaret de Graham married William de Douglas. In light of the confusion, numerous independent pedigrees list the wife of William de Douglas as "Elizabeth or Margaret" de Graham.[443]

4) It is easy to confuse this Margaret de Graham, daughter of Sir John de Graham of Dalkeith, the elder, and wife of Hugh de Ross with her cousin Margaret de Graham-- the Countess of Menteith, daughter of John Graham, ninth earl of Menteith, and likely also of Abercorn.[444] (Figure 43)

---

[440] John P. Ravilious, "Queen Euphemia and Her Ancestry," 49-50.

[441] Sir Robert Douglas, *The Peerage of Scotland: containing an historical and genealogical account of the nobility of that kingdom,* 1694-1770 (Edinburgh: R. Fleming, 1764), 47. https://archive.org/details/peerageofscotlan00doug/page/46/mode/2up?q=graham+dalkeith

[442] Sir James Balfour Paul, *The Scots Peerage, Founded on Wood's Edition,* Vol. VI, 196-197.

[443] Joseph Lindsay Bass and Becky Bonner, "My Southern Family," RootsWeb, 18 January 2000. https://freepages.rootsweb.com/~mysouthernfamily/genealogy/myff/d0030/g0000069.html

[444] William Fraser, *The Red Book of Menteith,* Vol. I (Edinburgh: 1880), 116-130. https://digital.nls.uk/histories-of-scottish-families/archive/96774276#?c=0&m=0&s=0&cv=217&xywh=-282%2C-337%2C5611%2C4159

## Origin of the Border Grahams

The library of documents from the Black Douglas "Land Grab" in Appendix F contains evidence of the origin of the Border Grahams. From a 1456 resignation charter: James Douglas, second Lord of Dalkeith, resigned the tenement of Hutton in favor of his son and heir: who was also named James, later the first Earl of Morton (1458). Witnesses: Robert de Grame, William de Grame, Richard de Grame, John de Grame.[445] Before this time, there is an undated King's letter compelling the "Grames to compear on 12th July and bring with them charters and documents to prove their rights to the lands of Hutton." The Grames claimed heritage for 100 years or more and complained of only twelve days' notice.[446] In 1361, Sir John "the Last" gifted lands in Southern Scotland (Elphinstone[447] and part of Elliston in Roxburghshire[448]) to John Grame, son of Richard. About this same time (approx. 1356), Sir John must have also granted to John, son of Richard, lands in Hutton given his heirs' insistence they received Hutton lands 100 years before 1456 and the assistance given them in 1463 by the Duke of Hamilton[449] to get them back. The original documents are presumed lost or destroyed.

The use of the unique name, "Richard de Grame," and the matching 100-year timeframes signify that the Grahams who were gifted land in 1361 were also progenitors of the Grahams losing land to the Douglas family in 1456. The name "Richard" is associated with the Border Grahams, specifically descendants of Lang Will Graham (1468-1540) of Mosskesswra, Parish of Hutton. Lang Will's eldest son was Richard Graham of Netherby (1490-1564),[450] perhaps a namesake of a Richard named above. See Figure 41 for the proposed descendancy of the Border Grahams from the elder line of William de Graham.

## Black Douglas "Land Grab"

Dr. William Knox, Professor of Scottish History, writes:

When the English threat disappeared, the Douglas family began to harbor ambitions to seize the throne of Scotland from the Stewarts. When James II acceded to the throne in 1437, the

---

[445] R.C. Reid, "The Border Grahams and Their Origins," 89.

[446] Royal Commission on Historical Manuscripts, *Historical Manuscripts Commission, Report on Manuscripts of Sir Archibald Edmonstone of Duntreath, Volumes 5 and 6* (Hereford: Anthony Brothers Limited, 1909), 77. https://archive.org/details/variousmanuscripts05greauoft/page/n83/mode/2up

[447] PoMS, "No. 10636-Elphinstone," accessed 19 October 2022. https://www.poms.ac.uk/record/source/10636/

[448] T.J. Carlyle, *The Debateable Land*, 10.

[449] Historical Manuscripts Commission, *The Manuscripts of the Duke of Hamilton, Knight, Eleventh Report, Appendix, Part VI*, 18.

[450] "First Graham of Netherby," Clan Graham Society, accessed 30 October 2022. https://clangrahamsociety.org/the-first-graham-of-netherby/

Black Douglases controlled three earldoms and were claiming a fourth. Their rule stretched over Galloway, Douglasdale, Annandale, Clydesdale, Lothian, Stirlingshire, and Moray.[451]

---

[451] William Knox, PhD, University of Saint Andrews, "Myth and History: The Case of the Black Douglases," *Scottish History for Dummies*, Wiley, 26 March 2016. https://www.dummies.com/article/academics-the-arts/history/scottish/myth-and-history-the-case-of-the-black-douglases-151986/

Figure 42: "County Abbreviations List," People of Medieval Scotland (PoMS), accessed 18 April 2023. https://www.poms.ac.uk/information/county-abbreviations-list/   Remaining sources provided in chronology in Appendix F, pages F-64 to F-70.

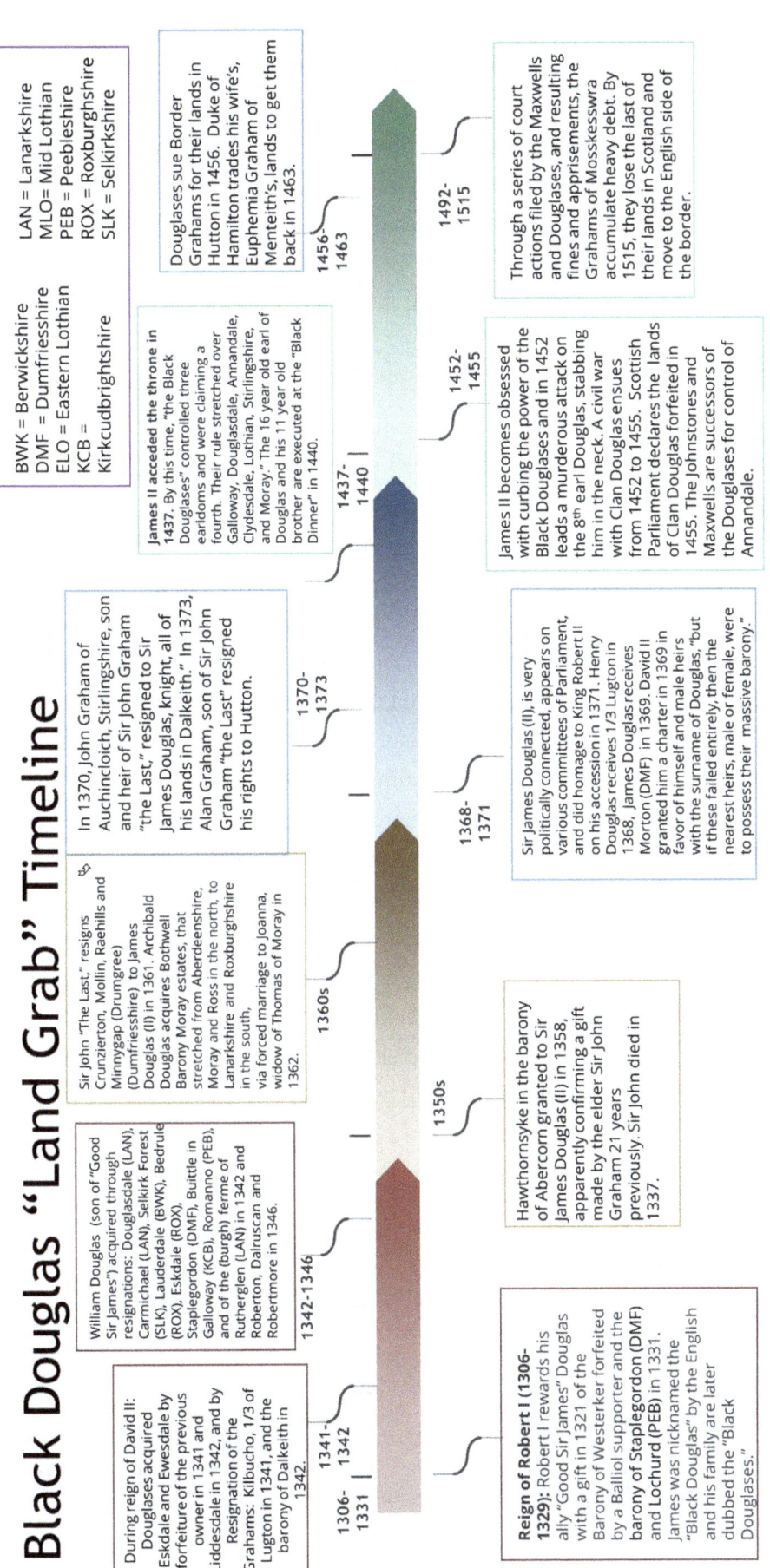

Figure 42: Timeline of Scotland's Internal Power Struggle Involving Clan Douglas (1331-1515).

The extensive documentary evidence of the multi-generational Black Douglas "Land Grab" against the Grahams, Murrays, and other clans can be found in the Abbreviated Historical Chronology of the Scottish Borderlands at the back of Appendix F. This "Land Grab" is essential to this search because published family histories have lost the evidence over time that Sir John de Graham "the Last" did have male heirs. However, it seems he was not up to dealing with the ambitious Douglas family or managing his many estates. For example, Sir John's father, the elder Sir John, had granted the rights of Tarbolton to his cousin, Robert Graham, Lord of Weyliston, in 1335. But in 1361, the younger Sir John also granted rights to Tarbolton in favor of Sir John Stewart, resulting in a legal dispute.[452]

## Sir William de Douglas

The Black Douglas "Land Grab" trail begins circa 1321 with Sir William de Douglas, who married Elizabeth de Graham, sister of Sir John "the Last." In December 1320, Sir John de Graham the elder, Lord of Eskdale, granted "Watistirkir" (Westerker/Westerkirk) barony in the valley of Esk to Sir William de Soulis, Knight of Liddesdale. Soulis soon forfeited the lands due to his part in the conspiracy against the king. When Soulis died in 1321, Robert I granted Soulis' half barony of Westerker to the monks of Melrose Abbey; however, curiously later that same year, Sir James Douglas was granted the same half-barony of "Wathstirker," and in a later charter, he is granted the entire barony of Westerker.[453] In 1342, the "John Graham, Lord of Abercorn" makes an overly generous gift by resigning the "total barony" of Dalkeith to William Douglas, Lord of Liddesdale.[454] William had already been granted Kilbucho and Newlands, presumably a tocher (dowry) upon marriage to Sir John of Dalkeith's sister Elizabeth Graham, in 1341.[455] Therefore, why did John also grant Sir William the entire barony of Dalkeith in 1342, which would be akin to granting him a modern-day county with a similar level of authority, more than just the Dalkeith lands themselves? Perhaps because before 1347 John Graham, Lord of Abercorn and Sir John Graham "the Last" of Dalkeith are two different people? The latter would have been a teenager and perhaps not ready to manage the barony without help from an elder relative? Michael A. Penman stated in the "The Scots at the Battle of Neville's Cross" that "John Graham, Lord of Abercorn" is actually the first Graham earl of Menteith who acquired the Menteith title (ninth earl of Menteith) by marriage to Countess Mary of Menteith.[456] The timing would then indicate "John Graham, Lord of Abercorn" was the son of Henry Graham of

---

[452] William Fraser, *The Scotts of Buccleuch, Volume II* (Edinburgh: 1878), 124-129. https://digital.nls.uk/histories-of-scottish-families/archive/96717116#?c=0&m=0&s=0&cv=123&xywh=0%2C-216%2C5049%2C3743

[453] Robert Bruce Armstrong, *The History of Liddesdale, Eskdale, Ewesdake, Wauchopedale and the debateable land, Part 1* (Edinburgh: David Douglas, 1883), 150. https://www.familysearch.org/library/books/viewer/425315/?offset=153266#page=177&viewer=picture&o=&n=0&q=

[454] *Registrum Honoris de Morton, Volume II: Ancient Charters*, 44-45.

[455] PoMS, "No. 4425-Kilbucho," accessed 19 October 2022. https://www.poms.ac.uk/record/source/4425/

[456] Michael A. Penman, "The Scots at the Battle of Neville's Cross, 17 October 1346," *The Scottish Historical Review*, Vol. 80, no. 210 (October 2001): 167. https://core.ac.uk/download/pdf/9048861.pdf

"Westirbyr" of Abercorn,[457] (Figure 41) and therefore a cousin to Sir John "the Last." The date of acquisition of Abercorn by sister Sybilla Graham and her husband Sir William More is ambiguous,[458] but is some time prior to 1363. Sybilla and William had received other lands that could have served as a dowry. They may have gained Abercorn in 1347 when Earl John Graham of Menteith, and possibly of Abercorn, was executed by order of Edward III of England. John and Mary Graham of Menteith had a single child, Countess Margaret of Menteith. We will revisit this Margaret shortly.

In 1343, David II granted lands in the valleys of Esk/Ewes to Sir William Douglas, lands which were previously held by Sir James Lovel. Sir James forfeited his lands for siding with the English in the wars of independence fifteen years previously.[459] Phil Graham notes these are suspicious circumstances, given the delayed timing and the pardoning of many others who had picked the wrong side in the wars. Sir William Douglas himself needed a pardon in 1345 for the murder of Alexander Ramsay. Douglas was angry the king had appointed Ramsay as Constable of Roxburgh and Sheriff of Teviotdale.[460] Historians believe that David II feared Douglas and his henchmen,[461] as Douglas had accumulated many estates and therefore power throughout Scotland by then. A search on the "Community of the Realm of Scotland, 1329-1424" land escheats and forfeiture lists reveals eighteen transfers of land to the Douglas family during the reign of David II and two more during the reign of Robert II. It seems there were a number of other estates the Douglases took over by "escheat": when the owners died without "apparent" heirs.[462] Historians have argued that William Douglas had become the most powerful man in Scotland, hence the pardon for the Ramsay murder.[463]

---

[457] Historical Manuscripts Commission, *The Manuscripts of the Duke of Hamilton, Knight, Eleventh Report, Appendix, Part VI*, 219.

[458] William Robertson, Esq. *An index, drawn up about the year 1629, of many records of charters, granted by the different sovereigns of Scotland between the years 1309 and 1413, most of which records have been long missing. With an introduction, giving a state, founded on authentic documents still preserved, of the ancient records of Scotland, which were in that kingdom in the year 1292* (Edinburgh: Murry and Cochrane, 1798), No. 13, 40.

[459] PoMS, "No. 10185-Eskdale and Ewesdale," accessed 8 November 2022. https://www.poms.ac.uk/record/source/10185/

[460] A.H. Millar, "Traditions and Stories of Scottish Castles, Hermitage Castle," Electric Scotland, accessed 6 March 2023. https://electricscotland.com/history/castles/hermitage.htm

[461] "The Great Historic Families of Scotland, The Douglases," Electric Scotland, accessed 8 November 2022. https://electricscotland.com/webclans/families/douglases.htm

[462] Matthew Hammond, "Resignations: David II (1329-71)," The Community of the Realm in Scotland, 1249-1424: History, Law and Charters in a Recreated Kingdom, 21 November 2019. https://cotr.ac.uk/social-network-analysis-political-communities-and-social-networks/forfeitures-resignations-and-escheats/resignations-david-ii-1329-71/

[463] Dr Callum Watson, "A Scourge of the English and a Wall to the Scots: A Life of Sir William Douglas of Liddesdale," Knights of the Two "L's," 17 July 2019. http://drcallumwatson.blogspot.com/2019/07/a-scourge-of-english-and-wall-to-scots.html

## Sir James Douglas

Sir James Douglas was the nephew of Sir William Douglas and son of Agnes Graham Monfode and Sir John Douglas. Agnes was another sister of Sir John "the Last."[464] (See Figure 41.) In 1358, Agnes of Monfode, nee Graham, was granted the land of Hawthornsyke in the barony of Abercorn.[465] The People of Medieval Scotland (PoMS) database shows twenty land charters where Sir James was the beneficiary, receiving large tracts of land all over Scotland. In 1361, Sir James acquired the lands of Crunzierton, Mollin, Raehills, Minnygap and others from his uncle, Sir John "the Last."[466] From 1368 onward, Sir James Douglas was very politically active, appeared on various committees of Parliament, and did homage to King Robert II on his accession in 1371.[467] Earlier in 1368, Sir James acquired permission from David II to repair Dalkeith castle,[468] which had been resigned under questionable circumstances to James' uncle, Sir William Douglas. Sir William and his wife, Elizabeth Graham, had only one child, a daughter named Mary. Mary died without heirs circa 1369,[469] so the Graham male heirs had a potential claim to Dalkeith. However, in 1369, David II signed the deed granting Dalkeith to Sir James Douglas.[470] David II not only confirmed the barony of Dalkeith to the Douglases, he made it illegal for any Douglas heirs to resign the barony and decreed that it must be inherited by a male surnamed Douglas, preventing the Graham heirs from making a claim.[471] Sir John "the Last's" son,

> **By the Way...**
> Between 1379 and 1387, during the reign of Robert II, Sir James Douglas used his political connections to elevate a number of his baronies, to include Dalkeith, Kilbucho and Roberton, to regalities. A regality would be akin to an American state with all its self-governing jurisdictional implications, and enforcement powers, growing Sir James' power and influence.

---

[464] John P. Ravilious, "Agnes De Graham, wife of (1) John de Monfode and (2) John de Douglas," *The Scottish Genealogist*, LXI No. 4, The Scottish Genealogy Society (December 2014): 129-133.
https://www.academia.edu/34967491/TSG_Agnes_de_Graham_wife_of_John_de_Monfode_and_Sir_John_de_Douglas_TSG_LXI_4_129_133

[By the Way...blurb] *Registrum Honoris de Morton, Volume II: Ancient Charters*, 138-139, 148-150, 154-157.

[465] PoMS, "No. 23347-Agnes of Monfode," accessed 28 December 2022.
https://www.poms.ac.uk/record/person/23347/

[466] PoMS, "No. 23552-James Douglas, Lord of Dalkeith (d. 1420)," accessed 20 October 2022.
https://www.poms.ac.uk/record/person/23552/

[467] Sir James Balfour Paul, *The Scots Peerage, Founded on Wood's Edition,* Vol. VI, 345.

[468] PoMS, "No. 23552-James Douglas, Lord of Dalkeith (d. 1420)," accessed 28 December 2022.
https://www.poms.ac.uk/record/person/23552/

[469] PoMS, "No. 23802-Mary Douglas, Daughter of William Douglas," accessed 28 December 2022.
https://www.poms.ac.uk/record/person/23802/

[470] PoMS, "No.10942-Renewal of Gift of Barony of Dalkeith to Sir James Douglas," accessed 4 December 2022.
https://www.poms.ac.uk/record/source/10942/

[471] PoMS, "No. 10942-Renewal of Gift of Barony of Dalkeith," accessed 4 December 2022.
https://www.poms.ac.uk/record/source/10942/

John Graham of Auchincloich, resigned his claim to Dalkeith in 1370.[472] Another son of Sir John, Alan de Graham, Lord of Morton, resigned his claim to Graham Hutton lands in 1373.[473] It was customary in medieval Scotland to require a re-submission of land charters when land was transferred.[474] In this case, the new charters reflect the superiority of the Dalkeith Barony and show the freeholders submitting to the new Lord Dalkeith, the nephew of Sir James Douglas "the Good," also named Sir James Douglas. The famous Sir James "the Good" died in battle in Spain in 1330 on a mission to take Robert I's heart on a Crusade and deliver it to Jerusalem.[475]

The Black Douglas "Land Grab" continued to successive generations. In 1456, the third Lord Douglas created the title "Earl of Morton" for his son. The same Lord Douglas successfully sued the Border Grahams for Hutton and Roxburghshire lands previously granted to their ancestors by Sir John "the Last" in 1361.[476] Later, Douglas fought against Douglas.[477] The conflict threw Lang Will Graham of the Border Grahams onto the wrong side, and his rights of hereditary fee were challenged and removed.[478] In comparison, his brother John Graham of Gillesbie's family appears to have fared better. The Gillesbies operated mills in Langholm, Hoddam, and along the River Dryfe and had approximately forty retainers raised from the Gillesbie/Hutton estates in 1541.[479]

The successors of the Douglases, the Johnstones, who were first granted Douglas lands that were forfeited circa 1455, continued the land grabbing against the Grahams[480] and other Border clans until many left Scotland altogether. For the rest of the story, see Appendix F: "Johnstone Land Takeover—The Disenfranchisement of the Grahams Chronology."

## The Connection between the Border Grahams and Menteiths

Early members of the present Netherby family, descendants of the Grahams of Plomp, claimed a relation to the Grahams of Menteith but could not provide conclusive proof.[481] They claimed descent from the earls of Menteith in a pedigree submitted in 1665 to William Dugdale, King of Arms, with a statement that their coat of arms were attested by the Earl of Menteith. This claim was based on

---

[472] John Reid, "Material for a Place Name Survey of East Stirlingshire," 109.
[473] *Registrum Honoris de Morton, Volume II: Ancient Charters*, 88-89, 119.
[474] Cynthia Neville, "Royal Mercy in Medieval Scotland," Vol. 29, *Florilegium* (2012): 12. https://www.academia.edu/15687472/Royal_Mercy_in_Medieval_Scotland
[475] William Fraser, *Douglas Book*, Vol. 1 (Edinburgh: T. and A. Constable, Edinburgh University Press, 1885), 172. https://digital.nls.uk/histories-of-scottish-families/archive/96806202?mode=transcription
[476] R.C. Reid, "The Border Grahams and Their Origins," 89-91.
[477] William Fraser, *Douglas Book*, Vol. 1, ii.
[478] R.C. Reid, "The Border Grahams and Their Origins," 89-91.
[479] Col William Rogerson, *Hutton Under the Muir*, 25.
[480] Jeffrey M. Johnstone, "History of the Clan," Clan Johnstone in America, accessed 9 November 2022. https://clanjohnstone.org/history-of-the-clan/
[481] Joseph Foster, *The Heralds' Visitations of the Counties of Cumberland and Westmoreland, made by Richard St. George, Norry, King of Arms in 1615, and by William Dugdale, Norry, King of Arms in 1666* (Carlisle: Charles Thurnam and Sons, 1891), 54. https://archive.org/details/pedigreesrecorde00sainrich

a previous claim by the Grahams of Nunnery, descendants of Lang Will. The referenced pedigree and *Peerage* writers attempted to connect the Border Grahams to the Earls of Menteith by asserting that they were descended from John Graham of Kilbride, the second son of Malise Graham, Earl of Strathearn and another Graham Earl of Menteith. *Peerage* later retracted the claim when they determined that John died in 1478 without male descendants.[482]

Upon further examination, it turns out there is a basis for the claim but quite different and more significant than originally thought. Apparently the first Graham to hold the title "earl of Menteith" was from the elder Graham line, not the younger. Evidence has been provided that the Border Grahams descend from the elder line of William de Graham, the Grahams of Dalkeith and Abercorn. The descendants of the previously mentioned Malise Graham (circa 1407-1490), Earl of Menteith, and the Montroses descend from the younger line. The very first Graham-styled Earl of Menteith occurred a century earlier.[483] Sir John de Graham of Abercorn," presumed son of Henry de Graham of West Byres/Binns in the Abercorn barony and nephew of Sir John de Graham of Dalkeith the elder, may have acquired the title of ninth Earl of Menteith circa 1334 via marriage to Mary, Countess of Menteith, only child of Alan, seventh Earl of Menteith[484] (Figure 43). The prevailing theory has been this John was from the younger Graham line, specifically the Montroses.

## What we know

John de Graham and Countess Mary of Menteith had to seek papal dispensation to marry since they were related within the four forbidden degrees of consanguinity[485] (third cousins or closer or step-cousins).[486] Pope John XXII issued the dispensation for John and Mary in May 1334 to the Bishop of Dunblane.[487]

Dunblane was the home diocese of Countess Mary. Since Countess Mary, great granddaughter of Sir Walter Stewart, needed a dispensation to marry Sir John Graham in 1334, this indicates they were third cousins or closer. Prior to 1334, the Stewarts had intermarried with the "elder line" Grahams of Dalkeith and Abercorn. (See Figure 41.) John was executed in 1347 by the order of Edward III for his part in the Battle of Neville's Cross.[488] Mary and John's daughter, Margaret Graham, also needed papal

---

[482] Sir Robert Douglas, *The Peerage of Scotland: containing an historical and genealogical account of the nobility of that kingdom,* 1694-1770, 47.
https://archive.org/details/peerageofscotlan00doug/page/46/mode/2up?q=graham+dalkeith
[483] William Fraser, *The Red Book of Menteith,* Vol. 1, 102-104.
[484] Michael A. Penman, "The Scots at the Battle of Neville's Cross, 17 October 1346," 167.
[485] Richard Burtsell, "Consanguinity (in Canon Law)." The Catholic Encyclopedia. Vol. 4. New York: Robert Appleton Company, 1908. 28 March 2023 http://www.newadvent.org/cathen/04264a.htm
[486] "Late Medieval Canon Law on Marriage," European Reformations, University of Oregon, accessed 290 December 2022. https://pages.uoregon.edu/dluebke/Reformations441/441MarriageLaw.html
[487] William Fraser, *The Red Book of Menteith,* Vol. 1, 128-129.
[488] Michael A. Penman, "The Scots at the Battle of Neville's Cross, 17 October 1346," 167.

dispensations to marry four times. However, by her fourth dispensation in 1362, her mother had also died, making Margaret the Countess of Menteith.[489] Her fourth and last dispensation was issued to the bishop of St. Andrews, the home diocese of the elder line/Dalkeith/Abercorn Grahams, not the diocese of Brechin, which was the home diocese of the Grahams of Montrose. If Margaret's father had been a Montrose Graham, the dispensation would have been granted to the bishop of Brechin.[490] See the Scottish Medieval Diocese map (Appendix B--Figure B-6).[491]

With the fourth marriage of Countess Margaret of Menteith to Robert Stewart, Duke of Albany, the earldom of Menteith passed to the Stewarts, who served as earls of Menteith until 1425. After a two-year break, Menteith passed to the younger line Grahams, possibly the grounds for the assumption that the ninth earl had also been of the younger line. In 1427, Malise Graham, son of Sir Patrick Graham and Euphemia Stewart, was styled Earl of Menteith by James I in exchange for taking Malise's Strathearn estates.[492] Further arguments supporting the claim that the ninth earl of Menteith, John de Graham, was an elder line Graham can be found in Appendix F.

---

[489] William Fraser, *The Red Book of Menteith*, Vol. 1, 116-130.
[490] John P. Ravilious, "Queen Euphemia and Her Ancestry," 50.
[491] Cushnie Enterprises, "Map of the Medieval Scottish Dioceses."
[492] William Fraser, *The Red Book of Menteith*, Vol. 1, 289-292.
[492] Figure 43: William Fraser, *The Red Book of Menteith*, Vol. I, 289-292. Wikimedia Commons contributors, "File:Menteith arms.svg," *Wikimedia Commons*, accessed 18 April 2023. CC BY-SA 4.0 https://commons.wikimedia.org/w/index.php?title=File:Menteith_arms.svg&oldid=460664027
[492] John P. Ravilious, "Queen Euphemia and Her Ancestry," *The Scottish Genealogist*, The Scottish Genealogy Society (June 2017): 49-50.
https://www.academia.edu/35370666/Queen_Euphemia_and_her_ancestry_TSG_LXIV_2_49_52
[492] John P. Ravilious, "Agnes De Graham, wife of (1) John de Monfode and (2) John de Douglas," *The Scottish Genealogist*, LXI No. 4, The Scottish Genealogy Society (December 2014): 129-133.
https://www.academia.edu/34967491/TSG_Agnes_de_Graham_wife_of_John_de_Monfode_and_Sir_John_de_Douglas_TSG_LXI_4_129_133

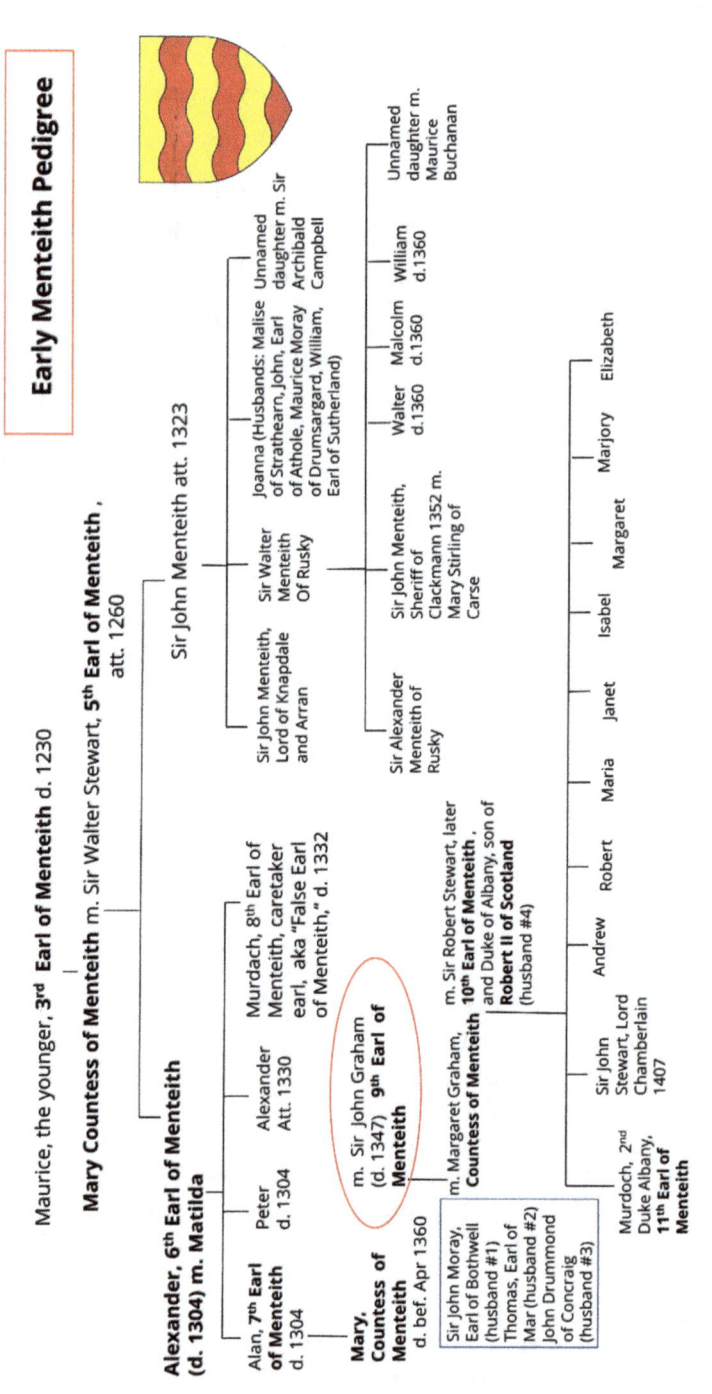

Figure 43: Descendants of the Menteith Earls based on the "Red book of Menteith," Volume I, by William Fraser and writings of John P. Ravilious [492]

## Chapter 6
## Y-DNA[xii]

Genetic testing of the male Y chromosome (Y-DNA) enables comparisons between males to determine very distant cousin matches and "long distance" direct paternal line inheritance. Y-DNA is especially useful as it can help us find ancestors as far back as they have been keeping records (1,000 years or more ago). In contrast, the more familiar autosomal DNA (aDNA), with kits for sale in local pharmacies, can only reliably trace back five to six generations. Even with advanced tools, aDNA might detect matches up to nine generations.[493] The "long distance" analysis works by examining Y-DNA test results in groupings of shared genetic sequences called "haplogroups" and "subclades." The order of subclades in a man's Y-DNA profile can be characterized as a family tree from parent subclades down to subsequent child subclades, which can assist in determining shared family lines.[494] See Appendix C.

What can Y-DNA say about the Grahams? The Grayville Graham men who have tested their Y-DNA have been reported as haplogroup J-M267 aka: "J1." This Y-DNA type is rare in Britain and unique to the Grahams who lived near the Scottish-English Border (a.k.a. the Border Grahams). J-M267 originated in the Middle East about 31,000 years ago in the Caucasus near the Black Sea. More recent child subclades originated in the Levant region, which includes Jordan, Israel, Syria, Lebanon, and southern Turkey (Anatolia). This area contained the great Phoenician cities of Tyre, Sidon, and Cicilia in Tarsus in modern-day Turkey.[495]

---

[493] Family Tree DNA (FTDNA), "Your DNA Guide, Which Y-DNA Test is Best?" accessed 1 November 2022. https://www.yourdnaguide.com/ydna#:~:text=YDNA%20is%20the%20DNA%20inherited,back%20than%20autosomal%20DNA%20tests.

[494] Debbie Kennett, "Haplogroup," International Society for Genetic Genealogy (ISOGG) Wiki, 27 June 2022. https://isogg.org/wiki/Haplogroup

[495] Maciamo Hay, Haplogroup J1 (Y-DNA), Eupedia, updated October 2021. https://www.eupedia.com/europe/Haplogroup_J1_Y-DNA.shtml

Per the Family Tree DNA (FTDNA) Graham Surname Project, the unique Y-DNA profile or subclade "tree" for the Graham J1s (and certain Jordans) is as follows:[496]

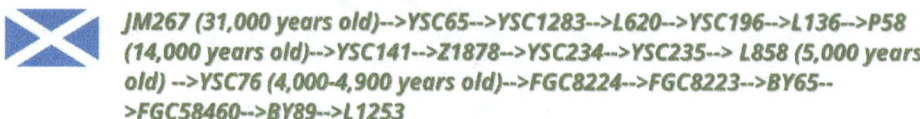
JM267 (31,000 years old)-->YSC65-->YSC1283-->L620-->YSC196-->L136-->P58 (14,000 years old)-->YSC141-->Z1878-->YSC234-->YSC235--> L858 (5,000 years old) -->YSC76 (4,000-4,900 years old)-->FGC8224-->FGC8223-->BY65-->FGC58460-->BY89-->L1253

*Figure 44: J1 Y-DNA Pedigree of Typical Border Grahams [497]*

P58, the Central Semitic branch of J1, appears to have expanded from the southern Levant (Israel, Palestine, Jordan) across the Arabian Peninsula during the Bronze Age, from approximately 3,500 to 2,500 B.C. However, existing data currently indicates that its fourth great-grandchild subclade, YSC76, was limited to the Lebanese region. From the subclades FGC8224 and FGC8223 descend child subclades that have been tied to Jewish groups.[497] It is possible that the ancestral migrants from the Middle East could have been tied to one of these haplogroups. However, it has not been confirmed if the "Graham L1253" is actually connected to one of the Jewish subclades. Not all of the Jewish subclades have been officially named and catalogued. The JewishDNA.net and Avotaynu DNA research projects have been working towards that goal since 2016.[498]

## Graham J1 Patriarch

Analysis indicates the J1 Grahams and J1 Jordans descend from a single patriarch. Based on Big Y results, which is the most in-depth Y-DNA test available, Dr. Iain McDonald of the FTDNA Scottish YDNA Project initially estimated that the J-L1253 haplogroup migrated from the Middle East to Scotland 500-1000 years ago, either directly or indirectly, via a third location. Dr. McDonald later updated his estimate in March 2021, determining that the common ancestor was born in the **1250-1550 A.D.** timeframe.[499] Dr. Robin Spencer projected a similar estimate for the mean Time to Most Recent Common Ancestor ( tMRCA), the estimated timeframe that the shared ancestor of the J1 Grahams was born, projecting a birth year in the middle of that time period: about 1400 A.D. Mean tMRCA is used in DNA analysis to rate the closeness of DNA matches.[500] As of 8 March 2023, FTDNA's

---

[496] FamilyTreeDNA, "Graham Surname DNA Project."
[497] Figure 44: Maciamo Hay, Haplogroup J1 (Y-DNA), Eupedia.
[498] Wim Penninx, "Jewish Group of Branches: J1-Other," JewishDNA.net, accessed 28 December 2022. https://jewishdna.net/J1-other.html
[499] FamilyTreeDNA, "Graham Surname DNA Project News," accessed 30 October 2022. https://www.familytreedna.com/groups/graham/about/news
[500] Robin Spencer, PhD. "Extending Time Horizons with DNA," video lecture, FamilySearch, 8 March 2022, 1:00:45. https://www.youtube.com/watch?v=wppXD1Zz2sQ

Discover™ tools estimated a 95% chance that the Most Recent Common Ancestor of the J1 Grahams and J1 Jordans was born between 1011 and 1357A.D.[501]

As detailed in Appendix F, "Border Graham Genealogy," the strongest candidates to be the J1 Graham Patriarch are Sir Andrew Murray of Manuel, armor bearer to King David II or his biological father. Sir Andrew (who died 1392) is the most likely possibility to be the Andrew who married Agnes de Graham before 23 March 1363, projecting his birth year between the late 1330s and the early 1340s.[502] See Table F-1 for the list of candidate Andrews recorded in the People of Medieval Scotland (PoMS) database.

*Figure 45: Map showing Dalkeith, "Elphinstoun I," Edmondstoun Castle, Atlas of Scotland, 1654; Joan and Cornelius Blaeu, Timothy Pont. CC-BY 4.0 Reproduced with the permission of the National Library of Scotland.*[503]

The theory depicted in Figure 41 is that Sir Andrew Murray of Manuel and Agnes de Graham had two sons: Sir William Murray who inherited the Murray lands of Touchadam and a younger son who inherited his mother's surname and lands, Graham lands such as Elliston, "Elphinstone I," and Nether Hutton. Agnes de Graham was the daughter and heir of "John de Grame, son of Richard,"

---

[501] FamilyTreeDNA, "Scientific Details Haplogroup J-L1253," Copyright 2022 Gene by Gene, Ltd., accessed 8 November 2022. https://discover.familytreedna.com/y-dna/J-L1253/scientific

[502] PoMS, "Person Search for Sixteen Andrews," accessed 30 October 2022. https://www.poms.ac.uk/search/?index_type=person&q=andrew&min_date=1315&max_date=1371

[503] Figure 45: Joan and Cornelius Blaeu and Timothy Pont, *Atlas of Scotland,* Lothian and Linlitquo / Joh. et Cornelius Blaeu exc., Amsterdam, Blaeu, 1654. https://maps.nls.uk/view/00000395

who received the Elliston, Roxburghshire[504] and "Elphinstone I," land gifts from suspected cousin Sir John de Graham "the Last" lord of Dalkeith between 1360 and 1363. In the latter land charter, David II confirms the grant of Elphinstone that Sir John "the Last" had previously gifted to her father, John, to "Agnes de Graham, spouse of Andrew de?" PoMS lists a question mark for this Andrew's surname.[505] *The Register of the Great Seal of Scotland* also leaves a blank spot for Andrew's surname.[506] It must have been illegible or the original document damaged. Of the sixteen candidate Andrews in Table F-1, Sir Andrew Murray of Manuel stands out as the strongest prospect to be the husband of Agnes de Graham. He is the right age to be married to Agnes, and while his second wife is known (Janet Kirkhalche or Kirkintilloch), his first wife is unknown.[507] Sir Andrew's Manuel, Polmaise and Touchadam estates on the eastern edge of Stirlingshire [508] are the closest to the Graham estates of "Elphinstone I" and Abercorn[509] of all the candidates in Table F-1. See Figure 46.[510]

---

[504] T.J. Carlyle, *The Debateable Land,* 10.

[505] PoMS, "No. 10636-Elphinstone in East Lothian confirmation to 'Agnes de Grame, wife of Andrew de ?'" accessed 19 October 2022. https://www.poms.ac.uk/record/source/10636/

[506] John Maitland Thomson, *Register of the Great Seal of Scotland, A.D. 1306-1424* (Edinburgh: H.M. General Register House, 1912), 29. https://www.google.com/books/edition/The_Register_of_the_Great_Seal_of_Scotla/ZbI3AQAAMAAJ?hl=en

[507] Author: "B," "The Chiefship of the Clan Murray," *The Scottish Antiquary, or, Northern Notes and Queries*, Vol. 15, No. 58 (Edinburgh University Press, October 1900): 72. https://www.jstor.org/stable/25516988

[508] Google (2022), "Stirlingshire, Scotland," accessed 28 December 2022. https://www.google.com/maps/place/Stirling,+UK/@56.2518488,-4.6063728,10z/data=!3m1!4b1!4m5!3m4!1s0x48886294ea24c6bd:0x5ea5c3dc8e20c553!8m2!3d56.1165329!4d-3.9369086

[509] Joan and Cornelius Blaeu and Timothy Pont, *Atlas of Scotland,* Sterlinshyr, Joan et Cornelius Blaeu exc., Amsterdam, Blaeu, 1654. https://maps.nls.uk/view/00000441

[510] Figure 46: Joan and Cornelius Blaeu and Timothy Pont, *Atlas of Scotland,* Lothian and Linlitquo / Joh. et Cornelius Blaeu exc., Amsterdam, Blaeu, 1654.

Figure 47: Google (2022), "Stirlingshire, Scotland," accessed 28 December 2022. https://www.google.com/maps/place/Stirling,+UK/@56.2518488,-4.6063728,10z/data=!3m1!4b1!4m5!3m4!1s0x48886294ea24c6bd:0x5ea5c3dc8e20c553!8m2!3d56.1165329!4d-3.9369086

*Figure 46: Map showing Dalkeith, "Elphinstoun 1," Abercorn, Manuel, Atlas of Scotland, 1654; Joan and Cornelius Blaeu, Timothy Pont. CC-BY 4.0 Reproduced with the permission of the National Library of Scotland.[510]*

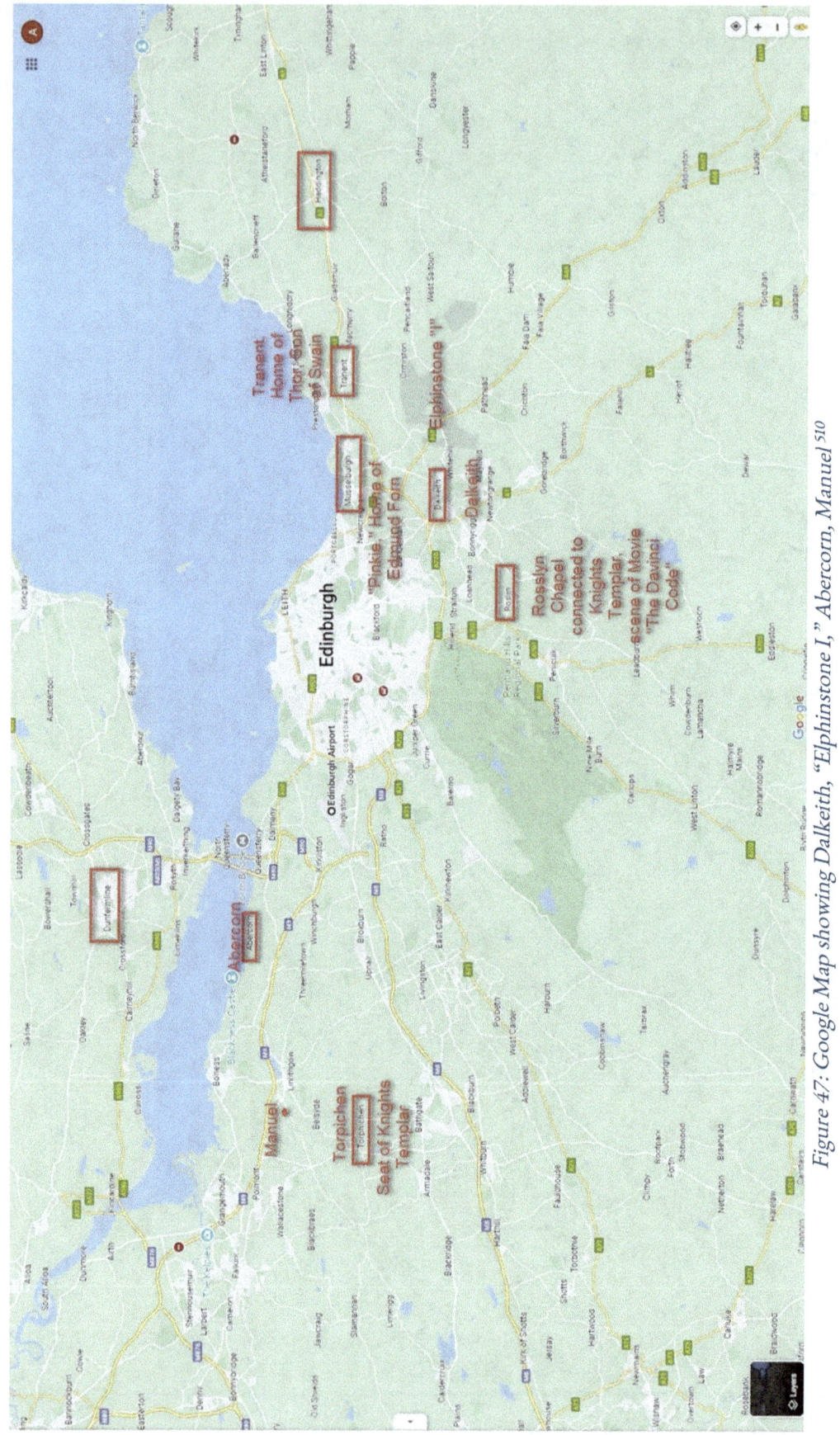

*Figure 47: Google Map showing Dalkeith, "Elphinstone I," Abercorn, Manuel* [510]

*Figure 48: Stirlingshire Map showing Northern Estates of Sir Andrew Murray of Manuel and "Elphinstoun II," Atlas of Scotland, 1654; Joan and Cornelius Blaeu and Timothy Pont. CC-BY 4.0, Reproduced with the permission of the National Library of Scotland.* [511]

PoMS records Sir Andrew Murray of Manuel as a relative to David II.[512] He was a descendant and heir of Sir Andrew de Moray the Regent (d. 1338) and Christian Bruce, sister of Robert I (d. circa 1358).[513] No record can be found to confirm Sir Andrew of Manuel as the son of the Regent, only an heir. Coincidentally, the Moray lands that should have been Sir Andrew's inheritance wound up in the hands of the Black Douglases in July 1362. The date of the papal dispensation to approve the forced marriage of the widow of Thomas de Moray (fifth Lord Bothwell), Joanna of Menteith, to Archibald

---

[511] Figure 48: Joan and Cornelius Blaeu and Timothy Pont, *Atlas of Scotland*, Sterlinshyr, Joan et Cornelius Blaeu exc., Amsterdam, Blaeu, 1654. https://maps.nls.uk/view/00000441

[512] PoMS, "No.23774-Sir Andrew Murray of Manuel, Armor Bearer, Cousin to David II," accessed 20 October 2022. https://www.poms.ac.uk/record/person/23774/

[513] Author: "B," "The Chiefship of the Clan Murray," 60, 63, 64, 72.

Douglas was 23 July 1362.⁵¹⁴ If Sir Andrew lost his inheritance to the Douglases in July 1362, that might explain his need, prior to March 1363, to marry an heiress with lands.

Figure 49: Shield of the Burgh of Dalkeith, showing the Graham Escallops, the Douglas Arms which Combined the Braveheart Symbol with the Murray Stars, St. Nicholas of Myra's symbols, Dalkeith Chapel and Center: Dalkeith Castle ⁵¹⁴

Sir Andrew of Manuel was significantly younger compared to the other sons of Sir Andrew the Regent. Sir John of Moray, died without heirs in 1351. Sir John's widow was the previously mentioned Margaret Graham of Menteith (and possibly Abercorn).⁵¹⁵ The elder son, Sir Thomas of Moray, fifth Lord Bothwell, died of the plague while serving as a hostage in England in 1361, also without heirs. His widow was Joanna of Menteith.⁵¹⁶

Coincidentally, there is a second estate named Elphinstone that is close to Manuel on the eastern edge of Stirlingshire. I call it "Elphinstone 'II'" to distinguish from the Elphinstone in Lothian first granted to Agnes de Graham and her husband Andrew of the unknown surname. Joan Blaeu's 1654 map in Figure 48 makes it appear as if Elphinstone II was carved from the Menteith estate of Airth.⁵¹⁷ Perhaps, Sir Andrew of Manuel inherited Elphinstone II lands from John and/or Thomas Moray, lands they had acquired from their Menteith wives? He might have named some of his new lands after the first Elphinstone estate in Lothian that he and Agnes de Graham received circa 1363? Since it seems Sir Andrew named his new home near Manuel "Ballenbreich" or "Ballynbruch"⁵¹⁸ after the Murray family's traditional residence by the same name in Morayshire,⁵¹⁹ it is possible he also named one of his and Agnes' new lands after their first home estate of Elphinstone. Coincidentally, prior to 1337, Sir John Graham the elder signed a charter renewing a grant of the lands of "Balnebuch" near "Elphinstone I" in Lothian to the monks of Newbattle with rights to quarry the

---

⁵¹⁴ William Fraser, *Douglas Book*, Vol. 1, 352.

Figure 49: John, Marquess of Bute, J.R.N. Macphail, and H.W. Lonsdale, *The Arms of the Royal and Parliamentary Burghs of Scotland* (Edinburgh: William Blackwood & Sons, 1897), 155. https://play.google.com/store/books/details?id=7VA4AQAAMAAJ&rdid=book-7VA4AQAAMAAJ&rdot=1

⁵¹⁵ Author: "B," "The Chiefship of the Clan Murray," 63.

⁵¹⁶ Sir James Balfour Paul, *The Scots Peerage, Founded on Wood's Edition*, Vol. II (Edinburgh: David Douglas, 1904), 130. https://www.electricscotland.com/books/pdf/scots_peerage.htm

⁵¹⁷ Joan and Cornelius Blaeu and Timothy Pont, *Atlas of Scotland*, Lothian and Linlitquo / Joh. et Cornelius Blaeu exc., Amsterdam, Blaeu, 1654. https://maps.nls.uk/view/00000395

⁵¹⁸ John Reid, "Feudal Land Divisions of East Stirlingshire," *Calatria*, No. 6 (Spring 1994): 27. https://falkirklocalhistorysociety.files.wordpress.com/2020/11/6.79-the-feudal-land-divisions-of-east-stirlingshire.pdf

⁵¹⁹ "Balnabreich," Canmore, National Record of the Historic Environment, 14 July 2021. https://canmore.org.uk/site/75789/balnabreich

slate rock.[520] The lands of the Murrays of Manuel near "Elphinstone II" were also known for their rock quarries.

Considering the Regent Sir Andrew's second wife, Christian Bruce, sister of Robert the Bruce (Robert I) was in her forties when she married him in 1323, and Sir Andrew of Manuel's birth year can be estimated to be approximately 1340-1344, he was likely a grandson rather than a son, perhaps via an unnamed daughter of the Regent and Christian Bruce.[521] That would explain how Sir Andrew of Manuel would be named as a cousin to David Bruce (David II). However, it does leave a mystery as to who was the biological father of Sir Andrew of Manuel. See Murray descendant chart, Figure F-3.

With the early deaths of John and Thomas Moray without heirs, the next in line to be named as heir would be a grandson, even via a daughter. If Sir Andrew of Manuel were in the direct male line to the famous Sir Andrew the Regent, one would expect that he would have a stronger claim to Murray lands than his sister-in-law and his father would be named in land charters, church records, and *Peerage* publications.[522] Since the Black Douglases were careful to get sons of Sir John "the Last" to relinquish their claims in writing, it seems they would have done the same if Sir Andrew of Manuel were the Regent's son. The Murray Y-DNA Surname Project is trying to recruit test subjects who are known descendants of Sir Andrew Murray of Manuel's eldest son, William Murray of Touchadam, to determine his paternal line.[523] Y-DNA can also help answer other historical questions.

## How did the Graham J1s get to Scotland?

The answer lies in the ages and geographic locations of the FGC58460, BY89 and J-L1253 subclades common to all J1 Grahams and Jordans. Fall 2022 analysis from FTDNA "Discover™ More" tools, based on the science pioneered by Dr. Iain McDonald,[524] and the SNP Tracker Tool, built by Dr. Robin Spencer of the England Groups EIJ Y-DNA Project,[525] initially indicated the unique J1 Y-DNA types first arrived in Britain in the late Bronze Age (circa 1400 B.C.). See "J1 Arrival in Scotland" scenarios in Appendix C. More recent analysis postulates that there may have been an

---

[520] PoMS, "No. 16488, accessed 26 December 2022." https://www.poms.ac.uk/record/person/16488/; PoMS, "No. 7444," accessed 26 December 2022. https://www.poms.ac.uk/record/source/7444/

[521] John Maitland Thomson, *Register of the Great Seal of Scotland, A.D. 1306-1424* (Edinburgh: H.M. General Register House, 1912), 461, 621. https://www.google.com/books/edition/The_Register_of_the_Great_Seal_of_Scotla/ZbI3AQAAMAAJ?hl=en

[522] Author: "B," "The Chiefship of the Clan Murray," 53-77.

[523] "Murray Clan DNA Reseach Project," Family Tree DNA, accessed 28 December 2022. https://www.familytreedna.com/groups/murray/about/background

[524] Family Tree DNA (FTDNA), "Scientific Details Haplogroup L1253."

[525] Robin Spencer, PhD. "SNP Tracker," Timelines Tab for SNP: L1253, Tracking Back-A Website for Genetic Genealogy Tools, Experimentation and Discussion, accessed 28 December 2022. http://scaledinnovation.com/gg/snpTracker.html (Discussion tab explains how to use site.)

earlier J1 group that arrived soon after the last Ice Age, but unlikely if any survived.[526] The Discover™ tools take into account archaeological DNA data, carbon dating, and present-day results of Y-DNA tests of volunteers. There are a few theories regarding how the J1 got to Scotland detailed in Appendix C. The best-known theory is laid out in Scotland's famous declaration of independence called the "Declaration of Arbroath."

## "From Scythia We Descend"

The Declaration of Arbroath was written in 1320 and signed by the Scottish land barons of the time, including the elder Sir John de Graham of Dalkeith,[527] as a plea to Pope John XXII to recognize Scotland's independence from England and their new king, Robert the Bruce.[528] Included in the document is the following claim (translated from the original Latin) on the origin of the Scottish people:

> Most Holy Father and Lord, we know and from the chronicles and books of the ancients we find that amongst other famous nations our own, the Scots, has been graced with widespread renown. They journeyed from **Greater Scythia by way of the Tyrrhenian Sea and the Pillars of Hercules, and dwelt for a long course of time in Spain** amongst the most savage tribes, but nowhere could they be subdued by any race, however barbarous. Thence they came, twelve hundred years after the people of Israel crossed the Red Sea, to their home in the west where they still live today. The Britons they first drove out, the Picts they utterly destroyed, and, even though very often assailed by the Norwegians, the Danes and the English, they took possession of that home with many victories and untold efforts; and, as the historians of old time bear witness, they have held it free of all bondage ever since. In their Kingdom there have reigned one hundred and thirteen Kings of their own Royal Stock, the line unbroken by a single foreigner.

Many historians have dismissed this claim as myth or legend, partly because the stories surrounding the origin were inconsistent and partly because of the lack of documented proof. However, in the fourteenth and fifteenth centuries B.C., most histories were oral, as written language was only just developing in parts of the world.[529] It is an interesting coincidence that the new Y-DNA results indicate this rare Middle Eastern J1 Y-DNA

> **Did you know?**
> The earliest written language known in the British Isles was the runic stone that represented the Scandinavian alphabet beginning in 200 A.D.

---

[526] England Great Britain Groups EIJ, "E I J G R T England Scotland Wales Ireland Norman & Diverse Others," Activity Feed, Family Tree DNA, accessed 28 December 2022. https://www.familytreedna.com/groups/england-gbgroups-eij/activity-feed

[527] Jane Brankstone Thomas, J.C. B. Sharp, and Michael Anne Guido, "A Cumberland Family with Medieval Roots in Scotland and Northern England: A Study Gilbert Fitz Richer and His Descendants," 368.

[528] "The Declaration of Arbroath," National Records of Scotland, accessed 8 November 2022. https://www.nrscotland.gov.uk/Declaration

[529] UKEssays, "History of Early Writing Systems in the British Isles," November 2018. https://www.ukessays.com/essays/history/early-writing-systems-of-british-isles-history-essay.php?vref=1

type arrived in Scotland circa 1417 B.C., the same timeframe as the arrival of the legendary Princess Scota of Egypt and her husband Gaythelos in Ireland referenced in the Declaration of Arbroath,[530] so warrant another look at the story. The legendary first king of Scotland, Fergus I (330-305 B.C.) allegedly descended from Princess Scota.[531] Despite the inconsistencies in the various versions, several chroniclers (e.g., John of Fordun, Manetho) have these story elements in common: the Scots were named after Scota, a daughter of an Egyptian Pharoah; Scota's husband was a Greek warrior of "Scythian ancestry" called "Gaythelos," whom the Gaels are named for; Scota and Gaythelos were driven from Egypt and settled in what is now Spain, then later left Spain and settled in Ireland.[532] Some of their descendants then migrated to Scotland. Of note: 1. Scota's alleged grave site is near Munster in County Kerry, Ireland.[533] 2. In ancient Egypt, succession was matrilineal,[534] wherein descent to the throne was determined through the female line. Ancient Celtic tribes also practiced matrilineal succession through the Iron Age.[535]

## Gaytheolos (Goídel Glas in Gaelic)

The oldest identified J1 sample (13,200 B.C.) was found in a cave in Satsurblia Cave Natural Monument in modern-day Kumistavi, Georgia, on the edge of what became Scythian territory.[536] The Scythians were an ancient equestrian nomadic people who lived in the region of modern-day Ukraine, north of the Black Sea. Scythia was a loose federation that originated as early as the eighth century B.C.,[537] composed mainly of people speaking Scythian languages,[538] and is usually regarded as the first of the nomad empires. While there is no evidence of the existence of Scythians prior to 900 B.C., the heritage of Gaythelos was possibly from nomadic peoples of the Eastern Mediterranean or nomads from the Black Sea region. Prior to the Middle Ages, ancient scribes used the term "Scythians" to refer

---

[530] Zteve T. Evans, "Founding Myths: Princess Scota, Goídel Glas and their Links to the Gaelic People," Under the Influence! 7 December 2021. https://ztevetevans.wordpress.com/2021/12/07/founding-myths-princess-scota-goidel-glas-and-their-links-to-the-gaelic-people/

[Did you know? Blurb] UKEssays, "History of Early Writing Systems in the British Isles."

[531] Jeffrey King, "Scotichronicon," *World History Encyclopedia*, 15 January 2019. https://www.worldhistory.org/Scotichronicon/

[532] The Scotsman, "The Pharaoh's Daughter Who was the Mother of all Scots," 13 September 2006. https://www.scotsman.com/whats-on/arts-and-entertainment/pharaohs-daughter-who-was-mother-all-scots-2507668

[533] Active Me Irelands Travel Guide, "Queen Scotia's Grave Walk, Scotia's Glen, Tralee, Kerry, Ireland," accessed 28 December 2022. https://www.activeme.ie/guides/queen-scotias-grave-walk-scotias-glen-kerry/

[534] Moustafa Gadalla, "Matrilineal/Matriarchial Society," Egyptian Wisdom Center, accessed 8 November 2022. https://egyptianwisdomcenter.org/matrilineal-matriarchal-society/

[535] Kathleen O'Connor, "Early and Iron Age Celtic Society," Women in Ancient Celtic Society, accessed 8 November 2022. https://ancientcelticwomen.weebly.com/society.html

[536] Maciamo Hay, "Haplogroup J1 (Y-DNA)," Eupedia.

[537] Tom Garlinghouse, "Who Were the Scythians?" LiveScience.com, updated 2 September 2022. https://www.livescience.com/who-were-the-scythians

[538] A. Chay and G. Dremin, "Scythian Vocabulary in the Sources, Introduction," Turkic History, TurkicWorld.org, 2002. http://s155239215.onlinehome.us/turkic/27_Scythians/ScythianWordListSourcesEn.htm

to early Eurasian nomads in general.⁵³⁹ There were numerous nomadic tribes in existence in the fourteenth and fifteenth centuries B.C., such as the Israelites dwelling in Egypt or Shasu mercenaries from the southern Levant. The legends say that Scota and Gaythelos were forced to leave Egypt for some reason.⁵⁴⁰ They would have taken servants, a crew and a military force with them. Some of this entourage could have included Jews, or other Middle Eastern ethnicities. The Shasu could have served them as mercenary soldiers.

> **Fun Fact**
> Ironically, when university students stole the Stone of Scone from Westminster Abbey on Christmas Day 1950, they smuggled it through former Graham haunts: Arthuret and Canonbie, and the back roads of Eskdale, eventually hidden in the undercroft of Graham's castle at Aberfoyle.

The Shasu were organized in clans such as that seen in the ancient Celts under a tribal chieftain, and were described as brigands active from the Jezreel Valley to Ashkelon and the Sinai.⁵⁴¹ Gaythelos' army may have included Shasu mercenaries. A connection to these nomads from the Eastern Mediterranean would increase the chances that Gaythelos or members of his household or army were J1 Y-DNA. In addition, the legend behind the Stone of Scone used to crown Scottish monarchs was that the stone was tied to the Prophet Jacob and that Gaythelos brought it from Syria to Egypt. While the origin of the stone itself has been in question, it is another story that ties Gaytheolos to the Eastern Mediterranean and coincidentally to the origin of the J1-YSC76 haplogroup with ties to Britain.

## Princess Scota

Per the legends, she was a daughter of an Egyptian pharaoh and ancestor of the Gaels. Some scholars believe her name origin may have been derived from the Scoti people, who were Milesians who came to Ireland from Northern Spain.⁵⁴² Determining the father of Princess Scota is a favorite discussion

*Figure 50: Relief of Akhenaten, Nefertiti and two daughters praying to Aten, the Egyptian sun god. Tell el-Amarna, Egypt, 18th dynasty, reign of Akhenaten (dated between 1372 and 1355 B.C.).* ⁵⁴⁴

---

⁵³⁹ Robert C. L. Holmes, "The Scythians: Who Were They?" The Collector, 13 September 2021. https://www.thecollector.com/who-were-the-scythians/

⁵⁴⁰ United Church of God, "Gathelus, Scota and the Exodus," Beyond Today, accessed 8 November 2022. https://www.ucg.org/bible-study-tools/ebooklet/the-throne-of-britain/appendix-8-gathelus-scota-and-the-exodus

⁵⁴¹ Titus Kennedy, "The Land of the SAsw (Shasu Nomads) of yhwA at Soleb," *Dotawo: A Journal of Nubian Studies* 6 (2019): 175–192.
https://escholarship.org/content/qt07x6659z/qt07x6659z_noSplash_b41d2cc59a80dd132c3838e7ec75c0f8.pdf?t=q2zg3k

⁵⁴² United Church of God, "Gathelus, Scota and the Exodus."

[Fun Fact blurb] "Aberfoyle, Did You Know?" The Scottish Banner, January 2018, 11.
https://www.scottishbanner.com/wp-content/uploads/2017/12/SB-4107-January-AU.pdf

topic of Egyptologists, but what follows is a summary of the two most promising candidates.

1. Using the timeline of fourteenth-century chronicler John of Fordun, Damian B. Bullen calculated, using Fordun's statement, that Princess Scota lived 760 years before the building of Rome. He concluded Scota's father would be Thutmose I (reign estimated to be 1525-1512 B.C.), and Scota would be Thutmose I's missing daughter, Nefrubity (Akhbetneferu). A hieroglyphic pictogram of Nefrubity exists in her sister's mortuary temple Dayr el-Bahari located near Luxor, together with her father Thutmose I and her mother Ahmose. However, she then seems to vanish from Egyptian history, implying she left Egypt.[543]

2. In "Scota, Egyptian Queen of the Scots," Ralph Ellis dissects the Princess Scota/Gaythelos story using "The History of Egypt," written in 300 B.C. by an Egypto-Greek historian called Manetho. Using Manetho's text, Ellis provides evidence that Scota was really Ankhesenamun (Princess Meriaten), one of the daughters of Pharoah Akhenaton and Queen Nefertiti[544] (their reign was 1353 to 1336 B.C.). See Figure 50. Tutankhamun may have been her step-brother and first husband. Manetho estimated that the number of people that accompanied the couple numbered 1,000.[545]

Other stories name various pharaohs as Scota's father—Ramses II, Friel, Nectanebo I, Necho II, and Neferhotep I [546]—however, the reigns of those pharaohs are far outside the time window indicated by Y-DNA results as of March 2023. It is possible with the accumulation of more Y-DNA test data, that this conclusion could change.

## Other evidence that may support the Princess Scota legend:

- Per the FTDNA Scottish DNA Project, J1-FGC58460 is also found in England and may have arrived in England prior to or the same timeframe that the J1-L1253 arrived in Britain (circa 1417B.C.). Some English J1 surnames include Corder, Crouch, Cuffley, Baker, Day, and Robinson. [547]
- Dr. Sean O'Riordan, an archaeologist of Trinity College, Dublin, during an excavation at the Hill of Tara in 1955, discovered skeletal remains dated to the Bronze Age believed to be

---

[543] Damian Beeson Bullen, "Nefrubity and Princess Scota," Academia.edu, accessed 28 December 2022. https://www.academia.edu/45466704/NEFERUBITY_and_PRINCESS_SCOTA

[544] Figure 50: Wikimedia Commons contributors, "File:La salle dAkhenaton (1356-1340 av J.C.) (Musée du Caire) (2076972086).jpg," Wikimedia Commons, the free media repository, accessed 28 December 2022. https://commons.wikimedia.org/w/index.php?title=File:La_salle_dAkhenaton_(1356-1340_av_J.C.)_(Mus%C3%A9e_du_Caire)_(2076972086).jpg&oldid=670985236

[545] The Scotsman, "The Pharaoh's Daughter Who was the Mother of all Scots."

[546] Henry Kwadwo Amoako, "Did Queen Scotia Really Exist in The Days of The Biblical Moses?" African Research Consult, 22 March 2022. http://african-research.com/research/did-queen-scotia-really-exist-in-the-days-of-the-biblical-moses/

[547] "Scottish Y-DNA Project," English J1s, Page 4, Family Tree DNA, accessed 28 December 2022. https://www.familytreedna.com/public/Scottishdna?iframe=ycolorized

those of a young prince.⁵⁴⁸ The Hill of Tara is an ancient ceremonial and burial site in County Meath, Ireland.⁵⁴⁹ Tradition identifies the hill as the inauguration place and seat of the High Kings of Ireland. Around the boy's neck was a rare necklace of faience beads made from a mixture of plants and minerals. The carbon dating results of the skeleton: <u>1359 B.C.</u> The design of the beads show them to be Egyptian. <u>Coincidentally, Tutankhamen, the boy king, was interred in Egypt about this same timeframe.</u> Even more surprising is the fact that both Tutankhamun's mummy and the Tara skeleton had the same golden collar around their neck, which was inlaid with matching conical, blue-green faience beads.⁵⁵⁰ A Bronze Age burial ground in Devon, England also yielded a similar necklace.⁵⁵¹

- In Kingdom of the Ark, Egyptologist Lorraine Evans claims the remains of ancient boats discovered in 1937 in North Ferriby, Yorkshire, belonged to ancient Egyptians. The boats were at first thought to be Viking longships, but do not match Viking longship descriptions. They are similar to a boat exhumed from the Great Pyramid of Giza in 1954 and relief pictures at the temple of Queen Hatshepsut in Luxor. According to radiocarbon dating, the boats found in Yorkshire were crafted around 1400 to 1350 B.C. ⁵⁵²

---

⁵⁴⁸ David Halpin, "Thoth's Storm: New Evidence for Ancient Egyptians in Ireland?" Ancient Origins®, 19 June 2021. https://www.ancient-origins.net/opinion-guest-authors/thoth-s-storm-new-evidence-ancient-egyptians-ireland-005187

⁵⁴⁹ Lorraine Evans, *Kingdom of the Ark: The Startling Story of how the Ancient British Race is Descended from the Pharaohs* (London: Simon & Schuster, 2000), 1.

⁵⁵⁰ Natalia Klimczak, "Exploring the Little Known History of Celtic Warrior in Egypt," Ancient Origins, 4 January 2016. https://www.ancient-origins.net/history/exploring-little-known-history-celtic-warriors-egypt-005100

⁵⁵¹ Heather Elizabeth Adams-Osborn, "The Story of Princess Scota, Atlantis, Egypt, and Ireland: The Story of Princess Scota," Ancient Mysteries, ARE, February 2007. https://www.researchgate.net/publication/277713025_'Atlantis_Egypt_and_Ireland_The_Story_of_Princess_Scota'_Ancient_Mysteries_ARE_Feb_2007 (Need to file a request with author.)

⁵⁵² Lorraine Evans, *Kingdom of the Ark: The Startling Story of how the Ancient British Race is Descended from the Pharaohs*, 1-17.

## Three other possible scenarios to explain the arrival of J1 in Britain in the Bronze Age:

### Phoenician Trader Option:

> **Did you know?**
> The purple dye manufactured in Tyre for the robes of royalty gave Phoenicia the name by which we know it today (from the Greek *Phoinikes* for Tyrian Purple). The reason the Phoenicians were known as 'purple people' by the Greeks is because the dye would stain the skin of the workers.

Phoenicia was an ancient Semitic-speaking, nautical civilization that originated in the Levant region of the eastern Mediterranean, primarily in/near modern-day Lebanon—which is also near the theorized origin of J-M267/YSC76. Famous for their mastery of ancient maritime navigation and shipbuilding, the Phoenicians were likely the first to survey the Mediterranean Sea and begin the modern field of geography, the first to use celestial navigation, and the first Mediterranean people to venture past the Strait of Gibraltar into the Atlantic Ocean. The Phoenicians also conducted a vital transit trade, especially in the manufactured goods of Egypt and Babylonia (Herodotus, i, 1).[xiii] From the lands of the Euphrates and Tigris, regular trade routes led to the Mediterranean. In Egypt, the Phoenician merchants soon gained a foothold; they alone maintained a profitable trade in the anarchic times of the 22nd and 23rd dynasties (circa 945-circa 730 B.C.).[553] Though there were never any regular colonies of Phoenicians in Egypt, the Tyrians (Phoenicians) had a large base in Memphis (Herodotus, ii, 112).[554]

According to author Salim Khalaf, "The Arabian caravan trade in perfume, spices, and incense passed through Phoenician hands on its way to Greece and the West (Herodotus, iii, 107)." The prophet Eziekiel was a witness. In Eziekiel Chapter 27 of the Bible, he gives a detailed account of the Phoenicians: "Thy wise men, O Tyre, were in thee—they were thy pilots. The ancients of Gebal, and their wise men, were thy calkers; All the ships of the sea, with their mariners, were in thee, That they might occupy thy merchandise." Comparing Figure C-15 (Phoenician Trade Routes)[555] with Figure C-7 (J1 P58 Y-Haplogroup Geographic Distribution), the higher concentrations of J1 (dark green) correlate well with Phoenician settlements. However, the earliest the Phoenicians may have been in Britain was about 700-800 B.C. based on the establishment of their trading base at Gibraltar circa 950 B.C.[556] and

---

[553] Ryan Schleeter, "First Rulers of the Mediterranean," National Geographic Resource Library, updated 20 May 2022. https://education.nationalgeographic.org/resource/first-rulers-mediterranean

[Did you know? Blurb] Joshua J Mark, "Phoenicia," *World History Encyclopedia*, 19 March 2018. https://www.worldhistory.org/phoenicia/

[554] Salim George Khalaf, "Phoenician Trade and Ships," Phoenicia.org, accessed 8 November 2022. https://phoenicia.org/trade.html

[Did you know? Blurb] Joshua J Mark, "Phoenicia," *World History Encyclopedia*, 19 March 2018. https://www.worldhistory.org/phoenicia/

[555] Salim George Khalaf, "Phoenician Trade and Ships," Phoenicia.org, accessed 8 November 2022.

[556] "A Brief History of Gibraltar," Gibraltar Timeline, accessed 8 November 2022. http://gibraltartimeline.com/brief-history-of-gibraltar/

Carthage in 813 B.C. Records of their distant voyages in search of tin,[557] and the discovery of Phoenician monuments and coins in Britain are dated as early as 400B.C. [558] This theory is at least 600 years later than the current Y-DNA estimate for the arrival of J1s in Britain.[559]

## Picts Option:

The Picts were an Iron-Age people who lived in eastern and northern Scotland, and were organized by tribes. St.Bede, an Anglo-Saxon monk, wrote in the eighth century that he believed the Picts sailed from Scythia, initially landed in Ireland, were turned away, and moved onto Scotland.[560] He also wrote that the Picts practiced matrilineal kingship succession,[561] a similar custom practiced in ancient Egypt.[562] The Picts and Egyptian origin legends now share a connection to Spain. Recent Y-DNA analysis indicates the Picts originated in Iberia, were perhaps relatives of the Basques, and were believed to have arrived in Scotland circa 7000-8000 B.C. There is an R1b/L1335 DNA marker of Pictish heritage that was recently discovered, but the entire Pictish civilization likely had more than one Y-DNA type. The R1b/L1335 is the one survivor that geneticists have identified so far.[563]

## The Syrian Archer Theory:

This theory is expounded in "Syrian Scots on the Borderlands" by Jim Farmer. Mr. Farmer theorizes that the J1 Y-DNA arrived in Scotland with Syrian Archer auxiliaries, remnants of the Roman army left behind when the Romans withdrew in 410 A.D.[564] See Figure 51. Thanks to Y-DNA cousin David Noble, I learned of a website on the extinction rates of male lines, run by Dr. Robin Spencer from the England Groups EIJ Y-DNA Project. It includes a tool based on fertility rates for calculating the extinction of male lines (Figure 52). If it assumed, on average, that there were two births per man in the period discussed, Dr. Spencer's model suggests that 98% of male lines go extinct after an average of 6.4 generations. Thus, estimating that there were 500 Syrian archers mustered and sent to British Isles

---

[557] Salim George Khalaf, "Phoenician Canaanite History Timeline," Phoenicia.org, accessed 8 November 2022. https://phoenicia.org/phoeniciatimeline.html

[558] Lawrence Austine Waddell, *The Phoenician Origins of Britons, Scots and Anglo-Saxons*, Chapter 2 (London: Williams and Norgate, 1924), 16-19. https://www.jrbooksonline.com/pob/pob_toc.html

[559] Department of Ancient Near-Eastern Art. "The Phoenicians 1500-300 B.C.," The Metropolitan Museum of Art, October 2004. https://www.metmuseum.org/toah/hd/phoe/hd_phoe.html

[560] Tom Garlinghouse, "Who were the Picts, the Early Inhabitants of Scotland?" LiveScience, updated August 2022. https://www.livescience.com/who-were-picts-scotland

Figure 51: "Teaching Romans, Anglo-Saxons, and Vikings in Britain," Historical Association, 25 January 2011. https://www.history.org.uk/primary/resource/3860/teaching-romans-anglo-saxons-and-vikings-in-brit

[561] Benjamin Hudson, *The Picts* (New York: John Wiley & Sons, 2014), 35.

[562] Moustafa Gadalla, "Matrilineal/Matriarchal Society," Egyptian Wisdom Center, accessed 23 January 2023. https://egyptianwisdomcenter.org/matrilineal-matriarchal-society-2/

[563] Roberta Estes, "You Might Be a Pict If ..." DNAeXplained-Genetic Genealogy, 24 August 2013. https://dna-explained.com/2013/08/24/you-might-be-a-pict-if/

[564] Jim Farmer, "Syrian Scots on the Borderlands," Academia.edu, 9 June 2009. (DOC) Syrian Scots on the Borderlands No Pics | Jim Farmer - Academia.edu

in the year 130 A.D., then after 6.4 generations (with an average generation of 30 years)—or 192 years total —only ten lines would have survived.[565] While it is technically possible that one Syrian Y-DNA line survived from 1900 years ago, it is unlikely. Furthermore, Y-DNA analysis in Appendix C, indicates the Scottish J1 progenitor was born circa 300 B.C., which is too early to match the time period that the Roman auxiliaries were in Britain (after 130 A.D.). [566]

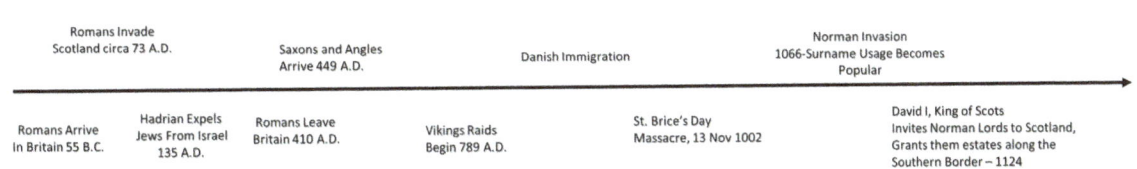

*Figure 51: A Brief Timeline of Early History in Britain* [560]

---

[565] Robin Spencer, PhD, "The Extinction of Lines," Tracking Back-A Website for Genetic Genealogy Tools, Experimentation and Discussion, 31 March 2020. http://scaledinnovation.com/gg/extinctionDemo.html.

[566] The Antonine Wall, "The Romans in Scotland," Antoninewall.org, accessed 15 December 2022. https://www.antoninewall.org/about-the-wall/the-romans-in-scotland

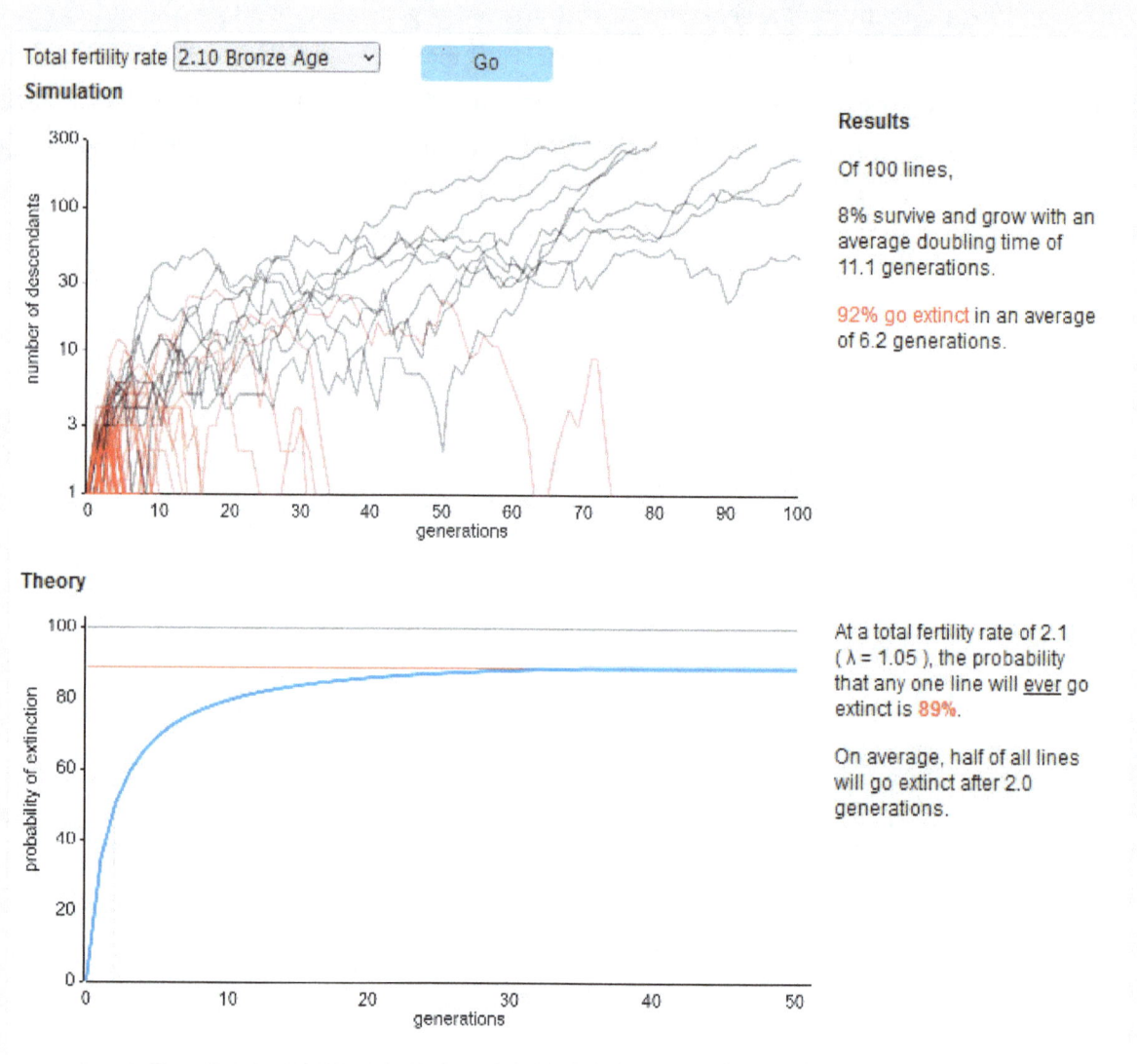

*Figure 52: Extinction Rate Tool from ScaledInnovation.com by Dr Robin Spencer* [567]

As more "Big-Y" testers come forward, these estimates can be refined and determine a more definitive age for the L1253 subclade, unique to the Border Grahams. Over 1300 have registered with the Graham Y-DNA Surname Project as of April 2023.[568] As of that time, there were 707 Y-DNA profiles reported in the Graham project results, and project administrators sorted them into about 96 groups. Those 96 groups were reduced to five major categories, depicted in Figure C-3 and described in Table C-1 in Appendix C.

---

[567] Figure 52: Robin Spencer, PhD, "The Extinction of Lines," Tracking Back-A Website for Genetic Genealogy Tools, Experimentation and Discussion.

[568] FamilyTreeDNA, "Graham Surname DNA Project News."

## Closest Y-DNA Match

Some clues come from the closest Y-DNA cousin match from Canada to determine the origin of Christopher Graham and his brothers, James, John, and William, in Scotland. The match is a five genetic distance (5 GD) match at 111 markers[569] which indicates a 90% chance that a common ancestor lived **13** generations before present, where "present" is defined as 1950, the birth year of the average Y-DNA tester.[570] This closest match can trace his Grahams to Westerkirk and nearby Langholm, Scotland, in the early 1700s; has Graham ancestors named Christopher, James, John, and William; and also has a number of Langholm Armstrongs in his family tree. Since the American immigrant brothers, Christopher, James, John, and William are **10** generations above the Grayville, Illinois, Graham test subjects, and our Canadian cousin's ancestors remained in Scotland until the nineteenth century, 11-13 generations[571] (circa 1521-1587) is before the time the families would have split—with one branch leaving for Ireland and the other staying in Scotland. Given that: 1) Captain Edward Armstrong left Langholm, Scotland, between 1635 and 1641)[572] 2) The Laird of the Gillesbie Grahams and much of his clan also left Scotland by 1641.[573] 3) Captain Edward Armstrong's family in County Fermanagh, Ireland, was closely tied to the Grahams in County Fermanagh[574], and 4) in 1642, the "deserted Tower of Grame," formerly owned by the Grahams of Gillesbie, was confidently used to keep a high-profile prisoner, a powerful judge, for three months by Edward's father, Colonel William Armstrong.[575] This suggested that Colonel Armstrong was familiar with the tower's previous owners and knew they weren't coming back, since an experienced military officer would not have used an unsecure location for such a risky mission. In this case, Colonel Armstrong knew the Grahams who owned the tower personally and was related to them by marriage. He also knew the circumstances prompting their departure for Ireland, after the unfortunate fight that left the laird of the Shaw

> **In the "Saints" Category**
> Another Y-DNA match to the Grayville Grahams is a paternal cousin of William Franklin "Billy" Graham Jr. (November 7, 1918 – February 21, 2018). He was an American evangelist and an ordained Southern Baptist minister who became well known internationally in the late 1940s. He was a prominent evangelical Christian figure, and according to a biographer, was "among the most influential Christian leaders" of the 20th century.

---

[569] Family Tree DNA (FTDNA) Y-DNA Matches for Barry Scott Graham, accessed 20 October 2022.
[570] Roberta Estes, "Concepts—Genetic Distance," DNAeXplained Genetic Genealogy, accessed 20 October 2022. https://dna-explained.com/2016/06/29/concepts-genetic-distance/
[571] Since the Grayville Grahams confidently know their paternal line to the 10th generation, that narrows the range of the match to above 10 generations.
[572] James Lewis Armstrong, M.D., *Chronicles of the Armstrongs*, 317-320, 309-310.
[573] Col William Rogerson, *Hutton Under the Muir*, 26-28, 39.
[574] James Lewis Armstrong, M.D., *Chronicles of the Armstrongs*, 317-320, 309-310.
[In the "Saints" Category Blurb] Geni.com, "Rev. William Franklin II," updated 22 April 2022. https://www.geni.com/people/Billy-Graham/6000000015742172128
[575] John G. Armstrong, "The Debatable Armstrongs and Their Graham Relations," 1-3.

Grahams dead, [576] and that they left about the same time as his adult sons Edward, John, Alexander, and Thomas.[577]

The collection of evidence ties the Grayville Grahams' ancestors to Lang Will's brother, John Graham of Gillesbie, Brackenwra, in the Parish of Hutton. The first year of a document attestation (att) or first year that John Graham was a document signatory, was 1470. The Gillesbie estate in the Parish of Hutton and Corrie included the deserted tower of Grame.[578]

Descending from John Graham of Gillesbie, brother to Lang Will Graham, would explain why the Grayville Grahams are more distantly related via Y-DNA to other J1 Grahams suspected of being Lang Will descendants (Figure C-8). In addition, the Grahams of Shaw, the previously referenced Gillesbie Graham cadet line, owned properties along the Wauchope Water, the primary river of Langholm Parish.[579, 580] Phil Graham believes this includes the Mill of Millholm which could explain how the Gillesbie Grahams developed close ties with the Langholm Armstrongs. The Brackenwra Grahams also operated the Mill of Hoddam Parish, near Graham's Hall.[581] See Dumfriesshire Map from Thomson's 1832 Atlas of Scotland in Figure 53. More confirmation of a bond between the Grahams of Gillesbie and the Armstrongs: per *The Register of the Privy Council of Scotland,* in 1623, Robert Graham of Gillesbie served as a cautioner (co-signed for a loan) jointly and severally with Francie Armstrong of Kinmont (near the town of Sark), [582] and David Quihippo in Boig, providing a bail bond of 500 merks for John Armstrong of Woodhouse (Kirkpatrick Fleming Parish in Dumfriesshire).

---

[576] Col. William Rogerson, *Hutton Under the Muir*, 26-28, 39.

[577] James Lewis Armstrong, M.D. *Chronicles of the Armstrongs*, 317-320, 309-310.

[578] *Registrum Honoris de Morton, Volume II: Ancient Charters,* 216-217.

[579] John and Robert Hylsop, *Langholm As it Was: A History of Langholm and Eskdale from the Earliest Times* (Sunderland: Hills and Company, 1912), 119, 292. https://archive.org/details/langholmasitwashhysl/mode/2up?q=shaw

[580] David Masson, *The Register of the Privy Council of Scotland. Volume XIV, Addenda A. D. 1545-1625* (Edinburgh: H.M. General Register House, 1898), 698. https://www.google.com/books/edition/The_Register_of_the_Privy_Council_of_Sco/5fcVHNMT5nIC?hl=en&gbpv=1&bsq=hoddam%20mill

[581] J. Bell Irving, Esq. "List of Armorial Bearings Noted in Dumfriesshire and Neighboring Counties," *Transactions of the Dumfries and Galloway Natural History and Archaeological Society (TDGNHAS)*, Third Series, Vol. 1 (1912-1913): 130-131. https://archive.org/details/transactionsjour31191213dumf/mode/2up?q=escallop

[582] "Tower-of-Sark, Kinmont's Tower," Canmore, National Record of the Historic Environment, accessed 28 December 2022. https://canmore.org.uk/site/67538/tower-of-sark

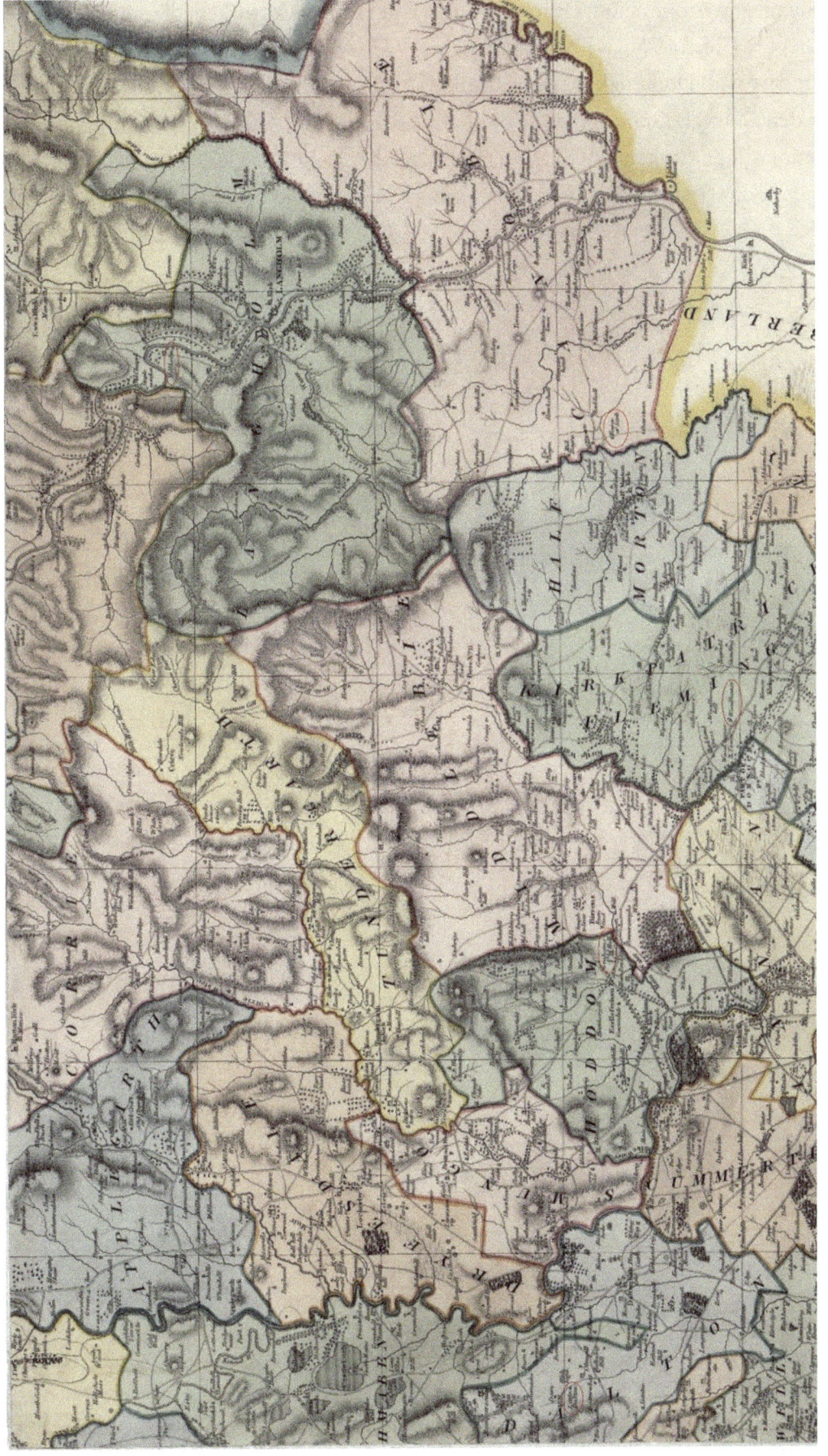

*Figure 53: Langholm, Hoddam, Dalton and Southern Hutton and Corrie Parishes in Dumfriesshire, as shown in John Thomson's 1832 Atlas of Scotland. CC-BY 4.0 Reproduced with the permission of the National Library of Scotland.* [584]

Hoddam gravestones show Hutton Graham and Hutton Corrie heraldic emblems circa 1700s, indicating they are Gillesbie/Shaw Graham relations.[583] Hoddam Parish is near Dalton Parish which shares a boundary with Dryfesdale,[584] which could explain why three men with the locational surname "Dalton" match Grayville Graham men at a 6-step GD-111-markers, indicating a common ancestor in 10-17 generations. John Graham of Gillesbie and his brother Lang Will Graham are 17 generations back from the present-day Grayville Grahams. These same Daltons do not match suspected Lang Will descendants.

---

[583] J. Bell Irving, Esq. "List of Armorial Bearings Noted in Dumfriesshire and Neighboring Counties," 128-131.
[584] Figure 53: John Thomson, "Dumfriesshire," *Atlas of Scotland, 1832.*

# Chapter 7
# Summary[xiv]

## American Immigrant Brothers

The oldest confirmed ancestor of the Grahams of Grayville, Illinois, is James Graham Sr. (1683-1745), who was likely born in County Fermanagh, Ireland, and traveled to America with his brothers, Christopher, John, and a fourth brother, likely named William, to Pennsylvania between June and October 1720. The family were known to be devout Presbyterians in Pennsylvania and Virginia and were associated with known covenanting families (e.g. Risks, Browns); however, no evidence of these Grahams can be found in the documented lists and court proceedings concerning Covenanters. Therefore, it can be surmised that the ancestors of the Grayville Grahams acquired their dedication to Presbyterianism from their wives.

## Irish Military Records

The elder brother of James Sr., Christopher Graham, served as a cavalry trooper in Colonel Wolseley's famous Regiment of Horse, known as the "Inniskilleners" during the Williamite Wars in Ireland (1688-1693). Christopher's first troop commander, Captain Martin Armstrong, a descendant of the Armstrongs of Langholm, Scotland,[585] is likely a relative. This conclusion can be drawn given that local militias of the time comprised families and close friends. This conclusion is further supported by the ties of the Langholm Armstrongs to other Grahams in County Fermanagh and the closest Y-DNA match to the Grayville Grahams, whose ancestry traces to eighteenth century Westerkirk and Langholm, Scotland. Furthermore, Grahams are buried in the Armstrong family crypt in Aghavea in County Fermanagh.[586] The Grahams of Gillesbie tower disappeared from Scotland about the same

---

[585] FindmyPast.com, "Beatty notebooks, v. 6-12," *Crosslé Genealogical Abstracts, 1620-1850*, FindmyPast, 240, accessed 27 December 2022. (Requires Account.) https://search.findmypast.com/record?id=S2%2FIRE%2FNAI%2F007634818%2F00600&parentid=IRE%2FNAI%2FGENABS%2F00602219%2F1

[586] James Lewis Armstrong, M.D., *Chronicles of the Armstrongs*, 317-320, 309-310.

time as the sons of Colonel Will Armstrong—about 1641. Colonel William Rogerson of Gillesbie wrote in 1908 of the local story of the lairds of Shaw and Gillesbie quarreling and one killing the other and the former fleeing the country. Colonel Rogerson interviewed a senior resident (who was a Graham) who said that the Tower of Gillesbie was deserted by 1641.[587] Both families missed being counted in the County Fermanagh Muster Roll of 1629,[588] indicating they arrived after 1629. The year 1635 is the last time a Graham of Gillespie is found in Scotland,[589] except for a John Graham, who mortgages the Gillesbie lands 33 years later.[590] By the time Colonel William Armstrong used the "deserted tower of Grame" to house a famous prisoner, Lord Durie, it was 1642.[591] I believe the John Graham of Gillesbie left behind in Scotland and who mortgaged Gillesbie lands from 1668 to 1670 is the ancestor of the Grayville Grahams' closest Y-DNA match whose ancestors remained in Scotland until the nineteenth century.

Additional historical research, a compilation of the unique male family name combination of Christopher-James-John-William present in the Grayville Graham ancestors, and the ancestors of their closest Y-DNA match and the Langholm Armstrongs lead us to conclude that the sixth Laird of Gillesbie, John Graham (Generation 13), is the most likely common ancestor of Christopher, James Sr., John, and William* Graham, later of the Lancaster area of Pennsylvania and of their closest Y-DNA cousin. John Graham, the sixth laird of Gillesbie, was born in circa 1580 and was reported among other border lairds in 1618. This Laird John Graham was the third-great grandson of the first John Graham of Gillesbie, brother to Lang Will Graham of the Border Grahams.[592]

We detangled the confusion of similar names, places, and errors from previous secondary sources and presented evidence for several other new theories:

---

[587] Col. William Rogerson, *Hutton Under the Muir*, 25, 31, 26.

[588] Robert John Hunter, "Families and Kinship," Muster Rolls c. 1630, Introduction, The R.J. Hunter Collection.

[589] R.C. Reid, "The Border Grahams and Their Origins," 93-94.

[590] Gillesbie Graham property owner mortgages lands until Scott family takes over

Scottish Record Office, *Index to Register of Deeds, 1668, Volume VIII* (Edinburgh: His Majesty's Stationery Office, 1924), 181. https://www.google.com/books/edition/Indexes/6ISQFt6Y5ekC?hl=en&gbpv=1&bsq=%20gillesbie

Scottish Record Office, *Index to Register of Deeds, 1669, Volume IX* (Edinburgh: His Majesty's Stationery Office, 1926), 177.
https://www.google.com/books/edition/Index_to_Register_of_Deeds_Preserved_in/C8wRAAAAIAAJ?hl=en&gbpv=1&bsq=graham

Scottish Record Office, *Index to Register of Deeds, 1670, Volume X* (Edinburgh: His Majesty's Stationery Office., 1926), 170.
https://www.google.com/books/edition/Index_to_Register_of_Deeds_Preserved_in/vsQRAAAAIAAJ?hl=en&gbpv=1

[591] John G. Armstrong, "The Debatable Armstrongs and Their Graham Relations," 3.

[592] Col. William Rogerson, *Hutton Under the Muir*, 26-28, 39.

1. The Corrie/Corry family was a previously unknown sept clan to the elder line of William de Graham. An unnamed daughter of the second Sir Henry de Graham and Christina Fitz Gilbert married a Ralph de Corrie.[593, 594] Their son, the fourth Sir Henry de Graham, who fought at the siege of Caerverlock, used a combined Corrie-Graham coat of arms that had the white saltire on a red background used by the Corries.[595]

> **Did you know?**
> A saltire (X-shaped cross) in a coat of arms in medieval Scotland, indicated service to the lords of Annandale, the Bruces. Three escallops in chief were commonly used by Grahams. "In chief" means the escallops were running along the top border of the shield. See Appendix E.

2. Sir John de Graham "the Last" Lord of Dalkeith is a misnomer, as Sir John was the father of at least two, possibly three sons: Alan de Graham, Lord of Morton, and Nether Hutton[596]; John Graham of Auchinloch and Lugton [597]; and a possibly a priest named Nicholas.[598] John, the heir, resigned his rights of Dalkeith to the Douglases in 1370. Alan resigned his rights to Nether Hutton (Hutton Sub Mora) to the Douglases in 1373.

3. Successive generations of Black Douglases managed to take control of most of the former empire of the elder line Grahams, in addition to lands belonging to others, including the Murrays and the Scottish church.[599] Their ambitions to seize power and the Scottish throne are a part of Scottish history. [600] They may have coerced the sons of Sir John "the Last" to resign their rights to the Dalkeith Barony, which included detached lands in the Dryfe Valley and Eskdalemuir, and are suspected of coercing David II to grant William Douglas a pardon for murder.

---

[593] *Registrum Honoris de Morton, Volume II: Ancient Charters*, 3.

[594] Ralph Corrie also witnessed a charter where the third Sir Henry de Graham, possibly his brother-in-law, gifted the lands of Upper Dryfe to Sir David of Torthorwald in the mid 1200s. PoMS no. 4859, accessed 3 March 2023. https://www.poms.ac.uk/record/source/4859/

[595] Walter of Exeter, Franciscan Friar and Witness to the Siege, The Siege of Carlaverock, 1300, accessed 18 October 2022. https://www.deremilitari.org/RESOURCES/SOURCES/carlaverock.htm

[Did you know? Blurb] Thomas Allen Bruce, "Bruce Heraldry Part III," *The Blue Lion*, Newsletter for the Family of Bruce International, Inc., Vol. 16, Issue 3 (September 2010): 7. https://familyofbruceinternational.org/wp-content/uploads/2020/02/SEPT-2010-BLUE-LION-E-VERSION.pdf

[596] *Registrum Honoris de Morton, Volume II: Ancient Charters*, 88, 115, 117-119.

[597] John Reid, "Material for a Place Name Survey of East Stirlingshire," 109.

[598] William Robertson Esq. *An index, drawn up about the year 1629, of many records of charters, granted by the different sovereigns of Scotland between the years 1309 and 1413, most of which records have been long missing. With an introduction, giving a state, founded on authentic documents still preserved, of the ancient records of Scotland, which were in that kingdom in the year 1292* (Edinburgh, Murry and Cochrane, 1798), No. 284, 93.

[599] Author: "B," "The Chiefship of the Clan Murray," 65-66.

[600] William Knox, PhD, "Myth and History: The Case of the Black Douglases."

4. There is a basis after all for the claims by the Fergus Graham of Nunnery, grandson of Lang Will and the new Grahams of Netherby (of Plomp),[601] that their families should have been able to use the Menteith coat of arms as there is evidence their ancestor was the ninth earl of Menteith, John Graham. The ninth earl of Menteith was the first Graham to hold the title, acquiring it by marriage to Mary, the Countess of Menteith. Church records show that these Grahams were from the Diocese of St. Andrews, the diocese of the elder line Grahams. If they were Montrose Grahams of the younger line, their diocese would have been declared as the Diocese of Brechin.[602]

5. The Border Grahams, whose Y-DNA is commonly J1/L1253, are likely descendants of the elder line of William de Graham via a female cousin of Sir John "the Last": Agnes de Grame and her husband, who was named simply as "Andrew de ?" in the People of Medieval Scotland (PoMS) database [603] (possibly Sir Andrew de Murray of Manuel). Agnes and Andrew were married shortly before 1363, so their birth years are estimated in the late 1330s/early 1340s. Sir Andrew or his biological father are strong candidates to be the patriarch of the J1 Grahams, given the March 2023 Y-DNA estimate from the FTDNA Discover™ tool that the L1253 patriarch was born between 1011 and 1357 A.D.[604]

6. March 2023 Y-DNA analysis indicates that the ancestors of the J1 Grahams may have arrived in the British Isles in the late Bronze Age, circa 1417 B.C.,[605] which coincides with the legends of the formation of Scotland and the arrival of an Egyptian princess named Scota, her husband Gaythelos, and their army. It is possible that Scota and Gaythelos brought servants and a mercenary army when, per the legends, they were forced to leave Egypt.[606] Some of the servants could have been Jews sojourning in Egypt or representatives of other Middle Eastern ethnicities. The mercenaries hired to fill out the ranks of Gaythelos' army may have been Shasu, mercenaries who were established in the Levant and the Sinai Peninsula at that time.

7. I believe William de Graham, the first documented Graham, was a younger son of an established family in Cumbria and northern England, called the Lords of Greystoke (Gristock), sons of Forne Sigulfson, who were themselves descendants of the Danes who formerly controlled

---

[601] Joseph Foster, *The Heralds' Visitations of the Counties of Cumberland and Westmoreland, made by Richard St. George, Norry, king of arms in 1615, and by William Dugdale, Norry, king of arms in 1666* (Charles Thurnam and Sons, Carlisle, 1891), 54. https://archive.org/details/pedigreesrecorde00sainrich

[602] John P. Ravilious, "Queen Euphemia and Her Ancestry," 49-50.

[603] PoMS, "No. 23643- Agnes Graham, 'Wife of Andrew de ?,'" accessed 20 October 2022. https://www.poms.ac.uk/record/person/23643/

[604] Family Tree DNA (FTDNA), "Scientific Details Haplogroup L1253."

[605] England Great Britain Groups EIJ, "E I J G R T England Scotland Wales Ireland Norman & Diverse Others," Activity Feed.

[606] Damian Beeson Bullen, "Nefrubity and Princess Scota."

Yorkshire.[607] Gris-stock is Norse for "home of the boars."[608] "*Gris*" is also Latin for "gray," and may explain how the name transitioned from Gristock to Greystoke and to "Gray-ham" when translated to/from Latin and Old English in land charters and other legal documents and why the boar was commonly used in many Graham armorials.[609] I also presented evidence from land charters and church records to show evidence of sons and a son-in-law of Forne Sigulfson in Scotland.

8. The use of escallops in the Graham armorials is derived from a saint popular amongst Normans, Saint Michael the Archangel, a patron saint of the military, whose escallop symbol was shared with Saint James the Greater, patron saint of Spain. As stated, the alternate symbol on many Graham armorials is the boar. The boar is the ancient Pictish, Celtic and Norse symbol for courage and strength in battle.[610] It can be argued that the Norman equivalent symbol of the boar would be the symbol of the patron saint of warriors, Saint Michael the Archangel—which is the escallop in heraldry terminology, aka: a scallop shell.[611]

In conclusion, after analyzing the FTDNA Graham Surname Project results, and investigating the origins of the many different Y-DNA categories in Appendix C, it appears that a majority of people born with the Graham surname descend from the twelfth century knight William de Graham, the first documented Graham. However, most of them (92%) have one or more Graham females in their lines. The many unofficial sept clans, where the surname was passed down the distaff (female) side, would account for 96 different Y-DNA types reported in the Graham Surname Project.[612] I argue the Grayville Grahams descend from John Graham of Gillesbie, who descended from Agnes de Graham and her husband Andrew, possibly surnamed Murray of Manuel. There are still many unknowns regarding the origin of the Border Grahams and also of the knight William de Graham. Hopefully, we have shed more light on the subject and with new Y-DNA data and more historical records being digitized, the origin questions will be answered in full.

---

[607] Stephen M. Lewis, "Forne Sigulfson-The Normans Come to Cumbria."
[608] Stephen M. Lewis, Université de Caen Normandie, "Grisdales of Matterdale, Grisdale 1332."
[609] Lloyd D.Graham, *House Graham, From the Antoine Wall to the Temple of Hymen*, 1-5.
[610] Symbols.com, "Boar," accessed 4 December 2022. https://www.symbols.com/symbol/boar
[611] Duane L.C.M. Galles, "Pilgrims and Heraldry."
[612] FamilyTreeDNA, "Graham Surname DNA Project News."

# Table of Figures

Figure 1: Descendants Chart of the Four Graham Brothers who emigrated to Pennsylvania from Ireland in 1720 along with their wives and children [11] ................................................................. 11

Figure 2: Original Figure drawn by Leon Spangler in Our Graham Family History depicting the locations of the Graham Farms in the newly established townships of Derry, Hanover and Paxton/Paxtang Pennsylvania. Enhanced by Elizabeth Graham Everett. ................................................................. 12

Figure 3: Old Derry Presbyterian Church, Hershey Pennsylvania, First Presbyterian Church in America, from Postcard Collection of U.S. Presbyterian Historical Society ................................................................. 16

Figure 4: Paxtang Presbyterian Church, Harrisburg, Pennsylvania from Postcard Collection of the U.S. Presbyterian Historical Society ................................................................. 17

Figure 5: Reverend John Thomson Grave Marker, Centre Presbyterian Church Cemetery, Mooresville, N.C. Photo by L. Nelson, 31 May 2020 [37] ................................................................. 18

Figure 6: Calfpasture Map in Augusta County, Virginia showing Family Land Patents as it appeared in the mid-1700s from the U.S. Library of Congress; Patents of Christopher Graham's sons are outlined in orange. © Copyright Meredith Leitch. ................................................................. 22

Figure 7: Clip of the Beverly Manor Land Patent of 1810 showing Family Land Patents From the U.S. Library of Congress © Copyright J.R. Hildebrand. ................................................................. 23

Figure 8: Original Figure drawn by Leon Spangler featured in Our Graham Family History of Buffalo Settlement in Amelia County, Virginia, showing Family Land Patents as it appeared in the mid-1700s. Lands of James Graham Jr.'s sons are marked in blue. ................................................................. 25

Figure 9: James Thornton Graham (1846-1889) of Grayville, Illinois (Generation 5). Photo provided courtesy of Ron Graham. ................................................................. 27

Figure 10: Depiction of Our Branch of the Grayville Grahams by Violet P. Graham ................................................................. 28

Figure 11: Paternal Pedigree of Grayville, Illinois Grahams ................................................................. 29

Figure 12: Co Fermanagh Deposition of Christopher Graham, gentleman, age 40, taken in November 1711 (from Crosslé Genealogical Abstracts). Image Courtesy of the National Archives of Ireland. [71] .. 32

Figure 13: Parish Magheraculmoney, Co Fermanagh, Ireland – Placename data from The Northern Ireland Place-Name Project' at Queen's University Belfast and licensed under CC BY 4.0. See Appendix A for more on Irish Geography. ................................................................. 35

Figure 14: Enniskillen Regiment Horse Personnel and Financial Records, circa 1692-1693, Crosslé Genealogical Abstracts. Images Courtesy of the National Archives of Ireland [92] ................................................................. 39

Figure 15: Lough Erne Looking WSW at Muckross, 25 April 2021. ................................................................. 40

Figure 16: Artist Rendering of King William III and the Inniskilling Regiment of Horse at the Battle of the Boyne, 11 July 1690, Artist: T.A. Mercer [99] ................................................................. 41

Figure 17: Map of the Scottish English Border showing divisions into Marches, by Tom Moss. Reproduced here under Creative Commons License BY. With additions. ................................................................. 52

Figure 18: Cumberland Map by Christopher Saxton, 1637, Showing Debatable Lands and Graham Towers Along the River Esk. Provided by Lloyd Reeds Map Collection, McMaster University Library 154 .................................................................................................................................................. 54

Figure 19: Map of the Dryfe Valley, Hutton and Corry Parish, in NW Dumfriesshire, Scotland; Ordnance Survey (map GB.) Landranger Series SCALE OF 1; 50 000, SHEET NO 79 HAWICK & ESKDALE (LANGHOLM) Ordnance Survey licence number 100066333. All rights reserved. © Copyright and database right 2022. ............................................................................................. 57

Figure 20: Armorial of the Grahams of Drumgoon, Ireland, By SurnameCoatsofArms.uk [176] ............ 58

Figure 21: Pedigree of the Grahams of Esk and Their Armstrong Relations-by John C. Armstrong. ....64

Figure 22: Notional Paternal Pedigree of James Graham Jr. to John Graham of Gillesbie and Brackenwra, Brother of Lang Will Graham of Stuble ........................................................................................ 65

Figure 23: Timeline from the Beginnings of the Border Grahams to the Arrival of their Descendants in Grayville, Illinois in 1818 ................................................................................................................. 67

Figure 24: Cumbrian Territory Boundaries Prior to 1124 [227] ............................................................... 70

Figure 25: Kingdoms of Britain circa 886 A.D. [262] ............................................................................... 76

Figure 26: St. Cuthbert Church, Edinburgh Castle in Background. Photo by Barry S. Graham. .......... 84

Figure 27: The Cross Pattée of the Knights Templar [332] ...................................................................... 84

Figure 28: St. Cuthbert's pectoral cross, from the 5th century, one of the few items of value to have survived from the shrine. It is made of gold and garnets. © Durham Cathedral and Jarold Printing [331] .................................................................................................................................................................. 84

Figure 29: The Ceremonial County of Cumbria in Northwest England. [347] ...................................... 87

Figure 30: Pre-April 2023 District Boundaries for Cumbria: Allerdale (orange), and Copeland (gold) and Carlisle (blue) Districts; Greystoke is located in the district of Eden (lime green), a few miles from the from the boundary with Allerdale. [347] .......................................................................................... 87

Figure 31: The Arms of Mont Saint-Michel, Art by Euryel. [352] ........................................................... 88

Figure 32: Armorial of Michel de Cambernon. ................................................................................... 89

Figure 33: Collar of the French Royal Order of Saint Michael the Archangel. CC-BY-SA 3.0 [361] ........ 89

Figure 34: Extracted image of Saint James from the altarpiece in church of Mount San Martino, Italy painted by Carlo Crivelli circa 1480. [366] ........................................................................................ 90

Figure 35: Boar's Head Couped (cut off)-Scottish style—A Complete Guide to Heraldry, by Arthur Charles Fox-Davies, published in 1909 .............................................................................................. 91

Figure 36: Arms of Fergus Graham of Mote [378] .................................................................................. 92

Figure 37: Proposed Ancestry of William de Graham, ..................................................................... 93

Figure 38: Amended William de Graham Tree Showing Line of his Elder son, Peter, Lord of Dalkeith .................................................................................................................................................................. 95

Figure 39: Coat of Arms of the Grahams of Dalkeith, Abercorn, Eskdale, First Used by the "Fourth Sir Henry de Graham," 1300; Newm30, CC BY-SA 4.0 [413] ................................................................. 97

Figure 40: Corrie of Newby Coat of Arms granted to Sir Walter de Corrie with the fief of Newby, 1296. This saltire (X-shaped cross) was used by vassals of the Bruces of Annandale. By Brianann MacAmhlaidh, ...................................................................................................................................97

Figure 41: Descendants of the 3rd Sir Henry de Graham of Dalkeith and Hutton and the Proposed Origin of the J1 Border Grahams.........................................................................................101

Figure 42: Timeline of Scotland's Internal Power Struggle Involving Clan Douglas (1331-1515). ........ 106

Figure 43: Descendants of the Menteith Earls based on the "Red book of Menteith," Volume I, by William Fraser and writings of John P. Ravilious [492]...................................................113

Figure 44: J1 Y-DNA Pedigree of Typical Border Grahams [497] ...........................................................115

Figure 45: Map showing Dalkeith, "Elphinstoun I," Edmondstoun Castle, Atlas of Scotland, 1654; Joan and Cornelius Blaeu, Timothy Pont. CC-BY 4.0 Reproduced with the permission of the National Library of Scotland. ...........................................................................................................116

Figure 46: Map showing Dalkeith, "Elphinstoun I," Abercorn, Manuel, Atlas of Scotland, 1654; Joan and Cornelius Blaeu, Timothy Pont. CC-BY 4.0 Reproduced with the permission of the National Library of Scotland.[510] ...................................................................................................118

Figure 47: Google Map showing Dalkeith, "Elphinstone I," Abercorn, Manuel [510] ............................119

Figure 48: Stirlingshire Map showing Northern Estates of Sir Andrew Murray of Manuel and "Elphinstoun II," Atlas of Scotland, 1654; Joan and Cornelius Blaeu and Timothy Pont................... 120

Figure 49: Shield of the Burgh of Dalkeith, showing the Graham Escallops, the Douglas Arms which Combined the Braveheart Symbol with the Murray Stars, St. Nicholas of Myra's symbols, Dalkeith Chapel and Center: Dalkeith Castle [514] ................................................................................121

Figure 50: Relief of Akhenaten, Nefertiti and two daughters praying to Aten, the Egyptian sun god. Tell el-Amarna,Egypt, 18th dynasty, reign of Akhenaten (dated between 1372 and 1355 B.C.). [544] ........... 125

Figure 51: A Brief Timeline of Early History in Britain [560] ................................................................ 130

Figure 52: Extinction Rate Tool from ScaledInnovation.com by Dr Robin Spencer ........................131

Figure 53: Langholm, Hoddam, Dalton and Southern Hutton and Corrie Parishes in Dumfriesshire, as shown in John Thomson's 1832 Atlas of Scotland. CC-BY 4.0 Reproduced with the permission of the National Library of Scotland. [584].................................................................................... 134

# Endnotes

[i] Chapter 1 Header, State Flag of Pennsylvania: Wikimedia Commons contributors, "File:Flag of Pennsylvania.svg," Wikimedia Commons, the free media repository, accessed 6 December 2022. https://commons.wikimedia.org/w/index.php?title=File:Flag_of_Pennsylvania.svg&oldid=710477618

[ii] Chapter 2 Header, State Flag of Virginia: Wikimedia Commons contributors, "File:Flag of Virginia.svg,"Wikimedia Commons, the free media repository, accessed 6 December 2022.
https://commons.wikimedia.org/w/index.php?title=File:Flag_of_Virginia.svg&oldid=710472536

iii Hurricane Symbol. Wikimedia Commons contributors, "File:Hurricane red.png," Wikimedia Commons, the free media repository, accessed 6 December 2022. CC BY-SA 4.0. https://commons.wikimedia.org/w/index.php?title=File:Hurricane_red.png&oldid=504996579

iv Chapter 3 Header, Coat of Arms of County Fermanagh, Ireland: Wikimedia Commons contributors, "File:Ferm arms.png," Wikimedia Commons, the free media repository, accessed 6 December 2022. CC BY-SA 3.0 https://commons.wikimedia.org/w/index.php?title=File:Ferm_arms.png&oldid=613848535

v Chapter 4 Header, National Flag of Scotland: Wikimedia Commons contributors, "File:Flag of Scotland.svg," Wikimedia Commons, the free media repository, accessed 6 December 2022. https://commons.wikimedia.org/w/index.php?title=File:Flag_of_Scotland.svg&oldid=710527396

vi William de Graham was a witness on a number of medieval land charters: Church of St.Cuthbert, Edinburgh in 1127, Holyrood Abbey Foundation in 1128. https://archive.org/details/libercartarumsan00bann/page/6/mode/2up , land gift to St.Mary and St.Cuthbert Priory at Coldingham in honor of the late Gospatric, brother of Dolfin in 1139, gift of Clerkington to St.Mary's Church in Haddington in 1141, gift by Prince Henry to St.Mary's Church in Haddington circa 1141, and transferring churches from Laudonie from the oversight of the Bishop of Glasgow to the Bishop of St.Andrews circa 1150. https://deeds.library.utoronto.ca/deeds-search?keywords=graham&search_field=all&date-start=&date-end=&q=deeds-search&fq%5B0%5D=issued_country%3A%22England%22

vii I estimate the date of the Holyrood land charter as 1125. Holyrood Abbey was founded in 1128, so the charter granting the land for it would have been at least three years prior. With a dedicated labor force provided by the king, it could take three to six years to build a castle in medieval times. So if they had finished a chapel in 1128, then they would have started it by 1125.

viii The first earl of Dunbar also "Normanized" his name from "Gospatric" to "Patrick." His father, the elder Gospatric, former earl of Northumberland, was not popular with the Normans given his role in uprisings in England. https://thewildpeak.wordpress.com/2013/04/01/who-was-the-cumbrian-earl-gospatric/

ix Saint Cuthbert was later adopted by the Roman Catholic Church.

x Chapter 5 Header, Heraldry: Escallop Seal of Patrick Graham of Lovat on Declaration of Arbroath, 1320. Wikimedia Commons contributors, "File:Heraldic Shell.svg," *Wikimedia Commons,* accessed 17 April 2023. https://commons.wikimedia.org/w/index.php?title=File:Heraldic_Shell.svg&oldid=463233327 CC BY-SA 4.0

Wikimedia Commons contributors, "File:Coa (blank).png," *Wikimedia Commons,* accessed 17 April 2023. https://commons.wikimedia.org/w/index.php?title=File:Coa_(blank).png&oldid=703278740

xi Note: Anno Regis 2$^{nd}$ = the 2$^{nd}$ year in the reign of King Robert II (1373).

xii Chapter 6 Header. Double Helix DNA Depiction: Wikimedia Commons contributors, "File:DNA Double Helix.png," Wikimedia Commons, the free media repository, accessed 6 December 2022. https://commons.wikimedia.org/w/index.php?title=File:DNA_Double_Helix.png&oldid=669935287

xiii Herodotus of Halicarnassus (circa 480-circa429 B.C.): Greek researcher, often called the world's first historian.

xiv Chapter 7 Header: Photo of Mugdock Castle by Barry S. Graham, July 2022. Mugdock Castle was a stronghold of Clan Graham in the thirteenth century.

# Appendix A: Irish Geography

## A Brief Lesson in Eighteenth Century Irish Geography

Tracing a family trail into Ireland is not possible without geography. Per Irish Genealogist, John Grenham, "the single most important item of information for Irish family history is a precise place of origin."[1] For those unfamiliar with Ireland, a short lesson on locating Irish counties, Anglican Dioceses, civil parishes, Roman Catholic parishes, baronies, and townlands is needed. Take it from me: limiting yourself to modern map engines to find locations mentioned in old records will send you in the wrong direction.

The first step is knowing the various spellings for your townland or placename as it changed and shifted over the centuries, as Irish Gaelic placenames were inconsistently anglicized--written phonetically using English spellings.

Secondly, like American states, Ireland is organized by counties. However, those counties are divided into baronies, which are then divided into civil parishes. Civil parishes are further divided into townlands. Civil parishes and Roman Catholic parishes differ, the latter usually being much larger than the former, so you need to check both sets of parish maps in your search.[2]

## Spelling Variations

As stated, it is critical to know the various spellings for your townland or placename as it shifted over the centuries. English spellings weren't consistent either, at least not until Richard John Griffith completed the first ordnance surveys of Ireland in the nineteenth century. For example, "Drumadraho" could be spelled "Drumadaragh," "Dromadraho," or "Dromadrenagh." The Gaelic sound "gh" represents the English "y." The Gaelic sound "bh" represents the English "v." This can corrupt the translation further to give something like Dromadravey or Drumdraghy. In 1851, there were two official placenames in County Fermanagh spelled like that: Drumadraghy in Parish Magheraculmoney and Drumdravey in Parish Derryvullan. Therefore, we would need additional clues to determine where "Drumadraho, Co. Fermanagh" from a 1721 will is actually located. Note also that the civil parish of Magheraculmoney was sometimes known as "Templemaghery" and is in roughly the same location as the Roman Catholic parish Magheraculmany (just to keep us on our toes).[3]

Placenamesni.org is a helpful website that can provide you with the various spellings of Northern Irish placenames over the centuries and, conveniently, displays them on a base map generated from current satellite imagery using ESRI's ArcGIS software, with various layers that can be toggled on/off. Their map engine can show the townland, parish and barony boundaries of Ireland in

---

[1] John Grenham, "Irish Placenames-search window," JohnGrenham.com, accessed 30 December 2022. https://www.johngrenham.com/places/

[2] John Grenham, "Irish Placenames-Details," JohnGrenham.com, accessed 31 December 2022. https://www.johngrenham.com/browse/retrieve_text.php?text_contentid=64#Property

[3] Queen's University Belfast, "Languages," Placenamesni.org, Northern Ireland Place-Name Project, accessed 31 December 2022. https://experience.arcgis.com/experience/9b31e0501b744154b4584b1dce1f859b/page/Useful-Information/?views=Languages

1851 as overlays, while allowing you to select the map background of your preference (e.g. various scales, terrain, topographics, navigation charts).[4]

Figure A-1: Placename data from *The Northern Ireland Place-Name Project* at Queen's University Belfast and licensed under CC BY 4.0.[4]

## Identifying an Irish Place Name

Most problems with Irish placenames involve peculiar phonetic renderings of the original Irish language names. When trying to identify the location of a name, keep in mind that English cannot cope with some of the sounds of Irish. Some imagination and persistence may be needed. The most common problems and solutions are listed below.

The most changeable sounds are vowels and vowel-like sounds— a, e, i, o, u, gh, ch. Thus the original Irish *Drum na Roghan* might be rendered as Drumrown, Drimnyrone, Drommnarone, Dramrowny, etc.[5]

---

[4] Figure A-1: Queen's University Belfast, "Discover the Origin of our Local Placenames," Placenamesni.org, Northern Ireland Place-Name Project, accessed 30 December 2022.
https://experience.arcgis.com/experience/9b31e0501b744154b4584b1dce1f859b

[5] John Grenham, "Irish Placenames."

John Grenham's list of Common Irish Placename elements is listed below.[6] For a more comprehensive list of placename components, go to: http://www.logainm.ie/en/glossary or see the simplified tables on Wikipedia: https://en.wikipedia.org/wiki/Place_names_in_Ireland

### Common Irish Placename Elements

| ELEMENT | TRANSLATION | VARIATION |
|---|---|---|
| Áth | ford | Agha-, Ath-, Aha-, Agh-, A- |
| Baile | town/homeplace | Bally-, Bal-, Ball-, Ballina-, Ballyna- |
| Carrig | rock | Carrig-, Carrick- |
| Ceathrú | quarter | Carra-, Carrow-, Curra-, Curragh-, Car-, Curry- |
| Cill | Church | Kil-, Kill- |
| Cluan | meadow | Cloon-, Clon- |
| Cnoc | hill | Knock- |
| Cúl | rear | Cool-, Cul |
| Domhnach | Sunday/Church | Donny-, Dunna-, Donna- |
| Dún | fort | Dun-, Don- |
| Drum | hillock | Drum-, Drim-, Drom- |
| Gort | field | Gurt-, Gort- |
| Inis | island | Inis-, Inish-, Inch-, Insh- |
| Leath | half | Le-, La- |
| Rath | fort | Rath-, Ra- |
| Tamhlagh | grave | Talla-, Tamla- |
| Tullach | hill | Tulla-, Tul-, Toll- |

*Figure A-2: Common Irish Placename Elements from John Grenham's "Irish Placenames" site* [6]

## Counties, Baronies, Parishes, Townlands and Dioceses

Secondly, like American states, Ireland is organized by counties. Those counties are divided into baronies (Figure A-3), which are further divided into civil parishes.[7] A popular way to navigate through the complex layers of Irish maps are with genealogist John Grenham's map tools: https://www.johngrenham.com/ and *Irish Townlands* which is based on OpenStreetMap: https://www.townlands.ie/

---

[6] Figure A-2: John Grenham, "Irish Placenames."

[7] Queen's University Belfast, "Land Units," Placenamesni.org, Northern Ireland Place-Name Project, accessed 30 December 2022. https://experience.arcgis.com/experience/9b31e0501b744154b4584b1dce1f859b/page/Land-Units/

## Baronies

While baronies are now obsolete, many historical Irish maps are organized by barony,[8] so it is important to learn about them. From Placenamesni.org: "The process of bringing Irish tribal kingdoms into the feudal system as baronies under chieftains owing allegiance to the English crown began during the medieval period, although the system was not extended throughout Ulster until the early 17th century...The barony system was revised and coordinated at the same time as the counties so that later baronies always fit inside the county bounds. Both counties and baronies appear on maps from 1590 onwards."[9]

## Counties

The present-day counties were planned in the early sixteenth century, although some existed long before this time.[10] Beginning with the Norman conquest, the English government created a new

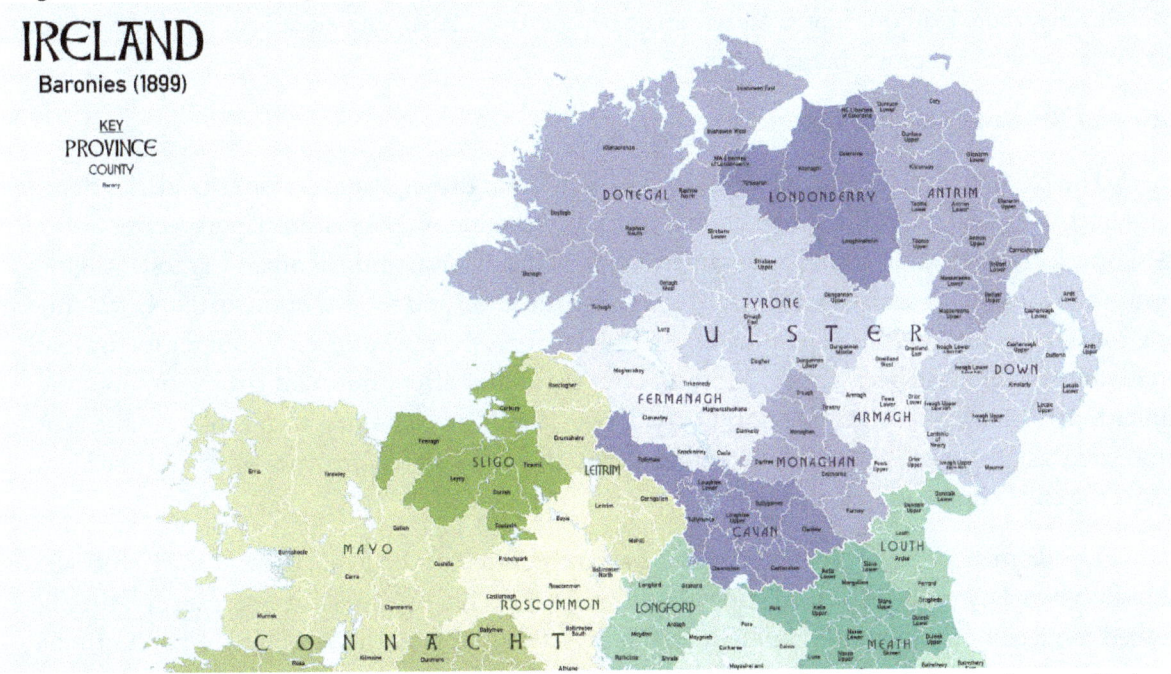

Figure A-3: Northern Irish Baronies by county as of 1899 by XrysD; Derived from the Ordnance Survey of Ireland: Baronies 2011, Ordnance Survey of Northern Ireland: Townlands, and National University of Ireland Galway: Barony Maps. This file is licensed under Creative Commons CC BY-SA 4.0.[8]

---

[8] "About PRONI Historical Maps Viewer," NIDirect Government Services, accessed 31 December 2022. https://www.nidirect.gov.uk/articles/about-proni-historical-maps-viewer

Figure A-3: Wikimedia Commons contributors, "File:IrelandBaronies1899Map.png," *Wikimedia Commons*, accessed 16 April 2023. https://commons.wikimedia.org/w/index.php?title=File:IrelandBaronies1899Map.png&oldid=649756752

[9] Queen's University Belfast, "Secular Administrative Divisions, Land Units," Placenamesni.org, Northern Ireland Place-Name Project, accessed 30 December 2022. https://experience.arcgis.com/experience/9b31e0501b744154b4584b1dce1f859b/page/Useful-Information/?views=Secular-Administrative-Divisions

[10] "About PRONI Historical Maps Viewer," NIDirect Government Services.

administrative system in Ireland, dividing each Irish province into counties. The counties were equivalent to the shire in England, where a sheriff exercised jurisdiction on behalf of the King.[11]

### Civil Parishes/Townlands.

Civil parishes are divided into townlands. For instance, County Fermanagh is divided into eight baronies, 23 civil parishes, and 2,302 townlands. Place names can be reused and can have multiple possible spellings. For example, there are four civil parishes in Co. Fermanagh with townlands named Carn or Carne. The civil parish of Templecarn in Co. Fermanagh and the Roman Catholic parish of Carn partially overlap. Co. Donegal also has a civil parish called Templecarn that has a townland named Carn.[12] Turns out that in medieval times, before the baronies and counties were established, what is now Templecarn in Co. Donegal and the Templecarn in Co. Fermanagh were a joined land called Tarmonmagrath.

Lastly, there is a Poor Law Union map of Ireland from 1851,[13] but since it doesn't apply to our timeframe, we won't explore them for now.

### Celtic and Roman Catholic Dioceses.[14]

The Roman Catholic Church in Ireland had different diocesan and parish boundaries than the Anglican church, and its parishes were known by multiple names.[15] The historical perspective on ecclesiastical administration from Placesnamesni.org: "The invasion of the Roman Catholic Anglo-Normans in the twelfth century encouraged the re-organization and reform of the native Celtic church along continental lines. By the beginning of the 14th century, the territories and boundaries for Irish bishops and dioceses had been settled. Most dioceses are named after important church or monastic foundations: Armagh, Clogher, Connor, Derry, Down, Dromore, Kilmore, and Raphoe in the North. The ancient secular province of Ulster was included in the ecclesiastical province of Armagh, which became the chief church in Ireland."[16]

The Roman Catholic diocesan structure was prohibited under Penal Laws at the Reformation, but bishops were consecrated abroad and visited Ireland in secret. By the eighteenth century, they had resumed residency. Although the Ecclesiastical Titles Act of 1851 made it illegal for Roman Catholic dioceses to use the same names as those of the Church of Ireland and England,[17] this was not enforced

---

[11] Queen's University Belfast, "Secular Administrative Divisions, Land Units."
[12] "Irish Townlands," Irish Open Street Map Community, accessed 31 December 2022. https://www.townlands.ie/
[13] John Grenham, "Poor Law Unions (1851)," JohnGrenham.com, accessed 31 December 2022. https://www.johngrenham.com/places/plu_index.php
[14] Queen's University Belfast, "Secular Administrative Divisions."
[15] FamilySearch, "Ireland Church Registers (National Institute)," Family Search Wiki, accessed 31 December 2022. https://www.familysearch.org/en/wiki/Ireland_Church_Registers_(National_Institute)
[16] Queen's University Belfast, "Ecclesiastical Administrative Divisions," Placenamesni.org, Northern Ireland Place-Name Project, accessed 30 December 2022. https://experience.arcgis.com/experience/9b31e0501b744154b4584b1dce1f859b/page/Useful-Information/?views=Ecclesiastical-Administrative-Divisions
[17] Great Britain, Parliament, House of Commons, *Report of the House of Commons Select Committee on Ecclesiastical Titles and Roman Catholic Relief Acts,* Vol. VIII (London: House of Commons, 2 August 1867), 89. https://books.google.com/books?id=RylcAAAAQAAJ&pg=PA89#v=onepage&q&f=false

*Appendix A: Irish Geography*

in Ireland.[18] Given baptism, marriage and death records were recorded and maintained by dioceses, it is the old diocesan maps that are especially important to genealogists.

**Roman Catholic Parishes.**

Irish vital records can also be linked to Roman Catholic parishes, therefore locating the parish within the civil county boundaries is essential to cross referencing church and civil records. Depending on the date of the record, it will be indexed to the Catholic Parish vs. the Civil Parish. The Catholic

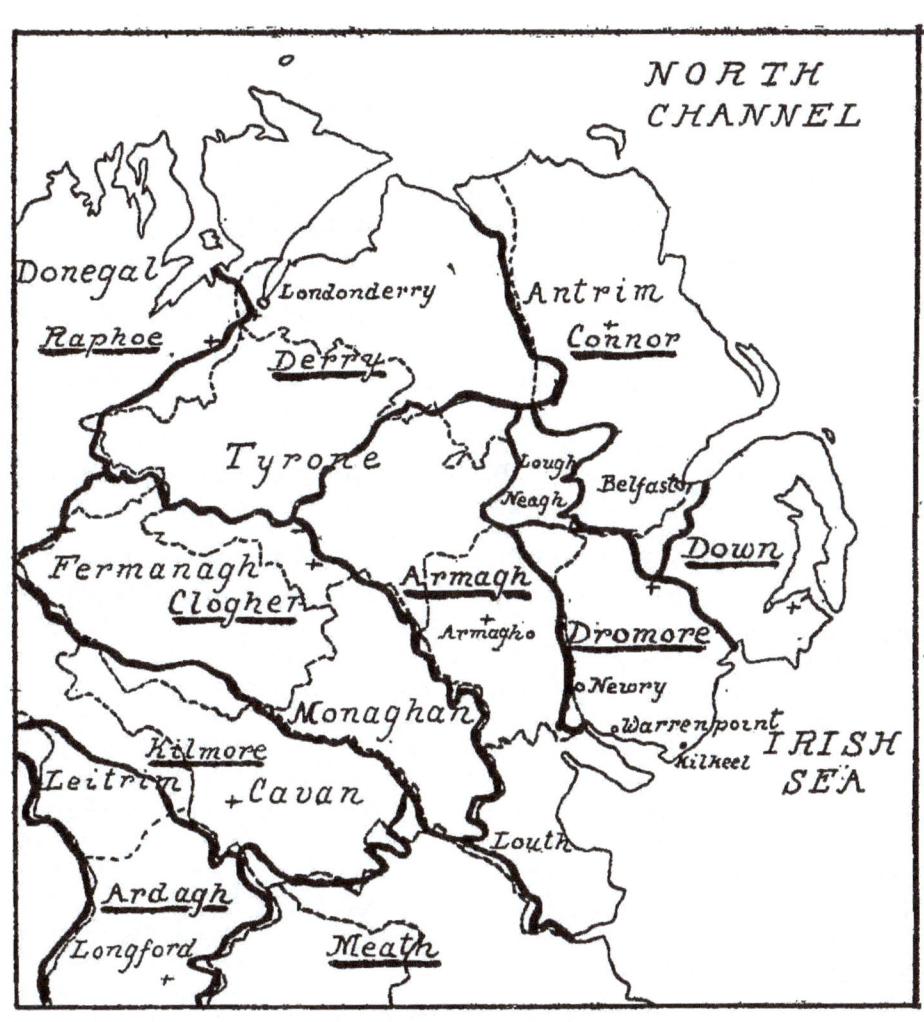

MAP OF N.E. IRELAND,
SHEWING DIOCESAN JURISDICTIONS.

(Dioceses indicated by heavy lines; county boundaries by broken lines.)

*Figure A-4: Anglican Diocese Map from Phillimore and Thrift Irish Will Index (1384-1858) overlaid on a Northern Irish County Map*[22]

---

[18] "Diocese of Ireland," Profilpelajar.com, accessed 31 December 2022. https://profilpelajar.com/article/Dioceses_of_Ireland

Parish names sometimes are the same as the Civil, but not always. You need to check both sets of parish maps in your search. John Grenham's handy map tools show both types of parishes and have other reference tools to assist in searches for Irish ancestors.[19]

**Anglican Dioceses.**

The Church of Ireland, which is Anglican, was the established church of Ireland prior to 1871 and its boundaries were used by the state for censuses, taxation and land surveying, i.e. the civil parishes.[20] The Anglican Church is organized by dioceses that jump county boundaries. Those dioceses were consolidated in 2019,[21] so you need to look at an eighteenth-century diocese map when studying the will indexes from that time, such as the map in Figure A-4 from the Irish Will Index, 1384-1858.[22] Note the diocese boundaries are indicated by heavy lines, and county boundaries by dashed lines. From Figure A-4, you can see how it is possible to be in the Diocese of Derry but not the county of Londonderry. The Diocese of Armagh, for example, includes portions of Co. Armagh, Co. Tyrone, Co. Londonderry, and Co. Louth. It is easy to mistake a will index that a genealogy site has indexed to "Armagh" for Co. Armagh. Sometimes the indexers make this mistake and mark records from eastern County Tyrone that are also in Diocese Armagh as "County Armagh." Be on the lookout for this common error when searching online.

## Griffith's Valuation

In the nineteenth century, the British Board of Ordnance commissioned Richard Griffith to produce a comprehensive series of property surveys and six-inch scale maps of Ireland, the first of its kind.[23] The maps and property valuations, which include property owners and tenant names, were published between 1847 and 1864.[24] John Grenham's site integrates Griffith Valuation placename searches using AskAboutIreland.ie.[25]

Per John Grenham, the most important tool in identifying Irish placenames is the *General Alphabetical Index to the Townlands and Towns, Parishes and Baronies of Ireland*.[26] [27]

---

[19] John Grenham, "Catholic Parishes in Ireland," JohnGrenham.com, accessed 30 December 2022. https://www.johngrenham.com/places/rcmap_index.php

[20] FamilySearch, "Ireland Church Registers (National Institute)."

[21] Gregg Ryan, "Church of Ireland Synod: Merger of two dioceses approved," *Church Times*, 28 May 2019. https://www.churchtimes.co.uk/articles/2019/24-may/news/uk/church-of-ireland-synod-merger-of-two-dioceses-approved

[22] Figure A-4: Ancestry.com. *Ireland, Indexes to Wills, 1384-1858*, Provo, UT: USA: Ancestry.com Operations, Inc., 2014. https://www.ancestry.com/search/collections/9144/

[23] "An Eye on the Survey," History Ireland, Summer 2001. https://www.historyireland.com/an-eye-on-the-survey/

[24] "Valuation Office Records," *National Archives of Ireland*, accessed 31 December 2022. https://www.nationalarchives.ie/article/valuation-office-records/

[25] "Griffith Evaluation," AskAboutIreland, accessed 31 December 2022. https://www.askaboutireland.ie/griffith-valuation/

[26] John Grenham, "Irish Placenames-search window," JohnGrenham.com.

[27] Census of Ireland, *General Alphabetical Index to the Townlands and Towns, parishes and Baronies of Ireland* (Dublin: Alexander Thom, 1861). https://archive.org/details/op1248631-1001

If you do a place name search on AskAboutIreland.ie, open the map and click on "Show Towns," moving the mouse so the cursor is over a town, and you will see a symbol over it. You can click on the town symbol to bring up a map at a finer scale.

# GENUKI

Another great resource is GENUKI.org.uk (GENealogical information for the United Kingdom and Ireland), a free virtual reference library organized by geography and topic. Its geography is organized by historic counties and ancient parishes, and the topics are based on a well-established system for genealogists. GENUKI is a non-commercial service maintained by a charitable trust and a group of volunteers.[28] It covers England, Ireland, Wales, Scotland, the Isle of Man, and the Channel Islands. The website showcases its offerings: "You can use the gazetteer to find the location of places, view online maps, and discover which GENUKI pages may contain information about that place and the genealogical resources available."[29] You can also refine your search if yours returns too many results using their built-in tools.[30]

# Public Record Office of Northern Ireland (PRONI)

PRONI provides historical Ordnance Survey of Northern Ireland (OSNI) maps and information on sites, buildings, and landmarks of historical interest.[31,32]

Per Roger Cousens: "In rural areas, for considerable precision, historical versions of Ordnance Survey maps (now online for some scales) also allow us to see how things have changed—as long as we are only interested in the mid-nineteenth century onwards… There is also PRONI's excellent collection of Ordnance Survey town maps, referenced under OS/9 in their catalog, but again only available at PRONI. But these maps do not show the household numbering system used in Griffith's."[33]

PRONI has around 40,000 Ordnance Survey maps, forming a sizeable proportion of their archives and map holdings in particular. From a research point of view, they have a great advantage in covering every mile of the country, so they are of universal interest to local historians. The maps are listed under "OS" rather than under their functional department as with other records, simply because of the size of the archive and its specialist nature. The maps are arranged and listed according to their original referencing system.[34] So after the OS class (which represents the particular series at a certain

---

[28] "Ireland," GENUKI, accessed 31 December 2022. https://www.genuki.org.uk/big/irl
"Scotland," GENUKI, accessed 31 December 2022. https://www.genuki.org.uk/big/sct
[29] "GENUKI Gazetteer-Find Places," Genealogy for the United Kingdom and Ireland (GENUKI), accessed 31 December 2022. https://www.genuki.org.uk/gazetteer#results
[30] "GENUKI Gazetteer-Refine Your Selection," Genealogy for the United Kingdom and Ireland (GENUKI), accessed 31 December 2022. https://www.genuki.org.uk/gazetteer#refine
[31] Public Record Office of Northern Ireland, "PRONI Historical Maps Viewer," NIDirect Government Services, accessed 8 December 2022. https://www.nidirect.gov.uk/services/search-proni-historical-maps-viewer
[32] PRONI Historical Maps, "Ordnance Survey of Northern Ireland® (OSNI)," NIDirect Government Services, accessed 8 December 2022. https://apps.spatialni.gov.uk/PRONIApplication/
[33] Roger Cousens, "Griffith's Valuation: Fermanagh Town Maps and Ordnance Survey Maps," Fermanagh Gold, accessed 31 December 2022. https://fermanagh-gold.com/_media/roger_cousens/town_maps_and_proni.pdf
[34] "About PRONI Historical Maps Viewer," NIDirect Government Services, accessed 31 December 2022. https://www.nidirect.gov.uk/articles/about-proni-historical-maps-viewer

scale), the county maps at 6" or 25" are arranged firstly by county (alphabetically), so the number after the OS class stands for the county. For example, the 6" county maps are to be found in OS/6, so OS/6/1 = Co. Antrim, OS/6/2 = Co. Armagh, OS/6/3 = Co. Down, etc. Similarly, in OS 10 (the 25" county series), OS/10/1 = Co. Antrim, and OS/10/2 = Co. Armagh.[35] The next number is the sheet number, so OS/6/1/1 is sheet 1 of the 6" map for Co. Antrim. When it comes to the Irish grid series, the same applies: the class and piece numbers reflect the plan numbers, except there is no county reference.[36]

| PRONI Reference | Title/Description | Date(s) | Digital Record |
|---|---|---|---|
| OS/1 | First Edition 6" (1:10560) maps  More | No Date | |
| OS/1A | 6" Ordnance Survey Maps: Cos Donegal, Cavan, Monaghan, Louth and Leitrim  More | 1836-1877 | |
| OS/1B | 6" Ordnance Survey Map Negatives  More | | |
| OS/2 | c.1900 Edition 6" (1:10560) maps  More | No Date | |
| OS/3 | Air Photographs  More | 1951-1955 | |
| OS/4 | Boundary Records, 1825-1830  More | 1825-1830 | |
| OS/5 | Sample Field Books, c.1900  More | c.1900 | |
| OS/6 | County Series 6" (1:10560) maps  More | c.1830-1959 | |
| OS/7 | Irish Grid Series 6" (1:10560) maps, 1950s-  More | c.1950-1959 | |
| OS/8 | Published Town Plans  More | No Date | |
| OS/9 | Manuscript Town Plans, 1828  More | 1828 - 1834 | |
| OS/10 | County Series, 1:2500 (25") plans, 1890s-1950s  More | 1893-1952 | |
| OS/11 | Irish Grid Series, 1:2500 (25") plans, 1950s  More | 1960-1978 | |
| OS/12 | County Series, 1:1250 (50") plans of towns (enlarged from 25" County Series)  More | No Date | |
| OS/13 | Irish Grid Series, 1:1250 (50") plans  More | No Date | |

*Figure A-5: PRONI Ordnance Survey Holdings[34] Open Government Licence 3.0.*

The FamilySearch Wiki for Irish maps has a complete list of online Irish map databases online.[37]

---

[35] Figure A-5: "Search eCatalogue," search on "OS," *Public Record Office of Northern Ireland*, accessed 22 February 2023. https://apps.proni.gov.uk/eCatNI_IE/BrowseSearchPage.aspx

[36] Public Record Office of Northern Ireland, "PRONI Historical Maps Viewer."

[37] FamilySearch Wiki contributors, "Ireland Maps," FamilySearch Wiki, accessed 8 December 2022. https://www.familysearch.org/en/wiki/index.php?title=Ireland_Maps&oldid=5063315

*Appendix A: Irish Geography*

# Table of Figures

Figure A-1: Placename data from The Northern Ireland Place-Name Project at Queen's University Belfast and licensed under CC BY 4.0.[4] ............... A-2

Figure A-2: Common Irish Placename Elements from John Grenham's "Irish Placenames" site [6] .... A-3

Figure A-3: Northern Irish Baronies by county as of 1899 by XrysD; Derived from the Ordnance Survey of Ireland: Baronies 2011, Ordnance Survey of Northern Ireland: Townlands, and National University of Ireland Galway: Barony Maps. This file is licensed under CC BY-SA 4.0. [8] ............... A-4

Figure A-4: Anglican Diocese Map from Phillimore and Thrift Irish Will Index (1384-1858) overlaid on a Northern Irish County Map [22] ............... A-6

Figure A-5: PRONI Ordnance Survey Holdings[34] Open Government Licence 3.0. ............... A-9

# Appendix B: Scottish Geography

*Figure B-1: River Esk Near Castle O'er, Dumfries and Galloway, Great Britain, © Copyright Richard Webb, CC BY-SA 2.0.* [1]

## Maps of Scotland

Like Ireland, Scotland's placenames and municipal boundaries changed over the years, so having a map to match the time period you are searching is key. In some cases, placenames disappear altogether in more recent maps, making the historical maps all the more important.

The most comprehensive source for historical and recent maps of Scotland are stored in the National Library of Scotland (NLS) database.[2] The website allows you to search graphically, chronologically, by modern place name, by mapmaker, by keyword and by place name used in the map. The NLS "Maps of Scotland, 1560s-1940s" section holdings include the first atlases of Scotland,

---

[1] Figure B-1: Richard Webb, "Photo of River Esk Downstream of the Black/White confluence," Geograph.org, 12 January 2019. https://www.geograph.org.uk/photo/6025183

[2] "Map Images, Guide to this Website," *National Library of Scotland*, accessed 31 December 2022. https://maps.nls.uk/guide/

a consistent set of maps of the entire country based on data collected by the same team at the same time: Joan Blaeu's Atlas of Scotland, 1654[3] and John Thomson's Atlas of Scotland, 1832.[4]

Blaeu's Atlas of Scotland of 1654, is known as the first atlas of Scotland and is also known for its quality. It is based on the work of Scottish cartographer Timothy Pont, who did much of the fieldwork in the 1580s and 1590s. Pont never quite finished. He did ask King James VI and I for financial support for an atlas in the 1610s, but he died in 1615 before he could finish. Due to a number of issues, it wasn't until 1654 that the Dutch mapmakers, Joan and Cornelius Blaeu were finally able to complete Pont's work, along with assistance from John Scot, Robert and James Gordon, George Buchanan and an Englishman surnamed Camden, and publish the first atlas of Scotland.[5]

*Figure B-2: Lothian and Linlithgow from Joan Blaeu's Atlas of Scotland, 1654 based on surveys by Timothy Pont. Creative Commons License CC-BY 4.0 Reproduced with the permission of the National Library of Scotland.[6]*

---

[3] Joan and Cornelius Blaeu, "Browse the Atlas," *Atlas of Scotland,* 1654, Joan et Cornelius Blaeu exc. (Amsterdam: Blaeu, 1654). https://maps.nls.uk/atlas/blaeu/index.html

[4] John Thomson, "John Thomson's Atlas of Scotland, 1832," Graphic Index, *National Library of Scotland*, accessed 31 December 2022. https://maps.nls.uk/atlas/thomson/index.html

[5] Christopher Fleet, "The history behind the publication of the Blaeu Atlas of Scotland," *National Library of Scotland*, accessed 31 December 2022. https://maps.nls.uk/atlas/blaeu/history_behind_publication.html

[6] Figure B-2: Joan and Cornelius Blaeu, and Timothy Pont, *Atlas of Scotland,* Lothian and Linlitquo / Joh. et Cornelius Blaeu exc., Amsterdam, Blaeu, 1654. https://maps.nls.uk/view/00000395

In 1832, John Thomson published the first large-scale atlas of Scotland organized by county.[7] Thomson's Atlas of Scotland was the first since Blaeu's Atlas to map the land from accurate surveys and collected information. He began the effort in 1820. The scale of the effort was so large it led to Thomson's bankruptcy in 1830 due to the high costs of gathering the latest surveys. He announced that: "…the New County Atlas of Scotland will either be derived from Actual Surveys; or where such cannot be obtained, from other authentic materials, so corrected by the Attestators, and their Assistants, as to ensure greater accuracy than is to be found in any book of the kind published in this or any other Country." [8]

Despite publication in 1832, Thomson declared bankruptcy a second time in 1835.[9]

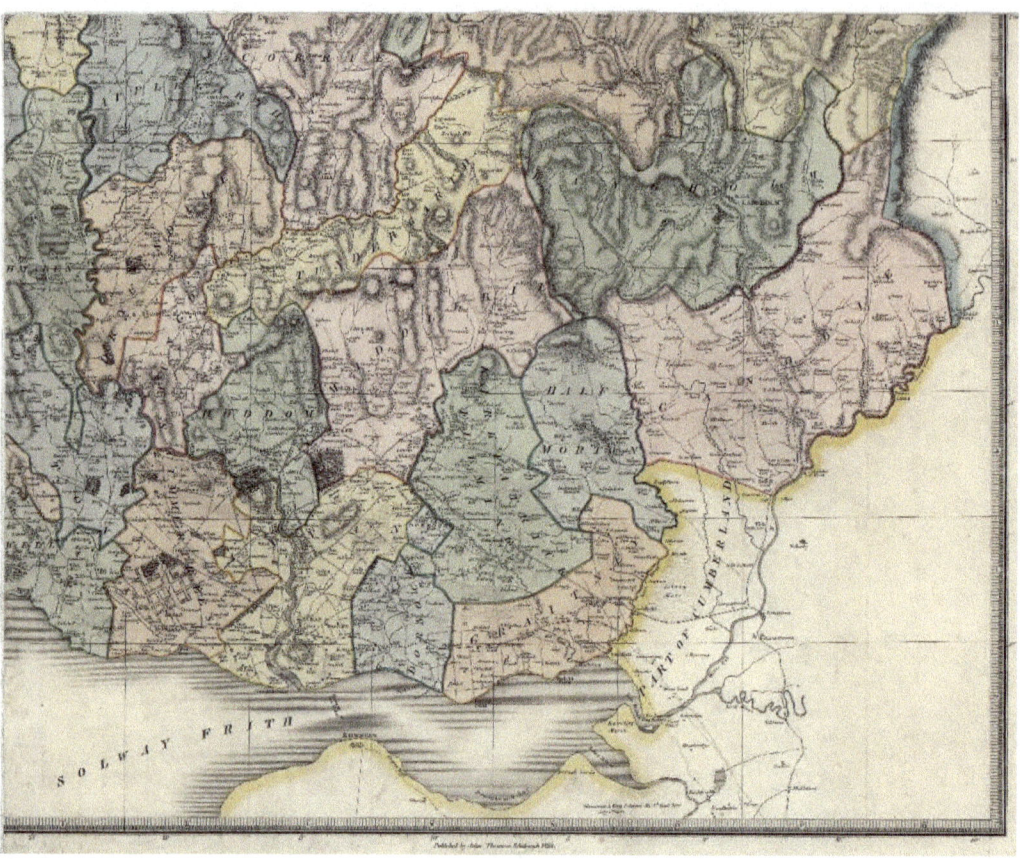

*Figure B-3: South West Dumfriesshire, as shown in John Thomson's 1832 Atlas of Scotland. CC-BY 4.0 Reproduced with the permission of the National Library of Scotland.* [10]

---

[7] John Thomson, *Atlas of Scotland, Containing Maps of Each County* (Edinburgh: John Thomson and Co., 1832), Table of Contents, iv. https://www.davidrumsey.com/luna/servlet/detail/RUMSEY~8~1~35384~1181010:Title-Page--Atlas-of-Scotland-?sort=Pub_List_No_InitialSort&qvq=q:Pub_List_No%3D%225748.000%22%20;sort:Pub_List_No_InitialSort;lc:RUMSEY~8~1&mi=3&trs=114

[8] "New Facsimile Publication – John Thomson's Atlas of Scotland (1832)," *CAIRT Newsletter of the Scottish Maps Forum*, Issue 13 (July 2008): 8. https://www.nls.uk/media-u4/1008031/cairt13.pdf

[9] Barry Lawrence Ruderman, "Antique Maps by John Thomson," Raremaps.com, accessed 31 December 2022. https://www.raremaps.com/gallery/detail/17741/united-states-and-additions-1832-thomson

[10] Figure B-3: John Thomson, "Dumfriesshire," *Atlas of Scotland, 1832, National Library of Scotland,* accessed 27 December 2022. https://maps.nls.uk/view/74400175

*Appendix B: Scottish Geography*

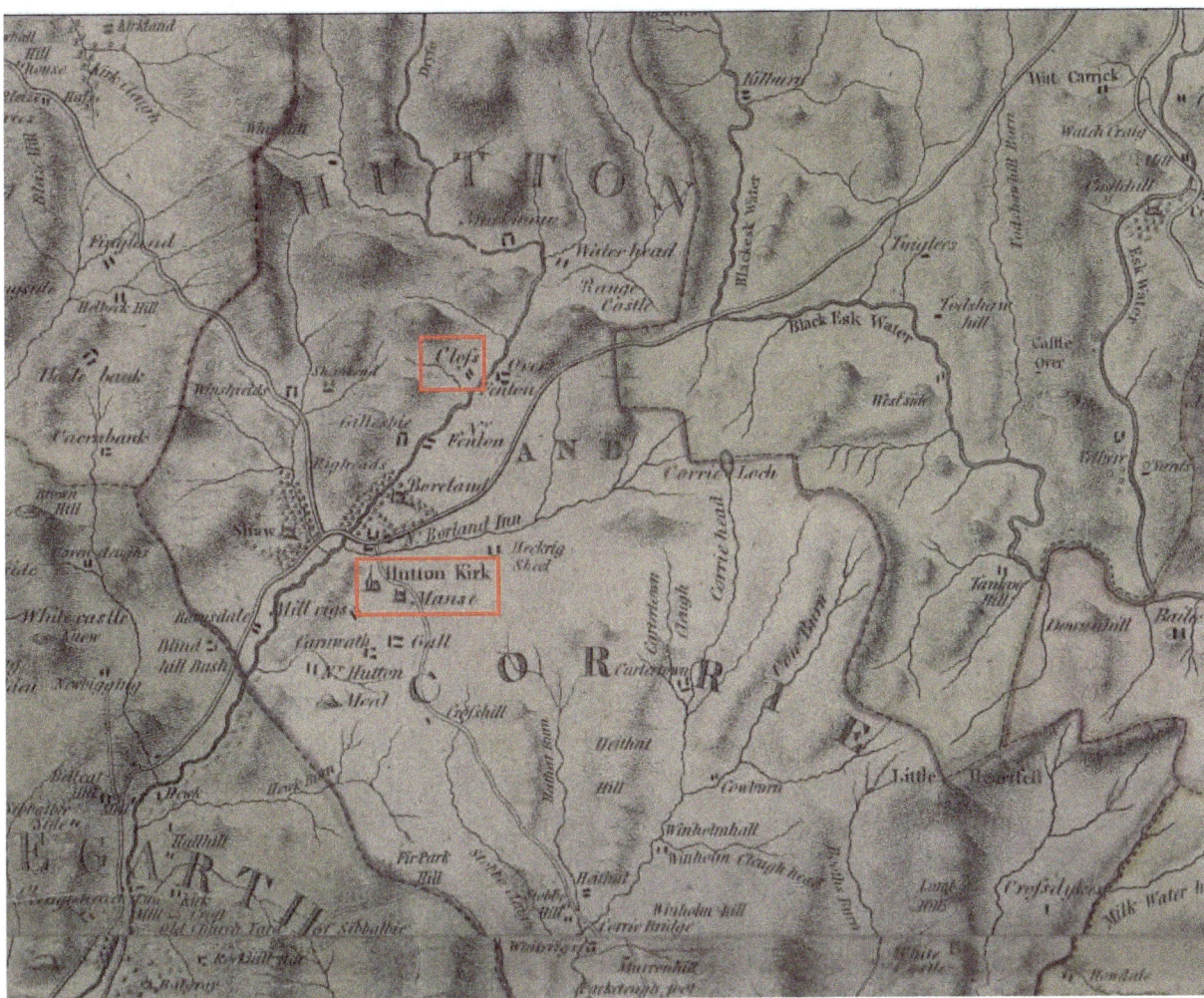

*Figure B-4: Moskesso Closs/Close, Hutton Parish, Dumfriesshire (Survey by Wm Crawford, 1804).* [11]
CC-BY 4.0 *Reproduced with the permission of the National Library of Scotland.*

Another mapmaker of immense utility in historical Scottish maps is William Crawford. His maps are based on actual land surveys made from 1774 to 1828. The minute detail in his map of Dumfriesshire[11] enabled us to finally locate the ancient medieval church dedicated to Saint Kessog, in Hutton Parish, the origin of Lang Will Graham of the Border Grahams. The location of the Moskesso (meaning "My Dear St. Kessog") Church close is shown at Figure B-4. A church **"close"** is the area immediately around the church, sometimes extending for a hundred meters or more from the main cathedral building. In Europe in the Middle Ages, and often later, it was usually all the property of the church or cathedral that was under the church's legal jurisdiction rather than that of the local government. It normally had gates which were closed and locked at night or when there were disturbances in the city, hence the name.[12]

---

[11] Figure B-4: William Crawford, *Map of Dumfries-shire from an actual survey by Wm. Crawford.*
[12] "Cathedral Close Tour (Self Guided), Salisbury," GPSMyCity, accessed 31 December 2022. https://www.gpsmycity.com/tours/cathedral-close-tour-5144.html

Further guidance on how to search the National Library of Scotland (NLS) databases is available at https://maps.nls.uk/guide/ and in an introductory video on the NLS Map Finder is at: https://maps.nls.uk/videos/?vid=Map-Finder-Help

## Structure of Scandinavian Place Names

In medieval times, the territories of the northern kingdoms were a melting pot of East Scandinavian (Danish), West Scandinavian (Old Norse, Norwegian, Icelandic), Gaelic, Welsh, and other peoples and the placenames reflect that. *Ordnance Survey's* "Introduction to Scandinavian" explains that like place names in most languages, Norse names are largely descriptive of the surroundings. Therefore some Norse placenames will refer to the shape of natural features, such as *Longa Berg*, 'long hill' or 'long rock.' Other placenames refer to location, such as in Isbister from the Old Norse (ON) *eystri*, meaning 'easterly.' Most Scandinavian place names are made up of more than one element, such as adjective-noun. Example: Deepdale which translates to 'deep valley', which was derived from the ON *djúpr*, 'deep', and the ON *dalr*, 'valley.'

One important group for those researching the genealogy of border clans are place names referring to farms or settlements, such as the "-bie or by" ending, as in Canobie, Lockerbie, Overby ("upper farm"), Middlebie ("middle farm"), Netherby ("lower farm")[13], and Newbie. The bie/by ending is derived from the ON word for farm: *býr*. The generic -sta is from the ON *staðir* meaning 'steading' or 'farm', as in Hoversta and Griesta.[14]

*Figure B-5: Looking from Kirkandrews, Across River Esk, at the Netherby Estate. © Copyright Jonathan Thacker CC BY-SA 2.0* [14]

---

[13] John and Robert Hyslop, *Langholm As it Was* (Sunderland: Hills and Company, 1912), 102. https://electricscotland.com/history/gazetteer/langholm.pdf

[14] "The Scandinavian Origins of Placenames in Britain," Ordnance Survey, accessed 31 December 2022. The Scandinavian origins of place names in Britain (ordnancesurvey.co.uk)

Figure B-5: Jonathan Thacker, "River Esk, Looking Across to the Netherby Estate," Geograph.org, 24 November 2018. https://www.geograph.org.uk/photo/5987096

To look up specific placename derivations, check the Scandinavian place names glossary at: https://getoutside.ordnancesurvey.co.uk/guides/the-scandinavian-origins-of-place-names-in-britain/

## Scottish Gaelic Placenames

In the Middle Ages, Scottish Gaelic or Scots was the main language of all of Scotland, Lowlands, Highlands and the islands. Gaelic lefts its mark on many familiar place names, such as "Auch- from *achadh*, Auchter- from *uachdar*," as in Auchterarder, former home of the Grahams of Kincardine,[15] "Bal- from *baile*, Dun- from *dùn*, Inver- from *inbhir*, Kin- from *ceann*, and Kil- usually from *cill* or *coille*."[16]

In the nineteenth century Ordnance Survey (OS) maps of Scotland, placenames were depicted in both English and Gaelic. This does not mean the place names were derived from Gaelic but reflects the areas in which Gaelic was spoken at the time of the creation of the Ordnance Survey maps. The Gaelic placename Glossary from Ordnancesurvey.co.uk focuses only on names based on Gaelic. The OS glossary is an update of the original Gaelic-Gaelic dictionary Brìgh nam Facal by Richard A V Cox (Gairm Publications, Glasgow 1991).[17]

Structure of Scots Place Names.

Place names usually describe a special feature of a place. From *Ordnance Survey*: "Place names can consist of a single generic element, usually a noun (Comar NH3331, Corran NS2193). These are often preceded by the Scottish Standard English definite article 'the', Gaelic an, am, a', plural na (An Dùnan NM8629, Am Fasgadh NN0169, A' Charraig NR8467, Na Croitean NM3721). Most place names, however, are made up of more than one element, with a linguistic relationship between the elements."[18]

See Gaelic spelling and pronunciation guide and Glossary of Terms at: https://getoutside.ordnancesurvey.co.uk/guides/the-gaelic-origins-of-place-names-in-britain/

## Introduction to Welsh Placenames

In the Middle Ages, the Britons of Cumbria (southern Scotland) spoke a language called "Cumbric," which some linguists believe could be a dialect of Old Welsh.[19] Influence of the Welsh language can be found in some Scottish placenames. For example: the name of the Borders town Peebles is derived from *pebyll* which is Welsh for tents." Author William Oxenham provides other examples: Cochrane comes from *coch rhen*, meaning red rivulet, Ogilvie from *uchel fai* (high plain or

---

[15] "Kincardine Castle, Built: 13th or 14th Century, Location: Auchterarder in Perth and Kinross, Scotland," Clan Graham Society, accessed 1 January 2023. https://clangrahamsociety.org/membership-donations/

[16] "The Gaelic Origins of Placenames in Britain," Ordnance Survey, accessed 31 December 2022. https://getoutside.ordnancesurvey.co.uk/guides/the-gaelic-origins-of-place-names-in-britain/

[17] Ibid.

[18] Ibid.

[19] Neil Whalley, "Cumbraek," Linguifex, accessed 1 January 2023. https://linguifex.com/wiki/Cumbraek

field), Leslie from *llys celyn* (courtyard of holly trees), and Abercrombie from *aber crwm bych* (mouth of the little curving stream).[20] Dalkeith is understood to be a Cumbric name, derived from the Welsh *ddôl* for meadow, plateau, valley and *coed* for "wood." [21]

A handy guide on spotting Welsh place names is available from *Ordnance Survey*: Welsh "place names can consist of a single generic element, usually a noun (Bryn, Talwrn or Dinas), but most comprise more than one element with a linguistic relationship between the elements." Generic elements can be: topographic, describe the settlement in which people lived (tref, pentref and bod); or by qualified by personal names (Tremadog, Pentremeurig, Bodorgan), size, or location.

See the full Welsh Placename Glossary at:
https://getoutside.ordnancesurvey.co.uk/guides/the-welsh-origins-of-place-names-in-britain/

## Gazetteer for Scotland Maps©

The Gazetteer for Scotland is supported by the School of GeoSciences, University of Edinburgh and The Royal Scottish Geographical Society. It is a vast geographical encyclopedia, featuring details of towns, villages, bens (mountains), and glens from the Scottish Borders to the Northern Isles.

Important guidance from the Gazetteer:

From medieval times until 1974, Scotland was divided into a system of counties for the purposes of local administration. You can search the Gazetteer for Scotland using these divisions, and link from these to parishes. Counties and parishes are particularly useful if your interests are in family history, because this is how historical records are arranged. Bear in mind that the boundaries of both have changed regularly throughout history. There were 34 counties until 1890, although the Gazetteer maps show the 33 counties as they were in 1951.[22]

## Imperial Gazetteer for Scotland

For historical place descriptions in Scotland, another good reference is *The Imperial Gazetteer* of Scotland, a topographical dictionary first published in two volumes between 1854 and 1857. On the front cover, it is described as: "A Dictionary of Scottish Topography compiled from the most recent authorities, and forming a complete body of Scottish Geography, Physical, Statistical and Historical." The Gazetteer contains a detailed description of Scotland and a brief article on each county, city,

---

[20] Rhodri Clark, "Glenfiddich Named by the Welsh," Wales Online, updated 31 March 2013. https://www.walesonline.co.uk/news/wales-news/glenfiddich-named-by-the-welsh-2377168

[21] Wikipedia contributors, "Dalkeith," Wikipedia, The Free Encyclopedia, accessed 29 April 2023. https://en.wikipedia.org/wiki/Dalkeith

[22] Bruce Gittings, "Gazeteer for Scotland," School of GeoSciences, University of Edinburgh and The Royal Scottish Geographical Society, accessed 1 March 2023. https://www.scottish-places.info/

borough, civil parish, and diocese, describing their political and physical features and naming the principal people of each place.[23]

*The Imperial Gazeteer* of Scotland was digitized in 2012 with funding from the National Library of Scotland. As of April 2023, it can be searched via the NLS website at https://digital.nls.uk/gazetteers-of-scotland-1803-1901/archive/97459138?mode=gallery_list&sn=326 or the full volumes can each be downloaded at:

Volume I: https://digital.nls.uk/gazetteers-of-scotland-1803-1901/archive/97459138

Volume II: https://digital.nls.uk/gazetteers-of-scotland-1803-1901/archive/97470686

## Typical Scots Phrases used in Maps and Medieval Land Charters

The People of Medieval Scotland (PoMS) database of land charters and related documents includes a glossary of terms commonly seen in documents from medieval Scotland. https://www.poms.ac.uk/information/glossary-of-terms/

Atlassian.net provides a comprehensive list of Scots words and phrases from the Registers of Scotland (RoS) that can be found in property records and other legal documents.[24] https://rosdev.atlassian.net/wiki/spaces/2ARM/pages/58690463/Scots+Phrases#:~:text=A%20ploughgate%20being%20a%20forty,than%20on%20its%20superficial%20area.

## Further information and references

- More information on the Scots language and Scots dictionaries can be found on the Scottish Language Dictionaries website. www.sldl.org.uk
- The Dictionary of the Scots Language, www.dsl.ac.uk, brings together the Dictionary of the Older Scottish Tongue and the Scottish National Dictionary.
- The Scottish Place-Name Society/Comann Ainmean-Àite na h-Alba is another great resource for those interested in studying and discussing the origin of Scottish place names: www.spns.org.uk

## Scottish Dioceses

The Medieval Church was characterized by the establishment of a Diocesan structure that included parishes, with well-defined geographic boundaries. Since vital records from that time are

---

[23] Rev. John Marius Wilson, *The Imperial Gazetteer of Scotland; or, Dictionary of Scottish Topography*, Vol. I (Edinburgh: Fullarton & Co., 1854), i-ii. https://archive.org/details/imperialgazette01wils/page/n15/mode/2up

[24] "Scots Phrases," atlassian.net/wiki/, 14 October 2014. https://rosdev.atlassian.net/wiki/spaces/2ARM/pages/58690463/Scots+Phrases#:~:text=A%20ploughgate%20being%20a%20forty,than%20on%20its%20superficial%20area.

church records, it is important to become familiar with maps of the old Scottish church dioceses. The "Early Church in Northern Scotland" website describes the early Scottish church organization:

> Since the twelfth century a continuous series of bishops can be traced in the thirteen dioceses which had become established in what is now Scotland. However, two of these dioceses were not part of *Alba* (Scotland) at all but were part of the Norwegian hegemony. The islands of Orkney and Shetland (the Northern Isles -Norðreyjar)[25] were staunchly Norwegian up to the time that the King of Norway ceded them to the Scottish King in 1472. [26]

---

[25] Wikipedia contributors, "Northern Isles," Wikipedia, The Free Encyclopedia, accessed 19 December 2022. https://en.wikipedia.org/w/index.php?title=Northern_Isles&oldid=1108130095

[26] Cushie Enterprises, "The Medieval Church in Alba," The Early Church in Northern Scotland, 14 December 2022. https://www.cushnieent.com/medievalchurch/medieval_portal.htm

Figure B-6: Cushie Enterprises, "Map of the Medieval Scottish Dioceses," accessed 16 April 2023. https://www.cushnieent.com/medievalchurch/map_scotland.htm

*Appendix B: Scottish Geography*

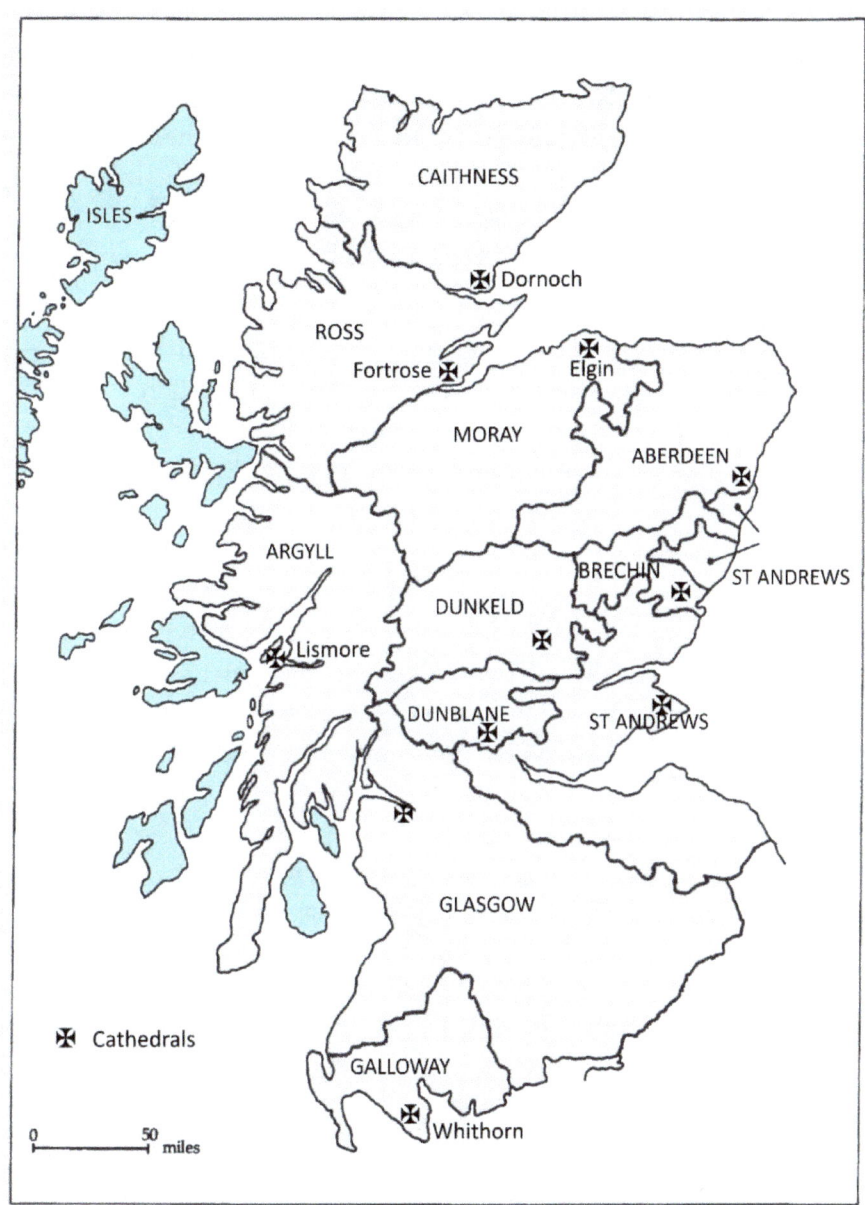

*Figure B-6: Map of Medieval Scottish Church Dioceses provided by ECNS (Early Church in Northern Scotland).* [26]

## Scottish and English Marches

The Marches[27] were established via treaty between Henry III of England and Alexander III of Scotland in 1249 as an attempt to control the English-Scottish border by establishing a buffer zone. Per Figure B-7, the area was divided into the West March, the Middle March and the East March. In the late thirteenth century, Edward I of England appointed the first Lord Warden of the Marches. Both countries encouraged cross-border raiding, and minor skirmishes.[28]

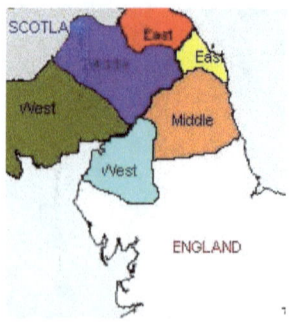

*Figure B-7: Scottish and English Marches* [27]
[CC-BY-SA 3.0](#)

The history of the Border Reivers and the Border Grahams are tied to the Scottish and English Marches. The Scottish Marches were disestablished in 1603. In an effort to institute central control of the border region and of Scotland, James VI of Scotland and I of England renamed the border region "Middle Shires." [29]

# GENUKI

Another great resource is GENUKI or GENealogical information for the United Kingdom and Ireland, is a free virtual reference library that is organized by geography (using historic counties and ancient parishes) and topic. GENUKI is a non-commercial service, maintained by a charitable trust and a group of volunteers.

GENUKI link for Ireland: https://www.genuki.org.uk/big/irl
GENUKI link for Scotland: https://www.genuki.org.uk/big/sct

The GENUKI Gazetteer is a good "first place to look" for research in England, Ireland, Wales, Scotland, Isle of Man, and the Channel Islands. The gazetteer can help find the location of obscure places, showing which GENUKI pages have information about that place and the corresponding genealogical resources available.

From GENUKI's "Find Places" page: "The place names in the gazetteer are generally for larger places. We have an additional set based upon names on Ordnance Survey maps dated around 1900

---

[27] Figure B-7: Scottish and English Marches Wikimedia Commons contributors, "File:Marches map.JPG," Wikimedia Commons, the free media repository, accessed 1 January 2023. https://commons.wikimedia.org/w/index.php?title=File:Marches_map.JPG&oldid=487528473

[28] R.C. Reid, "The Office of Warden of the Marches; its Origin and Early History," *The English Historical Review*, Volume XXXII, Issue CXXVIII (October 1917): 479–496. https://doi.org/10.1093/ehr/XXXII.CXXVIII.479
(Restricted access)

[29] Anna Groundwater, "The Chasm between James VI and I's Vision of the Orderly 'Middle Shires' and the 'Wickit' Scottish Borderers between 1587 and 1625." *Renaissance and Reformation / Renaissance et Réforme* 30, no. 4 (2007): 105–132. http://www.jstor.org/stable/43445941

which can be accessed via the 'Place search' tab near the top of many of our pages. This can help in searching for farms and hamlets."[30]

## ©OpenStreetMap

©OpenStreetMap is an open source mapping database whose contributors use aerial imagery, GPS devices, and field maps. ©OpenStreetMap is cross referenced to the open source GeoNames geographical database which covers all countries and contains over eleven million placenames.[31] ©OpenStreetMap has been particularly helpful as it offers a free source of locations of landmark buildings such as "Boreland House" and archaeological landmarks such as the medieval church close of Saint Kessog, the first home of Lang Will Graham of the Border Grahams, as well as the village of Gillesbie, all on a current map, enabling an in-person visit to the location.[32]

*Figure B-8: OpenStreetMap depiction of the Village of Boreland and Surrounding Area [32] CC-BY-SA 3.0*

---

[30] "Find Places," UK & Ireland Genealogical Information Service (GENUKI), accessed 1 January 2023. https://www.genuki.org.uk/gazetteer#results

[31] "Geonames search window," Geonames.org, accessed 1 January 2023. http://www.geonames.org/

[32] Figure B-8: ©OpenStreetMap contributors, "About OpenStreetMap," OpenStreetMap.org, accessed 1 January 2023. https://www.openstreetmap.org/about

## Table of Figures

Figure B-1: River Esk Near Castle O'er, Dumfries and Galloway, Great Britain, © Copyright Richard Webb, CC BY-SA 2.0. ................................................................................................................................ B-1

Figure B-2: Lothian and Linlithgow from Joan Blaeu's Atlas of Scotland, 1654 based on surveys by Timothy Pont. ................................................................................................................................ B-2

Figure B-3: South West Dumfriesshire, as shown in John Thomson's 1832 Atlas of Scotland............................B-3

Figure B-4: Moskesso Closs/Close, Hutton Parish, Dumfriesshire (Survey by Wm Crawford, 1804). [11] CC-BY 4.0 Reproduced with the permission of the National Library of Scotland. ................................................................B-4

Figure B-5: Looking from Kirkandrews, Across River Esk, at the Netherby Estate. © Copyright Jonathan Thacker CC BY-SA 2.0 [14] ................................................................................................................................ B-5

Figure B-6: Map of Medieval Scottish Church Dioceses provided by ECNS (Early Church in Northern Scotland). [26] ................................................................................................................................ B-10

Figure B-7: Scottish and English Marches [27] ................................................................................................ B-11

Figure B-8: OpenStreetMap depiction of the Village of Boreland and Surrounding Area [32] CC-BY-SA 3.0 ... B-12

# Appendix C: Y-DNA

## Table of Contents

Graham Surname Project Results ................................................................................................ C-1

Ancient Origins.............................................................................................................................. C-21

J1 Arrival in Scotland .................................................................................................................... C-24

Could the Legends Be Based on Fact? ......................................................................................... C-25

What We Do Know. ...................................................................................................................... C-25

King Fergus I .................................................................................................................................. C-26

Three other possible scenarios to explain the arrival of J1 in Britain in the Bronze Age: .................. C-26

Arguments against Arabic origin for J1-L1253 ........................................................................... C-28

Border Graham J1 Patriarch......................................................................................................... C-30

Fergus the Rascal .......................................................................................................................... C-31

Graham Origins ............................................................................................................................ C-34

Time to Most Recent Common Ancestor (tMRCA) and the Grayville Grahams........................ C-35

Summary ....................................................................................................................................... C-36

Other Related Y-DNA Surname Projects: ................................................................................... C-37

Table of Figures............................................................................................................................. C-42

Endnotes ....................................................................................................................................... C-42

## Graham Surname Project Results

Y-DNA, analysis of the male chromosome, is useful as it can help us find ancestors as far back as they have been keeping records (1,000 or more years ago), whereas the popular autosomal DNA (aDNA) testing we see advertised is based on analysis of the 22 pairs chromosomes called autosomes. The 23rd pair of chromosomes are the sex chromosomes. Autosomal testing can only reliably get us back five to six generations, maybe further with advanced tools. However, use of those advanced tools required accurate, verified trees of distant cousins that also go back to the 1600s and 1700s (a rare occurrence). Assuming we find distant matches with verified trees, aDNA might get us back as far as nine or ten generations.

*Appendix C: Y-DNA*

On the other hand, analysis of the male sex chromosome and female mitochrondrial DNA, can provide valuable historical information. In the case of the male Y chromosome, useful groupings of genetic codes called haplogroups and their associated child subgroups or subclades, are revealed. A term for the referenced genetic codes used to determine haplogroups is Single Nucleotide Polymorphisms (SNPs). The SNPs, haplogroups and subclades enable comparisons between males to determine cousin matches and "long-distance" direct paternal line inheritance. The sequence of subclades in one's Y-DNA profile can be characterized as a family tree from parent subclades down to subsequent child subclades, which can assist in determining shared family lines.[1]

The more technical explanation: Y-DNA haplogroups are defined by the presence of a series of Single nucleotide polymorphisms, or SNPs (pronounced "snips"). Individual SNPs mutate every hundred years on average. After a series of mutations, new subclades are created.[2] Subclades are subgroups of the haplogroups, defined by a terminal SNP-- the most recent SNP in one's Y genetic tree. Finally, STRs are Short Tandem Repeat markers that can change from one generation to the next.[3] An analogy provided by James M. Irvine and Kevin Irvin is that STRs identify the leaves of a tree, SNPs identify the twigs, and subclades and haplogroups identify the main branches.[4]

The Houston-based company, Family Tree DNA (FTDNA), hosts many Y-DNA surname, geographic and demographic projects to enable open research into the origins of family groups, ethnic groups and geographic areas. Early Britain is the subject of a number of these projects as it saw the merging of different ethnic groups. After the Romans left about 410A.D., the Saxons and Angles arrived soon after 449 A.D.[5] Viking raids began 789 A.D., followed by a wave of Danish immigration, the Danish conquest of England from 991 to 1016,[6] and the St Brice's Day Massacre (a genocide of Danes ordered by King Æthelred the Unready in retaliation for Danish attacks) in November of 1002 A.D.[7] The Normans invaded England in 1066A.D. Then beginning in 1124, Norman land barons and their knights began to arrive in Scotland at the invitation of David I, King of Scots.[8] See timeline in Figure C-1 below.[9]

---

[1] "Y-DNA Test, Which Y-DNA Test is Best?" Your DNA Guide (blog), accessed 29 December 2022. https://www.yourdnaguide.com/ydna#:~:text=Y-DNA%20is%20the%20DNA%20inherited,back%20than%20autosomal%20DNA%20tests

[2] Debbie Kennett, "Haplogroup," International Society for Genetic Genealogy (ISOGG) Wiki, 27 June 2022. Haplogroup - ISOGG Wiki

[3] Family Tree DNA Learning Center, "Subclade," FamilyTreeDNA.com, accessed 29 December 2022. https://learn.familytreedna.com/faq-items/subclade/

[4] James M. Irvine and Kevin Irvin, "Interpreting yDNA Test Results," Clan Irwin Surname DNA Study, accessed 29 December 2022. https://www.clanirwin-dna.org/interpreting-ydna-test-results

[5] Dr. Catherine Hills, "The Anglo-Saxon invasion and the beginnings of the 'English,'" Ourmigrationstory.org.uk, accessed 15 December 2022. https://www.ourmigrationstory.org.uk/oms/anglo-saxon-migrations

[6] Joanna Story, "The Viking Raid on Lindisfarne," English Heritage, accessed 15 December 2022. https://www.english-heritage.org.uk/visit/places/lindisfarne-priory/History/viking-raid/

[7] EditorBee, "The St Brice's Day Massacre," The Armchair Anglophile, 13 November 2011. http://www.armchairanglophile.com/st-brices-day-massacre/

[8] Ruth M. Blakely, "The Brus Family in England and Scotland, 1100-c. 1290" (PhD Thesis, University of Durham, 2000), 35-36. http://etheses.dur.ac.uk/1594/

[9] Figure C-1: A Brief Timeline of Early History in Britain  Anglo-Saxon History Timeline (softschools.com)

*Appendix C: Y-DNA*

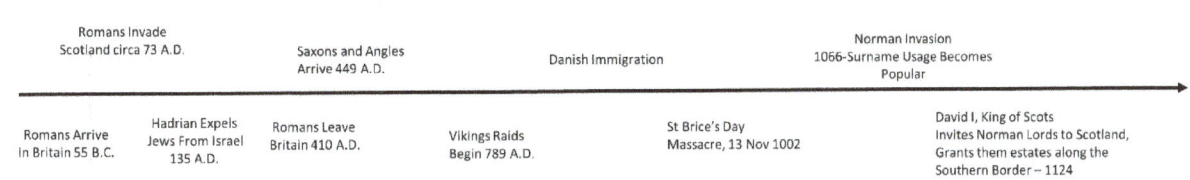

*Figure C-1: A Brief Timeline of Early History in Britain* [9]

Over 1300 have registered with the Graham Y-DNA surname project as of April 2023. There are 707 Y-DNA profiles currently reported in the Graham project results and project administrators have sorted them into 96 groups. The project results are posted at: https://www.familytreedna.com/public/Graham?iframe=ycolorized.

Those 96 groups were reduced to the five major categories depicted in Figure C-3 and described in Table C-1. There are multiple theories on the origins of each group, some with more evidence than others. It does appear, however, that a majority of the Y-DNA groups were formed before hereditary surnames were required. While hereditary surnames became more customary with the arrival of the "Normans" in 1066, they were not mandatory for everyone. It wasn't until the sixteenth century that hereditary surnames for all became common with the introduction of parish registers.[10]

---

[10] J. E. Corrie, *Records of the Corrie Family, 802-1899 A.D.* (London: Mitchell and Hughes, 1899), 133. https://archive.org/details/recordsofcorrief01corr

*Appendix C: Y-DNA*

By taking advantage of the latest archeological and DNA discoveries and looking at the entire Graham Surname project fresh, we can sort the project members into five Major Groups—which implies multiple patriarchs. As of April 2023, at the 12-marker match level, there were 707 Graham Y-DNA profiles reported.[11] While the 12-marker match level is of limited utility when seeking to find one's own genetic lineage, it is useful here for an <u>aggregate analysis</u> as shown in the chart in Figure C-3.

1. **Group 1: R-M269 (R1b)** is the largest group in the Graham surname project. R-M269 is found in all of mainland Europe from Poland to France and parts of Scandinavia.[12] 331 of 707 participants (**46.82%**) are in this group.[13] Y-DNA analysis of skeletons and other archeological evidence published in September 2020 in "Population genomics of the Viking world," in the journal *Nature,* a result of 6 years of work by Margaryan, A., Lawson, D.J., Sikora, M. *et al.*, provides additional supporting evidence to help us further divide this largest group, into **1A., Pre-Norman Conquest** (which I define as being present in Britain before 1066A.D.), and **1B., Post-Norman Conquest** (present in Britain after 1066A.D.). The 442 Viking skeletons found outside Scandinavia were sequenced by Eske Willerslev's lab, producing whole genome sequences for both men and women from sites in Scotland, Ukraine, Poland, Russia, the Baltic, Iceland, Greenland, and elsewhere in continental Europe. They were compared to known Viking samples from Scandinavia. The Normans or "North Men" were originally Viking pirates from Denmark, Norway, and Iceland who began raids on European coastal settlements in the eighth century and secured a permanent foothold in Northern France (later named Normandy) by the year 900 A.D. However, caution must be exercised in utilizing the term "Normans" for people who arrived in Britain at the time of conquest or afterward. In fact, those who arrived in Britain with William the Conqueror were not exclusively of Scandinavian ancestry.[14] The new arrivals were not just from Normandy, but from all over France and Flanders.[15] Much of this subdivision is guesswork, tying Group 1B members to the Y-DNA of known Norman families. <u>The point of this exercise is to show the relatively small contribution of the Normans to the gene pool of Scotland and provide evidence against *Peerage's* claim from 1909 that William de Graham was "of Norman stock."</u>[16]

2. **Group 2: J-M267 (J1).** The second largest group in the Graham surname project are the J-M267s or J1s (218 of 707 members or **30.83%**).[17] It is a rare haplogroup in Britain and its L1253 subclade is peculiar to Grahams and some Jordans <u>indicating, a single J1 Scottish patriarch, and</u>

---

[11] FamilyTreeDNA, "Graham DNA Surname Project Background," FamilyTreeDNA.com, accessed 29 December 2022. https://www.familytreedna.com/groups/graham/about/background

[12] Maciamo Hay, "Haplogroup R1b (Y-DNA)," Eupedia.com, last updated October 2021. https://www.eupedia.com/europe/Haplogroup_R1b_Y-DNA.shtml

[13] FamilyTreeDNA, "Graham DNA Surname Project Results," FamilyTreeDNA.com, accessed 29 December 2022. https://www.familytreedna.com/public/Graham?iframe=ycolorized

[14] "Wars of the Normans," Heritage History, accessed 17 April 2023. https://www.heritage-history.com/index.php?c=resources&s=war-dir&f=wars_norman

[15] C. P. Lewis, "Companions of the Conqueror (act. 1066–1071)," *Oxford Dictionary of National Biography,* 24 May 2007. https://doi.org/10.1093/ref:odnb/95594

[16] Sir James Balfour Paul, *The Scots Peerage, Founded on Wood's Edition,* Vol. VI (Edinburgh: David Douglas, 1909), 191. https://archive.org/details/scotspeeragefoun06pauluoft/page/n5/mode/2up?q=graham

[17] FamilyTreeDNA, "Graham DNA Surname Project Results."

a patriarch who was able to pass his surname to his heirs,[18] which implies a patriarch who was born after the Normans arrived in Scotland, sometime after 1124 A.D.

J-M267/YSC76 is most concentrated in Eastern Anatolia (Turkey) and the Levant region (near modern-day Lebanon), its theorized origin. However, the oldest identified J1 sample was found in a cave in Satsurblia Cave Natural Monument, in modern-day Kumistavi, Georgia, about 70 miles east of the eastern shore of the Black Sea, and was dated 13,200 B.C.[19]

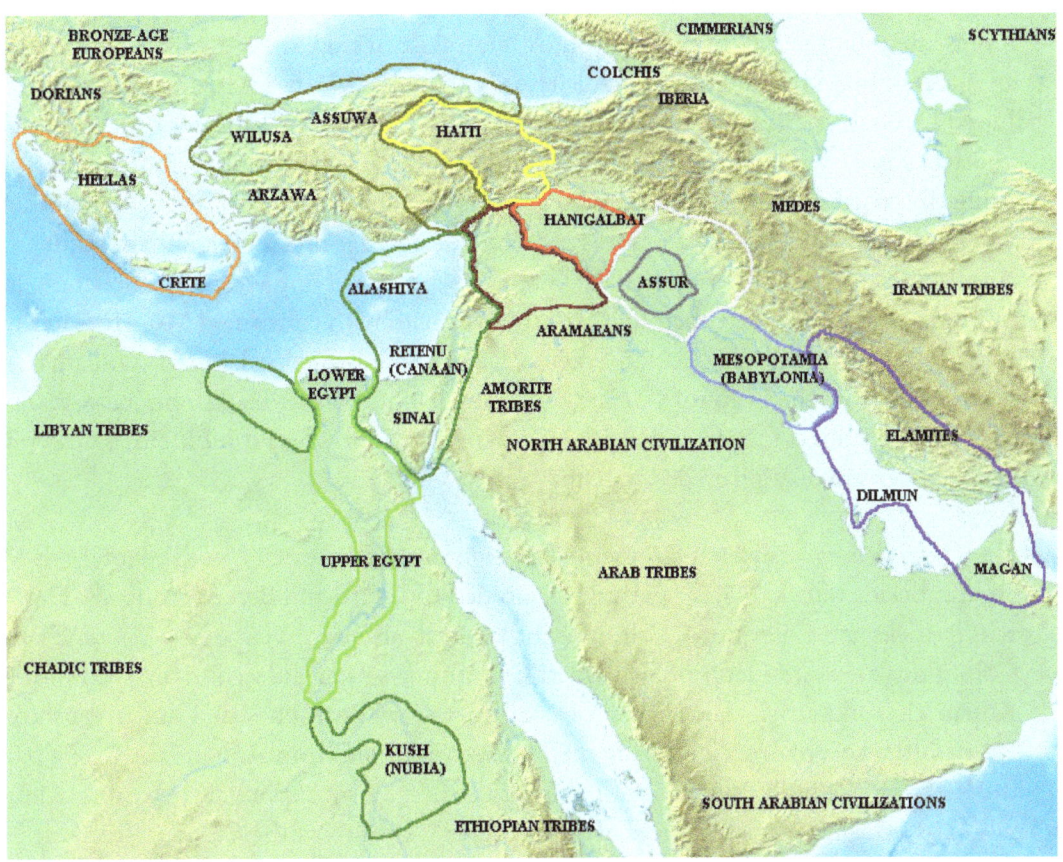

*Figure C-2: Map of Ancient Babylonia, Egypt, and Scythian Territory by Brian Gotts. This file is licensed under Creative Commons CC BY 4.0.* [19]

My husband, Barry Graham, and therefore his male line, is J-M267- L1253. Tracing his father's family nine generations, I could only find marriages with other farming families of Scots, English, Welsh, and Cornish heritage in isolated rural areas in America, and no marriages with other groups until 1959. Barry, his brother, and his father's autosomal DNA reports show them to be mostly Scottish/English (no surprise there). However, what is a surprise is recently

---

[18] FamilyTreeDNA, "Graham DNA Surname Project News," FamilyTreeDNA.com, accessed 29 December 2022. https://www.familytreedna.com/groups/graham/about/news

[19] Maciamo Hay, "Haplogroup J1 (Y-DNA)," Eupedia.com, updated October 2021. https://www.eupedia.com/europe/Haplogroup_J1_Y-DNA.shtml

Figure C-2: Brian Gotts, "Map of the ancient Near East during the Amarna Period," World History Encyclopedia, Last modified April 26, 2012. https://www.worldhistory.org/image/171/map-of-the-ancient-near-east-during-the-amarna-per/

revised autosomal ethnicity estimates on the major DNA sites, now also show small (2-5%) percentages of ethnicity from Italy, Greece, Turkey, and/or the Levant area. Only their Y chromosomes should have those markers as the family intermarried with Scots/English/Welsh/Irish as far back as we know, and no Mediterranean ethnicity can be found in their close Graham female cousins.

3. **Group 3: IM253/DF29 (I1)** is represented by 59 project members, or 8.35% of the total, and is a Nordic group.[20] Haplogroup I1 is the most common type of haplogroup I in northern Europe (Figure C-9). It is found mostly in Scandinavia and Finland, where it is typically represented in over 35% of the Y chromosomes. Associated with Norse ethnicity, I1 is found in all places invaded by ancient Germanic tribes and by the Vikings.[21] In *House Graham*, Dr. Lloyd D. Graham provides evidence that "Noble Grahams," male descendants of Alan, the younger son of William de Graham, were of the I-M253 haplogroup.[22] This conclusion was primarily based on a male Graham who was a confirmed descendant of the Grahams of Glenny and Gartmore, who also tested as I-M253. Burke's *Peerage* lists these Graham families as descendants of the Earls of Menteith. Thanks to the tenacity of Mr. Rob Sinclair in searching out test subjects, in November 2021, another Graham with confirmed Montrose heritage via the Graemes of Inchbrakie,[23] Alex Graeme, was also confirmed as I-M253. William de Graham descending from the Lords of Greystoke/Gristock who were of Danish heritage would be supported by this evidence, as both the Grahams of Montrose and Menteith[24] descend from the younger son of William de Graham, Alan de Graham.

4. **Group 4: E-M35 (E1b1b)** is represented by eight members, or 1.13% of the total.[25] E-M35, a child subclade of E-M215, is an ethnic group tied to Jewish and Berber groups.[26] The Kirkpatricks and Coloquons (Calhouns in America) also have a large E-M35 branch. The Coloquons are descendants of Sir Robert Coloquon, son of the second Sir Humphrey Kilpatrick/Kirkpatrick. The Kirkpatricks of Luss near Port Menteith, Dunbartonshire use the Bruce saltire coat of arms indicating their ancestor's origin from Annandale.[27] The patriarch of the Kirkpatricks and Coloquons of Luss was the first Sir Humphrey Kirkpatrick/Kilpatrick who was a neighbor of the Bruces of Annandale.[28] Analysis of the Calhoun surname project

---

[20] FamilyTreeDNA, "Graham DNA Surname Project Results."

[21] Maciamo Hay, "Haplogroup J1 (Y-DNA)," Eupedia.com.

[22] Lloyd D. Graham, *House Graham, From the Antoine Wall to the Temple of Hymen* (Lulu.com, 2020), 31-32. https://clangrahamsociety.org/wp-content/uploads/2020/09/House-GRAHAM-eBook.pdf

[23] Darrin Lythgoe, "Graemes of Inchbrakie" Clan Macfarlane and Associated Clans Genealogy, accessed 29 December 2022. https://www.clanmacfarlanegenealogy.info/genealogy/TNGWebsite/getperson.php?personID=I23489&tree=CC

[24] Sir James Balfour Paul, *The Scots Peerage, Founded on Wood's Edition,* Vol. VI (Edinburgh: David Douglas, 1909), 147-149, 224-225. https://archive.org/details/scotspeeragefoun06pauluoft/page/148/mode/2up?q=glenny

[25] FamilyTreeDNA, "Graham DNA Surname Project Results."

[26] Jayne Ekins, "Y-DNA Haplogroup: E1b1b and E1b1a," Your DNA Guide (blog), accessed 14 December 2022. https://www.yourdnaguide.com/ydgblog/ydna-haplogroup-e

[27] Joseph Irving, *The Book of Dumbartonshire, Volume II, Parishes* (Edinburgh and London: W. and A. K. Johnston, 1879, 244-245. https://deriv.nls.uk/dcn23/9539/95398878.23.pdf

[28] Amanda Beam, John Bradley, Dauvit Broun, John Reuben Davies, Matthew Hammond, Neil Jakeman, Michele Pasin and Alice Taylor (with others), People of Medieval Scotland (PoMS) 1093-1371 (Glasgow and London: 2019), PoMS "No. 3884," accessed 29 December 2022. https://www.poms.ac.uk/record/source/3884/

shows the Colquhouns (Calhouns) of Dunbartonshire sharing the same Y-DNA profile as the Kirkpatricks of Dumfries.[29] A connection to the Grahams may be through the great-grandson of the first Sir Humphrey, who was the second Sir Humphrey Kirkpatrick who acquired the Graham lands of Over Dryfe upon marriage circa 1321 to Isobel of Torthorwald, daughter of Christine Graham (Figure 41). A second possibility could be via the marriage of the second Sir Humphrey's son, Sir John Coloquon to Lady Lilias Graham, sister to the famous Marquis of Montrose in 1620 and his subsequent affair with her sister, Catherine Graham.[30] A third more recent possibility is through the Grahams of Nether Glenny, Port Menteith who were related to the Coloquons via marriage.[31] One candidate of the Nether Glenny Grahams is Hugh Graham (1788-1880)[32] who was the father of ten known children.[33] He served in the Queen's Regiment and his portrait was included in "The Highlanders of Scotland Volume II," commissioned by Queen Victoria.[34]

5. **Group 5: Remaining project members.** Each subgroup, which includes haplogroups E1b1a, G2, I, I2, J2, N, Q, and R1a, together comprise the remaining 12%. E1b1a (2.8%), I2 (2.55%), R1a (2.4%), J2 (1.56%), G (1.41%), Q (.42%), N (.28%), and C (.14%) are the remaining haplogroups in the Graham surname project.

---

[29] FamilyTreeDNA, "Calhoun/Colquhoun Y-DNA Surname Project Results," FamilyTreeDNA.com, accessed 30 December 2022. https://www.familytreedna.com/public/calhoun/default.aspx?section=ycolorized

[30] Joseph Irving, *The Book of Dumbartonshire, Volume II, Parishes* (Edinburgh and London: W. and A. K. Johnston, 1879), 252-253. https://deriv.nls.uk/dcn23/9539/95398878.23.pdf

[31] Ryk Brown, "Duncan Graham of Nether Glenny (1708-1759)," Brown's Genealogy Database and Stewarts of Balquhidder, 16 November 2022. https://rykbrown.net/TNG/getperson.php?personID=I7082&tree=BROWN

[32] FamilySearch, "Scotland Births and Baptisms, 1564-1950," "Hugh Graham, 1788," FamilySearch.org, accessed 11 February 2020. https://familysearch.org/ark:/61903/1:1:X14T-6XS (Requires account.)

[33] "Hugh Graham (28 July 1788-20 July 1880)," Familysearch.org, accessed 30 December 2022 (restricted). https://www.familysearch.org/tree/person/sources/97RX-DKK (Requires account.)

[34] Kenneth Macleay, *Highlanders of Scotland. Portraits illustrative of the principal clans and followings, and the retainers of the royal household at Balmoral, in the reign of her majesty Queen Victoria*, Vol. II (London: Mr. Mitchell, 1870), "Hugh Grahame," Plate 24. https://www.splrarebooks.com/collection/view/highlanders-of-scotland.-portraits-illustrative-of-the-principal-clans-and-

*Appendix C: Y-DNA*

This study focuses on Major Groups 1-4 which have the higher percentages of members assigned.[35] See Table C-1 for study observations.[36, 37]

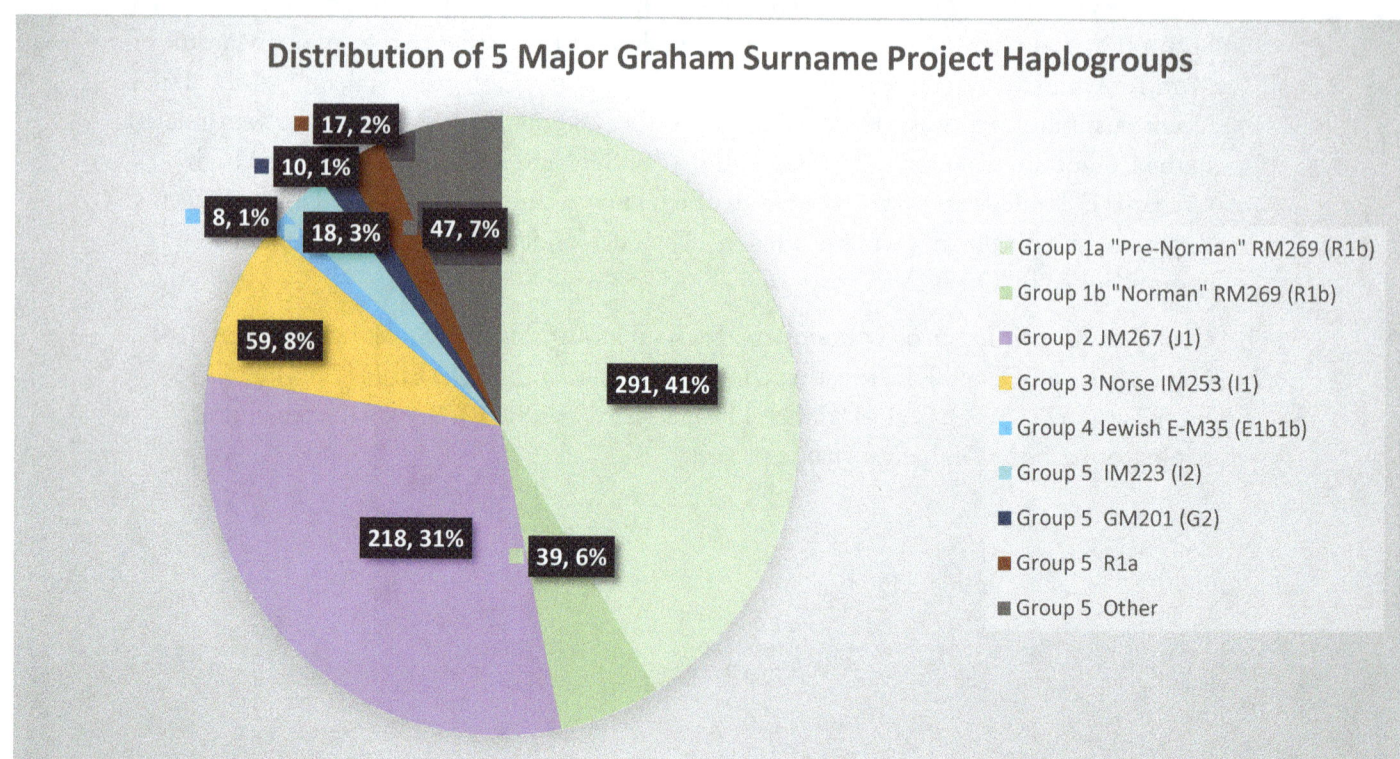

*Figure C-3: Distribution of the Five Major Graham Surname Project Groups as of April 2023* [35]

---

[35] Figure C-3: FamilyTreeDNA, "Graham DNA Surname Project Results."

[36] A note about Y-DNA subclade notation, which consists of one to three letters followed by a string of numbers (e.g., R-M222). The first letter is the haplogroup, the remaining letters identify the laboratory that discovered the subclade. If more than one lab lays claim to a subclade, it can be known by more than one notation, causing confusion. The numbers refer to the next number available in that lab's registration index.

[37] Hunter Provyn, "What Do All These Codes Mean?" PhyloGeographer.com, 25 April 2020. https://phylogeographer.com/what-do-all-these-codes-mean/

## TABLE C-1: INITIAL SORT OF FTDNA GRAHAM Y-DNA SURNAME PROJECT MEMBERS RESULTS OVERVIEW

[collapsing 96 groups to 5]

| | |
|---|---|
| **Group 1: R1b (R-M269) Haplogroup** — Largest group in the project (41%). R-M269 is found in all of mainland Europe and Scandinavia | Y-DNA Matches Groups from the FTDNA Graham Surname Project[38] |
| **Group 1a: PRE-NORMAN (BEFORE 1066 A.D.)** | **R1b Subclade: R1b1a2a1a1a: (R-U106)** Britain's DNA labeled this branch: Germanic.[39] Ancient DNA sample RISE94 from Sweden. Also identified in 9th/10th century Viking skeletons in Bødkergarden, Langeland, Denmark and Telemark, Norway.[40] |
| The R-L48 subclade matches a Viking skeleton found in Oxford, England, from 880-1000 A.D. This Viking may have been a victim of the St. Brice's Day massacre on 13 November 1002.[41] The Nethery participants in the project are L48, as are Sinclairs and certain Lyons and Grahams/Grimes.[42] | **R1b Group: Nethery/Nedry: R-L48:** The R-L48 subclade matches a Viking skeleton found in Oxford, England from 880-1000A.D.[43] |
| | **R1b Subclade: R1b1a2a1a1b5b: (R-L165)** This subclade is defined by the presence of the marker S68, also known as L165. It is found in England, Scandinavia, and Scotland (in this country it is mostly found in the Northern Isles and Western Isles). It has been suggested, therefore, that it arrived in the British Isles with the Vikings. Britain's DNA labeled this branch: Hebridean Viking.[44] |

---

[38] FamilyTreeDNA, "Graham DNA Surname Project Results."

[39] "Ancestral DNA Marker Pedigree Display for R-U106," GeneticHomeland.com, accessed 14 December 2022. https://www.genetichomeland.com/welcome/dnapedigree.asp?snp=r-u106&Chromosome=Y&snp2=&DB=0

[40] Roberta Estes, "442 Ancient Viking Skeletons Hold DNA Surprises – Does Your Y or Mitochondrial DNA Match?" DNAeXplained-Genetic Genealogy (blog), 18 September 2020.
https://dna-explained.com/2020/09/18/442-ancient-viking-skeletons-hold-dna-surprises-does-your-y-or-mitochondrial-dna-match-daily-updates-here/comment-page-1/

[41] Nadia Durrani, "Mass burials in England attest to a turbulent time, and perhaps a notorious medieval massacre," *ARCHAEOLOGY magazine (online),* November/December 2013. https://www.archaeology.org/issues/109-1311/features/1421-viking-england-st-brices-day

[42] Family Tree DNA, "Lyons Surname Y-DNA Project Results," FamilyTreeDNA.com, accessed 15 December 2022. https://www.familytreedna.com/public/lyon?iframe=ycolorized

[43] Roberta Estes, "442 Ancient Viking Skeletons Hold DNA Surprises – Does Your Y or Mitochondrial DNA Match?" DNAeXplained-Genetic Genealogy (blog), 18 September 2020.

[44] "Ancestral DNA Marker Pedigree Display for R-L165," GeneticHomeland.com, accessed 14 December 2022. https://www.genetichomeland.com/welcome/dnapedigree.asp?snp=R-L165&Chromosome=Y&snp2=&DB=0

| | |
|---|---|
| R-M269 members whose profile includes the R-M222 subclade total 28 or 4.4%. R-M222 includes the DF105 subclade. DF105 matches Viking skeletons found in the British Isles dated between the 7th and 9th centuries.[45] GeneticHomeland.com shows the subclade tree for the DF-105 group: R-M269--> R-L51--> R-L151--> R-U106-->R-S263--> R-S499--> R-L48/S162.[46] [Note: R-U106 is also known as R-S21, and R-M405, (Figure C-4). 23andMe utilizes the subclade notation "R-M405."[47]] | 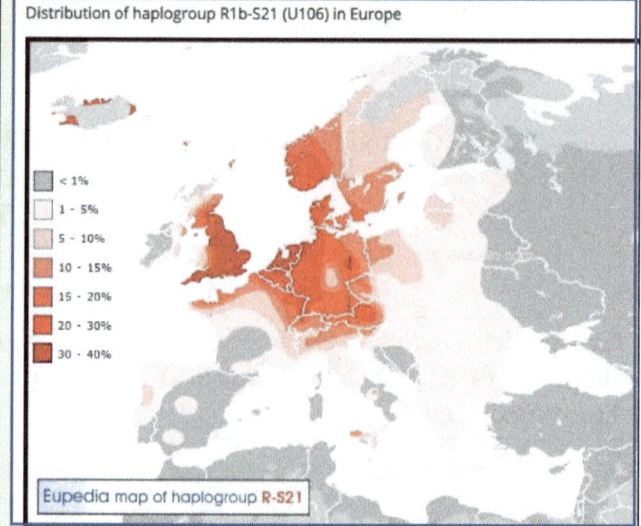<br><br>*Figure C-4: Eupedia's R1b-RS21 (a.k.a. R1b-U106 and R1b-M405) Geographic Distribution* [48] |
| | **R1b Subclade: R1b1a2a1a1b4b: (R-M222)** [49]<br><br>Sometimes called Northwest Irish, concentrated in Ireland and western Scotland. Associated with Niall of the Nine Hostages and Ui Neill clans. Britain's DNA labeled this branch: Ancient Irish.[50] Niall of the Nine Hostages, an Irish king, was the ancestor of the Uí Néill dynasties that dominated the northern half of Ireland from the 6th to the 10th centuries.[51] |
| According to the O'Neill Y-DNA Project, the king's probable lineage was: R1b-L21 –> DF13 –> DF49 –> Z2980 –> Z2976 –> DF23 –>Z2961 –> S645 –> Z2965 –> M222–>Y2605 –> Y2841 –>DF104 –>DF109 (a.k.a. DF105), which split into 29 branches. | |
| | **R1b Group: R-M222>DF105**<br><br>DF105 matches Viking skeletons found in the British Isles dated between the 7th and 9th centuries.[52] |

---

[45] Roberta Estes, "442 Ancient Viking Skeletons Hold DNA Surprises – Does Your Y or Mitochondrial DNA Match?"

[46] "Ancestral DNA Marker Pedigree Display for R-DF105," GeneticHomeland.com, accessed 14 December 2022. https://www.genetichomeland.com/welcome/dnapedigree.asp?snp=DF105&Chromosome=Y&snp2=&DB=0

[47] Edison Williams, "Did you see that Family Tree DNA has made public the world's largest yDNA Haplotree?" WikiTree.com, 28 September 2018. https://www.wikitree.com/g2g/691651/that-family-tree-made-public-worlds-largest-ydna-haplotree

[48] Figure C-4: Maciamo Hay, "Haplogroup R1b (Y-DNA)," Eupedia.com, last updated October 2021. https://www.eupedia.com/europe/Haplogroup_R1b_Y-DNA.shtml

[49] FamilyTreeDNA, "Graham DNA Surname Project Results."

[50] "Ancestral DNA Marker Pedigree Display for R-M222," GeneticHomeland.com, accessed 14 December 2022. https://www.genetichomeland.com/welcome/dnapedigree.asp?snp=R-m222&Chromosome=Y&snp2=&DB=0

[51] Wu Mingren, "Niall of the Nine Hostages, One of the Most Fruitful Kings in History," Ancient Origins, accessed 22 April 2023. https://www.ancient-origins.net/history-famous-people/niall-nine-hostages-0011410

[52] "Ancestral DNA Marker Pedigree Display for R-DF105," GeneticHomeland.com, accessed 14 December 2022. https://www.genetichomeland.com/welcome/dnapedigree.asp?snp=DF105&Chromosome=Y&snp2=&DB=0

*Appendix C: Y-DNA*

| | |
|---|---|
| | **R1b Subclade: R1b1a2a1a1b4: (R-L21)**<br><br>Largest European group under R1b P312. Highly correlated with the geography of ancient Celts. "Britain's DNA labeled this branch: Pretani." [53] |
| | **R1b Group: R-L21>DF13>ZZ10.1>Z255. ("Irish Sea Group").** [54]<br><br>DF13 is a major branch of L21 in haplogroup R1b found primarily in Ireland. Originated about 2200 B.C. A child subclade of ZZ10, L066, matches a 9th century Viking skeleton found in Sweden and a modern-day match in England. [55] |
| *Figure C-5: Eupedia's R1b-L21 Geographic Distribution* [56] | **R1b Group: R-FT38313**<br><br>R-FT38313 is a child subclade of R-P312/L21 (Beaker Folk or Bell Beaker). |
| **Group 1b: POST-NORMAN (AFTER 1066 A.D.).**<br><br>It appears that several of the groups from the R-M269 haplogroup in the Graham surname project have ties to Normandy, Northwestern France, and Iberia. | |

---

[53] "Ancestral DNA Marker Pedigree Display for R-L21," GeneticHomeland.com, accessed 14 December 2022. https://www.genetichomeland.com/welcome/dnapedigree.asp?snp=R-l21&Chromosome=Y&snp2=&DB=0

[54] FamilyTreeDNA, "Graham DNA Surname Project Results."

[55] "Ancestral DNA Marker Pedigree Display for R-Z255," GeneticHomeland.com, accessed 14 December 2022. https://www.genetichomeland.com/welcome/dnapedigree.asp?snp=R-z255&Chromosome=Y&snp2=&DB=0

[56] Figure C-5: Maciamo Hay, "Haplogroup R1b (Y-DNA)," Eupedia.com, last updated October 2021. https://www.eupedia.com/europe/Haplogroup_R1b_Y-DNA.shtml

| | |
|---|---|
| BY42299 is marked and represented by the tree:<br><br>R-M269>L23>L51>PF7589>CTS6689>S1141>FGC24138>FGC24158>BY11999>BY12006>BY42299. A match to the parent subclade, FGC24138, is found in an ancient bone sample called "CL53" from a 6th-century Longobard grave in Collegno, Italy. Collegno is near Turin, about 60 miles from the French border. The Longobards, or Lombards, were a Germanic tribe that originated in Scandinavia and ruled the Italian peninsula from 568 until 774 when Charlemagne, King of the Franks, conquered Northern and Central Italy. The Lombards were also allies of the Normans, so it is feasible that some Lombards fled to Normandy once they lost their territory in Italy to the Franks.[57] | R1b Group R-M269>L23>L51>PF7589>CTS6689>S1141>FGC24138>FGC24158>BY11999>BY12006>BY42299<br><br>(Longobards or Lombards) |
| R-P25 matches a Viking skeleton from 900-1050 A.D. found in Sweden. | **R1b Group R-P25:** Associated with Normandy via the Y-DNA Normandy Project.[58] P25 matches a Viking skeleton from 900-1050 A.D. found in Sweden. The Normans were also Vikings from this time period.[59] |
| | **R1b Subclade: R1b1a2a1a1: R-P310:** Shares parent subclades with Lyons surname project participants, a surname associated with the Normans, particularly the Bruces. A match to this subclade tree is found in an ancient bone sample called "CL53" from a 6th- century Longobard grave in Collegno, Italy.[60] |
| | **R1b Subclade: R1b1a2a1a1b: (R-P312) (Beaker Folk):** Shares parent subclades with Bruce surname participants as well as Normandy and Iberian Y-DNA projects. |
| R1b Groups R-BY40815, R-BY36344, and R-BY21596 descend from the DF-27 parent subclade, (Figure C-6) as do several groups from the Bruce, Lyons, and Normandy Y-DNA Surname Projects. DF-27 concentrated in and is therefore thought to originated from Spain, Portugal, and Southern France.[61, 62] | **R1b Group: R-BY40815:** R-BY40815 is a child subclade of R-P312/DF-27. DF-27 is peculiar to Spain, Portugal, and France.[63] |

---

[57] Maciamo Hay, "Genetic History of the Italians," Eupedia.com, last updated December 2017. https://www.eupedia.com/genetics/italian_dna.shtml

[58] FamilyTreeDNA, "Normandy Y-DNA Project Results," FamilyTreeDNA.com, accessed 15 December 2022. https://www.familytreedna.com/public/Normandy?iframe=ycolorized

[59] "Ancestral DNA Marker Pedigree Display for R-P25," GeneticHomeland.com, accessed 14 December 2022. https://www.genetichomeland.com/welcome/dnapedigree.asp?snp=R-p25&Chromosome=Y&snp2=&DB=0

[60] Roberta Estes, "442 Ancient Viking Skeletons Hold DNA Surprises – Does Your Y or Mitochondrial DNA Match?"

[61] Diana have Gale Matthiesen, Lyon(s) Families Association, "Results of Y-DNA Testing for Surname LYON and Its Variations, Haplogroup R1b Links Hub," Diana, Goddess of the Hunt—For Ancestors! accessed 30 December 2022. http://dgmweb.net/DNA/Lyon/LyonDNA-results-R1b-Hub.html

[62] FamilyTree DNA, "Lyon(s) Surname DNA Project Results," FamilyTreeDNA.com, accessed 30 December 2022. https://www.familytreedna.com/public/lyon?iframe=ycolorized

[63] Neus Solé-Morata, Patricia Villaescusa, Carla García-Fernández, et al., "Analysis of the R1b-DF27 haplogroup shows that a large fraction of Iberian Y-chromosome lineages originated recently in situ," *Scientific Reports* (4 August 2017): 1. https://www.nature.com/articles/s41598-017-07710-x

*Appendix C: Y-DNA*

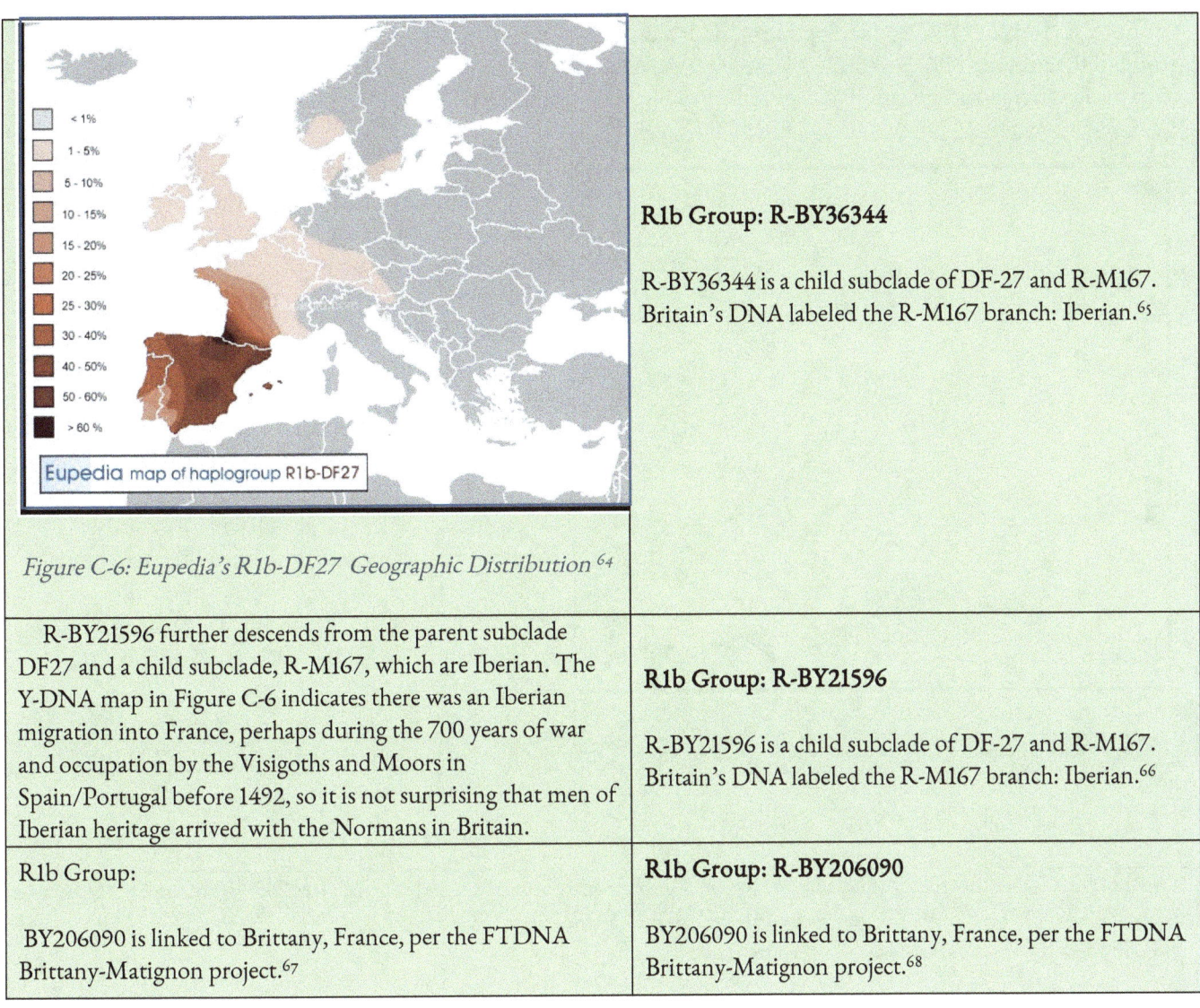

| | R1b Group: R-BY36344 |
|---|---|
| | R-BY36344 is a child subclade of DF-27 and R-M167. Britain's DNA labeled the R-M167 branch: Iberian.⁶⁵ |

*Figure C-6: Eupedia's R1b-DF27 Geographic Distribution ⁶⁴*

| | |
|---|---|
| R-BY21596 further descends from the parent subclade DF27 and a child subclade, R-M167, which are Iberian. The Y-DNA map in Figure C-6 indicates there was an Iberian migration into France, perhaps during the 700 years of war and occupation by the Visigoths and Moors in Spain/Portugal before 1492, so it is not surprising that men of Iberian heritage arrived with the Normans in Britain. | **R1b Group: R-BY21596**<br><br>R-BY21596 is a child subclade of DF-27 and R-M167. Britain's DNA labeled the R-M167 branch: Iberian.⁶⁶ |
| **R1b Group:**<br><br>BY206090 is linked to Brittany, France, per the FTDNA Brittany-Matignon project.⁶⁷ | **R1b Group: R-BY206090**<br><br>BY206090 is linked to Brittany, France, per the FTDNA Brittany-Matignon project.⁶⁸ |

---

⁶⁴ Figure C-6: Maciamo Hay, "Haplogroup R1b (Y-DNA)," Eupedia.com, last updated October 2021. https://www.eupedia.com/europe/Haplogroup_R1b_Y-DNA.shtml

⁶⁵ "Ancestral DNA Marker Pedigree Display for R-BY21596," GeneticHomeland.com, accessed 22 April 2023. https://www.genetichomeland.com/welcome/dnapedigree.asp?snp=R-BY21596&Chromosome=Y&snp2=&DB=0

⁶⁶ Ibid.

⁶⁷ FamilyTreeDNA, "R-BY3265, R-BY3266 Subclade & Brittany > Matignon > Grouazel and other families Y-DNA Classic Chart," FamilyTreeDNA.com, accessed 30 December 2022 https://www.familytreedna.com/public/Grouazel_Pays_de_Matignon/default.aspx?section=yresults

⁶⁸ Ibid.

**Group 2: J1 (J-M267/YSC76) Haplogroup–2nd largest group in the project (31%)** J1/YSC76's origin is postulated to be in the Levant region (modern-day Lebanon).

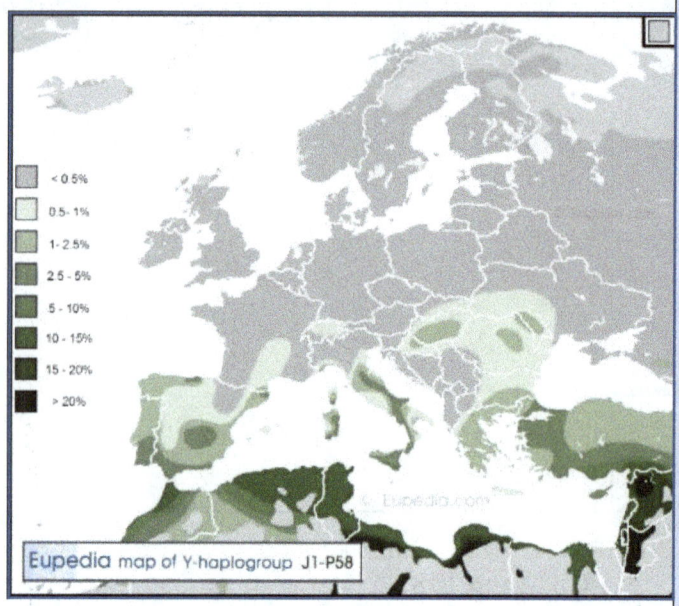

*Figure C-7: Eupedia's J1-P58 Geographic Distribution* [69]

### J1 L1253

This subclade is uniquely Scottish and tied to the Graham surname. As for the arrival of the J1s in Scotland, analysis of the Beta FTDNA Discover™ More SNP tool and Dr. Robin Spencer's SNP Tracker predict the J1s arrived in Scotland in **the late Bronze Age, in about the 1400s B.C.** [Dr. Spencer subsequently updated his analysis on 25 September 2022 to report that G, T, and J, especially J1, first arrived in Britain much earlier, soon after the last Ice Age, but it is unlikely these groups survived. Then more arrived later in the Bronze and Iron Ages.][70] This supports the claim that the paternal ancestors of these J1s may have arrived in Scotland from Egypt and the eastern Mediterranean in the 1400s B.C. per the legend of the foundation of Scotland included in the Scottish "Declaration of Independence," called the Declaration of Arbroath,[71] written in 1320.

The unique Y-DNA profile or subclade tree for the Graham and Jordan J1's is as follows: **J-M267 ->YSC65 -> YSC1283 -> L620--> YSC196-->L136-->P58-->YSC141-->Z1878-->YSC234-->YSC235-->L858-->YSC76-->FGC8224--> FGC8223-->BY65-->FGC58460 --> BY89-->L1253**

Analysis indicates the J1 Grahams and Jordans descend from a single patriarch. Per Dr. Iain McDonald of the FTDNA Scottish Y-DNA Project in March 2021:
"As a rough estimate, the BigY results indicate a common ancestor around 500-1000 years ago for J-L1253 and around 1500-2500 years ago for J-BY89. This puts the migration from the Middle East to Scotland sometime between 2500 and 500 years ago."[72] Dr. McDonald later refined his estimate on the Border Graham patriarch birth year to: "closer to 400-700 years ago or (taking into account the age of the average tester) around 1250-1550 A.D." Dr. Robin Spencer has a tighter estimate for the Time to Most Recent Common Ancestor (tMRCA)—in the middle that that time period: circa

---

[69] Figure C-7: Maciamo Hay, "Haplogroup J1 (Y-DNA)," Eupedia.com, last updated October 2021. https://www.eupedia.com/europe/Haplogroup_J1_Y-DNA.shtml

[70] Robin Spencer, PhD. "SNP Tracker," Timelines Tab for SNP: L1253, Tracking Back-A Website for Genetic Genealogy Tools, Experimentation and Discussion, Scaled Innovation, accessed 28 December 2022. http://scaledinnovation.com/gg/snpTracker.html (See Discussion tab for instructions on site use.)

[71] "The Declaration of Arbroath," *National Records of Scotland*, accessed 8 November 2022. https://www.nrscotland.gov.uk/Declaration

[72] FamilyTreeDNA, "Graham DNA Surname Project News."

1400 A.D. The Beta FTDNA Discover™ More SNP tool, as of April 2023, estimated the mean tMRCA as 1200 A.D. with a 95% probability that he was born between 1010 and 1356 A.D.[73]

Figure C-8 is a notional breakout of the GrahamJ1 Big Y results. It is meant to visually organize the results available as of April 2023 and will continue to change as new information is available. These estimates support the theory that the Border Graham ancestors were maternal cousins of "the Last" Graham lord of Dalkeith and Mosskesswra and Figure 41, Descendants of the Grahams of Dalkeith and Proposed Origin of the Border Grahams. In 1362/63, John de Graham, "the last" Lord of Mosskeswra, gifts lands in southern Scotland, apparently including lands in Hutton parish, to Graham cousins, believed to be the ancestors of the Border Grahams, who are believed to be J1. Lang Will Graham, chief of the Border Grahams was from the parish of Hutton and several of his suspected descendants have tested as J1. If so, the unofficial "J1 Graham Sept clan" would have originated with a child born to J1 male and a Graham female within a generation of 1362. By "sept clan" we mean a family line that branched off the main line via an ancestral daughter. In medieval times, husbands and/or sons of these ancestral daughters, usually heiresses, might also take the woman's surname. Also, this was a time when younger sons would have changed their surnames to match the estates of the families they married into.[74]

The estimated age of the FT24860 subclade roughly matches the father (or possibly grandfather) of Lang Will Graham and John Graham of Gillesbie as shown in Figure C-8 and 41. Note: Figure C-8 is a notional first guess at the structure of the Border Graham Big Y breakout based on available data as of April 2023 and is likely to change as Y-DNA data is updated.[75]

**J1 L1253>FT24860 Postulated Y-DNA breakdown of Border Grahams**

---

[73] Family Tree DNA, "Scientific Details Haplogroup J-L1253," Copyright 2022-2023 Gene by Gene, Ltd., accessed 28 April 2023. https://discover.familytreedna.com/y-dna/J-L1253/scientific

[74] J.E. Corrie, *Records of the Corrie Family, 802-1899 A.D.* (London: Mitchell and Hughes, 1899), 133. https://archive.org/details/recordsofcorrief01corr

[75] YFull, "YTree v10.07.00 Classic Chart for the J1/Y3441/L1253 Haplogroup," YFull.com, 16 November 2022. https://www.yfull.com/chart/tree/J-Y3441/

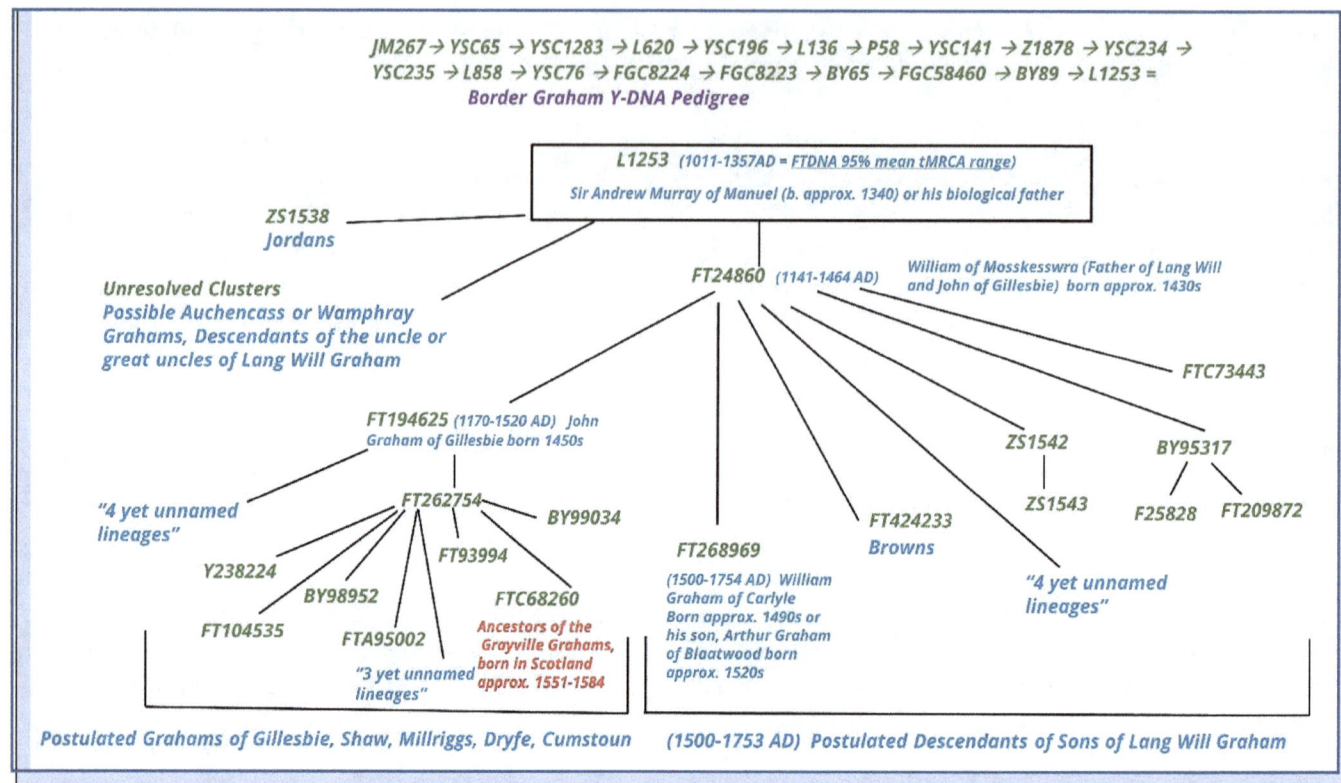

*Figure C-8: NOTIONAL J1 Big Y Breakout-First Guess[76, 77] Note: My candidate patriarchs are consistently 110 to 140 years to the right (more recent) than FTDNA estimates.[78]*

| Projected descendants of John Graham of Gillesbie (born circa 1450s), brother of Lang Will Graham. | J1 L1253>FT24860>FT194625[79] |
|---|---|

---

[76] FamilyTreeDNA, "Graham DNA Surname Project Results."

[77] FamilyTreeDNA, "J-FT24860 Haplogroup Story," Copyright 2022-2023 Gene by Gene, Ltd., accessed 15 April 2023. https://discover.familytreedna.com/y-dna/J-FT24860/story

[78] It is possible that the Graham J1s are atypical, like the Royal Stewarts (R-S781), and do not fit the FTDNA algorithmic assumptions as suggested by Belinda Dettmann, Graham Project co-administrator.

[79] Tom Field, Co-Administrator of the FTDNA England GB EIJ Y-DNA Project, has stated some concerns regarding FT194625 as it is in the centronomic region of the Y chromosome. That means it is located on a portion of the Y that connects to the X chromosome and is considered unreliable by at least one testing company (YSEQ). Tom has embarked on an independent study of Graham/Jordan/Noble J1 Big Y results to verify test members' relations to each other. For more information, join the England Great Britain Groups EIJ, E I J G R T England Scotland Wales Ireland Norman & Diverse Others" project: https://www.familytreedna.com/groups/england-gbgroups-eij/activity-feed

*Appendix C: Y-DNA*

| | |
|---|---|
| Ancestors of the Grayville Grahams and closest Y-DNA cousin, born in Scotland approx. 1551-1584 (based on genetic distance on the cousin match). Ancestors of Grayville Grahams left Scotland for Ireland circa 1641, while ancestors of closest Y-DNA cousin remained in Scotland until the 19th century. | J1 L1253>FT24860>FT194625 >FT262754>FTC68260 [80] |
| Projected descendants of a son of Lang Will Graham, known as the chief of the Border Grahams. | J1 L1253>FT24860>FT424233 "Browns and relatives." [81] |
| Possible descendants of the Grahams of Blaatwood, descendants of William Graham of Carlisle, younger son of Lang Will Graham. [82] | J1 L1253>FT24860>FT268969 |
| Theorized descendants of a son of Lang Will Graham, known as the chief of the Border Grahams. | J1 L1253>FT24860>ZS1542 |
| | J1 L1253>FT24860>BY95317 [83] |
| Unofficial Jordan sept clan of Clan Graham may have been formed by the marriage of a Jordan heiress to a Graham male between 1300 and 1518. | J1 L1253>ZS1538 "Jordans and relatives." [84] |
| Need Big Y test to determine detailed ancestry of this group. | J1-L1253: Typical Border Grahams. J-M267>YSC0000076>FGC8224>BY65>BY89>L1253 /Z18194. "Suggest BigY test." [85] |
| Projected descendants of a son of Lang Will Graham, known as the chief of the Border Grahams. | J1-L1253 "Typical Border Grahams." ZS1542. [86] |
| **Group 3: IM253 (Nordic) Haplogroup Represents 7% of the project members** | **I Group Type 1**<br><br>I-M253 is associated with Scandinavia. I-M253 skeletons were found in Oxford, England, from 880-1000A.D. Suspected victims of St Bryce's Day Massacre, 13 November 1002 A.D. Also found in Viking graves in Norway (8th-16th century), Estonia (8th century), and Russia (11-12th century). [87] |

---

[80] FamilyTreeDNA, "Big Y-DNA Barry Scott Graham," FamilyTreeDNA, accessed 30 December 2022. https://www.familytreedna.com/my/ydna/matches/detail-view (Restricted access)

[81] FamilyTreeDNA, "Graham DNA Surname Project Results."

[82] Alicia Graham, "Fergus Graham of Mossknowe, a.k.a.: Fergus the Rascal," *Clan Graham Society Newsletter*, November 2022. https://clangrahamsociety.org/news-resources/#archive (Restricted access)

[84] FamilyTreeDNA, "Graham DNA Surname Project Results."

[85] Ibid.

[86] Ibid.

[87] Roberta Estes, "442 Ancient Viking Skeletons Hold DNA Surprises – Does Your Y or Mitochondrial DNA Match?"

| | |
|---|---|
| 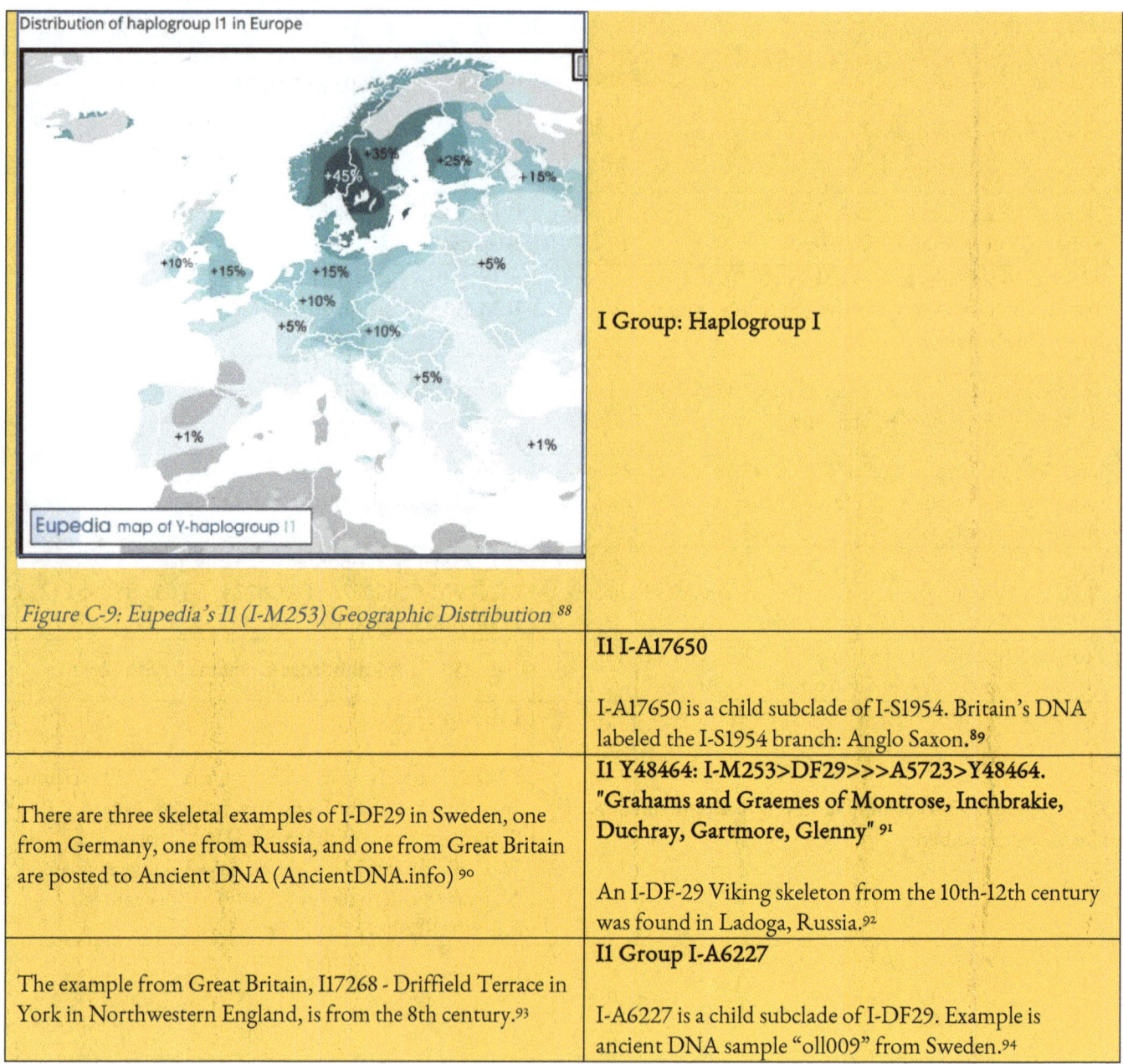<br><br>Figure C-9: Eupedia's I1 (I-M253) Geographic Distribution [88] | **I Group: Haplogroup I** |
| | **I1 I-A17650**<br><br>I-A17650 is a child subclade of I-S1954. Britain's DNA labeled the I-S1954 branch: Anglo Saxon.[89] |
| There are three skeletal examples of I-DF29 in Sweden, one from Germany, one from Russia, and one from Great Britain are posted to Ancient DNA (AncientDNA.info) [90] | **I1 Y48464:** I-M253>DF29>>>A5723>Y48464. "Grahams and Graemes of Montrose, Inchbrakie, Duchray, Gartmore, Glenny" [91]<br><br>An I-DF-29 Viking skeleton from the 10th-12th century was found in Ladoga, Russia.[92] |
| The example from Great Britain, I17268 - Driffield Terrace in York in Northwestern England, is from the 8th century.[93] | **I1 Group I-A6227**<br><br>I-A6227 is a child subclade of I-DF29. Example is ancient DNA sample "oll009" from Sweden.[94] |

---

[88] Figure C-9: Maciamo Hay, "Haplogroup I1 (Y-DNA)," Eupedia.com, last updated October 2021. https://www.eupedia.com/europe/Haplogroup_I1_Y-DNA.shtml

[89] "Ancestral DNA Marker Pedigree Display for I-A17650," GeneticHomeland.com, accessed 14 December 2022. https://www.genetichomeland.com/welcome/dnapedigree.asp?snp=A17650&Chromosome=Y&snp2=&DB=0

[90] Carlos Quiles, Jari Kinnunen, and Jean Manco, "Ancient DNA: https://ancientdna.info. Map based on public dataset on www.haplogroup.info. (www.indo-european.eu)," *Haplotree Information Project* (parameters: I-DF-29), accessed 30 December 2022. https://haplotree.info/maps/ancient_dna/slideshow_samples.php?searchcolumn=Y_Haplotree_Variant&searchfor=I-DF29&ybp=500000,0

[91] FamilyTreeDNA, "Graham DNA Surname Project Results."

[92] "Ancestral DNA Marker Pedigree Display for Y48464," GeneticHomeland.com, accessed 14 December 2022. https://www.genetichomeland.com/welcome/dnapedigree.asp?snp=Y48464&Chromosome=Y&snp2=&DB=0

[93] Carlos Quiles, Jari Kinnunen, and Jean Manco, "Ancient DNA: https://ancientdna.info. Map based on public dataset on www.haplogroup.info. (www.indo-european.eu," Haplotree Information Project, I-DF-29.

[94] "Ancestral DNA Marker Pedigree Display for I-A6227," GeneticHomeland.com, accessed 14 December 2022. https://www.genetichomeland.com/welcome/dnapedigree.asp?snp=A6227+&Chromosome=Y&snp2=&DB=0

| | |
|---|---|
| A Viking skeleton in Lagdoga, Russia, is DF29 from the 10th-12th centuries.<br><br>A second Viking skeleton was identified in Ladoga, Russia, and classified as IM253 from the 11th-12th centuries.<br><br>Since the oldest I-DF29 skeletal samples are the three from Sweden, it appears the origin of I-DF29 may be Sweden.[95] | **I1 Group I-BY172227**<br><br>I-BY172227 is a child subclade of I-DF29. Example is ancient DNA sample "oll009" from Sweden.[96] |
| | **I1d1 Subgroup: Haplogroup I1d1(I-P109) "Scandinavian"**<br><br>Example is ancient DNA sample "VK549" from 8th century Viking grave in Salme, Estonia.[97] |
| | **I1 Group I-Y4741**<br><br>I-Y4741 is a child subclade of Y-4738 and P109. Y4738 is believed coincident with Y4735. Example is ancient DNA sample "VK295" from 10th century Viking grave in Hessum, Funen, Denmark.[98] |
| | **I1b1 Group I-FGC21735**<br><br>I-FGC21735 is a child subclade of I-P109. Example is ancient DNA sample "VK549" from 8th century Viking grave in Salme, Estonia.[99] |
| | **I1b1 Group I-L1483**<br><br>L1483 is a child subclade of I-Y8334. Example is ancient DNA sample "VK327 "from 11th century Viking grave in Ribe, Denmark.[100] |

---

[95] Carlos Quiles, Jari Kinnunen, and Jean Manco, "Ancient DNA: https://ancientdna.info. Map based on public dataset on www.haplogroup.info. (www.indo-european.eu," Haplotree Information Project, I-DF-29.

[96] "Ancestral DNA Marker Pedigree Display for I-BY172227," GeneticHomeland.com, accessed 14 December 2022. https://www.genetichomeland.com/welcome/dnapedigree.asp?snp=BY172227+&Chromosome=Y&snp2=&DB=0

[97] Carlos Quiles, Jari Kinnunen, and Jean Manco, "Ancient DNA: https://ancientdna.info. Map based on public dataset on www.haplogroup.info. (www.indo-european.eu," Haplotree Information Project, I-P109, accessed 30 December 2022. https://haplotree.info/maps/ancient_dna/slideshow_samples.php?searchcolumn=Y_Haplotree_Variant&searchfor=I-P109&ybp=500000,0

[98] Carlos Quiles, Jari Kinnunen, and Jean Manco, "Ancient DNA: https://ancientdna.info. Map based on public dataset on www.haplogroup.info. (www.indo-european.eu," Haplotree Information Project, I-Y4738, accessed 30 December 2022. https://haplotree.info/maps/ancient_dna/slideshow_samples.php?searchcolumn=Y_Haplotree_Variant&searchfor=I-Y4738&ybp=500000,0

[99] Carlos Quiles, Jari Kinnunen, and Jean Manco, "Ancient DNA: https://ancientdna.info. Map based on public dataset on www.haplogroup.info. (www.indo-european.eu," Haplotree Information Project, I-P109.

[100] Carlos Quiles, Jari Kinnunen, and Jean Manco, "Ancient DNA: https://ancientdna.info. Map based on public dataset on www.haplogroup.info. (www.indo-european.eu," Haplotree Information Project, I-BY463, accessed 30 December 2022. https://haplotree.info/maps/ancient_dna/slideshow_samples.php?searchcolumn=Y_Haplotree_Variant&searchfor=I-BY463*&ybp=500000,0

*Appendix C: Y-DNA*

| | |
|---|---|
| **Group 4: EM35 Haplogroup. Represents 2% of project members.** "A significant proportion of Jewish male lineages are M35. M35, which accounts for approximately 18% to 20% of Ashkenazi and 8.6% to 30% of Sephardi Y-chromosomes. It appears to be one of the major founding lineages of the Jewish population."[101] Per Phil Graham: could be descendants of Jerusalem rescuees brought back from the Crusades by Knights such as the Kirkpatricks. | Detailed Y-DNA analysis is needed to determine when this Kirkpatrick-Graham split may have occurred to determine which Graham branch is connected to this group.<br><br>**E Group E1b1a:** Historical and Y-DNA evidence suggest these Grahams may be genetically Colquhons/Calhouns and Kirkpatricks.[102] |
| | **E Group: Haplogroup E1b1b1.**[103] Britain's DNA labeled this branch: Elmenteitan.[104] |
| **Group 5: Remaining project members. Each subgroup is under 2%**[105] | **G Group G2a2b.** A child subclade of L1259, believed to have originated in Anatolia during the Neolithic Age.[106] |
| | **J2 Group:** J1 and J2 split from the J Haplogroup 30,000 years ago. Of Middle Eastern origin. Join the "England GB Group EIJ" project page to participate in discussions on J1, J2, as well as the E and I haplogroups and others and their presence in Britain.[107] |
| | **N Haplogroup:** Britain's DNA labeled this branch: Siberian.[108] |
| | **Q Group:** Britain's DNA labeled this branch: Altai and formerly Yenisei.[109] |
| | **R1a: Haplogroup R1a:** R1a and R2 split about 22,000 years ago. Ancient R1a samples can be found throughout Asia.[110] |

---

[101] Jayne Ekins, "Y-DNA Haplogroup: E1b1b and E1b1a," Your DNA Guide (blog), accessed 29 December 2022. https://www.yourdnaguide.com/ydgblog/ydna-haplogroup-e

[102] FamilyTreeDNA, "Calhoun/Colquhoun Y-DNA Surname Project Results," accessed 30 December 2022. https://www.familytreedna.com/public/calhoun/default.aspx?section=ycolorized

[103] FamilyTreeDNA, "Graham DNA Surname Project Background."

[104] "Ancestral DNA Marker Pedigree Display for E1b1b1," GeneticHomeland.com, accessed 22 April 2023. https://www.genetichomeland.com/welcome/dnapedigree.asp?snp=E1b1b1&Chromosome=Y&snp2=&DB=0

[105] FamilyTreeDNA, "Graham DNA Surname Project Results."

[106] "Ancestral DNA Marker Pedigree Display for G2a2b," GeneticHomeland.com, accessed 22 April 2023. https://www.genetichomeland.com/welcome/dnapedigree.asp?snp=G2a2b&Chromosome=Y&snp2=&DB=0

[107] England Great Britain Groups EIJ, E I J G R T England Scotland Wales Ireland Norman & Diverse Others," Activity Feed, FTDNA Surname Project, accessed 22 April 2023. https://www.familytreedna.com/groups/england-gbgroups-eij/activity-feed (Requires account.)

[108] "Ancestral DNA Marker Pedigree Display for N(M231)," GeneticHomeland.com, accessed 22 April 2023. https://www.genetichomeland.com/welcome/dnapedigree.asp?snp=n&Chromosome=Y&snp2=&DB=0

[109] "Ancestral DNA Marker Pedigree Display for Q(M242)," GeneticHomeland.com, accessed 22 April 2023. https://www.genetichomeland.com/welcome/dnapedigree.asp?snp=q&Chromosome=Y&snp2=&DB=0

[110] "Ancestral DNA Marker Pedigree Display for R1a(L657.1)," GeneticHomeland.com, accessed 22 April 2023. https://www.genetichomeland.com/welcome/dnapedigree.asp?snp=r1a&Chromosome=Y&snp2=&DB=0

*Appendix C: Y-DNA*

# Ancient Origins

**R-M269-R1b**. Of the 330 members in the R1b/R-M269 group, a large majority are in the "Pre-Norman" category (e.g. Ancient Celt, Ancient Viking, Germanic). This would reflect the population of the time. The locals outnumbered the Norman arrivals. William II (William Rufus) and Henry I of England were concerned about their Norman deputies being spread thin in the northern territories. As a result, Henry I deputized 30 trusted local men in Yorkshire to serve as a northern extension of his royal court. One of the "trusted men" was Forne Sigulfson, a descendant of the Danes who had previously controlled Yorkshire.[111] On another note, of the eight subgroups in the "Post-Norman Conquest" or Norman R1b category, three were of Iberian origin, indicating that the "Norman" families who immigrated to Britain after the conquest came from all over France and bordering regions, such as Spain and Flanders.

**J-M267-J1 L1253**. The latest Y-DNA results indicate this rare Middle Eastern J1 Y-DNA type may have arrived in Scotland during the late Bronze Age (circa 1400 B.C.).[112] Arriving at this timeframe required us to first dissect the unique Y-DNA profile or subclade/ SNP tree for the Border Graham and Jordan J1s:

*Figure C-10: Haplogroup Tree/Y-DNA Pedigree of Graham J1s and Jordan J1s (J-YSC76 Highlighted)* [113]

## Levant Ancient Origin.

Starting with the YSC76 in the J1 Graham "Y-DNA family tree" above, genealogists are in general agreement this subclade originated in the Levant region (Israel, Lebanon, Southern Turkey) 4,000 to 4,900 years ago.[113] Skeletal samples of YSC76's child subclades, FGC8224 and FGC8223,[114] support this hypothesis.

*Figure C-11: Haplogroup Tree/Y-DNA Pedigree of Graham J1s and Jordan J1s (J-FGC8224/8223 Highlighted)* [113]

---

[111] Paul Dalton, "Feudal Politics in Yorkshire, 1066 x 1054," (PhD Thesis, University of Sheffield, 1990), 11, 47, 50. https://etheses.whiterose.ac.uk/1870/

[112] Robin Spencer, "Comments on determining age of the J1-L1253 Haplogroup, England Great Britain Groups EIJ, E I J G R T England Scotland Wales Ireland Norman & Diverse Others," Activity Feed, FTDNA Surname Project, accessed 20 October 2002. https://www.familytreedna.com/groups/england-gbgroups-eij/activity-feed (Requires account.)

[113] Maciamo Hay, "Haplogroup J1 (Y-DNA)," Eupedia.com.

[114] Carlos Quiles, Jari Kinnunen, and Jean Manco, "Ancient DNA: https://ancientdna.info. Map based on public dataset on www.haplogroup.info. (www.indo-european.eu)," Haplotree Information Project (parameters: J-FGC8224/FGC8223), accessed 30 December 2022. https://haplotree.info/maps/ancient_dna/slideshow_samples.php?searchcolumn=Y_Haplotree_Variant&searchfor=J-FGC8224&ybp=500000,0

## Appendix C: Y-DNA

AncientDNA.info by the Haplotree Information Project, an effort by volunteer and professional geneticists to organize Ancient DNA data in a single, easy-to-use database,[115] documents six ancient J1 skeletal samples discovered in Jordan and Lebanon in the early 1990s. The skeletal samples are FGC8224 and its child subclade FGC8223. Two of the FGC8223 samples and three of the FGC8224 samples were found in northwestern Jordan, in Baqah, which is near the modern border with Israel and considered "Southern Levant" in the archaeological catalogues. The skeletons found in Jordan were dated 3200-3300 years before present (ybp) where "present" is defined as 1950, as that is the average birth year of the typical Y-DNA test subject, which means 1350 B. C. - 1250 B. C. The sixth skeleton (FGC8223) which was found near Beirut, Lebanon was dated 2415 ybp.[116] Of note: both FGC8224 and FGC8223 were simultaneously found in the Levant region, the Arabian peninsula, and Iberia, which suggests an event or closely spaced cluster of events that spread those similar groups far apart.[117] We will come back to the discussion of what events could have caused this spreading out or "diaspora," but we first need to look at what happened in Britain.

Country Frequency of FTDNA Test Members

As recommended by Dr. Robin Spencer, let's look at the nationalities of the test volunteers starting with the BY65 subclade. According to the FTDNA Discover™ page as of April 2023 for this type, BY65 is the first subclade going down the Graham J1 tree where there is a significant drop in test subjects from Middle Eastern countries as

Figure C-12: Haplogroup Tree/Y-DNA Pedigree of Graham J1s and Jordan J1s Showing Timeframe of British-Middle Eastern Split [118],[119],[121]

compared to those from English speaking countries. It is a decrease from 44% (FGC8223) down to 12.7% (BY65).[118] Going further down the Graham J1 tree, the FGC58460,[119] BY89 and L1253 types have even fewer (12.4%, 5%, 0% respectively)[120] test subjects remaining who identify as originating from Middle Eastern countries.[121] This indicates the geographic split between the British J1 branches and its Middle Eastern cousins happened between the beginning of

---

[115] Carlos Quiles, Jari Kinnunen, and Jean Manco, "Ancient Y-DNA and mtDNA," Indo-European.eu, accessed 30 December 2022. https://indo-european.eu/ancient-dna/

[116] Carlos Quiles, Jari Kinnunen, and Jean Manco, "Ancient DNA: https://ancientdna.info. Map based on public dataset on www.haplogroup.info. (www.indo-european.eu)," Haplotree Information Project (parameters: J-FGC8224/FGC8223), accessed 30 December 2022. https://indo-european.eu/ancient-dna/

[117] Abu-Amero, Khaled K., Hellani, Ali, González, Ana M. et al. Saudi Arabian Y-Chromosome diversity and its relationship with nearby regions. BMC Genet 10, 59 (2009). https://doi.org/10.1186/1471-2156-10-59

[118] FamilyTreeDNA. "Scientific Details Haplogroup J-BY65," Country Frequency, Copyright 2022-2023 Gene by Gene, Ltd., accessed 8 April 2023. https://discover.familytreedna.com/y-dna/J-BY65/frequency?view=table

[119] FamilyTreeDNA, "Scientific Details Haplogroup J-FGC58460," Copyright 2022-2023 Gene by Gene, Ltd., accessed 8 April 2023. https://discover.familytreedna.com/y-dna/J-FGC58460/story

[120] There is a large error margin in using the self-reported country of the test subjects as up to 40% of test subjects did not report their country.

[121] FamilyTreeDNA. "Scientific Details Haplogroup J-BY89," Copyright 2022-2023 Gene by Gene, Ltd., accessed 8 April 2023. https://discover.familytreedna.com/y-dna/J-BY89/story

BY89 and the point just before the Scottish L1253 branched off from BY89.[122] This equates to **2050 B.C. to 300 B.C.** which is a wide spread. By studying the English J1s, and making the assumption the English and Scottish J1s are derived from the same patriarch, we can narrow down the timeframe of the J1 arrival in Britain and also determine the time of the subsequent English-Scottish split.[123]

## English J1s.

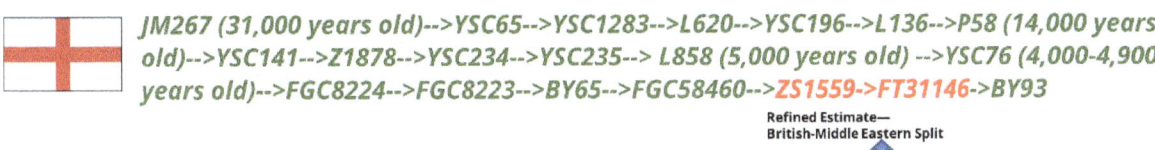

Figure C-13: *Haplogroup Tree/Y-DNA Pedigree of English J1s Showing Refined Estimate of British-Middle Eastern Split* [126, 127]

English J1 surnames include[124] Baker, Corder, Crouch, Cuffley, Day, and Robinson[125] per the FTDNA Scottish DNA Project. See English J1 pedigree in Figure C-13. The FTDNA Discover™ page for the next subclade down the English J1 tree, ZS1559, shows 21% of its test members[120] who identified as from the Middle East.[126] Its child, FT31146, has zero members[i] that identified from Middle Eastern countries.[127] Therefore, we can conclude that ZS1559 did not originate in Britain, but its child subclade FT31146 did originate in Britain, and estimate that the J1 arrival from the Middle East occurred around the time of the formation of FT31146, when it breaks off from ZS1559, which is after 1950 B.C. The FTDNA Discover page then further estimates that the most recent common ancestor of this line is estimated to have been born (tMRCA) around **1417 B.C.**

In other words, current Y-DNA analysis, based on the assumption that the Scottish and English J1s descended from the same patriarch, indicates the J1 progenitors arrived in Britain approximately **1417 B.C.**

---

[122] Robin Spencer, PhD, "Comments on determining age of the J1-L1253 Haplogroup," England Great Britain Groups EIJ, FamilyTreeDNA.com, accessed 30 December 2022. https://www.familytreedna.com/groups/england-gbgroups-eij/activity-feed (Requires account.)

[123] Robin Spencer, PhD, "Extending Time Horizons with DNA," FamilySearch.org, 8 March 2022. 1:00:45. https://www.youtube.com/watch?v=wppXD1Zz2sQ

[124] FamilyTreeDNA, "Scottish Y-DNA Project Results," FamilyTreeDNA.com, accessed 30 December 2022. https://www.familytreedna.com/public/Scottishdna?iframe=ycolorized

[125] FamilyTreeDNA, "JL1253 News," FamilyTreeDNA.com, accessed 30 December 2022. https://www.familytreedna.com/groups/j-1c-3d-with-snp-l1253/about/news

[126] FamilyTreeDNA, "Scientific Details Haplogroup J-ZS1559," Copyright 2022-2023 Gene by Gene, Ltd., 8 April 2023. https://discover.familytreedna.com/y-dna/J-ZS1559/story

[127] FamilyTreeDNA, "J-FT31146 Haplogroup Story," Copyright 2022-2023 Gene by Gene, Ltd., accessed 8 April 2023. https://discover.familytreedna.com/y-dna/J-FT31146/story

## J1 Arrival in Scotland

If the J1 arrived in England around 1417 B.C., when did it arrive in Scotland?

Scenario 1: the J1-FGC58460/ZS1559/FT31146 that is found in England arrived in England first and then the English J1s migrated to Scotland.

Scenario 2: the J1s arrived in Scotland and England concurrently. In this scenario: two distantly related J1 men from the Middle East could have arrived together as a part of the army or navy that arrived in Britain about 1417 B.C. The first man would have had the BY89 (Scottish) mutation and the other the ZS1559 (English) mutation. The remains of ancient Egyptian boats discovered in 1937 in North Ferriby, Yorkshire, that were radiocarbon dated to approximately **1400 to 1350 B.C.**[128] would support the concurrent scenario. The Yorkshire boats could have been part of a larger fleet heading further north to Scotland.

*Figure C-14: Scota and Gaedel Glas (Gaythelos) in a 15th century manuscript of Bower's Scotichronicon*[128]

Scenario 3: the J1s arrived in Scotland with the Romans circa 73 A.D.

Using the FTDNA Discover™ Haplogroup Story summaries, the Scottish J1 progenitor would have arrived in Scotland <u>after</u> the formation of subclade BY89, which means after 2050 B.C.,[129] but before L1253 branched off of BY89 -- circa 300 B.C.[130] This progenitor was probably born towards the end of this time period (closer to 300 B.C.), which is a still a little bit too early to match Scenario 3, Roman arrival timeline[ii] (55 B.C. in England to circa 73 A.D. in Scotland).[131] These results are a slightly better match for Scenario 2 where they arrived concurrently or Scenario 1, where the J1s arrived in England first, and then migrated to Scotland. As more data is collected, the optimum scenario should become clearer.

---

[128] Lorraine Evans, *Kingdom of the Ark: The Startling Story of how the Ancient British Race is Descended from the Pharaohs* (London: Simon & Schuster, 2000), 1-17.

Figure C-14: Wikimedia Commons contributors, "File:Scota & Gaedel Glas.jpg," *Wikimedia Commons,* accessed 14 April 2023. https://commons.wikimedia.org/w/index.php?title=File:Scota_%26_Gaedel_Glas.jpg&oldid=307368053

[129] FamilyTreeDNA, "Haplogroup Story J-L1253," FamilyTreeDNA.com, accessed 8 February 2023. https://discover.familytreedna.com/y-dna/J-L1253/story

[130] FamilyTreeDNA, "Scientific Details Haplogroup J-L1253."

[131] The Antonine Wall, "The Romans in Scotland," Antoninewall.org, accessed 15 December 2022. https://www.antoninewall.org/about-the-wall-the-romans-in-scotland

*Appendix C: Y-DNA*

## Could the Legends Be Based on Fact?

The 1417 B.C. timeframe for arrival in Britain projected by Y-DNA analysis lines up with the arrival in Ireland in the legends of Princess Scota of Egypt, her husband Gaythelos, and their army. Princess Scota and Gaythelos are key figures in the story of the Foundation of Scotland. Despite inconsistencies in the various story versions, several ancient chroniclers (e.g., author of *Historia Brittonum*, Manetho, John of Fordun) have these story elements in common[132]: the Scots were named after Scota, a daughter of an Egyptian Pharoah; Scota's husband, was a Greek warrior, of "Scythian" ancestry,[133] called "Gaythelos," whom the Gaels are named for; Scota and Gaythelos were driven from Egypt and settled in what is now Galicia in Northern Spain, and then later left Spain and settled in Ireland. Scota's alleged grave site is near Munster in County Kerry, Ireland.[134] The stories tell how Scota and Gaythelos' descendants later migrated to Scotland.

## What We Do Know.

In ancient Egypt, succession[135] was matrilineal, wherein descent to the throne was determined through the female line. Ancient Celtic and Pictish tribes also practiced matrilineal succession through the Iron Age.[136] Coincidentally, the Pictish tribes from ancient Scotland also share Y-DNA with the Basques of Northern Spain. (R1b-S530).[137]

During a 1955 dig at the Hill of Tara in County Meath, Ireland, Dr. Sean O'Riordan, an archaeologist of Trinity College, Dublin, discovered skeletal remains dated to the Bronze Age believed to be those of a young prince.[138] The Hill of Tara is an ancient ceremonial and burial site in County Meath, Ireland.[139] Tradition identifies the hill as the inauguration place and seat of the High Kings of Ireland. Around the boy's neck was a rare necklace of faience beads made from a mixture of plants and minerals. Carbon dating results of the skeleton: **1359 B.C.** The design of the beads shows them to be Egyptian. Coincidentally, Tutankhamun, the boy king, was interred in Egypt during this timeframe. Both Tutankhamun's mummy and the Tara skeleton had the same golden collar around their neck, which was inlaid with matching conical, blue-green faience beads.[140] An excavation at a Bronze Age burial ground in Devon, England, also yielded a similar necklace.[141]

---

[132] Damian Beeson Bullen, "Nefrubity and Princess Scota," Academia.edu, accessed 28 December 2022. https://www.academia.edu/45466704/NEFERUBITY_and_PRINCESS_SCOTA

[133] Robert Alexander Stewart Macalister, *Lebor gabála Érenn: The book of the taking of Ireland*, Part IV (Dublin: Educational Company of Ireland, Ltd., 1941), 207. https://archive.org/details/leborgablare04macauoft

[134] ActiveMe, "Queen Scotia's Grave Walk, Scotia's Glen, Tralee, Kerry, Ireland," Active Me Irelands Travel Guide, accessed 15 December 2022. https://www.activeme.ie/guides/queen-scotias-grave-walk-scotias-glen-kerry/

[135] Moustafa Gadalla, "Matrilineal/Matriarchial Society," Egyptian Wisdom Center, accessed 8 November 2022. https://egyptianwisdomcenter.org/matrilineal-matriarchal-society/

[136] Kathleen O'Connor, "Early and Iron Age Celtic Society," Women in Ancient Celtic Society, accessed 8 November 2022. https://ancientcelticwomen.weebly.com/society.html

[137] Roberta Estes, "You Might Be a Pict If ..." DNAeXplained-Genetic Genealogy (blog), 24 August 2013. https://dna-explained.com/2013/08/24/you-might-be-a-pict-if/

[138] David Halpin, "Thoth's Storm: New Evidence for Ancient Egyptians in Ireland?" Ancient Origins, 19 June 2021. https://www.ancient-origins.net/opinion-guest-authors/thoth-s-storm-new-evidence-ancient-egyptians-ireland-005187

[139] Lorraine Evans, *Kingdom of the Ark: The Startling Story of how the Ancient British Race is Descended from the Pharaohs*, 1.

[140] Natalia Klimczak, "Exploring the Little Known History of Celtic Warrior in Egypt," Ancient Origins, 4 January 2016. https://www.ancient-origins.net/history/exploring-little-known-history-celtic-warriors-egypt-005100

[141] Heather Elizabeth Adams-Osborn, "The Story of Princess Scota, Atlantis, Egypt, and Ireland: The Story of Princess Scota," Ancient Mysteries, ARE, February 2007.

## Appendix C: Y-DNA

The main book presented the two strongest theories for the parents of Princess Scota: Thutmose I whose reign is estimated at 1525-1512 B.C. and Pharoah Akhenaton and Queen Nefertiti (their joint reign was 1353 to 1336 BC). Other stories name pharaohs: Ramses II, Friel, Nectanebo I, Necho II, and Neferhotep I as Scota's father.[142] However, the reigns of those five pharaohs are much further away in time as indicated by Y-DNA results as of April 2023. Once Y-DNA analysis is updated, the new age estimates of the haplogroups may better suggest which theory is the best fit.

Figure C-15: Phoenician Trade Routes and Trading Bases [144] Creative Commons License CC BY-SA 3.0

### King Fergus I.

According to the *Scotichronicon,* a chronicle of the early kings of Scotland, the first king of Scotland was Fergus I (**330 B.C. to 305 B.C.**). He traveled to Scotland from Ireland to help the local Scots fight the Picts and Britons and was a descendant of Princess Scota.[143] Coincidentally, the appearance of Fergus I fits within the arrival time estimate for the J1 haplogroup in Scotland.

### Three other possible scenarios to explain the arrival of J1 in Britain in the Bronze Age:

1. Phoenician Trader option: Phoenicia was an ancient Semitic-speaking, nautical civilization that originated in the Levant region of the eastern Mediterranean, primarily in/near modern-day Lebanon—which is also the theorized origin of J-M267 (J1)/YSC76. Famous for their mastery of ancient maritime navigation and shipbuilding, the Phoenicians were likely the first to survey the Mediterranean Sea, beginning the modern field of geography, the first to use celestial navigation, and they were the first Mediterranean people to venture past

---

https://www.researchgate.net/publication/277713025_'Atlantis_Egypt_and_Ireland_The_Story_of_Princess_Scota'_Ancient_Mysteries_A RE_Feb_2007 (Must request copy from author.)

[142] Henry Kwadwo Amoako, "Did Queen Scotia Really Exist in The Days of The Biblical Moses?" African Research Consult, 22 March 2022. http://african-research.com/research/did-queen-scotia-really-exist-in-the-days-of-the-biblical-moses/

[143] Jeffrey King, "Scotichronicon," *World History Encyclopedia*, 15 January 2019. https://www.worldhistory.org/Scotichronicon/

the Strait of Gibraltar into the Atlantic Ocean. The Phoenicians also conducted an important transit trade, especially in the manufactured goods of Egypt and Babylonia. From the lands of the Euphrates and Tigris, regular trade routes led to the Mediterranean. In Egypt, the Phoenician merchants soon gained a foothold. They alone were able to maintain a profitable trade in the anarchic times of the 22nd and 23rd dynasties (circa 945 to circa 730 B.C.).[144] **The earliest the Phoenicians may have been in Britain was about 700-800 B.C.** based on the establishment of their trading bases in Gibraltar circa 950 B.C.,[145] and Carthage in 813 B.C.,[146] records of their distant voyages in search of tin, and discovery of Phoenician monuments and coins in Britain dated as early as 400 B.C.[147] This theory is at least 650 years later than the April 2023 Y-DNA estimate for the arrival of J1s in Britain.[148]

2. <u>Picts option.</u> The Picts from North and Eastern Scotland are assumed to have been the descendants of the Caledonii and other Iron Age tribes that were mentioned by Roman historians. Per Irish legends and a statement in Bede's[149] history, the Picts apparently practiced matrilineal kingship succession,[150] a similar custom practiced in ancient Egypt. There is also the connection to Spain that the Picts and Egyptian origin legends have in common. Recently, **Y-DNA analysis indicates the Picts originated in Iberia, perhaps were relatives of the Basques, and believed to have arrived in Scotland circa 7000-8000 B.C.** There is an R1b/L1335 marker of Pictish heritage that was recently discovered,[151] but the entire Pictish civilization likely had more than one Y-DNA type. The R1b/L1335 is the one survivor that genealogists have identified so far.

3. The <u>Syrian Archer Theory</u> is expounded in "Syrian Scots on the Borderlands" by Jim Farmer. Mr. Farmer theorizes that the J1 Y-DNA arrived in Scotland with Syrian Archer auxiliaries to the Roman army left behind when the Romans withdrew in 410 A.D.[152] Thanks to Y-DNA cousin David Noble, I learned of a website called "Scaled Innovation" on the extinction rates of male lines. The site is run by Dr. Robin Spencer from the England Groups EIJ Y-DNA Project and includes a tool for calculating the extinction of male lines and is based on fertility rates. If it is assumed, on average, that there were two births per man in the period we are talking about, Mr. Spencer's model suggests that 98% of male lines go extinct after an average of 6.4 generations. So, estimating that there were 500 Syrian archers mustered and sent to the British Isles in the year 130 A.D., then after 6.4 generations (average generation of 30 years)--or 192 years, only 10 lines would have survived.[153] So,

---

[144] Ryan Schleeter, "First Rulers of the Mediterranean," *National Geographic Resource Library*, updated 20 May 2022. https://education.nationalgeographic.org/resource/first-rulers-mediterranean

Figure C-15: Wikimedia Commons contributors, "File:Phoenician trade routes (eng).svg," *Wikimedia Commons*, accessed 14 April 2023. https://commons.wikimedia.org/w/index.php?title=File:Phoenician_trade_routes_(eng).svg&oldid=694327570

[145] "A Brief History of Gibraltar," Gibraltar Timeline, accessed 8 November 2022. http://gibraltartimeline.com/brief-history-of-gibraltar/

[146] Salim George Khalaf, "Phoenician Canaanite History Timeline," Phoenicia.org, accessed 8 November 2022. https://phoenicia.org/phoeniciatimeline.html

[147] Lawrence Austine Waddell, *The Phoenician Origins of Britons, Scots and Anglo-Saxons*, Chapter 2 (London: Williams and Norgate, 1924), 16-19. https://www.jrbooksonline.com/pob/pob_toc.html

[148] Department of Ancient Near-Eastern Art, "The Phoenicians 1500-300 B.C.," The Metropolitan Museum of Art, October 2004. https://www.metmuseum.org/toah/hd/phoe/hd_phoe.html

[149] Tom Garlinghouse, "Who were the Picts, the Early Inhabitants of Scotland?" Live Science, updated August 2022. https://www.livescience.com/who-were-picts-scotland

[150] Benjamin Hudson, *The Picts* (New York: John Wiley & Sons, 2014), 35.

[151] Roberta Estes, "You Might Be a Pict If ...."

[152] Jim Farmer, "Syrian Scots on the Borderlands," Academia.edu, 9 June 2009. https://www.academia.edu/36354861/Syrian_Scots_on_the_Borderlands_No_Pics

[153] Robin Spencer, PhD, "The Extinction of Lines," Tracking Back-A Website for Genetic Genealogy Tools, Experimentation and Discussion, Scaled Innovation, 31 March 2020. http://scaledinnovation.com/gg/extinctionDemo.html

while it is technically possible that one Syrian Y-DNA line survived from 1900 years ago, it is not as likely. In addition, this theory is 1,547 years later than the April 2023 Y-DNA estimate for the arrival of J1s in Britain.

## Arguments against Arabic origin for J1-L1253.

The peoples known as Arabs did not exist in the Bronze Age (3300 B.C. to 1200 B.C.), the age that includes the estimated arrival timeframe of the J1 in Britain. Even if the L1253 creation estimate is revised to more recent Roman times, YFull shows that the primary Arab subclade, FGC12, is too young to be a "fifth great-grandparent" of L1253. FGC12 was formed 3300 years before present.[154]

JM267 (31,000 years old)-->YSC65-->YSC1283-->L620-->YSC196-->L136-->P58 (14,000 years old)-->YSC141-->Z1878-->YSC234-->YSC235--> L858 (5,000 years old) -->YSC76 (4,000-4,900 years old)-->FGC8224-->FGC8223-->BY65-->FGC58460-->BY89-->L1253

A reminder that the unique Y-DNA profile or subclade tree for the Border Graham and Jordan J1s is as follows:

*Figure C-16: Haplogroup Tree/Y-DNA Pedigree of Graham J1s and Jordan J1s (With Ancient Subclades P58 and L858 Highlighted)* [155]

Important notes from Eupedia.com, which is based on several Y-DNA analytical papers, concerning J1-P58: Looking at their map in Figure C-7.

It is easy to assume that P58 is a marker of Arabic ancestry because it reaches its maximum frequency in and around the Arabian peninsula. That would be an oversimplification. It is important to make a clear distinction between people who speak Arabic and those who are genetically Arabic. The confusion comes from the fact that the Arabic language as we know it today, appeared a little more than 1,500 years ago.[155]

Arabic is a language that originates from the Arabian peninsula, where many different dialects used to exist. With the birth of the Islamic religion, the Arabic language became fixed to the dialect that was used[156] to write the Quran in approximately 500 A.D.

More clarification from Eupedia.com: Arabic is "much more recent than the haplogroup J1 (31,000 years old) or even the P58 subclade (14,000 years old). Even the J1-L858 subclade (5,000 years old), associated with Southwest Asian people, predates the Arabic language. The common ancestor of the J1-L858 men alive today dates back to approximately 4,500 years ago, a time that corresponds to the development of the oldest Semitic languages." "L858 covers all the region

> **Did you know?**
> Sephardic Jews were from Iberia, "Sepharad" being the Hebrew word for Spain. Ashkenzai Jews were from Germany and Eastern France, "Ashkenaz" being the Hebrew word for Germany.

---

[154] Yfull, "Yfull Tree for J-FGC11," YFull.com, accessed 30 December 2022. https://www.yfull.com/tree/J-FGC11/

[155] Maciamo Hay, "Haplogroup J1 (Y-DNA)," Eupedia.com.

[Did you know? Blurb] Tracey R.Rich, "Ashkenazic and Sephardic Jews," Judaism 101, accessed 16 December 2022. https://www.jewfaq.org/ashkenazic_and_sephardic

[156] Mille Larsen, "How Old is the Arabic Language, and Where Did it Come From, A Look at Three Historical Arabic Languages," Autolingual, accessed 16 December 2022. https://autolingual.com/arabic-how-old/

where ancient Semitic languages were spoken, well before Arabic existed. That is why *L858 should be seen as more widely Semitic and not just Arabic, even if the many Levantines and Mesopotamians were later Arabicized."* i.e. The British J1s were not descendants of Arabs, as the peoples known as "Arabs" did not exist when the British J1 ancestors left the Middle East.

The subclade that belongs to the historic Arab people who settled in the Syrian Desert, which includes Jordan, Lower Mesopotamia, and Saudi Arabia[157] is **J1-FGC12**, a "grandchild" subclade of J1-L858. All branches of J1-L858 (S640, YSC76 and FGC11) can be found in Europe. Per Eupedia, the time of divergence of the L858 branches in the Late Bronze Age to Iron Age suggests that "they would have arrived in Europe with the Phoenicians (Sicily, Sardinia, Spain), and later in greater numbers with the Jewish diaspora." [158]

Regarding the Jewish diaspora, which occurred as a result of Roman evictions in the first and second centuries: the analysis of Y-DNA samples in the Jewishdna.net database, which has verified the Jewish heritage of all participants, indicates the presence of subclades FGC8224 and FGC8223 in Spain.[159] For similar Y-DNA to be spread so far in multiple directions (Lebanon, Spain, Arabia, Iran, Turkey, Greece) about the same timeframe indicates an event that would have caused such a quick dispersal, such as the Roman evictions in Israel.[160] Of note, FGC8224 is also a parent subclade of known Jewish subclades, specifically Cohanim.[161] The Iberian Ashkenaz Y-DNA project also classifies descendants of the FGC8223 subclade as "Possible Sephardic" Jews.[162]

More arguments against Arabic origin: The authors of "Origin and Diffusion of Human Y Chromosome Haplogroup J1-J-M267," who performed extensive analysis of Y-DNA samples from West Asia, Mesopotamia, and the Levant, concur with the summary from Eupedia.com. They disagree with previous studies that attributed J1 geographic distribution to Arab conquests connected to the spread of Islam. They cite the absence of representatives of other Arab populations in the same areas and timeframes as the J1 locations. They argue that the J1 distribution was already shaped before the Arab conquests, also noting that autosomal DNA studies support their conclusion that the J1/YSC76 origin was in the region of N. E. Syria, S. E. Turkey, and N. W. Iran.[163] The founders then migrated south to the Arabian peninsula, Southern Levant, and southern Mesopotamia, where the P58 branch evolved in the early Holocene period (11,700 years before the present, after the last glacial period). Per the authors of "Saudi Arabian Y-Chromosome diversity and its relationship with nearby regions," the J1/J-M267 diversities found in southern Saudi Arabia and Yemen are comparatively high relative to Turkey." This southwards decreasing trend is more compatible with a Neolithic (Stone Age: 12,000 years ago) arrival to Arabia via the Levant, as proposed by others."[164]

---

[157] C.E. Bosworth, "'ARAB i. Arabs and Iran in the pre-Islamic period," *Encyclopaedia Iranica*, II/2, 201-203, accessed 30 December 2012. http://www.iranicaonline.org/articles/arab-i

[158] Maciamo Hay, "Haplogroup J1 (Y-DNA)," Eupedia.com.

[159] Wim Penninx, "Jewish Group of Branches: J1-Other," JewishDNA.net, accessed 28 December 2022. https://jewishdna.net/J1-other.html

[160] H. Sahakyan, A. Margaryan, L.Saag, *et al.*, "Origin and diffusion of human Y chromosome haplogroup J1-M267," *Scientific Reports* 11, 6659 (2021). https://doi.org/10.1038/s41598-021-85883-2

[161] Maciamo Hay, "Haplogroup J1 (Y-DNA)," Eupedia.com.

[162] FamilyTreeDNA, "Iberian Ashkenaz Background," FamilyTreeDNA.com, accessed 8 April 2023. https://www.familytreedna.com/groups/iberian-surnamesof-ashkenaz/about/background

[163] H. Sahakyan, A. Margaryan, L.Saag, et al., "Origin and diffusion of human Y chromosome haplogroup J1-M267."

[164] Khaled K. Abu-Amero, Ali Hellani, Ana M. González, *et al.*, "Saudi Arabian Y-Chromosome diversity and its relationship with nearby regions," BMC Genetics **10**, 59 (2009). https://doi.org/10.1186/1471-2156-10-59

*Appendix C: Y-DNA*

## Border Graham J1 Patriarch.

Analysis indicates the J1 Grahams and J1 Jordans descend from a single patriarch. As detailed in Appendix F, "Border Graham Genealogy," the strongest candidate to be the J1 Graham Patriarch is Sir Andrew Moray/Murray of Manuel, armor bearer to King David II or his biological father. Sir Andrew was likely born between the 1330s and 1340s, as he first married around 1363 and is the suspected spouse of Agnes de Graham. Agnes was the daughter and heir of John de Graham, son of Richard, who received land gifts from Sir John de Graham "the Last" lord of Dalkeith circa 1360-1362. The Brackenwra and Hutton lands and former Dalkeith Graham advowson rights were later found in the custody of the Border Grahams.[165] Per the People of Medieval Scotland (PoMS) database, Agnes married an Andrew with an unknown surname in or just before 1363. Andrew Murray of Manuel is the best fit among the 16 possible Andrews (Table F-1).[166] Andrew de Murray is the right age, and while his second wife is known, Janet Kirkintilloch (Kirkhalche), his first wife is unknown.[167]

Coincidentally, the Moray lands that should have been Sir Andrew's inheritance wound up in the hands of the Douglases in July 1362,[168] so that might explain his immediate need in 1362/1363 to seek an heiress. His estates are the closest to the Graham estates of Elphinstone and Abercorn of the "Andrew candidates." Sir Andrew Murray of Manuel is recorded as a cousin to David II and a descendant and heir of Sir Andrew de Moray, the Regent (d. 1338), and his second wife Christian Bruce, sister of Robert I (d. about 1358). No record can be found to confirm Sir Andrew of Manuel as a biological son of the Regent, only a descendant. Sir Andrew of Manuel is significantly younger in age compared to the other sons of Sir Andrew the Regent (Sir John of Moray died without heirs in 1351, and Earl Thomas of Moray died of the plague while serving as a hostage in England in 1361,[169] also without heirs). Considering Christian Bruce would have been in her forties, nearing the end of her childbearing years, when she married the elder Sir Andrew in 1323,[170] she was likely too old to be the biological mother of Sir Andrew of Manuel. Therefore, Sir Andrew of Manuel was more likely a grandson versus a son of Sir Andrew the Regent, perhaps via an unnamed daughter. With the early deaths of Sir John and Sir Thomas de Moray without children, the next in line to be named as heir would be a grandson, even via a daughter. If Sir Andrew of Manuel was in the direct male line to the famous Sir Andrew the Regent, one would expect history to preserve his father's name and for him to have a stronger claim to the Murray lands transferred to the Douglases in July 1362. The Murray Y-DNA Surname Project confirms the Morays, the earls of Sutherland and the "Black and Red Douglases," [171] were descendants of Freskin de Moravia, were R-M269/DF-27

---

[165] T.J. Carlyle, *The Debateable Land* (Dumfries, W.R. McDarmid and Co., 1868), 10. https://ia600206.us.archive.org/0/items/debateablelandr00carlgoog/debateablelandr00carlgoog.pdf

[166] PoMS, "Person Search for Sixteen Andrews," accessed 30 October 2022. https://www.poms.ac.uk/search/?index_type=person&q=andrew&min_date=1315&max_date=1371

[167] Figure C-17: Author: "B," The Chiefship of the Clan Murray,' *The Scottish Antiquary, or, Northern Notes and Queries*, Vol. 15, No. 58 (Edinburgh University Press, October 1900): 72. https://www.jstor.org/stable/25516988

[168] William Fraser, *Douglas Book*, Vol. 1 (Edinburgh: T. and A. Constable, Edinburgh University Press, 1885), 352. https://digital.nls.uk/histories-of-scottish-families/archive/96806202?mode=transcription

[169] David Dalrymple, *Annals of Scotland from The Accession of Robert I, Surnamed Bruce, to The Accession of the House of Stewart* (Edinburgh: Balfour and Smellie, 1879), 249. https://www.google.com/books/edition/Annals_of_Scotland_From_the_Accession_of/POMUSyU9KfoC?hl=en&gbpv=1&dq=thomas+moray+died+1361&pg=PA249&printsec=frontcover

[170] John Maitland Thomson, *Register of the Great Seal of Scotland, A.D. 1306-1424* (Edinburgh: H.M. General Register House, 1912), 461. https://www.google.com/books/edition/The_Register_of_the_Great_Seal_of_Scotla/ZbI3AQAAMAAJ?hl=en

[171] Morvern French, "The Barony of Kervale and its Links with some Key Moray Families," University of St. Andrews, 20 March 2015. https://flemish.wp.st-andrews.ac.uk/2015/03/20/the-barony-of-kerdale-and-its-links-with-some-key-moray-families/

(Iberian) in origin. The project administrators are trying to recruit test subjects who are known descendants of Sir Andrew Murray of Manuel's eldest son William Murray of Touchadam to determine his paternal line.[172]

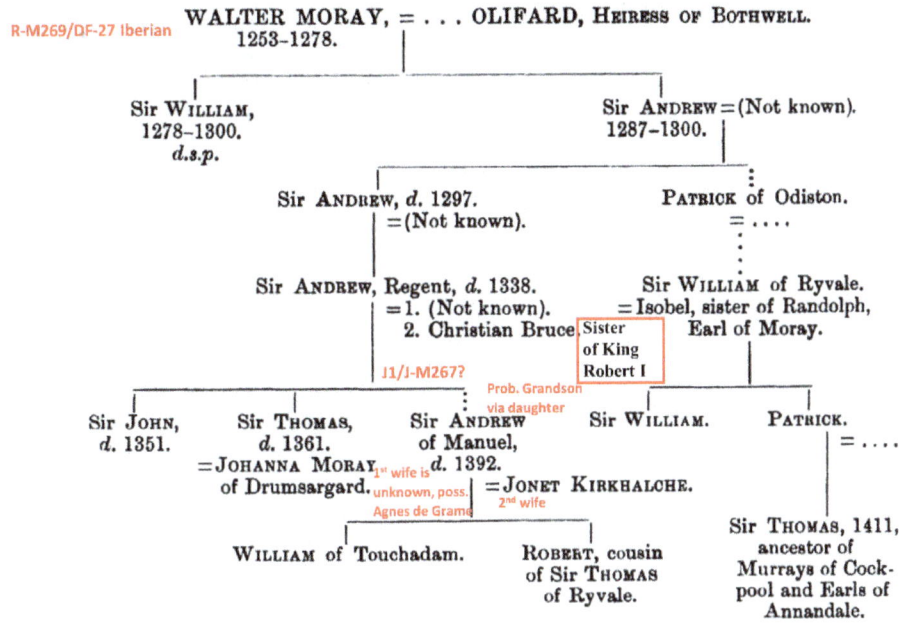

*Figure C-17: Pedigree of Sir Andrew de Murray of Manuel, J1 Graham Patriarch Candidate from The Chiefship of the Clan Murray, Author: "B." The Scottish Antiquary, or, Northern Notes and Queries, Oct., 1900, Vol. 15, No. 58 with modifications in red.* [167]

## Fergus the Rascal.

An Aside regarding Rev. William Graham and his Grandson Fergus Graham of Mossknowe, a.k.a.: "Fergus the Rascal." While illegitimate children can throw a monkey wrench into Y-DNA studies, researchers hope that the illegitimacy rates are low enough to allow the productive study of paternal lines. The Grahams of Mossknowe, particularly Fergus Graham of Mossknowe, a.k.a. "Fergus the Rascal," were so exceptional in the numbers of illegitimate children produced that they require a mention. Fergus Graham of Mossknowe, born circa 1690, was the son of William and grandson of Rev. William Graham.[173] When Rev. William Graham married Margaret Irving/Irvine, "David Irvine of Moskow," Margaret's father, assigned on 26 July 1657 to William Graham, 40s lands of old extent of Mossknow, and 40s lands of Righeids; and of an apprising of the lands of Skaillis led by Irvine against Arthur Irvine of Skaillis." In other words, William Graham received as a dowry for marriage to Margaret Irvine, 40 shillings worth of land in Mossknowe, 40 shillings of land in Righeids, and the promise of lands in Skaillis[174] if the foreclosure against Arthur Irvine was successful.

---

[172] "Murray Clan DNA Research Project," FamilyTreeDNA.com, accessed 28 December 2022. https://www.familytreedna.com/groups/murray/about/background

[173] Alicia Graham, "Fergus Graham of Mossknowe, a.k.a.: Fergus the Rascal."

[174] Figure C-18: John Thomson, "Dumfriesshire," *Atlas of Scotland, 1832, National Library of Scotland*, accessed 27 December 2022. https://maps.nls.uk/view/74400175

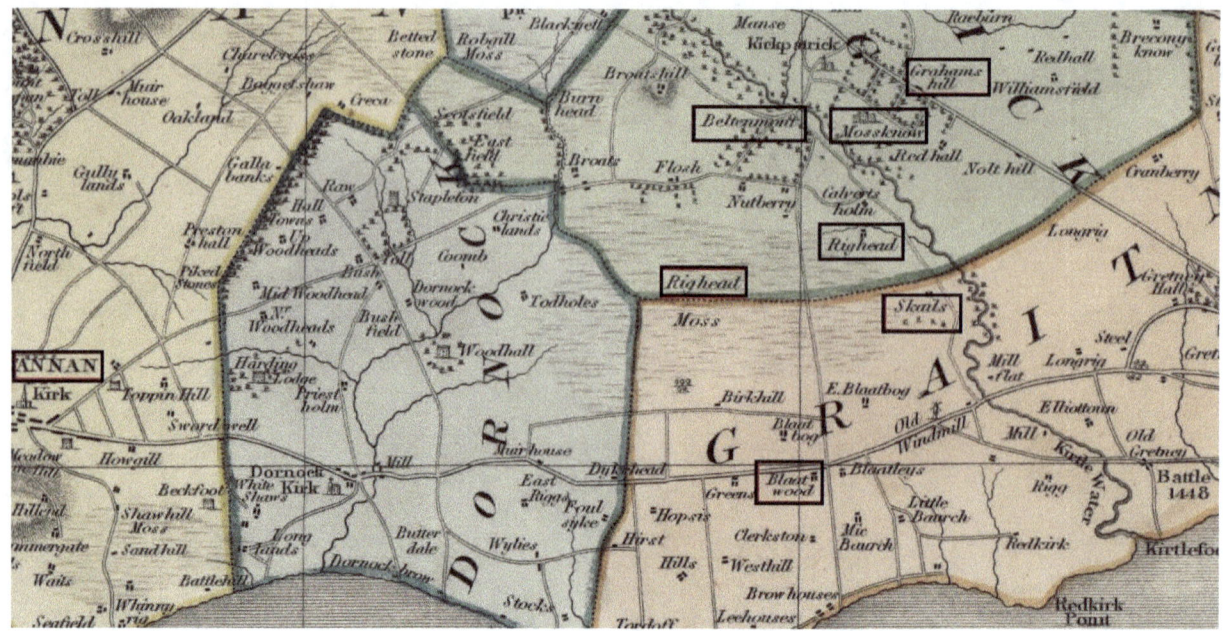

*Figure C-18: Kirkpatrick-Fleming and Graitney Parishes, John Thomson's 1832 Atlas of Scotland* [174]
*Creative Commons License* CC-BY 4.0 *Reproduced with the permission of the National Library of Scotland.*

In the Mossknowe Papers, T. Carlyle Aitken claims that Rev. William Graham was the son of Fergus Graham of Blaatwood[175] (namesake of the 12th century Lord Fergus of Galloway) and, therefore a great-great-grandson of Lang Will Graham (1468-1540) of the Border Grahams from Appendix F. The reverend was more likely the son of Fergus' brother, William Graham of Blaatwood and Rosina Scott of Beltenmont. Beltenmont is next to Mossknowe and was part of the Graham of Mossknowe estate by 1875. Fergus of Blaatwood's son William was the provost of Annan (1669/1683), and therefore he did not live near Mossknowe.[176]

Per the minutes of the Middlebie Presbytery in southern Dumfriesshire, Fergus was in continual trouble with the Presbytery from 1710 to the 1720s for living in sin/fornicating with a number of ladies. Luckily the Presbyterian minutes name the females also being charged along with Fergus Graham of Mossknowe: first Janet Irving, then Mary Irving (mother of four children by Fergus), Janet Fullerton (three children by Fergus, who "removed to England"), Mary McCubbin (one child), and Katherine Douglas. These ladies may have married and taken their husband's surnames for themselves and their children, which could account for other surnames in the mix like Noble, Bennett, Irving, etc. From the minutes, we also know that Fergus' brother-in-law was David Graham, a minister from Langholm, and that Fergus was a Jacobite who was involved in the "Rising of 1715," [177] a failed revolt of Jacobites in an attempt to put a Stuart back on the throne.

The Jacobites were taken prisoner, convicted, and deported to the American colonies as indentured servants. They were required to work under indenture to reimburse the Crown for their ship passage. We have an affirmation signed on 14 January 1716 by Captain Edward Trafford of the Elizabeth and Anne that he left Fergus Graham from

---

[175] National Records of Scotland, Graham of Mossknowe Papers (GD1/403/25) (see also GD1/403/45).

[176] C.L. Johnstone, *The Historical Families of Dumfriesshire and the Border Wars*, CHAPTER XII, Ancient Provosts of Annan (Dumfries: Anderson & Son, 1889), 61, 168, 202. https://archive.org/details/historicalfamili00grah

[177] W. F. Cormack, "Fergus Graham of Mossknow, and the Murder at Kirkpatrick," *Transactions of the Dumfries and Galloway Natural History and Archaeological Society (TDGNHAS)* No. 3064, Vol 64 (1989): 94-97. https://dgnhas.org.uk/sites/default/files/transactions/3064.pdf

"Kilpatrick," Scotland, in Yorktown, Virginia, with 111 other "rebell prisoners." By "Kilpatrick," they likely meant "Kirkpatrick Fleming," as Kilpatrick and Kirkpatrick were used interchangeably.[178] There was also a separate record of a David Graham from "Kilpatrick" who arrived in Yorktown on the ship Goodspeed in July 1716,[179] but his indenture was sold to a man from Maryland.[180] The Yorktown prisoners were transferred to Fort Christianna, near current-day Brunswick County, Virginia. Fort Christianna was shut down in 1718,[181] the same year Fergus surprised the Middlebie Presbytery with his presence, as documented in their August 1718 minutes.[182] So Fergus was definitely in Virginia starting in January 1716, and he definitely returned to Scotland by August 1718.

Fergus' time in Virginia (1716-1718) is important, as it explains why an American member of the Graham Surname Project, who is a J1, with ancestral ties to Brunswick County, Virginia from before the American Revolution, is a "very tightly related" match (zero genetic distance at 67 markers) to other J1 men whose families apparently never left Britain. None of them are surnamed "Graham" but share the J1/L-1253 Y-DNA profile unique to Grahams. The first British settlers, in what was to become Brunswick County, swarmed into the relatively protected lands near Fort Christianna during its four years of operation (1714–1718), i.e. a source of females for "Fergus the Rascal."[183] Females of the local native Sapony tribe near Ft. Christianna were "very true to their husbands" and "wouldn't let you touch them," per the observation of traveler John Fontaine in his journal in 1716.[184] Therefore, it is unlikely that Fergus would have been able to take a Sapony mistress during his stay as a prisoner at Ft. Christianna.

More recent Big Y analysis indicates Fergus' descendants may fall within FT268969, (Figure C-8) which is a child subclade of FT24860 (theorized subclade of the father of Lang Will Graham) and a grandchild subclade of L1253. In summary, there is enough evidence to warrant deeper investigations into Fergus and his grandfather, Rev. William Graham, as potential ancestors of J1 Graham surname project members who are not surnamed "Graham."[185]

---

[178] Kirkpatrick of Closeburn, (London: George Norman, 1863), 2. https://archive.org/details/kirkpatrickofclo00kirk/page/n6/mode/1up?ref=ol&view=theater&q=kilpatrick

[179] Hugh Tornabene, "Jacobite Rebellion Ships," Immigrant Ships Transcribers Guild, 1 August 2007. https://immigrantships.net/jacobite/indexjacobite.html

[180] David Dobson, *Directory of Scots Banished to the American Plantations, 1650-1775* (Baltimore: Genealogical Publishing Co., 1984), 61. https://www.google.com/books/edition/Directory_of_Scots_Banished_to_the_Ameri/QZDSAQ9CRGQC?hl=en&gbpv=1&bsq=graham

[181] John & Alexander Fontaine and Edward Porter, *The journal of John Fontaine; an Irish Huguenot son in Spain and Virginia*, 1710-1719 (Williamsburg, Virginia: Colonial Williamsburg Foundation, 1972; distributed by the University Press of Virginia).

[182] *Fergus Graham of Mossknow, and the Murder at Kirkpatrick*, by W. F. Cormack, DGNHAS, Vol 64, 1989.

[183] Alicia Graham, "Fergus Graham of Mossknowe, a.k.a.: Fergus the Rascal."

[184] John Fontaine, and Edward Porter Alexander, *The journal of John Fontaine; an Irish Huguenot son in Spain and Virginia*, 1710-1719 (Williamsburg, Virginia: Colonial Williamsburg Foundation, 1972), 92.

[185] FamilyTreeDNA, "Graham DNA Surname Project Results."

*Appendix C: Y-DNA*

# Graham Origins

The name "Graham" has over 300 documented spelling variations, as well as Sept and Cadet clans: Airth, Allardice, Allardyce, Bonar, Bonnar, Bontein, Bontine, Buntain, Bunten, Buntine, Bunting, Graeme, Grahame, Grahym, Grayham, Grim, Grymn, Hadden, Haldane, Macgibbon, Macgilvernock, McIlverock, Macgrime, Maharg, Menteith, Monteith, Pitcairn, Pye, Pyott, Warnock.[186] Some were known by the location or name of their estate (e.g., Gillespie, Kirkpatrick, Montrose, Moffat, Dalton, Menteith, Nethery/Netherby).[187]

## Proposed origin of the first man surnamed Graham, William de Graham:

Danish Theory. Per my theory on the origin of William de Graham summarized in the main book, the father of William de Graham was the first lord of Greystoke, Forne Sigulfson. Forne was one of Henry I's trusted men in the northern territories, an extension of his royal court.[188] Forne was a descendant of the Danes who had formerly controlled Yorkshire.[189] The surname Greystoke may have very well started out as "Gristock," as the barony contains the ancient village of Grisdale, which is Norse for "valley of the boars."[190] Gristock is a variant of Greystoke seen in early documents. "Gris" is Norse for boar or pig.[191] "Stoc" was used for house or

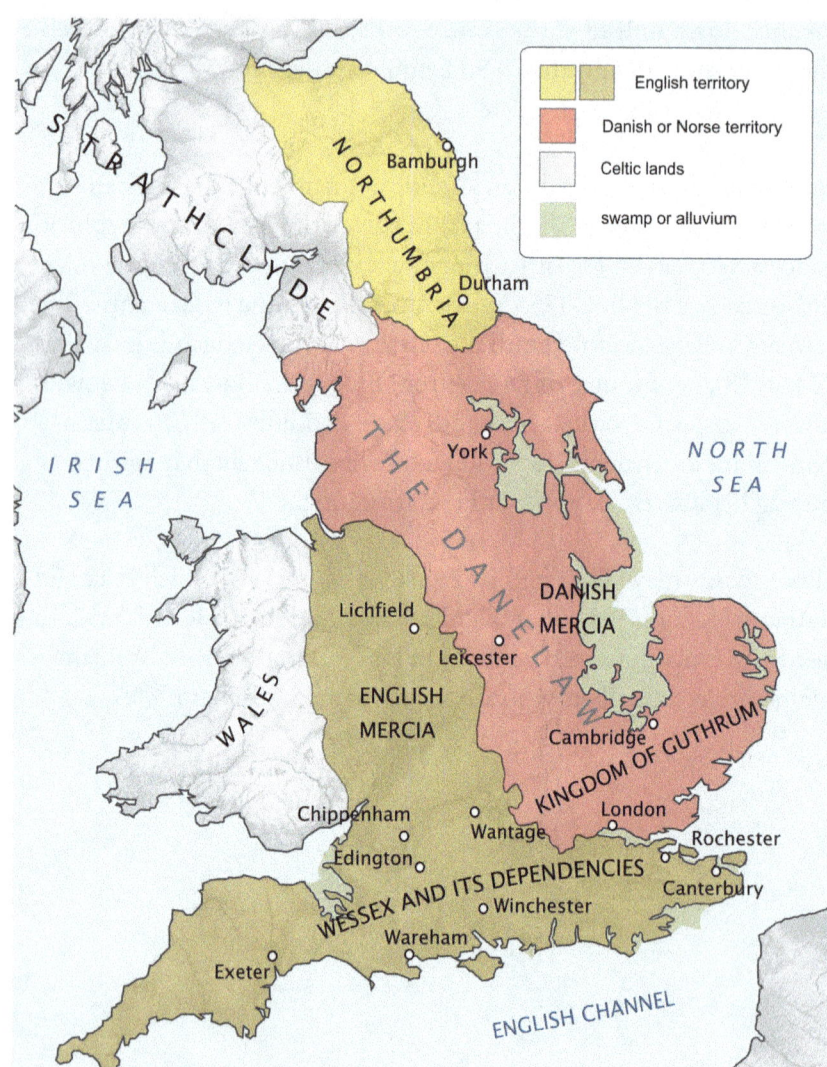

*Figure C-19: Ethnicities in Britain Prior to the Norman Invasion (878 A.D.)[186] Creative Commons License CC BY-SA 3.0*

---

[186] Figure C-19: Ethnicities in Britain Prior to the Norman Invasion (878 A.D.) Wikimedia Commons contributors, "File:England 878.svg," *Wikimedia Commons, the free media repository,* accessed 6 December 2022. https://commons.wikimedia.org/w/index.php?title=File:England_878.svg&oldid=702681650

"Graham," Electric Scotland, accessed 30 December 2022. https://electricscotland.com/webclans/dtog/graham.html

[187] George Fraser Black, and Mary Elder Black, *The Surnames of Scotland: Their Origin, Meaning, and History* (New York: New York Public Library, 1946), 323-324. https://babel.hathitrust.org/cgi/pt?id=mdp.39015011274175&view=1up&seq=415&q1=graham

[188] Paul Dalton, "Feudal Politics in Yorkshire, 1066 x 1054," (PhD Thesis, University of Sheffield, 1990), 11, 47, 50. https://etheses.whiterose.ac.uk/1870/

[189] Stephen M. Lewis, Université de Caen Normandie, Forne Sigulfson-"The 'First' Lord of Greystoke in Cumbria," The Wild Peak (blog), 2013. https://thewildpeak.wordpress.com/2013/03/30/forne-sigulfson-the-first-lord-of-greystoke-in-cumbria/

[190] Stephen M. Lewis, Université de Caen Normandie, "Grisdales of Matterdale, Grisdale 1332," The Wild Peak (blog), 2013. https://grisdalefamily.wordpress.com/tag/barons-of-greystoke/

[191] Wiktionary contributors, "gris," *Wiktionary, The Free Dictionary,* accessed 4 November 2022. https://en.wiktionary.org/w/index.php?title=gris&oldid=69567367

farm.[192] However, "gris" is also Latin and French for "gray," so it is understandable how scribes writing documents in Latin could have translated "Gristock" to "Gray-ham." "Ham" is Old English for a "village without a church," hence the word "hamlet." Normans preferred to use "ham" for place, or hamlet.[193] Of note, some Graham family armorials, such as that of Fergus Graham of Mote, include a boar.[194] Y-DNA of a confirmed Menteith and a Montrose descendant, direct male line descendants of William de Graham, have been classified as I-M253, which is Scandinavian,[195] supporting the Danish theory.

## Time to Most Recent Common Ancestor (tMRCA) and the Grayville Grahams.

tMRCA is used in DNA analysis to rate the closeness of DNA matches and estimate the timeframe during which their shared ancestor lived.[196] The MRCA calculator by Bruce Walsh, Department of Ecology and Evolutionary Biology, University of Arizona, published June 2001 by the Genetics Society of America, provides statistical likelihoods for common ancestors of matches in terms of generations vs. years. It compares 67 chromosome marker Y-DNA cousin matches.[197]

The Grayville Graham test subjects, Barry Graham and Ron Graham, are third cousins. Ron and Barry are confirmed descendants of James Thornton Graham (four generations to common ancestor). Barry is a genetic distance (GD) 1 match to Ron. For comparison, the MRCA calculator predicts a 69% chance that for a GD1 (66/67 marker) match, the common ancestor will be within four generations (which it is). Their shared closest Y-DNA match, who is from Canada, is a GD 3 (64 of 67 markers) match to Ron but a GD 4 to Barry. In addition, he is also a GD 5 match of 111 markers to Ron, while a GD 6 of 111 markers to Barry. I learned from Garth Graham, administrator for the Clan Graham Y-DNA Project, that Barry's line had recent mutations, which is confirmed by an examination of his Big Y results. So for comparison purposes, we will use Ron's closer genetic distance results.

The closest Y-DNA match for the Grayville Grahams is from Canada, and like Barry and Ron, took the Big Y test and was matched to **Haplogroup variant J-FTC68260** (Figure C-8). They are currently the only three members of this group. This confirms a tight male-line connection.[198] FTDNA Discover™ More tools estimate a tMRCA at 95% confidence between 1082 and 1724 A.D. for J-FTC68260.[199] However, the records of both families show that their shared ancestor couldn't have been born much after 1640, given when the families split.

---

[192] Wiktionary contributors, "stoc," Wiktionary, The Free Dictionary, accessed 4 November 2022. https://en.wiktionary.org/w/index.php?title=stoc&oldid=68776363

[193] "Hamlet," AlphaDictionary.com, accessed 28 December 2022. https://www.alphadictionary.com/goodword/word/hamlet#:~:text=This%20ham%20was%20borrowed%20from,borrowed%20back%20as%20English%20haunt

[194] Robert Riddle Stodart, *Scottish Arms, Being a Collection of Armorial Bearings A.D. 1370 – 1678* Vol. I, William Patterson (Edinburgh: 1881), n206 (Plate 79A). https://archive.org/details/ScottishArmsV1/page/n205/mode/2up?q=79A

[195] FamilyTreeDNA, "Graham DNA Surname Project Activity Feed."

[196] Robin Spencer, PhD. "Extending Time Horizons with DNA," (video lecture), FamilySearch, 8 March 2022. 1:00:45. https://www.youtube.com/watch?v=wppXD1Zz2sQ

[197] Bruce Walsh, University of Arizona, "Most Recent Common Ancestor Calculator," Genetics Society of America, June 2001. http://www.moseswalker.com/mrca/calculator.asp?q=1

[198] Family Tree DNA (FTDNA) Y-DNA Matches for Barry Scott Graham, FamilyTreeDNA.com, accessed 20 October 2022. https://www.familytreedna.com/my/ydna/matches/detail-view (Restricted access)

[199] FamilyTreeDNA. "Scientific Details Haplogroup J-FTC68260," Copyright 2022-2023 Gene by Gene, Ltd., accessed 8 April 2023. https://discover.familytreedna.com/y-dna/J-FTC68260/story

For a GD3 (64/67 match), the MRCA calculator predicts an 83.9% chance the common ancestor will be in 10 generations, 88.7% in 11 generations, 92.2% in 12 generations, and 94.7% in 13 generations. The GD 5 match (106/111 markers) has more fidelity and indicates a **98.7% chance of a common ancestor in 13 generations.**[200] Barry and Ron confidently know their ancestry to the 10th generation (immigrant James Graham Sr (abt. 1683-1729)). Therefore, the common ancestor shared with their Canadian cousin is more than ten generations back, given the Grayville Graham ancestors arrived in the U.S. from Ireland in 1720 and their Canadian cousin's ancestors remained in Scotland… until migrating to Canada between 1852 and 1861. The results of the GD 5 of 111 markers indicate that the common ancestor is very likely in 11 to 13 generations.[201] If the Grayville Graham ancestors moved to County Fermanagh, Ireland, between 1635 and 1642, as discussed in Chapter 3, then the timing indicates it was probably the grandfather of the immigrant brothers, Christopher, James, William, John, who moved (with the Langholm Armstrongs) to Ireland. Given that our Canadian cousin's ancestors remained in Scotland, the common ancestor between his line and the Grayville Grahams had to be at least one more generation back—i.e., the great-grandfather of the immigrant brothers, or 13 generations. **This common ancestor would likely have been born between 1570 and 1590.** See Figure 22 for the resulting pedigree that reflects the common ancestor between the Grayville Grahams and their closest Canadian cousin.

## Summary

Looking at the four largest groups of the Graham Surname project, which includes the Pre/Post Norman subgroups 1A and 1B (both R1b), and knowing of the inconsistency with surname inheritance before the 1500s, we can conclude that: 1) It is unlikely that the first Graham, William de Graham, was Norman and 2) There were multiple Graham patriarchs.[202] The Clan Graham Society's website explains that "Sept Clans" arose when sons-in-law swore allegiance to their father-in-law's more powerful clan.[203] We have learned that the another way to form a sept, would be through younger sons inheriting their mother's lands or husbands marrying heiresses, who sometimes took the name of the estate, which would be the woman's surname. Regarding the Border Grahams (J1), there is still some debate on the arrival timeframe of J1s in Britain, more specifically in Scotland, and also when the common J1 Graham patriarch was born. As more Y-DNA test subjects come forward and more participate in the Big-Y tests, we may find the answers.

---

[200] Bruce Walsh, University of Arizona, "Most Recent Common Ancestor Calculator."
[201] Roberta Estes, "Concepts—Genetic Distance," DNAeXplained Genetic Genealogy, accessed 20 October 2022. https://dna-explained.com/2016/06/29/concepts-genetic-distance/
[202] FamilyTreeDNA, "Graham DNA Surname Project Background."
[203] Ann Belanger, "Cadets and Septs of the Grahams," Clan Graham Society, accessed 18 October 2022. https://clangrahamsociety.org/about/#septs

## Other Related Y-DNA Surname Projects:

The **Correy** Y-DNA Surname project shows that the Correy/Corrie patriarchs are primarily pre-Norman R-M269, specifically pre-Norman/"Norse Viking" and pre-Norman/"Ancient Celt." More participants in the Correy/Corrie project would be needed to determine specifics. As of June 2021, there are five common Y-DNA pedigrees in the Corey surname project:

1) R-BY91254 (child subclade of L151/P312/U152) Alpine
2) R-FT343957 R1a Vikings
3) R-DC362 (child subclade of L151/P312/Z17669) Triangulation of descendants with the Irish annals suggests this would be a marker of King Lorcan of the Dal Cais of Ireland circa 900 A.D.
4) R-BY158550 (child subclade of L151/P312/U152) Alpine; Corrie of South Africa: R-FGC3222 (child subclade of L151/P312/L21) Beaker Folk/Ancient Celts.[204]

## Cunningham

There are three primary groups in the Cunningham surname project: 1. IM253 (Norse), 2. R-M269/P312/RM222's (Ancient Irish), and 3. the R-M269/U106/**L48's** (Viking), the largest group.[205]

## Dalton

Dalton is a locational surname. Dalton is the parish just to the south of Lochmaben in Dumfriesshire. See John Thomson's 1832 Atlas of Scotland.[206] Looking at the Dalton Surname project,[207] the Dalton participants are mostly R-M269/RM222, Ancient Celts, but there is a 6 GD (105/111 marker) and two more 37 marker matches surnamed Dalton with the Grayville Grahams, indicating the common ancestor once owned land in neighboring Dalton Parish. The closest Dalton match is J-FT262754, the parent subclade of the Grayville Grahams FTC68260.

## Gillespie

Gillespie/Gillesbie is another locational surname. Gillespie was located in Dumfriesshire, just west of the village of Boreland in the Parish of Hutton. See Figure C-20. Grahams in the Calendar of Border Papers and Scottish Privy Council records in the 1500/1600s of Gillespie, Shaw, Dryfe, Millriggs, and Boreland are likely related.[208] In the

---

[204] FamilyTreeDNA, "Corey/Cory Y-DNA Surname Project Results," FamilyTreeDNA.com, accessed 30 December 2022. https://www.familytreedna.com/public/CoryorCorey?iframe=ycolorized

[205] FamilyTreeDNA, "Cunningham Y Chromosome DNA Surname Project Results," FamilyTreeDNA.com, accessed 30 December 2022. https://www.familytreedna.com/public/cunningham?iframe=ycolorized

[206] John Thomson, "Dumfriesshire," *Atlas of Scotland, 1832, National Library of Scotland,* accessed 27 December 2022. https://maps.nls.uk/view/74400175

[207] FamilyTreeDNA, "Dalton America DNA Surname Project Results," FamilyTreeDNA.com, accessed 30 December 2022. https://www.familytreedna.com/public/dalton?iframe=ycolorized

[208] Scotland. *The Register of the Privy Council of Scotland*. Edinburgh, First Series, Volume 9 (H.M. General Register House, 1877), 712-713, 808-809. https://catalog.hathitrust.org/Record/100404514

Gillespie surname project, the primary groups are R-M269/P312/RM222 (Ancient Irish) and, secondly, R-M269/U106/L48 (Viking).[209]

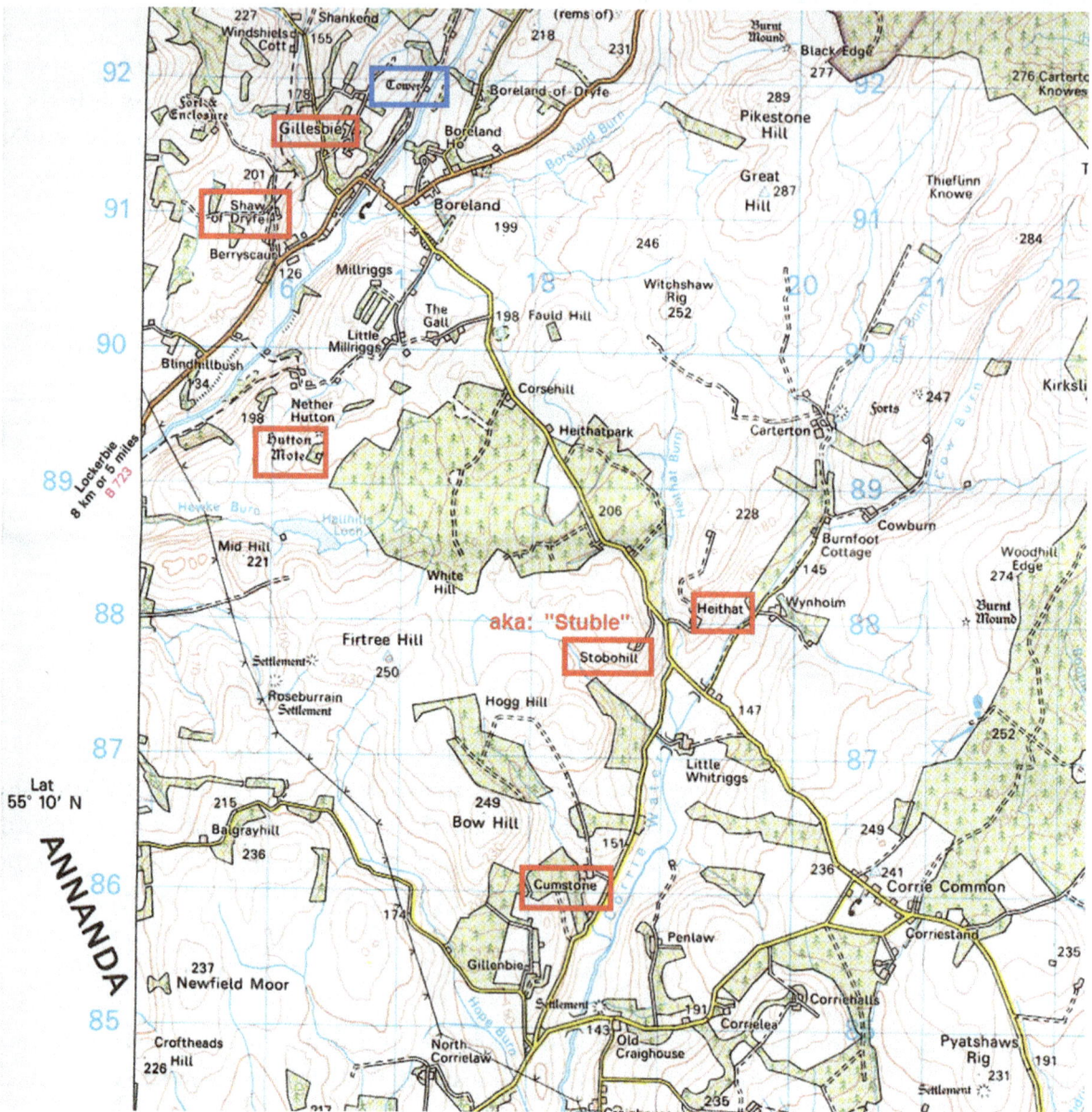

Figure C-20: Map of the Dryfe Valley, Hutton and Corry Parish, in NW Dumfriesshire, Scotland; Ordnance Survey (map GB.) Landranger Series SCALE OF 1; 50 000, SHEET NO 79 HAWICK & ESKDALE (LANGHOLM) Ordnance Survey licence number 100066333. All rights reserved. © Copyright and Database right 2022.

---

[209] FamilyTreeDNA, "Gillespie Y-DNA Surname Project Results," FamilyTreeDNA.com, accessed 30 December 2022. https://www.familytreedna.com/public/GillespieDNAProject?iframe=ycolorized

*Appendix C: Y-DNA*

## Jordan/Jardine

There are four primary groups of Jordans in the Jordan Surname Project: one group of R-M269/DF27s (parent subclade of Iberian child subclades), a second group of R-M269/FCG24158 (Lombards-Norman allies), a third group that shares a Y-DNA profile with the J1 Grahams (J-M267/L1253), and a fourth huge group with members that are unrelated to each other.[210] It became popular about the time of the Crusades (1095-1291 A.D.) to use the surname Jordan,[211] which explains the fourth huge group of unrelated Jordans. The third group of J1 Jordans (and one Jardine) share a Y-DNA profile with the J1 Grahams. Considering the nearly 300 spelling variations of the name "Graham," it isn't too far of a leap to postulate that the French name "Jardine" was corrupted into "Jordan," given the other variations like Jarden, Jardin, Gardener, Jourden, etc. This would explain why a few Jardines also share a J1 Y-DNA profile with some J1 Jordans and J1 Grahams. Of note: the Jardines were granted the lands of Applegarth in Dumfriesshire,[212] which is surrounded by parishes known to be home to Grahams: Lochmaben, Wamphray, Dryfesdale, and Corrie.

## Kirkpatrick

The major Y-DNA groups in the Kirkpatrick project are E-M35 (likely Jewish and match the Coloquons/Calhouns), R-M269/R-P312/ (Beaker Folk-Ancient Celt or Alpine/Saxon, called "Celto-Germanic" by Eupedia.com) and R-M269/R-M222 (Ancient Irish). The last two categories are pre-Norman.[213]

From the historical manuscripts of the Duke of Buccleugh, published in 1897, we read that "The Kirkpatrick traditions have connected this family with Nithsdale at an earlier date than is warranted by charter evidence. The earliest known Kirkpatricks were: 'Ivo' who afterwards circa 1194-1214 became 'Ivo de Kirkpatrick,' and Roger Kirkpatrick who witnessed several charters in Annandale as early as 1194[214] to include a 1218 charter signed by Robert de Brus (IV) granting Roger Crispin the lands of Cuoculeran.[215] The Kirkpatricks appear to have settled in Annandale contemporaneously with the Bruces in the twelfth century, and were certainly closely connected with the Bruces as lords of Annandale."[216]

"The foundation charter of the family of Kirkpatrick" is by the second Robert de Brus of Annandale to one Ivo, without a surname, and conveyed to him and his heirs a place between the fishing of "Blatwod by Annan" and the water of Sark, for the purpose of fishing and spreading of nets. The charter is undated, but Sir William Fraser places it at approximately 1190.[217] A few years later, between 1194 and 1214, William Brus grants another charter to the same

---

[210] FamilyTreeDNA, "Jordan Family Surname DNA Project Results," FamilyTreeDNA.com, accessed 30 December 2022. https://www.familytreedna.com/public/Jordan-Surname-Project?iframe=ycolorized

[211] SurnameDB, "last name: Jordan," SurnameDB.com, accessed 29 December 2022. https://www.surnamedb.com/Surname/Jordan

[212] "Clan Jardine," Scottish American Society, accessed 29 December 2022. http://www.scottishamericansociety.org/id23.html

[213] "Kirk(Kil)patrick/Kilpatrick Results," FamilyTreeDNA.com, accessed 27 December 2022. https://www.familytreedna.com/public/kirkpatrick?iframe=ycolorized

[214] J. Bain, *Calendar of Documents Relating to Scotland preserved in Her Majesty's Public Record Office*, Vol. I, (1108-1272) (London, Edinburgh: H.M. General Register House, 1881), 107, 108, 124.

[215] Sir William Fraser Facsimiles of Scottish Charters and Letters, "Charter by Robert de Brus to Roger Crispin of the lands of Cuoculeran c. 1218," *School of History, Classics and Archaeology Teaching Collections*, University of Edinburgh, accessed 27 February 2023. http://Col.lections.shca.ed.ac.uk/items/show/36

[216] Ruth M. Blakely, "The Brus Family in England and Scotland, 1100-c. 1290," 36.

[217] PoMS, "No. 4645-Ivo de Kirkpatrick person summary," accessed 26 December 2022. https://www.poms.ac.uk/record/person/4645/

man, this time bearing a surname-Ivo de Kirkpatrick. Ivo married Euphemia Bruce, daughter of Robert de Brus, second lord of Annandale.[218]

Sir Roger de Kilpatrick, "Roger de Cella Patricii," was one of those who famously attended to King Robert I in Dumfries when the "perfidious Red Comyn" was slain in Grey Friar's Church in Dumfries.[219] See the "Knights of Annandale" section in Appendix F.

## Moffat

Considered a locational name tied to Scots from Moffat Hills in Dumfriesshire, Scotland.[220] Per the Moffat-Rutherford DNA Surname Project: "All project members of the Moffat-Rutherford Y-DNA project have the R-L21 mutation that characterizes haplogroup R1b1b2a1a2f. They share a common origin with the Ui Neill and Dalcassian Royal Families between 1,500 and 4,500 years ago in northwest Ireland… It is likely that the common ancestor of certain project members came to Lowland Scotland from Ulster during the Dalriadan migrations from around 500 to 700 A.D. These project members share a common ancestor in the last few hundred years and an extremely rare DYS marker value of 7 at 385a. This rare value probably arose after the thirteenth century A.D., when surnames were adopted, as it appears to be associated distinctly with Moffat and Rutherford males."[221]

## Nethery

Nethery/Netherby is a locational surname. Netherby is located in Cumberland, England, just south of the Scottish/English border. The Netherby estate was the home of Lang Will Graham's eldest son, Richard Graham of Netherby. The current family of Netherby are descendants of the Grahams of Plomp. See Appendix G for more on the Grahams of Plomp. From the Graham surname project, it appears the Nethery participants are R-M269/L48,[222] which is a subclade of L151/U106 and matches a Viking skeleton exhumed in Oxford, a possible victim of the St Brice's Day Massacre in Nov 1002 A.D.[223]

Phylogenetic Children: A6703, A6704, BY30290, CTS3104, L47, S21809, Y10968, Y37962, Z9 [224]

---

[218] PoMS, "Transaction Factoid 40943-Confirmation of a fishery at Torduff for monks of Holm Cultram Abbey," accessed 26 December 2022. https://www.poms.ac.uk/record/factoid/40943/

[219] "Events The Shaped The Kirkpatrick Family: 1300-1499," The House of Kirkpatrick, accessed 29 December 2022. https://pppat.tripod.com/index.html

[220] "Moffat Surname Definition," Forebears, accessed 28 April 2023. https://forebears.io/surnames/moffat

[221] FamilyTreeDNA, "Moffat-Rutherford DNA Surname Project—About Us," FamilyTreeDNA.com, accessed 30 December 2022. https://www.familytreedna.com/groups/moffittmoffett/about/results (Requires account.)

[222] FamilyTreeDNA, "Graham DNA Surname Project Results."

[223] Roberta Estes, "442 Ancient Viking Skeletons Hold DNA Surprises – Does Your Y or Mitochondrial DNA Match?"

[224] "DNA Marker Index Data for Marker: R-A6703 on Chromsome: Y," GeneticHomeland.com, accessed 30 December 2022. https://www.genetichomeland.com/welcome/dnamarkerindex.asp?chromosome=Y&snp=A6703
"DNA Marker Index Data for Marker: R-A6704 on Chromsome: Y," GeneticHomeland.com, accessed 30 December 2022. https://www.genetichomeland.com/welcome/dnamarkerindex.asp?chromosome=Y&snp=A6704
"DNA Marker Index Data for Marker: R-BY30290 on Chromsome: Y," GeneticHomeland.com, accessed 30 December 2022. https://www.genetichomeland.com/welcome/dnamarkerindex.asp?chromosome=Y&snp=BY30290
"DNA Marker Index Data for Marker: R-CTS3104 on Chromsome: Y," GeneticHomeland.com, accessed 30 December 2022. https://www.genetichomeland.com/welcome/dnamarkerindex.asp?chromosome=Y&snp=CTS3104
"DNA Marker Index Data for Marker: R-L47 on Chromsome: Y," GeneticHomeland.com, accessed 30 December 2022. https://www.genetichomeland.com/welcome/dnamarkerindex.asp?chromosome=Y&snp=L47

*Appendix C: Y-DNA*

## Royal Stewarts

From the Stewart/Stuart Surname project, the major groups are:

R-M269/L151/P312/Z290/L21/DF13/Z39589.1/R-DF41>S775>S310(L746) **Ancient Celts**, R-Y138948, Earl of Monteith **Ancient Celts,** and

R-DF41>S775>S310(L746)>Z38845>Z17581 **Ancient Celts**, branch of the descendants of James Stewart, 5th High Steward of Scotland. [225]

## Sinclair

The title of First Earl of Sinclair was awarded by King Håkon on 2 August 1379 to a family from Rosslyn who moved north to Orkney and Caithness to accept the title. The St. Clair Research Project is attempting to determine the origins of the first Sinclair family and all its branches.

From the Sinclair Y-DNA Surname project, while there are fourteen different groups,[226] they are all child subclades of R-M269/L151, and all but three include the **L48** (Viking) subclade. R-M269/**L48** is a subclade of L151/U106 and matches a Viking skeleton exhumed in Oxford, a possible victim of the St Brice's Day Massacre in Nov 1002 A.D.[227]

- Sinclairs of Caithness R-U106>Z381>**L48**>Z9 (Z30-)[228]
- Sinclairs of Argyll R-U106>S21>Z381>S263>Z301>S499>**L48**>Z9>Z30>S271>Z2> ~22277095--A >S9342>PF5143>PH765>Y20215
- Sinclairs of Argyll R-U106> Z2265> BY30097> Z381> Z301> **L48**> Z9>Z30>Z27>Z345>Z2>FGC31495>FGC31514>S9342>Y16505>PH3240>Y20215G8i.
- Sinclairs of Argyll R-U106>Z381>**L48**>Z9>Z30>Z2 'negative for Z7'

---

"DNA Marker Index Data for Marker: R-S21809 on Chromsome: Y," GeneticHomeland.com, accessed 30 December 2022. https://www.genetichomeland.com/welcome/dnamarkerindex.asp?chromosome=Y&snp=S21809

"DNA Marker Index Data for Marker: R-Y10968 on Chromsome: Y," GeneticHomeland.com, accessed 30 December 2022. https://www.genetichomeland.com/welcome/dnamarkerindex.asp?chromosome=Y&snp=Y10968

"DNA Marker Index Data for Marker: R-Y37962 on Chromsome: Y," GeneticHomeland.com, accessed 30 December 2022. https://www.genetichomeland.com/welcome/dnamarkerindex.asp?chromosome=Y&snp=Y37962

"DNA Marker Index Data for Marker: R-Z9 on Chromsome: Y," GeneticHomeland.com, accessed 30 December 2022. https://www.genetichomeland.com/welcome/dnamarkerindex.asp?chromosome=Y&snp=Z9

[225] FamilyTreeDNA, "Stewart Stuart (royal) Y-DNA Project Results," FamilyTreeDNA.com, accessed 30 December 2022. https://www.familytreedna.com/public/Stuart?iframe=ycolorized

[226] FamilyTreeDNA, "St Clair Sinclair Y-DNA Study Results," FamilyTreeDNA.com, accessed 30 December 2022. https://www.familytreedna.com/public/Sinclair?iframe=ycolorized

[227] Roberta Estes, "442 Ancient Viking Skeletons Hold DNA Surprises – Does Your Y or Mitochondrial DNA Match?"

[228] "Sinclair Groupings, our Caithness, Shetland, and Orkey Families," St Clair Research, accessed 30 December 2022. http://www.stclairresearch.com/content/groupingsCaithness.html

*Appendix C: Y-DNA*

## Table of Figures

Figure C-1: A Brief Timeline of Early History in Britain [9] .................................................. C-3
Figure C-2: Map of Ancient Babylonia, Egypt, and Scythian Territory by Brian Gotts. This file is licensed under Creative Commons CC BY 4.0. [19] .................................................. C-5
Figure C-3: Distribution of the Five Major Graham Surname Project Groups as of April 2023 [35] .............. C-8
Figure C-4: Eupedia's R1b-RS21 (a.k.a. R1b-U106 and R1b-M405) Geographic Distribution ................ C-10
Figure C-5: Eupedia's R1b-L21 Geographic Distribution .................................................. C-11
Figure C-6: Eupedia's R1b-DF27 Geographic Distribution .................................................. C-13
Figure C-7: Eupedia's J1-P58 Geographic Distribution .................................................. C-14
Figure C-8: NOTIONAL J1 Big Y Breakout-First Guess, Note: My candidate patriarchs are consistently 110 to 140 years to the right (more recent) than FTDNA estimates. .................................................. C-16
Figure C-9: Eupedia's I1 (I-M253) Geographic Distribution .................................................. C-18
Figure C-10: Haplogroup Tree/Y-DNA Pedigree of Graham J1s and Jordan J1s (J-YSC76 Highlighted) [113] ...... C-21
Figure C-11: Haplogroup Tree/Y-DNA Pedigree of Graham J1s and Jordan J1s (J-FGC8224/8223 Highlighted) [113] C-21
Figure C-12: Haplogroup Tree/Y-DNA Pedigree of Graham J1s and Jordan J1s Showing Timeframe of British-Middle Eastern Split [118],[119],[121] .................................................. C-22
Figure C-13: Haplogroup Tree/Y-DNA Pedigree of English J1s Showing Refined Estimate of British-Middle Eastern Split [126],[127] .................................................. C-23
Figure C-14: Scota and Gaedel Glas (Gaythelos) in a 15th century manuscript of Bower's Scotichronicon [128] .......... C-24
Figure C-15: Phoenician Trade Routes and Trading Bases [144] Creative Commons License CC BY-SA 3.0 ............ C-26
Figure C-16: Haplogroup Tree/Y-DNA Pedigree of Graham J1s and Jordan J1s (With Ancient Subclades P58 and L858 Highlighted) [155] .................................................. C-28
Figure C-17: Pedigree of Sir Andrew de Murray of Manuel, J1 Graham Patriarch Candidate from The Chiefship of the Clan Murray, Author: "B." The Scottish Antiquary, or, Northern Notes and Queries, Oct., 1900, Vol. 15, No. 58 with modifications in red. [167] .................................................. C-31
Figure C-18: Kirkpatrick-Fleming and Graitney Parishes, John Thomson's 1832 Atlas of Scotland [174] ............ C-32
Figure C-19: Ethnicities in Britain Prior to the Norman Invasion (878 A.D.) [185]   Creative Commons License CC BY-SA 3.0 .................................................. C-34
Figure C-20: Map of the Dryfe Valley, Hutton and Corry Parish, in NW Dumfriesshire, Scotland; Ordnance Survey (map GB.) Landranger Series SCALE OF 1; 50 000, SHEET NO 79 HAWICK & ESKDALE (LANGHOLM) Ordnance Survey licence number 100066333. All rights reserved. © Copyright and Database right 2022. ................ C-38

## Endnotes

[i] Its child, FT31146, has <u>zero</u> members that identified from Middle Eastern countries, although thirteen members did not identify a country of origin.

[ii] Of course, if the FTDNA estimates are updated as new test data becomes available and shifts 67 years to the right, then the Roman scenario is back in play.

# Appendix D: A Primer on the Ancient British and Roman Catholic Churches in Scotland

## Table of Contents

**Celtic Culdee History** .................................................................................................................. **D-2**
    Characteristics of the Early Celtic Church ................................................................................. D-3
    Church Organization After the Arrival of the Normans and David I ........................................ D-4
    History of Tithes in Scotland ....................................................................................................... D-9
    History of Worship in the Scottish Borders Region ................................................................. D-11

**The Grahams and the Knightly Orders (Templar, Hospitaller, Trinitarian)** ....................... **D-12**
    Knights Templar ........................................................................................................................ D-12
        Temple Properties in Scotland ............................................................................................ D-14
        Temple Lands in Dumfriesshire and Annandale ................................................................ D-14
    Knights Hospitaller .................................................................................................................... D-15
    1534 – 1689 Templars Operate in Secret ................................................................................. D-17
    Trinitarians ................................................................................................................................ D-17

**GLOSSARY** ................................................................................................................................. **D-21**
    Lands with Culdee Connections ............................................................................................... D-21
    Culdee Place Name Etymology ................................................................................................ D-33
    Key Norman Church Establishments ....................................................................................... D-34
    Abbreviated Glossary of Native British Saints (Alphabetical Order) ...................................... D-37
    Glossary of Relevant Roman Catholic Saints (Alphabetical Order) ........................................ D-46
    Graham Scottish Church Leaders .............................................................................................. D-54
    Saints Patronages and Dedications that are Connected to the Grahams .................................. D-56
    Relevant Scottish Church Land Charters ................................................................................. D-62
    Table of Figures ........................................................................................................................ D-65
    Endnotes .................................................................................................................................... D-66

*Appendix D: A Primer on the Ancient British and Roman Catholic Churches in Scotland*

The church was the single most dominant institution in medieval life. It influenced nearly every aspect of people's lives, played a role in government, and were major landowners.[1] Since family records from medieval times are church records, it is not possible to investigate family history from that era without first studying church history. Maps depicting the church organizations of the times are also needed to locate our ancestors' origins.

Those who are unfamiliar with Scottish History may not recognize that the name of the wizard's hospital called "St. Mungo's," in J.K. Rowling's *Harry Potter* series shares its name with a real Culdee Christian saint. Prior to the arrival of the Roman Catholic Normans in Scotland, about 1124 A.D., the Culdee church was established throughout Ireland, Scotland, and Wales. The Culdees or Keledei (Irish: *Céilí Dé*, lit."Spouses of God") were members of Celtic Christian monastic communities of Britain.

> **FYI...**
> Many authors and historians believe that Culdee practices and saints are shared with and possibly derived from the Egyptian Coptic Church.

**An Aside on Prayer and Saints.** First, one difference amongst Christian denominations that is relevant to our studies is prayer. The etymology of the word "pray" comes from the Latin "to ask."[2] While the Culdees did honor their saints, they did not pray to them. They prayed in memory of and in gratitude to their founding patrons, but they did not pray for the dead.[3] In the case of evangelical Protestants, they will ask the living to pray for them. They also do not pray for the dead. Those of the Catholic, Anglican, and Orthodox faiths ask both the living and the "non-living" to pray for them, and they pray for the souls of the departed. The non-living seen with the most "pull" with the Almighty are the saints, hence the prayers to ask them to *intercede* on one's behalf.[4]

# I. Celtic Culdee Church History

The early Celtic church was first organized such that bishops were subordinate to the abbot of the nearest monastery. The "Early Church in Northern Scotland" website describes the early Culdee church structure:

---

[1] Alixe Bovey, "The Medieval Church: From Dedication to Dissent," *The British Library*, accessed 30 April 2015. https://www.bl.uk/the-middle-ages/articles/church-in-the-middle-ages-from-dedication-to-dissent

[blurb on connection to Coptic Church] "The Coptic Church," Coptic Orthodox Diocese of Los Angeles, Southern California, and Hawaii, accessed 9 January 2023. https://stpeterandstpaul.org/coptic-church/

"Coptic Influence in the Early British Church," St. George Orthodox Ministry, 30 January 2018. http://www.stgeorgeministry.com/coptic-influence-early-british-church/

Abba Seraphim, "On the Trail of the Seven Coptic Monks in Ireland," The British Orthodox Church, accessed 9 January 2023. https://britishorthodox.org/miscellaneous/on-the-trail-of-seven-coptic-monks-in-ireland/

[2] "pray (v)," Etymology Online Dictionary, accessed 19 January 2023. https://www.etymonline.com/word/pray

[3] James Taylor, *The Pictorial History of Scotland* Vol. I (London: James S. Virtue, 1859), 55. https://www.electricscotland.com/books/pdf/pictorialhistory01tayluoft.pdf

[4] The Boise Center Papers on Religion in the United States, "Introduction to Christian Theology," Boston College, accessed 19 January 2023. https://www.bc.edu/content/dam/files/centers/boisi/pdf/bc_papers/BCP-Christianity.pdf

"In the very earliest days, priests were supported 'voluntarily' by the tribes-people with whom they lived and served. These voluntary gifts were mostly in the form of produce and labor. But this was a tenuous means of support because it was very reliant on the abundance of the seasons and the generosity of the tribes-people (and perhaps also on the 'quality' of the priest and his 'popularity')... The first move was to incorporate the priest into an agricultural partnership with the village community and to encourage this he was awarded a plot of land which came to be known as his *glebe*..."[5]

## Characteristics of the Early Celtic Church.

1. The Culdee Church was both tribal and hereditary. Each kingship or clan would patronize its own saints and sponsor their own hereditary priests. The monastery with its endowments belonged to a particular family. Author Frank Adam provided examples: "St. Columba, abbot of Iona, named his own cousin as his successor and 120 years passed before there was any free election of an abbot... Six centuries later, we find that the Abbot of Abernethy is also lord of Abernethy, and that he not only grants tithes out of his property there, but asserts that property to be the inheritance of himself and his heirs."[6]

2. Culdees were known for their distinctive round tower style churches, prevalent throughout Britain. One such church is Dunkeld, Gaelic for "Fort of the Culdees."[7] Dunkeld was first built by Constantine, son of Fergus, King of the Picts, circa 790 A.D. for Culdee monks.[8]

*Figure D-1: The round bell towers of Dunkeld Cathedral* [7]
Photo by DAVID ILIFF. License: CC BY-SA 3.0

---

[5] Cushie Enterprises, "The Medieval Church in Alba," The Early Church in Northern Scotland, 14 December 2022. https://www.cushnieent.com/medievalchurch/medieval_portal.htm

[6] James Taylor, *The Pictorial History of Scotland* Vol. I (London: James S. Virture, 1859), 167.

[7] Figure D-1: Wikimedia Commons contributors, "File:Dunkeld Cathedral Exterior, Dunkeld, UK - Diliff.jpg," *Wikimedia Commons,* accessed 10 April 2023. https://commons.wikimedia.org/w/index.php?title=File:Dunkeld_Cathedral_Exterior,_Dunkeld,_UK_-_Diliff.jpg&oldid=529380313

[8] William F. Skene, *Chronicles of the Picts, Chronicles of the Scots* (Edinburgh: H.M. General Register House, 1867), clxii, 150, 173. https://ia600903.us.archive.org/20/items/chroniclesofpict00sken/chroniclesofpict00sken.pdf

3. Eventually, the Church in southern Scotland inherited the parish system from England where a mother church would support a group of smaller churches. With the steep terrain and islands, the parish system did not spread into the rest of the country.[9]

**Church Organization after the Arrival of the Normans and David I.** David I established a Diocesan structure of thirteen dioceses that did include parishes, but with well-defined geographic boundaries and throughout all of Scotland. However, this did not include the islands of Orkney and Shetland (the Northern Isles -Norðreyjar)[10] that were under the control of the King of Norway until he ceded them to the Scottish King in 1472.[11]

Traditionally, Saint Ninian is credited as the first bishop in Scotland. He is mentioned by sixth century English monk and historian, Bede, who states that around 397 A.D., Ninian set up his base at Whithorn in the south-west of Scotland. The first confirmed contact between the Celtic Church and the church based in Rome was two hundred years later with the arrival of Benedictine missionary St. Augustine in Kent, England in 597 A.D., after the Celtic Church was well-established.[12]

The general Christianization of the Strathclyde region (Figure D-2) began about 500 A.D. This Celtic version of Christianity began earlier in Scotland and Ireland.[13] The Culdee church continued until about the year 1250 A.D., when Scotland officially converted to Roman Catholicism.[14] During the "Western Schism" from 1378 to 1417, where both Avignon and Rome claimed the papacy of the Catholic Church, Scotland sided with Avignon.[15] As such, papal documents relating to Scotland will be found in the libraries of the Avignon popes [(Clement V (1305-1314), John XXII (1316-1334), Benedict XII (1334-1342), Clement VI (1342-1352), Innocent VI (1352-1362), Urban V (1362-1370), Gregory XI (1370-1378), Clement VI (1378-1394), Benedict XIII (1394-1419))].[16]

In the eleventh and twelfth centuries,[17] it was uncommon for patrons of Culdee monasteries and priories (convents) to be Normans. Beginning with the marriage of Malcolm Canmore, Malcolm III of Scotland to Queen Margaret[i] circa 1070, the bishoprics in Scotland came under the control of the

---

[9] Cushie Enterprises, "The Medieval Church in Alba," *The Early Church in Northern Scotland*, 14 December 2022.

[10] Cushie Enterprises, "Map of the Medieval Scottish Dioceses," *The Early Church in Northern Scotland*, accessed 14 February 2023. https://www.cushnieent.com/medievalchurch/map_scotland.htm

[11] Cushie Enterprises, "The Medieval Church in Alba," *The Early Church in Northern Scotland*, 14 December 2022. https://www.cushnieent.com/medievalchurch/medieval_portal.htm

[12] Dugald Butler and Herbert Story, *Scottish Cathedrals and Abbeys* (London: A&C Black, Edinburgh: R&R Clark Ltd, 1901), 3. https://www.gutenberg.org/files/21688/21688-h/21688-h.htm

[13] Rev. James Rankin, "Celtic Saints and Ancient Churches of Strathearn," *Chronicles of Strathearn* (Crieff: David Philips, 1896). https://www.gutenberg.org/files/26342/26342-h/26342-h.htm

[14] Rev. J.A. Wylie, *The History of the Scottish Nation*, Vol. 3 (London: Hamilton, Adams and Co., 1886), 203-204, 298. https://www.originofnations.org/books,%20papers/history%20of%20the%20scots/scothistvol3.pdf

[15] A. Francis Steuart, "Scotland and the Papacy during the Great Schism," *The Scottish Historical Review* 4, no. 14 (1907): 144–58. http://www.jstor.org/stable/25517825

[16] Melissa Snell, "The Avignon Papacy-When the Popes Resided in France," ThoughtCo, 24 June 2020. https://www.thoughtco.com/the-avignon-papacy-1789454

[17] St. Cuthbert of Lindisfarne (634-687)," CatholicIreland.net, accessed 14 February 2023. https://www.catholicireland.net/saintoftheday/st-cuthbert-of-lindisfarne-634-687/

*Appendix D: A Primer on the Ancient British and Roman Catholic Churches in Scotland*

Roman Catholic monarchy. The practices of the Roman Catholic Church, whose priests were celibate and received their authority from bishops appointed by the pope in Rome, differed from the early Celtic Church. The new policy advocated by Queen Margaret introduced the orders of the Roman Catholic Church to Scotland. However, the Canmores did embrace certain Culdee/Native British saints, specifically St. Cuthbert, St. Columba, and St. Patrick, and also Celtic traditions in an effort to avoid a schism between the native Celtic Church and Rome.[18] Theorized Graham ancestor, Forne Sigulfson, was a benefactor to the Priory of Hexham, known for its connection to St. Cuthbert.[19] St. Cuthbert was a Christian saint in the Celtic Culdee tradition. He was also Anglo-Saxon and the patron saint of Northumbria.[20]

Scottish Culdees were first joined by Augustinian canons from St. Oswald Priory in Nostell, Yorkshire,[21] when one of Queen Margaret's elder sons, Alexander I, founded Scone Priory in Perthshire about 1114.[22] Canons from Nostell helped her younger son, David I, found Holyrood Abbey in 1128.[23] For a

*Figure D-2: Monasteries of Scotland Prior to the Eighth Century. Map from "A Handbook of the Church of Scotland" by James Rankin.*[18]

---

[18] Catholic News World, "St. Margaret of Scotland, Queen of Scotland," last updated 13 November 2015. http://www.catholicnewsworld.com/2015/11/saint-november-16-st-margaret-of.html

Figure D-2: James Rankin, *A Handbook of the Church of Scotland* (Edinburgh and London: Blackwood and Sons, 1888), inside cover. https://ia600703.us.archive.org/22/items/handbookofchurch188800rank/handbookofchurch188800rank.pdf

[19] James Raine, *The Priory of Hexham, Its Chroniclers, Endowments and Annals*, Vol. I (Durham England: Andrews and Co, 1864), 59. https://archive.org/details/prioryofhexham01rain

[20] "St. Cuthbert," Catholic Online, accessed 11 April 2023. https://www.catholic.org/saints/saint.php?saint_id=491

[21] John Jamieson, *An Historical Account of the Ancient Culdees of Iona* (Edinburgh: John Ballantyne and Company, 1811), 207. https://archive.org/details/historicalaccoun00jami/page/n6/mode/1up?ref=ol&view=theater

[22] PoMS "no. 786," accessed 17 January 2023. https://www.poms.ac.uk/record/source/786/

[23] "Holyrood Abbey: Edinburgh Old Town," Truly Edinburgh, accessed 17 January 2023. https://trulyedinburgh.com/things-to-do-in-edinburgh/holyrood-abbey/

*Appendix D: A Primer on the Ancient British and Roman Catholic Churches in Scotland*

concise list of cathedral sites in Great Britain, from before the conquest and after, Wikipedia has an easy-to-read reference table.[24]

David I (1082-1153) and Bishop Jocelin of Glasgow, and their successors, gradually changed the patronages of Scottish churches. For example, the patronage of Old Melrose Abbey was St. Cuthbert, but New Melrose Abbey founded by David I was the Blessed Virgin Mary.[25] At the same time, David and Bishop Jocelin promoted St. Cuthbert as a Roman Catholic Saint.[26] Evenso, the new Scottish Church stubbornly maintained independence from Rome and York. This independence, manifested itself on several important historical occasions, finally resulting in the Reformed Church (Presbyterian) of 1560.[27]

*Figure D-3: Bishoprics of Scotland during Reign of David I (1124-1153). Map from "A Handbook of the Church of Scotland" by James Rankin* [23]

---

Figure D-3: James Rankin, *A Handbook of the Church of Scotland* (Edinburgh and London: Blackwood and Sons, 1888), 62.

[24] Wikipedia contributors, "List of former cathedrals in Great Britain," Wikipedia, The Free Encyclopedia, accessed 9 January 2023. https://en.wikipedia.org/w/index.php?title=List_of_former_cathedrals_in_Great_Britain&oldid=1127504741

[25] James Murray MacKinlay, *Ancient Church Dedications in Scotland* (Edinburgh: David Douglas, 1914), 246, 250-253. https://archive.org/stream/cu31924092331242/cu31924092331242_djvu.txt

[26] Sally Crumplin, "Rewriting History in the Cult of St. Cuthbert, from the Ninth to the Twelfth Centuries," (PhD Thesis, The University of St. Andrews, 10 December 2004), 251-255. https://core.ac.uk/download/pdf/1154335.pdf

[27] "The Declaration of Arbroath," National Records of Scotland, accessed 8 November 2022. https://www.nrscotland.gov.uk/Declaration

D-6

*Appendix D: A Primer on the Ancient British and Roman Catholic Churches in Scotland*

While Robert I, who reigned 1306-1329, promoted both Culdee and Roman Catholic saints in his lifetime, he may have been partial to the Celtic saints. Michael Penman writes: "Bruce sought to revive a kingship and royal household that by 1306 had been stripped of its spiritual heritage."[28] His seal included the Culdee St. Serf dragon[29] of his mother's Carrick family. As king, Bruce intervened in a number of disputes between the independent Scottish Culdees of St. Serf and the new Roman Catholic houses particularly the Graham dispute with the "New" (Cistercian) Melrose Abbey for appropriating their ancestral gifts[ii] previously made to the "Old" (Culdee) Melrose Abbey.[30] In 1314, Bruce led his soldiers into the battle of Bannockburn in the name of the Dumbarton patron saint, "Our Blessed St. Kessog,"[iii] while they carried the talismanic relics of St. Fillan.[31] Before his death, he traveled on a pilgrimage to St. Ninian's Cave on the southern Scottish coast in Whithorn[32] and made specific funeral instructions that his body be carried to the battlefield at Bannockburn, then to St. Serf's Chapel in Culross, Fifeshire, and, finally, buried at Dunfermline Abbey.[33]

> **FYI...**
> King Robert the Bruce (Robert I) had three different burial sites, a medieval custom called the *viator*:
>
> His organs were interred in Levengrove Park, St. Serf's Kirk in Cardross, Dumbarton (Figure D-4); His body lies in Dunfermline Abbey; And his heart was to be buried at New Melrose Abbey in Roxburghshire. He later requested his heart be carried on a Crusade before its final burial in the Church of the Holy Sepulchre in Jerusalem.[203] Sir James Douglas died in Spain during this undertaking. Bruce's "Brave Heart" and "Good Sir" James' body were returned to Scotland.

Per Dugald Butler and Herbert Story in *Scottish Cathedrals and Abbeys*, the old Celtic Church of Scotland was brought to an end by a number of factors:

1. A tribal system (vs. territorial) where bishops were subject to the abbot of the nearest monastery. The Culdee recluses were not pledged to celibacy. Many of them were married and

---

[28] Michael Penman, "'Sacred Food for the Soul': In Search of the Devotions to Saints of Robert Bruce, King of Scotland, 1306-1329." *Speculum* 88, no. 4 (2013): 1041. http://www.jstor.org/stable/43576866

[29] "St. Serf," *Undiscovered Scotland*, accessed 10 January 2023. https://www.undiscoveredscotland.co.uk/usbiography/s/stserf.html

[30] Douglas MacQueen, "Marjorie, Countess of Carrick and Mother of Scottish King Robert the Bruce," *Transceltic*, 27 June 2017. https://www.transceltic.com/blog/marjorie-countess-of-carrick-and-mother-of-scottish-king-robert-bruce

[31] Michael Penman, "Robert the Bruce, the Piety of the of the Victor of Bannockburn," History Scotland, 18 June 2014. https://www.historyscotland.com/history/robert-the-bruce-the-piety-of-the-victor-of-bannockburn/

[32] "Visit Dunfermline, Scotland's Ancient Capital," Unique Travel Photo, 5 June 2021. https://www.uniquetravelphoto.com/visit-dunfermline-scotlands-ancient-capital/

[33] "The Funeral Procession of King Robert the Bruce," *Dumbarton and Vale of Leven Reporter*, 12 March 2013. https://www.dumbartonreporter.co.uk/opinion/13957969.the-funeral-procession-of-king-robert-the-bruce/

[blurb on Robert the Bruce burial] Danielle Dray, "The Melrose Casket and Robert the Bruce," Historic Environment Scotland (blog), 24 June 2018. https://blog.historicenvironment.scot/2018/06/melrose-casket-robert-bruce/

*Figure D-4: Drawing by John Slezer of "Dumbarton Castle - His Majesties Castle from the West of Dumbritton" with Cardross medieval chapel dedicated to St. Serf, burial place of King Robert I's organs, in foreground across the River Leven from the Castle. From the David Laing Bequest to the Royal Scottish Academy transferred 1910. [33, 34] Image licensed by the National Galleries of Scotland.*

were succeeded in office by their own sons. They were not dedicated for life to their calling, but were free at any time to change it for another.[34]

2. Frequent Danish invasions, where Celtic churches and monasteries were destroyed. The church lands then fell into the hands of a few lay families who acted as the ***custodiers*** **(custodians) of the pastoral staff. They made the lands hereditary in their families, and exercised jurisdiction over the ancient sanctuary boundaries.**[35]

3. External factors—the policy adopted towards the Celtic Church by Queen Margaret, later known as Saint Margaret of Scotland, and her sons in the eleventh and twelfth centuries: **(1) placing the Church upon a territorial vs. tribal basis, organizing into dioceses; (2) founding great monasteries and cathedrals; (3) absorbing the Culdees or Columban clergy**

---

[34] "Culdees," McClintock and Strong Bible Clopedia, accessed 9 January 2023. https://www.biblicalcyclopedia.com/C/culdees.html

Figure D-4: Drawing by John Slezer, "Dumbarton Castle—His Majesty's Castle at Drumbritton from the West," Scottish National Gallery of Modern Art, David Laing Bequest to the Royal Scottish Academy, transferred 1910. https://www.nationalgalleries.org/art-and-artists/6332/dumbarton-castle-his-majestys-castle-drumbritton-west

And National Libraries of Scotland (NLS) https://maps.nls.uk/view/91169108

[35] Dugald Butler and Herbert Story, *Scottish Cathedrals and Abbeys* (London: A&C Black, Edinburgh: R&R Clark Ltd, 1901), 3. https://www.gutenberg.org/files/21688/21688-h/21688-h.htm

into the Roman Catholic system, by first converting them from secular into regular (celibate) canons.[36]

### History of Tithes in Scotland.

In the Celtic church, beginning about the sixth century, payment of teinds, also known as tithes or tenths, was made chiefly to monasteries and occasionally to laymen clergy. With the Norman system, David I founded fifteen religious houses, including the abbeys of Holyrood, Melrose,[37] Dryburgh, Newbattle, Cambuskenneth, Kelso, Dundrennan Abbey in Galloway in 1142; Kinloss Abbey in Moray, and Holm Cultram Abbey in Cumbria in 1150,[38] and established a new structure for tithing. James Rankine explains: "Teinds constituted a burden on the land. The owner of the estate was not a complete owner. The Church was a joint owner with each, but this joint ownership did not consist in separating a certain percentage of acres, but only a certain percentage of crop or rent." David I also made grants of land directly to abbeys and churches. David II sponsored a law that excommunicated those refusing to pay tithes.[39] Forne Sigulfson, one of Henry I's "trusted men" in the Northern Territories,[iv] acted as an enforcer when the canons of St. Peter's York complained to Henry I of the failure of the local landowners to pay tithes and their seizure of church lands.[40]

Medieval records show Grahams in various roles in the Celtic Culdee church, including bishops and Archdeacon, indicating Grahams or Graham ancestors were already in Scotland prior to the Norman invasion. If the first Grahams were Normans as claimed by *Peerage*, we would expect them all to be Roman Catholic and the profession of clergymen not to be the "family business," given that by 1124 Roman Catholic priests took vows of celibacy. There were assuredly others, but of the 25 pre-Norman (before 1124) Culdee properties that I could locate in Scotland,[41] Grahams were associated with fourteen of them, plus Arthuret in Cumberland.[42] In Strathclyde, the Culdee patronage of St. Patrick became Chapel Royal,[43] and with St. Kessog these transitioned to Graham Temple foundation[44] (Graham properties donated to the Knights Templar, Knights Hospitaller, and

---

[36] Dugald Butler and Herbert Story, *Scottish Cathedrals and Abbeys* (London: A&C Black, Edinburgh: R&R Clark Ltd, 1901), 3.

[37] Roberta Gilchrist, "Monastic Archaeology and National Identity: The Scottish Monastic Experience," *Cambridge University Press* (20 December 2019): 52. https://www.cambridge.org/core/books/sacred-heritage/monastic-archaeology-and-national-identity-the-scottish-monastic-experience/6BD6F88E5222E126AFF581466E3D9F75

[38] James Rankin, *A Handbook of the Church of Scotland* (Edinburgh and London: Blackwood and Sons, 1888), 348-349. https://ia600703.us.archive.org/22/items/handbookofchurch188800rank/handbookofchurch188800rank.pdf

[39] James Rankin, *A Handbook of the Church of Scotland* (Edinburgh and London: Blackwood and Sons, 1888), 348-349.

[40] Charles Johnson and H.A. Cronne, *Regesta Regum Anglo-Normannorum*, Vol. II, 1100-1135 (Oxford: Clarendon Press, 1956), 216. https://deeds.library.utoronto.ca/cartularies/0378

[41] John Jamieson, *An Historical Account of the Ancient Culdees of Iona* (Edinburgh: John Ballantyne and Company, 1811), v-viii. https://archive.org/details/historicalaccoun00jami/page/n6/mode/1up?ref=ol&view=theater

[42] Ninian Hill, *The Story of the Scottish Church From Earliest Times* (Glasgow: James Maclehose and Sons, 1919), 6, 45. https://www.forgottenbooks.com/en/download/TheStoryoftheScottishChurch_10216219.pdf

[43] William Fraser, *The Red Book of Menteith*, Vol. II (Edinburgh: 1880), 256-257. https://digital.nls.uk/histories-of-scottish-families/archive/97146821

[44] Sir James Balfour Paul, *The Scots Peerage, Founded on Wood's Edition,* Vol. VI (Edinburgh: David Douglas, 1909), 213. https://archive.org/details/scotspeeragefoun06pauluoft/page/148/mode/2up?q=glenny

Trinitarians) lands by the thirteenth century.[45] <u>Knights Hospitaller (and sometimes the other orders) were exempt from paying teinds</u>.[46]

    The glossary at the back of this appendix provides documents of Grahams and their Corrie cousins in possession of many former Culdee church lands from the eleventh to fourteenth centuries. This indicates that they were descendants of the previously referenced <u>custodiers (custodians) of the pastoral staff, who had made lands hereditary in their families and exercised "jurisdiction over the ancient sanctuary boundaries."</u>[47] The practice of collecting teinds continued even after the Culdee clergy fled and the church buildings were destroyed by invaders, the lands falling into the hands of laymen.[48]

    Disputes frequently occurred between the conventual houses and the incumbents of their churches and chapels regarding the allocation of the teinds. For example, such a dispute arose about the year 1360 between the rector of Westerkirk and the monks as to the appropriation of the teinds of the "seculars" who lived on the Abbey's land of Watcarrick in Eskdale. By 1550, Lord Maxwell held the *advocatioun/advowson* (the position of guardian or patron of a church[49]) of the kirks of Eskdale. In 1609, William, Earl of Morton, received a grant of the church, vicarage, and the teinds of the parish, out of which he had to pay the minister a stipend of 500 merks and provide him with a manse and glebe. By 1653, the teinds were the property of Countess Mary of Buccleuch, whose successors retained the patronage."[50]

    The Border Grahams and their Corrie cousins, who were lay residents of church lands, continued this custom of collecting teinds until Lang Will Graham and his kinsman John Corrie were forfeited of former church lands in 1517.[51] Grahams possessed former church lands in Wamphray,[52] Kirkpatrick, Dryfe (Mosskesswra), Corrie and Sibbaldbie[53] and the kirk in Sibbaldbie.[54]

---

[45] William J. Dillon, "The Trinitarians at Failford," *Ayrshire Archaeological and Natural History Society* Vol 4 (1957): 76, 91-93. https://aanhsorg.files.wordpress.com/2018/08/the-trinitarians-of-failford.pdf

[46] Rev. James Hutchison Cockburn, B.D., "Papal Collections and Collectors in Scotland in the Middle Ages," *Scottish Church History Society* (1945): 175. https://electricscotland.com/history/middleages/middleages03a.pdf

[47] Dugald Butler and Herbert Story, *Scottish Cathedrals and Abbeys* (London: A&C Black, Edinburgh: R&R Clark Ltd, 1901), 3. https://www.gutenberg.org/files/21688/21688-h/21688-h.htm

[48] "Teinds," Scottish Archive Network, accessed 16 January 2023. https://www.scan.org.uk/researchrtools/glossary_t.htm

[49] "Advocatioun," *Dictionaries of the Scots Language*, accessed 13 January 2023. https://dsl.ac.uk/entry/dost/advocatioun

[50] "Dryfe, Old Parish Church and Churchyard," Archaeology Notes, Canmore-National Record of the Historic Environment, accessed 9 January 2023. https://canmore.org.uk/site/67816/bentpath-westerkirk-old-parish-church?fbclid=IwAR3A0F74PCA1gcl775XfpT0dVw-xzwvBj7wJImEQhQ-w0EcP4eHfsacrcfQ

[51] R.C. Reid, "The Border Grahams and Their Origins," *Transactions of the Dumfries and Galloway Natural History and Archaeological Society (TDGNHAS)* No. 3038 (1961): 91. https://dgnhas.org.uk/sites/default/files/transactions/3038.pdf

[52] "Wamphray Church," Archaeology Notes, Canmore-National Record of the Historic Environment, accessed 9 January 2023. https://canmore.org.uk/site/66905/wamphray-church

[53] J. E. Corrie, *Records of the Corrie Family, 802-1899 A.D.* (London: Mitchell and Hughes, 1899), 136-137.

[54] PoMS "no. 9120, Church of Sibbaldbie," accessed 10 April 2023. https://www.poms.ac.uk/record/person/9120/

*Appendix D: A Primer on the Ancient British and Roman Catholic Churches in Scotland*

## History of Worship in the Scottish Borders Region.

Evidences of religious worship can be found in the area dating back to the year 1290 B.C. Priests carried out their religious activities at the Girdle Stones situated in Eskdalemuir, where they greeted the rising sun with great ceremony. Coincidentally, the ancient Egyptians used Girdle Stones in their worship of the sun god Ra.[55] The Romans began settling in large numbers in Scotland during the time of Emperor Hadrian, 117-138 A.D. and first introduced the Christian faith.[56] However, the real source of Scottish Christianity was the Irish Mission established by St. Columba on Iona in 523 A.D., a Church independent of both Rome and England.[57]

---

[55] Bruno Coursol, "The endless fights between Sun god Ra and the Great Serpent god Apep (Apophis) in the Underworld are representations of the grand gallery impactor operating cycle of the Great Pyramid of Khufu," 1001 Tasses, 24 September 2021. https://www.milleetunetasses.com/amp/blog/the-great-pyramid-of-khufu/sun-god-ra-and-the-great-serpent-god-apep-apophis-fights-in-the-underworld.html

[56] "The Roman Empire Part Two," Mr. Giotto's Online Textbook, Penfield CSD, accessed 13 April 2023. https://www.penfield.edu/webpages/jgiotto/onlinetextbook.cfm?subpage=1678803

[57] "Iona Abbey and Nunnery," Historic Environment Scotland, accessed 13 April 2023. https://www.historicenvironment.scot/visit-a-place/places/iona-abbey-and-nunnery/history/

## II. The Grahams and Military Orders of Knights (Templar, Hospitaller, Trinitarian)

### Knights Templar.

The Knights of the Temple, commissioned by Pope Gelasius II, began work in the year 1119.[58] A French knight named Hugues de Payens founded the military order along with eight relatives and acquaintances, calling it the "Poor Fellow-Soldiers of Christ and the Temple of Solomon" (later known as the Knights Templar).[59] With the support of Baldwin II, the king of Jerusalem, they set up headquarters on the sacred Temple Mount and pledged to protect pilgrims destined there. Reverend Alfred Coutts synopsizes the history in *The Knights Templar in Scotland*:

*Figure D-5: Red Cross Pattée of the Knights Templar* [58]

*Figure D-6: Cross Pattée on Columns that surround the front of the Church of the Holy Sepulchre in Jerusalem which was added during the Crusader Period. Photo by Alicia Graham.*

"At first all the Knights were required to live in Palestine. They took the usual vows of a monk: poverty, chastity and obedience. In Jerusalem there were probably never more than 500 Knights, but they were leaders who were everywhere recognised as the finest soldiers in Christendom. The average life of a Templar was very short, for in a battle with the Moslems the Knights would often lose one-half of their number… Acre was held as the last Christian stronghold in Palestine till 1291… It was not long before the Order rapidly extended its influence in Europe. Besides the regular Knights, wealthy men of good position were admitted under the name of Sergeant (O.F. for servant), and to them were assigned places of high rank in the Order…. After 1163 the Knights were authorised by Pope Alexander III to have their own Chaplains, who must also be of noble descent, and were declared to be free from the jurisdiction of all Bishops and to be under the direction of the Pope alone."[60]

In 1305, Pope Clement V in Avignon disbanded the Knights Templar, bowing to pressure from King Phillip IV of France who was deeply in debt to the Templars. On 14 September 1307, Philip IV signed an order to arrest all Knights Templar for heresy and seize all their lands and wealth. While some knights were arrested, tortured, and killed, many escaped. A large number sailed to Portugal and Argyll, Scotland. The Scottish king, Robert I, had been excommunicated, and was sympathetic to their

---

[58] Rev. Alfred Coutts, *The Knights Templar in Scotland* (Scottish Church History Society, 1941), 127. https://archive.org/details/rschsv07p2coutts/page/126/mode/2up

Figure D-5: Wikimedia Commons contributors, "File:Cross-Pattee-red.svg," *Wikimedia Commons*, accessed 17 April 2023. https://commons.wikimedia.org/w/index.php?title=File:Cross-Pattee-red.svg&oldid=642366812

[59] Jennie Cohen, "History of the Knights Templar," History.com, 3 September 2018. https://www.history.com/news/who-were-the-knights-templar-2

[60] Rev. Alfred Coutts, *The Knights Templar in Scotland* (Scottish Church History Society, 1941), 127.

situation. In addition, Scotland had a tradition of strongly supporting the knightly orders for two centuries.[61] [62]

Under the influence of Henry I, David I of Scotland had established the Knights Templar

*Figure D-7: Ruins of the Church of the Paralytic, built by Crusaders over part of the Ruined Basilica at the Pools of Bethesda. Columns are marked with the Cross Pattée associated with the Templars. Ruins are located next to St. Ann's Church, traditional birthplace of the Virgin Mary, which was also built by Crusaders and also features the Cross Pattée. Photos by Alicia Graham.*

Order in Scotland in 1128, with its main Preceptory at Ballantrodoch, now the Midlothian village of Temple.[63] With the support of succeeding Scottish kings, the Order came to possess considerable property in Scotland.[64] While still Prince David, David became Lord of Huntingdon, a substantial estate in Northumberland, upon marriage to Matilda of Huntingdon in 1113.[65] Therefore, it is not surprising that King David I claimed the patron saint of Northumbria, St. Cuthbert, as the first patron saint of the Templars in Scotland in 1128. Coincidentally, the Templar cross was a red cross pattée, the same as St. Cuthbert's cross.

---

[61] "The Templars and other Monastic Military Orders," MedievalWarfare.info, accessed 10 January 2023. https://www.medievalwarfare.info/templars.htm

[62] "Clan Carruthers: The Carruthers Chiefs and the Templar Link," Clan Carruthers Society, 12 September 2020. https://clancarrutherssociety.org/2020/09/12/clan-carruthers-the-carruthers-chiefs-and-the-templar-link/

[63] "Temple History-Brief," TempleVillage.org.uk, accessed 9 January 2023. http://www.templevillage.org.uk/temple-village/temple-village-history/

[64] "The Order of the Temple in Scotland," The Knights Templar, accessed 12 March 2023. https://www.theknightstemplar.org/scottish-templars/

[65] Richard Oram, *David: The King Who Made Scotland* (Stroud, Gloucestershire, UK: Tempus Publishing Limited, 2004), 41, 63-70.

Another man under the influence of Henry I was Forne Sigulfson of Yorkshire, who was named a "taini regis" or thegn of the king in the Domesday book of 1086.[66] He was one of Henry I's "new men," of the "Northern Territories," which included Yorkshire and Northumberland, from circa 1086 to 1129.[67] He and his successor, his eldest son Ivo, would have implemented Henry I's wishes to establish knightly orders. Forne was also a benefactor to the Priory of Hexham in Northumberland, known for its connection to St. Cuthbert.[68] He helped mediate the claim of the monks of St. Cuthbert to Tynemouth Priory and the first charter his theorized younger son, William de Graham, witnessed was for a church dedicated to St. Cuthbert.

### Temple Properties in Scotland.

The Templars owned **over 500 sites in Scotland**. Their Scottish assets included preceptories at Adamtoun and at Maryculter at Garvock in Aberdeenshire[69] and the Templar houses in: Aboyne, Balantrodoch on the South Esk, Denny, Holy Mount in Edinburgh, Hoddam, Inchinnan, Liston, Red Abbey Stead in Roxburghshire, St. German's House near Seton, Stanhouse, Temple on Southesk near Edinburgh, Thankerton, Tulloch in Aberdeenshire, Turriff and Urquhart Bay on Loch Ness.[70] In the context of the Templars, the term preceptory refers not only to a building, but to the entire estate.

### Templar Lands in Dumfriesshire and Annandale.

St. Cuthberts Chapel in Moffat was built in the late twelfth century by the Knights Templar who protected travelers on holy pilgrimages, including those travelling to the Holy Land and Jerusalem.[71] The complete list of properties in Dumfriesshire and Annandale is extensive and includes: Shaw,[72] Becktoun in Dryfesdale, Bridge-end, Carnsalloch, Dalgarno,[73] Dinwoodie, Durisdeer,[74] Glen of Lag, Ingleston in Glencairn, the Chapel of Kirkbride in Kirkpatrick, lands beside Lincluden College,

---

[66] Stephen M. Lewis, "A Likely Story - Eleanor Grisdale and the King of Mardale," Grisdales of Matterdale (blog), 30 August 2014. https://grisdalefamily.wordpress.com/tag/william-the-conqueror/

[67] Stephen M. Lewis, "Forne Sigulfson-The 'First' Lord of Greystoke in Cumbria," The Wild Peak Blog, 30 March 2013. https://thewildpeak.wordpress.com/2013/03/30/forne-sigulfson-the-first-lord-of-greystoke-in-cumbria/

[68] James Raine, *The Priory of Hexham, Its Chroniclers, Endowments and Annals*, Vol. I (Durham: The Surtees Society, Andrews and Co, 1864), 59. https://archive.org/details/prioryofhexham01rain

[69] Francis H. Groome, *Ordnance Gazetteer of Scotland*, Vol. V (Edinburgh: Thomas C. Jack, Grange Publishing Works, 1884), 97. https://digital.nls.uk/gazetteers-of-scotland-1803-1901/archive/97385114?mode=transcription

[70] James Rankin, *A Handbook of the Church of Scotland* (Edinburgh and London: William Blackwood & Sons, 1888), 133-134.
https://ia800703.us.archive.org/22/items/handbookofchurch188800rank/handbookofchurch188800rank.pdf

[71] "Moffat History Trail," The Merlin Trail, accessed 9 January 2023. http://merlintrail.com/the-moffat-history-trail/

[72] Col. William Rogerson, *Hutton Under the Muir* (Dumfries, Scotland: Dumfries and Galloway Courier and Herald, 1908), 4, 7, 30.
https://www.google.com/books/edition/Hutton_under_the_muir_notes_on_the_past/BiwVAAAAQAAJ?hl=en&gbpv=1

[73] Dumfriesshire and Galloway Natural History and Antiquarian Society, *The Transactions and Journal of Proceedings of the Dumfriesshire and Galloway Natural History and Antiquarian Society: Session 1908-1909* (Dumfries, Scotland: Dumfriesshire and Galloway Natural History and Antiquarian Society, 1910), 138.
https://dgnhas.org.uk/sites/default/files/transactions/2021.pdf#page=138

[74] Ibid.

*Appendix D: A Primer on the Ancient British and Roman Catholic Churches in Scotland*

Lochmaben,[75] Moffat, Muirfad near Moffat, Reidhall, Sibbaldbie, Templand in Lochmaben, Torthorwald, and Trailtow south of Hoddam.[76, 77]

### Knights Hospitaller.

The great military Order of Knights of the Hospital of Saint John of Jerusalem, or Knights Hospitaller, originated in old Jerusalem,[78] where the knights operated the hospital of St. John the Baptist for the care of travelers to the Holy Land. These knights wore a uniform displaying an eight-pointed cross[v] of white on a black mantle. David I invited the Knights Hospitaller to Scotland in 1132.[79] They established their Scottish headquarters in a church in the village of Torphichen, West Lothian, Scotland. While Torphichen was always considered the order's chief house in Scotland, and usually its only preceptory, the order's estates were sometimes split between different brethren or lay administrators.[80] William McDowall writes in *The History of the Burgh of Dumfries*: "Hospitallers had not so much landed property as their fellow knights, but they seem to have possessed a large number of foundations." Hospitaller establishments in Scotland numbered eighty-five and included: Ballantyne's Hospital between Edinburgh and Dalkeith, Brechin, Maison Dieu established in 1264, Dalkeith in 1396,[81] numerous properties

*Figure D-9: Black and White Maltese Cross of the Knights Hospitaller[76] by Heratlas*
[CC BY-SA 3.0](#)

*Figure D-8: Marker Identifying location of the First Hospital of the Knights Hospitaller in Muristan (Christian Quarter of Old Jerusalem). By tradition, the site of a hospital founded during the Maccabean era in the second century B.C. [76] Photo by Alicia Graham*

---

[75] Ibid.

[76] "The Templars in Annandale-Carruthersland," Clan Carruthers—Warriors, 13 January 2007. https://clancarruthers228187931.wordpress.com/tag/ruthwell/

Figure D-8: Wikimedia Commons contributors, "File:Amalfi-Cross-Heraldry.jpg," *Wikimedia Commons*, accessed 18 April 2023. https://commons.wikimedia.org/w/index.php?title=File:Amalfi-Cross-Heraldry.jpg&oldid=481576796

Figure D-9: Wikipedia contributors, "Muristan," Wikipedia, The Free Encyclopedia, accessed 28 April 2023. https://en.wikipedia.org/wiki/Muristan

[77] "The Order of the Temple in Scotland," TheKnightsTemplar.org, accessed 10 January 2023. http://www.theknightstemplar.org/scottish-templars/

[78] Edwin James King, *The Knights Hospitallers in the Holy Land* (London: Methuen & Co. Ltd., 1931), 4-5.

[79] "Torphichen Preceptory," Undiscovered Scotland, accessed 13 April 2023. https://www.undiscoveredscotland.co.uk/torphichen/preceptory/index.html

[80] Ian B. Cowan, P.H.R. Mackay and Alan Macquarrie, *Knights of St. John of Jerusalem in Scotland*, Vol. 19 (Edinburgh, Clark Constable, 1983), xxxix. https://digital.nls.uk/126638043

[81] James Rankin, *A Handbook of the Church of Scotland* (Edinburgh and London: William Blackwood & Sons, 1888), 135-138.

in Renfrewshire,[82] Kirkstyle, in the parish of Ruthwell, Spitalfield, about a mile southeast of Dumfries, Ladyfield on Kelton Road, a hospital adjacent to Howspital and Spitalridding,[vi] and another hospital in Annandale at Trailtrow. The masters of both orders in Dumfriesshire submitted to Edward I after the English Invasion of Scotland in 1296 and were confirmed in their possessions by precepts addressed to the Sheriff by the King."[83]

In 1312, Clement V signed a papal bull transferring Templar assets in Europe to the Knights Hospitallers. In Scotland, the Order has never been banned or abolished. On the contrary, it remained under the protection of the King of Scotland as an Autonomous Grand priory.[84] However, many Scottish Temple holdings gradually transferred to the Knights Hospitaller, making it difficult to determine which properties originally belonged to which order. Mary, Queen of Scots, refers to Hospitaller properties in documents dated as late as 1564.[85] Both orders lost their properties during the Reformation: Murray of Cockpool acquired Hospitaller land in Ruthwell; Lord Herries their house and lands at Trailtrow[86] while, the Spitalfield of Dumfries was acquired before 1666 by the M'Brairs of Almagill. Regarding Temple lands in Hutton: the Grahams of Gillesbie acquired the Temple lands of Shaw in 1626[87] and Ross Rosile acquired in a 1677 sasine: "The Closs,"[88] Broomhills and the Chapel Croft in Hutton.[89] This implies the previous owners of "the Closs," the Grahams of Mosskesswra, were involved in the Temple order. A Mosskesswra Graham descendant was later presented a ring with a Templar emblem by Elizabeth I prior to 1603.[90]

*Figure D-10: John Graham of Claverhouse, "Bonnie Dundee"* [84]

---

[82] T.C. Welsh, "The Renfrewshire Templelands," *Renfrewshire Local History Forum (RLHF) Journal* Vol. 3 (1991/2,): 5-11. https://rlhf.info/wp-content/uploads/3.1-Templelands-Welsh.pdf

[83] William McDowall, *History of the Burgh of Dumfries* (Edinburgh: Adam & Charles Black, 1874), 231-233. https://books.google.com/books/about/History_of_the_Burgh_of_Dumfries.html?id=MD0PAAAAYAAJ

[84] James Burnes, *Sketch of the History of the Knights Templar*, Second Edition (Edinburgh: William Blackwood and Sons, London: Payne & Foss, Dublin: John Cumming, 1840), 33, 34, 52, 60-63. https://ia600200.us.archive.org/18/items/sketchofhistoryo00burn/sketchofhistoryo00burn.pdf

Figure D-10: Wikimedia Commons contributors, "File:John Graham, visc Dundee David Paton.jpg," *Wikimedia Commons*, accessed 13 April 2023. https://commons.wikimedia.org/w/index.php?title=File:John_Graham,_visc_Dundee_David_Paton.jpg&oldid=706874417

[85] T.C. Welsh, "The Renfrewshire Templelands," *Renfrewshire Local History Forum (RLHF) Journal* Vol. 3 (1991/2,): 3. https://rlhf.info/wp-content/uploads/3.1-Templelands-Welsh.pdf

[86] William McDowall, *History of the Burgh of Dumfries* (Edinburgh: Adam & Charles Black, 1874), 231-233.

[87] T.J. Carlyle, "The Debatable Land," *Transactions of the Dumfries and Galloway Natural History and Archaeological Society (TDGNHAS)* No. 1004 (1868): 29. https://dgnhas.org.uk/sites/default/files/transactions/1004.pdf

[88] "The Closs" is the close of the medieval church of Mosskesswra.

[89] Col. William Rogerson, *Hutton Under the Muir* (Dumfries, Scotland: Dumfries and Galloway Courier and Herald, 1908), 5.

[90] *Notes and Queries*, Series 6, Vol. 2 (London: John Francis, 1881), 71. https://archive.org/details/s6notesqueries02londuoft/page/70/mode/2up?q=fergus

*Appendix D: A Primer on the Ancient British and Roman Catholic Churches in Scotland*

### 1534 – 1689 Templars Operate in Secret.

The Reformation in Britain began in 1534 with the withdrawal of Henry VIII from the Roman Catholic Church and lasted until 1603 with the death of Elizabeth I.[91] During the Reformation and afterwards, the order drew back from public view. This secret functioning was not compromised until 1689 when John Graham of Claverhouse known as "Bonnie Dundee" was killed in the battle of Killiecrankie. Historian and French priest, Dom Antoine Augustin Calmet, claimed the cross of the Order (Pectoral) was found under Claverhouse's breast plate at Killiecrankie, removed by his brother David, who later left it with Calmet for safekeeping. Calmet also stated that Claverhouse was a "Grand master of Templars in Scotland."[92]

Several years later, just prior to 1603, Sir Richard Graham of Brackenhill and Whitechurch, Ireland, son of Fergus Graham of Mote, was granted a signet ring by Elizabeth I for "military service." Membership in a knightly order is not mentioned in the award. However, this ring included the Templar Sword emblem.[93]

After 1689, there was little known Templar activity in Scotland until the order was revived by Charles Edward Stuart "Bonnie Prince Charlie" in a ceremony in Holyrood Abbey in 1745. "Bonnie Prince Charlie" used the mystique of the order to recruit followers called "Jacobites" in memory of his father, James II. The goal of the Jacobites of 1745, like the Jacobites of 1715 under James II, was to put a Stuart back on the British throne. Both rebellions, the Rising of 1715 and the Rising of 1745, were unsuccessful and the Jacobites were captured and imprisoned.

### Trinitarians.

The third knightly order established in Scotland that we will address was the Order of the Trinitarians (Order of the Most Holy Trinity for the Redemption of the Captives) first founded in 1197 A.D. to exchange prisoners. Pope Innocent III consented to the request by St. John of Matha and St. Felix of Valois, to erect a new religious order, and declared St. John the first general

*Figure D-11: Red and Blue Cross Pattée of the Order of the Trinitarians* [91]

---

[91] "The English Reformation," Study.com, accessed 15 March 2023. https://study.com/learn/lesson/english-reformation-timeline-summary.html

Figure D-11: Wikimedia Commons contributors, "File:Trinitarians - old cross.jpg," *Wikimedia Commons*, accessed 17 April 2023. https://commons.wikimedia.org/w/index.php?title=File:Trinitarians_-_old_cross.jpg&oldid=534648834

[92] Daniel J. Clausen, "Origins of Masonic Templarism in the French Ordre du Temple," Academia.edu, accessed 13 March 2023. https://www.academia.edu/53226567/Origins_of_Masonic_Templarism_in_the_French_Ordre_du_Temple

[93] *Notes and Queries*, Series 6, Vol. 2 (London: John Francis, 1881), 71. https://archive.org/details/s6notesqueries02londuoft/page/70/mode/2up?q=fergus

minister.[94] The Bishop of Paris, and the abbot of St. Victor, were ordered to draw up their rules, which the pope approved by a bull on 17 December 1198. He ordered the religious to wear a white habit, with a red and blue cross on the breast, and to take the name of the order of the Holy Trinity. He added new privileges through a second bull, dated 1209. The Trinitarians of Failford in Ayrshire, were not monks, friars or canons. They were a minor branch of the great Military Orders which came into being during the early Crusading period. The order had become exceedingly popular, with the result that it was formally recognized by Pope Innocent III on 17 December 1198. The main house of the order in Scotland was at Failford in Ayrshire.

The Wallace, Lindsay of Craigie and Thurston, and Kyle-Stewart families all claimed membership in the Trinitarians. These Lindsays witnessed the donation by **Sir John Graham**, the elder of Dalkeith, Lord of Tarbolton, to Failford Ministry of his right of patronage to the church of Tarbolton in 1337. Later, Sir John Graham the younger bestowed it on Robert Graham of Weyliston, who in 1342 transferred it to Melrose Abbey, which resulted in a dispute. The dispute must eventually have been settled by a compromise, because in 1414 the patronage of Tarbolton Kirk was held jointly by the triple patron, Failford, Melrose and the lord of Tarbolton, shortly before the church became a prebend of Glasgow Cathedral.[95] In this case, the prebend was property that provided a regular stipend to the canons of Glasgow Cathedral.[96] The Bosco (Bois) family were major sponsors of the temple in England, providing at least four patrons who donated many acres of land in Oxfordshire and other support such as pasturage rights from 1190-1269, suggesting that the Boscos who moved to Scotland also were strong supporters of the order.[97] Phil Graham believes the family also served as Masters of the Temple, given examples like John de Bosco of Hoddom, who was a Culdee Doctor from Trinitarian Scots College;[98] Richard de Bosco, who served as attorney to the Templars in the thirteenth century;[99] and Ralph De Boys,[vii] who was the parson of Hutton when the Grahams of Mosskesswra came into possession of Hutton, circa 1220-58.[100]

Lesser orders came into being about the same time with similar purposes. Among these were: the *Fratres Pontifices,* who built roads and bridges and gave shelter to pilgrims; the Mercedarians, or

---

[94] Rev Alban Butler, *The Lives or the Fathers, Martyrs and Other Principal Saints*, Vol. 4 (Derby, England: D. & J. Sadlier, & Company, 1864), 380-381. https://archive.org/details/livesoffathersma04butl/page/380/mode/2up?q=matha

[95] William J. Dillon, "The Trinitarians at Failford," *Ayrshire Archaeological and Natural History Society* Vol. 4 (1957): 76, 91-93. https://aanhsorg.files.wordpress.com/2018/08/the-trinitarians-of-failford.pdf

[96] "Prebend," *Dictionary.com*, accessed 13 January 2023. https://www.dictionary.com/browse/prebend

[97] John Walker, "The Patronage of the Templars and the Order of St. Lazarus in England in the Twelfth and Thirteenth Centuries" (Ph.D. Thesis, University of St. Andrews, 1990), 110-113. https://core.ac.uk/download/pdf/9045114.pdf

[98] Mackenzie E.C. Walcott, *Scoti Monasticon-The Ancient Church of Scotland* (London: Virtue, Spalding and Daldy, 1874), 333. https://ia600309.us.archive.org/22/items/scotimonasticona00walc/scotimonasticona00walc.pdf

[99] John Walker, "The Patronage of the Templars and the Order of St. Lazarus in England in the Twelfth and Thirteenth Centuries" (Ph.D. Thesis, University of St. Andrews, 1990), 113. https://core.ac.uk/download/pdf/9045114.pdf

[100] PoMS "no. 4164, person summary," accessed 21 January 2023. https://www.poms.ac.uk/record/person/4164/

*Appendix D: A Primer on the Ancient British and Roman Catholic Churches in Scotland*

*Order of Our Lady of Mercy for the Redemption of Captives,* founded in 1218;[101] and the Trinitarians. The Mercedarians and Trinitarians devoted all their energies and resources to purchasing freedom for those who had been captured by the Turks.[102] Lastly, the Mathurins or *Red Friars* were a religious order instituted circa 1004 by St. Jean de Matha and Felix de Valois for the redemption of Christian slaves in Barbary. The Mathurin friars first emerged at Notre Dame in Paris before the Norman Conquest, then merged with the Trinitarians in 1153.[103] Former Graham church lands in Torthorwald[104] and Moffat were also connected to Trinitarians or the Red Friars.[105] About the beginning of the sixteenth century, the Earl of Lennox gifted St Mary's Chapel of the Dumbarton Collegiate Church connected to the Montrose Grahams[106] to the Abbey of Kilwinning.[107] About that same time, Kilwinning became the Mother Lodge for the Freemasons.[108]

> **Important Note...**
> One of the first patrons of Newbattle Abbey, was "William, son-in-law of Sorn (Forn)." Forn was the theorized father of William de Graham and also a signatory on the foundation charter of Scone Abbey.

**Summary of Grahams with Suspected Connections to (Provided Financial/Logistical Support or were Members of) one of the Knightly Orders:**

Templar Connections: William de Graham,[109] Ralph de Graham[110], Henry of Braid,[111] David Graham of Dundaff [noted as " David Graham (III)" in the People of Medieval Scotland (PoMS)],[112]

---

[101] "Our History," Order of the Blessed Virgin Mary of Mercy, Mercedarian Friars USA, accessed 16 January 2023. https://www.orderofmercy.org/our-history

[102] Daniel Hershenzon, "Ransom: Between Economic, Political, and Salvific Interests," *The Captive Sea: Slavery, Communication, and Commerce in Early Modern Spain and the Mediterranean* (Philadelphia: University of Pennsylvania Press, 2019), 41-67. https://doi.org/10.9783/9780812295368-004

[103] Ebeneezer Cobham Brewer, *Historic Note Book* (Philadelphia: Lippincott, 1892), 575. https://www.google.com/books/edition/Historic_Note_book/YmwUAAAAYAAJ?hl=en&gbpv=1&dq=order+of+mathurin+first+established+in+scotland&pg=PA575&printsec=frontcover

[104] George Chalmers, *Caledonia or an Historical and Topographical Account of North Britain*, Vol. VI (Paisley: Alexander Gardner, 1890), 492. https://www.electricscotland.com/books/pdf/caledoniaorhisto06chal.pdf

[105] William McDowall, *History of the Burgh of Dumfries* (Edinburgh: Adam and Charles Black, 1867), 231. https://www.seibelfamily.net/uploads/1/1/6/5/116501719/history_of_the_burgh_of_dumfries.pdf

[106] Sir James Balfour Paul, *The Scots Peerage, Founded on Wood's Edition,* Vol. VI (Edinburgh: David Douglas, 1909), 213. https://archive.org/details/scotspeeragefoun06pauluoft/page/148/mode/2up?q=glenny

[107] David MacGibbon and Thomas Ross, The ecclesiastical architecture of Scotland from the earliest Christian times to the seventeenth century, Vol. 3, (Edinburgh: George Waterson and Sons, 1897), digitized/produced by Chuck Greif, Project Gutenberg, 423. https://www.gutenberg.org/files/65014/65014-h/65014-h.htm#page_423

[108] Iain D. McIntosh, "Scottish Freemasonry and England 1700- 1750," *Grand Lodge of Scotland*, accessed 6 March 2023. http://www.pglforfarshire.org/Scottish_Freemasonry_and_England_Part02.html

[109] PoMS no. 1038 , place summary, Clerkington, accessed 6 March 2023. https://www.poms.ac.uk/record/place/1038/

[110] PoMS, "no.5942, factoid," accessed 13 February 2023. https://www.poms.ac.uk/record/factoid/5942/

[111] PoMS, "no. 4388," accessed 8 February 2023. https://www.poms.ac.uk/record/source/4388/

[112] PoMS, "no. 2005-David Graham (III), Sheriff of Berwick," accessed 12 November 2022. https://www.poms.ac.uk/record/person/2005/

[blurb] PoMS, "No. 374," accessed 18 October 2022. https://www.poms.ac.uk/record/source/374/

*Appendix D: A Primer on the Ancient British and Roman Catholic Churches in Scotland*

William Graham of Claverhouse (Bonnie Dundee),[113] David Graham of Claverhouse,[114] the Grahams of Mosskesswra, Sir Richard Graham of Ireland (great-grandson of Fergus of Mote), and the 324 entries with the surname "Graham" in FindmyPast's database of prisoners from the Jacobite Rising of 1745, which include several Grahams of Dundee.[115]

A search on David Graham of Dundaff (III), Sheriff of Berwick in PoMS, from 1247 to 1259 reveals 50 different transactions involving land gifts. This was an unusually high number for anyone except the king. Coincidentally, the Seventh Crusade began in 1248 and lasted until 1254,[116] supporting the claim that David Graham served as a finance officer for the order and that they were making preparations for the Crusades.[117] The Dalkeith Grahams (elder line) were a primary sponsor of Newbattle Abbey in Dalkeith,[118, 119] a base of the Knights Templar.[120] Newbattle's first abbot (1140-1150), known as "Ralph,"[121] may be an uncle to the Ralph Graham (Figure 38) who gifted the temple lands of Clifton, Curry, and Gogor to the abbey between 1170 and 1174.[122]

Hospitaller Connections: Alexander Graham of Denny,[123] Sir Nicholas de Graham (d. 1306) was a member of the Order of Knights of the Hospital of Saint John of Jerusalem, given he held advowson rights for the Hospital of St. Mary Magdalene.[124]

Trinitarian Connections: Sir John de Graham, the elder (d. 1337)[125]

---

[113] If Bonnie Dundee was connected to the Templars, some of his relatives may also have been involved. James Graham, ninth Laird of Fintry, commissioned a major in the Forfar Regiment in support of Charles II, and Dundee's friend, may have been responsible for the latter agreeing to serve under Charles II. The Marquis of Montrose, grandson of the Great Marquis, wrote Dundee in 1678 to persuade him to join a troop of horse the Marquis was raising "for the King of Scotland." Sir Francis Mude and David M. Walker, "Mains Castle and the Grahams of Fintry." *Abertay Historical Society* No. 9 (1964): 14-15. https://abertay.org.uk/wp-content/uploads/2017/08/MainsCastle&Grahams.pdf

[114] "John Graham of Claverhouse," *The Order of the Fleur de Lis*, accessed 30 November 2021. https://www.orderofthefleurdelys.org.uk/order-history/john-graham-of-claverhouse/

[115] Iain Gray, "Masonic Parable and the Legend of the Pillar," *The Herald*, 4 October 1989. https://www.heraldscotland.com/news/11929072.masonic-parable-and-legend-of-the-pillar/

[116] "Crusades Timeline, *World History Encyclopedia*, accessed 16 January 2023. https://www.worldhistory.org/timeline/Crusades/

[117] PoMS "No. 2005," person summary, accessed 13 December 2022. https://www.poms.ac.uk/record/person/2005/

[118] PoMS "no. 7444," accessed 1 March 2023. https://www.poms.ac.uk/record/source/7444/

[119] PoMS "no. 1764," person summary, accessed 1 March 2023. https://www.poms.ac.uk/record/person/1764/

[120] Jim McQuiston, "Templars," ILoveScotland.net, accessed 1 March 2023. http://www.ilovescotland.net/templars.html

[121] PoMS, "no. 339, person summary," accessed 1 March 2023. https://www.poms.ac.uk/record/person/339/

[122] PoMS, "no. 1286, person summary," accessed 1 March 2023. https://www.poms.ac.uk/record/person/1286/

[123] Ian B. Cowan, P.H.R. Mackay and Alan Macquarrie, *Knights of St. John of Jerusalem in Scotland*, Vol. 19 (Edinburgh, Clark Constable, 1983), 8. https://digital.nls.uk/126638043

[124] Joseph Bain, *Calendar of Documents Relating to Scotland*, Vol. IV, 1357 A.D. – 1509 (Edinburgh: H.M. General Register House, 1888), 362. https://www.electricscotland.com/history/records/bain/calendarofdocuments04.pdf

[125] William J. Dillon, "The Trinitarians at Failford," *Ayrshire Archaeological and Natural History Society* Volume 4 (1957): 76, 91-93.

*Appendix D: A Primer on the Ancient British and Roman Catholic Churches in Scotland*

## III. GLOSSARY

### A. Lands with Culdee Connections in Scotland (in Alphabetical Order):

Examples of church properties where Grahams of Hutton were found in possession include Moskesso Barony (St. Kessog), Old Melrose Abbey (St. Cuthbert), Westerkirk (St. Cuthbert-a subordinate church to Melrose), Wamphray (St. Cuthbert), Kirkpatrick, Redkirk and Rampatrick (St. Patrick), Hutton (St. Cuthbert-a subordinate church to Jedburgh Abbey[126]), Dryfe (St. John of Jerusalem), Gretna (St. Patrick), Hoddam and Lochmaben (St. Mungo, aka St. Kentigern).

Ancestors of the Grahams of Hutton, the Corries, were established all throughout Hoddam,

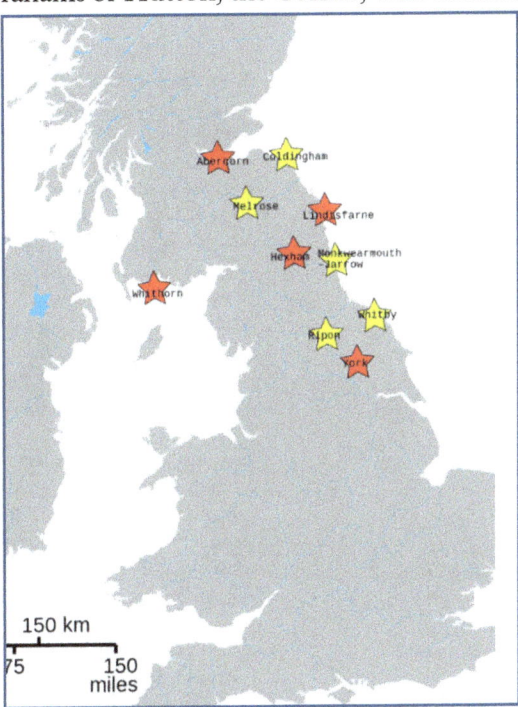

*Figure D-12: Northumbrian Bishoprics and Monasteries, circa 680 A.D. By Angus McLellan* [126] *Note: Bishoprics are in Red, Monasteries are in Yellow. This file is licensed under Creative Commons CC-BY 3.0.*

Redkirk, Langholm and Lochmaben in Dumfriesshire before the arrival of the Normans circa 1124. The property records listed in the chronology at the end of Appendix F, show the circumstances

---

[126] Jane Brankstone Thomas, J.C. B. Sharp, and Michael Anne Guido, "A Cumberland Family with Medieval Roots in Scotland and Northern England: A Study Gilbert Fitz Richer and His Descendants," *Foundation for Medieval Genealogy, Foundations* (2008): 360. https://fmg.ac/phocadownload/userupload/foundations2/JN-02-05/358Richer.pdf

Figure D-12: Wikimedia Commons contributors, "File:Northumbrian bishoprics and monasteries, 680s.svg," *Wikimedia Commons,* accessed 17 April 2023. https://commons.wikimedia.org/w/index.php?title=File:Northumbrian_bishoprics_and_monasteries,_680s.svg&oldid=484058331

leading up to Lang Will Graham and his kinsman John Corry being forfeited of these same former church lands in 1517.[127]

Wikiwand provides a comprehensive collection of historical information on monasteries in Scotland.[128] Rev James Rankin provided a brief list in *A Handbook of the Church of Scotland* in 1888.[129] See Figure D-13.

```
CELTIC MONASTERIES.                                    31

Seats of Celtic Monasteries.—Fifty institutions.
Aberdour, in Buchan.  S. Drostan's settlement.
Abernethy.  Long dispute of Culdees there with the monks
    of Arbroath.
Applecross, Monastery of S. Maelrubha.
Aberelliot or Arbirlot, Forfarshire.
Blair, in Gowrie.
Brechin.  Culdees continued long after it was a bishop's see.
Cloveth, in parish of Auchindoir or Cabrach, a cell of Mortlach.
Culross on Forth, said to be founded by S. Serf, but existed
    earlier.
Deir.  The Book of Deer of ninth century connects it with
    Columba and Drostan.
Dull, an Abthane, S. Adamnan.  Had "smith" street and
    "mason" street.
Dunblane.  Lower part of tower of Culdee date.  They
    struggled on to thirteenth century.
Dunfermline.  Had buildings for Culdees under Malcolm III.
Dunkeld.  S. Adamnan's foundation after plunder of Iona.
Ecclesgrig or S. Cyrus, at Kirkside.
Edzell, in Glenesk, founded by S. Drostan.
Falkirk or Varia Capella, centre of S. Modan's work.
Glasgow, S. Kentigern's foundation.
Glendochart, S. Fillan's monastery.  Bell, crosier, pool.
Govan, on site of the Parish Church.  See S. Constantine.
Hoddam.  Kentigern spent eight years here on return from
    Wales.
Iona or Hy, planted by Columba and twelve disciples 563.
Kettins, in south-west corner of Forfarshire, had six ancient
    chapels.
Kilgouerin, Kilgour or Falkland, an old religious seat.
Kilmuir, in Ross.
Kilmund.  See Mund in list of Celtic Saints.
Kilspindy, near Aberlady, which belonged to Dunkeld.
Kineff, in Kincardine, where is S. Arnty or Adamnan's cell.
Kingarth or Cenn Garad, in Bute.  S. Blane.

32                                    CELTIC MONASTERIES.

Kinghorne, an old Abthanery, implying a monastery.
Kirkcaldy, old Kyre-aldyn.  Chalmers's Caledonia, i. 439.
Kirkmichael, an Abthanedom under Dunkeld.
Lesmahago.  Culdees settled at Kirkfield on Abbey Green be-
    fore David I.
Lismore, a settlement of Molocus which prepared for see of
    Argyle.
Lochleven.  In 842 King Brude founded on S. Serf's Isle a
    college of Culdees.
Madderty, an Abthanedom, site of Inchaffray Abbey.
Melginch or Megginch, in parish of Errol.
Monifieth, an Abthanedom, and had Keledei before 1242.
Monymusk.  Twelve Culdees under a prior preceded Church
    of SS. Mary and John.
Mortlach, original of see of Aberdeen.
Muthill.  Tower of tenth or eleventh century.  Had monastery
    on Estate "Culdees," and had Keledei from 1178 to 1214.
Old Dornoch, in earldom of Caithness.  Had Culdees till
    1222.
Old Mailros, under Eata, Boisil, and Cuthbert.  Had monks
    from Lindisfarne.
Old Montrose, Munros, Celurka or Salorky.
Ratho, S. Mary's, near Edinburgh.
Rosmarky, Fortrose, S. Boniface, 716.  Culdees afterwards.
Rossin or Rossinclerach, Rossie in Inchture, north bank of
    Tay.
Scone, representing the earldom of Gowrie.  Had an earlier
    monastery.
Selkirk, a monastery before the Abbey of SS. Mary and John,
    1113.
S. Andrews.  Had Celtic monks under S. Cainnech in 598,
    and at first elected the bishop.
Turriff, overlooking valley of Dee, founded by S. Congan.
```

Figure D-13: List of Celtic (Culdee) Monasteries from "A Handbook of the Church of Scotland" by Rev. James Rankin, published in 1888 [129]

---

[127] R.C. Reid, "The Border Grahams and Their Origins," *Transactions of the Dumfries and Galloway Natural History and Archaeological Society (TDGNHAS)* No. 3038 (1961): 91.
https://dgnhas.org.uk/sites/default/files/transactions/3038.pdf

[128] "List of Monastic Houses in Scotland," Wikiwand, accessed 9 January 2023.
https://www.wikiwand.com/en/List_of_monastic_houses_in_Scotland

[129] Figure D-13: James Rankin, *A Handbook of the Church of Scotland* (Edinburgh and London: William Blackwood & Sons, 1888), 31-32.
https://ia800703.us.archive.org/22/items/handbookofchurch188800rank/handbookofchurch188800rank.pdf

1. **Abercorn, West Lothian (681–685 A.D.):** A monastery dedicated to St. Serf was founded circa 675 by St. Wilfrid near the northern extremity of the newly expanded Anglo-Saxon Kingdom of Northumbria.[130] In 681 A.D., St. Trumwine from Lindisfarne was appointed "Bishop of those Picts who were then subject to English rule," i.e., those north of the River Forth paying tribute to Northumbria." The church at Abercorn was converted to an Anglian kirk under Lindisfarne (St. Cuthbert) in 854.[131] With the arrival of the Normans in Scotland, Abercorn and the Celtic bishopric of Abercorn, the oldest bishopric in Scotland, Figure D-12 , came under the Avenel family. David I later transferred the Abercorn bishopric to the bishop of St. Andrews. The lands transferred in marriage from the Avenels to the Grahams of Dalkeith about 1248.[132] While the official date of Scotland's conversion to Roman Catholicism is given as 1250A.D.,[133] some still followed Culdeeism through the age of the Royal Stewarts circa 1427.[134]

2. **Abernethy, (Perthshire), Perth, and Kinross (early eighth century – eleventh century):** The capital of the Picts, a Columban monastery was established there in the sixth century. By 1100, Abernethy became an important center for Culdee monks.[135] Their churches had the characteristic round towers of Culdee churches. The Picts appointed their own bishops and stubbornly refused to submit to bishops outside their kingdom.[136] By 1100, the Abbot of Abernethy asserted that the church property was the inheritance of himself and his heirs.[137] A small Augustinian priory of 1272 in Abernethy likely included Culdees, given construction of round towers in the eleventh to twelfth centuries.[138]

3. **Brechin, Angus Cathedral of the Holy Trinity (*ante* 1150):** The former cathedral building, now Brechin High Kirk, dates from the thirteenth century. The site was formerly occupied by a Culdee monastery, possibly derived from Abernethy. After the Reformation, the building was abandoned. A much-criticized reconstruction completed in 1806 was followed by a more sensitive restoration

---

[130] "Records of Abercorn / Abercorn North Kirk Session," *National Records of Scotland*, accessed 9 January 2023. https://catalogue.nrscotland.gov.uk/nrsonlinecatalogue/browseDetails.aspx?reference=CH2/835&

[131] Mackenzie E.C. Walcott, *Scoti Monasticon-The Ancient Church of Scotland* (London: Virtue, Spalding and Daldy, 1874), 239. https://ia600309.us.archive.org/22/items/scotimonasticona00walc/scotimonasticona00walc.pdf

[132] "Death of Bishop Trumwine, 2nd December 704," Engliscan Gesiðas (The English Companions), accessed 16 January 2023. https://www.tha-engliscan-gesithas.org.uk/events-in-anglo-saxon-times/on-this-day/on-this-day-in-december/

[133] Rev J.A. Wylie, *The History of the Scottish Nation*, Vol. 3 (London: Hamilton, Adams and Co., 1886), 203-204, 298. https://www.originofnations.org/books,%20papers/history%20of%20the%20scots/scothistvol3.pdf

[134] "Culdees," McClintock and Strong Bible Clopedia, accessed 11 April 2023. https://www.biblicalcyclopedia.com/C/culdees.html

[135] "Abernethy," Undiscovered Scotland, accessed 16 January 2023. https://www.undiscoveredscotland.co.uk/abernethy/abernethy/index.html

[136] Archibald B. Scott, *The Pictish Nation, Its People and Its Church* (Edinburgh and London: T.N. Foulis, 1918), 263, 480-482. https://archive.org/details/pictishnationits00scotrich

[137] James Taylor, *The Pictorial History of Scotland*, Vol. I (London: James S. Virture, 1859), 167.

[138] "Abernethy 'Culdees' Monastery," Canmore: National Record of the Historic Environment, accessed 16 January 2023. https://canmore.org.uk/site/27936/abernethy-culdees-monastery

1900–1902.¹³⁹ Original parts remaining include the western gable and massive square tower, parts of the choir, the nave pillars and clerestory. Next to the church is a fine round tower dating circa 1000 and strange creature carved around doorways in Celtic style.¹⁴⁰

4. **Closeburn (founded twelfth century)**: "In the parish of Closeburn there was formerly a chapel which was dedicated to St. Patrick, and which gave its name of Kirkpatrick to a nearby farm, whereon stand its ruins. From this place the family of Kirkpatrick assumed their surname in the twelfth century. The Kirkpatricks were the proprietors of Closeburn from the twelfth to the eighteenth century."¹⁴¹

5. **Dryfesdale (founded 1116)**: The parish church was built in 1671. This is the second of two churches on Kirkhill. The earliest document of the first church, which was dedicated to Saint Cuthbert, is in 1116. It was swept away by the river in 1670 and replaced by another church at Lockerbie in 1757.¹⁴²

6. **Dunkeld (Perthshire), Cathedral of St. Columba (founded ninth century)**: Tradition tells of a monastery founded by the early seventh century after a visit by St. Columba, who was based at Iona. By the ninth century the site had a stone-built Culdee monastery possessing relics of St. Columba. About 869, its abbot was described as the chief bishop of the kingdom, but very soon after St. Andrews became the chief bishopric of the Scottish church. The cathedral was re-founded in the twelfth century, though most surviving fabric dates from the fifteenth century (there are traces of Culdee stonework). In the Reformation the nave was unroofed, but the thirteenth-century choir has been used ever since as the parish kirk.¹⁴³

7. **Glasgow Cathedral of St. Kentigern/St. Mungo (founded 1114)**: Tradition holds a church settlement founded here by St. Mungo (also known as St. Kentigern) in the sixth century, from which Glasgow developed. The diocese began with the appointment of Bishop John (1114–1147). Most of the fabric is thirteenth-century, the central tower and spire are fifteenth-century, and the Blackadder Aisle is from circa 1500. What is unusual for a pre-Reformation Scottish cathedrals, Glasgow's was never unroofed, which helps explain its good and complete condition. St. Mungo's tomb is in the crypt.¹⁴⁴

8. **Gretna (before tenth Century)**: The Church had its origins in Pictish times at St. Brigids Well on Gretna Hill. There was an early Christian connection with the district as an adjoining parish,

---

¹³⁹ "History," Brechin Cathedral, accessed 11 April 2023. https://brechincathedral.org.uk/about/history/

¹⁴⁰ P.H. Ditchfield, *The Cathedrals of Great Britain, Their History and Architecture* (London: J&M Dent and Co., 1902), 442. https://www.gutenberg.org/files/43402/43402.txt

¹⁴¹ James Murray MacKinlay, *Influence of the Pre-Reformation Church on Scottish Placenames* (Edinburgh and London: Blackwood and Sons, 1904), 136-137. https://archive.org/details/cu31924028080566/page/n159/mode/2up?q=closeburn

¹⁴² "Dryfe, Old Parish Church and Churchyard," Archaeology Notes, Canmore: National Record of the Historic Environment, accessed 9 January 2023. https://canmore.org.uk/event/729149

¹⁴³ "Dunkeld Cathedral," Historic Environment Scotland, accessed 11 April 2023. https://www.historicenvironment.scot/visit-a-place/places/dunkeld-cathedral/

¹⁴⁴ "The St. Kentigern Way, Following the Saint's Journey from Hoddom to Glasgow," Kentigern Way, accessed 9 January 2023. http://kentigernway.com/page22.html

named Reinpatrick, indicating that it was probably an outpost of St. Patrick's mission field. By the sixteenth century, the church at Reinpatrick, or the Red Kirk, had fallen into decay and was joined to the Parish of Graitney. The parishes of Gretna and Redkirk were united in 1609.[145] Dumfries and Galloway Gretna's old parish church probably lies on the site of its medieval precursor, first recorded in 1170. The churchyard contains a number of medieval grave-slabs. The grave-slabs are probably 'hogback' stone, so-called because of its distinctive arched back and tapered shape. Hogback stones appear to have developed in northern England in the tenth century, influenced by the house-shaped shrines used to hold the relics of Christian saints. In Scotland, early examples can be seen at Govan, Meigle, and on Inchcolm Island on the Firth of Forth.[146]

9. **Halkirk (Caithness), Highland (founded eighth century):** Tradition tells of a church founded here by St. Fergus in the early eighth century before Caithness fell under Norse control. Claims that the cathedral of the Bishop of Caithness was located here are unresolved. Halkirk was one part of the large parish of Skinnet until the thirteenth century.[147]

10. **Hoddom (Dumfriesshire) (founded sixth century):** In Dumfries and Galloway, a cathedral was said to have been founded here in the late sixth century by St. Mungo (Kentigern).[148] The cathedral seems not to have survived his death in 612. The Old Churchyard of St. Kentigern, a graveyard and a medieval church, was built there in the twelfth century. In 1851, archaeologists discovered the remains of a bronze crozier or staff in the ruins of the church, a symbol of St. Kentigern/St. Mungo.[149] In 1991 the remains of a large eighth century monastery were discovered on the high ground behind the churchyard.[150]

11. **Staplegordon, Langholm (founded twelfth century):** It was originally included in the ancient parish of "Staplegortoun." William de Cunnigburc, who possessed the manor of Staplegortoun in the Twelfth Century, granted it to the Monks of Kelso "the Church of Staplegortoun with all the lands belonging to it." The Kelso Monks held the church until the Reformation when it was transferred to the Earl of Roxburgh. Sometime later, the King bought the parish titles and, in 1637, transferred them to the Bishop of Glasgow.[151]

---

[145] Gerald England, "Old Gretna Parish Church," Geography.org, accessed 9 January 2023. https://www.geograph.org.uk/photo/5511143

[146] "View of coped graveslab to SE of church bearing two parallel graves in its upper surface, Gretna Old Church and Parish Church," Canmore: National Record of the Historic Environment, accessed 9 January 2023. https://canmore.org.uk/collection/382638

[147] "St. Fergus the Pict," Cushnieent.com, accessed 11 April 2023. https://www.cushnieent.com/saints/stfergus.html

[148] "Churchyard of St. Kentigern," VisitScotland, accessed 9 January 2023. https://www.visitscotland.com/info/see-do/churchyar Zd-of-st-kentigern-p254441

[149] C.A. Ralegh Radford, "Two Reliquaries Connected with South-West Scotland," *Transactions of the Dumfries and Galloway Natural History and Archaeological Society (TDGNHAS)* No. 3032 (1955): 116. https://dgnhas.org.uk/sites/default/files/transactions/3032.pdf

[150] "St. Mungo (or Castlemilk) Parish in Annandale," GENUKI.org.uk, accessed 9 January 2023. https://www.genuki.org.uk/big/sct/DFS/St.Mungo

[151] "Langholm Old Parish Church (1846-1946)," Langholm Archive Group, accessed 11 April 2023. https://www.langholmarchive.com/pchistory/pchistory.php

12. **Kingarth, Isle of Bute, Argyll, and Bute Monastery of St. Blane (founded sixth century):** A monastery was reputedly built here by Saint Cathan. He was succeeded as bishop by his nephew Saint Blane. It was a cathedral until St. Blane's death circa 590. The monastery was destroyed by Viking raids circa 790. A new church was built on the site in the twelfth century but fell out of use after 1560.[152]

13. **Lochmaben, St. Kentigern/St. Mungo (late sixth century):** Nuath, son of Coel Godhebog, a Cumbrian prince who flourished before 300, owned lands in Annandale and Clydesdale. It is said these lands were named after him—Caer-nuath, or Carnwath. One of Nuath's descendants, Loth, a Pictish king, formed an encampment along the base of the Tynwald hills. The second son, Gwallon, built a chain of forts extending from Dryfesdale to the vicinity of Lochmaben. Gwallon's sister, Thenelis, was the mother of the celebrated Kentigern, or St. Mungo, whose name is retained by a Dumfriesshire parish.[153]

14. **Melrose Abbey ("Old Melrose"- St. Cuthbert) (650A.D. – 1609 A.D.):** An ancient monastery of Melrose had existed since the seventh century on the Tweed River in Roxburghshire. It was established about 650A.D. by St. Aidan, the Culdee missionary from Iona, who preached in Northumbria, and founded the abbey of Lindisfarne. St. Cuthbert spent much of his early life at this monastery later referred to as "Old Melrose," and later in life at Hexham and Lindisfarne. Figure D-12. The monks of Lindisfarne fled a Danish raid with St. Cuthbert's body in 875 A.D, which ultimately found its final resting-place at Durham. By the eleventh century "Old Melrose" had become a ruin.[154] The "New Melrose" Abbey was founded further up the River Tweed by David I in 1136. See Figure D-14. He granted the abbey to the Cistercian Order of monks, previously instituted in France.[155]

---

[152] Helen Armet, "Saint Blaine's Chapel," The Orkney News, 18 September 2019. https://theorkneynews.scot/2019/09/18/st-blanes-chapel/

[153] William McDowall, *History of the Burgh of Dumfries* (Edinburgh: Adam and Charles Black, 1867), 21. https://archive.org/details/cu31924028091357/page/20/mode/2up?q=lochmaben

[154] James Augustine Wade, *The History of St. Mary's Abbey, Melrose, The Monastery of Old Melrose and the Town and Parish of Melrose* (Edinburgh: Thomas C. Jack, 1841), 82-120. https://archive.org/details/historyofstmarys00wadeiala/page/n7/mode/2up

[155] Peta Stamper, "Melrose Abbey," History Hit, 26 May 2021. https://www.historyhit.com/locations/melrose-abbey/

Appendix D: A Primer on the Ancient British and Roman Catholic Churches in Scotland

Figure D-14: Joan Blaeu's 1654 Atlas of Scotland, Based on surveys by Timothy Pont, showing Old and New Melrose. CC-BY 4.0 Reproduced with the permission of the National Library of Scotland.

a. **Melrose Abbey-Graham Connections**
   i. The oldest heraldic memorial of the ancient family of Avenel is the seal of Sir Robert Avenel, the Norman benefactor of "New" Melrose, which is appended to one of the Abbey charters. Robert Avenel, the first Lord of Eskdale, and ancestor of the Grahams of Hutton, received his lands from King David I, whom he accompanied from England to Scotland. In the reign of King Malcolm IV (1141-1165), Robert de Avenel gave the monks of Saint Mary's Abbey at Melrose parcels of land in Eskdale, reserving to himself the right of hunting in the forests of Selkirk (now called Ettrick Forest) and Traquair, also a yearly rent of five marks. One of these marks he remitted for maintaining a light to burn perpetually before the altar of the Blessed Virgin Mary in remembrance of his wife, Sybilla. He entered this same monastery in his old age and died in 1185.[156]
   - 1235: Robert's son, Roger Avenel, confirmed the land gift to "New Melrose" Abbey[157]
   - 1306-1329: The Grahams of Dalkeith were at loggerheads so much with "New" Melrose that King Robert the Bruce, Robert I, had to

---

[156] Monsignor Seton, *An Old Family or The Setons of Scotland and America* (New York: Bretano's, 1899), 8-9. https://deriv.nls.uk/dcn23/9572/95729930.23.pdf

[157] PoMS, "no.2223, person summary," accessed 9 February 2023. https://www.poms.ac.uk/record/person/2223/

mediate a settlement. The family had claimed back all the gifts their ancestors had previously given to "Old Melrose."[158] The basis of the argument would have been that the gifts to "Old Melrose" and the foundations of Celtic Culdee Saints Cuthbert and Aidan did not transfer to "New" Melrose (and Saint Mary) under Anglo-Norman rule.[viii] Robert I was obliged to mediate between Grahams/Corries and the new Prior of Melrose Abbey, which was not the same house as the original Celtic Orthodox Culdee foundation. That would explain why the Grahams and their Corrie cousins were keepers of many Culdee Establishments in Scotland.[159] [160]

- 1308: Grant in dedication to Mary the Blessed Virgin.
- Before 1337: "New" Melrose Abbey, Devotee: Sir John de Graham (the elder) of Dalkeith, Abercorn, and Eskdale, born circa 1278, died 25 April 1337. Son of Sir Nicholas de Graham (died circa 1304).[161]
- Circa 1335: Sir John de Graham (the elder) forcibly resumed land at Eskdale given earlier to the abbey.[162]
- 1360: Letter of Protection by William Earl of Douglas (Graham brother-in-law) in favor of the Monks of Melrose, 24th April 1360[163]

15. 1361-62: Sir John the Graham of Dalkeith gifts the lands of "Elsystone" or "Ellastown" to John, son and heir of Richard de Graham." I believe this "Ellastown" is "Elliston" on the estate of Melrose Abbey.[164] **Mortlach, (now Dufftown), (Banffshire), Moray St. Moluag's Cathedral 1011 to 1131:** The *Chronicle of* John of Fordun records the establishment of an episcopal seat in Mortlach aided by Malcolm II of Scotland, circa 1011. The see was translated to Aberdeen in 1131. The placename of Mortlach was superseded by

---

[158] PoMS, "no. 16488, person summary," accessed 14 February 2023. https://www.poms.ac.uk/record/person/16488/

[159] "Melrose Abbey," Undiscovered Scotland, accessed 9 January 2023. https://www.undiscoveredscotland.co.uk/melrose/melroseabbey/index.html

[160] James Augustine Wade, *The History of St. Mary's Abbey, Melrose, The Monastery of Old Melrose and the Town and Parish of Melrose* (Edinburgh: Thomas C. Jack, 1841), 82-120. https://archive.org/details/historyofstmarys00wadeiala/page/n7/mode/2up

[161] "Survey of Dedications to Saints in Medieval Scotland," *University of Edinburgh, School of History, Classics and Archaeology*, accessed 10 January 2023. http://www.shca.ed.ac.uk/Research/saints/Project.htm

[162] PoMS, "no.7761," accessed 9 February 2023. https://www.poms.ac.uk/record/source/7761/

[163] "Letter of Protection by William Earl of Douglas in favour of the Monks of Melrose, 24th April 1360," School of History, Classics and Archaeology Teaching Collections, *accessed* 10 February 2023. 2023. http://collections.shca.ed.ac.uk/items/show/100

[164] T.J. Carlyle, "The Debatable Land," *Transactions of the Dumfries and Galloway Natural History and Archaeological Society (TDGNHAS)*, No. 1004 (1868): 28. https://dgnhas.org.uk/sites/default/files/transactions/1004.pdf

*Appendix D: A Primer on the Ancient British and Roman Catholic Churches in Scotland*

Dufftown in 1817 (the church is located in the Dufftown district known as Kirktown of Mortlach).[165]

16. **Mosskesswra:** The barony also spelled "Moskesso" in the Dryfe Valley of Dumfriesshire and juxta (nearby) and "Mossknow Kirk" in the parish of Kirkpatrick-Fleming are derived from "Mo Kesso," which means "my dear St. Kessog."[166] Lang Will Graham of the Border Grahams was from the Moskesso (Mosskesswra) Barony before he re-settled in England. The Kirkpatrick-Fleming parish church, erected in 1778, is located next to Mossknowe. The ancient church was given to the monks of Gisburn by Robert I and includes the ancient parishes of Kirkconnel, Kirkpatrick, and Irvine. It received the adjunct to its name from the Fleming family, who possessed several towers on the border.[167]

> **FYI...**
> David I promised the Annandale parishes of Hoddam, Wamphray, and as far north as Moffat to the Glasgow Diocese around 1124 A.D., but Bishop Ingram of Glasgow required royal mediation to finally secure them from the Bruces in 1185.

17. **Paisley:** Sir William Wallace himself was likely educated at the Culdee school of the Paisley Clunaics, and the influence of the abbey may have helped to mold within him the character which Fordun thus describes:— "He [Wallace] venerated the church and respected the clergy; his greatest abhorrence was for falsehood and lying; his uttermost loathing for treason, and therefore the Lord was with him, through whom he was a man whose every work prospered in his hand." The monks of Paisley during the times of Wallace and Bruce were on the Scottish patriotic side.[168]

18. **Rampatrick and Redkirk:** The parish church of Redkirk, also known as Raynpatrick or Rampatrick, dedicated to St. Patrick, was probably built in the late twelfth century. It was granted to the monks of Guisborough Priory circa 1170 by Robert de Brus. Redkirk ownership was frequently in dispute between Guisborough and the bishops of Glasgow to whom it was ceded in 1223, but it was still connected with the priory in 1330. Eventually it became an independent parsonage under Glasgow. The parish was united to Gretna in 1609. This church and its burial-ground originally stood at the head of Redkirk Point overlooking the Solway, but was eroded away entirely and the church fell into the sea in 1675.[169]

---

[165] James E. Cumming, "Saint Moluag of Mortlach," June 1966. https://dufftown.info/2022/05/28/saint-moluag-of-mortlach-1966/

[166] James Murray Mackinlay, "St. Kessog and His Cultus in Scotland," *Transactions of the Glasgow Archaeological Society* 3, no. 2 (1899): 347. http://www.jstor.org/stable/24680608

[167] "Kirkpatrick-Fleming," GENUKI.org.uk, accessed 9 January 2023. https://www.genuki.org.uk/big/sct/DFS/KirkpatrickFleming

[FYI..blurb] PoMS, "no.4192," accessed 19 February 2023. https://www.poms.ac.uk/record/source/4192/

[168] Dugald Butler and Herbert Story, *Scottish Cathedrals and Abbeys* (London: A&C Black, Edinburgh: R&R Clark Ltd, 1901), 153. https://www.gutenberg.org/files/21688/21688-h/21688-h.htm

[169] "Dryfe, Old Parish Church and Churchyard," Archaeology Notes, Canmore: National Record of the Historic Environment, accessed 9 January 2023. https://canmore.org.uk/site/67469/redkirk-old-parish-church

*Appendix D: A Primer on the Ancient British and Roman Catholic Churches in Scotland*

19. **Rosemarkie, (Ross), Highland Cathedral of St. Peter (and St. Boniface):** A monastic cathedral was probably founded by St. Curetán (also known as St. Boniface), Bishop of Ross, and St. Moluag about 716. St. Moluag was probably buried here. The Diocese of Ross was restored by David I in 1124.[170]

20. **Tarbolton:** A dependency of Mauchline Priory under Melrose and St. Michael the Archangel.[171] Given to Failford in Ayrshire in 1337 by the elder Sir John de Graham.[172]

21. **Wamphray:** Per Tradition, St. Mungo, protégé of St. Serf, established the first Christian church in the Annandale region at Wamphray as a base church in pagan territory near the end of the sixth century.[173] By medieval times, Wamphray and Hutton were under the St. Cuthbert branch of Culdees: "Old Melrose" monastery and the Lindisfarne bishopric.[174] The church is known for the mysterious "Wamphray Dragon" now located above its western entrance. It was used as a Christian cross grave stone that curiously combined a distinctly Norse dragon with a pattern derived from Anglian leaf scrolls, and a Celtic Wheel used in Celtic Wheel Crosses[175] dated 950-960 A.D.[176] Coincidentally, the Corrie-Grahams inherited a dragon well beside Hutton Kirk and with a dragon cross shaft.

*Figure D-15: Wamphray Dragon on the Western Door of St. Cuthbert's Church in Wamphray, Scotland, dated 950-960A.D. CC-BY-SA/2.0 - © Chris Newman - geograph.org.uk/p/831825*

What is confusing is that the dragon symbology is also connected to St. Serf, as well as the seals of David I and his father Malcolm III, and St. Michael of Archangel.[177] Phil Graham notes that the "Triple Cult of the Dragon" was later branded Trinity when King Robert the Bruce merged St. Serf with the Norse and Temple dragon of Saint Michael. He also notes given the

---

[170] "Monastic Settlement, Rosemarkie, Church Place," Highland Historic Environment Record, accessed 14 February 2023. https://her.highland.gov.uk/monument/MHG25214

[171] "St. Michael's Church Mauchline," Saints in Scottish Place-Names, accessed 16 January 2023. https://saintsplaces.gla.ac.uk/place.php?id=1325863152

[172] James Rankin, *A Handbook of the Church of Scotland* (Edinburgh and London: William Blackwood & Sons, 1888), 78. https://ia800703.us.archive.org/22/items/handbookofchurch188800rank/handbookofchurch188800rank.pdf

[173] Alexander Porteous, *The Town Council Seals of Scotland* (Edinburgh and London: W & A.K. Johnston, Ltd, 1906), 81. https://electricscotland.com/council/wamphray3.pdf

[174] James Murray MacKinlay, *Ancient Church Dedications in Scotland* (Edinburgh: David Douglas, 1914), 252. https://archive.org/details/churchdedication02mackuoft

[175] The side of the Wamphray Dragon stone is decorated with a modified two-cord plait, and the back-built into the church wall, the exposed side shows two more dragons.

[176] Anne T., "St. Cuthbert's Church (Wamphray)," The Megalithic Portal, 5 April 2019. https://www.megalithic.co.uk/article.php?sid=51598

[177] St. Serf and St. Mungo patronages after 1124 were "Culdee revival" gifts of David I and the Bruces.

*Appendix D: A Primer on the Ancient British and Roman Catholic Churches in Scotland*

shared ancient dragon symbology and its much earlier establishment timeframe, that Wamphray may have originally been the mother house for the church of Hutton under the Celtic Church.[178]

22. **Westerkirk Dumfriesshire:** Westerkirk parish was originally known as Wester Ker or Wester Caer "Western Fort," from its situation to the west of an ancient fortress on the river Megget, near its influx into the Esk.[179] Westerkirk was granted to Melrose by John de Graham (the elder), Lord of Westerkirk, and confirmed to the abbey by Robert I in 1321. This church with all its teinds was granted to the uses of the abbey in that same year by the chapter of Glasgow cathedral. Apparently John de Graham retained *advocatioun/advowson* (the position of guardian or patron of a church[180]), given in 1476 descendants of his heirs, William de Graham (Lang Will's father) and Thomas de Graham served on an assize (jury panel[181]) regarding terce (Church issues/tithes) from Dalduran in Langholm (later known as Westerhall in Parish Westerkirk).[182]

22. **Whithorn, (Wigtownshire), Dumfries and Galloway Cathedral of St. Martin of Tours and St. Ninian circa 1130 – 1690):** The *Candida Casa*, Figure D-3, ("White House") was the name given to the small stone church which by tradition was built circa 397 by the local Briton, Saint Ninian, "apostle to the southern Picts." The stone used was probably white-washed, and the name became attached to the locality (Whithorn). The church became a cathedral and monastery and was dedicated to St. Martin of Tours between the fifth century and early ninth century. Its list of bishops ended in 731 when it fell under Northumbrian control and protection ceased. The See of Whithorn was refounded in 1128 within the English province of York until 1472; afterwards in the Diocese/Archdiocese of Glasgow.[183] The Whithorn Way, is a 143-mile pilgrimage trail inspired by St. Ninian, the first Christian missionary to Scotland, from Glasgow to Whithorn in Dumfriesshire.[184]

---

[178] James Rankin, *A Handbook of the Church of Scotland* (Edinburgh and London: Blackwood and Sons, 1888), 65, 76, 77.

[179] FamilySearch Wiki contributors, "Westerkirk, Dumfriesshire, Scotland Genealogy," FamilySearch Wiki, accessed 9 January 2023.
https://www.familysearch.org/en/wiki/index.php?title=Westerkirk,_Dumfriesshire,_Scotland_Genealogy&oldid=5140745

[180] "Advocatioun," *Dictionaries of the Scots Language*, accessed 13 January 2023.
https://dsl.ac.uk/entry/dost/advocatioun

[181] "Assize," *Dictionaries of the Scots Language*, accessed 13 January 2023. https://dsl.ac.uk/entry/snd/assize

[182] R.C. Reid, "The Border Grahams and Their Origins," 90.

[183] J.A. Wylie, History of the Scottish Nation (London: Hamilton and Adams Co., 1887), 68-89.
https://books.google.com/books/about/History_of_the_Scottish_Nation.html?id=ITCykuEcgFwC

[184] "Whithorn Way," The British Pilgrimage Trust, accessed 9 January 2023.
https://britishpilgrimage.org/portfolio/whithorn-way/

*Appendix D: A Primer on the Ancient British and Roman Catholic Churches in Scotland*

IV. **Lands with Culdee Connections in Northumberland (in Alphabetical Order):**

1. **Arthuret (Ard ' e ryd):** Named after Arthur, King of the "Brito-Picts," who ruled in the Strathclyde area in the sixth century. He was known to be a Christian and died in 537 A.D. in hand-to-hand combat.[185] The kingdom of Strathclyde came into existence after the Battle of Arthuret in 573 A.D. between the Christian and pagan inhabitants of the area. After this battle, Saint Mungo was recalled to Strathclyde from Wales.[186]

2. **Chester-le-Street, County Durham, Collegiate Church of St. Mary and St. Cuthbert (circa 883 – circa 995):** Initial location that the monks of Saint Cuthbert escaped to, with the saint's coffin and relics, after Viking raids forced them to evacuate Lindisfarne.[187] The oldest parts of the current structure that can be dated, are to 1056, when a stone church was built to replace the original wooden shrine to St. Cuthbert.[188]

3. **Durham, County Durham, The White Church (Alba Ecclesia) (circa 998 – circa 1104):** Towards the end of the tenth century the community of St. Cuthbert (that had settled at Chester-Le-Street since 883) feared renewed Viking attacks. Carrying Saint Cuthbert's body, they once again sought safety, and journeyed south to arrive in 995 at Durham, which provided a secure site. By 998 A.D., the community began building a stone "white" church, into which Cuthbert's relics were transferred the next year. The cruciform stone Anglo-Saxon cathedral, with a central and a western tower was completed circa 1020. In 1083 the Norman bishop, William de St. Calais, replaced the monks of St. Cuthbert with Benedictine monks from

*Figure D-16: Durham Cathedral with Durham Castle in Background, photo by Vik Walker.* [185] CC-BY-2.0.

---

[185] Archibald B. Scott, *The Pictish Nation, Its People and Its Church* (Edinburgh and London: T.N. Foulis, 1918), 176, 191, 192, 216, 217. https://archive.org/details/pictishnationits00scotrich
Figure D-16: Wikimedia Commons contributors, "File:Durham Cathedral and Castle.jpg," *Wikimedia Commons,* accessed 17 April 2023.
https://commons.wikimedia.org/w/index.php?title=File:Durham_Cathedral_and_Castle.jpg&oldid=733129338
[186] James Murray MacKinlay, *Ancient Church Dedications in Scotland* (Edinburgh: David Douglas, 1914), 178-179. https://archive.org/details/churchdedication02mackuoft
[187] "Cuthbert's Move to Durham: Two Stories," Durham World Heritage Site, accessed 16 January 2023. https://www.durhamworldheritagesite.com/learn/history/st-cuthbert/body/durham
[188] "Chester-le-Street SS. Mary & Cuthbert," Bells of the Northeast of England, A Bellringer's Guide, accessed 12 April 2023. https://northeastbells.co.uk/chester-le-street/

Evesham. By 1093 Bishop William began construction of the Norman cathedral that underlies today's cathedral.[189]

4. **Hexham, Northumberland Priory and Parish Church of St. Andrew (678 – circa 821):** A monastery founded circa 674 A.D. by St. Wilfrid, the first native Saxon to hold the position of Bishop of York. It became the site of a cathedral in 678, but was destroyed in ninth-century Viking raids. It is known for its influence by St. Cuthbert. An Augustinian priory was founded in 1113 on the earlier site, sustained damage due to attacks by Sir William Wallace in 1296, and was dissolved by Henry VIII in 1537.[190] The priory's chancel was saved as the parish church, and a new nave was added later, being finally completed in 1907–08. The present church includes some Anglo-Saxon material, notably St. Wilfrid's original crypt.[191]

*Figure D-17: Holy Island in Northumberland by Sandy Gemmill* [189] CC-BY-2.0.

5. **Lindisfarne, Northumberland (Holy Island) (635–875):** A monastery was founded in 635 by King Oswald for St. Aidan as the site for a cathedral for the northern part of the kingdom of Northumbria. Viking raids that began in 793, led to its destruction in 875. The monks fled with the body and relics of Saint Cuthbert, later settling at Chester-Le-Street in 883, then Durham in 995.[192]

## B. Culdee Place Name Etymology

The Gaelic prefix Mael/Maol meaning "bare," and the Gaelic Gil/Gille meaning servant, usually denote Culdees.[193] For example: Mael Bethad (Macbeth) de Libertona, Gaelic landowner, Thor, son of Swain and William de Graham, Earl Henry, son of David I, sign an 1127 charter for St. Cuthbert church in Edinburgh.[194] Macbeth of Libertona, who flourished early in David's reign, later

---

[189] "William of St. Calais," Durham World Heritage Site, accessed 13 January 2023. https://www.durhamworldheritagesite.com/learn/history/prince-bishops/early-bishops/william-calais
Figure D-17: Wikimedia Commons contributors, "File:St Cuthbert's Isle - geograph.org.uk - 2977711.jpg," *Wikimedia Commons,* accessed 17 April 2023. https://commons.wikimedia.org/w/index.php?title=File:St_Cuthbert%27s_Isle_-_geograph.org.uk_-_2977711.jpg&oldid=706094378

[190] Michael Muncaster, "How Hexham Abbey was Built and Survived Attacks from the Vikings and the Scots," Chronicle Live, 4 March 2017. https://www.chroniclelive.co.uk/news/north-east-news/how-hexham-abbey-built-survived-12678086

[191] "List of Former Cathedrals in Great Britain," Kiddle, accessed 13 January 2023. https://kids.kiddle.co/List_of_former_cathedrals_in_Great_Britain

[192] "List of Former Cathedrals in Great Britain," Kiddle.

[193] H. Cameron Gillies, M.D., *The Place-Names of Argyll* (London: David Nutt, 1906), xvii, 113. https://www.electricscotland.com/books/placenames/placenamesofargy00gill.pdf

[194] Michael Gervers, *Documents of Early England Dataset (DEEDS)*, University of Toronto Libraries, accessed 9 January 2023. https://deeds.library.utoronto.ca/charters/05130072

granted to the church of St. Cuthbert the tithes and oblations of Legbernard.[195] No Norman land barons sign this charter, implying that the signatories are followers of St. Cuthbert from Northumbria or Yorkshire. This also implies that: William de Graham was a follower of Christian Culdeeism and St. Cuthbert, like Forne Sigulfson was before him, considering that Scotland did not officially convert to Roman Catholicism until 1250A.D.[196] Examples of place names using "gille:" Gillslands, Gillesbie, Gillebride and Gillechomedy.

## C. Key Norman Church Establishments

1. **Dunfermline Abbey:** The Benedictine Abbey of the Holy Trinity and St. Margaret, was founded in 1128 by David I of Scotland, but the monastic establishment was based on an earlier foundation dating back to the reign of his father King Máel Coluim mac Donnchada, i. e. "Malcolm III" or "Malcolm Canmore" (regnat 1058–93), and Queen Margaret. At its head was the Abbot of Dunfermline, the first of which was Geoffrey of Canterbury, former Prior of Christ Church, Canterbury. At the peak of its power, it controlled four burghs, three burghs with courts[197] of regality,[198] and a large portfolio of lands from Moray in the north, and south to Berwickshire. Sir John de Graham (the elder) added gifts to Dunfermline in honor of the Holy Trinity and St. Matthew the Apostle in 1317 to sponsor a perpetual memorial for his father, Sir Nicholas de Graham.[199]

*Figure D-18: Dunfermline Abbey by Paul McIlroy [195] CC-BY-2.0.*

> ***Note from Phil Graham:*** Per family tradition: Sir Nicholas Graham was the keeper of the real cross of Margaret, or "holy rood," receiving it from Margaret Drummond.

2. **Holyrood Abbey (Holy Cross):** Holyrood Abbey in Edinburgh was founded in 1128 by David I of Scotland. The abbey was originally served by a community of Augustinian Canons from Merton Priory. In 1189, the nobles and prelates of Scotland met

---

[195] Sir William Fraser, *The Melvilles and the Leslies, the Earls of Melville and the Earls of Leven,* Vol. I (Edinburgh: 1900),xl. https://deriv.nls.uk/dcn23/9666/96660715.23.pdf

Figure D-18: Wikimedia Commons contributors, "File:Dunfermline Abbey Geograph.jpg," *Wikimedia Commons,* accessed 17 April 2023.
https://commons.wikimedia.org/w/index.php?title=File:Dunfermline_Abbey_Geograph.jpg&oldid=533171930

[196] Rev J.A. Wylie, *The History of the Scottish Nation*, Vol. 3 (London: Hamilton, Adams and Co., 1886), 203-204, 298. https://www.originofnations.org/books,%20papers/history%20of%20the%20scots/scothistvol3.pdf

[197] Burghs of Regality and Barony," *Scottish Archive Network,* accessed 14 February 2023.
https://www.scan.org.uk/knowledgebase/topics/burgh.htm#:~:text=These%20were%20burghs%20granted%20by,in%20criminal%20and%20civil%20law.

[198] James Moir Webster, *Notes on the Burgh of Dunfermline* (Dunfermline: Pitcairn Publications, 1949), 8, 29. http://www.royaldunfermline.com/Resources/notes_on_dunfermline_burgh.pdf

[199] Ebeneezer Henderson, *The Annals of Dunfermline and Vicinity* (Glasgow: John Tweed, 1879), 15, 40, 41. https://archive.org/details/cu31924091208359/page/n9/mode/2up?q=four+burghs

*Appendix D: A Primer on the Ancient British and Roman Catholic Churches in Scotland*

at the abbey to discuss raising a ransom for William the Lion.[200] In the church was preserved an object in a golden receptacle, said to be a fragment of the True Cross brought by David's mother, Saint Margaret, from Waltham Abbey (that she had previously brought from her home in Hungary[201]), and known thereafter as the Black Rood of Scotland or the "Holyrood," a.k.a "Holy Cross"). At the battle of Neville's Cross, in 1346, the cross reportedly fell into the hands of the English, and it was placed in Durham Cathedral, from where it disappeared at the Reformation.[202]

3. **"New Melrose:"** A monastery founded in 1136 by David I, and granted by royal charter to the Cistercian Order of monks, which had a short time previously be instituted in France. It was a mother church to the all the Cistercian order in Scotland, controlling Cavers Magna, Dunscore, Ettrick, Hassendean/Hazeldean (estate of Nicholas de Graham), Mauchline, Melrose, Ochitree, Tarbolton (estate of Sir John de Graham), Westerkirk (estate of Sir John de Graham) and Wilton churches. The Abbey is known for being the last resting place of the "Heart of Robert the Bruce." Bruce directed that his heart should be buried in Melrose Abbey. But subsequently, he asked instead that his heart be sent to Jerusalem and buried in the Church of the Holy Sepulchre. Sir James Douglas set sail with the sacred deposit, but encountered the Saracens in Spain and fell. His body was recovered with the heart of his master, which was then interred at Melrose Abbey.[203]

*Figure D-19: "New Melrose" Abbey from the Burial Ground, photo by Walter Baxter.* [200] CC-BY-SA/2.0

4. **Church of St. Michael.** St. Michael's Parish Church, dedicated to St. Michael the Archangel, dominates the skyline of Linlithgow due to its size and distinctive tower. It is almost of cathedral proportions and considered one of the finest medieval churches in Scotland. The earliest record of the Great

---

[200] Marjorie Ogilvie Anderson, *Chronicle of Holyrood* (Edinburgh: University Press, 1938), 122, 158. https://deriv.nls.uk/dcn23/1266/1376/126613769.23.pdf

Figure D-19: Wikimedia Commons contributors, "File:Melrose Abbey from the burial ground - geograph.org.uk - 781601.jpg," *Wikimedia Commons,* accessed 17 April 2023. https://commons.wikimedia.org/w/index.php?title=File:Melrose_Abbey_from_the_burial_ground_-_geograph.org.uk_-_781601.jpg&oldid=716760017

[201] Medieval Hungary and their royal family had a strong tie to Byzantine Christianity, a tie through which they claimed to have acquired a number of holy Christian relics. Gyula Moravcsik, "The Role of the Byzantine Church in Medieval Hungary," *American Slavic and East European Review* 6, no. 3/4 (1947): 134–51. https://doi.org/10.2307/2491705

[202] D. O. Hunter Blair, "Holyrood Abbey," Mary Foundation, accessed 14 February 2023. https://www.catholicity.com/encyclopedia/h/holyrood_abbey.html

[203] James Augustine Wade, *The History of St. Mary's Abbey, Melrose, The Monastery of Old Melrose and the Town and Parish of Melrose* (Edinburgh: Thomas C. Jack, 1841), 42, 46, 224, 277, 281. https://archive.org/details/historyofstmarys00wadeiala/page/n7/mode/2up

Church of Linlithgow is its gift, in 1138, to the Bishop of St. Andrews by King David I (circa 1080 - 1153).[204,205]

5. **Newbattle Abbey.** David founded Newbattle Abbey, a Cistercian monastery, in the barony of Dalkeith in 1140.[206] Newbattle was associated with the Knights Templar.[207] The Graham family were one of its primary patrons. Newbattle is famous for hosting the meeting of Scottish nobles in the Spring of 1320 to draft a letter asking the Pope to recognize Scotland's independence and their king. The letter was known as the Declaration of Arbroath.[208]

---

[204] The Editors of The Gazetteer for Scotland, "St. Michael's Parish Church," Gazetteer for Scotland, accessed 9 January 2023. https://www.scottish-places.info/features/featurefirst1011.html
[Did you know? Blurb] Gail Delahunt, "Everything you need to know about St. James the Greater," Follow the Camino, 27 December 2019. https://followthecamino.com/en/blog/history-of-the-apostle-saint-james/

[205] The Church of St. Michael in Linlithgow is near Manuel, estate of theorized patriarch of the Graham J1s and the Church of St. Michael in Inveresk, near the estate of Edmund, son of Forn, theorized brother of the first Graham, William de Graham. St. Michael is associated with the escallop prevalent in Graham armorials. See Appendix E.

[206] PoMS, "no. 127, person summary," accessed 1 March 2023. https://www.poms.ac.uk/record/person/127/

[207] PoMS, "no. 61866, factoid," accessed 12 April 2023. https://www.poms.ac.uk/record/factoid/61866/

[208] "History, Tours and Filming," Newbattle Abbey, accessed 14 January 2023. https://newbattleabbey.com/filming-historical-tours-scotland/

## D. Abbreviated Glossary of NATIVE BRITISH SAINTS (Alphabetical Order)

Below is a short summary of Culdee Saints relevant to Graham family history. Most have Celtic origins and were later recognized by the Roman Catholic Church and the Orthodox Churches. For a complete list of Celtic Culdee Saints see the alphabetical index on the Celtic Christianity website:

http://www.celticchristianity.infinitesoulutions.com/saints_alpha.html [209]

> *Did you know?*
> A patron saint is considered to be a defender of a specific group of people or a nation.

1. **St. Adrian of May (died 875):** Martyr and saint of ancient Scotland. He may have been an Irish monk and bishop, with the Gaelic name of Ethernan, and also Bishop of St. Andrews, who had built a series of monasteries and hermitages on the Isle of May. May is five miles out to sea in the Firth of Forth. About 875 A.D., marauding Vikings invaded May, and slaughtered the entire population of the monastery, traditionally numbered at six thousand six hundred.[210] A small chapel was soon built on May presumably to house the relics of Saint Adrian. The island was abandoned until 1145, when David I gifted the island to Reading Abbey in Berkshire.[211]

2. **St. Bega:** Irish princess who was promised in marriage to a Viking prince who was the "son of the king of Norway." Bega escaped across the Irish sea and landed at St. Bees on the Cumbrian coast sometime after 850 A.D. The name of the village *Kirkeby Becok* used in the charters of St. Bees Priory from the times of Henry II and Richard I, and the tenth century stone cross, provide evidence the priory was a pre-Norman religious site.[212] The name "Kilbucho" (Scottish Gaelic: *Cille Bheagha*) of the village in Peeblesshire owned by the Dalkeith Grahams is derived from the church dedicated to St. Bega.[213] Several monasteries in Cumbria were also dedicated to St. Bega, and also in Scotland at Kilbagie in Clackmannanshire, and Kilbegie in Argyllshire.[214]

3. **Saint Blane (died 590):** His name is from the Old Irish *Bláán*. Blane was a Bishop and Confessor in Scotland, born on the Isle of Bute. Late (medieval) Scottish texts relate that his mother was Irish and that St. Cathan was her brother. It was his uncle, Cathan, who saw to Blane's education. Blane became a monk and left for Scotland, where he became a bishop among the Picts. Several miracles

---

[209] "Celtic Saints Alphabetic References," Celtic Christianity, accessed 16 January 2023. http://www.celticchristianity.infinitesoulutions.com/saints_alpha.html

[210] Rev. Alban Butler, *The Lives of the Fathers, Martyrs, and Other Principal Saints*, Vol. III (Dublin: James Duffy, 1866; Bartleby.com, 2010). https://www.bartleby.com/210/3/043.html

[211] "Isle of May, St. Adrian's Chapel," Canmore: National Record of the Historic Environment, accessed 17 February 2023. https://canmore.org.uk/site/57873/isle-of-may-st-adrians-chapelv

[212] Rev. Alban Butler, *The Lives of the Fathers, Martyrs, and Other Principal Saints*, Vol. IX (Dublin: James Duffy, 1866; Bartleby.com, 2010). https://www.bartleby.com/210/9/063.html

[Did you know? Blurb] "Kircudbright (Surveyed 1850)," National Library of Scotland, accessed 17 April 2023. https://maps.nls.uk/townplans/background/kirkcudbright_1.html

[213] Rev. John Marius Wilson, *Imperial Gazeteer of Scotland Volume 2* (London and Edinburgh: A. Fullarton and Co., 1868), 189-190. https://digital.nls.uk/gazetteers-of-scotland-1803-1901/archive/97473162

[214] Dmitry Lapa, "St. Bega, The Anchoress of Cumbria," Pravoslavie, accessed 17 February 2023. https://pravoslavie.ru/82258.html

are attributed to him, among them, the restoration of a dead boy to life. There was a church of St. Blane in Dumfries and another at Kilblane. The place names Kilblane, and Dunblane were derived from the saint's name.[ix] The ruins of his church at Kingarth, Bute, where his remains were buried, still stand. The bell of his monastery is believed to be preserved at Dunblane Cathedral, which was founded on the site allegedly first used by St. Blane.[215]

4. **St. Columba (circa 521-597 A.D.):** Born in Tyrconnell (now County Donegal), Ireland. He was of the northern branch of the Uí Néill (aka: "Niall of the Nine Hostages"). Considered to be a patron saint of Ireland (along with St. Patrick and St. Brigid),[216] credited with spreading Christianity throughout Scotland. Around 563, he and his twelve companions settled on the island of Iona, where they founded a base for spreading Celtic Christianity among the northern Pictish kingdoms who were pagan. Three surviving medieval Latin hymns are attributed to him.[217, 218]

5. **St. Cuthbert (died 687):** Considered the patron saint of Northumberland. Missionary, former prior of "Old Melrose" and bishop of Lindisfarne (Holy Island).[219] St. Cuthberts Way is a pilgrimage trail built circa 634 from Dumbarton to Abercorn, and to Lindisfarne, named after St. Cuthbert.[220] In 698A.D., the relics of Cuthbert were removed and carried as a talisman in Northumberland. In 1095 A.D., King Edgar, son of Malcom III and St. Margaret, was founder of St. Cuthbert gifts, including a castle at Bamburgh overlooking Lindisfarne.[221]

*Figure D-20: St. Cuthbert Statue on Holy Island in Lindisfarne Priory in Northumberland, photo by Nilfanion.* [220] *CC-BY-3.0.*

> **Did you know?**
> Kirkcudbright is derived from the Gaelic for "Church of St. Cuthbert."

Other Northumbrian saints were patrons of Scottish churches, notably Aidan and Oswald, founders of Cuthbert's Church, and Æbbe, sister of Oswald and abbess of Coldingham in Berwickshire. King Edgar rebuilt Coldingham and dedicated it to Cuthbert and Æbbe along with the Virgin

---

[215] "St. Blane, St. Blaan," Gazeteer for Scotland, accessed 17 February 2023. https://www.scottish-places.info/people/famousfirst1606.html

[216] "Saint Columba of Iona," CatholicNews.net, accessed 17 January 2023. https://www.catholicnewsagency.com/saint/st-columba-of-iona-722

[217] William Reeves, *Life of St. Columba, written by Adamnan,* (Edinburgh: Edmonston and Douglas, 1874), xxix, xl, 34. https://archive.org/details/lifeofsaintcolum00adamuoft/page/n11/mode/2up .

[218] Rev. Alban Butler, *The Lives of the Fathers, Martyrs, and Other Principal Saints,* Vol. VI (Dublin: James Duffy, 1866; Bartleby.com, 2010). https://www.bartleby.com/210/6/092.html

[219] "St. Cuthbert," Catholic Online, accessed 11 April 2023. https://www.catholic.org/saints/saint.php?saint_id=491

[220] "Saint Cuthbert," Undiscovered Scotland, accessed 11 April 2023. https://www.undiscoveredscotland.co.uk/usbiography/c/stcuthbert.html

Figure D-20: Wikimedia Commons contributors, "File:Lindisfarne Priory 8.JPG," *Wikimedia Commons,* accessed 17 April 2023. https://commons.wikimedia.org/w/index.php?title=File:Lindisfarne_Priory_8.JPG&oldid=488822884

[221] Wikisource contributors, "Dictionary of National Biography, 1885-1900/Cuthbert (d.687)," Wikisource, accessed 10 January 2023. https://en.wikisource.org/wiki/Dictionary_of_National_Biography,_1885-1900/Cuthbert_(d.687)

*Appendix D: A Primer on the Ancient British and Roman Catholic Churches in Scotland*

Mary. In these church dedications one begins to see the complex links among Northumbrian saints and southern Scotland.²²²

### The Lindisfarne Gospels.

The Lindisfarne Gospels are an illuminated manuscript probably produced around the years 710–721 in the monastery at Lindisfarne, off the coast of Northumberland. The manuscript combines Mediterranean, Anglo-Saxon and Celtic elements. The Lindisfarne Gospels are presumed to be the work of a monk named Eadfrith, who became Bishop of Lindisfarne in 698 and died in 721. It is believed they were produced in honor of St. Cuthbert.²²³

*Figure D-21: Image of St. Matthew from the Lindisfarne Gospels, The Yorck Project (2002) 10.000 Meisterwerke der Malerei* ²²³

Each gospel begins with what is called a carpet page that has an intricate and colorful pattern. The rest of each gospel contains the text done in elaborate calligraphy, and with illustrations throughout. The monks finally left Lindisfarne in 875, after nearly a century of Viking raids, arriving at Chester-le-Street in 995, when they moved to Durham Priory, where they stayed, except for a brief period when they returned to Lindisfarne because of the Norman invasion around 1066.²²⁴ In 1104, the body of St. Cuthbert, the Lindisfarne Gospels and the other treasures of the monastery were installed in Durham.²²⁵ The symbols of the four Gospel Writers used in the Lindesfarne Gospels and also in ancient Celtic art and carvings were: Matthew (a man), Mark (a lion), Luke (a bull) and John (an eagle).²²⁶ An example can be seen in the Ruthwell Cross located in Priestside in Annandale, Scotland, hewn from stone in the eighth century.²²⁷

---

²²² Hew Scott, *Fasti Ecclesiae Scoticanae*, Vol. II (Edinburgh: Oliver and Boyd, 1917), 36. https://www.forgottenbooks.com/en/download/FastiEcclesiScotican_10248383.pdf

²²³ "Lindisfarne Gospels," British Library, accessed 12 April 2023. https://www.bl.uk/collection-items/lindisfarne-gospels

Figure D-21: Wikimedia Commons contributors, "File: Book of Lindisfarne, Szene: Hl. Matthäus," Wikimedia Commons, accessed 12 April 2023. https://commons.wikimedia.org/wiki/File:Meister_des_Book_of_Lindisfarne_001.jpg

²²⁴ Jennifer Shaw, "Where are the Lindisfarne Gospels?" Study.com, accessed 12 April 2023. https://study.com/academy/lesson/what-are-the-lindisfarne-gospels-writer-facts.html#:~:text=The%20monks%20were%20chased%20out,invasion%20of%20William%20the%20Conqueror

²²⁵ Jessica Brain, "The Lindisfarne Gospels," HistoricUK.com, 8 March 2021. https://www.historic-uk.com/HistoryUK/HistoryofEngland/Lindisfarne-Gospels/#:~:text=A%20famous%20illuminated%20manuscript%20created,beauty%2C%20ornate%20detail%20and%20design

²²⁶ Katherine Taggart and Erin Devine, "Exploring Meaning—The Lindisfarne Gospels," Longwood University-Incite, accessed 17 February 2023. https://blogs.longwood.edu/incite/2011/09/08/exploring-meaning-%E2%80%93-the-lindisfarne-gospels/

²²⁷ Éamonn Ó Carragain, "Christian Inculturation in Eighth-Century Northumbria: The Bewcastle and Ruthwell Crosses," Institute of Sacred Music, Yale University: 19, accessed 12 April 2023. https://ism.yale.edu/sites/default/files/files/Christian%20Inculturation%20in%20Eighth.pdf

*Appendix D: A Primer on the Ancient British and Roman Catholic Churches in Scotland*

6. **St. Declan**: A fifth century Irish saint remembered for converting the Déisi and for having founded the monastery of Ardmore (*Ard Mór*) in what is now County Waterford. He was regarded as a patron saint of the Déisi of East Munster who preceded Saint Patrick in bringing Christianity to Ireland.[228] St. Patrick has been credited with introducing the Celtic Cross to Ireland; however, there are some claims that it was St. Declan who introduced the cross.[229] See Appendix E for more information on the Celtic Cross symbolism.

7. **Saint Fillan:** St. Fillan (Foelan) lived in the eighth century. He was born in Ireland. His mother was St. Kentigerna and his uncle was St. Comgan. In approximately 717A.D., he moved with his family to Scotland. There he became a monk and preached to the local Picts until the end of his life. In 1314, the forces of Robert the Bruce took a relic of the saint with them into the Battle of Bannockburn and attributed his victory over the English to Fillan's intercession. He funded the building of a church in Fillan's name in 1329. Fillan was buried in Strathfillan, in West Perthshire, near to where he lived, worked and possibly built a church.[230]

*Figure D-22: Celtic Cross in Fintry Churchyard,* [228] © Robert Murray CC-BY-SA/2.0.

8. **Saint Kessog— (circa 460 – 520):** Saint Kessog, also known as Saint Makkessog, was the patron saint of Lennox[231] and Scotland's first patron saint. There is an old joke that points out the irony that Ireland's patron saint was a Scot (St. Patrick) and Scotland's first patron saint was an Irishman (St. Kessog).[232] Kessog was the son of the king of Cashel in Munster, Ireland. Per tradition, he was the nephew of the legendary King Arthur.[233] He was recognized for his piety and miracles at an early age and

---

[228] Rev. P. Power, *Life of St. Declan of Ardmore*, (London: Irish Texts Society, 1914). https://www.ccel.org/d/declan/life/declan.html
   Figure D-22: Robert Murray, "Celtic Cross in Fintry Churchyard," 9 September 2015. https://www.geograph.org.uk/more.php?id=4652987

[229] "The Symbolic Meaning of the Celtic Cross," Irish Central, accessed 10 January 2023. https://www.irishcentral.com/roots/history/the-symbolic-meaning-of-the-celtic-cross

[230] Dmitry Lapa, "A Family of Saints: Sts. Kentigerna, Fillan and Comgan of Scotland," Orthodox Christianity, accessed 10 January 2023. https://orthochristian.com/76644.html

[231] "Saint Kessog of Lennox, March 10," Omnium Sanctorum Hiberniae, 10 March 2014. http://www.omniumsanctorumhiberniae.com/2014/03/saint-kessog-of-lennox-march-10.html#:~:text=St.,%2C%20Patron%20of%20Lennox%2C%20Scotland.&text=This%20holy%20bishop%20is%20venerated,living%20for%20ever%20in%20heaven.

[232] Hamish MacPherson, "The History of Scotland's First Patron Saint, Saint Kessog," The National, 8 March 2020. https://www.thenational.scot/news/18288418.history-scotlands-first-patron-saint-saint-kessog/

[233] "Saint Kentigern-Patron Saint of Glasgow, Nephew of King Arthur," Clan Arthur, accessed 6 March 2023. http://clanarthur.org/history/arthur-the-chieftain/st-kentigern-patron-saint-of-glasgow-nephew-of-king-arthur/

*Appendix D: A Primer on the Ancient British and Roman Catholic Churches in Scotland*

was educated in a monastery under St. Machaloi. He left Ireland and became a missionary bishop in Scotland about 510 A.D. Using Inchtavannach (Monks' Island) in Loch Lomond as his base, he evangelized the surrounding area until he was martyred there in 520A.D. Kessog was murdered either on Inchtavannach or at nearby at Bandry, marked by a heap of stones known as Saint Kessog's Cairn. He may have been killed by brigands or mercenaries, paid by pagans jealous of his success in converting the locals, thereby making Kessog one of the first Christian martyrs in Scotland.[234]

Soldiers had a special connection to St. Kessog. He was sometimes portrayed in military dress with a bended bow and arrow. King Robert the Bruce's gift in honor St. Kessog is recorded in the University of Edinburgh database. Bruce led his soldiers into the battle of Bannockburn in the name of "Our Blessed St. Kessog."[235] As late as 1695, the saint's bell, a sacred relic was listed among the funeral investitures of the Earldom of Perth. Numerous places throughout Scotland bear his name. For example: a nineteenth century church in Callander is named St. Kessog's and a nearby circular mound by the River Teith is named in pseudo-Gaelic as "Tom na Chessaig," meaning "the Hill of Kessog." The Kessock area of Inverness and the Kessog oil field in the North Sea bear his name.[236] The Graham's former barony named **"Mosskesso"** in Dumfriesshire means "my dear Saint Kessog."[237] The barony took its name from the medieval church and lands dedicated to St. Kessog. Figure D-23. Lang Will Graham of the Border Grahams was from the Mosskesso (Mosskesswra) Barony before he re-settled in England.[238]

---

[234] "Saint Kessog," Undiscovered Scotland, accessed 10 January 2023. https://www.undiscoveredscotland.co.uk/usbiography/k/stkessog.html

Figured D-23: Dumfriesshire Sheet XXXIV, GB Ordnance Survey six inch first edition 1843-1882, performed 1857, published 1861, National Library of Scotland. https://maps.nls.uk/view/228777274

[235] "Sir William Fraser Facsimilies of Scottish Charters and Letters," School of History, Classics and Archaeology Teaching Collections.

[235] "Sir William Fraser Facsimilies of Scottish Charters and Letters," School of History, Classics and Archaeology Teaching Collections.

[236] The Editors of The Gazetteer for Scotland, "Saint Kessog, c460-520," *The Gazetteer of Scotland.*

[237] James Murray Mackinlay, "St. Kessog and His Cultus in Scotland," *Transactions of the Glasgow Archaeological Society* 3, no. 2 (1899): 347. http://www.jstor.org/stable/24680608

[238] Col William Rogerson, *Hutton Under the Muir* (Dumfries, Scotland: Dumfries and Galloway Courier and Herald, 1908), 24.

Figure D-24: Wikimedia Commons contributors, "File:Glasgow Coat of Arms 1996.svg," *Wikimedia Commons*, accessed 13 April 2023.
https://commons.wikimedia.org/w/index.php?title=File:Glasgow_Coat_of_Arms_1996.svg&oldid=749695552

*Appendix D: A Primer on the Ancient British and Roman Catholic Churches in Scotland*

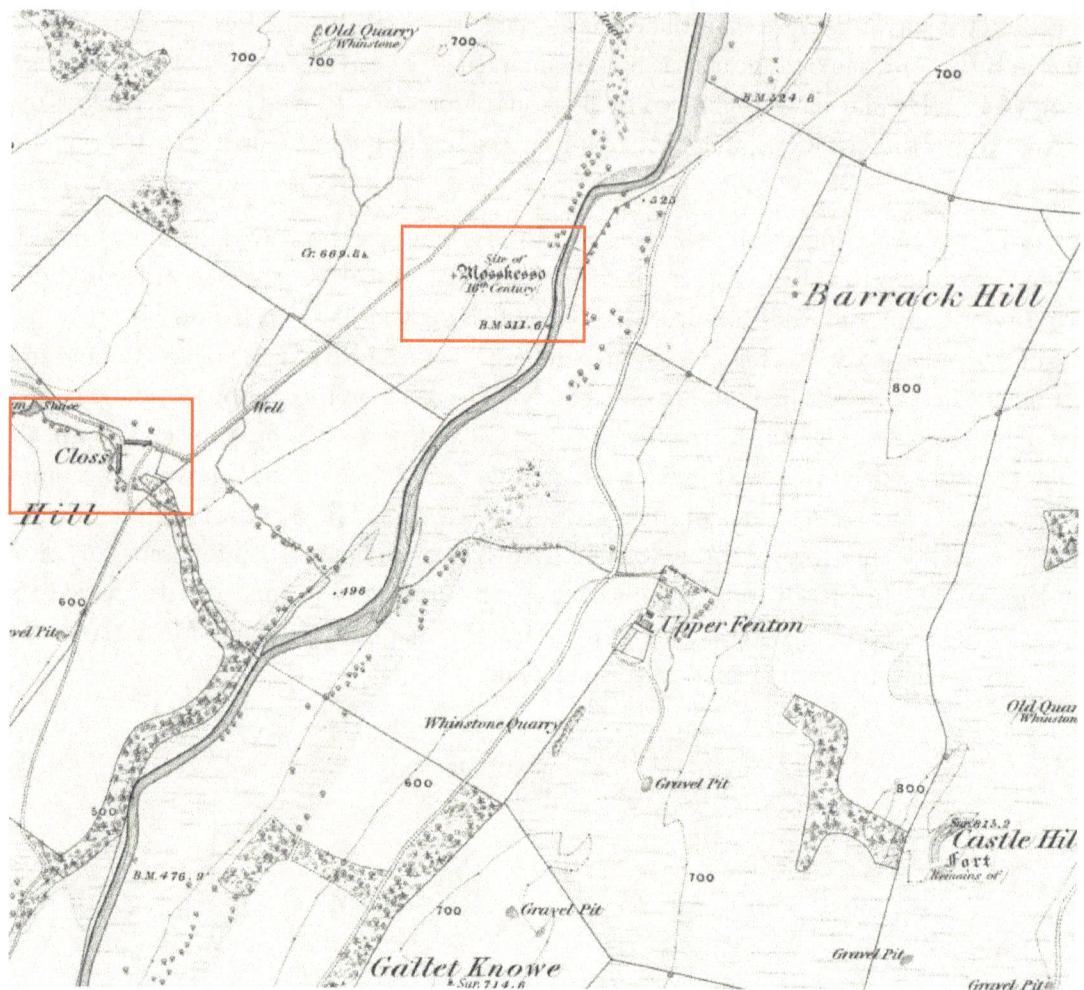

*Figure D-23: Site of Moskesso, and the Moskesso Closs/Close in Hutton Parish, Dumfriesshire (GB Ordnance Survey performed 1857, published 1861).* [234] *CC-BY-4.0 Reproduced with the permission of the National Library of Scotland.*

*Appendix D: A Primer on the Ancient British and Roman Catholic Churches in Scotland*

9. **St. Ninian (born *circa* 360, Britain—died *circa* 432):** bishop generally credited as the first Christian missionary to Scotland, responsible for widespread conversions among the Celts and possibly the Southern Picts.[239]

10. **St. Mungo (Died between 603-612):** St. Mungo (Kentigern) was born in Culross in Lothian to Saint Thenaw, a British princess. He was a missionary in the Brittonic Kingdom of Strathclyde in the late sixth century, and the founder and patron saint of the city of Glasgow and Strathclyde.[240]

*Figure D-24: Coat of Arms of the City of Glasgow by TillmanR [238] CC-BY-4.0*

According to Jocelyn of Furness,[x] Mungo was gifted the land in Hoddam by the king of Cumbria, however the church built there in St. Mungo's memory was dated centuries later.[241] He was consecrated the first bishop of Strathclyde by an Irish bishop.[242] He may have begun his missionary efforts at Cathures on the Clyde, founding the church at Glasgow. Political unrest drove him into exile in Carlisle and then into Wales. At some point, at the request of the Cumbrian king, he left Wales and lived in Hoddam for seven years. Then he moved his bishopric to Glasgow, where he died of natural causes. He was buried in Glasgow Cathedral,[243] which is also known as St. Mungo's Cathedral.[244] As a saint, he is venerated by the Church of Scotland, the Scottish Episcopalian Church,[245] the Anglican Church, the Church in Wales, the Roman Catholic Church, the Eastern Orthodox Churches, and other denominations.[246]

> *Did you know?*
> The rings and fish displayed on the heraldic arms of the city of Glasgow refer to a legend about Saint Mungo, in which he miraculously saves an unfaithful wife from the anger of her royal husband. The queen had given her husband's ring to her lover. The king discovered it, threw it into the sea and told his wife she must find it again in three days. Mungo told her not to worry: One of his monks had extracted the ring from a salmon he caught.

---

[239] Editors of Encyclopaedia Brittanica, "St. Ninian." *Encyclopedia Britannica*, accessed 10 January 2023. https://www.britannica.com/biography/Saint-Ninian

[240] S. Baring Gould and John Fisher, *The Lives of British Saints*, Vol. II (London: Charles J. Clark, 1908), 231-240. https://archive.org/details/livesofbritishsa02bariuoft/page/240/mode/2up?view=theater&q=kentigern

[241] Cynthia Whiddon Green, University of Houston, "Saint Kentigern, Apostle to Strathclyde: A Critical Analysis of a Northern Saint," Fordham University, December 1998. https://sourcebooks.fordham.edu/basis/cynthiawhiddengreen-saintkentigern1998.asp

[242] "The Saint with Two Names: St. Kentigern/St. Mungo," Idle Speculations, 25 December 2006. http://idlespeculations-terryprest.blogspot.com/2006/12/saint-with-two-names-st-kentigernst.html

[243] "Route Heritage," St. Kentigern Way, accessed 10 January 2023. http://kentigernway.com/page22.html

[244] David Roberts, "St. Mungo's Cathedral," National Galleries of Scotland, accessed 12 April 2023. https://www.nationalgalleries.org/art-and-artists/91251/st-mungos-cathedral-glasgow

[245] "St. Mungo, Alexandria, Scottish Episcopal," GENUKI, accessed 12 April 2023. https://www.genuki.org.uk/big/sct/DNB/Alexandria/StMungo

[246] Dmitry Lapa, "Holy Hierarch Kentigern (Mungo) of Strathclyde, Bishop of Glasgow," Orthodox Christianity, accessed 12 April 2023. https://orthochristian.com/67850.html

11. **St. Oswald (604-642A.D.):** King of Northumbria from 634 to 642. Oswald was the son of Æthelfrith of Bernicia and came to rule after a time in exile. After defeating the British ruler Cadwallon ap Cadfan, Oswald unified the two Northumbrian kingdoms of Bernicia and Deira, and promoted the spread of Christianity throughout Northumbria. He ruled for eight years and was the most powerful ruler in Britain of his time. Oswald was killed in the Battle of Maserfield in 642. The historian Bede, writing nearly a century after Oswald's death, regarded Oswald as a saintly king and is the main source for historical knowledge of him.[247]

12. **Saint Patrick (373-461A.D.):** The man known to us as Saint Patrick was originally called - Maewyn Succat or Magonus Saccatus, and was born in "Roman Britain" (per tradition in Dumbarton, Scotland) in the year 373. His mother was Conchessa, and his father Calpurnius, had been a deacon and a decurion, [a Roman officer in command of a *turma* (ten men) of cavalrymen] and his grandfather was a priest. St. Patrick is known from his own writings. According to the *Confession of Saint Patrick*, at the age of sixteen he was captured by a group of Irish pirates. They took him to Ireland where he was enslaved and held captive for six years.[248] Patrick writes in the *Confession* that the time he spent in captivity was critical to his spiritual development. He said the visions he had during this time re-enforced his faith. During one of these visions he heard voices that told him where he could find a getaway ship. He escaped, went to France where he later returned to become a priest and returned again to become a bishop. Pope Celestine gave Maewyn Succat/Magonus Saccatus the name of Patrick. He was sent to Ireland and became known as the 'Apostle of Ireland.'[249]

Patronages of St. Patrick in Old Strathclyde are too numerous not to be Culdee, albeit some Norman Plantations also claim St. Patrick for Norman Temple foundations. He had a greater influence in Dumfriesshire than even Saint Columba himself. The Grahams of Dumbarton and the Grahams of Dumfriesshire were in possession of former Culdee properties connected to Saint Patrick to include: Saint Patrick Chapel Royal in Dumbarton Castle,[250] Kirkpatrick-Fleming,[251] Kirkpatrick-Juxta, Old Rampatrick and Redkirk[252] and Hoddam.[253] In the thirteenth century, a fountain known as the Fountain of Saint Patrick and Saint Bridget/Saint Bride is recorded in the

---

[247] Rev. Alban Butler, *The Lives of the Fathers, Martyrs, and Other Principal Saints,* Vol. VIII (Dublin: James Duffy, 1866; Bartleby.com, 2010). https://www.bartleby.com/210/8/052.html

[248] "Saint Patrick," Biography.com, 15 March 2023. https://www.biography.com/religious-figures/saint-patrick

[249] "St. Patrick, Bishop, Apostle of Ireland," Vatican News, accessed 16 January 2023. https://www.vaticannews.va/en/saints/03/17/st--patrick--bishop--disciple-of-ireland-.html

[250] William Fraser, *The Red Book of Menteith*, Vol. II (Edinburgh: 1880), 256-257. https://digital.nls.uk/histories-of-scottish-families/archive/97146821

[251] Alicia Graham, "Fergus Graham of Mossknowe, aka: Fergus the Rascal," *Clan Graham Society Newsletter*, November 2022.

[252] A. W. Cornelius Hallen. "The Grahams of the Border," *The Scottish Antiquary* or *Northern Notes and Queries 9*, no. 36 (1895): 162. https://www.google.com/books/edition/The_Scottish_Antiquary/Zdyk2WG8ILQC?hl=en&gbpv=1&bsq=netherby

[253] J. Bell Irving, Esq. "List of Armorial Bearings Noted in Dumfriesshire and Neighboring Counties," *Transactions of the Dumfries and Galloway Natural History and Archaeological Society (TDGNHAS)*, Third Series, Vol. 1 (1912-1913): 130-131. https://archive.org/details/transactionsjour31191213dumf/mode/2up?q=escallop

*Appendix D: A Primer on the Ancient British and Roman Catholic Churches in Scotland*

neighborhood of Staplegordon. It was dedicated by what was probably the earliest church in Eskdale--St. Bride's Chapel and St. Bride's Hill in Wauchope.[254]

13. **St. Serf:** Saint Serf lived from about 490 to 550. Per legend, Serf was the son of the King of Canaan, and a daughter of a King of Arabia. He was elected pope, and served in Rome for seven years. He then journeyed across Europe, eventually landing in Scotland. Here he established a religious community, first on St. Serf's Inch, an island in Loch Leven in Perth and Kinross. Later, he established a church at Dunning in Perth where, according to legend, he slew a dragon with his staff, then finally settled at Culross in Fife, where he established another religious community.[255] The Celtic dragon symbol is associated with St. Serf. Saint Serf is also said to have been a contemporary of Saint Mungo (St. Kentigern). A legend states that when the Scottish princess Theneva (Thenaw) became pregnant, her family threw her from a cliff. She survived the fall unharmed, and was soon met by an unmanned boat,[256] which took her across the Firth of Forth to Culross where she was cared for by Saint Serf;[257] who became foster-father of her son, Saint Mungo (Saint Kentigern).[258]

King Robert the Bruce adopted a St. Serf patronage. Archbishop Patrick Graham (of Fintry), the first archbishop of St. Andrews, therefore the first head of the Scottish Church, also had a strong connection to St. Serf, having led the parish church of Kinneil, dedicated to St. Serf[259] for many years and was buried at St. Serf's Inch in Lochleven.[260, 261]

Abercorn is the oldest Bishopric in Scotland, its ancient monastery dating to the seventh century and its twelfth century church dedicated to St. Serf.[262] It served as a base for Bishop Trumwine, missionary to the Picts, mentioned by historian Bede circa 696.[263]

---

[254] John and Robert Hylsop, *Langholm As it Was: A History of Langholm and Eskdale from the Earliest Times* (Sunderland: Hills and Company, 1912), 138-139. https://archive.org/details/langholmasitwashhysl/mode/2up?q=shaw

[255] Rev J.A. Wylie, *The History of the Scottish Nation*, Vol. 3 (London: Hamilton, Adams and Co., 1886), 181-182, 295. https://www.originofnations.org/books,%20papers/history%20of%20the%20scots/scothistvol3.pdf

[256] S. Baring Gould and John Fisher, *The Lives of British Saints*, Vol. II, (London: Charles J. Clark, 1908), 232-234. https://archive.org/details/livesofbritishsa02bariuoft/page/240/mode/2up?view=theater&q=kentigern

[257] "St. Serf," Undiscovered Scotland, accessed 10 January 2023. https://www.undiscoveredscotland.co.uk/usbiography/s/stserf.html

[258] S. Baring Gould and John Fisher, *The Lives of British Saints*, Vol. II, (London: Charles J. Clark, 1908), 231-240. https://archive.org/details/livesofbritishsa02bariuoft/page/240/mode/2up?view=theater&q=kentigern

[259] Geoff Bailey, "History of Kinneil Kirk," Kinneil.org, 9 September 2019. https://kinneil.org/2019/09/09/history-of-kinneil-kirk-by-geoff-bailey/

[260] "About Patrick Graham (bishop)," DBPedia.org, accessed 9 January 2023. https://dbpedia.org/page/Patrick_Graham_(bishop)

[261] Sir John Herkless, *The Archbishops of St. Andrews*, 1855-1920 (Edinburgh: W. Blackwood, 1907), 255. https://archive.org/details/thearchbishopsof05herkuoft

[262] "Records of Abercorn, North Kirk Session, 1691-1945," Reference CH2/835, *National Records of Scotland*, accessed 20 January 2023. https://catalogue.nrscotland.gov.uk/nrsonlinecatalogue/browseDetails.aspx?reference=CH2/835&

[263] "A History of Abercorn," Seton Residences, accessed 20 January 2023. http://www2.thesetonfamily.com:8080/gallery/Abercorn_History.htm

*Appendix D: A Primer on the Ancient British and Roman Catholic Churches in Scotland*

## E. GLOSSARY OF RELEVANT ROMAN CATHOLIC SAINTS (Alphabetized)

Here is a short list of the Roman Catholic saints relevant to our investigations. A more complete online list can be found at www.Catholic.org. The full list, called *Index ac status causarum beatificationis servorum dei et canonizationis beatorum*, is available in hard copy only, updated by the Congregation for the Causes of Saints annually.

1. **Saint Andrew the Apostle (died 60 A.D.):** Brother to Saint Peter and one of Christ's Twelve Apostles. He is the patron saint of Scotland and fishermen. The Scottish Flag bears the cross of St. Andrew. Per Christian tradition, he was martyred by crucifixion at the city of Patras in Achaea in 60 A.D. on an "X-shaped" cross (saltire) at his own request. The same tradition says that, like his brother Peter, he did not feel worthy of being crucified on the same type of cross that Christ was crucified upon.[264] The coats of arms of the Norman Bruce and Jardin families, as well as vassals of the Bruces of Annandale such as the Corries of Newby, Kirkpatricks, Johnstons and Moffats are based on saltires. Saint Andrew was initially an ancient Anglo-Saxon patronage in Hexham in Northumberland. His relics arrived in Scotland in the eighth or ninth centuries. Andrew's connection with Scotland may have been reinforced following the Synod of Whitby in 664,[265] where Celtic Church leaders wrote that "Columba had been outranked by Peter." By this, they meant that since the patron saint of the Church based in Rome was Peter, they needed a higher ranking patron saint than Columba (or Kessog).[266] The political compromise to switch to St. Andrew, brother of St. Peter, as patron is attributed to Kenneth MacAlpin,[267] who united the kingdoms of Dalraida and Pictlands in the ninth century. The Picts had adopted St. Peter as patron a hundred years previously.[268] MacAlpin, the first king of the combined kingdom called "Alba," (Scotland), reigned from 843-858.[269] The Declaration of Arbroath written to Pope John XXII in 1320, claimed Scotland's conversion to Christianity was by Andrew, "the first to be an Apostle." Numerous churches in Scotland are named after St. Andrew.[270]

*Figure D-25: Flag of Scotland Photo by Smooth_O [265] CC-BY-2.0*

---

[264] "Ancient Wisdom, Modern Mission-Saint Andrew Complete Resource Guide," The Church of England: 24, accessed 20 January 2023. https://www.churchofengland.org/sites/default/files/2020-10/ST%20ANDREW%20COMPLETE%20RESOURCE%20PDF.pdf

[265] "Synod of Whitby," Whitby Abbey, North Yorkshire, UK, accessed 16 January 2023. https://www.whitbyabbey.co.uk/whitby-abbey/synod-whitby/

Figure D-25: Wikimedia Commons contributors, "File:Flag of Scotland.jpg," *Wikimedia Commons,* accessed 13 April 2023. https://commons.wikimedia.org/w/index.php?title=File:Flag_of_Scotland.jpg&oldid=685868464

[266] Michael T.R.B. Turnbull, "A History of St. Andrew," Scotland.org, 20 November 2016. https://www.scotland.org/events/st-andrews-day/a-history-of-st-andrew

[267] Craig Borland, "Eye on Millig: Remembering St. Kessog of Luss," *Helensburgh Advertiser*, 14 March 2017. https://www.helensburghadvertiser.co.uk/news/15156671.eye-on-millig-remembering-st-kessog-of-luss/

[268] James Rankin, *A Handbook of the Church of Scotland* (Edinburgh and London: Blackwood and Sons, 1888), 50-51.

[269] "King Kenneth I," Undiscovered Scotland, accessed 21 January 2023. https://www.undiscoveredscotland.co.uk/usbiography/monarchs/kennethi.html

[270] "How Apostle Andrew Became the Patron Saint of Scotland," The Catalogue of Good Deeds, 13 December 2017. https://catalogueofstelisabethconvent.blogspot.com/2017/12/how-apostle-andrew-became-patron-of.html

*Appendix D: A Primer on the Ancient British and Roman Catholic Churches in Scotland*

2. **Catherine of Alexandria (died c. 305 A.D.):** Saint Catherine of Alexandria is a saint in the Orthodox, Coptic and Roman Catholic churches. She was the daughter of Costus, pagan governor of Alexandria. Roman Emperor Maxentius, ordered her executed on a "breaking wheel," an instrument of torture, for refusing to recant her faith. The nucleus of attention on Saint Catherine in the Middle Ages was an Orthodox monastery at the foot of Mount Sinai, which claimed to have acquired her tomb and her relics by miraculous means. The monks reported her hair was still growing.[271] Since Catherine's tomb exuded an oil with healing powers that could be sold to pilgrims, it became a major source of fame and revenue for the monastery, aided by advertisements by pilgrims' retelling of her legend. By the end of the Middle Ages, she had become one of the most popular saints in Europe. When the crusaders first arrived in the Holy Land in 1099, they took possession of Bethlehem, before taking Jerusalem.[272] Bethlehem was traditionally the site where Jesus Christ appeared to Catherine and told her of her martyrdom. The medieval chapel named after St. Catherine of Alexandria built next to the famous Church of the Nativity in Bethlehem, may have been the first chapel built by the crusaders in the region.[273]

*Figure D-26: St. Catherine of Alexandria shown with a crown and the "Breaking Wheel" painting by Antonio de Solario in 1514, courtesy The National Gallery, London* [271]

St. Catherine of Siena, who is sometimes confused with St. Catherine of Alexandria, lived a thousand years later, in Italy and was known for her writings.[274] However, connections to both St. Catherines can be found in Edinburgh and both are associated with the Grahams and their kindred. In art, Catherine of Alexandria is dressed as a princess in rich clothes, often with a crown, long blonde hair, and sometimes with the wheel.[275] The expression: "To braid St. Catherine's hair" means to emulate St. Catherine and live life as a virgin. The analogy can be explained that it would take a lifetime to braid her hair when it has been growing since she died.[276] The Braids Nunnery, southwest of Edinburgh, was dedicated to St. Catherine of Alexandria, and estates

---

[271] "Marian Apparition to Saint Catherine," Roman Catholic Saints, accessed 10 January 2023. https://www.roman-catholic-saints.com/apparition-to-saint-catherine.html

Figured D-26: Wikimedia Commons contributors, "File:Antonio Solario (active 1502-1518) - Saint Catherine of Alexandria - NG646 - National Gallery.jpg," *Wikimedia Commons,* accessed 13 April 2023. https://commons.wikimedia.org/w/index.php?title=File:Antonio_Solario_(active_1502-1518)_-_Saint_Catherine_of_Alexandria_-_NG646_-_National_Gallery.jpg&oldid=703497733

[272] Father Sean Connolly, "The Church that Stands at the Spot of Christ's Birth," The Catholic World Report, 23 December 2019. https://www.catholicworldreport.com/2019/12/23/the-church-that-stands-at-the-spot-of-christs-birth/

[273] Diana Von Glahn, "St. Jerome and Bethlehem's Church of St. Catherine," Spiritual Direction, 30 September 2014. https://spiritualdirection.com/2014/09/30/st-jerome-bethlehems-church-st-catherine

[274] Rev. Alban Butler, *The Lives of the Fathers, Martyrs, and Other Principal Saints,* Vol. IV (Dublin: James Duffy, 1866; Bartleby.com, 2010). https://www.bartleby.com/210/4/301.html

[275] "Marian Apparition to Saint Catherine," Roman Catholic Saints, accessed 10 January 2023. https://www.roman-catholic-saints.com/apparition-to-saint-catherine.html

[276] Rebekah Curtis, "Contemplaiting," First Things, 27 June 2017. https://www.firstthings.com/web-exclusives/2017/06/contemplaiting

*Appendix D: A Primer on the Ancient British and Roman Catholic Churches in Scotland*

connected to that nunnery also called "Braids,"[277] to include the Lincolnshire Nunnery Priory.[278] Radulpho (Ralph) de Graham was granted the heritable lands of Cousland, Pentland[279] and Gogar[280] (later associated with the knightly orders[281]) by William the Lion about 1170.[282] See Figure 38. By the late thirteenth century, the Pentlands Forest region was noted as part of the estate of the Sir Henry of Braid, Sheriff of Edinburgh (the first Sir Henry de Graham) in a charter where Sir Henry provides support of the "Chapel of the Blessed Katherine."[283]

3. **St. John the Baptist (died 36 A.D.):** St. John the Baptist was known for evangelization and for baptizing Jesus Christ. He is recognized as a saint in many denominations and a prophet in others.[284] The great Military Order of St. John originated in Jerusalem circa 1080 during the Crusades where the knights operated the Hospital of St. John the Baptist for the care of travelers to the Holy Land.[285] These knights wore a uniform displaying an eight-pointed cross of white on a black mantle.[xi] The Scottish chapter of the Knights Hospitaller of the Order of St. John of Jerusalem was established at Torphichen in 1132.[286] The Order maintained only two bases in Britain. The other was in London. The knights were famous for the occupation of Malta in the face of Turkish siege in 1565 and later continued as the Sovereign Military Order of Malta after 1798.[287] Phil Graham speculates

*Figure D-27: HRH Prince Richard, Duke of Gloucester, Grand Prior of the Most Venerable Order of the Hospital of Saint John of Jerusalem processing at the Investiture Service of the Priory in the United States at Saint Michael and All Angels Episcopal Church in Dallas [278] CC0 1.0*

---

[277] A caution, "Braids" can also be a reference for "St. Bride," a nickname for St. Bridget.

[278] William Page, *A History of the County of Lincoln: Volume 2.* ( London: Victoria County History Online, accessed April 13, 2023. http://www.british-history.ac.uk/vch/lincs/vol2

Figure D-27: Wikimedia Commons contributors, "File:HRH Duke of Gloucester Processing.jpg," *Wikimedia Commons,* accessed 13 April 2023. https://commons.wikimedia.org/w/index.php?title=File:HRH_Duke_of_Gloucester_Processing.jpg&oldid=691540756

[279] William Robertson, Esq., *An index, drawn up about the year 1629, of many records of charters, granted by the different sovereigns of Scotland between the years 1309 and 1413, most of which records have been long missing. With an introduction, giving a state, founded on authentic documents still preserved, of the ancient records of Scotland, which were in that kingdom in the year 1292,* No. 180 (Edinburgh: Murry and Cochrane, 1798), 83. https://www.familysearch.org/library/books/viewer/365596/?offset=&return=1#page=1&viewer=picture&o=&n=0&q=

[280] Sir James Balfour Paul, *The Scots Peerage, Founded on Wood's Edition,* Vol. VI (Edinburgh: David Douglas, 1909), 198. https://archive.org/details/scotspeeragefoun06pauluoft/page/198/mode/2up?q=graham

[281] Ian B. Cowan, P.H.R. Mackay and Alan Macquarrie, *Knights of St. John of Jerusalem in Scotland,* Vol. 19 (Edinburgh, Clark Constable, 1983), lvii, 20, 23-24, 220. https://digital.nls.uk/126638043

[282] PoMS, "no.5942, factoid," accessed 13 February 2023. https://www.poms.ac.uk/record/factoid/5942/

[283] PoMS, "no. 4388," accessed 8 February 2023. https://www.poms.ac.uk/record/source/4388/

[284] "St. John the Baptist," Vela de Jerusalen, accessed 6 March 2023. https://santosepulcro.co.il/en/saints/st-john-the-baptist/

[285] "History," Sovereign Order of St. John of Jerusalem, Knights Hospitaller, accessed 31 March 2023. https://www.sosjinternational.org/history/

[286] "Torphichen Preceptory," Undiscovered Scotland, accessed 13 April 2023. https://www.undiscoveredscotland.co.uk/torphichen/preceptory/index.html

[287] Ian B. Cowan, P.H.R. Mackay and Alan Macquarrie, *Knights of St. John of Jerusalem in Scotland,* Vol. 19 (Edinburgh, Clark Constable, 1983), xxxix. https://digital.nls.uk/126638043

*Appendix D: A Primer on the Ancient British and Roman Catholic Churches in Scotland*

that Johnstone Kirk in old Dryfe ties to St. John of Jerusalem--that the surname "Johnstone" may have been derived from "St. John."

4. **St. Catherine of Siena (25 March 1347 – 29 April 1380):** She was a lay member of the Dominican Order from Siena, Italy, activist, and author. She was instrumental in the return of Pope Gregory XI from Avignon to Rome, brokered peace deals amongst the Italian city states, and carried out many missions entrusted by the pope, something rare for a woman of her time. Her *Dialogue*, includes hundreds of letters, and dozens of prayers, is considered a prominent part of Italian literature.[288] Canonized in 1461, she was only the second woman to be named "Doctor of the Church."[289] There is a Chapel of St. Catherine of Siena on the Grahams of Kincardine land and a nunnery in Edinburgh dedicated to her.[290]

*Figure D-28: Saint Catherine of Siena. From chiesa di Santa Maria del Rosario in Prati, Roma. Shown as Dominican nun in white with a black over-robe.* [289]

4. **Saint Gilbert of Dornoch (died 1245):** He was born "Gilbert of Moravia," later known as Saint Gilbert of Dornoch, or Gilbert of Caithness, and was the most famous Bishop of Caithness and the founder of Dornoch Cathedral. He was known as a dragon slayer,[291] hence the use of dragon symbology in churches connected to him.[292] He has a number of "Gilbert" namesakes amongst the lords of Strathearn and Kilbucho (e.g. Gilbert fitz Richer), the Avenels but also Graham cousins, particularly the Morays/Murrays, Johnstones and Armstrongs.[293]

---

[288] Paul Halsall, "Internet Medieval Sourcebook, Saints' Lives," Fordham University, accessed 10 January 2023. https://sourcebooks.fordham.edu/sbook3.asp

[289] "Saint Catherine of Siena," Catholic Online, accessed 19 January 2023. https://www.catholic.org/saints/saint.php?saint_id=9

Figure D-28: Wikimedia Commons contributors, "File:Catherine of Siena.jpg," *Wikimedia Commons,* accessed 13 April 2023. https://commons.wikimedia.org/w/index.php?title=File:Catherine_of_Siena.jpg&oldid=634487842

[290] "Survey of Dedications to Saints in Medieval Scotland," search on "Catherine of Siena," University of Edinburgh, School of History, Classics and Archaeology, accessed 13 February 2023. http://www.shca.ed.ac.uk/Research/saints/Project.htm

[291] Marcus Pitcaithly, "The Dragon Slaying Bishop of Caithness," Home Page of Author Marcus Pitcaithly, accessed 17 February 2023. https://www.marcus-pitcaithly.com/single-post/2018/03/16/st-gilbert-and-the-dragon

[292] Wikisource contributors, "The Folk-Lore Journal/Vol. 6/Folk-Lore of Sutherlandshire (September)," Wikisource, accessed 19 January 2023. https://en.wikisource.org/w/index.php?title=The_Folk-Lore_Journal/Volume_6/Folk-Lore_of_Sutherlandshire_(September)&oldid=10058354

[293] PoMS, Search on "Gilbert," accessed 15 January 2023. https://www.poms.ac.uk/search/?q=gilbert&index_type=person&page=11&min_date=1093&max_date=1371

5. **St. James the Greater (died 44 A.D.):** Saint James the Apostle is the patron saint of pilgrims and of Spain, as well as the patron of the Scottish Stewarts. University of Edinburgh's Survey of Dedications to Saints in Medieval Scotland database shows a number of Graham saint dedications in recognition of "Saint James the Greater." James, along with his brother John, left his life as a fisherman when Jesus called him to be a "fisher of men." Following the crucifixion of Jesus Christ, James made a pilgrimage to the Iberian Peninsula to evangelize. When he returned to Judea, he was beheaded by King Herod Agrippa I in the year 44A.D. "And he killed James the brother of John with the sword." (Acts 12:2 American Standard Version) The remains or relics, of St. James the Greater, were transported by his followers to the Iberian Peninsula and per tradition are buried in Santiago de Compostela in Galicia where scallop shells are common. Hence the reason the scallop shell symbol has become associated with St. James.[294] See Appendix E.

6. **Saint Malachy (1094– 2 November 1148):** He is an Irish saint who was Archbishop of Armagh. To his intercession were attributed several miracles, including healing the son of David I.[295] His connection to Annandale concerns the legend of his visit with Robert de Brus II, ancestor of King Robert I. From the Medieval Bruce Heritage Trust: "The Bruces ruled Annandale from motte and bailey castles at Lochmaben and Annan. Annan was initially their main stronghold… Malachy O'Moore (St. Malachy) passed through the town on his way to Rome probably about 1140. He stayed with Robert the Bruce II, as his guest. During the stay, he overhead servants talking about a robber who was awaiting sentence… Malachy asked Bruce to spare the life of the man. Bruce said he would and Malachy blessed the Bruce household. Later …when he saw the robber hanging from gallows, he put a curse on the household. The story goes that soon after a flood swept away a large section of Annan Motte forcing the Bruces to transfer their headquarters to Lochmaben."[296]

*Figure D-29: Extracted image of Saint James from the altarpiece in church of Mount San Martino, Italy painted by Carlo Crivelli circa 1480.* [294]

7. **Saint Mary the Virgin:** As the mother of Jesus Christ, Mary is a central figure in Christianity, and is given titles such as "Virgin" and "Queen."[297] She is by far the most popular saint of medieval times. While dedications to Mary were rare or non-existent in the Celtic Church, they became commonplace with the arrival of the Roman Catholic Normans.[298] A search on "Mary the Blessed Virgin" in University of Edinburgh's Survey of Dedications to Saints in Medieval Scotland database yields 1340

---

[294] Gail Delahunt, "Everything You Need to Know About the Apostle St. James the Greater," Follow the Camino, 27 December 2019. https://followthecamino.com/en/blog/history-of-the-apostle-saint-james/

Figure D-29: Wikimedia Commons contributors, "File:Carlo Crivelli 064.jpg," *Wikimedia Commons,* accessed 13 April 2023. https://commons.wikimedia.org/w/index.php?title=File:Carlo_Crivelli_064.jpg&oldid=706789331

[295] "St. Malachi," Catholic.org, accessed 20 January 2023. https://www.catholic.org/saints/saint.php?saint_id=4431

[296] "Overview," Medieval Bruce Heritage Trust, accessed 16 January 2023. http://www.brucetrust.co.uk/places-events.html

[297] "Mary, the Blessed Virgin," Catholic.org, accessed 20 January 2023. https://www.catholic.org/saints/saint.php?saint_id=4967

[298] James Rankin, *A Handbook of the Church of Scotland* (Edinburgh and London: Blackwood and Sons, 1888), 50-51.

occurrences, 84 of which belong to the Bruce family,[xii] five times more than any other saint. With the arrival of the Normans in Scotland, there was a significant increase in patronages and dedications to Saint Mary.[299] Patrons of religious houses dedicated to Saint Mary usually can be connected to Norman families, such as the Avenels, patrons of St. Mary's Abbey of "New Melrose."[300]

8. **Saint Michael the Archangel:** He is considered a patron saint of warriors[301] and the town of Dumfries in Scotland.[302] In the Christian Old Testament and Hebrew Torah, the Archangel Michael is the protector of Israel. In the Book of Revelation, Michael leads the armies of heaven against Satan.[303] He was often depicted as a warrior clad in armor slaying a dragon.[304] Figure D-30. In some parts of France, mainly Normandy, Brittany, and Poitou, **the scallop shell was associated not with the Apostle James but with the Archangel Michael**. The shell thus appears prominently in the arms of the Norman Abbey of Mont Saint Michel, the French Royal Order of Saint Michael the Archangel,[305] as well as the Graham Coat of Arms. The popularity of the scallop shell and its association with St. Michael the Archangel in Normandy may be due to the legend that St. James of Compostela visited Charlemagne in a dream and urged him to liberate his forgotten tomb in Spain from the Saracens. St. Michael the Archangel, as the patron saint of warriors, would have been tied to the campaign to liberate Spain.[306] Wikipedia has a comprehensive collection of imagery of the insignia of the Most Distinguished Order of Saint Michael and Saint George in Britain, featured in the 007 movies. The order, to include its chapel inside Saint Paul's Cathedral in London, is named in honor of two military

DUMFRIES.
*Figure D-30 : Arms of the Burgh of Dumfries from "The Arms of the Royal and Parliamentary Burghs of Scotland," by H.R.N. Macphail and H.W. Lonsdale, 1897* [299]

---

[299] "Survey of Dedications to Saints in Medieval Scotland," University of Edinburgh, School of History, Classics and Archaeology, accessed 10 January 2023. http://www.shca.ed.ac.uk/Research/saints/Project.htm
Figure D-30: John, Marquess of Bute, J.R.N. Macphail, and H.W. Lonsdale, *The Arms of the Royal and Parliamentary Burghs of Scotland* (Edinburgh: William Blackwood & Sons, 1897), 99.
https://play.google.com/store/books/details?id=7VA4AQAAMAAJ&rdid=book-7VA4AQAAMAAJ&rdot=1

[300] PoMS, "no. 7813, factoid," accessed 16 January 2023. https://www.poms.ac.uk/record/factoid/7813/

[301] Dr. Geraldine Rohling, "St. Michael the Archangel: Warrior and Protector," The Basilica of the National Shrine of the Immaculate Conception, 9 November 2021. https://www.nationalshrine.org/blog/st-michael-the-archangel-warrior-and-protector/

[302] G.W. Shirley, "Notes of the Arms of the Royal Burgh of Dumfries," *Transactions of the Dumfries and Galloway Natural History and Archaeological Society (TDGNHAS)* No. 3011 (1925): 162-165.
https://dgnhas.org.uk/sites/default/files/transactions/3011.pdf

[303] Mark Russell, "Why is Saint Michael so Important to Airborne Troops?" The Veterans Site, accessed 20 January 2023. https://blog.theveteranssite.greatergood.com/saint-michael/

[304] G.W. Shirley, "Notes of the Arms of the Royal Burgh of Dumfries," *Transactions of the Dumfries and Galloway Natural History and Archaeological Society (TDGNHAS)* No. 3011 (1925): 162-165.

[305] Duane L.C.M. Galles, "Pilgrims and Heraldry," The Heraldry Society, *Coats of Arms* No. 145 (Spring 1989), accessed 27 December 2022. https://www.theheraldrysociety.com/articles/pilgrims-and-heraldry/

[306] "History of Charlemagne and Roland, Compostela and the Legend of the Milky Way," Compostela, Joining Heaven and Earth, accessed 7 March 2023. https://compostela.co.uk/mythology/charlemagne-and-the-legend-of-the-milky-way/

saints, Saint Michael and Saint George, and features an image of Saint Michael subduing Satan.[307] See Appendix E.

9. **Saint Peter the Apostle (died 64 A.D.):** Also known as Simon Peter of Cephas, he was one of Christ's twelve apostles, and is recognized as the first pope. While he is a saint in many Christian denominations, his position as the first pope in Rome is a strong connection to the Roman Catholic Church. He is considered a patron saint of fishermen, net makers and ship builders. His symbol is an upside-down cross[308] as he was crucified upside-down at his request as he did not feel worthy to be crucified in the same manner as Christ.[309] As the keeper of the keys to heaven, Peter is also symbolized by a set of keys crossed in the shape of an "X."[310] When Edwin, king of Northumbria, converted to Christianity in 627, he was baptized at York in a new wooden church dedicated to Saint Peter. A school, a hospital run by the Knights Hospitaller, and a cathedral all dedicated to St. Peter were added in York over the centuries. The cathedral called the "York Minster" was completed in 1472 and became the powerful seat of the Archbishop of York. William de Graham's theorized father, Forne Sigulfson, was tasked by Henry I in the 1120s to rectify the complaints of the canons of St. Peter's York that the locals had not paid tithes nor returned church lands in Aldborough.[311] His successor, King Stephen, also gave St. Peter's York similar protections.[312] Kings of England getting personally involved in the complaints of a religious house in York indicates an elevated status amongst their peers. In addition, the Northumbrian influence on the Picts cause them to also adopt Peter around the eighth century.[313] The name "Peter" was likely chosen to have the same status as Saint Peter's York and Saint Peter's Basilica in Rome,[314] implying that religious houses dedicated to Saint Peter have an elevated leadership role.

10. **Saint Sebastian (255-288 A.D.):** He was an early Christian martyr and patron of soldiers. He is known for surviving the Romans' first attempt to kill him by shooting him repeatedly with arrows. He was later killed by club.[315] King Robert I adopted St. Sebastian as patron for his body guard Archers.[316]

---

[307] Wikipedia contributors, "Order of St. Michael and St. George," Wikipedia, The Free Encyclopedia, accessed 10 January 2023. https://en.wikipedia.org/w/index.php?title=Order_of_St._Michael_and_St._George&oldid=1131968343

[308] "St. Peter," Catholic Online, accessed 16 January 2023. https://www.catholic.org/saints/saint.php?saint_id=5358

[309] Hector Molina, "What Does an Upside Down Cross Mean?" Catholic Answers, 17 July 2014. https://www.catholic.com/magazine/online-edition/the-upside-down-cross-satanic-or-symbolic

[310] Friedrich Rest, *Our Christian Symbols* (Cleveland: The Pilgrim Press, 1954), 29. https://archive.org/details/ourchristiansymb00fred/mode/2up?q=peter

[311] Charles Johnson and H.A. Cronne, *Regesta Regum Anglo-Normannorum*, Vol. II, 1100-1135 (Oxford: Clarendon Press, 1956), 216. https://deeds.library.utoronto.ca/cartularies/0378

[312] Paul Dalton, "Feudal Politics in Yorkshire, 1066 x 1054" (Phd Thesis, University of Sheffield, 1990), 74, 129. https://etheses.whiterose.ac.uk/1870/

[313] James Rankin, *A Handbook of the Church of Scotland* (Edinburgh and London: Blackwood and Sons, 1888), 50-51.

[314] David Simpson, "Kingdom of Northumbria 450 AD to 866AD, Edwin's Conversion," England's Northeast, accessed 16 January 2023. https://englandsnortheast.co.uk/kingdom-northumbria/

[315] "Saint Sebastian," Catholic Online, accessed 16 January 2023. https://www.catholic.org/saints/saint.php?saint_id=103

[316] William P. Bruce, "The Bowmen of Saint Sebastian," Family of Bruce International, February 2017. https://familyofbruceinternational.org/the-bowmen-of-saint-sebastian/

*Appendix D: A Primer on the Ancient British and Roman Catholic Churches in Scotland*

11. **Saint Thomas Becket (1118-1170):** He was the Archbishop of Canterbury at the time he was murdered in Canterbury Cathedral for putting church needs ahead of the directives of Henry II.[317] William the Lion of Scotland, a friend of Becket, dedicated the famous Arbroath Abbey in his memory.[318] Becket's assistant, a monk named Edward Grim (a variant of "Graham") was with him the night he was murdered and attempted to defend him.[319]

12. **Saint Walthorf of Melrose (1095-1115):** He was the son of Simon St. Liz of Huntington, and a stepson of David I. He was the second Abbot of New Melrose, and joined the newly established Cistercian order at Reivaulx in 1143.[320] He was known for his kindness to the poor and miracle healings of the sick and blind.[321] He was never officially canonized.[322] St. Waltheof was a grandson of Waltheof, earl of Northumberland, and brother to Simon a successor earl. Earl Simon built a number of castles in Tynedale to defend against invasions by the Scots. The castle and estate of Simonburn is named for him. St. Mungo founded the church in Simonburn.[323] The elder line Grahams, who had inherited the Wooler barony in Northumberland via marriage to the Muschamps heiress, apparently acquired Simonburn (Figure F-8) about the time the Scots acquired Tynedale in a 1237 treaty with Henry II. Like the elder line Grahams, the Muschamps supported St. Waltheof's "Old Melrose" and some were buried there.[324]

---

[317] "Thomas Becket, Archbishop of Canterbury, Martyr, b. 1118, died December 29, 1170," Saint Thomas Church, Fifth Avenue, New York City, accessed 16 January 2023. https://www.saintthomaschurch.org/liturgical_date/thomas-becket/

[318] "William the Lion penny," Historic Environment Scotland, accessed 16 January 2023. https://www.historicenvironment.scot/archives-and-research/archives-and-collections/properties-in-care-collections/object/william-the-lion-penny-1165-1214-medieval-arbroath-abbey-1254

[319] Rev. Alban Butler, *The Lives of the Fathers, Martyrs, and Other Principal Saints,* Vol. XII (Dublin: James Duffy, 1866; Bartleby.com, 2010). https://www.bartleby.com/210/12/291.html

[320] "Saint Waltheof of Melrose," Catholic.net, accessed 16 January 2023. https://catholic.net/op/articles/3008/cat/1205/st-waltheof-of-melrose.html

[321] James A. Wade, *History of St. Mary's Abbey, Melrose and the Monastery of Old Melrose* (Edinburgh: Thomas C. Jack, 1861), 196-197. https://books.google.mu/books?id=-BEFAAAAYAAJ&printsec=frontcover#v=onepage&q&f=false

[322] The Laird O'Thistle, "Royal Saints of the British Crown," Unofficial Royalty, 26 October 2008. https://www.unofficialroyalty.com/columnists/the-laird-othistle/royal-saints-of-the-british-crown/

[323] "The Great Parish of Simonburn, from Hadrian's Wall to Carter's Bar," Hallbarns-Simonburn, accessed 19 January 2023. http://www.hallbarns-simonburn.co.uk/simonburn.htm

[324] M.C. Dixon, "The Knightly Families of Northumberland: A Crisis in the Fourteenth Century" (Masters Thesis, Durham University, 2000), 1, 16, 17, 18. http://etheses.dur.ac.uk/4373/1/4373_1893.pdf

*Appendix D: A Primer on the Ancient British and Roman Catholic Churches in Scotland*

## F. Grahams who are Scottish Church Leaders

1. **Patrick Graham, First Archbishop of St. Andrews (circa 1420-1478):** The first Bishop of Brechin. Patrick was elected Bishop of St. Andrews 1465; and the first Archbishop of St. Andrews in 1472. He was a younger son of Robert Graham of Fintry and grandson of Sir William Graham of Kincardine by Lady Mary Stewart, daughter of King Robert III of Scotland.[325] Before rising to the rank of bishop, Patrick, for many years, led the parish church of Kinneil, which had strong ties to the Culdee missionary St. Serf.[326] Patrick's career as the first Archbishop of St. Andrews, and therefore the <u>**first head of the Church in Scotland**</u> was marked with conflict between the Scottish government and Rome. The Scottish crown and parliament refused all papal directives subjecting Scottish bishops to the authority of the Archbishops of York and Canterbury, protested taxes from Rome, and imposed their own taxes on the Scottish church.[327]

   The position of Scotland's first Archbishop was created to give the Scottish Church freedom from the English Church and gave Patrick authority over Scotland's bishops. Archbishop Graham's rival and ultimate successor, William Schevez, orchestrated charges of blasphemy and later insanity against him, after Patrick cautioned James III against listening to astrological advice provided by Schevez. Pope Sixtus IV ordered an enquiry into Patrick's conduct and subsequently ordered his confinement, first at Inchcolm, then Dunfermline Abbey. Graham was formally removed from office on 9 January 1478. Schevez imprisoned Graham in Loch Leven Castle, moved him to Inchholm, then back to Loch Leven due to fears he would be freed by the English, where he died that year.[328] Given the timing and circumstances, we speculate Patrick did not die of natural causes. Fittingly, the archbishop was buried near the site of a medieval monastery dedicated to St. Serf, at St. Serf's Inch in Lochleven.[329]

2. **Robert Graeme, Archdeacon of Ross, of the Grahams of Drynie (1513-1602):** Robert, the younger son of Patrick, first laird of Inchbrakie, and grandson of the earl of Montrose, was educated for the church. His wife was Marjorie Dunbar of Albrach. In 1567, when he served as the Prebendary (church administrator) of Alyth, he received a deed for the lands belonging to the Alyth cathedral from the Bishop of Dunkeld. His career was also marked with continual accusations of dereliction of duty brought about by his enemies, of which he was fully acquitted shortly before his death in 1602. Graeme acquired the lands of Drynie from the MacKenzies some time after 1578. James VI presented the Archdeanery of Ross to Robert Graeme 2 August 1573. He

---

[325] "Graham, Patrick (d. 1478)," *Dictionary of the National Biography*, accessed 20 January 2023. https://en.wikisource.org/wiki/Dictionary_of_National_Biography,_1885-1900/Graham,_Patrick

[326] Geoff Bailey, "History of Kinneil Kirk," Kinneil.org, 9 September 2019. https://kinneil.org/2019/09/09/history-of-kinneil-kirk-by-geoff-bailey/

[327] John Herkless and Robert Kerr Hannay, *The Archbishops of St. Andrews*, Vol. I (Edinburgh and London: William Blackwood and Son, 1907), 12, 13, 62-65, 75-77, 82. https://www.familysearch.org/library/books/viewer/197574/?offset=&return=1#page=5&viewer=picture&o=&n=0&q=

[328] "Graham, Patrick (d. 1478)," *Dictionary of the National Biography*.

[329] John Herkless and Robert Kerr Hannay, *The Archbishops of St. Andrews*, Vol. I (Edinburgh and London: William Blackwood and Son, 1907), 12, 13, 62-65, 75-77, 82.

was confirmed by the General Assembly 6 March 1574. In 1597, his eldest son, George is styled "son and heir of the Archdeacon of Ross."[330]

The archdeacon also shared a caution of 5000 pounds Scots for David Graham, sixth Laird of Fintry, along with his kinsmen: John, Earl of Montrose, Robert Graeme of Thornick, and William Graham of Claverhouse. Fintry was a Jacobite, and supporter of Mary, Queen of Scots, during her lifetime. Even following her execution in 1587, plots to overthrow Protestant rule continued. Fintry was executed in 1592 for his role in the "Spanish Blanks Plot," an attempt to invite Spanish forces to Scottish and English shores to bolster a Counter-Reformation.[331, 332]

3. **Andrew Graham, Bishop of Dunblane:** The son of the Laird of Morphie. He was granted the temporalities of the bishopric on 28 July 1575. He resigned the see early in 1603, making way for his kinsman George Graeme. His episcopate fell in a time when the role of bishops had been significantly reduced.[333]

4. **George Graeme (1565–1643), Bishop of Dunblane and Bishop of Orkney:** The younger son of George Graeme 2nd of Inchbrakie and Marion/Mary Rollo, daughter of Rollo of Duncrub, and a great-grandson of William Graham, first Earl of Montrose. In 1595, he married Marion Crichton, daughter of Sir Robert Crichton of Eliock and Cluny, Perthshire, Lord Advocate of Scotland, and his wife Elizabeth Stewart.[334]

   George was minister of Scone, and then in February 1603, he received a crown provision to the bishopric of Dunblane, vacated by Andrew Graham. George was consecrated by 3 May 1611. On 26 August 1615, he was transferred to the bishopric of Orkney. He held that bishopric for more than three decades. Graeme, along with all other bishops of Scotland, was deprived of his see on 18 November 1638. He renounced his rights to the bishopric a few months later, on 11 February 1639, after being threatened by the Assembly at Glasgow. By this action, he avoided excommunication, and retained his estate at Gorthie.[335]

5. **Archibald Grahame, (Alias: Archibald McIlvernock of Oib), Bishop of Argyle and the Isle, 1682:** From the Graham family of Kilbride who claimed descent from the Lords of Galloway. He became a Church of Scotland minister, and was parson of Rothesay before becoming Bishop of the Isles in 1680. After the Revolution of 1688 (a.k.a Glorious Revolution), all Church of Scotland bishops, including Grahame, lost their sees. He bequeathed to the poor of Rothesay, a valuable theological library, alleged to contain Culdee historical records, consisting over 169 volumes. The

---

[330] Louisa Grace Graeme, *Or and Sable : a Book of Graemes and Grahams* (Edinburgh: William Brown, 1903), 10-18. https://archive.org/details/orsablebookofgra00grae/page/642/mode/2up?q=archdeacon

[331] Cathy Marsden, "An Unfortunate End, The Rebellious David Graham's Album Amicorum," Lyon and Turnbull, accessed 9 January 2023. https://www.lyonandturnbull.com/news/article/an-unfortunate-end/

[332] Louisa Grace Graeme, 620.

[333] Louisa Grace Graeme, xl-xli.

[334] Louisa Grace Graeme, 35, 41-44.

[335] Hew Scott, *Fasti Ecclesiae Scoticanae*, Vol. VII (Edinburgh: Oliver and Boyd, 1928), 353. https://ia802904.us.archive.org/31/items/fastiecclesiaesc00scot/fastiecclesiaesc00scot.pdf

### G. Saint Patronages and Dedications Connected to the Grahams

local kirk in Rothesay sold a small amount for the poor, but retained the majority. He died in Edinburgh on 23 June 1702, leaving no male heirs.[336]

The University of Edinburgh, School of History, Classics and Archaeology sponsored the "Survey of Dedications to Saints in Medieval Scotland," a three-year project (2004-2007) funded by a Major Research Grant from the Arts and Humanities Research Council (AHRC). While the project was completed in 2007, the database is still updated annually. The survey defines an 'act of dedication' in a broad way as the invocation or use of a saint's name occurs in multiple situations. The database incorporates not just the straightforward categories of church or altar dedications, but also a variety of less obvious indications of interest in, or familiarity with, a particular saint. The categories of dedication type include: the association of a saint's name with landscape features (for example, hills, wells or springs, bays); the naming of ships, streets, buildings, rooms, liturgical or domestic objects; or the use of a saint's feast day to date charters or other documents.[337]

Homepage: http://www.shca.ed.ac.uk/Research/saints/
Search page: http://saints.shca.ed.ac.uk/index.cfm?fuseaction=home.adhocform

**Saint Dedications from Dumfriesshire:** Selected Culdee Dedications in Dumfriesshire from the University of Edinburgh database are listed below. Of note: Culdee Saint dedications still occurred after 1124, the time of arrival of David I and Norman land barons in Scotland, and also after 1250, the date of Scotland's official conversion to Roman Catholicism.[338]

**Early Culdee Dumfriesshire Dedications Found in the University of Edinburgh Database:**

- St. Cuthbert in Ewesdale before 1274
- St. Kessog Grant in Luss, Dumbarton -March 1314; Grant in dedication of St. Kessog by the Earl of Lennox and King Robert the Bruce, June 1315, Auchterarder Chapel in Perth, dedication 1542
- St. Patrick Kirkpatrick Juxta Moffat before 1274
- St. Patrick Kirkpatrick Fleming (vicarage of Kirkpatrick Fleming Gretna) before 1274
- St. Patrick Redkirk before 1274
- St. Fechan in Ecclefechan before 1274
- St. Osbern in Closeburn before 1274

---

[336] James King Hewison, *The Isle of Bute in the Olden Time: With Illustrations, Maps, and Plans*, Vol. 2 (Edinburgh and London: W. Blackwood and sons, 1895), 290-291. https://archive.org/details/isleofbuteinolde02hewiuoft/page/290/mode/2up?q=graham

[337] "Survey of Dedications to Saints in Medieval Scotland," University of Edinburgh, School of History, Classics and Archaeology, accessed 10 January 2023. http://saints.shca.ed.ac.uk/index.cfm?fuseaction=home.adhocform

[338] Rev J.A. Wylie, *The History of the Scottish Nation*, Vol. 3 (London: Hamilton, Adams and Co., 1886), 203-204, 298. https://www.originofnations.org/books,%20papers/history%20of%20the%20scots/scothistvol3.pdf

*Appendix D: A Primer on the Ancient British and Roman Catholic Churches in Scotland*

- St. Patrick Kirkpatrick Irongray near Closeburn 1315
- St. Ninian in Lochmaben from 1502 to 1505[339]

## Scottish Temple/Hospital Saints adopted by Cistercians and Norman Church Foundations.

- Saint Andrew the Apostle was an Anglo-Saxon patronage before the Norman Conquest.[340]
- Saint Peter was an Anglo-Saxon patronage in York before the Norman Conquest.[341]
- Saint Peter was a Pictish patronage before the Norman conquest.[342]
- Saint Patrick, an old Strathclyde patronage, culminating in the Chapel Royal of Scotland.[343]
- Virgin Mary was adopted by Simon de St. Liz (Senlis), Earl of Huntingdon, at Simonburn, (St. Mary's Well)[344] and Hexham[345] and Dumbarton[346] and by Bruce in Annandale.[347]
- Saint Columba outranked by the Anglo-Saxons at the Synod of Whitby 664.[348]
- Saint Adrian and the Culdee Hermits of The Forth killed by Vikings 875.[349]
- Saint Adrian McGabrain, the Culdee of Lindisfarne and Hexham, father of King Arthur at Arthuret.[350]
- Saint Bega was an Anglo-Saxon Saint circa 850 whose Kilbucho lands passed to the Dalkeith Grahams, ancestors of the Grahams of Corry and Hutton.[351]

---

[339] "Survey of Dedications to Saints in Medieval Scotland," University of Edinburgh, School of History, Classics and Archaeology, accessed 10 January 2023. http://saints.shca.ed.ac.uk/index.cfm?fuseaction=home.adhocform

[340] "Synod of Whitby," Whitby Abbey, North Yorkshire, UK, accessed 16 January 2023. https://www.whitbyabbey.co.uk/whitby-abbey/synod-whitby/

[341] Charles Johnson and H.A. Cronne, *Regesta Regum Anglo-Normannorum*, Vol. II, 1100-1135 (Oxford: Clarendon Press, 1956), 216. https://deeds.library.utoronto.ca/cartularies/0378

[342] James Rankin, *A Handbook of the Church of Scotland* (Edinburgh and London: Blackwood and Sons, 1888), 50-51.

[343] Erik McLeary, "Saint Patrick," The Dumbarton Castle Society, accessed 6 March 2023. https://www.dumbartoncastle.co.uk/saint-patrick

[344] Robert Charles Hope, *The Legendary Lore of the Holy Wells of England* (London: Elliott Stock, 1894), 104. https://insearchofholywellsandhealingsprings.files.wordpress.com/2014/03/legendaryloreofholywellshope.pdf

[345] Wikisource contributors, "Catholic Encyclopedia (1913)/Devotion to the Blessed Virgin Mary," Wikisource, accessed 6 March 2023. https://en.wikisource.org/w/index.php?title=Catholic_Encyclopedia_(1913)/Devotion_to_the_Blessed_Virgin_Mary&oldid=10729898

[346] "Dumbarton, St. Mary's Collegiate Church," Canmore: National Record of the Historic Environment, accessed 6 March 2023. https://canmore.org.uk/site/42351/dumbarton-st-marys-collegiate-church

[347] "Survey of Dedications to Saints in Medieval Scotland," University of Edinburgh, School of History, Classics and Archaeology, accessed 10 January 2023. http://saints.shca.ed.ac.uk/index.cfm?fuseaction=home.adhocform

[348] "Synod of Whitby," Whitby Abbey, North Yorkshire, UK, accessed 16 January 2023. https://www.whitbyabbey.co.uk/whitby-abbey/synod-whitby/

[349] Rev. Alban Butler, *The Lives of the Fathers, Martyrs, and Other Principal Saints*, Vol. III (Dublin: James Duffy, 1866; Bartleby.com, 2010). https://www.bartleby.com/210/3/043.html

[350] Archibald B. Scott, *The Pictish Nation, Its People and Its Church* (Edinburgh and London: T.N. Foulis, 1918), 176, 191, 192, 216, 217. https://archive.org/details/pictishnationits00scotrich

[351] Rev. John Marius Wilson, *Imperial Gazetteer of Scotland Volume 2* (London and Edinburgh: A. Fullarton and Co., 1868), 189-190. https://digital.nls.uk/gazetteers-of-scotland-1803-1901/archive/97473162

*Appendix D: A Primer on the Ancient British and Roman Catholic Churches in Scotland*

- Saint Cuthbert was connected to the Knights Templar. Coldingham Priory,[352] Wamphray[353] and Dryfe[354] whose religious houses were under the order of St. Cuthbert, became Temple lands.[355]

### Scottish Temple Norman Related Patronages.

- Saint Michael the Archangel (and the Dragon) in Dumfries Royal Burgh and Linlithgow Royal Burgh.[356] There were also dedications to St. Michael in Dalgarnock, Nithsdale before the year 1200, in Dumfries about 1504 and 276 others throughout *Scotland in the Survey of Dedications to Saints in Medieval Scotland* database.[357]
- Saint James the Greater, a patron saint and therefore protector of pilgrims, was popular with knights engaging in the Crusades.[358,359]
- Hospital Foundation at Torphichen in Scotland was established in 1132 (not 1128).[360]
- Saint John of Jerusalem "Black Mantle" Temple Foundation founded 1119.
- Saint John of Jerusalem "Red Cross" Temple Foundation founded in Jerusalem 1146.[361]
- The first known William de Graham witnessed King David's foundation of Holyrood Abbey in 1125[xiii] and St. Cuthbert's (the saint whose cross became the symbol of the Templars) Church in Edinburgh in 1127.[362] This William de Graham of Dalkeith, may have been in possession of the Templar property of Clerkstoun (Clerkington)[xiv] of Mont Lothian before the

---

[352] Dmitry Lapa, "Saint Aebba of Coldingham," *The Postil Magazine*, 1 July 2021. https://www.thepostil.com/saint-aebba-of-coldingham/

[353] "Wamphray Church," Canmore National Record of the Historic Environment, accessed 6 March 2023. https://canmore.org.uk/site/66905/wamphray-church

[354] Col William Rogerson, *Hutton Under the Muir* (Dumfries, Scotland: Dumfries and Galloway Courier and Herald, 1908), 5.

[355] "The Templars in Annandale-Carruthersland," Clan Carruthers--Warriors, 13 January 2007. https://clancarruthers228187931.wordpress.com/tag/ruthwell/

[356] John, Marquess of Bute, J.R.N. Macphail, and H.W. Lonsdale, *The Arms of the Royal and Parliamentary Burghs of Scotland* (Edinburgh: William Blackwood & Sons, 1897), 99, 100, 256, 257. https://play.google.com/store/books/details?id=7VA4AQAAMAAJ&rdid=book-7VA4AQAAMAAJ&rdot=1

[357] "Survey of Dedications to Saints in Medieval Scotland," University of Edinburgh, School of History, Classics and Archaeology, accessed 10 January 2023. http://saints.shca.ed.ac.uk/index.cfm?fuseaction=home.adhocform

[358] "Military Commandery of St. James the Greater," Grand Priory of the Knights Templar in the United Kingdom, accessed 6 March 2023. https://www.osmthgpuk.org/military

[359] "The Legends of Saint James," St. James Cathedral, Seattle, accessed 6 March 2023. https://www.stjames-cathedral.org/prayer/jameslegend.aspx

[360] "Torphichen Preceptory," Undiscovered Scotland, accessed 13 April 2023. https://www.undiscoveredscotland.co.uk/torphichen/preceptory/index.html

[361] Charles G. Addison, *The History of the Knights Templar, the Temple Church and the Temple* (London: Longman, Brown, Green, Longmans, 1842), 38, 54, 55. https://archive.org/details/historyofknights00addiuoft

[362] Michael Gervers, *Documents of Early England Data Set (DEEDS)*, **Charter Numbers:** 05130072, accessed 6 March 2023. https://deeds.library.utoronto.ca/charters/05130072

*Appendix D: A Primer on the Ancient British and Roman Catholic Churches in Scotland*

creation of the Scottish Hospital and Temple foundations circa 1136 to 1140.[363] In 1140, William de Graham is the perambulator (land surveyor) for David I in the gift of Clerkington (Temple lands in the barony of Dalkeith[364]) to St. Mary's in Haddington.[365, 366] David II granted Clerkington to the Collegiate Church of Corstorphine before 1371. Temple Parish, erected later in 1618, combined the ancient Chapelry of Balantrodoch with the Chapelries of Clerkington and Moorfoot.[367]

- The connection of the Lindisfarne Gospels housed at Durham 995-1536 [368] and an increase in patronages of Saints Matthew, Mark, Luke and John during this time period.[369]
- David I, son of Queen Margaret Canmore, founded Holyrood (Holy Cross) Abbey and the Benedictine Abbey of the Holy Trinity and St. Margaret at Dunfermline both in 1128. Queen Margaret and King Malcolm III were buried at Dunfermline[370] while Holyrood housed Margaret's "True Cross" of Christ.[371] King Alexander II established the Scottish chapter of the Order of the Most Holy Trinity and of the Captives (Trinitarians) at Failford circa 1198 [372] because it was there that he recovered Margaret's "True Cross" relic.[373]
- Saint Nicholas was adopted by Sir James Douglas for Dalkeith Chapel in 1369 and for his new Dalkeith Collegiate Church in 1406.[374]

---

[363] Midlothian Ordnance Survey Name Books, 1852-1853, Midlothian Volume 52, OS1/11/52/15, Scotlands Places, accessed 14 March 2023. https://scotlandsplaces.gov.uk/digital-volumes/ordnance-survey-name-books/midlothian-os-name-books-1852-1853/midlothian-volume-52/15

[364] Joan Blaeu and Timothy Pont, "Provinciae Edinburgenae Description," Atlas of Scotland, 1654, *National Library of Scotland.* https://maps.nls.uk/view/00001284

[365] PoMS no. 1038, place summary, Clerkington, accessed 6 March 2023. https://www.poms.ac.uk/record/place/1038/

[366] Michael Gervers, *Documents of Early England Data Set (DEEDS),* University of Toronto, 1975-present, Charter Number: 05130134, accessed 27 December 2022. https://deeds.library.utoronto.ca/charters/05130134

[367] Rev. Alfred Coutts, *The Knights Templar in Scotland* (Scottish Church History Society, 1941), 127. https://archive.org/details/rschsv07p2coutts/page/126/mode/2up

[368] Jessica Brain, "The Lindisfarne Gospels," HistoricUK.com, 8 March 2021. https://www.historic-uk.com/HistoryUK/HistoryofEngland/Lindisfarne-Gospels/#:~:text=A%20famous%20illuminated%20manuscript%20created,beauty%2C%20ornate%20detail%20and%20design

[369] "Survey of Dedications to Saints in Medieval Scotland," University of Edinburgh, School of History, Classics and Archaeology, accessed 5 March 2023.

[370] "King David I, Dunfermline Abbey," English Monarchs, accessed 6 March 2023. https://www.englishmonarchs.co.uk/dunfermline_abbey.html

[371] Turgot, Bishop of Saint Andrews, translated by William Forbes-Leith, *The Life of St. Margaret, Queen of Scotland* (Edinburgh: William Patterson, 1884), 77. https://archive.org/details/lifeofstmargaret00turguoft/page/n9/mode/2up

[372] William J. Dillon, "The Trinitarians at Failford," *Ayrshire Archaeological and Natural History Society* Vol 4 (1957): 76, 91-93. https://aanhsorg.files.wordpress.com/2018/08/the-trinitarians-of-failford.pdf

[373] Mackenzie E.C. Walcott, *Scoti Monasticon-The Ancient Church of Scotland* (London: Virtue, Spalding and Daldy, 1874), 36. https://ia600309.us.archive.org/22/items/scotimonasticona00walc/scotimonasticona00walc.pdf

[374] "Survey of Dedications to Saints in Medieval Scotland," University of Edinburgh, School of History, Classics and Archaeology, accessed 5 March 2023.

- Saint Sebastian was adopted by King Robert the Bruce for his body guards known as the "Guards de Ecosse." [375]
- Saint Leonard adopted by the hospital in Edinburgh. [376]
- Saint Catherine of Alexandria was adopted by Graham son-in-law, Henry of Braid in Pentland before 1300, (Figure 38) and of "William of Dalkeith" [377] in Peebleshire in 1334. [378]
- Robert the Bruce created The Order of the Scottish Rosy Cross at Bannockburn in 1314. [379] At the same time, Bruce is also said to have united the Templars and the Royal Order of Heredom with the guilds of working masons, who had also fought in his army. He founded the famous Lodge at Kilwinning in 1286. [380] Phil Graham believes one of the Rosicrucian early masters was William More, husband of Sybilla (Isabella) Graham of Abercorn, and the son Sir Reginald More, justiciar to Robert I and chamberlain to David II. [381] Both Reginald and William were named as guardians of the Knights Hospitaller. [382]

**Norman Saints contemporary with the first Grahams, listed in order of appearance:**

- Saint Wilfred (1095-1115) was born in Lindisfarne and studied there. He was first the Abbot of Old Melrose Abbey of St. Cuthbert, then Bishop of Hexham and then Archbishop of York. [383] Since Forne Sigulfson, was a benefactor to the Priory of Hexham in Northumberland during this timeframe, he would have been well acquainted with Bishop Wilfred. [384]
- Forne Sigulfson, Lord of Greystoke was a benefactor to the Priory of Hexham in Northumberland, known for its connection to St. Cuthbert. [385] He helped mediate the claim of

---

[375] William P. Bruce, "The Bowmen of Saint Sebastian," Family of Bruce International, February 2017. https://familyofbruceinternational.org/the-bowmen-of-saint-sebastian/

[376] Ian Borthwich Cowan, *Medieval Religious Houses, Scotland: with an appendix on the Houses on the Isle of Man*, second edition (London and New York: Longman Group Limited, 1976), 175, 176. https://archive.org/details/medievalreligiou0000cowa/page/174/mode/2up

[377] Likely Sir William Douglas, future Graham brother-in-law, who had already acquired lands in Peebleshire prior to 1334. https://www.poms.ac.uk/record/person/22909/

[378] "Survey of Dedications to Saints in Medieval Scotland," University of Edinburgh, School of History, Classics and Archaeology, accessed 5 March 2023.

[379] R.W. BRO. C.C. Nisbet, "Historical Sketch," The Provincial Grand Lodge U.S.A. accessed 8 March 2023. https://roosusa.org/about-us/

[380] S. Linton, "Mount Heredom and the Holy Grail," 16, Academia.edu, November 2010. https://www.academia.edu/25560426/Mount_Heredom_And_the_Holy_Grail

[381] PoMS no.23454, person summary, Reginald More, accessed 13 March 2023. https://www.poms.ac.uk/record/person/23454/

[382] Rory MacLellan, PhD, "Templars and Hospitallers: the military-religious Orders in Scotland, 1128-1564," Pressreader, accessed 13 March 2023. https://www.pressreader.com/uk/history-scotland/20210101/282136409152361

[383] Rev. Alban Butler, *The Lives of the Fathers, Martyrs, and Other Principal Saints*, Vol. III (Dublin: James Duffy, 1866; Bartleby.com, 2010). https://www.bartleby.com/210/10/121.html

[384] James Raine, *The Priory of Hexham, Its Chroniclers, Endowments and Annals*, Vol. I (Durham: The Surtees Society, Andrews and Co, 1864), 59. https://archive.org/details/prioryofhexham01rain

[385] James Raine, *The Priory of Hexham, Its Chroniclers, Endowments and Annals*, Vol. I (Durham: The Surtees Society, Andrews and Co, 1864), 59. https://archive.org/details/prioryofhexham01rain

*Appendix D: A Primer on the Ancient British and Roman Catholic Churches in Scotland*

the monks of St. Cuthbert to Tynemouth Priory.[386] Perhaps his theorized son, William de Graham, was living on one of Forne's holdings in Northumberland[387] or Tynedale before moving to Scotland and witnessing the foundation charter for St. Cuthbert Church in Edinburgh in 1127? St. Cuthbert is the patron saint of Northumberland.[388] Forne also witnessed the Scone Abbey foundation charter between 1114 and 1122. The Abbey was dedicated to Saints Mary, Michael, John, Laurence, and Augustine.[389]

- Saint Margaret (Queen Margaret Canmore) was canonized by the Pope Innocent IV in 1250.[390]
- Saint David of Scotland (David I) is recognized as a Roman Catholic saint,[391] although he was never formally canonized.[392]
- Saint Malachy was canonized by Pope Clement III in 1199.[393]
- Saint Duthac (d. 1065), was the bishop of Ross (d. 1065) and patron saint of Tain in Scotland. Per tradition Euphemia, Countess of Ross, later Queen Consort of Scotland and daughter of Margaret Graham Ross, was involved in the construction of a church in Saint Duthac's honor in the 1390s.[394]
- Saint Gilbert of Moray, the Dragon slaying Bishop of Caithness and Dornock who died 1245,[395] was the last pre-Reformation Scotsman to be canonized by the Roman Catholic Church.[396] He is also related to the Moray family who became the earls of Bothwell.[397]
- Saint Thomas Becket, who was murdered in Canterbury in 1170, was a friend of William the Lion of Scotland. As a result, a number of religious houses were dedicated in his memory:

---

[386] Stephen M. Lewis, "Forne Sigulfson-The 'First' Lord of Greystoke in Cumbria."

[387] Forne held estates in Coquetdale in Northumberland. Paul Dalton, "Feudal Politics in Yorkshire, 1066 x 1054" (Phd Thesis, University of Sheffield, 1990), 68.

[388] "St. Cuthbert of Lindisfarne (634-687)," CatholicIreland.net, accessed 14 February 2023. https://www.catholicireland.net/saintoftheday/st-cuthbert-of-lindisfarne-634-687/

[389] PoMS No. 7988, "Foundation of Scone Priory," accessed 5 March 2023. https://www.poms.ac.uk/record/factoid/7988/

[390] "Turgot, Bishop of Saint Andrews," translated by William Forbes-Leith, *The Life of St. Margaret, Queen of Scotland* (Edinburgh: William Patterson, 1884), 81.

[391] "Saint David I of Scotland," Catholic Online, accessed 5 March 2023. https://www.catholic.org/saints/saint.php?saint_id=5790

[392] "David I (1124-1153)," Scot Clans, accessed 5 March 2023. https://www.scotclans.com/pages/david-i-1124-1153

[393] "St. Malachy," Catholic Online, accessed 5 March 2023. https://www.catholic.org/encyclopedia/view.php?id=7429

[394] Thomas J. M. Turpie, "Scottish Saints Cults and Pilgrimage from the Black Death to the Reformation, c. 1349-1560" (PhD thesis, University of Edinburgh, 2011), 119, 147. https://era.ed.ac.uk/bitstream/handle/1842/5983/Turpie2011.pdf?sequence=2

[395] Marcus Pitcaithly, "The Dragon Slaying Bishop of Caithness," *Home Page of Author Marcus Pitcaithly*, accessed 17 February 2023. https://www.marcus-pitcaithly.com/single-post/2018/03/16/st-gilbert-and-the-dragon

[396] The last Scottish saint to be canonized was Catholic priest John Ogilvie (1579-1615), executed for refusing to accept James I's claims over the Church. He was beatified in 1929 and canonized in 1976 by Pope Paul VI. "Society of Jesus Celebrates St. John Ogilvie, SJ," Jesuits.org, accessed 6 March 2023. https://www.jesuits.org/stories/society-of-jesus-celebrates-feast-of-st-john-ogilvie-sj/

[397] Author: "B," "The Chiefship of the Clan Murray," *The Scottish Antiquary, or, Northern Notes and Queries*, Vol. 15, No. 58 (Edinburgh University Press, October 1900): 53. https://archive.org/details/scottishantiqua00unkngoog/page/n8/mode/2up?q=chiefship

Arbroath Abbey, the chapel of the Royal Burgh of Dumfries in 1188, Maxwellheugh Chapel at Kelso Abbey in Roxburghshire in 1195, and the Chapel at Harelaw Hospital in Canonbie in 1254[398], as well as the church in Applegarth prior to 1300.[399]

## H. Saint Dedications that Name Grahams [400]:

- Mary the Blessed Virgin, grant in dedication of the saint in thirteenth century. Kelso Abbey in Roxburghshire moved from Selkirk in circa 1128. Cowan and Easson, *Medieval Religious Houses: Scotland*, 68. Devotee: David de Graham, son of David de Graham (half-brother of Richard de Faunes).
- St. James the Greater, payment on the saint's feast day, 1232, Roxburgh. Devotee: David de Graham, son of David de Graham (half-brother of Richard de Faunes).
- Mary the Blessed Virgin, Grant in dedication of the saint in 1308, Melrose Abbey. Devotee: Sir John de Graham (the elder) of Dalkeith, Abercorn and Eskdale, born circa 1278, died 25 April 1337. Son of Sir Nicholas de Graham (died circa 1304).
- Blessed John the Baptist, Grant in dedication of the saint between 1314 and 1325, Beauly Priority, Kilmorack, Inverness. Devotee: Patrick Graham, landowner.
- Mary the Blessed Virgin, Grant in dedication of the saint between 1314 and 1325, Beauly Priority, Kilmorack, Inverness. Devotee: Patrick Graham, landowner.
- Holy Trinity, Grant in dedication of, 1317, Dunfermline Abbey, Fife. Devotee:
- Sir John (the elder) de Graham of Dalkeith, Abercorn and Eskdale, born circa 1278, died 25 April 1337. Son of Sir Nicholas de Graham (died circa 1304).
- St. Matthew the Apostle, Grant in dedication of the saint, 1317, Dunfermline Abbey, Fife. Devotee: Sir John de Graham (the elder) of Dalkeith, Abercorn and Eskdale, born circa 1278, died 25 April 1337. Son of Sir Nicholas de Graham (died circa 1304).
- Mary the Blessed Virgin, Altar dedication 1492, Dundee Church, Forfar. Devotee: Robert Graham of Fintry.
- St. James the Greater, Pilgrimage in 1512. Devotee: Malcolm Graham, Cook at the court of James IV.

## I. Relevant Scottish Church Land Charters

A majority of the <u>early</u> land charter activity, particularly gifting lands to the church, is tied to families from the Borderlands in southern Scotland where the Norman land barons were first established by David I circa 1124. The <u>later</u> charters are for lands in northern and central Scotland (e.g. Kilpoint, Montrose, Fintry).

---

[398] Hew Scott, *Fasti Ecclesiae Scoticanae*, Vol. II (Edinburgh: Oliver and Boyd, 1917), 199. https://play.google.com/store/books/details?id=l3_ZAAAAMAAJ&rdid=book-l3_ZAAAAMAAJ&rdot=1

[399] Michael Penman, "'Sacred Food for the Soul': In Search of the Devotions to Saints of Robert Bruce, King of Scotland, 1306-1329." *Speculum* 88, no. 4 (2013): 1047. http://www.jstor.org/stable/43576866

[400] "Survey of Dedications to Saints in Medieval Scotland," University of Edinburgh, School of History, Classics and Archaeology, accessed 5 March 2023.

*Appendix D: A Primer on the Ancient British and Roman Catholic Churches in Scotland*

Family relationships: The Douglas family charters are included here as they acquired Graham lands in Dalkeith and Eskdale between 1341 and 1370. See "Black Douglas Land Grab" in Appendix F. The Grahams had previously inherited Avenel lands (Abercorn) and Comyn lands (Tarbolton, Kilbucho) through marriage. The Kirkpatricks had intermarried with the Auchencass Grahams so were close cousins to Sir John "the Last." Figure 41.

- "Charter by Robert de Graham, Lord of Weyliston, to the Church of St. Mary of Melrose, of the patronage of the Church of Tarbolton, 11 July 1342.
- Deed of Mortification by Robert Avenel, and Gervase, his heir, renouncing four merks paid by the Monks of Melrose for the lands of Eskdale, in their favor, 1180-1198.[401]
- Charter by King William the Lion confirming to the Monks of Melrose their charters of the lands of Eskdale, 1180-1201.[402]
- Charter by John, son of Michael, to the Monks of Melrose, of the lands of Pensheil in the Lammermoors, circa 1230.[403]
- Charter by King Alexander II to the Abbey of Melrose, of the waste of Ettrick, 21 February 1235-36.[404]
- Letter by King John Baliol, in favour of the Abbot of Melrose, as to a right-of-way through Douglas, 13 April 1294.[405]
- Sir John Graham's (the elder) gift of Newlands in Tweedale to the Crown Memorials in Dunfermline, circa 1317. [406]
- Charter by King Robert the Bruce to the Carmelite Friars near Banff, of ground for building their Church, 1 August 1324.[407]
- Charter by William, Abbot of Kelso, to Sir William of Douglas, of the lands of Dowglen in Eskdale, 21 December 1343.[408]
- Letter of Protection by William Earl of Douglas in favor of the Monks of Melrose, 24 April 1360.[409]
- Deed by Patrick [Graham], Bishop of Brechin, recognizing an annuity from Montrose to the Priory of Restinot, 1 May 1361.[410]

---

[401] "Sir William Fraser Facsimiles of Scottish Charters and Letters," School of History, Classics and Archaeology Teaching Collections, accessed 19 January 2023. http://collections.shca.ed.ac.uk/collections/show/1
[401] "Sir William Fraser Facsimiles of Scottish Charters and Letters."
[402] Ibid.
[403] "Sir William Fraser Facsimiles of Scottish Charters and Letters"
[404] Ibid.
[405] Ibid.
[406] The Bannatyne Club, *Registrum de Dunfermelyn* (Edinburgh: 1842), 236-237. https://ia600901.us.archive.org/31/items/registrumdedunfe00bann/registrumdedunfe00bann.pdf
[407] "Sir William Fraser Facsimiles of Scottish Charters and Letters."
[408] Ibid.
[409] Ibid.
[410] Ibid.

- Deed of Excambion by Robert Scott, Lord of Rankilburn, to the Monastery of Melrose, of his lands of Glenkery in exchange for Bellenden. Melrose, 28 May 1415.[411]
- Letter by James, Earl of Morton, Regent, to David Wemyss of that Ilk, for the liberation of a borderer in his keeping. Holyrood, 2 February 1574.[412]
- Letter by Sir Walter Scott, first Lord Scott of Buccleuch, dated Dieppe, 1 March 1584.[413]

---

[411] Ibid.
[412] Ibid.
[413] Ibid.

*Appendix D: A Primer on the Ancient British and Roman Catholic Churches in Scotland*

# Table of Figures

Figure D-1: The round bell towers of Dunkeld Cathedral [7] ................................................................. 3

Figure D-2: Monasteries of Scotland Prior to the Eighth Century. Map from "A Handbook of the Church of Scotland" by James Rankin. [18] ................................................................. 5

Figure D-3: Bishoprics of Scotland during Reign of David I (1124-1153). Map from "A Handbook of the Church of Scotland" by James Rankin [23] ................................................................. 6

Figure D-4: Drawing by John Slezer of "Dumbarton Castle - His Majesties Castle from the West of Dumbritton" with Cardross medieval chapel dedicated to St. Serf, burial place of King Robert I's organs, in foreground across the River Leven from the Castle. From the David Laing Bequest to the Royal Scottish Academy transferred 1910. [33, 34] Image licensed by the National Galleries of Scotland... 8

Figure D-5: Red Cross Pattée of the Knights Templar [58] ................................................................. 12

Figure D-6: Cross Pattée on Columns that surround the front of the Church of the Holy Sepulchre in Jerusalem which was added during the Crusader Period. Photo by Alicia Graham. ................................................................. 12

Figure D-7: Ruins of the Church of the Paralytic, built by Crusaders over part of the Ruined Basilica at the Pools of Bethesda. Columns are marked with the Cross Pattée associated with the Templars. Ruins are located next to St. Ann's Church, traditional birthplace of the Virgin Mary, which was also built by Crusaders and also features the Cross Pattée. Photos by Alicia Graham. ................................................................. 13

Figure D-8: Marker Identifying location of the First Hospital of the Knights Hospitaller in Muristan (Christian Quarter of Old Jerusalem). By tradition, the site of a hospital founded during the Maccabean era in the second century B.C. [76] Photo by Alicia Graham ................................................................. 15

Figure D-9: Black and White Maltese Cross of the Knights Hospitaller [76] by Heratlas ................................................................. 15

Figure D-10: John Graham of Claverhouse, "Bonnie Dundee" [84] ................................................................. 16

Figure D-11: Red and Blue Cross Pattée of the Order of the Trinitarians [91] ................................................................. 17

Figure D-12: Northumbrian Bishoprics and Monasteries, circa 680 A.D. By Angus McLellan [126] Note: Bishoprics are in Red, Monasteries are in Yellow. This file is licensed under Creative Commons CC-BY 3.0. ................................................................. 21

Figure D-13: List of Celtic (Culdee) Monasteries from "A Handbook of the Church of Scotland" by Rev. James Rankin, published in 1888 [129] ................................................................. 22

Figure D-14: Joan Blaeu's 1654 Atlas of Scotland, Based on surveys by Timothy Pont, showing Old and New Melrose. CC-BY 4.0 Reproduced with the permission of the National Library of Scotland. ....... 27

Figure D-15: Wamphray Dragon on the Western Door of St. Cuthbert's Church in Wamphray, Scotland, dated 950-960A.D. CC-BY-SA/2.0 - © Chris Newman - geograph.org.uk/p/831825 .......... 30

Figure D-16: Durham Cathedral with Durham Castle in Background, photo by Vik Walker. [185] CC-BY-2.0. ................................................................. 32

Figure D-17: Holy Island in Northumberland by Sandy Gemmill [189] CC-BY-2.0. ................................. 33

Figure D-18: Dunfermline Abbey by Paul McIlroy [195] CC-BY-2.0. ................................................................. 34

Figure D-19: "New Melrose" Abbey from the Burial Ground, photo by Walter Baxter. [200] CC-BY-SA/2.0 .................................................................................................................................... 35

Figure D-20: St. Cuthbert Statue on Holy Island in Lindisfarne Priory in Northumberland, photo by Nilfanion. [220] CC-BY-3.0. ................................................................................................... 38

Figure D-21: Image of St. Matthew from the Lindisfarne Gospels, The Yorck Project (2002) 10.000 Meisterwerke der Malerei [223] ................................................................................................ 39

Figure D-22: Celtic Cross in Fintry Churchyard, [228] © Robert Murray CC-BY-SA/2.0. ........ 40

Figure D-23: Site of Moskesso, and the Moskesso Closs/Close in Hutton Parish, Dumfriesshire (GB Ordnance Survey performed 1857, published 1861). [234] CC-BY-4.0 Reproduced with the permission of the National Library of Scotland..................................................................................................42

Figure D-24: Coat of Arms of the City of Glasgow by TillmanR [238] CC-BY-4.0...................43

Figure D-25: Flag of Scotland Photo by Smooth_O [265] ........................................................ 46

Figure D-26: St. Catherine of Alexandria shown with a crown and the "Breaking Wheel" painting by Antonio de Solario in 1514, courtesy The National Gallery, London [271] ................................47

Figure D-27: HRH Prince Richard, Duke of Gloucester, Grand Prior of the Most Venerable Order of the Hospital of Saint John of Jerusalem processing at the Investiture Service of the Priory in the United States at Saint Michael and All Angels Episcopal Church in Dallas [278] CC0 1.0...................48

Figure D-28: Saint Catherine of Siena. From chiesa di Santa Maria del Rosario in Prati, Roma. Shown as Dominican nun in white with a black over-robe. [289] ...............................................................49

Figure D-29: Extracted image of Saint James from the altarpiece in church of Mount San Martino, Italy painted by Carlo Crivelli circa 1480. [294] ....................................................................................50

Figure D-30 :Arms of the Burgh of Dumfries from "The Arms of the Royal and Parliamentary Burghs of Scotland," by H.R.N. Macphail and H.W. Lonsdale, 1897 [299] ......................................... 51

## Endnotes

[i] Queen Margaret of Canmore was canonized as a Catholic saint by Pope Innocent IV in 1250. Margaret was known for her piety and founding a number of churches, including Dunfermline Abbey, which held her greatest treasure that she brought from her home in Hungary: a relic of the true Cross. https://www.newadvent.org/cathen/09655c.htm

[ii] For example, the Grahams of Dalkeith were at loggerheads so much with "New" Melrose that King Robert the Bruce, Robert I, had to mediate a settlement. The family had claimed back all the gifts their ancestors had previously given to "Old Melrose."

[iii] In 1322, Robert I granted a charter to John of Luss "for the reverence and honour of our patron, the most holy man, the blessed Kessog" and also for his assistance in feeding Bruce's army eight years previously.
https://www.helensburghadvertiser.co.uk/news/15156671.eye-on-millig-remembering-st-kessog-of-luss/

[iv] Phil Graham Note: Given that Forne Sigulfson began his career as an enforcer of tithes to the religious houses, this adds weight to the argument that he was an ancestor of the first Grahams who were hereditary Clerks of Church, Temple, and in the Royal Households.

*Appendix D: A Primer on the Ancient British and Roman Catholic Churches in Scotland*

---

[v] The eight-pointed Maltese cross of white on a blank mantle used by the Knights Hospitaller or the "Knights of the Order of Saint John of Jerusalem" symbolizes the eight Beatitudes which include the eight virtues knights must possess, including care for the sick and poor. Order of Malta, accessed 30 March 2023. https://www.orderofmalta.int/history/the-eight-pointed-cross/

[vi] Any location name in Scotland that contains "spital," short for "hospital," implies a connection to the Knights Hospitaller.

[vii] While Boys is a spelling variant of Bois, and "Bosco" is the Latin form, these names should not be confused with the Boyville family of Levington (Kirklinton) in Cumberland.

[viii] Old Melrose (Culdee) being replaced by the Cistericien New Melrose Abbey (also Scottish Temple) was the source of the conflict. New Melrose was no longer under the jurisdiction of Rome after 1309 when the papacy moved to Avignon in France and the Scottish clergy recognized Robert I as king in 1310, despite his excommunication from the Roman Catholic Church from 1306 to 1328. https://www.san.beck.org/7-12-England.html

[ix] Phil Graham note: Strathblane became Temple lands dedicated to St. Kessog of Luss. https://digital.nls.uk/histories-of-scottish-families/archive/95337607?mode=transcription

[x] There are two clerics of the name "Jocelyn" are that often confounded: Jocelin/Jocelyn, bishop of Glasgow (1175-1199), and Jocelyn, a monk of Furness Abbey in Cumberland. They lived about the same time which contributes to the confusion. https://www.jstor.org/stable/24681431

[xi] The eight-pointed white cross on a black background that is the emblem of the Knights Hospitallers is known as a "Maltese Cross" which is preserved in certain flags of Malta. https://www.maltauncovered.com/malta-history/maltese-cross/

[xii] In addition, King Robert the Bruce established a special link to St. Mary between Dumbarton and Kilwinning Abbey in Ayrshire. The Exchequer Rolls reveal Bruce Memorials in Dumbarton, Stirling, and Dunfermline. Countess Lennox and Robert Dumbarton were the hereditary keepers of St. Mary for Bruce. https://electricscotland.com/history/dumbarton/The_Book_of_Dumbartonshire_Parishes.pdf

[xiii] I estimate the date of the Holyrood land charter as 1125. Holyrood Abbey was founded in 1128, so the charter granting the land for it would have been at least three years prior. With a dedicated labor force provided by the king, it could take three to six years to build a castle in medieval times. So if they had finished a chapel in 1128, then they would have started it by 1125.

[xiv] At the Reformation, Clerkington was renamed New Ancrum, then Nicolson, again Clerkington, and now Rosebery. Moorfoot was a Chapelry of the Abbey of Newbattle.

# Appendix E: Heraldry

The symbols in family coats of arms, particularly Scottish coats of arms, have significant historical meaning. By studying the history behind each symbol, we can learn more about the origins of those families. But first—a few basic heraldic terms.

## Heraldic Terminology

**Charge**: any symbol on a shield or coat of arms. Charges can be animals, objects, or geometric shapes. The cross, including hundreds of variations, is the most frequent charge, along with the lion and eagle.

Animals are found in various stereotyped positions or "attitudes." Quadrupeds are often **rampant**—standing on one or both hind feet. Another frequent position is ***passant***, or walking, like the lions of the coat of arms of England. Eagles are almost always shown with their wings spread, or **displayed**. If the animal looks towards the viewer, it is ***guardant***, or "on guard." It is **regardant** if it is looking at the viewer over its shoulder.[1]

**Cadet branches**: cadet branches are 'descendants" of younger brothers vs. the primary line of eldest male heirs in a primogeniture system. In British heraldry, the crescent, mullet, martlet, annulet, fleur-de-lis, and rose may be added to a shield to distinguish cadet branches of a family from the primary line. The cadet branches of the Grahams of Montrose[2] and Drumgoon[3] use the rose in their armorials.

**Cinquefoil**: the trefoil (three leaves or petals), quatrefoil (four leaves or petals), and cinquefoil (five leaves or petals) are a class by themselves. Despite the derivation of their names, the quatrefoil and cinquefoil were probably intended to be flowers rather than leaves.[4] The cinquefoil is sometimes "blazoned fraise" (depicted as a strawberry flower), most notably in Fraser heraldry.[5]

---

[1] English Heritage, "Our Guide to Heraldry," accessed 16 December 2022. https://www.english-heritage.org.uk/easter/preparing-for-easter-adventure-quests/our-guide-to-heraldry/.

[2] Angus J. Ray Associates, "The Grahams: These are Your People," Clan Graham Society, accessed 23 January 2023. https://clangrahamsociety.org/the-grahams-these-are-your-people/

[3] "Graham (Ireland) Coat of Arms," SurnameCoatofArms.uk, accessed 23 January 2023. https://surnamecoatsofarms.uk/shop/?s=drumgoon

[4] Arthur Charles Fox-Davies, "Trees, Leaves, Fruits, and Flowers" in *A Complete Guide to Heraldry* (Edinburgh, UK: T.C. & E.C. Jack, 1909), 262-280, accessed December 17, 2022 via Wikisource. https://en.wikisource.org/w/index.php?title=A_Complete_Guide_to_Heraldry/Chapter_18&oldid=6647208.)

[5] International Heraldry and Heralds, accessed 16 December 2022. https://www.internationalheraldry.com/

The basic heraldry elements, except for the field (background layer), are shown in Figure E-1[6]:

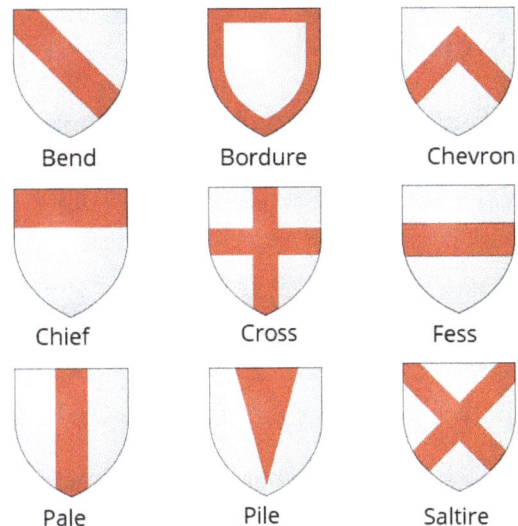

*Figure E-1: The Basic Elements of Heraldry, by Ipankonin, Balmung0731, and Kontributor 2K .* [6]
*These files are licensed under CC BY-SA 3.0*

The traditional heraldic colors are:

- Red = *Gules*
- Blue = *Azure*
- Green = *Vert*
- Black = *Sable*
- Purple = *Purpure*
- Gold or yellow = *Or*

---

[6] Figure E-1: Wikimedia Commons contributors, "File:Pale demo.svg," *Wikimedia Commons*, accessed 18 April 2023. https://commons.wikimedia.org/w/index.php?title=File:Pale_demo.svg&oldid=673452274
Wikimedia Commons contributors, "File:Pile demo.svg," *Wikimedia Commons*, accessed 18 April 2023. https://commons.wikimedia.org/w/index.php?title=File:Pile_demo.svg&oldid=573971966
Wikimedia Commons contributors, "File:Bordure demo.svg," *Wikimedia Commons*, accessed 18 April 2023. https://commons.wikimedia.org/w/index.php?title=File:Bordure_demo.svg&oldid=573971902
Wikimedia Commons contributors, "File:Bend demo.svg," *Wikimedia Commons*, accessed 18 April 2023. https://commons.wikimedia.org/w/index.php?title=File:Bend_demo.svg&oldid=708584808
Wikimedia Commons contributors, "File:Chief demo.svg," *Wikimedia Commons*, accessed 18 April 2023. https://commons.wikimedia.org/w/index.php?title=File:Chief_demo.svg&oldid=751036167
Wikimedia Commons contributors, "File:Blason-argent-fasce-gueules.svg," *Wikimedia Commons*, accessed 18 April 2023. https://commons.wikimedia.org/w/index.php?title=File:Blason-argent-fasce-gueules.svg&oldid=745296083
Wikimedia Commons contributors, "File:Saltire demo.svg," *Wikimedia Commons*, accessed 18 April 2023. https://commons.wikimedia.org/w/index.php?title=File:Saltire_demo.svg&oldid=733537186
Wikimedia Commons contributors, "File:Cross demo.svg," *Wikimedia Commons*, accessed 18 April 2023. https://commons.wikimedia.org/w/index.php?title=File:Cross_demo.svg&oldid=678157612
Wikimedia Commons contributors, "File:Chevron demo 2.svg," *Wikimedia Commons*, accessed 18 April 2023. https://commons.wikimedia.org/w/index.php?title=File:Chevron_demo_2.svg&oldid=741937183

- Silver or white = *Argent* [7]

## Ancient Celtic and Pictish Symbology

Celtic symbols in Scottish family coats of arms indicate potential Celtic heritage. The **Picts** were a confederation of Celtic tribes that lived in Northern Britain and Scotland until a thousand years ago. Their language has been lost save for fragments. However, they left behind a wealth of "picture stones," large monoliths carved with mysterious symbols whose meanings are mostly unknown.[8] Pictish animal signs may have been related to gods and goddesses and included typical Celtic themes of boars, salmon, wolves, and birds. Some of the most famous Pictish carvings are of mythical beasts like dragons and centaurs and also water horses, mermaids, and other sea creatures.[9]

**A short list of the relevant symbols to our investigations of the Grahams:**

*Figure E-2: Celtic Boar [10]* CC BY-SA 3.0

**Boar.** Wild boars are fearsome, dangerous animals prized for their meat, a favorite game animal of the Celts and the ancient Picts who lived in Scotland before them. It symbolizes fertility, courage, strength in battle, and hunting prowess. It also, however, represents stubbornness, war, and chaos. It is frequently found in Celtic chieftains' burial places.[10]

A number of Grahams,[11] including Lang Will's son, Fergus Graham of Mote, included a boar's head in his coat of arms.[12] The theorized origin of the Grahams is in the barony of Greystoke, which is also spelled "Gristock." "*Gris*" **is Norse**

---

**Did you know?**

Between the Hutton Kirk and the Moskesso Closs/Close, ten miles northwest of Lochmaben Castle, is a town named Boreland (Figure G-1). The name "Boreland" and "Boarland" could refer to the mensal land granted to the feudal superior to furnish food, boar hunting grounds for his castle or dwelling. "Boor" meant "serf" and Norman lords sometimes apportioned lands near their castles for their servants.

---

[7] English Heritage, "Our Guide to Heraldry," accessed 16 December 2022.

[8] Groam House Museum, "Pictish People," accessed 16 December 2022. https://openvirtualworlds.org/omeka/exhibits/show/groam-house-museum/pictish-people

[9] "Symbols Live On When Language is Lost—Archetypes of the Picts in Scotland," StOttilien, accessed 9 April 2023. https://stottilien.com/2013/09/17/symbols-live-on-when-language-is-lost-archetypes-of-the-picts-in-scotland/

[10] Jesse Brauner, "Boar," accessed 4 December 2022. https://www.symbols.com/symbol/boar

Figure E-2: Wikimedia Commons contributors, "File:KMM - Eber.jpg," *Wikimedia Commons,* accessed 13 April 2023. https://commons.wikimedia.org/w/index.php?title=File:KMM_-_Eber.jpg&oldid=575045457

[blurb] From Wikipedia: "Lands of Borland, Barony of Cumnock, accessed 7 March 2023. https://en.wikipedia.org/w/index.php?title=Lands_of_Borland,_Barony_of_Cumnock&oldid=996145471

[11] William Rae Macdonald, *Scottish Armorial Seals* (Edinburgh, UK: William Green and Sons, 1904), 140-143. https://www.electricscotland.com/books/pdf/scottisharmorial00macd.pdf.

[12] Robert Riddle Stodart, *Scottish Arms, Being a Collection of Armorial Bearings A.D. 1370 – 1678* (Edinburgh, UK: W. Paterson, 1881) n206 (Plate 79A). https://archive.org/details/ScottishArmsV1/page/n205/mode/2up?q=79A

for boar,[13] and "*stoc*" is sometimes Norse/Old English for "place."[14] The family crest of the Greystoke cousins, the Grimthorpes, includes a boar,[15] as well as the family armorials for the Grimstons and Grimbys, who may also be relatives, include boars.[16] It is understandable how scribes who knew Latin and French could erroneously translate "Gris" to "Gray," hence variants like Greystoke and Graystone.

**Dragon**. The Celtic Dragon represents sovereignty, power, or a chief or leader of a clan. "Pendragon" is the Celtic word meaning "chief."[17] Celtic dragons are usually used as a symbol of power and wisdom among leaders. In Celtic lore, there are two main types of dragons: large, winged creatures with four legs and large, serpent-like creatures with either small or no wings but no legs. Yordan Zhelyazkov writes: "Dragons were depicted in numerous ways, but a common portrayal is of dragons with their tails in (or near) their mouths, effectively creating a circle, which demonstrates the cyclical nature of the world and life."[18]

*Figure E-3: Celtic Dragon[18]* CC-BY-SA 3.0

The seal of Peter Currie (Petri de Curri) on an 1179 A.D. charter of the lands of Dalheagun and Bargower in Kyle to Melrose Abbey was described as thus: "A **dragon**, not on a shield." Use of a dragon indicates that the Corrie family was of Celtic heritage.[19] Appendix C indicates the Y-DNA of a significant number of Corrie males are of Ancient Celtic origins (R-M269/R-M222).[20]

---

[13] Wiktionary, "gris," accessed 4 November 2022. https://en.wiktionary.org/w/index.php?title=gris&oldid=69567367.

[14] Wiktionary, "stoc," accessed 5 December 2022. https://en.wiktionary.org/w/index.php?title=stoc&oldid=68776363.

[15] My Family Silver, "Grimthorpe Family Crests," accessed 8 November 2022. https://www.myfamilysilver.com/crestfinder-search/grimthorpe-family-crest. Family crest of the Grimthorpes includes a boar.

[16] *Debrett's Peerage, Baronetage, Knightage, and Companionage* (London: Dean & Son, Limited, 1903), 383. https://archive.org/details/b24883797/page/n427/mode/2up?ref=ol&q=grimthorpe

[17] Wiktionary contributors, "pendragon," Wiktionary, The Free Dictionary, accessed 23 January 2023. https://en.wiktionary.org/w/index.php?title=pendragon&oldid=70936150

[18] Figure E-3: Tim Lazaro, "Dragons, Celts and Druids," Dragon Dreaming Blog, accessed 16 December 2022. https://dragondreaming.wordpress.com/dragons-celts-druids/

[19] Henry Laing, *Impressions from Ancient Scottish Seals* (Edinburgh: Bannatyne and Maitland Clubs, 1850), 43. https://ia902606.us.archive.org/22/items/descriptivecatal00bann/descriptivecatal00bann.pdf

Figure E-4: Celtic Knot Wikimedia Commons contributors, "File:Celtic-knot-insquare-39crossings.svg," *Wikimedia Commons, the free media repository*, accessed 19 December 2022. https://commons.wikimedia.org/w/index.php?title=File:Celtic-knot-insquare-39crossings.svg&oldid=489958086

[20] My FamilyTree DNA Project Website, "Corey/Cory Surname - Y-DNA Colorized Chart," accessed 20 December 2022. https://www.familytreedna.com/public/CoryorCorey?iframe=ycolorized

Figure E-5: Celtic Cross Wikimedia Commons contributors, "File:Celtic Cross.jpg," *Wikimedia Commons, the free media repository*, accessed 19 December 2022. https://commons.wikimedia.org/w/index.php?title=File:Celtic_Cross.jpg&oldid=489954222

*Appendix E: Heraldry*

**Celtic Cross**. St. Patrick, a Christian Culdee from Scotland, has been credited with introducing the Celtic Cross when converting pagans in Ireland to Christianity (Although some claim that it was St. Declan who introduced the cross). See Appendix D. Theologians surmise that by placing the cross on top of the circle represents Christ's supremacy over the sun, which was worshiped by the pagans. The presence of the Celtic Cross in Coats of Arms or at burial sites indicates association with the Culdees, which means the family was present in Scotland before the arrival of the Normans. Examples include the Carricks (Robert I's mother was a Carrick), Campbells of Argyll, and St. John's Monastery, in Iona, Scotland.[21]

*Figure E-4: Celtic Knot* [19]

*Figure E-5: Celtic Cross* [20]

**Celtic knots** are elaborate, interwoven patterns that the Celts used for decorative purposes. The most common forms are spirals, step patterns, and key patterns.[22]

A good illustration of the use of Celtic symbols is the *Book of Kells* (sometimes known as the *Book of Columba*). The *Book of Kells* is an illuminated Latin manuscript containing the four New Testament Gospels together with various prefatory texts and tables. It was created in a Columban monastery circa 800 A.D. The manuscript takes its name from the Abbey of Kells, County Meath in Ireland, which was its home for centuries. Figures of humans, animals, and mythical beasts—primarily dragons—and heavy use of Celtic knotworking in vibrant colors decorate the manuscript's pages.[23]

*Figure E-6: Sample from the Book of Kells (St. Columba)* [23]

---

[21] Irish Central Staff, "The Symbolic Meaning of the Celtic Cross," Irish Central, 27 May 2017. https://www.irishcentral.com/roots/history/celtic-cross-meaning

[22] Dani Rhys, "Popular Celtic Symbols-A-List (with images)," SymbolSage, accessed 16 December 2022. https://symbolsage.com/popular-celtic-symbols-a-list/

[23] Laura King, "The Book of Kells," Color Theory Virginia Commonwealth University, accessed 22 December 2022. http://www.people.vcu.edu/~djbromle/color-theory/color04/laura/bookofkells.htm

Figure E-6: Wikimedia Commons contributors, "File:KellsDecoratedInitial.jpg," *Wikimedia Commons,* accessed 19 April 2023. https://commons.wikimedia.org/w/index.php?title=File:KellsDecoratedInitial.jpg&oldid=387931486

## Norman Symbols

These favored symbols are commonly found in Norman family coats of arms:

**Lion.** It traditionally symbolizes courage, nobility, royalty, strength, stateliness, and valor because, historically, the lion has been regarded as the "king of beasts." The lion also carries Judeo-Christian symbolism. The Lion of Judah stands in the coat of arms of William the Conqueror[24] and of Jerusalem. Lions have many varying positions in heraldry. Wikipedia has an excellent look-up table for researchers.[25] Lions can be:

Figure E-7: Arms of William the Conqueror [24] CC-BY-SA 3.0

- Rampant– standing on one or both hind paws, with forepaws raised
- Passant– walking, with the right fore paw raised and all others on the ground
- Statant– standing, all four feet on the ground
- Salient– leaping, with both hind legs together on the ground and both forelegs together in the air
- Sejant Sitting or Sejant Erect– sitting on his haunches, with both forepaws on the ground. Sejant Erect is the same, except both forepaws are raised.[26]
- Couchant– lying down, head raised
- Dormant– lying down with its eyes closed and head lowered[27]

Figure E-8: Fleur de lis [28]

**Fleur de lis.**[28] The symbol is a legend in itself—a lasting emblem of royalty, power, honor, grandeur, faith, and unity. Legend has it that an angel descended from heaven with the Holy Ampulla (flask of sacred oil) in the shape of a fleur-de-lis when King Clovis of France was proclaimed. It thus signified the French kings' direct link to God.[29]

---

[24] Figure E-7: Wikimedia Commons contributors, "File:Arms of William the Conqueror (1066-1087).svg," *Wikimedia Commons*, accessed 9 April 2023. https://commons.wikimedia.org/w/index.php?title=File:Arms_of_William_the_Conqueror_(1066-1087).svg&oldid=698182248

[25] "Lion (heraldry)," Wikipedia, modified 9 November 2022, accessed 17 December 2022. https://en.wikipedia.org/w/index.php?title=Lion_(heraldry)&oldid=1120931771.

[26] Edward S. Holden, *A Primer of Heraldry for Americans* (New York: The Century Co, 1898), 140. https://upload.wikimedia.org/wikipedia/commons/8/89/A_primer_of_heraldry_for_Americans_%28IA_primerofheraldry00holdrich%29.pdf

[27] "Lion (heraldry)," Wikipedia, modified 9 November 2022, accessed 17 December 2022.

[28] Figure E-8: Wikimedia Commons contributors, "File:Fleur-de-lis-gold.svg," *Wikimedia Commons*, accessed 9 April 2023. https://commons.wikimedia.org/w/index.php?title=File:Fleur-de-lis-gold.svg&oldid=732168671

[29] Sir George Bellow, "The Fleur de Lys," *Coat of Arms*, no. 6 (1951). https://www.theheraldrysociety.com/articles/the-fleur-de-lys/

**The Saltire.** A diagonal cross, also called Saint Andrew's Cross[30] or the crux decussata, is a heraldic symbol in the shape of the letter "X." St. Andrew was sentenced to death by crucifixion by the Romans in Patras, Greece, but asked to be crucified on a diagonal cross as he felt he wasn't worthy to die on the same shape of the cross as Jesus.[31] While the initial adoption of St. Andrew as the patron saint of Scotland was at the Synod of Whitby in 664 A.D,[32] the Canmores, the Scottish royal family until 1286, are known for widely endorsing St. Andrew as the patron.[33] St. Andrew's image and the saltire were used on seals in Scotland from about 1180 onwards. In 1286, when the Guardians of Scotland ruled Scotland in the absence of a king, the saint was depicted on the Guardians' seal used to authenticate legal documents. The word comes from the Middle French *sautoir* and the Middle Latin *saltatorial* ("stirrup"). From its use as a field sign, the saltire came to be used in a number of flags: in the 16th century for Scotland and Burgundy, in the 18th century also as the ensign of the Russian Navy, and for Ireland, Jamaica, and the Canary Islands.[34]

Figure E-9: Saltire or Saint Andrew's Cross [30] CC0 1.0

Figure E-10: Saint Peter's Cross or Inverted Latin Cross [35]

**The Cross of St. Peter** is an inverted Latin Cross.[35] St. Andrew's brother, St. Peter, was also crucified oddly, but upside down, in Rome and at his own insistence, also announcing that he did not feel worthy of being crucified in the same manner as Christ.[36] As the keeper of the keys to heaven, Peter is also symbolized by a set of keys crossed in the shape of an "X."[37]

**The Cross of St. Patrick** is a red saltire on a field of white.[38] The origin of the saltire is disputed. While one account dates the use of the cross in association with Saint Patrick to 1612, another dates its creation to 1783, when the Anglo-Irish Order of Saint Patrick adopted it as an emblem. This was a

Figure E-11: Cross of Saint Patrick [38]

---

[30] Figure E-9: Wikimedia Commons contributors, "File:Saint Andrew's cross.svg," *Wikimedia Commons,* accessed 9 April 2023. https://commons.wikimedia.org/w/index.php?title=File:Saint_Andrew%27s_cross.svg&oldid=649384401

[31] "About St Andrew and the Saltire," VisitScotland, accessed 16 December 2022. https://www.visitscotland.com/about/uniquely-scottish/st-andrews-the-saltire/

[32] "Synod of Whitby," Whitby Abbey, North Yorkshire, UK, accessed 16 January 2023. https://www.whitbyabbey.co.uk/whitby-abbey/synod-whitby/

[33] "How Apostle Andrew Became the Patron Saint of Scotland," The Catalogue of Good Deeds, 13 December 2017. https://catalogueofstelisabethconvent.blogspot.com/2017/12/how-apostle-andrew-became-patron-of.html

[34] "Saint Andrew," National Records of Scotland, accessed 16 December 2022. https://www.nrscotland.gov.uk/research/image-gallery/hall-of-fame/saint-andrew

[35] Figure E-10: Wikimedia Commons contributors, "File:Peter's Cross.svg," *Wikimedia Commons,* accessed 9 April 2023. https://commons.wikimedia.org/w/index.php?title=File:Peter%27s_Cross.svg&oldid=726064628

[36] Daniel Esparza, "Was Saint Peter Really Crucified Upside Down?" Aleteia, 26 August 2021. https://aleteia.org/2021/08/26/was-saint-peter-really-crucified-upside-down/

[37] Friedrich Rest, *Our Christian Symbols* (Cleveland: The Pilgrim Press, 1954), 29. https://archive.org/details/ourchristiansymb00fred/mode/2up?q=peter

[38] Figure E-11: Wikimedia Commons contributors, "File:Saint Patrick's Saltire.svg," *Wikimedia Commons,* accessed 9 April 2023. https://commons.wikimedia.org/w/index.php?title=File:Saint_Patrick%27s_Saltire.svg&oldid=723337795

British chivalric order established in 1783 by George III. St. Patrick is the patron saint of Ireland.[39]

Figure E-13: Cross of Saint George [42]
CC-BY-SA 3.0

**The Cross of St. George** is a red cross on a white background.[40] In England, St. George is considered a patron saint of the military. In heraldry, Saint George's Cross a red cross on a white background, became associated with Saint George in the Late Middle Ages. He was often depicted as a crusader. St. George is also the patron saint of England, Catalonia, and Georgia.[41]

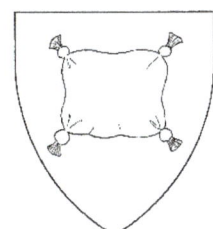

Figure E-12: Heraldic Cushions [40]
CC-BY-SA 3.0

### Cushions.

Heraldic cushions[42] were signs of authority.[43]

For the Johnstones of Annandale to carry three cushions in chief, they must have descended from the Chamberlain of Annandale.[44] Figure F-18.

### Scallop Shells or the "Escallop."

St. James, the Apostle and fisherman, also known as "St. James the Greater," is the patron saint of Spain. Scallop shells are most famously associated with St. James and are common in Galicia,

Figure E-15: Armorial of the Blason family of Bourbers [48]
CC-BY-SA 3.0

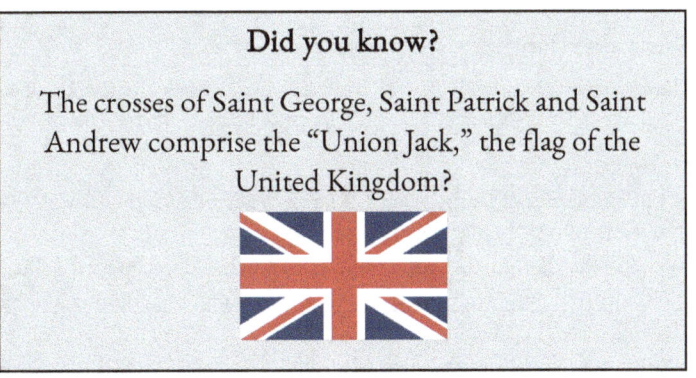

**Did you know?**

The crosses of Saint George, Saint Patrick and Saint Andrew comprise the "Union Jack," the flag of the United Kingdom?

Figure E-14: The Arms of Mont Saint-Michel; Art by Euryrel [48]
CC-BY-SA 3.0

---

[39] Colin Mansom, "Saint Patrick Saltire History," My Secret Northern Ireland, 23 October 2018. https://my-secret-northern-ireland.com/saint-patrick-saltire-html/

[40] Figure E-12: Wikimedia Commons contributors, "File:St George's Cross.png," *Wikimedia Commons,* accessed 9 April 2023. https://commons.wikimedia.org/w/index.php?title=File:St_George%27s_Cross.png&oldid=488301674

[41] "Saint George's Cross," Wikipedia, modified 22 October 2022, accessed 17 December 2022. https://en.wikipedia.org/w/index.php?title=Saint_George%27s_Cross&oldid=1117555278

[blurb] "The First Union Flag," Squaducation, accessed 20 March 2023. https://www.squaducation.com/blog/first-union-flag ; Wikimedia Commons contributors, "File:Flag of the United Kingdom (3-5).svg," *Wikimedia Commons, the free media repository,* accessed 9 April 2023. https://commons.wikimedia.org/w/index.php?title=File:Flag_of_the_United_Kingdom_(3-5).svg&oldid=688543217

[42] Figure E-13: Bruce Draconarius, "Cushion," Mistholme-Heraldry, Illumination and Random Jottings, 12 January 2014. https://mistholme.com/dictionary/cushion/

[43] "Symbolism of Heraldry A-K," accessed 16 December 2022. https://www.heraldryandcrests.com/pages/symbolism-of-heraldry

[44] Arthur Charles Fox-Davies, *A Complete Guide to Heraldry* (London: T.C and E.C. Jack, 1909) 290, 300. https://www.gutenberg.org/files/41617/41617-h/41617-h.htm#page290

where the saint is thought to be buried.⁴⁵ The Camino of St. James starts in Galicia and leads to Mont Saint-Michel, a monastery dedicated to Saint Michael the Archangel.⁴⁶

Per Duane Galles of the Heraldry Society, in Normandy, Brittany, and Poitou, the shell was associated not with the Apostle James, but with Saint Michael the Archangel. St. Michael is primarily depicted as a warrior clad in armor and is a **patron saint of <u>warriors</u> and the military**. The shell appears prominently in the arms of the Norman abbey of Mont Saint Michel (Figure E-14 ⁴⁷). The escallop was especially popular in family coats of arms⁴⁸ from Normandy, Brittany, and Poitou.⁴⁹, ⁵⁰

**Wyvern** (sometimes spelled wivern) is a legendary dragon that has two legs instead of four. It was popular amongst the Saxons, but also the Normans. The word "wyvern," derived from Middle English "wyvere" meaning viper, is more descriptive of the elongated shape of earlier standards.⁵¹

*Figure E-16: Wyvern Erect by Arthur Charles Fox-Davies ⁵¹*

The Anglo-Saxons did not make such a fine distinction between two and four-legged beasts on top of their spears, but the practice became popular with the Normans. From BritishCountyFlags.com: "The depiction of a two-legged dragon with a serpentine body is the recognized emblem of Wessex."⁵² The Norman Avenel family last used the Wyvern seal in Eskdale charters, linking the Border Grahams to the Avenels circa 1230. Sir John de Graham the elder (d. 1337) used the wyvern seal on a 1309 charter regarding the barony of Westerker (land inherited from his Avenel ancestor).⁵³

*Figure E-17: Description of the Seal of Gervase Avenel from 'Impressions from Ancient Scottish Seals' 1850, by Henry Laing ⁵³*

---

⁴⁵ Charles Moeller, "Order of Saint James of Compostela," *The Catholic Encyclopedia*, Vol. 13 (New York: Robert Appleton Company, 1912), 8 November 2022. http://www.newadvent.org/cathen/13353a.htm

⁴⁶ Rev. Mary Lessman, "Walking the Camino de Santiago: A Saint Michael Pilgrimage," Saint Michael and All Angels Episcopal, accessed 23 January 2023. https://www.saintmichael.org/blog/walking-the-camino-de-santiago-a-saint-michael-pilgrimage/

⁴⁷ Figure E-14: Wikimedia Commons contributors, "File:Arms of Mont-Saint-Michel Abbey.svg," *Wikimedia Commons, the free media repository,* accessed 9 April 2023. https://commons.wikimedia.org/w/index.php?title=File:Arms_of_Mont-Saint-Michel_Abbey.svg&oldid=702109558

⁴⁸ Figure E-15: Wikimedia Commons contributors, "File:Blason famille fr de Bourbers.svg," *Wikimedia Commons, the free media repository,* accessed 9 April 2023. https://commons.wikimedia.org/w/index.php?title=File:Blason_famille_fr_de_Bourbers.svg&oldid=702056434

⁴⁹ Duane L.C.M. Galles, "Pilgrims and Heraldry," *Coat of Arms* no. 45 (Spring 1989). https://www.theheraldrysociety.com/articles/pilgrims-and-heraldry/

⁵⁰ The popularity of the scallop shell and its association with St. Michael the Archangel in Normandy may be due to the legend that St. James of Compostela visited Charlemagne (747-814) in a dream and urged him to liberate his forgotten tomb in Spain from the Saracens. St. Michael the Archangel, as the patron saint of warriors, would have been tied to the campaign to liberate Spain. "History of Charlemagne and Roland, Compostela and the Legend of the Milky Way," Compostela, Joining Heaven and Earth, accessed 7 March 2023. https://compostela.co.uk/mythology/charlemagne-and-the-legend-of-the-milky-way/

⁵¹ Figure E-16: Arthur Charles Fox-Davies, *A Complete Guide to Heraldry*, 226, Figure 430.

⁵² Vexilo, "Wessex," British County Flags, 20 September 2013. https://britishcountyflags.com/2013/09/20/wessex-flag/

⁵³ Figure E-17: Henry Laing, *Impressions from Ancient Scottish Seals* (Edinburgh: Bannatyne and Maitland Clubs, 1850), 24, 67. https://ia902606.us.archive.org/22/items/descriptivecatal00bann/descriptivecatal00bann.pdf

## Pre-Norman Symbols

The use of Christian Culdee and early Anglo-Saxon Christian symbols in family coats of arms also indicates the heritage of pre-Norman peoples, such as the Celts, Picts, and Norse. The Picts and Norse were also known to have practiced Culdeeism. For example, King Constantine of the Picts retired from office to become Abbot of the Culdee settlement at St. Andrews in the tenth century. See Appendix D for more information.[54]

### Anglican/Anglian Symbols.

These Anglo-Saxon symbols have been found at burial sites in Dumfriesshire and Northumberland, sometimes mixed with Celtic Symbols.

**The Ruthwell Cross** is a stone Anglo-Saxon cross from about the eighth century, when the village of Ruthwell, now in Scotland, was part of the Anglo-Saxon Kingdom of Northumbria.[55] It is the most famous Anglo-Saxon sculpture and contains possibly the oldest surviving text in Old English. Nikolaus Pevsner has described it as such: "The crosses of Bewcastle and Ruthwell are the greatest achievement of their date in the whole of Europe." The figure of St. John and the lamb on both the Bewcastle and Ruthwell crosses may have been the first to introduce the design to the area.[56]

Figure E-18: Ruthwell Cross [56]
CC BY-SA 2.0

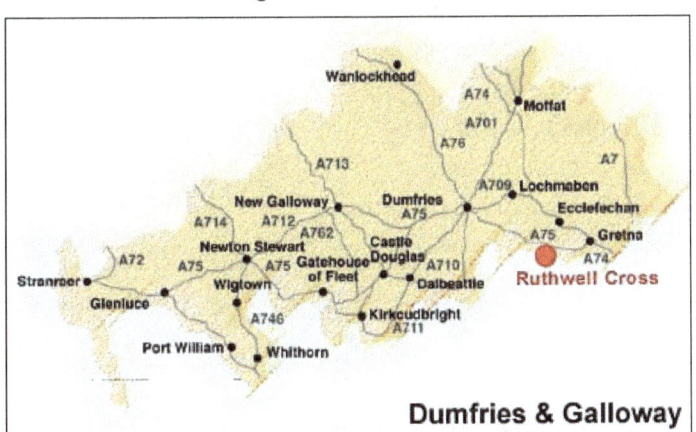

Figure E-19: Map showing location of Ruthwell Cross [55]

---

[54] Jackie Queally, *The Culdees: An Ancient Religious Enigma in Scotland* (United Kingdom: Celtic Trails, 2007), 18. http://www.earthwise.me/wp-content/uploads/culdeebook.pdf

[55] Figure E-19: "Ruthwell Cross," Birth of a Nation, BBC, accessed 9 April 2023. https://www.bbc.co.uk/history/scottishhistory/darkages/tourist_guide/darkages_ruthwell_cross.html

[56] Figure E-18: "Ruthwell Cross," Wikipedia, modified 9 June 2022, accessed 17 December 2022. https://en.wikipedia.org/w/index.php?title=Ruthwell_Cross&oldid=1092344422

Figure E-20: Bewcastle Cross [57] CC-BY-SA 3.0

**Bewcastle.** The Bewcastle Cross is also an Anglo-Saxon cross with some Celtic influences. It is still in its original position within the churchyard of St. Cuthbert's church at Bewcastle, in the English county of Cumbria.[57] The cross, which probably dates from the seventh or early eighth century, features reliefs and inscriptions in the runic alphabet. From Bewcastle.com: "There are three figures on the cross: the top one is John the Baptist, holding the Lamb of God and walking on the desert hills, proclaiming Christ in the wilderness. Below is Christ as King and law-giver, with the animals of the wilderness at his feet. And then, below the long inscription, comes the famous and controversial figure of a man with a falcon or eagle on a perch beside him. It would be remarkable at this date to have a lay portrait, and of such size, on a memorial, though the figure clearly has echoes of an Anglo-Saxon nobleman." [58, 59]

**Closeburn.** Closeburn is 16 miles north of the town of Dumfries in southwestern Scotland. A section of a medieval Anglian cross was found in Closeburn, near the churchyard. Date: ninth century.[60] From the description on Canmore.org: "Only the upper part of the cross shaft and a small part of the lower arm of the cross-head survives, and the carving is very worn. This fragment belonged to a cross with a substantial shaft, all four faces carved in relief. The central panel shows a frontal-robed figure with foliage on either side. Face C has panels of animals surrounded by bands of two-cord twist. Face D is carved with a single long panel of spiral vine scroll, inhabited by birds in profile."[61] Closeburn was the home of the Kirkpatrick family. St. Patrick was a well-known Christian Culdee saint. The first documented Kirkpatricks, Roger and Ivo de Kirkpatric, likely took their surname from the lands they occupied connected to the church of St Patrick.[62]

Figure E-21: Anglian Monument Fragments Found in Closeburn, Dumfriesshire [60]

---

[57] Figure E-20: Wikimedia Commons contributors, "File:Bewcastle cross - south and east faces.jpg," *Wikimedia Commons, the free media repository,* accessed 9 April 2023. https://commons.wikimedia.org/w/index.php?title=File:Bewcastle_cross_-_south_and_east_faces.jpg&oldid=417466143

[58] James King Hewison, *The Runic Roods of Ruthwell and Bewcastle* (Glasgow: John Smith & Son, 1914), 40-48. https://www.electricscotland.com/books/pdf/runic.pdf

[59] W.G. Collingwood, *Northumbrian Cross of the Pre-Norman Age* (London: Faber & Gwyer, 1927), 113. https://iiif.wellcomecollection.org/pdf/b31350987

[60] Figures E-21, E-22: W.G. Collingwood, "The Early Church in Dumfriesshire and Its Monuments," *TDGNHAS,* Vol 12, 3012 (1926): 56-58. https://dgnhas.org.uk/sites/default/files/transactions/3012.pdf

[61] R.C. Reid and W.F. Cormack, "Two Medieval Crosses at Kirkpatrick Fleming," *TDGNHAS,* Vol 62, 3038 (1987): 17-20. https://dgnhas.org.uk/sites/default/files/transactions/3038.pdf

[62] "Closeburn Old Church," Historic Environment Scotland (Canmore), modified 2019, accessed 20 December 2022. https://canmore.org.uk/site/319020/closeburn-old-church

*Appendix E: Heraldry*

**Wamphray.** Wamphray church was dedicated to St. Cuthbert. It was an independent parsonage, the patronage of which was granted by John of Corrie/de Grahame to his cousin, Roger de Kirkpatrick, in 1357. The church continued to be unappropriated but was under the local lords of the barony, who, from 1549 onwards, were the Johnstones of Wamphray. Wamphray Parish Church is a superb example of medieval carvings. The church is most famous for the spiraling "Wamphray Dragon" carved in stone above the tower door.[63] W.G. Collingwood describes this sample in "Northumbrian Cross of the Pre-Norman Age" as "an interesting example of the Scandinavian dragon side-by-side with a pattern derived from Anglian leaf-scroll, and not at all Danish or Norse in character." The dragon resembles Hiberno-Saxon manuscript animals. The scroll is similar to the Closeburn monument and is arranged like the spiral roundels of early Hiberno-Saxon manuscripts.[64]

*Figure E-22: Wamphray Dragon* [60]

**Hexham Scroll.** Another important example of ancient heraldry styles in the Borders region is the Hexham Scroll. Rosemary Cramp from the University of Durham provides this description: "Plant-scrolls found in Hexham are a distinctive feature of early Northumbrian sculpture and betray Mediterranean or near eastern contacts or models... A group of crosses which have a medallion scroll on the broader face and a spiral or simple scroll on the narrower is found in Hexham and along the Tyne valley. The Hexham scrolls are carved in a distinctive finely cut style with delicate modelling of detail, which resembles embossed metalwork." [65, 66]

*Figure E-23: Armorial of the Hexham Scroll in Northumberland* [66]

---

[63] "Wamphray Church," Historic Environment Scotland (Canmore), accessed 20 December 2022. https://canmore.org.uk/site/66905/wamphray-church

[64] W.G. Collingwood, *Northumbrian Cross of the Pre-Norman Age*, 19, 31-35, 55.

[65] Rosemary Cramp, "Sequence of Ornament," in *Northumbrian Crosses of the Pre-Norman Age*, Vol. 1 (London: Faber & Gwyer Limited, 1927) via the University of Durham, accessed 16 December 2022. https://iiif.wellcomecollection.org/pdf/b31350987

[66] Figure E-23: R. Cramp ,"The Anglian Sculptured Crosses of Dumfriesshire," *TDGNHAS*, Vol 62, 3038 (1961): 12-13, Figure 2. https://dgnhas.org.uk/sites/default/files/transactions/3038.pdf

## How Heraldry can help us in our family history investigation of the Grahams:

**Heraldry and the trail of the scallop shells.** The Graham coat of arms includes three scallop shells. Figure E-24 below is an example. For a full listing of Graham coats of arms see "The Mitchell Rolls"[67] and *House Graham* by Dr. Lloyd Graham.[68] As stated, the iconic Scallop Shell symbol is most famously connected with the Patron Saint of Spain, St James, the Apostle and fisherman.

*Figure E-24: Escallop Seal of Patrick Graham of Lovat, Signatory of the Declaration of Arbroath, 1320* [67]
CC BY-SA 4.0

There were many dedications by Norman families to St. James from 1124-1400 and a pilgrimage by Sir Patrick Grahame of Dundaff in the name of St. James de Compostella in 1361.[69] Both Saint Michael and the use of scallop shells in coats of arms, including the Graham Coats of Arms, became popular in Britain after the arrival of the Normans.[70] In fact, the use of the shells in heraldry and dedications to St. James and St. Michael the Archangel are indicators that can be used to help identify families and vassals of the first Norman Barons in England and Scotland as well as supporters of the Crusades.[71]

---

[67] Alexander Nisbet, *A System of Heraldry* (Edinburgh: Printed for W. Blackwood, 1722). http://www.heraldry-scotland.co.uk/nisbets.html

Figure E-24: Wikimedia Commons contributors, "File:Heraldic Shell.svg," *Wikimedia Commons,* accessed 17 April 2023. https://commons.wikimedia.org/w/index.php?title=File:Heraldic_Shell.svg&oldid=463233327 Wikimedia Commons contributors, "File:Coa (blank).png," *Wikimedia Commons,* accessed 17 April 2023. https://commons.wikimedia.org/w/index.php?title=File:Coa_(blank).png&oldid=703278740

[68] Lloyd D. Graham, *House Graham, From the Antoine Wall to the Temple of Hymen* (Lulu.com, 2020), 1-5. https://clangrahamsociety.org/wp-content/uploads/2020/09/House-GRAHAM-eBook.pdf

[69] Gail Delahunt, "Everything you need to know about St. James the Greater," Follow the Camino, 27 December 2019. https://followthecamino.com/en/blog/history-of-the-apostle-saint-james/

[70] Anthony Foljambe, "Chaptre the 17th, The Scallop Shells Crusades," in *1615-1669: An English Normand in America, Anthony Foljambe Blog,* accessed 17 April 2023. https://anthonyfoljambe.blogspot.com/2017/01/chaptre-17th-scallop-shells-crusades.html

[71] *The Great, Parliamentary, or Bannerets' Roll, c. 1312,* The British Museum's manuscript collection: MS. Cotton, Caligula A. XVIII, ff. 3-21b, accessed 13 November 2022. http://www.aspilogia.com/N-Parliamentary_Roll/N-0592-0701.html

## The Seal of King Robert "the Bruce" (Robert I) of Scotland.

In the seal of the Robert de Brus, sixth Lord of Annandale (1243-1304) (Figure E-26), from a 1285 charter dated at Melrose Abbey, in which Bruce gave twenty-two acres of land in Writtle to Nicholas Bannintone, a knight.

Figure E-26: Seal of Robert Bruce VI, Earl of Carrick, 1285 [72]

Rachel Meredith Davis from the University of Missouri provides this description: "The seal bears a saltire and on a chief a lion passant guardant. On each side of the shield is a lizard or wyvern. The legend reads, S' ROBERTI DE BRUS COMITIS DE CARRIK [The seal of Robert de Bruce, earl of Carrick].[72] His claim to Carrick was by right of his wife, Marjorie, countess of Carrick."[73] Their son was Robert I of Scotland, also known as King Robert the Bruce or "Braveheart." After this seal's appearance, we find the chief vassals of Annandale and of Bruce using the saltire in their coats of arms: Jardine, Johnstone,[74] Kirkpatrick, Carruthers, Corrie (Figure E-25)[75], Maxwell, Moffat, and Graham.[76] St. Andrew's image and the 'saltire' (diagonal cross) associated with him were used on seals in Scotland from about 1180 onwards. In 1286, when the Guardians of Scotland ruled Scotland in the absence of a king, St. Andrew was depicted on the Guardians' seal, used to authenticate their legal documents and communications to the rest of Europe.[77] However, given the association of the Bruce estates in Dunbartonshire with St. Patrick, Phil Graham believes

Figure E-25: Corrie of Newby Coat of Arms granted to Sir Walter de Corrie with the fief of Newby, 1296. By Brianann MacAmhlaidh. [75]
CC-BY-SA 3.0

> **Did you know?**
> While the 1995 movie "Braveheart" was based on Scottish history and the military leader from the first war of Scottish independence, Sir William Wallace, the actual "Braveheart" was King Robert the Bruce. Upon his death, the king requested his heart be taken on a crusade, hence the nickname.

---

[72] Henry Laing, *Impressions from Ancient Scottish Seals*, 30.
Figure E-25: Wikimedia Commons contributors, "File:Robert Bruce VI (seal 1).png," *Wikimedia Commons*, accessed 29 April 2023.
https://commons.wikimedia.org/w/index.php?title=File:Robert_Bruce_VI_(seal_1).png&oldid=242611045

[73] Rachel Meredith Davis, "Commentary on *No. 21 Robert Bruce, sixth lord of Annandale*," modified 27 June 2022, accessed 20 December 2022. https://scalar.missouri.edu/vm/vol3-plates26-30-scottish-seals-plate28

[74] William Rae Macdonald, *Scottish Armorial Seals*, 140 143, 180-181.

[75] Figure E-26: Wikimedia Commons contributors, "File:Arms of Corrie (or Currie) of Newbie.svg," *Wikimedia Commons*, accessed 9 April 2023.
https://commons.wikimedia.org/w/index.php?title=File:Arms_of_Corrie_(or_Currie)_of_Newbie.svg&oldid=592588667

[76] Henry Laing, *Impressions from Ancient Scottish Seals*, 83, 98, 220, 223.

[77] National Records of Scotland, "Saint Andrew," accessed 20 December 2022.
https://www.nrscotland.gov.uk/research/image-gallery/hall-of-fame/saint-andrew

[Did you know? Blurb] Genevieve Carlton, "Sorry William Wallace, In Real Life, Robert the Bruce Was the True Violent Hero Called Braveheart," Ranker.com, 19 October 2020. https://www.ranker.com/list/life-of-robert-the-bruce/genevieve-carlton

more investigation is needed to confirm which saint the Annandale Bruce saltire was honoring.

## Clan Armstrong Heraldry

A quick look at Armstrong heraldry is needed, given the close familial ties of the Co Fermanagh Ireland Armstrongs and our Co. Fermanagh Grahams: Per the Clan Armstrong website:

> A traditional story claims that the Armstrong clan progenitor was Fairbairn, an armour bearer to a king of Scotland, who rescued his master when he had his horse killed under him in battle. Fairbairn allegedly grasped the king by his thigh and set him on his own horse.[78]

Thus the surname "Armstrong" and the inclusion of a "strong arm" in all Armstrong Family Coats of Arms:

*Figure E-27: Seal of the Armstrongs of Terwinney, Ireland [80]*

The Terwinney Armstrongs in Ireland are descendants of the famous Col. William Armstrong and his son, Capt. Edward Armstrong. They left Langholm, Scotland by 1642 and first settled in Ireland, in Macguiresbridge in southeastern County Fermanagh. The Chronicles of the Armstrongs includes illustrations of the Armstrong burial memorials near Macguiresbridge, which include a "strong arm" and the motto "Valida Manu" (Latin for "Strong Hand") grasping a sword (Figure E-27).[79] Several Grahams are also buried at the Armstrong Macguiresbridge burial grounds.[80]

The coat of arms of the Grahams of nearby Drumgoon (the town next to Macguiresbridge) also includes a "strong arm," but grasping a red raguly (ragged staff) in addition to the traditional Graham scallop shells. It also includes a heraldic rose, added to distinguish this cadet branch of the Graham family from the senior line. (Figure E-28)

*Figure E-28: Armorial of the Grahams of Drumgoon, Ireland, [81] By SurnameCoatsofArms.uk*

**Grahams of Drumgoon Crest:** An arm embowed, vested blue and cuffed silver grasping a red staff raguly.

---

[78] Armstrong Clan Association, "Armstrong Clan History: Armstrong Origins," accessed 20 December 2022. https://www.armstrongclan.info/clan-history.html .

[79] Figure E-27: James Lewis Armstrong, M.D., *Chronicles of the Armstrongs* (Jamaica, Queensborough, N.Y: The Marion Press, 1902), 317-330. https://archive.org/details/chroniclesofarms00arms/mode/2up?ref=ol&view=theater

[80] Maguire, Noel. "Inscriptions from Aghavea Cemetery, Co. Fermanagh." *Clogher Record* 4, no. 1/2 (1960): 95–112. https://doi.org/10.2307/27695508

**Arms:** A gold shield with a red rose, barbed and seeded proper, and three gold escallops on a black chief.

**Grahams of Drumgoon Motto:** "Ratio Mihi Sufficit," meaning "Reason is sufficient for me." This motto is the same for the Netherby and Menteith branches of Clan Graham. (The Montrose motto is "Ne Oublie," or "Never Forget.")[81]

**Coat of Arms Origin:** Drumgoon, County Fermanagh, Ireland. Irish Gaelic spelling: Greachán [GRAY uh khawn]. "The staff *raguly*" or "*ragged staff*" frequently occurs in heraldry and is intended to show a rough-hewn branch for use as a walking aid or club, sometimes appearing in flame at the top.[82] The strong arms on Armstrong shields are clad in armor and are red or bare.

## Grahams of Mote.

Fergus Graham of Mote was an elder son of the famous Lang Will of Stuble (Appendix F) who served the English king Henry VIII as governor of an English garrison in Castlemilk, Scotland. In 1553, Henry VIII conferred upon Fergus of Mote the coat of arms described below[83] for services to the King during the civil war.[84]

> "A Barry of six Argent and Gules stripes. Over all a bend, a branch of an oak root branched with a bordure engrailed sable. On the first bar gules. A boars head cooped. Argent. His crest was on a wreath or (and gules. An arm bendy in four pieces gules and azure. Holding in the hand carnal, a branch of the bend." [85]

*Figure E-29: Fergus of Mote Coat of Arms issued in 1553 by Henry VIII [85] By Robert R. Stodart*

---

[81] Figure E-28: Surname Coats of Arms UK, "Graham Coat of Arms," accessed 20 December 2022. https://surnamecoatsofarms.uk/shop/product/graham-ireland-coat-of-arms-family-crest-instant-download/

[82] John Lehman, "The Aikman Coat of Arms— Its elements, history, and geographical distribution," modified 12 August 2017, accessed 20 December 2022. https://victorianweb.org/history/heraldry/aikman.html

[83] William A. l'Anson, "The Lass of Richmond Hill" in *Notes and Queries, Oxford Journals* 6, Vol. 2 (July-December 1880), 112. https://www.google.com/books/edition/Notes_and_Queries/nhf4FlLFM3wC?hl=en&gbpv=1&dq=fergus+greyme+coat+of+arms+1553&pg=PA112&printsec=frontcover

[84] His Majesty's Stationery Office, *Calendar of the Patent Rolls: Edward VI* (United Kingdom: H.M. Stationery Office, 1926), 380. https://www.google.com/books/edition/_/Olg4AQAAMAAJ?hl=en&sa=X&ved=2ahUKEwjvtsLhpYP8AhWYlmoFHYdPAwIQ7_IDegQIDRAE

[85] Figure E-29: Robert Riddle Stodart, *Scottish Arms,* n206 (Plate 79A).

The "arm bendy" is the Armstrong symbol. Phil Graham is of the opinion this barry six, the oak tree, and the arm bendy originate from Armstrong of Faulds, who assisted Fergus of Mote in the 1545 battle with Warden Maxwell.[86]

It is significant that the boar, the ancient Pictish, Celtic and Norse symbol for courage and strength in battle, is the primary symbol in some Graham armorials. Figure E-29. I believe the Norman equivalent symbol is the symbol of the Normans' patron saint of warriors, Saint Michael the Archangel. In Normandy, the escallop is used for St. Michael. The scallop shell is the primary symbol in most other Graham armorials.

Likewise, if we follow the trail of the use of the boar's head and the escallop, we may find a few lost relations. For example:

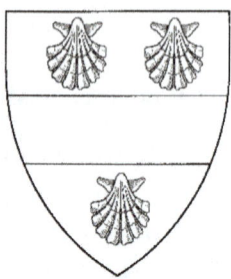

*Figure E-30: Seal of Nicol Graham of "Meskeswaye" (1543)* [87]

Long after William the Graham (Lang Will) left Hutton, plenty of the clan still lived there. On the 8th of May, 1543, a Nicol Graham of "Meskeswaye" gave a bond of manrent to John Johnston of that Ilk. A notary had to sign for him, but a portion of his seal is still attached to the document. Significantly, it shows a fess between three scallops, two and one.[87] The use of scallops at that time/place and the use of a variant of the elder line name, "Nicholas," indicates Nichol descended from Henry Graham, Lord of Hutton.

---

[86] *The Book of Carlaverock, Volume 1: Memoriors of the Maxwells, Earls of Nithsdale, Lords Maxwell & Herries* (Edinburgh, 1873), 216. https://electricscotland.com/webclans/m/bookofcarlaverv100fras.pdf

[87] William Fraser, *The manuscripts of J. J. Hope Johnstone, esq. of Annandale* (London: Eyre and Spotswood, 1897), 19. https://archive.org/details/manuscriptsofjjh00grea/page/18/mode/2up?q=nichol

Figure E-30: Arthur Charles Fox-Davies, *A Complete Guide to Heraldry* (London: T.C and E.C. Jack, 1909) 117, 300. https://www.gutenberg.org/files/41617/41617-h/41617-h.htm#page290

# Table of Figures

Figure E-1: The Basic Elements of Heraldry, by Ipankonin, Balmung0731, and Kontributor 2K .[6] These files are licensed under CC BY-SA 3.0 .................................................................. 2

Figure E-2: Celtic Boar [10] CC BY-SA 3.0 ........................................................................................ 3

Figure E-3: Celtic Dragon[18] CC-BY-SA 3.0 ................................................................................... 4

Figure E-4: Celtic Knot [19] ............................................................................................................. 5

Figure E-5: Celtic Cross [20] ............................................................................................................ 5

Figure E-6: Sample from the Book of Kells (St. Columba) [23] ..................................................... 5

Figure E-7: Arms of William the Conqueror [24] CC-BY-SA 3.0 .................................................... 6

Figure E-8: Fleur de lis [28] ............................................................................................................. 6

Figure E-9: Saltire or Saint Andrew's Cross [30] CC0 1.0 ............................................................... 7

Figure E-10: Saint Peter's Cross or Inverted Latin Cross [35] ....................................................... 7

Figure E-11: Cross of Saint Patrick [38] .......................................................................................... 7

Figure E-12: Heraldic Cushions [40] ............................................................................................... 8

Figure E-13: Cross of Saint George [42] ......................................................................................... 8

Figure E-14: The Arms of Mont Saint-Michel; Art by Euryrel [48] ............................................... 8

Figure E-15: Armorial of the Blason family of Bourbers [48] ....................................................... 8

Figure E-16: Wyvern Erect by Arthur Charles Fox-Davies [51] ..................................................... 9

Figure E-17: Description of the Seal of Gervase Avenel from 'Impressions from Ancient Scottish Seals' 1850, by Henry Laing [53] ....................................................................................... 9

Figure E-18: Ruthwell Cross [56] .................................................................................................. 10

Figure E-19: Map showing location of Ruthwell Cross [55] ....................................................... 10

Figure E-20: Bewcastle Cross [57] CC-BY-SA 3.0 ......................................................................... 11

Figure E-21: Anglian Monument Fragments Found in Closeburn, Dumfriesshire [60] ............. 11

Figure E-22: Wamphray Dragon [60] ........................................................................................... 12

Figure E-23: Armorial of the Hexham Scroll in Northumberland [66] ...................................... 12

Figure E-24: Escallop Seal of Patrick Graham of Lovat, Signatory of the Declaration of Arbroath, 1320[67] ......................................................................................................................... 13

Figure E-25: Corrie of Newby Coat of Arms granted to Sir Walter de Corrie with the fief of Newby, 1296. By Briann MacAmhlaidh. [75] ............................................................................... 14

Figure E-26: Seal of Robert Bruce VI, Earl of Carrick, 1285 [72] ................................................ 14

Figure E-27: Seal of the Armstrongs of Terwinney, Ireland [80] ............................................... 15

Figure E-28: Armorial of the Grahams of Drumgoon, Ireland, [81] By SurnameCoatsofArms.uk ........... 15

Figure E-29: Fergus of Mote Coat of Arms issued in 1553 by Henry VIII [85] .......................... 16

Figure E-30: Seal of Nicol Graham of "Meskeswaye" (1543) [87] .............................................. 17

# Appendix F: Genealogy of the Border Grahams

## *From William de Graham to Border Grahams*

### Table of Contents

| | |
|---|---|
| Examples of Sept Families descending from Younger Sons | F-3 |
| Elder Line and the Younger Line | F-4 |
|     Elder Line | F-4 |
|     Younger Line | F-4 |
| Background on the Corries, a Previously Unknown Sept of Clan Graham | F-5 |
| Discussion on the Border Grahams' Descent from the Elder Line | F-9 |
| Patriarch of the Graham J1s—Supporting Data | F-10 |
| More Discussion on the Connection between the Border Grahams and the Menteiths | F-13 |
|     Sir John Graham, Ninth Earl of Menteith = Sir John Graham of Abercorn? | F-13 |
|     Witnesses Dalkeith Graham Charters | F-13 |
|     Guardianship | F-14 |
|     Royal Stewart Connection | F-15 |
|     Home Diocese | F-15 |
|     Euphemia Graham of Menteith | F-16 |
|     Quote from Lord Cecil Burghley, minister to Elizabeth I | F-16 |
|     Heraldry | F-16 |
|     Knightly Orders | F-16 |
|     Multiple Menteiths by the Same Name, Who is Who? | F-18 |
| Background on Lang Will Graham | F-19 |
| The Eight Sons of Lang Will and Their Tribes | F-21 |
|     1.  Richard Graham of Netherby | F-21 |
|     2.  Fergus Graham of Mote | F-21 |
|     3.  George Graham of the Fauld | F-22 |
|     4.  Arthur Graham of Canobie | F-22 |
|     5.  John Graham of Medoppe "of The Braids" | F-22 |

6. Thomas Graham of Kirklanders ...........................................................................F-23

7. Hugh/Hutchin Graham of the Gards ..................................................................F-23

8. William Graham of Carlisle ..................................................................................F-23

    8a. Fergus Graham of Nunnery ............................................................................F-23

    8b. Arthur Graham of Blaatwood .......................................................................F-24

Gillesbie Grahams ...............................................................................................................F-25

Where is Mosskesswra/Moskessen? .................................................................................F-26

    Geography ....................................................................................................................F-26

    Where did lands of the Graham "elder line" come from, and what happened to them?....F-28

The Knights of Annandale, Who's Who and Where? ....................................................F-32

    Motte and Bailey Timber Castles ............................................................................F-32

    Searching For Bruce's Knights... Witnesses on Robert de Brus (II), Second Lord of Annandale, Charters (pre-1194): ..............................................................................F-34

    Other Candidate Knights of Annandale or Knights Who Later Shared Subdivisions of the Original Ten Knights Fee Estates ...........................................................................F-39

    Connections to Cumberland .....................................................................................F-42

    Searching for Lands Assigned to the First Knights of Annandale ......................F-45

Johnstone Land Takeover ..................................................................................................F-52

    Battle of Dryfe Sands, 6 December 1593 ...............................................................F-54

Scottish Naming Pattern ....................................................................................................F-55

Abbreviated Historical Chronology of the Scottish Borderlands ..................................F-58

"Black Douglas" Land Grab Begins ..................................................................................F-63

Table of Figures ...................................................................................................................F-76

Endnotes ...............................................................................................................................F-77

## From William de Graham to the Border Grahams

The hypothesis described on pages 75-87 argues that the patriarch of the Grahams of Scotland, William de Graham, who arrived in Scotland circa 1124 with David I, originated from the Greystoke Barony in Cumberland near the Scottish-English Border. His paternal ancestors of Danish descent were established in Yorkshire and also Northumberland before the arrival of the Normans. The theory on the origin of various Graham families identified in Appendix C, is that younger sons of the established families married Graham heiresses, acquired Graham estates in the process, and became known as "de Graham," thereby creating Graham sept branches, but also growing the Grahams into a large and powerful clan. There are approximately 96 different Y-DNA groupings in the Family Tree DNA (FTDNA) Graham surname project which implies a large number of unidentified sept clans. As stated previously, while the use of hereditary surnames became popular with the arrival of the Normans, it was the eldest son who inherited the father's estates and surname. The younger sons were at liberty to take whichever surname was expedient.[1] It wasn't until the sixteenth century, with the introduction of parish registers,[2] that hereditary surnames for all became common.[3]

## Examples of Sept Families descending from Younger Sons

It was common for a son-in-law to swear fealty to his father-in-law's clan if it was more powerful than his own, which was one way to create a sept clan. Another was for a younger son who inherited his mother's lands or who married an heiress to take the surname connected with the estates, the female's surname. Here are examples from other families:

1. Thomas Muschamp [d. 1190] of Wooler, Northumberland, ancestor of Sir Nicholas de Graham's wife, Maria/Marjorie de Strathearn. "Thomas de Muscampo," held land by the service of one knight's fee of Robert de Cauz, 1166 of Wooler. As his mother's heir,[4] he took his mother's patronymic.[5]
2. Land charters from 1125-1135 to St. Mary of York indicate the second son of Guy Balliol was named William Bertram, "William the Fair." [6]
3. Of the sons of Norman knight Guillaume de Mallet, his eldest son inherited the surname "Mallet," meaning "hammer," a nickname given to Guillaume for his exploits on the battlefield. Guillaume's son who inherited the Graville estate in Normandy was

> **FYI...**
> A "tenement" is land occupied under some form of tenure that includes structures (homes, barns).

---

[1] J. E. Corrie, *Records of the Corrie Family, 802-1899 A.D.* (London: Mitchell and Hughes, 1899), 130. https://archive.org/details/recordsofcorrief01corr

[2] FamilySearch Wiki contributors, "Researching Ancestors with Patronymic Surnames (National Institute)," FamilySearch Wiki, accessed November 17, 2022.
https://www.familysearch.org/en/wiki/index.php?title=Researching_Ancestors_with_Patronymic_Surnames_(National_Institute)&oldid=1853326

[3] Ellen Castelow, "Surnames," HistoricUK, accessed 1 January 2023. https://www.historic-uk.com/CultureUK/Surnames/

[4] Robert Bartlett, "England Under the Norman and Angevin Kings, 1075-1225" (Oxford: Oxford University Press, 2000), 543.
https://archive.org/details/englandundernorm00bart_0/page/426/mode/2up?q=muschamps

[FYI..blurb] "Tenement," *Dictionaries of the Scots Language*, University of Glasgow, accessed 17 November 2022. https://www.dsl.ac.uk/entry/snd/tenement

[5] Hubert Hall, F.S.A., ed., "The Red Book of the Exchequer" (London: Printed for Her Majesty's Stationery Office by Eyre and Spottiswoode, 1896), Vol. I, 343.
https://archive.org/details/redbookofexchequ9911grea/page/342/mode/2up?ref=ol&view=theater&q=muschamp

[6] William Farrer, Hon.D.Litt., Editor, *Early Yorkshire Charters,* Vol. II (Edinburgh: Ballantyne, Hanson & Co., 1915-1916):*127-128*. https://archive.org/details/earlyyorkshirech02farruoft/page/126/mode/2up?q=bertram

known as "de Graville." A third son took the surname "Curry-Mallet," when he married a Curry heiress in Somerset, and acquired Curry estates in the process.[7]

It seems that by the late 1300s, most of the lands in England and Scotland owned by the descendants of William de Graham's elder son, Peter, were either lost to the Douglas family in Scotland or to the crown in England. However, a century later, we find Grahams well established in southern Scotland. The Abbreviated Chronology later in this Appendix shows families surnamed Graham in control of large sections of the West Marches (Dumfriesshire) beginning in the fifteenth century to include: Brackenwra, the tenement of Hutton, Nether (Lower) Dryfe, Over (Upper) Dryfe which is defined in a thirteenth century charter as "as the marches of Eskdale run, the marches of Wamphray to Dryfsheid and thence descending by the marches of Eskdalemuir to Patrickshaw," Figure F-9, Croftend of Dryfe, Meikle ("greater") Hutton, Thornik, Langbedholm, and Gillespie (Gillesbie)." The Upper Dryfe lands (Mosskesswra Barony) were 23,000 acres.[8] Corrie cousin possessions in Corrie and Torthorwald,[9] and Graham possessions in Dryfe, Wamphray, Corry Hutton, Gillesbie, Brackenwra, Mosskesswra and Langholm,[10] put half of south Annandale in control of the Border Grahams and their relations by 1515, making them one of the most powerful clans in the border lands. This made them a target of clans wanting their fertile lands. In a feudal economy, lands = wealth.

## "The Elder Line" and "The Younger Line"

**Elder Line.** The first recorded Graham in Scotland was the knight William de Graham, who received from David I the lands of Dalkeith between 1124-1127. These estates were inherited by his elder son Peter, Lord of Dalkeith. The lands passed to Peter's son, Sir Henry and then Peter's grandson, the second Sir Henry de Graham, Lord of Dalkeith and Hutton. Figure 38. The second Sir Henry acquired the lands of Hutton, Tarbolton and Kilbucho via marriage to Christina, daughter of Idonea Comyn and Adam Fitz Gilbert.[11]

**Younger Line.** The "younger line" descends from the younger son of William de Graham, Alan. *Peerage* initially misrecorded his name as "John."[12] It is the "younger line" that is also known as the "noble line," as they retained their lands and titles when the elder line lost theirs. The primary house of

---

[7] "Laidman Family History," Robert, Lord of Curry Mallet in Somerset, Guild of One-Name Studies, 7 June 2022. https://laidman.one-name.net/getperson.php?personID=I32627&tree=Laidman

[8] "Map Area calculator-used to calculate acreage of Figure F-9" CalcMaps, accessed 17 November 2022. https://www.calcmaps.com/map-area/

[9] J.E. Corrie, *Records of the Corrie Family, 802-1899 A.D.*, 133.

[10] *Registrum Honoris de Morton, Volume II: Ancient Charters*, 138-139, 148-150, 154-157.

[11] Amanda Beam, John Bradley, Dauvit Broun, John Reuben Davies, Matthew Hammond, Neil Jakeman, Michele Pasin and Alice Taylor (with others), People of Medieval Scotland (PoMS) 1093-1371 database, Graham lands of Tarbolton, Kilbucho, and Hutton, D.C. 1272, *King's Digital Lab*, accessed 18 October 2022; PoMS, "No. 5972, Tarbolton," https://www.poms.ac.uk/record/source/5972/; PoMS "No. 4425, Kilbucho," https://www.poms.ac.uk/record/source/4425/; PoMS "No. 11964, Hutton," https://www.poms.ac.uk/record/person/11964/.

[12] Sir James Balfour Paul, *The Scots Peerage, Founded on Wood's Edition*, Vol. VI (Edinburgh: 1909), 193-194. https://archive.org/details/scotspeeragefoun06pauluoft/page/194/mode/2up?q=montrose

the younger line is the Grahams of Montrose. The Duke of Montrose is the Graham clan chief.[13] Montrose cadets families include: Menteith, Inchbrakie, Fintry, Claverhouse, Garvock, Balgovan, Knockdolian, and Gartmore.[14] Among the ancient documents found in the possession of the Duke of Montrose in 1871 is the earliest land charter for the younger line. It is a charter by William the Lion, probably from 1175, granting to David de Graham, second son of Alan, the lands of Kynnabre, Charlton, and Barrow-field, in the county of Forfar, and of the fishing of the Water of Northesk. Later they acquired the lands of Kincardine, Inchbrakie, Dundaff, Montrose, and Menteith.[15]

## Background on the Corries, a Previously Unknown Sept of Clan Graham

A charter from circa 1214, Henry Graham, Lord of Hutton, grants a lease of the lands of Over Dryfe to Sir David of Torthorwald, and names witnesses Sir Nicholas de Graham and "Henricus de Graham, filius Radulpho de Corry," Henry de Graham, son of Ralph Corry.[16] This Henry de Graham is labeled the "fourth Sir Henry de Graham" in Figure F-1.

The fourth Sir Henry used a banner with the white saltire (X-shaped cross) on a gules field (red background) and three red scallop shells in chief (across the top) at the Siege of Caerlaverock in 1300.[17] This banner combined the Corrie and Graham coats of arms.[18] Four years prior in 1296, a close relative, Sir Walter de Corrie, was granted the fief of Newby and adopted the Bruce family armorial with the white saltire on a gules field, indicating the Corries were in the service of the Bruces. The Corries were keepers of the Bruce castles[19] while the Carruthers served as hereditary stewards of Lochmaben for the Bruces.[20]

Sir Walter Curry (Corrie) was keeper of the castles of Wigton, Kirkcudbright and Dumfries in 1292 while his cousins Adam and Gilbert served as keepers of Lochmaben and Lochdoon respectively. Ralph de Corrie, father of the fourth Sir Henry Graham, must also be related to Sir Walter Corrie, given Henry Graham[21] and Walter Corrie were co-heirs in 1274 to the Boyville lands that later became the Parishes of Corrie and Sibbaldbie.[22] The shield in Figure 39 combined the saltire of the Corries with

---

[13] Lloyd D. Graham, *House Graham, From the Antoine Wall to the Temple of Hymen* (USA:Lulu.com, 2020), 1-2. https://clangrahamsociety.org/wp-content/uploads/2020/09/House-GRAHAM-eBook.pdf

[14] Ann Belanger, "Cadets and Septs of the Grahams," Clan Graham Society, accessed 18 October 2022. https://clangrahamsociety.org/about/#septs

[15] James Taylor, *The Great Historic Families of Scotland*, Vol. 2 (London: J.S. Virtue & Co. Ltd, 1889), 142. https://play.google.com/store/books/details?id=-0xHAQAAMAAJ&rdid=book--0xHAQAAMAAJ&rdot=1

[16] J. E. Corrie, *Records of the Corrie Family, 802-1899 A.D.* (London: Mitchell and Hughes, 1899), 130.

[17] Nicholas Harris Nicolas, *The Siege of Caerverlock, with the Earls, Barons and Knights Who Were Present for the Occasion* (London: J.B. Nichols, 1878), 69, 73, 331. https://archive.org/details/siegecarlaveroc00waltgoog/page/n370/mode/2up?ref=ol&view=theater&q=graham

[18] Walter of Exeter, Franciscan Friar and Witness to the Siege, *The Siege of Carlaverock*, 1300, accessed 18 October 2022. https://www.deremilitari.org/RESOURCES/SOURCES/carlaverock.htm

[19] J. E. Corrie, *Records of the Corrie Family, 802-1899 A.D.* (London: Mitchell and Hughes, 1899), 130-134, 139, 156.

[20] "Carruthers," Clan Douglas Society of North America, accessed 2 January 2023. http://clandouglassociety.org/carruthers/

[21] Jane Brankstone Thomas, J.C. B. Sharp, and Michael Anne Guido, "A Cumberland Family with Medieval Roots in Scotland and Northern England: A Study Gilbert Fitz Richer and His Descendants," Foundation for Medieval Genealogy, *Foundations* (2008): 359. https://fmg.ac/phocadownload/userupload/foundations2/JN-02-05/358Richer.pdf

[22] J. E. Corrie, *Records of the Corrie Family, 802-1899 A.D.* (London: Mitchell and Hughes, 1899), 136.

the scallop shells of the Grahams. Heirs of the Dalkeith Grahams later used the combined Corrie-Graham coat of arms when signing documents for former Corrie lands.[23]

---

[23] William Fraser, *The Annandale Family Book of the Johnstones, Earls and Marquises of Annandale*, Vol. I (Edinburgh: 1894), 10-11. https://archive.org/details/annandalefamilv100fras/page/10/mode/2up

*Appendix F: Genealogy of the Border Grahams*

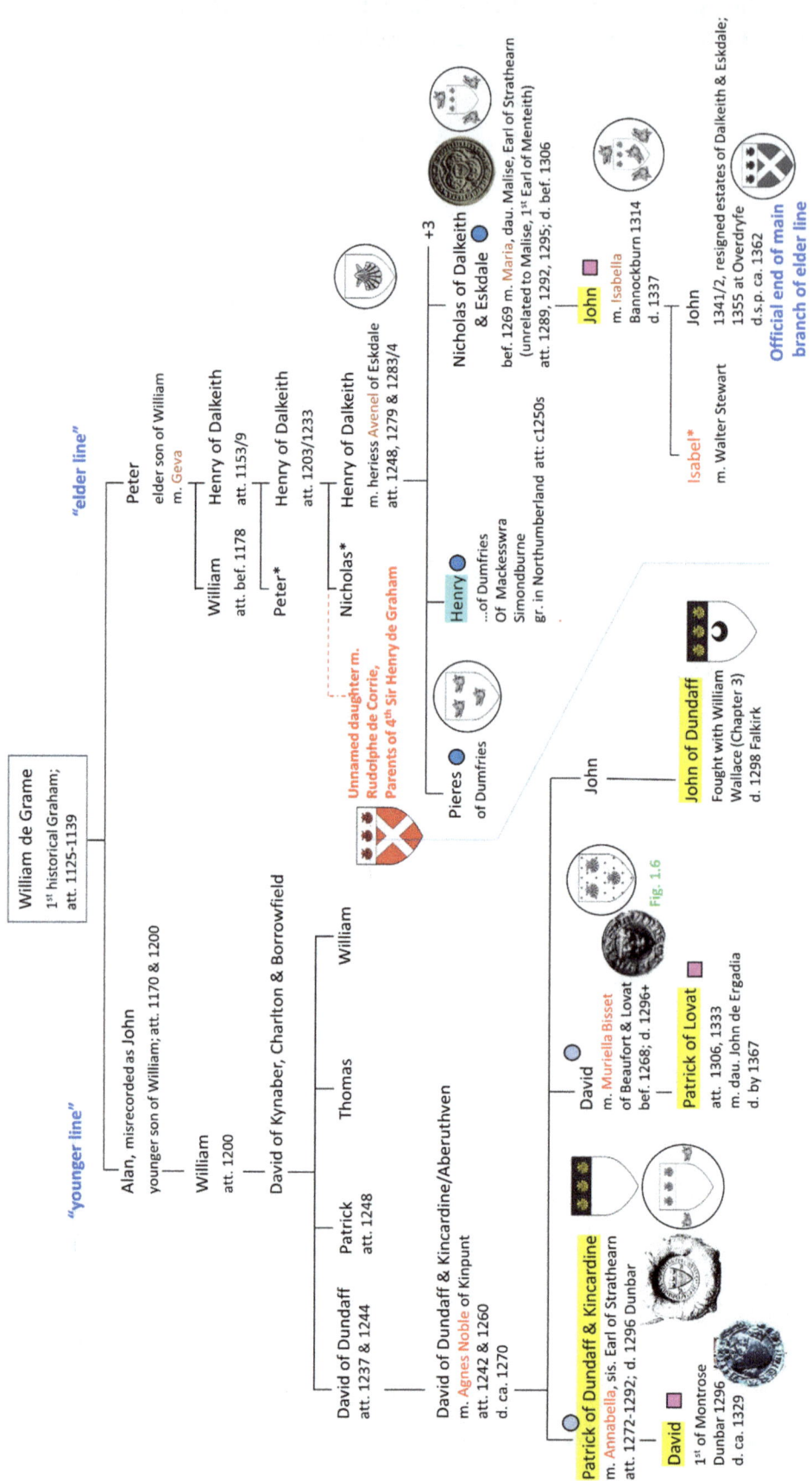

*Figure F-1: Amended Pedigree of William de Graham (Original Figure provided by Dr. Lloyd D. Graham in "House Graham" which can be found at https://clangrahamsociety.org/wp-content/uploads/2020/09/House-GRAHAM-eBook.pdf)*

*Appendix F: Genealogy of the Border Grahams*

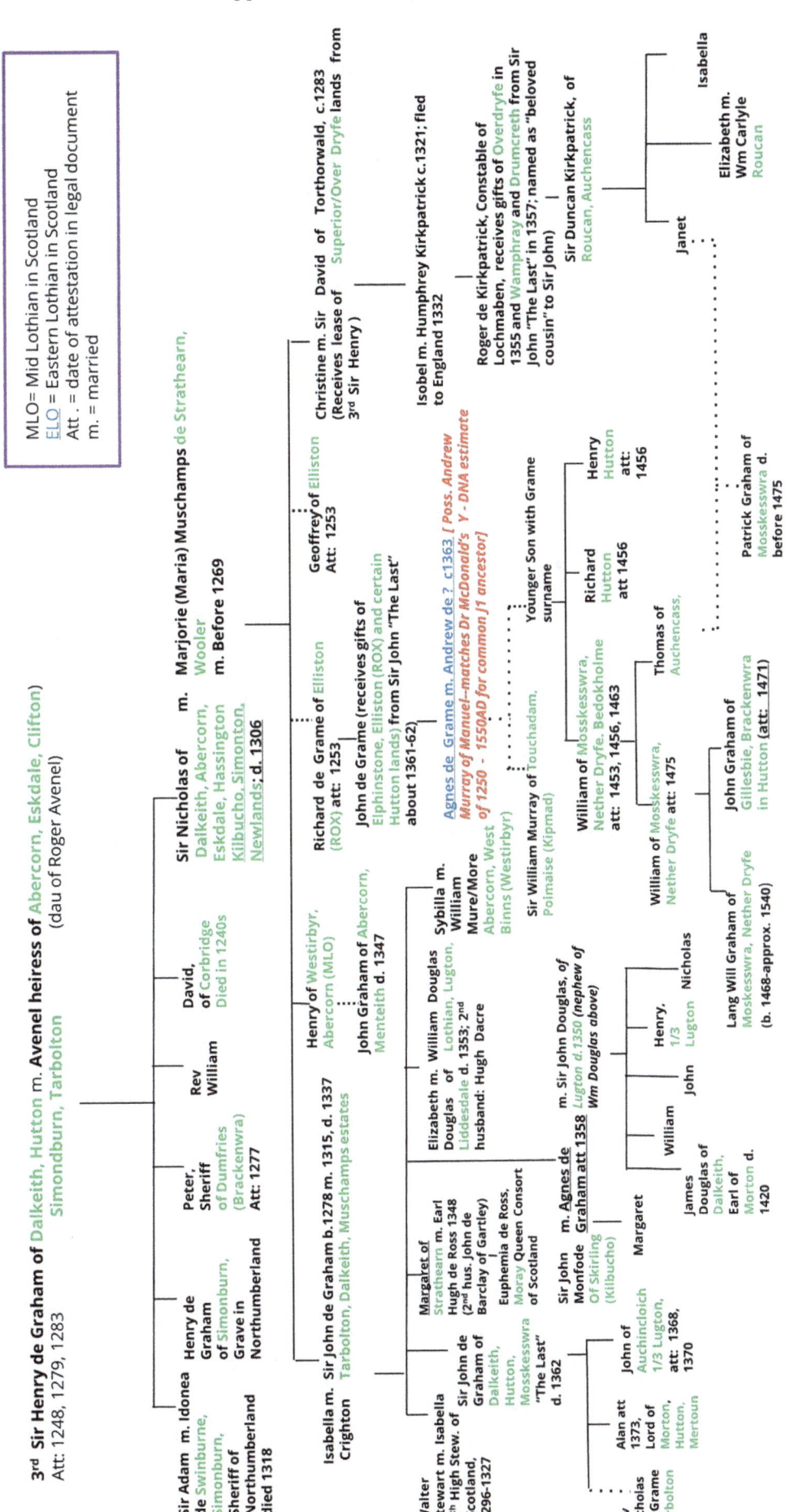

*Figure F-2: Pedigree of the Third Sir Henry de Graham and the Proposed Origin of the J1 Border Grahams*

## Discussions on the Border Grahams' Descent from the "Elder Line" of William de Graham:

I believe the Border Grahams descended from the elder line of William de Graham. The Grahams named in the 1361 and 1456 land charters associated with Elphinstone, Elliston of Roxburghshire and Hutton lands are the progenitors of the Border Grahams. The younger Sir John the Grame of Dalkeith a.k.a.: Sir John "the Last" gifted the lands of Elystone or Ellastown in 1361 to John, son and heir of Richard de Graham. I believe this "Ellastown" was the Elliston from the estates of Melrose Abbey. Elliston was originally part of Eskdale lands inherited from Sir John "the Last's" Avenel ancestors.[24] In 1363, David II confirmed the gift of Elphinstone in East Lothian, made by "John Graham, son and heir of John Graham of Dalkeith" to "John Graham son of Richard Graham;" held by "Agnes Graham, spouse of Andrew de ? [surname not given] nearest heir of the said John, as contained in John Graham's letter or charter." [25]

In 1456, the Douglases challenged the Border Grahams' claim to the lands of Hutton. Robert, Richard, William and John Graham insisted their family had held Hutton for 100 years or more, implying an ancestor received Hutton about the 1356 timeframe. Use of the name "Richard," unique to the Border Grahams, and the matching timeframes signify that the Grahams who were gifted elder line Graham lands 1356 to 1363, were also progenitors of the Grahams losing Hutton lands to the Douglas family in 1456.

*Note:* To clarify potential confusion between estates of the similar names held by the elder line Grahams and the younger line Grahams:

I. Elphinstone in East Lothian (ELO) is from the Graham elder line, lands inherited from the lords Bamburgh of Lindisfarne[26] via Marjorie Muschamps,[27] wife of Sir Nicholas de Graham.[28]

II. Elliston in West Lothian (WLO) is from David Graham of Kincardine (younger line) who acquired this Elliston via a tocher (dowry) by marriage to Agnes Noble.[29]

III. Elliston in Roxburghshire. The same David Graham of Kincardine also got this Elliston (y-liston) from Philip Elliston dated 27 Dec 1253.[30]

IV. Elliston Castle in the Johnstone Ward in Renfrewshire is also known as Eliestoun Castle and Elliotstone Tower.[31]

---

[24] T.J. Carlyle, *The Debateable Land* (Dumfries: W.R. McDarmid and Co., 1868), 10. https://ia600206.us.archive.org/0/items/debateablelandr00carlgoog/debateablelandr00carlgoog.pdf

[25] PoMS, "No. 10636-Elphinstone," accessed 19 October 2022. https://www.poms.ac.uk/record/source/10636/

[26] George Tate, *History of the Borough, Castle and Barony of Alnwick* (Alnwick: Henry Blair, 1866), 78, 408, 409, 413. https://books.google.com/books?id=CgkNAAAAYAAJ&pg=PA397&lpg=PA397&dq=v..#v=onepage&q=v..&f=false

[27] Sir James Balfour Paul, *The Scots Peerage, Founded on Wood's Edition*, Vol. VI, 195.

[28] J. Bain, *The Border Papers: Calendar of letters and papers relating to the affairs of the borders of England and Scotland preserved in Her Majesty's Public Record Office*, Vol. II (London, Edinburgh: H.M. General Register House, 1881), 134. https://archive.org/details/calendarofdocume02grea/page/134/mode/1up?q=graham

[29] PoMS, "No. 12834, person summary," accessed 9 January 2023. https://www.poms.ac.uk/record/person/12834/

[30] PoMS, "No. 925," accessed 9 January 2023. https://www.poms.ac.uk/record/source/925/

[31] "Elliston Castle," Stravaiging Around Scotland, accessed 9 January 2023. http://www.stravaiging.com/history/castle/elliston-castle/

## Patriarch of the Graham J1s-Supporting Data

Who is the Andrew of the unknown surname, *spouse of* Agnes de Graham, named in the March 1363 confirmation of the lands of Elphinstone? Reviewing all Andrews in the People of Medieval Scotland (POMS) database who were recorded between 1310 and 1371,[32] we arrive at Table F-1 below:

### TABLE F-1: Evaluation of Candidate Andrews to be the "Spouse of Agnes de Grame" as referenced in a 23 March 1363 Elphinstone Land Charter

| Est. Birth Year | Andrews Who Were Alive in Scotland circa 1363 | Notes |
|---|---|---|
| 1330s-1340s | Andrew de Campbell, knight, cousin to David II. Held lands in Angus to include Red Castle and Inverbervie in Kincardine in the 1360s.[33] Sheriff of Ayr who married Susanna Crawford of Louden per Clan MacFarlane Genealogy site. His son, Duncan, took possession of Red/Reid Castle lands in Angus.[34] | Married Susanna Crawford. Far from Edinburgh. |
| 1330s-1340s | Andrew Spring, burgess of Aberdeen[35] | Far from Edinburgh. |
| 1330s-1340s | Andrew de Urwell inherited lands of Sanquhar, Tulloch and Drumine in Morayshire in 1362.[36] | Far from Edinburgh. |
| 1330s-1340s | Andrew de Kirkcaldy, chaplain of St. Mary of Anderston, Edinburgh. | Chaplain Andrew de Kirkcaldy would have taken a vow of celibacy and remained unmarried. |
| 1330s-1340s | Andrew de Murray of Manuel, cousin to David II and his armor bearer.[37] His second wife is known, Janet Kirkintilloch (Kirkhalche). His first wife is unknown.[38] | <u>Strongest candidate:</u> Lost inheritance to Douglases in July 1362,[39] so would have been in need of a marriage to an heiress 1362-1363. |

---

[32] PoMS, Person Search for Sixteen Andrews, accessed 30 October 2022. https://www.poms.ac.uk/search/?index_type=person&q=andrew&min_date=1315&max_date=1371

[33] PoMS, "No. 23541," accessed 15 November 2022. https://www.poms.ac.uk/record/person/23541/

[34] "Andrew de Campbell (1319-after 1367)," Clan Mac Farlane and Associated Clans Genealogy, accessed 2 January 2023. https://www.clanmacfarlanegenealogy.info/genealogy/TNGWebsite/getperson.php?personID=I2295&tree=CC

[35] PoMS, "No. 23585," accessed 15 November 2022. https://www.poms.ac.uk/record/person/23585/

[36] PoMS, "No. 23613," accessed 15 November 2022. https://www.poms.ac.uk/record/person/23613/

[37] PoMS, "No. 23774," accessed 15 November 2022. https://www.poms.ac.uk/record/person/23774/

[38] Figure F-3: Author: "B," "The Chiefship of the Clan Murray," *The Scottish Antiquary, or, Northern Notes and Queries*, Vol. 15, No. 58 (Edinburgh: Edinburgh University Press, October 1900): 72. https://www.jstor.org/stable/25516988

[39] William Fraser, *Douglas Book*, Vol. 1 (Edinburgh: T. and A. Constable, Edinburgh University Press, 1885), 352. https://digital.nls.uk/histories-of-scottish-families/archive/96806202?mode=transcription

| | | |
|---|---|---|
| 1320s-1340s | Andrew de Landells resigned his lands of Ardross in Fifeshire in 1366 and died without heirs.[40] | Died without issue (without heirs). |
| 1320s-1330s | Andrew de Cunningham, cousin to David II. His lands (Drumcarn, Esstchom, Renruth, Gartheyr, Drumcheane, Drumquharne) in the earldom of Lennox in Lanarkshire were confirmed by David II in 1357. Received lands of Kildinny in Perthshire in 1369.[41] The Cunninghams of Drumquhassle were descended from one of the younger sons of Sir Robert Cunningham of Kilmaurs, and then through one of the younger sons of Andrew Cunningham of Polmaise, named Alexander.[42] Clan MacFarlane Genealogy page believes he married a Stewart.[43] | Married a Stewart. |
| 1330s-1340s | Andrew de Bet receives burgage (rental) lands in Edinburgh and Stirling from Richard de Roxburgh and his daughter and heiress, Eviota in 1370. Assumed tocher (dowry) for Eviota.[44] | Married Eviota de Roxburgh |
| 1280s-1300s | Andrew Russell, baillie of Aberdeen, att 1311 in a quit claim deed. | Too old. |
| 1280s-1310s | Andrew Grant, witnesses Inverness land charter between 1314 and 1325 | Too old. |
| 1280s-1300s | Andrew Gray, Knight, receives lands in Perthshire and in Angusshire in February 1315 | Too old. |
| 1250s-1280s | Andrew of Crawford, Knight, seems to be deceased by Nov 1303 | Too old. |
| 1280s-1300s | Andrew Murray, Pantler of Scotland, **died 1338**. Regent, Guardian of David II. First wife is unknown. | Too old. |
| 1280s-1300s | Andrew, clerk to Robert I. Receives lands in the sheriffdom of Banff in 1327. | Too old. |

---

[40] PoMS, "No. 23801," accessed 15 November 2022. https://www.poms.ac.uk/record/person/23801/

[41] D. Rixson, "Killearn Table-Eschend," Land Assessment Scotland, accessed 2 January 2023. http://las.denisrixson.com/2016/11/killearn-table/

[42] "The Scottish Nation, Cunningham," Electric Scotland, accessed 13 February 2023. https://electricscotland.com/history/nation/cunningham.htm

[43] "Andrew de Cunningham of Drumquhassil," Clan MacFarlane and Associated Clans Genealogy, accessed 2 January 2023. https://www.clanmacfarlanegenealogy.info/genealogy/TNGWebsite/getperson.php?personID=I38279&tree=CC

[44] PoMS, "No. 23920," accessed 15 November 2022. https://www.poms.ac.uk/record/person/23920/

| 1310s-1320s | Andrew of Buttergask, Knight, resigns lands of the Hill in West Lothian in favor of Thomas of the Hill in 1342. | Too old. |
|---|---|---|
| 1310s-1320s | Andrew Vallance (Valognes), lord of Dalginch, serves as a witness in an inspection of a Fife land charter of his daughter-in-law Agnes de Crambeth, along with his son James Vallance in 1353.[45] | Too old. His son James is married by 1353. |

Of the sixteen candidate Andrews in Table F-1, I believe that Sir Andrew de Murray of Manuel is the most viable candidate to be the husband of Agnes de Graham. The other candidates were discounted due to age differences, geographic distance, ordination as a Roman Catholic priest, confirmation of marriage to other people, or died without heirs. Sir Andrew was likely a grandson (versus son) of Sir Andrew de Moray of Bothwell, the Regent, and Christian Bruce, sister to King Robert I. Figure F-3. He was named in land charters as a "dear relative" to David Bruce (David II).[46]

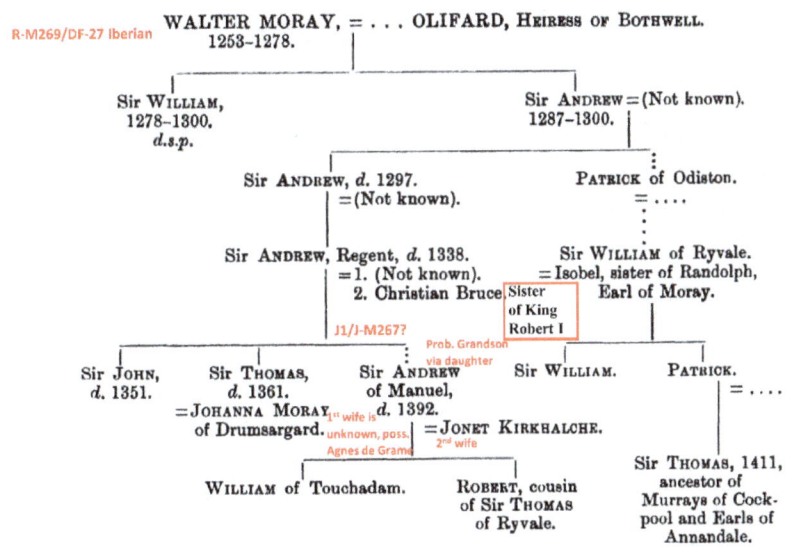

Figure F-3: Pedigree of Sir Andrew de Murray of Manuel, J1 Graham Patriarch Candidate from The Chiefship of the Clan Murray, Author: "B." The Scottish Antiquary, or, Northern Notes and Queries, Oct., 1900, Vol. 15, No. 58, [38] with modifications in red

A case can be made that Sir Andrew Murray of Manuel was not only the husband of Agnes de Graham, but also the patriarch (or son of the patriarch) of the Graham J1s later found concentrated near the Scottish-English border. Based on Y-DNA analysis of Graham surname project members, Dr. Iain McDonald of the FamilyTreeDNA Scottish Y-DNA project, initially estimated the Graham J1s descend from a single patriarch and the Time to Most Recent Common Ancestor (tMRCA) or the

---

[45] PoMS, "No. 10307," accessed 15 November 2022. https://www.poms.ac.uk/record/source/10307/
[46] PoMS, "No. 23774," accessed 15 November 2022. https://www.poms.ac.uk/record/person/23774/

timeframe the common J1 Graham ancestor was born was **1250-1550 A.D.**[47] Sir Andrew Murray of Manuel who would have first married circa 1363[48] and who was likely born about 1330-1340, and his biological father fit this timeframe.[49]

## More Discussion on the Connection between the Border Grahams and Menteiths

The male line of William de Graham, the first recorded Graham in Scotland, was carried on by descendants of his younger son, Alan, when the elder line officially "ended" circa 1362.[50] The evidence provided in the main book indicates that the Border Grahams are descendants of this "elder line." The very first Graham who was styled Earl of Menteith, Sir John de Graham, lived in the fourteenth century. "John de Graham of Abercorn," presumed son of Henry de Graham of West Byres (West Binns) in the Abercorn Barony, and nephew of Sir John de Graham of Dalkeith the elder, may have been the Sir John de Graham[51] who acquired the title of ninth earl of Menteith upon marriage to Mary, Countess of Menteith, circa 1332.[52] See Figure F-6.

Regardless whether the ninth earl was a Graham from Abercorn or not, a case still can be argued that the ninth earl was an elder line Graham.

## Sir John Graham, Ninth Earl of Menteith = Sir John Graham of Abercorn?

I. **Witnesses Dalkeith Graham Charters.** Between 1334 and 1340, John Graham, ninth earl of Menteith, witnesses the grant of lands called Bondingston, Ernseyth and Drumcros that were in the Barony of Dalkeith

*Figure F-4: Menteith Coat of Arms* [47] *Reproduced here under CC BY-SA 4.0.*

---

[47] FamilyTreeDNA, "Graham Surname DNA Project News," accessed 30 October 2022. https://www.familytreedna.com/groups/graham/about/news

Figure F-4: Wikimedia Commons contributors, "File:Menteith arms.svg," *Wikimedia Commons, the free media repository,* accessed 17 April 2023.
https://commons.wikimedia.org/w/index.php?title=File:Menteith_arms.svg&oldid=460664027

[48] PoMS, "No. 23643- Agnes Graham, 'Wife of Andrew de ?,'" accessed 20 October 2022. https://www.poms.ac.uk/record/person/23643/

[49] FTDNA Discover™ Tools estimate a J1 Graham common ancestor was born between 1011 and 1357 A.D., with a mean of 1201 A.D. However, it seems all our candidate ancestors, including the ones with the highest confidences, run consistently 100 to 140 years to the "right" of the Discover™ mean estimates, implying the Graham J1s may be atypical and do not fit the Discover™ assumptions.

[50] Lloyd D. Graham, *House Graham, From the Antoine Wall to the Temple of Hymen,* 2.

[51] Michael A. Penman, University of Stirling, "The Scots at the Battle of Neville's Cross, 17 October 1346," *The Scottish Historical Review,* Vol. 80, no. 210 (October 2001): 167. https://core.ac.uk/download/pdf/9048861.pdf

[52] William Fraser, *The Red Book of Menteith,* Vol. I (Edinburgh: 1880), 128-129, https://digital.nls.uk/histories-of-scottish-families/archive/96774276#?c=0&m=0&s=0&cv=217&xywh=-282%2C-337%2C5611%2C4159

to William Douglas by Robert, Stewart of Scotland.[53] A witness surnamed Graham to the transfer of Dalkeith lands, would typically have been a Graham of Dalkeith (elder line). If the transfer occurred towards the end of that window—between 1337 and 1340, it would have been soon after the death of the elder Sir John Graham of Dalkeith in 1337, and before the heir, the younger teenage Sir John Graham of Dalkeith (a.k.a.: "the Last") took full control of managing the estates of the massive Dalkeith Barony. An elder relative would have stepped in to help manage the estates until the heir was capable.

II. **Guardianship.** When her father, John de Graham, ninth Earl of Menteith, was executed in March 1347, having been captured by the English at the battle of Neville's Cross, Margaret Graham was about thirteen years old. As occurred for her mother, Countess Mary, whose own father died when she was very young, a guardian or caretaker earl from among her male relatives would likely have been appointed, particularly to avoid royal guardianship or involvement of the crown in the selection of a future spouse, a practice common when a powerful earldom such as Menteith was "up for grabs." The likely candidate to be appointed guardian as there were no close male relatives of her mother remaining, would be a relative of Margaret's father. I argue this caretaker was John de Graham "the Last" Lord of Dalkeith. One of the duties of the guardian was to arrange the ward's marriage.[54] From the Red Book of Menteith, Volume I:

> The death of her (Margaret's) father had an important bearing on the destinies of the young heiress, and led to events which might not have taken place had he lived. Deprived of her natural protector, even though her mother still lived, she was at the mercy of circumstances, and exposed to the schemes of intriguers, who were never wanting when so great an earldom was to be acquired by marriage. To escape their schemes, and following the custom then in vogue, it was arranged in 1348, while as yet Lady Margaret had only attained her fourteenth year, that a marriage should be celebrated between her and Sir John Moray, Lord of Bothwell. The proposals for the union were favorably received at (Royal) Court. One obstacle, however, stood in the way; the contracting parties were related to each other within the forbidden degrees, and to remove that impediment recourse was had by petition to the supreme pontiff for a dispensation. The Queen of Scotland interested herself in the marriage to such an extent that her Majesty presented a separate petition to the Pope to induce him to grant the necessary dispensation. Pope Clement gave the necessary apostolic authority to the Bishop of Moray to permit the marriage.[55]

As Margaret was not yet a countess, her first husband, John of Moray, son of Andrew of Moray, acting Regent of Scotland during the minority of David II, was of higher noble rank, hence the reason the dispensation was granted to his home diocese of Moray. After Sir John of

---

[53] Sir James Balfour Paul, *The Scots Peerage, Founded on Wood's Edition,* Vol. VI (Edinburgh: David Douglas, 1909), 138. https://archive.org/details/scotspeeragefoun06pauluoft/page/n5/mode/2up?view=theater&q=bondingston

[54] Janine Honey Sutter, "Assets to the Country: Countesses in 14th Century England" (MA Thesis, Clemson University, 2017), 45-46. https://tigerprints.clemson.edu/cgi/viewcontent.cgi?article=3683&context=all_theses

[55] William Fraser, *The Red Book of Menteith*, Vol. I, 116-130.

*Appendix F: Genealogy of the Border Grahams*

Moray died in England while serving as a hostage for David II in 1351, Margaret married her second husband, Thomas, Earl of Mar. Mar campaigned directly with the Vatican to marry Margaret, denying Margaret's guardians an opportunity to object. After Mar divorced her, she married her third husband John Drummond of Concraig circa 1359 to help quell a feud. Drummond died the following year.[56]

III. **Royal Stewart Connection.** When Margaret married her third husband in 1360 and fourth husband in September 1361, she was named the Countess of Menteith in marriage documents, indicating her mother had passed prior to 1360. Her third and fourth marriages again required papal dispensations due to a third cousin or closer relationship. Her fourth husband was Robert Stewart, son of Robert II. Sir John "the Last's" sister, Isabella, had married the sixth High Steward of Scotland, Walter Stewart (father of Robert II, by his first wife Marjorie Bruce). This relationship and the shared Strathearn ancestors between the Menteiths and elder line Grahams would have been enough to require the dispensation. Robert Stewart gained the title "Earl of Menteith" circa 1362 and the title first Duke of Albany in 1398.[57] Coincidentally, 1362 is the same year that Sir John de Graham "the Last" of Dalkeith died.[58] One of his final acts might have been to help arrange the marriage of his ward to a Stewart relative, especially since Margaret's other protector, her mother, was now deceased.

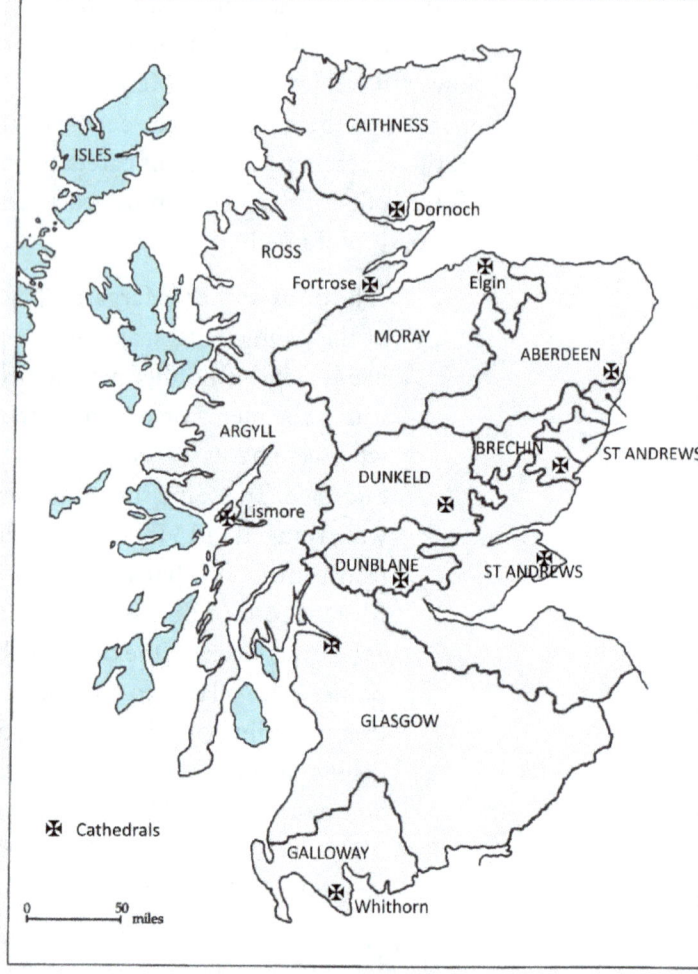

*Figure F-5: Map of Medieval Scottish Church Dioceses provided by ECNS [Early Church in Northern Scotland]* [59]

IV. **Home Diocese.** In 1362, Margaret Graham, now Countess of Menteith, "outranked" husband number four, Robert Stewart, at the time of the nuptials. Therefore, the papal dispensation approving the marriage would have been issued to her home diocese. The dispensation was issued to the Diocese of St. Andrews, the home diocese of the Grahams of Dalkeith. If Margaret were a daughter of a Graham of Montrose (younger line), her church-related documents would have listed her diocese as Brechin. The map in Figure F-5 shows

---

[56] William Fraser, *The Red Book of Menteith*, Vol. I, 117.
[57] William Fraser, *The Red Book of Menteith*, Vol. I, 127-130.
[58] Lloyd D. Graham, *House Graham, From the Antoine Wall to the Temple of Hymen*, 2.

Abercorn and Dalkeith were also located in the Diocese of St. Andrews.[59] For example, Agnes de Monfode nee Graham, sister of Sir John de Graham "the Last," was identified as being of St. Andrews in the dispensation for her marriage to Sir John Douglas.[60]

V. **Euphemia Graham of Menteith.** She assisted in returning Hutton Lands to the Border Grahams. In July 1456, the Douglases successfully sued William, Robert, Richard and John Graham, regarding their claims to certain lands in Hutton, lands the Grahams claimed had been in their family's possession for over a hundred years.[61] In May 1463, Euphemia Graham, sister of Malise Graham, earl of Menteith resigned some of her estates in a trade for the lands of Mosskesswra, Nether Dryfe and Bedokholme in Hutton, so they could be granted to "William the Grahame," presumably to return them.[62] See Abbreviated Historical Chronology of the Border Grahams, p. F-58.

VI. **Quote from Lord Cecil Burghley, minister to Elizabeth I.** He writes in 1596: "William Graham, alias Long Will of Scotland about 80 yeiris since (i.e., circa 1515) came into England and brought with him eight sonnes whom he planted neare the said river of Eske. By this William doe the Earls of Mounteth and Montrose in Scotland claims interest of the service of all Grames as descended out of their houses." [63]

VII. **Heraldry.** The Menteiths and Border Grahams as well as the Grahams of Drumgoon in County Fermanagh, Ireland and the Grahams of Galway, Ireland (Border Graham descendants), share the same motto: "Ratio mihi sufficit" or "Reason is sufficient for me" or "Right and Reason." The Montrose motto is "Ne Oublie" or "Do not forget."[64]

VIII. **Knightly Orders.** Given that Fergus of Mote and his great-grandsons, and the Grahams of Dalkeith, the Grahams of Menteith, the Grahams of Claverhouse, Grahams of Fintry, and the Grahams of Dundaff, were supporters of the knightly orders (Templar, Hospitaller, Trinitarian), they would have been acutely aware of their individual families' contributions of lands. They would have learned the family tradition of the connections between their clans and the knightly orders.[65] See Appendix D for information on Templar/Hospitaller/Trinitarian land gifts.

---

[59] Figure F-5: Cushie Enterprises, "Map of the Medieval Scottish Dioceses," *The Early Church in Northern Scotland*, accessed 14 February 2023. https://www.cushnieent.com/medievalchurch/map_scotland.htm

[60] John P. Ravilious, "Queen Euphemia and Her Ancestry," *The Scottish Genealogist*, The Scottish Genealogy Society (June 2017): 50. https://www.academia.edu/35370666/Queen_Euphemia_and_her_ancestry_TSG_LXIV_2_49_52

[61] Royal Commission on Historical Manuscripts, *Historical Manuscripts Commission, Report on Manuscripts of Sir Archibald Edmonstone of Duntreath, Volumes 5 and 6* (Hereford: Anthony Brothers Limited, 1909), 77. https://archive.org/details/variousmanuscripts05greauoft/page/n83/mode/2up

[62] Historical Manuscripts Commission, *The Manuscripts of the Duke of Hamilton, Knight, Eleventh Report, Appendix, Part VI* (London: Her Majesty's Stationery Office, 1887), 18. https://archive.org/details/manuscriptsofduk00greauoft/page/18/mode/2up?ref=ol&view=theater&q=moskeswra

[63] R.C. Reid, "The Border Grahams and Their Origins," *Transactions of the Dumfries and Galloway Natural History and Archaeological Society (TDGNHAS)* No. 3038 (1961): 86. https://dgnhas.org.uk/sites/default/files/transactions/3038.pdf

[64] Lloyd D. Graham, *House Graham, From the Antoine Wall to the Temple of Hymen*, 13.

[65] PoMS, "No. 2005-David Graham (III), Sheriff of Berwick," accessed 12 November 2022. https://www.poms.ac.uk/record/person/2005/

*Appendix F: Genealogy of the Border Grahams*

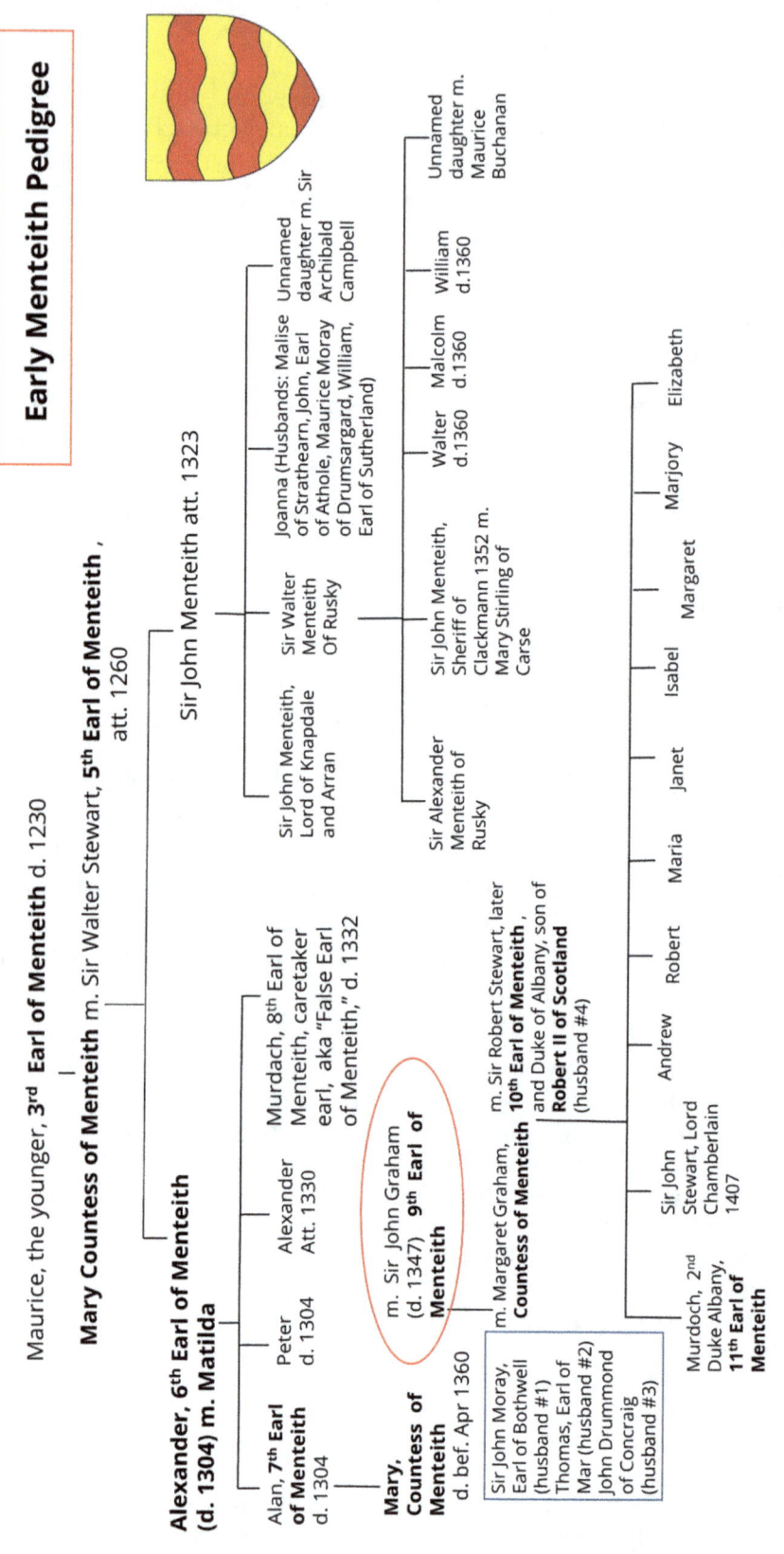

Figure F-6: *Thirteenth and Fourteenth Century Pedigree of the Menteith Earls of Menteith from the "Redbook of Menteith," Volume 1, by William Fraser[66] and the writings of John P. Ravilous.[60,67] CC BY-SA 4.0.*

## V. Multiple Menteiths by the Same Name: Who is Who?

There has been confusion among several earls and countesses of Menteith named John and Mary or similar names. To clarify using Figure F-6 as a reference:

1. John Graham of Rusky was the guardian of the earldom of Menteith, and the granduncle of Countess Mary of Menteith. When her father, Alexander the seventh earl, died in 1304 when she was a baby, John was named guardian to Mary and the earldom. It is this John who died in 1323, who is remembered as playing a role in the capture of Sir William Wallace. Mary's uncle Murdoch, the son of the above-named John, then served as caretaker earl, and claimed the title the eighth earl of Menteith, from 1323 until his death in 1332. Murdoch has been called the "False Earl of Menteith," since he wasn't heir to the title, but a caretaker.[66]

2. Sir John de Graham, ninth Earl of Menteith, acquired the title via marriage to Mary, Countess of Menteith and was executed by the English in 1347. Countess Mary likely died sometime between August 1352 and April 1360. This is determined by the reviewing the marriage dispensation documents of daughter Margaret. In the dispensation of her first marriage on 21 November 1348, her daughter is named as "Margaret, daughter of John Graham, Earl of Menteith." In the second dispensation dated 15 August 1352, she is named "Margaret, widow of John of Moray." In the third dispensation dated 29 April 1360 and later the fourth dated 9 September 1361, she is named "Margaret, Countess of Menteith."[67]

3. Sir John Stewart of Menteith, son of Sir Walter Menteith of Rusky, was the grandson of the guardian earl John of Rusky mentioned in the first paragraph of this section. Sir John Stewart was the second husband of Mary/Marjorie Stirling, daughter of Sir John of Stirling. Sir John Stewart, who succeeded his father-in-law as Sheriff of Clackmann, died circa 1348.[68] It is confusing with two Johns father-in-law and son-in-law, both in the barony of Kerse of the river Carron estate and both in the barony of Alva Clackmanan. Mary (Marjorie) Stirling was also known as Lady Roberton. She resigned the Barony of Roberton to William Douglas of Liddesdale in 1349.[69] In 1382, she signed over the barony of Kerse, a Stirling inheritance, to her son, Sir William Stewart upon marriage to Elizabeth Graham.[70] Elizabeth may have been the daughter of John Graham of Auchencloich, son of Sir John de Graham, "the Last" lord of Dalkeith (elder line). Auchencloich was in Herbertshire, about 16 miles south of Kerse, is geographically situated in the right place and John of Auchencloich is the right age to be the father of the Elizabeth Graham who married Sir William Stewart of Kerse. Futher, there is a

---

[66] William Fraser, *The Red Book of Menteith*, Vol. I, 289-292, 458-461.
[67] William Fraser, *The Red Book of Menteith*, Vol. I, 116-129.
Figure F-6: John P. Ravilious, "Agnes De Graham, wife of (1) John de Monfode and (2) John de Douglas," *The Scottish Genealogist*, LXI No. 4, The Scottish Genealogy Society (December 2014): 129-133. https://www.academia.edu/34967491/TSG_Agnes_de_Graham_wife_of_John_de_Monfode_and_Sir_John_de_Douglas_TSG_LXI_4_129_133
[68] William Fraser, *The Red Book of Menteith*, Vol. I, 458-461.
[69] PoMS, "No. 23260, person summary," accessed 7 January 2023. https://www.poms.ac.uk/record/person/23260/
[70] William Fraser, *The Red Book of Menteith*, Vol. I, 460-461.

shared judicial family profession common to the elder line Grahams and this branch of Stewarts : sheriffs, "justiciars" (judges) or justiciar clerks.[71]

4. John of Swinton (possibly a Graham kinsman) married Lady Margaret of Menteith after 1390. After the death of her first husband, Lady Margaret remarried Robert Stewart of Lorne. She had issue by both husbands.[72]

5. Sir John de Graham "the Last", Lord of Dalkeith, whose wife may have been named Mary or Margaret. He may have served as caretaker earl of Menteith upon the death of his relative, John de Graham, the ninth earl of Menteith, in 1347 until his own death in 1362.

## Background on Lang Will Graham

Lang Will was identified as the patriarch of the Grahams residing at the Scottish-English border by Lord Thomas Scrope of Bolton, the English Warden of the Western March in a 1583 letter to William Cecil, first Baron Burghley (Burleigh), Chancellor for Elizabeth I. Scrope refers to Will as "William Graham, Laird of Mosskesswra, who had a daughter married to David Graham of Netherby."[73] This David Graham of Netherby who was already living in Cumberland prior to 1515 may have been a distant cousin, a descendant of David Graham of Corbridge d. 1278, of Northumberland, brother of Sir Nicholas de Graham of Dalkeith.[74] See Figure 38.

> **Phil Graham Note on the "Elder Line"**
>
> The Grahams, like the Bruces, were on both sides throughout the Wars of Scottish Independence which ended with Grahams supporting Sir William Wallace, King Robert the Bruce (Robert I) and King David Bruce (David II). These Grahams (elder line) were subsequently forfeited of their extensive estates in Northumberland and Cumberland. They then focused on establishing their Scottish estates in Esk, Annan, Torthorwald, Dryfe, Hutton, Corrie, Mossknowe and parts of Galloway.

### English Graham Origins.

It is noteworthy that Sir Nicholas de Graham of Dalkeith and his siblings all had ties to Northumberland with the exception of brother Peter, hence the reason there seemed to be Grahams living on the English side of the border ready to assist Lang Will when he first arrived. It is through Sir Nicholas' wife Marjorie de Muschamps, that the Grahams acquired Northumberland lands in the Barony of Alnwick (Wooler, Chillingham).[75] Nicholas' brother William was an "ecclesiastic,"[76] meaning he was a monk or priest, likely serving at nearby Hexham Abbey.[i] His brother Henry de Graham gave his Northumberland

---

[71] POMs, "No. 896, person summary," accessed 6 January 2023. https://www.poms.ac.uk/record/person/896/ ; POMs, "No. 2005, person summary," accessed 6 January 2023. https://www.poms.ac.uk/record/person/2005/ ; POMs, "No. 10987, person summary," accessed 6 January 2023. https://www.poms.ac.uk/record/person/10987/

[72] William Fraser, *The Red Book of Menteith*, Vol. I, 238.

[73] A. W. Cornelius Hallen, "The Grahams of the Border," *The Scottish Antiquary* or *Northern Notes and Queries 9*, no. 36 (1895): 160–166. https://www.google.com/books/edition/The_Scottish_Antiquary/Zdyk2WG8ILQC?hl=en&gbpv=1&bsq=netherby

[74] PoMS, "No. 4185," accessed 19 January 2023. https://www.poms.ac.uk/record/source/4185/

[75] George Tate, *History of the Borough, Castle and Barony of Alnwick* (Alnwick: Henry Blair, 1866), 78, 408, 409, 413.

[76] Sir James Balfour Paul, *The Scots Peerage, Founded on Wood's Edition,* Vol. VI (Edinburgh: David Douglas, 1909), 197. https://archive.org/details/scotspeeragefoun06pauluoft/page/196/mode/2up?q=graham

estates of Simonburn and Swinburne to his sister Idonea and her husband, Adam de Swinburne.[77] Henry was buried in Northumberland.[78] Their brother David held lands in Corbridge.[79] Two centuries later, members of the Graham clan returned to Northern England with the arrival of Lang Will Graham. He was formally granted a lease of the lands of Netherby and Kirk Andrews by Henry VIII in 1537.[80]

The chief seat of Lang Will's branch of the family was Netherby. Cornelius Hallen writes that by the time he reached old age, "William Graham, ' Lang Willie ' as he was usually styled, had eight sons and thirty-three adult grandsons ready to join in the foray." They had more dependents and allies through marriage who regarded the Lairds of Netherby and Mote as the chiefs of the guards of the western borders.[81] John Maxwell, Lord Herries in his *Discourse on the Borders*, states that the "thieves of the March" with English assistance had slain the Lord Carlisle, as well as the lairds of Mouswald, Kirkmichael, Kirkconnel (Kirkpatrick-Fleming) and Logane and "many other landit men."[82] Per R.C. Reid: "In 1542 the Grahams were not more than 20-30 at most; by 1578 they were 16-18 score (320-360) and well horsed." [83]

### The Grahams of Esk and Netherby descend from "Lang Will."

According to Lord Burghley's report, by 1516 William Graham the younger ("Lang Will") and his family, had initially taken up residence along with six sons and other kinsmen in the Debatable Land' on the south bank of the Esk River near the Solway Firth. His residences in the Debatable Land included the English towns of Arthuret, Netherby, and Longtown,[84] which was also called "Lang" town, per Phil Graham, the likely reason behind his new nickname.

Lang Wills' eight famous sons were: Richard Graham of Netherby, Fergus Graham of Mote, George Graham of the Fauld, Arthur Graham of Canobie, John Graham of Medoppe, "the Braid," Thomas Graham of Kirklanders, William Graham of Carlisle, and Hutchin Graham of the Guard/Gard.[85] Several of them became leaders of the Border Reivers (robbers) who were accused of cattle and sheep rustling, and other crimes.[86] The family was singled out as the key instigators among

---

[77] Andy King, "War, Politics, and Landed Society in Northumberland, c1296-c1408" (PhD Thesis, Durham University, 2001), 6. http://etheses.dur.ac.uk/1729/

[78] Lloyd D. Graham, *House Graham, From the Antoine Wall to the Temple of Hymen*, 2.

[79] PoMS, "No. 4185," accessed 12 February 2023. https://www.poms.ac.uk/record/source/4185/

[80] *Letters and Papers, Foreign and Domestic, Henry VIII, Volume 12 Part 1, January-May 1537*, Edited by James Gairdner (London: Her Majesty's Stationery Office, 1890), 560, *British History Online*, accessed December 28, 2022. http://www.british-history.ac.uk/letters-papers-hen8/vol12/no1

[81] A. W. Cornelius Hallen, "The Grahams of the Border," 166.

[82] Royal Commission on the Ancient and Historical Monuments and Constructions of Scotland, *Seventh Report with Inventory of Monuments and Constructions in the County of Dumfries* (Edinburgh:1920), 41. https://scotlandsplaces.gov.uk/digital-volumes/rcahms-archives/inventories/dumfries-1920

[83] R.C. Reid, "The Border Grahams and Their Origins," 105.

[84] Great Britain. Record Commission, *State papers, published under the authority of His Majesty's Commission. King Henry the Eighth*, Vol. 5 (London: G. Eyre and A. Strahan, printers to the King's Most Excellent Majesty, 1836), 195-196. https://archive.org/details/statepaperspubli05grea/page/194/mode/2up?q=bishop+stewart

[85] John O'Hart, *Irish Pedigrees Volume II* (Dublin: James Duffy and Co Limited, 1892), 231-234. https://ia600202.us.archive.org/12/items/irishpedigreesor01ohar/irishpedigreesor01ohar.pdf

[86] A. W. Cornelius Hallen, "The Grahams of the Border," 160–166.

Border Reivers and in 1606, as advocated by Lord Burghley, were ordered "banished" to Roscommon, Ireland, along with their families.[87] However, in 1614 the commissioners issued a proclamation for the apprehension of the Grahams because "divers of them have returned into the middle shires, and are beginning to revive their old courses of robbing and riding armed to the great terror of our loving subjects." The rector of Arthuret reported in 1618 that numerous Grahams had crept back to their old haunts, including the chief, Walter Graham of Netherby, Grahams of Mote, Bankhead, Fauld, Brackenhill, Closegap, Mossband, Bankhead, Millees, Laird Place, Debatable Lands, Longtown, Easton, Burnfoot, and Nicholforest. William Graham of Guards must have also returned as he left a will, as did Robert Graham of Howend who witnessed it.[88] The Grahams of Plomp re-purchased the old Graham Lordship of Arthuret from the earl of Cumberland in 1629.[89] See Appendix G for more on the Grahams of Plomp.

## The Eight Sons of Lang Will Graham and Their Tribes

### 1. Richard Graham of Netherby.

Eldest son of Lang Will Graham and clan chief according to Lord Burghley in 1596. Richard succeeded in clearing himself of a treason charge in 1528 by proving that a member of the Storey family had informed Johnnie Armstrong of Lord Dacre's raid. After the Storeys fled, Lang Will's sons promptly divided up their land amongst themselves. The lands of Netherby were retained by eldest son Richard who built eight Pele (peel) towers. Richard had daughters and at least three sons: 1. Richard (Richie's Dick) Graham of Netherby (att. 1541), married a daughter of his cousin Arthur Graham of Carlisle; 2. William who first married a daughter of Mangerton, and second married Robin Elliott of Liddesdale; 3. Richard's third known son was George Graham of Ranpatrick/Rampatrick who married Katherine Maxwell and lived at the Redkirk in Scotland.[90] In 1579, George was called on to present his sons, Christopher and George, before the Scottish Privy Council as they had been implicated in the slaughter of William Johnston of Hayhill. [91]

### 2. Fergus Graham of Mote.

Fergus Graham of Mote, believed to be the second eldest son of Lang Will, was under the employ of Henry VIII serving as Governor of the Castlemilk fortress in Scotland with an English Garrison in 1547. The Castles of Mote and Milk covered a large area: Upper Esk, Upper

---

[87] J. Bain, *The Border Papers: Calendar of letters and papers relating to the affairs of the borders of England and Scotland preserved in Her Majesty's Public Record Office,* Vol. I, 1560-1594,Vol. II 1595-1603 (London, Edinburgh: H.M. General Register House, 1894), 123, 124, 135, 136, 176, 177, 270, 751, 778, 779, 807. https://archive.org/details/borderpaperscale02grea/mode/2up?q=burghley

[88] Richard T. Spence, "The Pacification of the Cumberland Borders, 1593-1628," *Northern History,* 13:1 (1977): 122.

[89] A. W. Cornelius Hallen, "The Grahams of the Border," 161.

[90] A. W. Cornelius Hallen, "The Grahams of the Border," 162.

[91] David Masson, *The Register of the Privy Council of Scotland.* Edinburgh, First Series (Edinburgh: H.M. General Register House, 1880), Vol. III, 246, 306.
https://www.google.com/books/edition/The_Register_of_the_Privy_Council_of_Sco/i7nUcH-JxsUC?hl=en&gbpv=1&bsq=graham

Dryfe, and Upper Annandale. In 1552, the Debateable Land on the English/Scottish border was divided, Canobie allotted to Scotland and Kirk Andrews to England.[92]

In 1553 Fergus had a grant of arms for military service.[93] He was the father of at least two daughters and eight sons: Francie of Canobie, Arthur, John/Jock, Christopher, (a.k.a.: Fergie's Christie or Creste), Hobbe, William, George and Richard of Breconhill. Richard of Breconhill founded the Kildare and Queens County of Ireland families, while Fergus' elder son and heir was Arthur Graham of Mote. Arthur's son and heir, Arthur (also of Mote), left two sons. The elder son was Colonel William Graham of Mote who died without heirs in 1657. The younger son, Arthur "the third," also left a son, Arthur Graham "the fourth," who went to Ulster in Northern Ireland in 1641 and there he had a confirmation of family arms documented circa 1643-1649.[94]

### 3. George Graham of the Fauld.

A younger son of Lang Will Graham from the Parish of Arthuret. George had at least two sons: Robert, and William,[95] as well as a daughter who married Christopher Armstrong of Barnegleish. Robert of the Fauld married a daughter of the laird of Hawmans and one of his daughters married Edward Irvine of Bonshaw, "young Edward," and the other daughter married Walter Graham, grandson of Richard of Netherby. William of the Fauld married a daughter of Hector Armstrong of Harlaw.[96]

### 4. Arthur Graham of Canobie.

Arthur was Lang Will's son who remained in Scotland, specifically in Canobie, when his father and brothers moved to England in 1515. He was killed at a young age in 1541 as the result of a feud with the Armstrongs. Arthur had a single daughter who later married Christopher Armstrong of Langholm.[97]

### 5. John Graham of Medoppe, "of the Braids."

---

[92] T.J. Carlyle, *The Debateable Land*, 13. Despite the new boundary, Kirkandrews was still ecclesiastically under Canobie, hence the number of church members from Kirkandrews who traveled to Canobie into the 18th century to have their children baptized such as the parents of Christopher Graham of Kirkandrews in 1707. Familysearch.org

[93] T.J. Carlyle, *The Debateable Land*, 150-151.

[94] John O'Hart, *Irish Pedigrees Volume II* (Dublin: James Duffy and Co Limited, 1892), 71, 231-234. https://ia600202.us.archive.org/12/items/irishpedigreesor01ohar/irishpedigreesor01ohar.pdf

[95] John Hill Burton, *The Register of the Privy Council of Scotland*. Edinburgh, First Series (Edinburgh: H.M. General Register House, 1878), Vol. I, 149. https://catalog.hathitrust.org/Record/100404514

[96] John G. Armstrong, "The Debatable Armstrongs and Their Graham Relations," pdf reprinted by permission of Armstrong Clan Association News (2009), 1-3. https://clangrahamsociety.org/wp-content/uploads/2020/01/TheDebatable-ArmstrongsandtheirGrahamRelations-JohnGArmstrong.pdf

[97] John G. Armstrong, "The Debatable Armstrongs and Their Graham Relations," pdf reprinted by permission of Armstrong Clan Association News (2009), 1-3.

John was full age in 1541. He had four sons: Richard, William, Robert, and John. The nickname "of the Braids" usually indicates a connection to St. Catherine of Alexandria[98] and perhaps the thirteenth century family of Braid, probable cousins of the Grahams of Dalkeith. Another more likely possibility is that like the Braids from Midlothian, the referenced Medoppe lands may also have been former church or priory lands connected to the saint.[99] John's son Richard, styled "Medhope," married a sister of Edward Irvine of Kirkpatrick. His son William married a sister of Johnstone of Gretna. Son John also known as "Braids' Jock," married a daughter of Edward Irvine of Bonshaw.[100]

### 6. Thomas Graham of Kirklanders.

Thomas was of full age in 1541 and had at least four sons: George, styled "Thomie's Gorth," Graham, David/Davie, styled "of the Bankhead," Arche, and Christopher Graham. George married a sister of William Armstrong of Kinmont and had a son, Alexander, who was of full age in 1592 plus a daughter who married Thomas Carleton.[101]

### 7. Hugh/Hutchin Graham of the Gards.

An illegitimate son of Lang Will Graham and of full age in 1541. He was implicated as a leader in the famous rescue of Kinmont Willie Armstrong from an English prison in Carlisle in 1596 and targeted for deportation to Ireland along with his wife and three children in 1606.[102] His son Andrew married a daughter of David Johnstone of Annandale. His son Robert married a daughter of Edward Irvine of Bonshaw. His son Richard married a daughter of Adam Carlisle in Annandale. He had a fourth son, named Arthur.[103]

### 8. William Graham of Carlisle.

Considered Lang Will's seventh and wealthiest son. His daughter married her cousin, Richard Graham of Netherby, the younger. His sons were: William of Rosetrees, Fergus, John, Walter, Arthur, and George (Gorth).[104] William Graham of Carlisle received Letters Patent on 9 March 1553 for service to the English crown, granting him the house and site of the late Priory of Armathwaite, a Benedictine nunnery.

### 8a. Fergus Graham of Nunnery.

---

[98] St. Catherine of Alexandria was known for her long hair and a legend that it continued to grow after her death. "Saint Catherine of Alexandria," Catholic Online, accessed 3 January 2023. https://www.catholic.org/saints/saint.php?saint_id=341

[99] Women of her time through medieval times would keep long hair in braids. Rosalie Gilbert, "Medieval Hairstyles," Rosalie's Medieval Woman, accessed 3 January 2023. https://rosaliegilbert.com/hairstyles.html

[100] A. W. Cornelius Hallen, "The Grahams of the Border," 165.

[101] A. W. Cornelius Hallen, "The Grahams of the Border," 165.

[102] John Graham, *Condition of the Border at the Union: Destruction of the Graham Clan* (London: George Routledge and Sons Ltd, 1907),175, 176, 188. https://archive.org/details/conditionofborde00grahuoft/page/n10/mode/1up?ref=ol&view=theater&q=hutchin

[103] A. W. Cornelius Hallen, "The Grahams of the Border." 165.

[104] R.C. Reid, "The Border Grahams and Their Origins," 106.

William of Carlisle left the nunnery lands to his second son, Fergus, later known as Fergus Graham of Nunnery.[105] Fergus went into business at Carlisle and may have become a burgess there. Fergus' sons William and Robert were "very good subjects," and permitted to keep the Nunnery lands at the Union of the Crowns (when the Scottish king James VI became James I of England) in 1603.[106]

### 8b. Arthur Graham of Blaatwood.

William Graham of Carlisle acquired Blaatwood in the aftermath of the 1542 Battle of Solway Moss. John Carruthers of Holmendis granted on 3 August 1544 the land of Blaatwood with the fishings of Skarris and Loupis (Coupis) to William Graham of Carlisle. To this was added on 6 November 1550, the nearby coastal land of Torduff by Michael, Lord Carlisle and Esota Carlisle, his spouse. William left Blaatwood to his son Arthur. Arthur of Blaatwood had one daughter and sons named: William, Fergus, David, Arche, Alexander, Johne, and Arthur (II).[107]

Arthur's son William Graham of Blaatwood married Rosina Scott of Beltenmont.[108] Beltenmont is next to Mossknowe and was part of the Graham of Mossknowe estate in 1875.[109]

Arthur's son Fergus of Blaatwood suffered financial difficulties. In 1619 he lent £80 to his brother-in-law, Robert Johnston of Howcleuch, and within six years found himself in prison. To appear in court in Edinburgh he had to obtain a crown protection which in 1631 was renewed to enable him to defend himself. In 1635, he sued his Johnston in-laws for a promised dowry via proxy. In 1638, he obtained further protection from his creditors for a year.[110]

In 1649 two Acts of Parliament were passed in favor of Fergus Graham of Blaatwood and his son William. Specifically mentioned in the acts: "William and Arthur his

> **FYI...**
>
> In 1657, the Postage Act was passed by Parliament. Fixed rates were established for the delivery of mail. Under this early scheme, the receiver had to pay the postage versus the sender. The rate was based on distance travelled. Those not wanting to pay the postage could refuse the letter.

---

[105] William Dugdale, *Monasticon Anglicanum: A History of the Abbies and Other Monasteries, Hospitals, Frieries, and Cathedral and Col.legiate Churches, with Their Dependencies, in England and Wales; Also of All Such Scotch, Irish, and French Monasteries, as Were in Any Manner Connected with Religious Houses in England*, Vol. 3 (London: Longman, Hurst, Rees, Orme and Brown, 1821), 270. https://quod.lib.umich.edu/e/eebo/A36798.0001.001?view=toc

[106] T.H.B. Graham, "Nunnery," *Transactions of the Cumberland and Westmoreland Antiquarian and Archaeological Society* (23 April 1915): 5-7. https://archive.org/details/transactionsofcu17cumb/page/6/mode/2up?q=fergus+graham

[107] William Fraser, *The Annandale Family Book of the Johnstones, Earls and Marquises of Annandale*, Vol. I, 124.

[108] R.C. Reid and W. F. Cormack, "Two Medieval Crosses at Kirkpatrick Fleming," *Transactions of the Dumfries and Galloway Natural History and Archaeological Society (TDGNHAS)* No. 3068, Vol 38 (1961): 118. https://dgnhas.org.uk/sites/default/files/transactions/3038.pdf

[109] C.L. Johnstone, *The Historical Families of Dumfriesshire and the Border Wars*, CHAPTER XII, Ancient Provosts of Annan (Dumfries: Anderson & Son, 1889), 61, 168, 202. https://archive.org/details/historicalfamili00grah See "Fergus the Rascal" in Appendix C.

[110] R.C. Reid, "The Border Grahams and Their Origins," 106-111.

[Postage Act blurb] Barbara J. Starmans, "Royal Mail History," The Social Historian, accessed 3 January 2023. https://www.thesocialhistorian.com/royal-mail-history/

sons, George Graham son of John Graham of Redkirk, William Graham son of George Graham called the Roust, and George Graham, son-in-law of the said Fergus." Per R.C. Reid, "The cost must have been ruinous for in 1650 Fergus and his wife, Sarah Johnston, and their 'eleven puir children' brought an action against Sarah's father, the earl for their sustenance." Fergus could not have survived long after 1650.

By 1657, Fergus's son, William Graham of Blaatwood was suing Archibald Johnston in Howcleuch for rights to deliver mail for Over Howcleuch. This William was provost of Annan as early as June 1677, and was a member of Parliament, 1669-72.[111]

## Gillesbie Grahams

The Grahams of Gillesbie are descendants of John Graham of Gillesbie, brother to Lang Will, who was granted the lands of Gillesbie in the region of Upper Dryfe. See Figure F-9. As shown in the historical documentary Chronology (p. F-70), the first record of someone by that name is in 1470, when John Graham of Gillesbie signs a deed at Dalkeith undertaking on 40 days notice to deliver to James Douglas, the first earl of Morton, the lands of Brackenwra, which are a part of Gillesbie, on payment of "four score merks."[112] Later we find a Robert Graham of Gillesbie mentioned in a land charter in 1508, and in 1515 John Graham of Gillesbie is accused along with his brother, Lang Will, of ingathering and failing to distribute the teinds (tithes) to the local vicarage.[113] We will address why the Grahams would feel they had a right to a portion of the tithes in the next section.

> *Did you know?*
> The bond of manrent was commonly an instrument in which a weaker man or clan pledged to serve, in return for protections, a stronger lord or clan—in effect becoming a vassal that rendered service to a superior, often made in the form of a covenant.

As we know, the Gillesbie Grahams were not financially impacted by the resulting fines like Lang Will was, for in 1541, James Graham of Gillesbie and Mosskesswra, headed forty retainers. In 1567, John Graham of Gillesbie, heir of James, is granted lands in Heithat and Branriggs. In 1579, forty-four Gillesbie Grahams entered into a bond of manrent with the laird of Johnstone which ensured their support at the Battle of Dryfe Sands between the Johnstones and Maxwells in 1593.[114]

Col. William Rogerson of Gillesbie wrote about a tradition well-known by elders living in Gillesbie in 1908. The story was of a battle on the Windshields Bog circa 1641 between the Graham lairds of Gillesbie and Shaw. One laird was left dead and the other fled the country with most of his clan. The Grahams of Shaw continued to be active in the area after 1641, implying it was the laird of

---

[111] R.C. Reid, "The Border Grahams and Their Origins," 111.

[112] *Registrum Honoris de Morton, Volume II: Ancient Charters* (Edinburgh: The Bannatyne Club, 1858), 216-217. https://archive.org/details/registrumhonoris02bann/page/n3/mode/2up?ref=ol&view=theater

[Manrent blurb] "Definitions for Manrent," Definitions.net, accessed 3 January 2023. https://www.definitions.net/definition/manrent

[113] R.C. Reid, "The Border Grahams and Their Origins," 93.

[114] Col. William Rogerson, *Hutton Under the Muir* (Dumfries, Scotland: Dumfries and Galloway Courier and Herald, 1908), 25, 26, 31. https://www.google.com/books/edition/Hutton_under_the_muir_notes_on_the_past/BiwVAAAAQAAJ?hl=en&gbpv=1&bsq=gillesbie

Shaw who was killed circa 1641 and the laird of Gillesbie was the one who fled. For example, in 1671, William Graham of Shaw is named as a heritor (wealthy elder) for the Presbyterian churches of Annandale[115] and in 1698 James Graham of Shaw married one of the Hunter of Ballagan co-heiresses.[116]

## Where is Mosskesswra/Moskessen?

There has been speculation of the specific location of the Mosskesswra Barony also known as Moskessen or Moskesso. First, a little behind the place name itself. In this usage, "Mo" is the Gaelic word for "my,"[117] a term of endearment, "Kesso" is short for the Celtic Culdee Saint Kessog.[118] "Mo kesso" likely means the "my dear Saint Kessog."[119] "Our Most Blessed Kessog," was reportedly shouted by King Robert the Bruce as he urged troops into battle in the name of St. Kessog at Bannockburn in 1314.[120] [See Appendix D for more on St. Kessog.] Archaeological evidence indicates Mosskesswra, located in the parish of Hutton and Corrie, started out as a Celtic Culdee church property, but became a barony sometime after the arrival of the Normans.[121]

**Geography.** The Closs, or Close, in Figure F-7 is a medieval church close or enclosure, which were lands surrounding a church. That means that in medieval times, there was a church "close to the close."[122] Given we know that Lang Will was in trouble for retaining church tithes in the **Kirk of Hutton**, which we know in other maps (Figure 19) is downstream of Gillesbie Tower on the Dryfe Water, that confirms Mosskesswra Barony[ii] includes the Hutton area as shown in Figure F-9. Figure F-7 is from the Ordnance Survey of Great Britain, first surveyed in 1857. It shows the site of Moskesso church, which included the St. Kessog Church and the lands connected to the referenced church Close (Closs), and the remains of Gillesbie tower.[123] With the Grahams and cousins in possession of lands that were former medieval Culdee church lands, and noted family members who were connected to the Culdee religion, implies the Graham ancestors were in Britain before the arrival of the Normans.

The Mosskesswra land would have had a watch tower along the Dryfe Water. Rivers were the fastest way to travel so required sentinels to keep watch.[124] Based on ages of the ruins, it seems the Grahams of Gillesbie replaced the Mosskesswra tower with the Gillesbie tower downstream in the early

---

[115] Col. William Rogerson, *Hutton Under the Muir*, 20, 26.

[116] T.J. Carlyle, *The Debateable Land* (Dumfries, W.R. McDarmid and Co., 1868), 12.

[117] "How to say 'my' in Scots Gaelic," WordHippo.com, accessed 3 January 2023. https://www.wordhippo.com/what-is/the/scots-gaelic-word-for-3ece1471f44f63177cbc35ba0b904e0c096b6783.html

[118] "About St. Kessog," Col.lege of St. Kessog, accessed 3 January 2023. http://kessog.lochac.sca.org/about.htm

[119] James Murray Mackinlay, "St. Kessog and His Cultus in Scotland," *Transactions of the Glasgow Archaeological Society* 3, no. 2 (1899): 347. http://www.jstor.org/stable/24680608

[120] "Was the "Bruce's 'Blessed Kessog' our Patron Saint before Andrew?" The Scotsman, 9 March 2008. https://www.scotsman.com/news/was-bruces-blessed-kessog-our-patron-saint-andrew-2480540

[121] R.C. Reid and W. F. Cormack, "Two Medieval Crosses at Kirkpatrick-Fleming," *Transactions of the Dumfries and Galloway Natural History and Archaeological Society (TDGNHAS)*, 3038 (1961): 114-127. https://dgnhas.org.uk/sites/default/files/transactions/3038.pdf

[122] "Cathedral Close Tour (Self Guided), Salisbury," GPSMyCity, accessed 31 December 2022. https://www.gpsmycity.com/tours/cathedral-close-tour-5144.html

[123] "GB Ordnance Survey 6-inch to 1 mile, Dumfriesshire, Sheet XXXIV," map, Survey date: 1857, Publication date: 1861. https://maps.nls.uk/view/228777274

[124] "Dictionary, Watchtower," educalingo.com, accessed 17 February 2023. https://educalingo.com/en/dic-en/watchtower

sixteenth century.¹²⁵ It was a pele (peel) tower, which was a fortified house for settlements that did not have a castle, Figure F-17, that were popular on both sides of the border.¹²⁶ When Gillesbie Tower was abandoned 1635-1640,¹²⁷ it would have been replaced by another tower by the remaining Shaw Grahams. It was probably the one downstream of Gillesbie, near Hewk Burn, as shown in the Aglionby Platt.¹²⁸

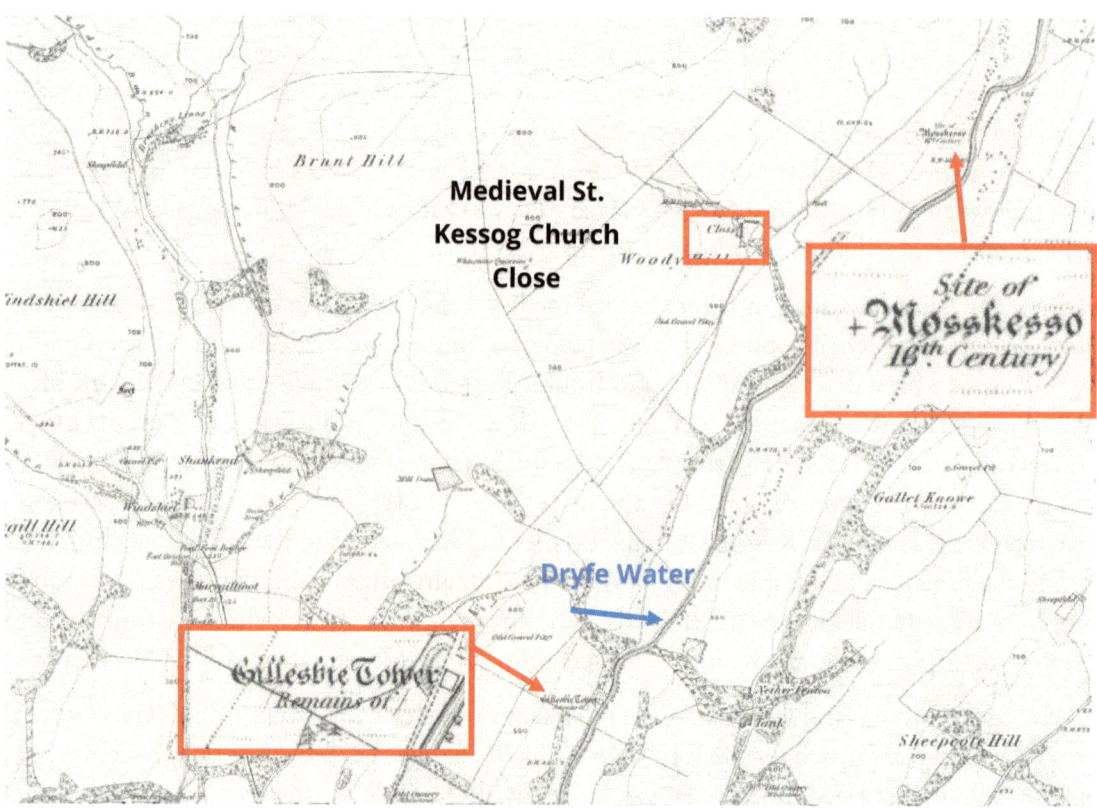

*Figure F-7: Site of Mosskesso Closs/Close, and the site of the Gillesbie Tower Remains Site of Mosskesso Closs/Close, and the site of the Gillesbie Tower Remains*
*GB Ordnance Survey 6-inch to 1 mile, Dumfriesshire, Sheet XXXIV," survey performed 1857, published 1861. ¹²⁷ CC-BY 4.0 Reproduced with the permission of the National Library of Scotland.*

---

¹²⁵ "GB Ordnance Survey, Dumfriesshire."
¹²⁶ "Pele Tower," Co-Curate, accessed 17 February 2023. https://co-curate.ncl.ac.uk/pele-tower/
¹²⁷ "Gillesbie Tower in Annandale North and Dumfries and Galloway," Ancient Monuments, Source ID: SM10433, accessed 4 January 2023. https://ancientmonuments.uk/123372-gillesbie-tower-annandale-north-ward#.Y0dVzXbMJPa
  Figure F-7: GB Ordnance Survey 6 in to mile, performed 1857, published 1861). This figure was derived from a cropping of the region Northwest of Upper Fenton from Ordnance Survey Maps - Six-inch 1st edition, Scotland, 1843-1882, Dumfriesshire, Sheet XXXIV, Survey date: 1857, Publication date: 1861.
  https://maps.nls.uk/view/228777274
¹²⁸ Edward Aglionby, "The Aglionby Platt of the Opposite Border of Scotland to Ye West Marches," map, December 1590, Gatehouse Gazeteer, accessed 27 December 2022. http://www.gatehouse-gazetteer.info/APHome.html

### Where did lands of the Graham "elder line" come from, and what happened to them?

Since the primary records available to us in medieval times are the land charters, tracking the transfers of land from parent to child, and between families as tochers (dowries) is key to completing a tree for the elder line of William de Graham, including all the previously "lost" or overlooked siblings and descendants. **Important to note that even if former church lands were transferred to another family through marriage, the rights of *custodiership* and the corresponding share of the church tithes were retained by the bride's family, hence the reason Lang Will and his brother John would have felt they had an ancestral right to retain a portion of the tithes.**[129] See Appendix D. Through service to the Scottish king and key marriages, by the mid-fourteenth century, the "elder line" Grahams had built a vast empire across southern Scotland and northern England. However, by the end of the century, that empire had dwindled.

Hexhamshire, Tynedale and Redesdale had been under Scottish control prior to 1286. The result of the Scottish Wars of Independence that began circa 1296 was that families were split. Land barons, like the "elder line" Grahams, who owned lands on both sides of the border, were forced to choose sides and surrender their lands on the other side.

In 1314, the English king, Edward II, ordered the Scottish lands of Sir John de Graham, the elder, (d. 1337), forfeited due to his participation on the Scottish side at Battle of Bannockburn.[130] Earlier, his father Sir Nicholas, lost his estates in Wooler and other lands in Tynedale and Northumberland in June 1300 after being a declared a rebel by the Edward I.[131] He did recover the Barony of Dalkeith in 1304.[132] Lastly, the marriages of Sir John "the elder's" five daughters required tochers[133] which resulted in dispersal of large portions of the remaining "elder line" Graham empire.

Mosskesswra (Mosskessen, Mosskesso) lands were part of the Kilbucho estates acquired through the second Sir Henry de Graham's marriage to Christina Fitz Gilbert, daughter of Idonea Comyn and Adam Fitz Gilbert, Lord of Kilbucho. Richer (Richard), Lord Kilbucho, Gilbert's father, retained his rights of custodiership of Hutton Sub Mora (Nether Hutton) and Mosskesswra and related tithes in Corry. The kirk or church of Nether Hutton was subject to the rights of the "mother house" i.e. "mother church" in Sibbaldbie. Christina's brother, Gilbert Fitz Adam Fitz Gilbert, Chaplain of Hutton, sought an exemption to free the church of Hutton from the mother church, Sibbaldbie. In 1193, the pope ordered an inquiry. As a result, Gilbert was turn over control of the

---

[129] Dugald Butler and Herbert Story, *Scottish Cathedrals and Abbeys* (London: A&C Black, Edinburgh: R&R Clark Ltd, 1901), 3. https://www.gutenberg.org/files/21688/21688-h/21688-h.htm

[130] J. Bain, *Calendar of Documents Relating to Scotland preserved in Her Majesty's Public Record Office*, Vol. III (1307-1357) (London, Edinburgh: H.M. General Register House, 1887), 69. https://archive.org/details/calendarofdocume03edin

[131] *Calendar of Patent Rolls, Edward I*: Vol. 3, 1292-1301, ed. H C Maxwell Lyte (London: 1895), 513, 577. https://babel.hathitrust.org/cgi/pt?id=mdp.39015031081154&view=1up&seq=627&q1=graham

[132] Grant G. Simpson and James D. Galbraith, *The Border Papers: Calendar of letters and papers relating to the affairs of the borders of England and Scotland preserved in Her Majesty's Public Record Office*, Vol. V (1108-1516) (London, Edinburgh: H.M. General Register House, 1881), 183. https://archive.org/details/calendarofdocume05grea/page/10/mode/2up

[133] "Tocher, Tochir," *Dictionaries of the Scots Language*, accessed 4 January 2023. https://www.dsl.ac.uk/entry/dost/tocher_n

church of Hutton to Jedburgh Abbey. It is unclear if this order was honored.[134] See Appendix D for explanations of mother and daughter houses.

These rights carried down to the third Sir Henry Graham and subsequently to his heirs. Even when the Kilbucho lands were turned over to Sir William Douglas in 1341[135], the custodiership rights, which included a portion of the tithes, would have been retained by the Grahams. The Border Grahams were in Hutton by right of the third Sir Henry Graham as heir to Richard of Kilbucho and both families track back to the first Graham lords of Tynedale.[136] Gillesbie Grahams are descendants of Lang Will's brother, John, and therefore descend from the same Grahams from old Mosskesswra, which is upper Hutton Parish (a.k.a.: Upper Dryfe in Figure F-9).[137]

> **Did you know?**
> Per old Scots Law, a *fiar* was the absolute possessor of a property as distinguished from a life-renter of it. A fiar retained rights of reversion, the right to resume possession of the land upon termination of the lease.

The Douglases who married sisters Agnes Graham Monfode, and Elizabeth Graham, later acquired the Dalkeith Barony, and styled James Douglas as earl of Morton in 1370.[138] The remaining Grahams still held a lordship of Morton. However, it was a different Morton—the one in Pentland Hills near Dalkeith.[139] The Douglases had attained the Morton lands in Dumfriesshire, the base of their new earldom, from George Dunbar, Earl of March in 1369. When they attained the Dalkeith Barony, they became *fiar* of the old Graham lands,[140] **but did not acquire rights to the tithes or patronages**.

Lang Will Graham and his brother John, as did their grandfather and great uncles in the 1456 petition to James II, Figure F-21, claimed the Hutton lands in "feu and heritage." They claimed the Hutton lands as their families' heritable lands,[141] to include the Hutton church land/income[iii] as carried to them from their father when they claimed the tithes.[142] However, a disagreement ensued, which ultimately resulted in the forfeit of Lang Will's lands along with his kinsman John Corrie in 1509. The

---

[134] Jane Brankstone Thomas, J.C. B. Sharp, and Michael Anne Guido, "A Cumberland Family with Medieval Roots in Scotland and Northern England: A Study Gilbert Fitz Richer and His Descendants," Foundation for Medieval Genealogy, *Foundations* (2008): 360-362. https://fmg.ac/phocadownload/userupload/foundations2/JN-02-05/358Richer.pdf

[135] Sir James Balfour Paul, *The Scots Peerage, Founded on Wood's Edition,* Vol. VI, 196-197.

[136] Jane Brankstone Thomas, J.C. B. Sharp, and Michael Anne Guido, "A Cumberland Family with Medieval Roots in Scotland and Northern England: A Study Gilbert Fitz Richer and His Descendants," 361.

[137] Royal Commission on Historical Manuscripts. *Historical Manuscripts Commission, Report on Manuscripts of Sir Archibald Edmonstone of Duntreath,* Vol. 5 and 6, 77.

[138] R.C. Reid, "The Border Grahams and Their Origins," 89.

[139] *Registrum Honoris de Morton, Volume II: Ancient Charters,* 88, 115, 117-119.

[140] "Fiar," *Dictionaries of the Scots Language,* accessed 4 January 2023. https://www.dsl.ac.uk/entry/snd/fiar_n1

[141] "Feu," *Dictionaries of the Scots Language,* accessed 12 February 2023. https://www.dsl.ac.uk/entry/snd/feu

[142] *Acts of the Lords of Council (Acta Dominorum Concilii),* 4 Oct. 1478 to 15 May 1532, National Records of Scotland, xx, frame 89v. https://www.nrscotland.gov.uk/research/research-guides/research-guides-a-z/court-of-session-records

Gillesbie Grahams, who remained in Scotland, continued litigation regarding the teinds of Hutton parish as late as 1551/1552.[143]

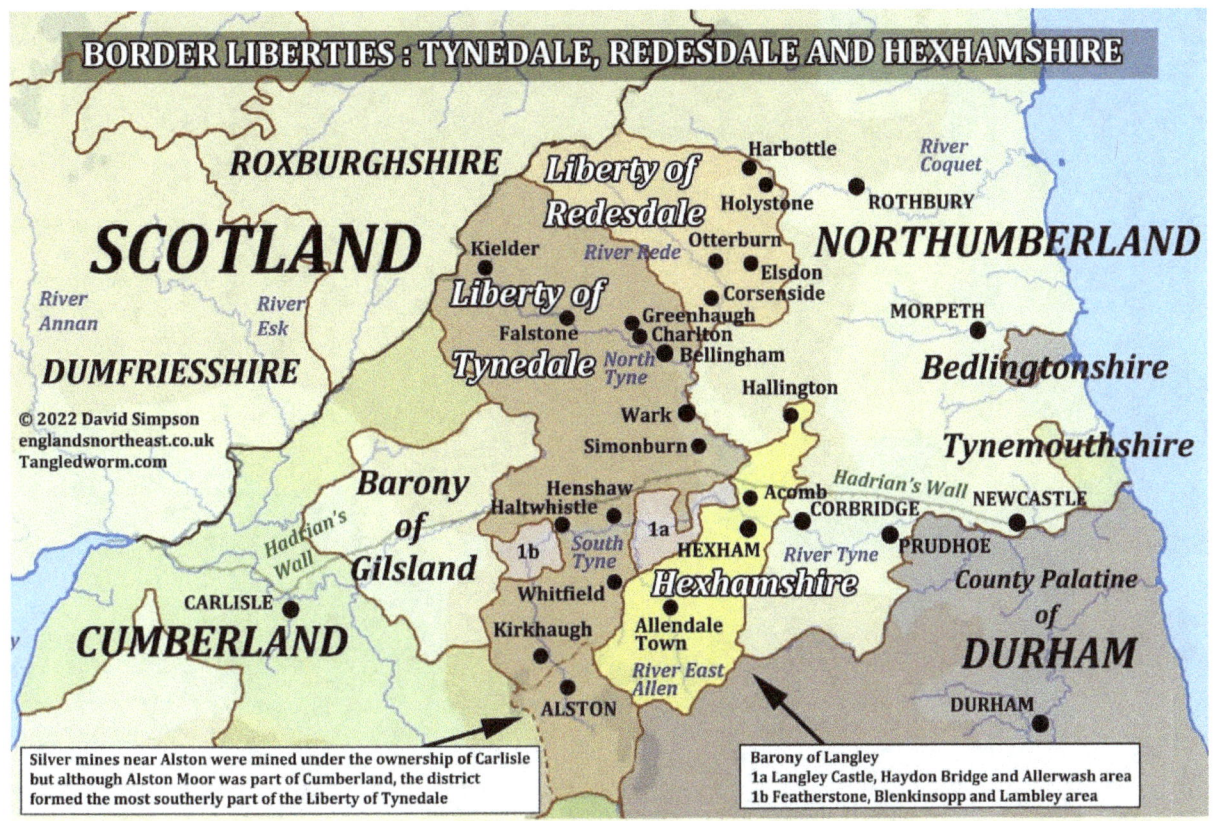

Figure F-8: Border Liberties (Free Territories) Under Scottish Control Prior to 1286.
©David Simpson 2022 englandsnortheast.co.uk. Reprinted with permission of David Simpson.

---

[143] *Acts and Decreets of the Lords of Council and Session*, 26 June 1542 to 26 February 1659, National Records of Scotland, vi, frame 155. https://digital.nls.uk/histories-of-scottish-families/archive/95649035?mode=transcription

*Appendix F: Genealogy of the Border Grahams*

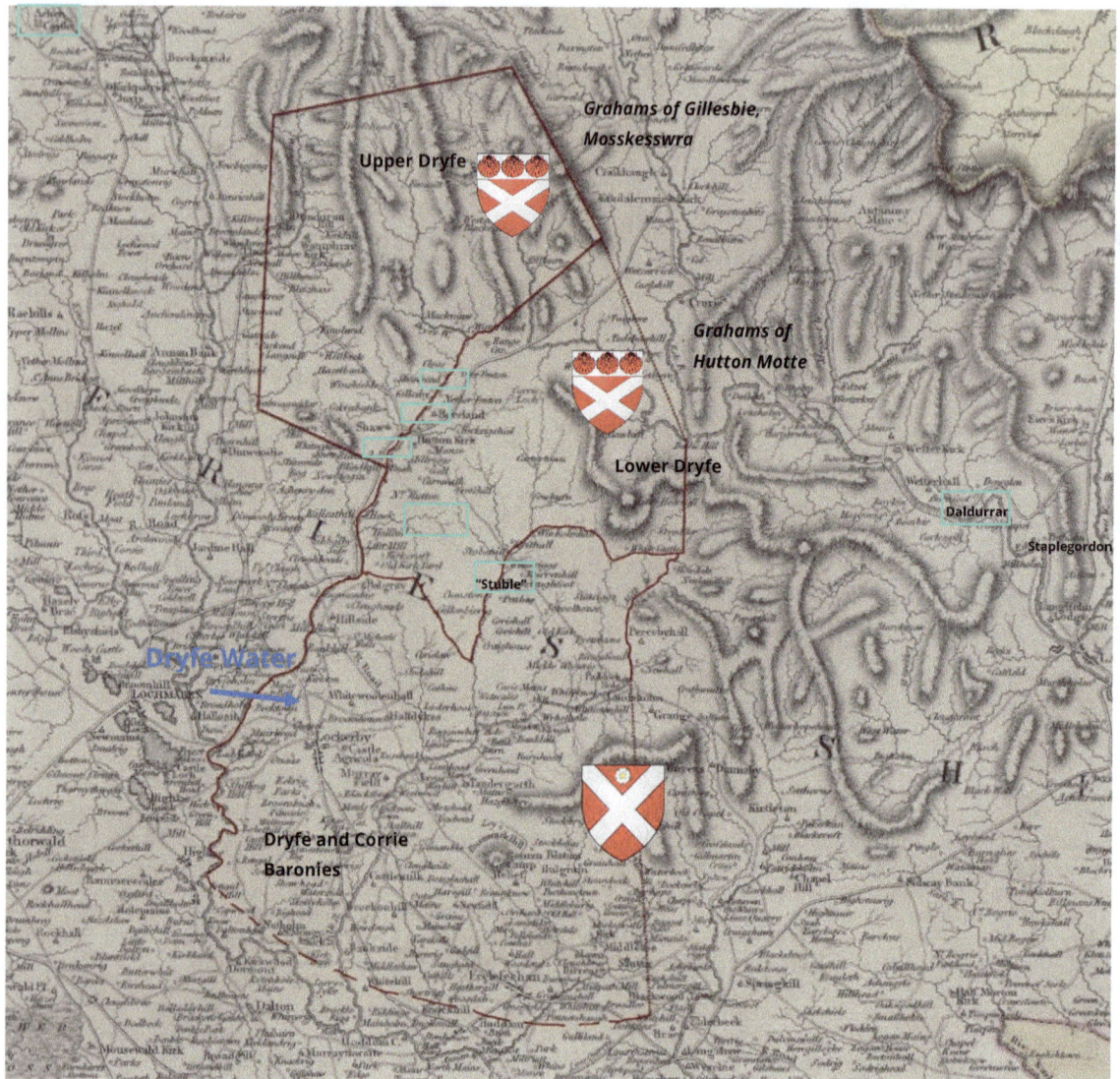

Figure F-9: Approximate Locations of Graham Estates in Hutton Parish. Upper Dryfe defined as "the marches of Eskdale run, the marches of Wamphray to Dryfehead and thence descending by the marches of Eskdalemuir to Patrickshaw," Lower Dryfe, which includes Nether Hutton (Hutton Sub Mora). The "barony" of Mosskesswra stretches below Cumstoun. The environs of Edinburgh, Haddington, Dunse, Kelso, Jedburgh, Hawick, Selkirk, Peebles, Langholm and Annan, making a complete map of the South East district of Scotland / by John Ainslie. Butterworth junt. script. 1821.[144] CC-BY 4.0 Reproduced with the permission of the National Library of Scotland.

## The Knights of Annandale-Who's Who and Where

Note that in Figure F-9 that within the Hutton lands (bordered in red) are the highest points between Roxburgh and Lochmaben. Graham castles would act as control barriers for all traffic between them. Stobohill or "Stuble" is marked in the south west corner of Lower Dryfe. The medieval Mote of Hutton, on the southern edge of Nether Hutton[144] would have been the domestic estate granted to the knight, who became the first lord of Dryfesdale. It embraced all the land between old Corry Kirk in the south and Wamphray Kirk in the north, bounded by the river Annan to the west. It is the mote or motte castle site locations that are our focus in Annandale.

Motte-and-bailey castles were wooden, and were built on elevated mounds called *mottes*. The motte overlooked a walled courtyard called a bailey, and was surrounded by a protective ditch (moat) and a wooden fence called a palisade.[145]

## Motte and Bailey Timber Castles.

From Historic Environment Scotland: Motte and bailey castles in medieval Scotland were initially made of timber. They are "associated with the spread of feudal society, and in Scotland are commonly associated with the attempts by 12th-century rulers to control the land through the settling of an immigrant aristocracy." Finding the surviving remains of these castles is somewhat rare, only 300 mottes have been located in Scotland.[146]

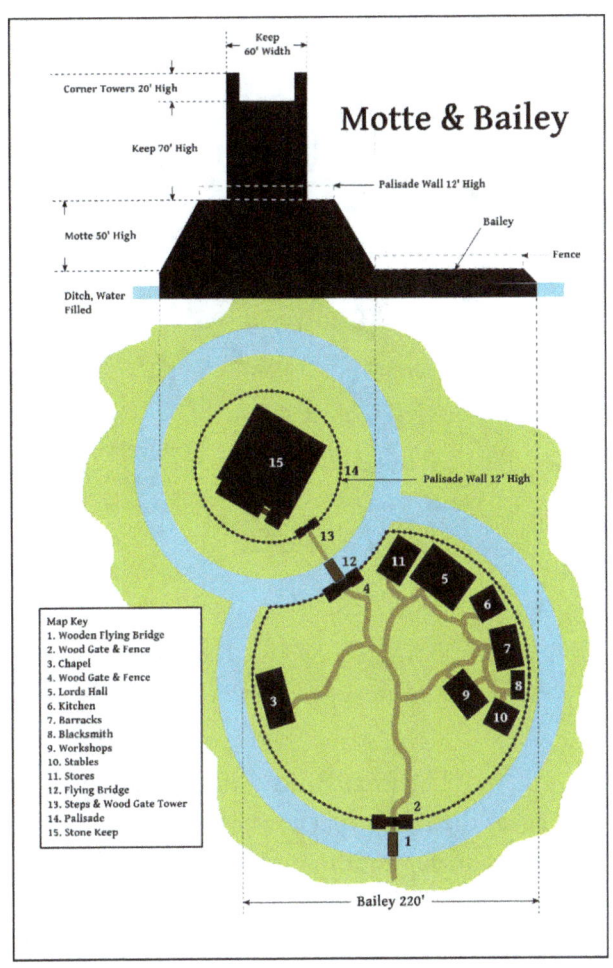

*Figure F-10: Medieval Motte and Bailey Castle Design* [144]
*Used here under* CC0 1.0 *License*

---

[144] Figure F-9: "GB Ordnance Survey 6-inch to 1 mile, Dumfriesshire, Sheet XXXIV," map, Survey date: 1857, Publication date: 1861. https://maps.nls.uk/view/228777274

Figure F-10: Wikimedia Commons contributors, "File:Motte & Bailey.png," *Wikimedia Commons*, accessed 17 April 2023. https://commons.wikimedia.org/w/index.php?title=File:Motte_%26_Bailey.png&oldid=454074656

[145] George Ghidrai, "Motte and Bailey Castles-The Original Castle Design," The World of Castles, accessed 5 January 2023. https://www.castlesworld.com/tools/motte-and-bailey-castles.php

[146] "Hutton Mote-motte," Historic Environment Scotland, accessed 6 January 2023. http://portal.historicenvironment.scot/designation/SM1

Early in his reign, David I gave to his mentor, the first Robert de Brus, the title of first Lord of Annandale. Robert de Brus' mission was to help contain Fergus, Lord of Galloway, and also to help secure the roads into Clydesdale.[147]

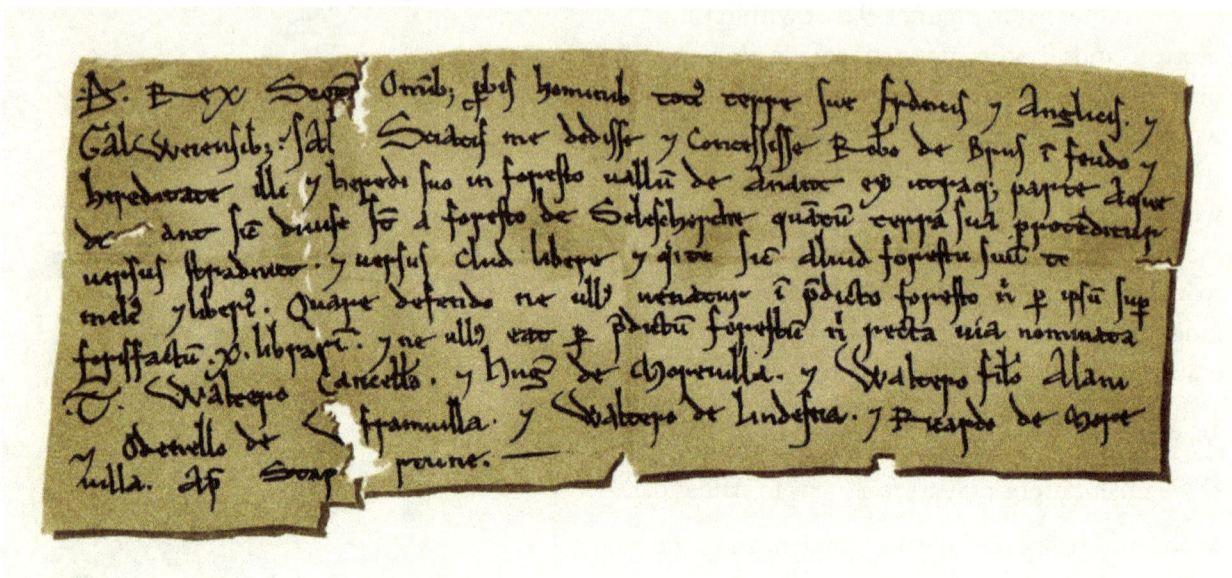

*Figure F-11: "Charter by King David I to Robert Bruce, of the lands of Annandale and Selkirk in Forest, circa 1125-1129," University of Edinburgh, School of History, Classics and Archaeology Teaching Collections* [147]

The Brus/Bruce family established large motte-and bailey castles at Annan and Lochmaben to act as their principal power bases.[148] Robert de Brus had twenty knights' fees in Yorkshire and ten in Annandale,[149] meaning his <u>ten knights would have been assigned individual demesnes around Annandale</u> to provide security. The demesne in this case were the domestic estates belonging to knights which later became baronies[150] for the manor or motte. This motte land was initially just a few acres and was also called a "bordland" or "boreland."[151, iv] The ten knights fees plus the lordship of Annan became eleven motte-and-bailey sites (Figure F-13 and Figure F-14). In addition, the Brus/Bruce family kept a contingent of household knights and officers who were resident in their castles.[v] As the estates

---

[147] Ruth M. Blakely, "The Brus Family in England and Scotland, 1100-c1290" (PhD Thesis, University of Durham, 2000), 165. http://etheses.dur.ac.uk/1594/

Figure F-11: Sir William Fraser Facsimiles of Scottish Charters and Letters, "Charter by King David I to Robert Bruce, of the lands of Annandale and Selkirk in Forest, circa 1125-1129," University of Edinburgh, School of History, Classics and Archaeology Teaching Collections, accessed 19 February 2023. http://collections.shca.ed.ac.uk/items/show/5

[148] "Hutton Mote/Motte," Ancient and Scheduled Monuments: History on the Ground, accessed 12 February 2023. https://ancientmonuments.uk/120722-hutton-mote-motte-annandale-north-ward#.Y7eqLxXMKUl

[149] Ruth M. Blakely, "The Brus Family in England and Scotland, 1100-c 1290," 46, 151.

[150] Sir Thomas Edlyne Tomkins, *The Law Dictionary Explaining the Rise, Progress and Present State of British Law*, Vol. I (London: J and W.T. Clarke, 1835), 25, 109, 110. https://www.google.com/books/edition/The_Law_dictionary_Explaining_the_Rise_P/Q0pKAAAAcAAJ?hl=en&gbpv=1&bsq=demesne

[151] Angus J. L. Winchester, "The Distribution and Significance of 'Bordland' in Medieval Britain," *The Agricultural History Review* 34, no. 2 (1986): 129–139. http://www.jstor.org/stable/40274465

were subdivided to accommodate more families, the mottes/motes were replaced with stone keep castles to improve defenses.[152] When the baronial system was implemented, this number grew to almost thirty sites. (Figure F-13).

By popular tradition, the "Anglo-Norman" knights brought to Annandale by the Bruces were: the Johnstons, Jardines, Maxwells, Kirkpatricks, and Crosbies. They became known as the "Knights of Annandale." They parceled out land amongst themselves, and became Scots loyal to Robert de Brus, Lord of Annandale.[153] However, upon further review, the Maxwells (Maccusweil) were not part of the original knights of Annandale. They were in Roxburghshire in the late twelfth century.[154] The first Maxwell to acquire land in Annandale was Sir John Maxwell who married a Herries heiress in 1548,[155] acquiring her lands in Hoddam.[156]

The son of the first Robert de Brus, Robert de Brus (II),[157] the second lord of Annandale, who died 1194, was the recipient of his father's Annandale estates, and therefore the first Brus who was exclusively Scottish. His father had extensive holdings in Yorkshire as well as Normandy and Scotland. Assuming the Knights of Annandale would be witnesses on Robert de Brus (II) land charters, let's examine the list of signatories.[158] The "non-Bruce" names are: Walter del Bois, Hugh de Corrie, Ivo de Crosby, Richard Fleming, Henry, son of Gerard, William Heriz, Robert of Hoddam, Peter de Humez, Hugh, son of Ingebald, Humphrey de Jardine,[159] Hugh Mauleverer, Adam and Ivo Seton, and Peter de Turp.[160] Some of these witnesses would have been household knights/officers of the Bruces in Annandale or Yorkshire.

## Searching for Bruce's Knights...

### Witnesses on Robert de Brus (II), Second Lord of Annandale, Charters (pre-1194):

1. **Bois/Boys/Bosco.** This family held lands in Middlebie. Walter Bois gave land to Durham Priory, St. Cuthbert's order in the latter half of the twelfth century.[161] The Bois family was of

---

[152] WyrdLight.com, "The Medieval Castle: Four Different Types," History on the Net, accessed 17 February 2023. https://www.historyonthenet.com/medieval-castle

[153] "The Jardine Clan," The Border Reivers, accessed 28 December 2022. http://www.borderreivers.co.uk/Border%20Families/Surnames/Jardine%201.htm

[154] "Maxwell History, Family Crest and Coat of Arms," House of Names, accessed 20 February 2023. https://www.houseofnames.com/maxwell-family-crest

[155] Sir John Maxwell's English relations were hanged for his Scottish marriage and "switching sides" in 1548. As a result, he built Repentance Tower onto Hoddam Castle. Figure F-14.

[156] Alex Maxwell Findlater, "Hoddam, A Medieval Estate in Annandale," *Transactions of the Dumfries and Galloway Natural History and Archaeology Society, (TDGNHAS)* No. 3082 (2008): 79. https://dgnhas.org.uk/sites/default/files/transactions/3082.pdf

[157] Using Dr. Ruth Blakely's notation: Robert de Brus I (d. 1142)--founder of the family; Robert de Brus II (d. c. 1194)—his younger son, recipient of his father's Scottish lands; Robert de Brus III (d. ante 1191)—son of Robert II, who predeceased his father, brother William became heir in his place; Robert de Brus IV (d. c. 1230)—son and heir of William de Brus; Robert de Brus V (d. 1295)—the "Competitor" claimant for the kingship in 1291-92; Robert de Brus VI (d. 1304)—earl of Carrick, father of King Robert I. "The Brus Family in England and Scotland, 1100-c. 1290," 9.

[158] PoMS, "No. 170, person summary," accessed 27 February 2023. https://www.poms.ac.uk/record/person/170/

[159] PoMS, "No. 3879," accessed 27 February 2023. https://www.poms.ac.uk/record/source/3879/

[160] PoMS, "No. 170, person summary," accessed 27 February 2023. https://www.poms.ac.uk/record/person/170/

[161] Ruth M. Blakely, "The Brus Family in England and Scotland, 1100-c 1290," 183, 184.

Norman origin. Several of them appear in the Domesday Book of 1086.[162] The family was prevalent throughout England, until a knight or knights of that surname, accompanied Robert de Brus on his journey to Scotland. Humphrey, Walter and Richard de Bois witnessed charters for Robert de Brus (II). Richard, the youngest of three, was an officer of the Brus household, named in the charter of Annan (1194-1211), using the Latin form "Richard de Bosco."[163] Master Ralph del Bois, persona of Hutton, is named in a 1258 charter where his possession of the Church of Hutton is confirmed for his lifetime. The arms of Sir Andrew de Bosco (Bois) in 1280 were the saltire and chief common to vassals of the lords of Annandale.[164] In 1296, "Sir Humphrey de Bosco, a knight in Annandale" gives homage to Edward I in the Ragman Roll. His seal is a "monster emerging from the waves."[165] The "monster" or "sea dragon" could be a representation of the dragon of St. Michael which would be a tie to the Temple order of the Dumfries Royal Burgh. Figure D-30. His English cousin, Lawrence de Bosco, used a lion rampant over a vanquished dragon.[166] A previous chancellor of the University of Oxford, William de Bosco,[167] is from the same family. The Bois family witnesses Bruce charters as late as 1230, after that it seems that the lands were assimilated into the Middlebie lands of Carruthers.[168]

2. **Corrie/Corry.** The Corries, who initially served in the Bruce household, acquired the lower portion of the Dryfesdale knights fee from their Levington relatives. Their lands included the Templar property Chapel Croft in Hutton.[169] Peter de Corrie witnessed several charters 1177-1204 regarding Ayshire lands to include gifts for Adam Fitz Gilbert and Melrose Abbey.[170] Hugh de Corri, likely Peter's son, witnessed numerous Bruce charters from 1194 to 1218.[171] By the end of the thirteenth century, this family was represented by Henry Graham of Duncorry, a.k.a.: the "fourth" Sir Henry de Graham, son of Ralph Corrie, whose cavalry unit sustained

---

[162] Duchess of Cleveland, *The Battle Abbey Roll*, Vol. I (London: John Murray, 1889), 88. https://books.google.com/books/about/The_Battle_Abbey_Roll.html?id=yV8JAAAAIAAJ

[163] Ruth M. Blakely, "The Brus Family in England and Scotland, 1100-c. 1290," 183.

[164] J.H. Stevenson, *Heraldry in Scotland*, Vol. I (Glasgow: James Maclehose and Sons, 1914), 158. https://ia800300.us.archive.org/14/items/heraldryinscotla01stev/heraldryinscotla01stev.pdf

[165] Bruce A. McAndrew, "The Sigillography of the Ragman Roll," *Proceedings of the Society of Antiquaries of Scotland*, (2000); 684. http://journals.socantscot.org/index.php/psas/article/view/10060

[166] John Robinson, *The Attwood Family* (Sunderland: 1903), 18. https://www.forgottenbooks.com/en/download/TheAttwoodFamily_10485733.pdf

[167] Anthony Wood, *Appendix to the History and antiquities of the Colleges and halls in the University of Oxford* (Oxford, Clarendon Press, 1790), 13. https://archive.org/details/appendixtohistor00wood

[168] Ruth M. Blakely, "The Brus Family in England and Scotland, 1100-c. 1290," 183.

[169] Col. William Rogerson, *Hutton Under the Muir* (Dumfries, Scotland: Dumfries and Galloway Courier and Herald, 1908), 5.

[170] PoMS, "No. 12737, person summary," accessed 27 February 2023. https://www.poms.ac.uk/record/person/12737/

[171] J. Bain, *Calendar of Documents Relating to Scotland preserved in Her Majesty's Public Record Office*, Vol. I, (1108-1272) (London, Edinburgh: H.M. General Register House, 1881), 107, 108, 112, 123, 124. https://www.electricscotland.com/history/records/bain/calendarofdocuments01.pdf

heavy casualties at the Siege of Caerlaverock in 1300.[172] Prior to 1304, Nicholas de Corrie served as seneschal under Robert de Brus (VI).[173]

3. **Crosby/Crosbie.** The first Crosbys in Scotland who may have originated from Cumberland, Ivo de Crosby and his son Richard, witnessed nearly every charter of Robert de Brus (II).[174] Euphemia Crosby married Robert de Brus, second Lord of Annandale.[175]

4. **French.** William Francis "the Frenchman," later known by the surname "French," became a knight when he was transferred to his own Motte of Frenchlands in Moffat in 1218.[176] He likely served as a household knight and came from Northumberland or York with the first Bruce.[177]

5. **Henry, son of Gerard.** This knight witnesses a single charter, regarding the fishery of Blaatwood in the late twelfth century. This indicates that he was a household knight who may not have lived long enough to procreate, as it appears he had no descendants.[178]

6. **Heriz/Herries.** First knight of this surname was William de Heriz, who witnessed a number of early Annandale charters. His descendant, Robert Herries, held the position of Senechal of Annandale during the time of Robert de Brus (V) who died in 1295.[179] William de Heriz was of Anglo-Norman origin, from Cumberland and was founder of the family that held Evandale and later Moffatdale[180] until the sixteenth century.[181] They were benefactors of Wetheral Priory, Holm Cultram Abbey and St. Bees, in Cumberland.

7. **Hoddom/Hoddam.** Men surnamed de Hoddom (Hodelme) served as witnesses to Annandale charters until the time of William de Brus (who died 1211). Their history is summarized in *Peerage* under "Lord Carlyle."[182] They also were known by "de Karliolo" as they descended from Hildred, Sheriff of Carlisle.[183] Odard (Udard) of Carlisle, son of Robert of Carlisle, was issued a fief in Hoddam[vi] after following Robert de Brus to Scotland and was afterwards

---

[172] *Registrum Honoris de Morton, Volume II: Ancient Charters* (Edinburgh: The Bannatyne Club, 1858), 2-3. https://archive.org/details/registrumhonoris02bann/page/n3/mode/2up?ref=ol&view=theater

[173] Ruth M. Blakely, "The Brus Family in England and Scotland, 1100-c 1290," 155.

[174] Ruth M. Blakely, "The Brus Family in England and Scotland, 1100-c. 1290," 188.

[175] Robert Edgar, *An Introduction to the History of Dumfries*, Vol. I (Dumfries: J. Maxwell and Sons, 1915), 167-168, 307. https://archive.org/details/cu31924028091233/page/n173/mode/2up?q=crosbie

[176] J. Bain, *Calendar of Documents Relating to Scotland preserved in Her Majesty's Public Record Office*, Vol. I, (1108-1272) (London, Edinburgh: H.M. General Register House, 1881), 124. https://www.electricscotland.com/history/records/bain/calendarofdocuments01.pdf

[177] PoMS, "No. 5226, person summary," accessed 19 February 2023. https://www.poms.ac.uk/record/person/5226/

[178] PoMS, "No. 3979," accessed 19 February 2023. https://www.poms.ac.uk/record/source/3879/

[179] Ruth M. Blakely, "The Brus Family in England and Scotland, 1100-c 1290," 187-188.

[180] William Fraser, *The Annandale Family Book of the Johnstones, Earls and Marquises of Annandale*, Vol. I (Edinburgh: 1894), xxii-xxiii. https://archive.org/details/annandalefamilv100fras/page/n61/mode/2up?q=hutton

[181] Ruth M. Blakely, "The Brus Family in England and Scotland, 1100-c1290," (Phd Thesis, University of Durham, 2000), 187.

[182] Sir James Balfour Paul, *The Scots Peerage, Founded on Wood's Edition*, Vol. II (Edinburgh: David Douglas, 1905), 369-376. https://archive.org/details/bub_gb_ELEEAAAAIAAJ/page/381/mode/2up?q=auchincass

[183] Alex Maxwell Findlater, "Hoddam, A Medieval Estate in Annandale," *Transactions of the Dumfries and Galloway Natural History and Archaeology Society, (TDGNHAS)* No. 3082 (2008): 77. https://dgnhas.org.uk/sites/default/files/transactions/3082.pdf

known as "Odard of Hodelme,"[184] or "Udard, knight of Hoddam." [185] Odard's son Robert received the lands of Lockerbie from Robert de Brus (II). William de Brus, third lord of Annandale was unhappy about the grant and after a court battle that took place in Westminster, London, Adam de Hodelme, grandson of Odard, quitclaimed Lockerbie to William de Brus[186] and in return received "Kinmount, and Braeansweit and a mill at Polranban on the Water Pow" in October of 1198. His successors supported St. Nicholas Hospital in Carlisle, Wetheral Priory, Abbey of Furness,[187] St. Mary Magdalene's church in Lochmaben,[188] and likely St. Mungo Kirk in Hoddam.[189] By 1189, Udard of Hodelme, the grandson, served as seneschal to Robert de Brus (II).[190]

8. **Hugh, Son of Ingebald.** Ingebald, a knight of Annandale, was granted lands in "Drivesdale"[191] by Robert de Brus, First Lord of Annandale, before 1142.[192] Author R.C. Reid believed these lands were located in the area around the motte at Applegarth [193, 194] in the portion of the Dryfesdale knights fee that became Parish Applegarth.[195]

9. **Humez/Hume/Home.** The Humez family held lands in Hartness in Yorkshire.[196] It does not appear they acquired lands in Annandale until the fifteenth century. Alexander Hume is witness to the old Corry Graham estate of Drumgree changing hands in 1408.[197]

10. **Jardine/Gardin/Gardyne.** There was a William Gardin from Northumberland holding land in Huntingdonshire in the late thirteenth century, so it is possible the Scottish Jardines descended from the Northumberland Jardines.[198]

---

[184] Sir James Balfour Paul, *The Scots Peerage, Founded on Wood's Edition,* Vol. II (Edinburgh: David Douglas, 1905), 371.

[185] PoMS, "No. 7418, person summary," accessed 19 February 2023. https://www.poms.ac.uk/record/person/7418/

[186] Ironically, Castlemilk Castle in Lockerbie became Isabel Graham of Dalkeith's in the fourteenth century by way of her marriage to Walter Stewart, being a dower of his first wife, the late Marjory Bruce, daughter of Robert I.

[187] Sir James Balfour Paul, *The Scots Peerage, Founded on Wood's Edition,* Vol. II (Edinburgh: David Douglas, 1905), 373-376.

[188] PoMS, "No. 3313," accessed 27 February 2023. https://www.poms.ac.uk/record/source/3313/

[189] "St. Mungo and His Galloway Connections," Kirkcudbright History Society, 13 January 2021. https://www.kirkcudbrighthistorysociety.org.uk/wp-content/uploads/2021/02/St-Mungo-talk.pdf

[190] J. Bain, *Calendar of Documents Relating to Scotland preserved in Her Majesty's Public Record Office,* Vol. I, (1108-1272) (London, Edinburgh: H.M. General Register House, 1881), 30. https://www.electricscotland.com/history/records/bain/calendarofdocuments01.pdf

[191] J. Bain, *Calendar of Documents Relating to Scotland preserved in Her Majesty's Public Record Office,* Vol. I, (1108-1272) (London, Edinburgh: H.M. General Register House, 1881), 112.

[192] PoMS, "No. 4635," accessed 19 February 2023. https://www.poms.ac.uk/record/source/4635/

[193] Alastair Maxwell Irving, "Towers, Hall-houses and Timber Superstructures," *The Castles Studies Group,* Journal no. 31 (2017-2018): 261. http://www.castlestudiesgroup.org.uk/CSGJournal2017-18-rev6-131-340Maxwellp.258-275.pdf

[194] "Applegarth Motte," Canmore-National Record of the Historic Environment, accessed 7 January 2023. https://canmore.org.uk/site/66813/applegarth-motte

[195] R.C. Reid "The Monastery at Applegarth," *Transactions of the Dumfries and Galloway Natural History and Archaeological Society, (TDGNHAS),* No. 3035 (1961): 158. https://dgnhas.org.uk/sites/default/files/transactions/3035.pdf

[196] Ruth M. Blakely, "The Brus Family in England and Scotland, 1100-c 1290," 189-190.

[197] William Fraser, *The Annandale Family Book of the Johnstones, Earls and Marquises of Annandale,* Vol. I, 12.

[198] Ruth M. Blakely, "The Brus Family in England and Scotland, 1100-c 1290," 189.

11. **Levington (Boyville).** Richard, Robert and William "Levinton" witness Annandale charters from 1210 to 1218.[199] This family was of Norman origin and had extensive holdings in Cumberland. Kirklinton was their base.[200] Phil Graham believes they originally held all of Annandale before the arrival of the Bruces and gradually transferred estates to the Bruce knights. Some of the transfers were via marriage, particularly when the family ran out of male heirs.[201] The patriarch of the Levingtons was Richer de Boyville who was granted lands in Cumberland by Henry I in the mid-twelfth century.[202] Richer was the father of Adam and Gilbert Fitz Richer, grandfather of Adam Fitz Gilbert,[203] great-grandfather of Christina Fitz Gilbert who married the second Sir Henry de Graham.[204] See Figure 38.

> **Phil's Note:**
> The Bruces did not establish a monastic house in Annandale. Annandale Plantation recruitment would have originated with the Bruce foundation of Guisburn/Gisborough Priory in Yorkshire. The six southern parishes of Annan assigned to Guisburgh Priory may account for the lack of Motte sites south of Lochmaben and east of Annan.

12. **Mauleverer.** This family was from Yorkshire. Both a Henry and Roger Mauleverer[205] are witnesses to Adam de Brus (II), Peter de Brus (I) and Peter de Brus (II) charters in Hartness.[206] Sir Humphrey de "Malleverer" is a witness to several charters in Annandale.[207] With the exception of a gift of a saltpan in Rainpatrick from their fellow knights circa 1207,[208] the Mauleverers did not possess lands in Annandale. The family continued to work for the Bruces as household knights, as demonstrated when John Mauleverer gets a pension when Bruce the King dies in 1329.[209]

---

[199] J. Bain, *Calendar of Documents Relating to Scotland preserved in Her Majesty's Public Record Office,* Vol. I, (1108-1272) (London, Edinburgh: H.M. General Register House, 1881), 107, 123, 124.

[200] Dr David B. Boles, "A Partly Hypothetical Pedigree of the Early Boyle Family of Kelburn, Ayrshire, Scotland," The Genealogist's Craft, 9 April 2020. https://bolesbooksblog.wordpress.com/tag/boyville/

[201] Jane Brankstone Thomas, J.C. B. Sharp, and Michael Anne Guido, "Further Addendum to the Five Odards: Eva de Hodelholm and her Step Children," Foundation for Medieval Genealogy, *Foundations* (2008): 360-362. https://fmg.ac/phocadownload/userupload/foundations3/JN-03-03/267Eva.pdf

[Phil's Note -blurb on monastic house of the Bruces] "Guisborough Priory," Moors Knowledge, accessed 19 February 2023. http://www.yorkshiremoors.co.uk/gazetteer/guisborough_priory.html

[202] Rev. James Wilson, "Some Extinct Cumberland Families," *The Ancestor Quarterly Review*, No. 3, (Oct 1902):80. https://archive.org/details/ancestorquarterl03unse/page/n5/mode/2up?q=levington

[203] J. Bain, *Calendar of Documents Relating to Scotland preserved in Her Majesty's Public Record Office,* Vol. I, (1108-1272) (London, Edinburgh: H.M. General Register House, 1881), 176.

[204] Jane Brankstone Thomas, J.C. B. Sharp, and Michael Anne Guido, "Further Addendum to the Five Odards: Eva de Hodelholm and her Step Children," Foundation for Medieval Genealogy, *Foundations* (2008): 360-362. https://fmg.ac/phocadownload/userupload/foundations3/JN-03-03/267Eva.pdf

[205] The surname Mauleverer might be the origin of the surname Maule.

[206] Ruth M. Blakely, "The Brus Family in England and Scotland, 1100-c. 1290," 192.

[207] J. Bain, *Calendar of Documents Relating to Scotland preserved in Her Majesty's Public Record Office,* Vol. I, (1108-1272) (London, Edinburgh: H.M. General Register House, 1881), 108, 112, 123, 124, 310. https://www.electricscotland.com/history/records/bain/calendarofdocuments01.pdf

[208] PoMS, "No. 3060," accessed 19 February 2023. https://www.poms.ac.uk/record/source/3060/

[209] John Stuart and George Burnett, *Rotuli Scaccarii Regum Scotorum,The Exchequer Rolls of Scotland* Vol. I (Edinburgh: H.M. Register House, 1878), 208-209. https://www.familysearch.org/search/catalog/192327?availability=Family%20History%20Library

13. **Richard le Fleming.**[vii] Richard was granted lands in Rainpatrick by Robert de Brus (II) between 1194 and 1200.[210] Fleming later served as chamberlain to William de Brus, third lord of Annandale[211] and may have assumed control of the Annan knight's fee when the Bruces moved to Lochmaben about the year 1200 when Annan Motte was damaged by flooding.[212]

14. **Seton.** The Setons held lands in Hartness in Yorkshire and Cumberland. While the Setons signed some charters for Robert de Brus (II) (before 1194), there isn't evidence of any of them holding land in Annandale until 200 years later.[213]

15. **Turp.** The Turps were tenants of the Bruces in Hartness in Yorkshire and Cumberland, but not in Annandale.[214] Turpin, the Culdee Bishop of Brechin (1178-1198), magister for William the Lion,[215] may be a related to the Turps in the Bruce household.[216]

**Other Candidate Knights of Annandale (or Knights who Later Shared Subdivisions of the Original Ten Knights Fee Estates):**

16. **Carnotto of that Ilk.** Patrick Carnotto, knight, had confirmation of a pension previously granted in 1329,[217] implying he had long served the Bruces as a household knight. Sir Adam de Carnoto witnessed a few Bruce Annandale charters between 1215 and 1245.[218]

17. **Corrie.** The Corries likely descended from a local family who derived their surname from the surrounding area. They were keepers of the Bruce castles,[219] were also heirs to the Levingtons and inherited Lower Dryfesdale that became the Corrie Barony.[220] The first knight surnamed Corrie was Hugh de Corrie who was present at William the Lion's court (1165-1214) and who witnessed over ten charters relating to the Bruces of Annandale.[221] The timing indicates the Grahams gained control of parts of the Corrie barony (Little Hutton/Lower Dryfe Figure F-9) through a marriage of a Graham daughter to Ralph de Corrie in the thirteenth century.[222]

---

[210] PoMS, "No. 8010, person summary," accessed 27 February 2023. https://www.poms.ac.uk/record/person/8010/
[211] PoMS, "No. 8010, person summary," accessed 19 February 2023. https://www.poms.ac.uk/record/person/8010/
[212] "Motte & Bailey," Annan, The History Town, accessed 6 January 2023. https://www.annanthehistorytown.org/defensive-annan-2/motte-bailey/
[213] Ruth M. Blakely, "The Brus Family in England and Scotland, 1100-c 1290," 189-190.
[214] Ruth M. Blakely, "The Brus Family in England and Scotland, 1100-c 1290," 189-190.
[215] Rev. John Dowden, *The Bishops of Scotland* (Glasgow: John Maclehose and Sons, 1912), 173-176, 194. https://archive.org/details/bishopsofscotlan00dowdrich/page/194/mode/2up?q=turpin
[216] Since Culdee priests were permitted to marry, and their positions were hereditary, the church was a "family business."
[217] John Stuart and George Burnett, *Rotuli Scaccarii Regum Scotorum, The Exchequer Rolls of Scotland* Vol. I (Edinburgh: H.M. Register House, 1878), 208-209.
[218] J. Bain, *Calendar of Documents Relating to Scotland preserved in Her Majesty's Public Record Office*, Vol. I, (1108-1272) (London, Edinburgh: H.M. General Register House, 1881), 309, 310. https://www.electricscotland.com/history/records/bain/calendarofdocuments01.pdf
[219] J. E. Corrie, *Records of the Corrie Family, 802-1899 A.D.* (London: Mitchell and Hughes, 1899), vi, 130-134, 139, 156.
[220] J. Bain, *The Border Papers: Calendar of letters and papers relating to the affairs of the borders of England and Scotland preserved in Her Majesty's Public Record Office*, Vol. II, 6-8.
[221] Christopher Johnston, PhD, "The Early History of the Corries of Annandale," *Transactions of the Dumfries and Galloway Natural History and Archaeological Society (TDGNHAS)* No. 3001 (1913): 86-87. https://dgnhas.org.uk/sites/default/files/transactions/3001.pdf
[222] J. E. Corrie, *Records of the Corrie Family, 802-1899 A.D.*, 133.

Ralph's son, the fourth Sir Henry de Graham, may have been the knight of Annandale in possession of Gillenbie of Parish Hutton and Corrie in 1296.[223]

18. **Dunwoodie/Dinwoodie** Place-derived name from a hill fort named "Dunwoodie" in the northern tip of Parish Applegarth (possibly in the knights fee of Wamphraydale). Figure F-14. "Dun" is Gaelic for "fort."[224] Alan English of Dunwoodie, served as Senechal of Annandale [225] and witnessed numerous early Annandale charters prior to 1212, implying he served the Bruce household.[226] The chapelry at Dinwoodie later became a Templar property.[227]

19. **Graham**. The elder line Grahams inherited Hutton and Upper Dryfe from a former chaplain of Hutton, Gilbert Fitz Adam Fitz Gilbert, a Levington heir. Gilbert may have also been related to the Bosco/Bois family who had acquired church lands in Hutton. Richard de Bosco served as an officer in the Bruce household in the late twelfth century. He is a witness on the charter of Annan (1194-1214).[228] Master Ralph del Bois, persona of Hutton, is named in a 1258 charter where his possession of the Church of Hutton is confirmed for his lifetime.[229] Master Richard and Master Ralph of Braid, suspected Graham cousins, appear together as witnesses on a 1255 Dunfermline charter,[230] and are likely Temple Hospital representatives.

20. **Jardine**. One surviving Annandale charter from between 1150 and 1194 shows a William de Jardine as a witness.[231] Humphrey de Jardine witnessed nine charters for the Bruces from 1188-1242.[232] The Scottish Jardines may descend from the Northumberland Jardines. If so, they may be one of the original ten Knights of Annandale, if not, household knights of the Bruce family.

21. **Johnstone**. The first of this surname was Gilbert son of John, later called "Gilbert de Joneston." He got Wormaby and a half carucate of land in Annan from Udard of Hoddam (1194-1214).[233] Phil Graham believes the surname may be derived from Saint John,[234] written "St. John."[235]

---

[223] PoMS, "No. 7591," accessed 27 February 2023. https://www.poms.ac.uk/record/source/7591/

[224] Thomas Somerill, "An Attempt at a Brief Family History of the Lairds of Dinwiddie," 1929, Electric Scotland, accessed 27 February 2023. https://electricscotland.com/webclans/dtog/dinwiddie4.html

[225] Thomas Somerill, "An Attempt at a Brief Family History of the Lairds of Dinwiddie," 1929, Electric Scotland, accessed 27 February 2023.

[226] PoMS, "No. 8014, person summary," accessed 27 February 2023 https://www.poms.ac.uk/record/person/8014/

[227] "Clan Carruthers: The Carruthers Chiefs and the Templar Link," Clan Carruthers Society International, 12 September 2020. https://clancarrutherssociety.org/2020/09/12/clan-carruthers-the-carruthers-chiefs-and-the-templar-link/

[228] J. Bain, *Calendar of Documents Relating to Scotland preserved in Her Majesty's Public Record Office*, Vol. I, (1108-1272) (London, Edinburgh: H.M. General Register House, 1881), 108.

[229] The Chapelry of Hutton may have still been a hereditary position in the latter half of thirteenth century.

[230] PoMS, "No. 5671," accessed 27 February 2023. https://www.poms.ac.uk/record/source/5671/

[231] PoMS, "No. 11323, person summary," accessed 27 February 2023. https://www.poms.ac.uk/record/person/11323/

[232] PoMS, "No. 7965, person summary," accessed 27 February 2023. https://www.poms.ac.uk/record/person/7965/

[233] J. Bain, *Calendar of Documents Relating to Scotland preserved in Her Majesty's Public Record Office*, Vol. I, (1108-1272) (London, Edinburgh: H.M. General Register House, 1881), 107, 123, 124.

[234] PoMS, "No. 20901, person summary," accessed 27 February 2023. https://www.poms.ac.uk/record/person/20901/

[235] Grant G. Simpson and James D. Galbraith, *The Border Papers: Calendar of letters and papers relating to the affairs of the borders of England and Scotland preserved in Her Majesty's Public Record Office*, Vol. V (1108-1516) (London, Edinburgh: H.M. General Register House, 1881), 221.

**22. Kirkpatrick.** Humphrey Kirkpatrick served as Senechal of Annandale (between 1215 and 1245).[236] He received lands called Colquhoun in Luss between 1225 and 1251.[237] Senechal was a position Dr. Blakely says was rotated amongst the household knights of the Bruces.[238] The earliest surviving charter[239] naming a Kirkpatrick was signed by William de Brus between 1194 and 1214. (Figure F-12) [240] granting Ivo Kirkpatrick lands in "feu" of "Pennersax" (Pennersaughs, near Ecclefechan) and the villa of Blackwood (Blaatwood).[241] There is some dispute whether Ivo Kirkpatrick or Roger Kirkpatrick was the first Kirkpatrick. Roger Kirkpatrick witnessed several charters in Annandale as early as 1194[242] to include a 1218 charter signed by Robert de Brus (IV) granting Roger Crispin the lands of Cuoculeran.[243] Given the years of the Ivo and Roger charters are imprecise ranges that overlap, hard to confirm who came first. In addition, an update to Alexander Nisbet's *System of Heraldry* published in 1892, indicated there was an earlier charter that Roger Kirkpatrick witnessed for the first Robert de Brus who died 1141.[244] I've not been able to verify this. If true, then Roger was the first Kirkpatrick. By 1544, the Border Grahams had acquired Blaatwood, Redkirk and Renpatrick/ Rampatrick, from John Carruthers of Holmendis.[245]

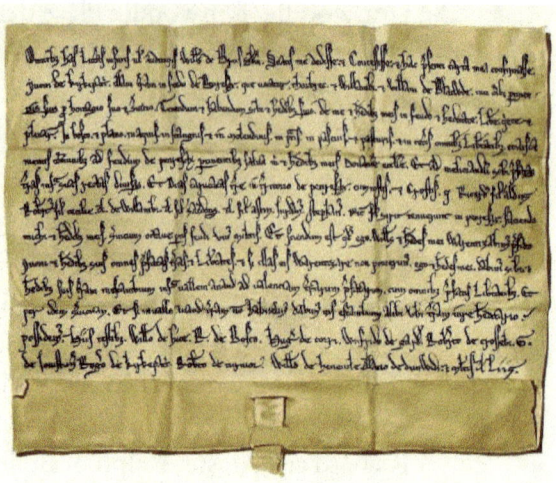

*Figure F-12: "Charter by William de Bruce to Ivo de Kirkpatrick, of the lands in Pennersax, called Thorbrec, and Williambi and Blacwde, 1194-1214," University of Edinburgh, School of History, Classics and Archaeology Teaching Collections.*[240]

---

[236] J. Bain, *Calendar of Documents Relating to Scotland preserved in Her Majesty's Public Record Office,* Vol. I, (1108-1272) (London, Edinburgh: H.M. General Register House, 1881), 308.

[237] PoMS, "No. 6171, person summary," accessed 27 February 2023. https://www.poms.ac.uk/record/person/6171/

[238] Ruth M. Blakely, "The Brus Family in England and Scotland, 1100-c 1290," 155, 192-193.

[239] Per Dr Ruth Blakey, the Blaatwood fishery charter granted to an "Ivo" in 1190 attributed to Ivo Kirkpatrick by some authors, may have actually been for Ivo de Crosby.

[240] Figure F-12: Sir William Fraser Facsimiles of Scottish Charters and Letters, "Charter by William de Bruce to Ivo de Kirkpatrick, of the lands in Pennersax, called Thorbrec, and Williambi and Blacwde, 1194-1214," University of Edinburgh, School of History, Classics and Archaeology Teaching Collections, accessed February 19, 2023. http://collections.shca.ed.ac.uk/items/show/25

[241] PoMS, "No. 4645, person summary," accessed 16 February 2023. https://www.poms.ac.uk/record/person/4645/

[242] J. Bain, *Calendar of Documents Relating to Scotland preserved in Her Majesty's Public Record Office,* Vol. I, (1108-1272) (London, Edinburgh: H.M. General Register House, 1881), 107, 108, 124.

[243] Sir William Fraser Facsimiles of Scottish Charters and Letters, "Charter by Robert de Brus to Roger Crispin of the lands of Cuoculeran c. 1218," *School of History, Classics and Archaeology Teaching Collections,* University of Edinburgh, accessed 27 February 2023. http://Col.lections.shca.ed.ac.uk/items/show/36

[244] Andrew Ross and Francis Grant, *Alexander Nisbet's Heraldic Plates Originally Intended for His System of Heraldry,* (Edinburgh: George Waterson & Sons, 1892), 42. https://www.familysearch.org/library/books/viewer/448766/?offset=0#page=1&viewer=picture&o=&n=0&q=

[245] R.C. Reid, "The Border Grahams and Their Origins," *Transactions of the Dumfries and Galloway Natural History and Archaeological Society (TDGNHAS)* No. 3038 (1961): 106-107. https://dgnhas.org.uk/sites/default/files/transactions/3038.pdf

23. **Levington/(Boyville).** The Levingtons were descendants of Richard de Boyville, a Norman and were based out of Kirklinton in Cumberland. Robert de Levington witnesses a William de Brus Annandale charter between 1194 and 1214. William de Levington witnesses one for Robert de Brus (IV) in 1218.[246]

24. **Loccard/Lockhart.** Simon Loccard, the earliest person of someone by that surname in Scotland, held land at The Lee and at Symington in Kyleshire. He witnessed William I's charter of Annandale to Robert de Brus at Lochmaben circa 1166.[247] His son, Malcom Loccard, witnessed Annandale charters from 1194 to 1214.[248] Loccard is a Flemish name that Lockerbie was named for.[249] Author Lauren Toorian states: "The *ecclesia de uilla Symonis Loccard*, also *de Symondstone*, which became the parish church of Symington [in Clydesdale], was circa 1189 the subject of controversy between Simon Loccard and the monks of Kelso (territory encroachment)." Perhaps "Symondstone" was actually the Simonburn in Tynedale, and Simon was a Graham relative migrating from north from Tynedale?

25. **Pearsby.** First known person in Annandale by the surname Pearsby, David de Pearsby, witnesses a charter signed by Laurence Avenel, between 1260 and 1267, gifting 40 shillings annually to Glasgow Cathedral.[250] Richard de Pearsby was taken prisoner at the Battle of Dunbar in 1296.[251]

**Connections to Cumberland.**

Phil Graham and Dr. Ruth Blakely note that other families may have originated from Cumberland, including the Carlisles, Hoddoms and Crosbies.[viii] Dr. Blakely writes: "Continuing links of the Bruses and their Annandale tenants with religious foundations in Cumberland demonstrates the affinity between the two regions, which was reinforced during David I's occupation of Carlisle between 1135 and 1153."[252] See Appendix D.

---

[246] J. Bain, *Calendar of Documents Relating to Scotland preserved in Her Majesty's Public Record Office,* Vol. I, (1108-1272) (London, Edinburgh: H.M. General Register House, 1881), 107, 123, 124.

[247] Lauren Toorians, "Flemish Settlements in Twelfth-Century Scotland," *Revue belge de philologie et d'histoire,* Tome 74 fasc. 3-4, (1996): 667, 684, 689. https://www.academia.edu/33460121/Lauran_Toorians_Flemish_Settlements_in_Twelfth_Century_Scotland

[248] J. Bain, *Calendar of Documents Relating to Scotland preserved in Her Majesty's Public Record Office,* Vol. I, (1108-1272) (London, Edinburgh: H.M. General Register House, 1881), 107, 108.

[249] Ruth M. Blakely, "The Brus Family in England and Scotland, 1100-c1290," (Phd Thesis, University of Durham, 2000), 184.

[250] PoMS, "No. 4331," accessed 27 February 2023. https://www.poms.ac.uk/record/source/4331/

[251] PoMS, "No. 7870," accessed 27 February 2023. https://www.poms.ac.uk/record/source/7870/

[252] Ruth M. Blakely, "The Brus Family in England and Scotland, 1100-c. 1290," 184-190.

Studying each Motte/Mote castle site, who got them and how they were destroyed during the Wars of Independence will help trace the knights of Annandale and their connection to the Border Grahams. With the subdividing of the estates over time, finding the original motte sites is a challenge as evidence has been destroyed over the centuries. Some Mottes/Motes were replaced with multiple castles when estates were subdivided. The castles of the knights of Annandale that have been unearthed correspond to the "Timber Castles" marked in Figure F-13.

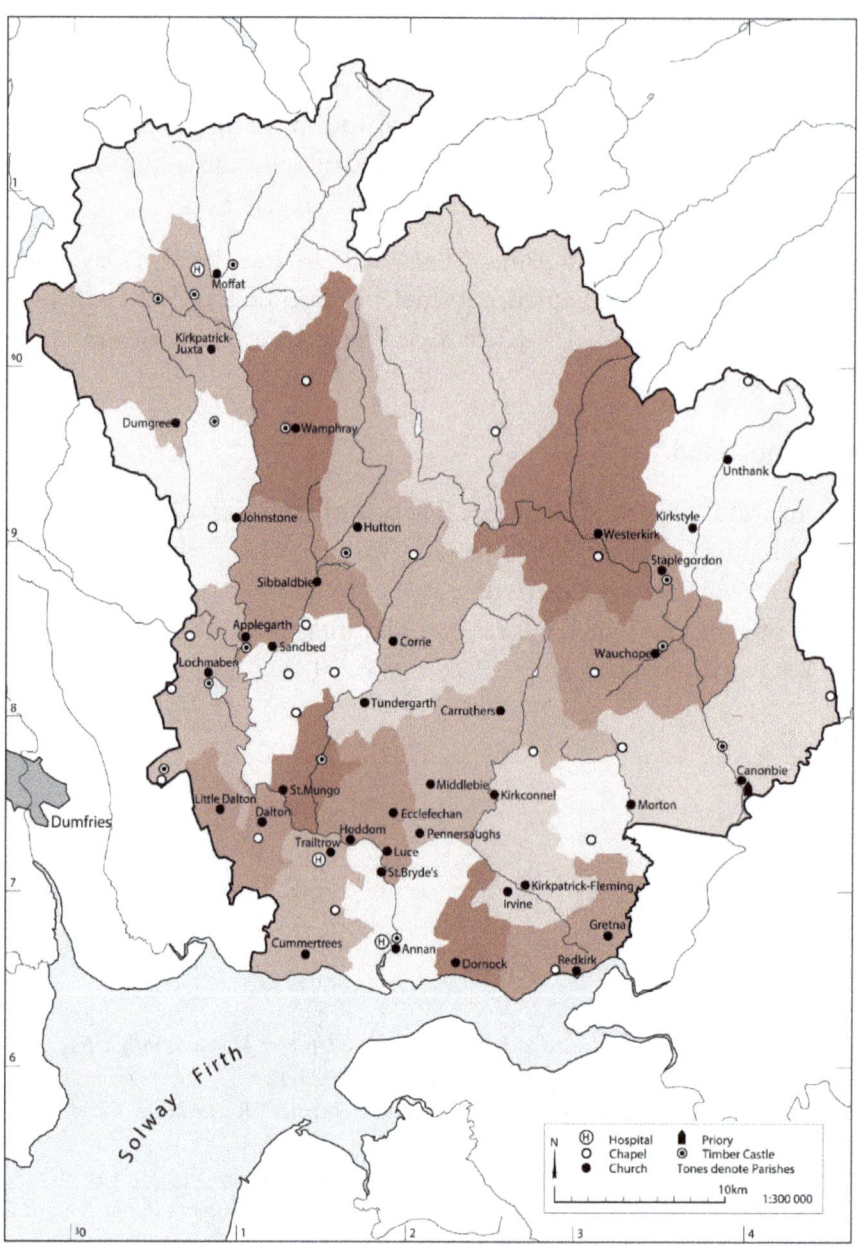

*Figure F-13: Map of Annandale Churches, Chapels, Priories, Hospitals and Timber Castles which correspond to the estates of the original Knights of Annandale © Crown Copyright: HES*
*https://canmore.org.uk/collection/1917793*

# Appendix F: Genealogy of the Border Grahams

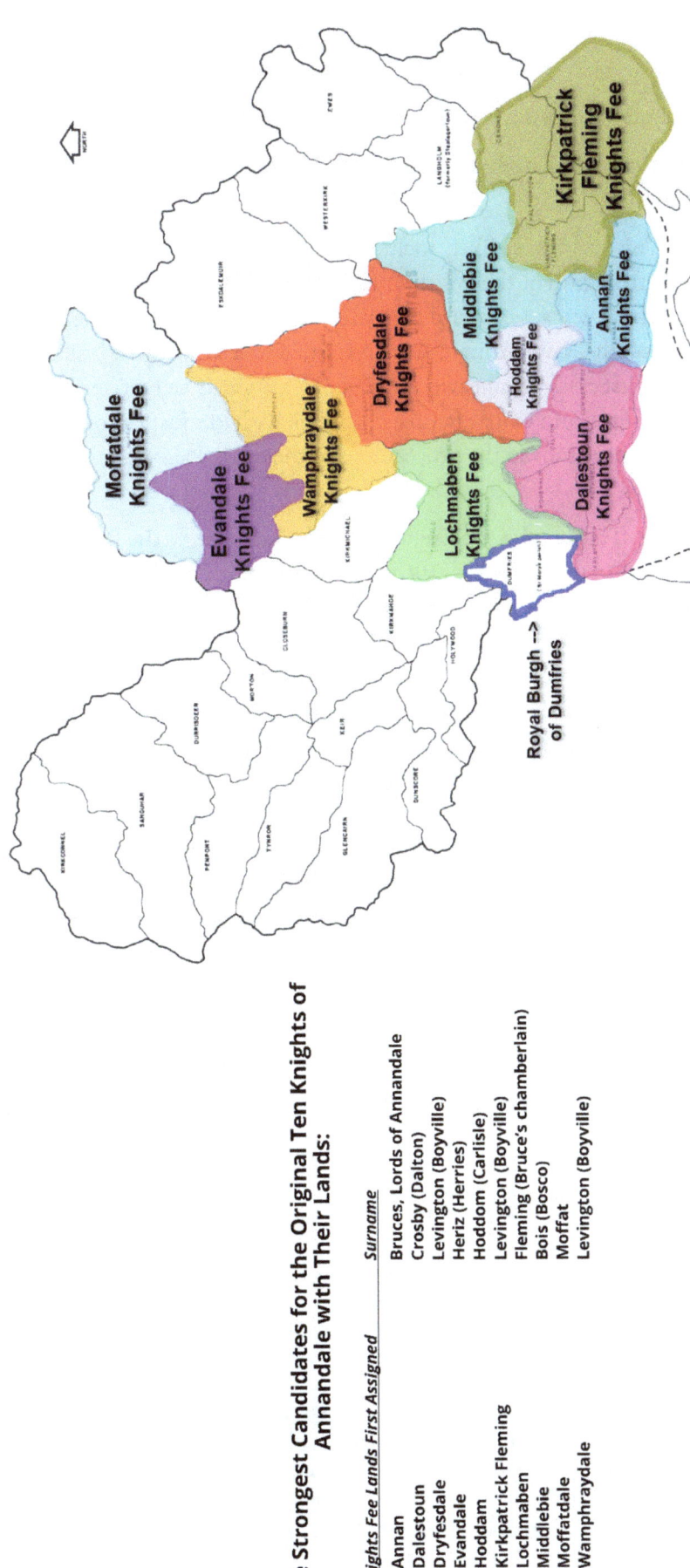

## The Strongest Candidates for the Original Ten Knights of Annandale with Their Lands:

| Knights Fee Lands First Assigned | Surname |
|---|---|
| 1. Annan | Bruces, Lords of Annandale |
| 2. Dalestoun | Crosby (Dalton) |
| 3. Dryfesdale | Levington (Boyville) |
| 4. Evandale | Heriz (Herries) |
| 5. Hoddam | Hoddom (Carlisle) |
| 6. Kirkpatrick Fleming | Levington (Boyville) |
| 7. Lochmaben | Fleming (Bruce's chamberlain) |
| 8. Middlebie | Bois (Bosco) |
| 9. Moffatdale | Moffat |
| 10. Wamphraydale | Levington (Boyville) |

Figure F-14: *Amended Map of the Original Ten Knights Fees of Annandale. With Author's annotations, and with gratitude to Aberdeen & North-East Scotland FHS for kind permission to reproduce their copyright map of Dumfriesshire.*

### Searching for the Lands Assigned to the First Knights of Annandale...

#### Proposed List of the Original Ten Knights Fee Estates (Figure F-14)[253] Assigned by Robert de Brus, First Lord of Annandale

1. **Annan Knights Fee.** This knights fee likely included what became the Parishes of Annan, Dornock and the western section of the Parish of Kirkpatrick-Fleming (the part that contained Rainpatrick). Annan Motte was a motte and bailey timber castle built by the de Brus family between 1124 and 1141 on the River Annan. Annan Castle was a stone castle built about 1245, about 45 years after the first castle was heavily damaged in a flood. The first hereditary stewards of Annandale, the Carruthers and Corrie families, would have had a justice court in the Motte of Annan, until flood damage moved the proceedings to the castle at Lochmaben in the year 1200.[254]

2. **Daletoun Knights Fee.** This knights fee likely included what became the Parishes of Mouswald, Caerlaverlock, Cummertrees, Dalton and Ruthwell. The first Crosbys in Scotland who likely originated from Cumberland, Ivo de Crosby and his son Richard, witnessed nearly every charter of Robert de Brus (II). The Crosbys held lands in Cummertrees as well as the "wood of Stableton" in nearby Annan.[255] While it appears that the Crosbys worked in the Bruce household, there were more than one of them, so possibly one was granted the Daletoun knights fee. Crosby knights' charters remained near Annan (fishing rights between Blaatwood and the Esk—Stableton in Dornock Parish).[256] The first Crosby came from Cumberland to join Bruce, Ivo de Crosby,[257] and was part of the household of the Motte of Annan. Adam de Crosby traded his lands in Cumertrees for lands in Gretna, and the Crosbys then served as keepers of the Bruce memorials in Gretna starting around 1204 to 1207.[258] Per Phil Graham, the Crosbys later migrated to Beattock in Moffat and Coats Motte became theirs, along with the hospital land.[259]

3. **Dryfesdale Knights Fee.** This knights fee likely included what became the Parishes of Dryfesdale, Applegarth (except the Northern tip that included Dinwoodie Hill), and Hutton and Corrie. The entire Dryfesdale enfeoffment was first held by a branch of the

---

[253] Figure F-14: Aberdeen and North East Scotland FHS, "The County of Dumfries," map, accessed 18 April 2023. http://www.scotlandsfamily.com/parish-map-dumfries.htm

[254] "Motte & Bailey," Annan, The History Town, accessed 6 January 2023. https://www.annanthehistorytown.org/defensive-annan-2/motte-bailey/

[255] Ruth M. Blakely, "The Brus Family in England and Scotland, 1100-c 1290," 188.

[256] PoMS, "No. 1434, Ivo of Crosby person summary," accessed 6 January 2023. https://www.poms.ac.uk/record/person/1434/

[257] PoMS, "No. 3879," accessed 27 February 2023. https://www.poms.ac.uk/record/source/3879/

[258] PoMS, "No. 4907," accessed 27 February 2023. https://www.poms.ac.uk/record/source/4907/

[259] Phil Graham believes that the Logan Hospital in Gretna and Coats Hospital in Moffat were hostels for travelers, similar to the New Hospital called "Annan Spital" at the river crossing and the Dumfries Spital at the old ford. These are St. John of Jerusalem Spitals. https://maps.nls.uk/view/00000402#zoom=5&lat=3489&lon=4316&layers=BT

Levington (Boyville) family,[260] ancestors to both the elder line Grahams and the Corries of Newby.[261] Dryfesdale was split into:

a. Greater Hutton.[ix] This subdivision included: Hutton Motte, Gillesbie Castle, Mosskesswra, a church and old manor site north of Graham Gillesbie Tower, Hutton Hospital, St. James Chapel, St. Michael Chapel in Sibbaldbie, and Sibbaldbie Temple lands. In 1193, Gilbert, son of Adam Fitz Gilbert, and Chaplain of Hutton, and also brother of Christina, wife of the second Sir Henry de Graham, agreed to transfer the chapel of Hutton under Jedburgh Abbey.[262] Chaplain Gilbert's father Adam and grandfather Gilbert were lords of Hutton, from the powerful Levington family, known for their leadership roles in the Knights Templar.[263, 264] Hutton was their seat of power.[265] The Dalkeith Grahams and their Border Graham heirs did not inherit Greater Hutton[266] (Upper Dryfe in Figure F-9) from their Avenel ancestors, former lords of Eskdale.[267, 268] The Grahams inherited Hutton/Upper Dryfe from their Levington/Fitz Gilbert ancestors.[269] Hutton Motte[270] was one of the minor timber castles of the Brus lordship, which would have been ascribed

---

[260] Alex Maxwell Findlater, "Hoddam, A Medieval Estate in Annandale," *Transactions of the Dumfries and Galloway Natural History and Archaeology Society, (TDGNHAS)* No. 3082 (2008): 80. https://dgnhas.org.uk/sites/default/files/transactions/3082.pdf

[261] Newby was marched (bounded) by Locher Water and River Annan. In 1296, Sir Walter de Corrie was granted the fief of Newby.
R.C. Reid, "The Early History of the Corries of Annandale," *Transactions of the Dumfries and Galloway Natural History and Archaeological Society (TDGNHAS)* No. 3004 (1916): 34. https://dgnhas.org.uk/sites/default/files/transactions/3004.pdf

[262] Jane Brankstone Thomas, J.C. B. Sharp, and Michael Anne Guido, "A Cumberland Family with Medieval Roots in Scotland and Northern England: A Study Gilbert Fitz Richer and His Descendants," 360-362.

[263] Royal Commission on Historical Manuscripts, *Historical Manuscripts Commission, Report on Manuscripts of Sir Archibald Edmonstone of Duntreath, Volumes 5 and 6* (Hereford: Anthony Brothers Limited, 1909), 80, 83, 84. https://archive.org/details/variousmanuscripts05greauoft/page/n83/mode/2up

[264] In 1274, Walter Corry was declared co-heir and cousin to Helewisa de Levington. Walter's mother was Agnes de Levington. These enfeoffment lands included Corry and Sibbaldbie, the domain stretched as far east as the River Esk, and south to the marches (border zones).

[265] T.H.B. Graham, "The de Levingtons of Kirklinton," *Transactions of the Cumberland and Westmoreland Antiquarian and Archaeological Society* (Carlisle: 1911): 63, 67-69. https://archive.org/details/transactionsofcu12cumb/page/60/mode/2up?q=graham

[266] J. Bain, *The Border Papers: Calendar of letters and papers relating to the affairs of the borders of England and Scotland preserved in Her Majesty's Public Record Office*, Vol. II, 6-8.

[267] Author T. L. Taylor wrote in 1933: "Sir Nicholas de Graham forfeited lands in Dumfriesshire for 'rebellion' during the English domination, and in 1307 Lord Hereford, the English Lord of Annandale, made a grant for life of lands in Hotone and Locardebi to Sir Bartholomew Denefand." Sir Nicholas did manage to recover a portion of the lands he lost as a result of siding with the Scots in the Wars of Scottish Independence.

[268] The Avenels did acquire lands in Hoddam, Tundergath, and Torthorwald by marriage. PoMS, "No. 4371," accessed 27 February 2023. https://www.poms.ac.uk/record/source/4372/
R.C. Reid, "The Scottish Avenels," *Transactions of the Dumfries and Galloway Natural History and Archaeological Society (TDGNHAS)* No. 3037 (1960): 76-77. https://dgnhas.org.uk/sites/default/files/transactions/3037.pdf

[269] Jane Brankstone Thomas, J.C. B. Sharp, and Michael Anne Guido, "A Cumberland Family with Medieval Roots in Scotland and Northern England: A Study Gilbert Fitz Richer and His Descendants," 360-362.

[270] T.L. Taylor, "Hutton Mote," *Transactions of the Dumfries and Galloway Natural History and Archaeological Society (TDGNHAS)* No. 3018 (1934): 384. https://dgnhas.org.uk/sites/default/files/transactions/3018.pdf

to his principal followers.[271] The surrounding land became known as "Hutton Below the Muir," or "Nether Hutton" and also recorded as "Hutton Sub Mora" in the Latin land charters.[272]

    b. "Little Hutton" or <u>Duncorry.</u> This partial knights fee included Corriebridge, Corrielaw, Little Hutton Kirk and Hospital,[273] the Corriehill, the old Kirk of Corrie,[274] and the Kirk of Cumstone (current location of Cumstone farm on the Ordnance Survey map, Figure 19). Little Hutton Kirk lands all lie on the north side of Corry Water which includes Stobhill (a.k.a.: "Stuble").[275]

    c. Applegarth. This portion passed to the Jardine clan. The first documented Jardine in Annandale is Humphrey Jardine, son of William, who witnesses Annandale charters beginning in 1215.[276]

4. **Evandale Knights Fee.** This knights fee is located on the land that became the Parish of Kirkpatrick-Juxta. Dr. Ruth Blakely notes the long standing presence of the Heriz/Herries family in the area until the sixteenth century.[277]

    a. Coats Hill Motte was on the east side of Beattock village (Kirkpatrick Juxta) and later became a Graham estate.[278]

    b. Auchen Castle (Auchencass) was on west side of Beattock village (Kirkpatrick Juxta) and later became a Graham estate when the lands passed to them in marriage to a Kirkpatrick heiress.[279]

---

[271] "Hutton Mote-motte," Historic Environment Scotland.

[272] Jane Brankstone Thomas, J.C. B. Sharp, and Michael Anne Guido, "A Cumberland Family with Medieval Roots in Scotland and Northern England: A Study Gilbert Fitz Richer and His Descendants," 360-362.

[273] *Monastic Annandale Caledonia*, Vol. III, Chapter 2, Dumfriesshire.

[274] The old kirk of Corrie is home to an ancient stone monument called the Dragon Stone. Corriehills is home to the legendary Dragon Well. https://draft.dgnhas.org.uk/sites/default/files/transactions/3074.pdf#page=112

[275] https://canmore.org.uk/site/search/result?NUMLINK=66755&view=map

[276] J. Bain, *Calendar of Documents Relating to Scotland preserved in Her Majesty's Public Record Office,* Vol. I, (1108-1272) (London, Edinburgh: H.M. General Register House, 1881), 123, 309.

[277] Ruth M. Blakely, "The Brus Family in England and Scotland, 1100-c. 1290," 187.

[278] "Coats Hill," Canmore National Record of the Historic Environment, accessed 27 February 2023. https://canmore.org.uk/site/48372/coats-hill

[279] "Auchen Castle," Stravaiging Around Scotland, accessed 7 January 2023. http://www.stravaiging.com/history/castle/auchen-castle

5. **Hoddam Knights Fee.** This land was first held by Odard de Carlisle. He changed his name to "Odard de Hoddam" upon acquiring the Hoddam lands. The old lands of Hoddom first held by the Herries family became a Bruce estate held by the Carlisles.[280] The west side of old Hoddom became Castlemilk in St. Mungo Parish, where a Bruce castle was built of stone at the castle guard.[281]

*Figure F-15: Hoddam Castle, View from Repentance Tower. Photo by Scot Hill, 2011. [280] This file is licensed under CC BY-SA 3.0.*

6. **Kirkpatrick-Fleming Knights Fee.** This knights fee was also controlled by the Levington (Boyville) family. It would have included the church lands of Redkirk and Gretna Kirk and also the parishes of Kirkconnel and Irvine, as well as the Chapel of Logan.[282] It is possible that this enfeoffment also included Kirkandrews in the Debateable Lands. The Levingtons were based out of nearby Kirklinton. Scotland controlled Kirkandrews until 1552 when it reverted to England.[283]

---

[280] "Clan Carruthers: The Secret Seat of the Templar," Clan Carruthers Society International, 10 August 2019. https://clancarrutherssociety.org/2019/08/10/clan-carruthers-the-secret-seat-of-the-templar/

Figure F-15: Wikimedia Commons contributors, "File:Hoddom Castle from Repentance Tower.jpg," *Wikimedia Commons,* accessed 17 April 2023. https://commons.wikimedia.org/w/index.php?title=File:Hoddom_Castle_from_Repentance_Tower.jpg&oldid=511429986

[281] J. Rafferty, "The Kirk and Parish of St. Mungo," *Transactions of the Dumfries and Galloway Natural History and Archaeological Society, (TDGNHAS),* No. 3033 (1956):170. https://dgnhas.org.uk/sites/default/files/transactions/3033.pdf

[282] James Rankin, *A Handbook of the Church of Scotland* (Edinburgh and London: Blackwood and Sons, 1888), 77. https://ia600703.us.archive.org/22/items/handbookofchurch188800rank/handbookofchurch188800rank.pdf

[283] James Rankin, *A Handbook of the Church of Scotland* (Edinburgh and London: Blackwood and Sons, 1888), 77.

7. **Lochmaben.** Lochmaben became the home of the Bruces, the Lords of Annandale, after their home base, the motte (timber) castle in Annan, was destroyed in flooding in approximately 1200.[284] The first Motte of Lochmaben was located on the East Nith and was called Rockhall. Robert Bruce, Lord of Annandale, replaced the Rockhall Motte with Lochmaben castle, his primary residence. The castle at Lochmaben was rebuilt by

*Figure F-16: Ruins of Lochmaben Castle from the Mid-Fourteenth Century. There was an Earlier Timber Structure on this Site.* [284] *Photo © Lynne Kirton (CC BY-SA/2.0), 2004.*

King Edward I in 1296, after he had all the others destroyed.[285] Knights surnamed Heriz, Kirkpatrick and Torthorwald held the position of Senechal of Annandale, a position Dr. Blakely says was rotated amongst the household knights of the Bruces. She states Dunwoodie was a Bruce household knight in the late thirteenth century.[286] Lochmaben lands were later subdivided in the western section for Dunwoodie some time prior to 1194,[287] and again for the knights fee of Torthorwald sometime after 1242.[288] The motte of Torthorwald stands just south of the confluence of the Torthorwald Burn and

---

[284] "Motte & Bailey," Annan, The History Town, accessed 6 January 2023. https://www.annanthehistorytown.org/defensive-annan-2/motte-bailey/
Figure F-16: Wikimedia Commons contributors, "File:Lochmaben Castle - geograph.org.uk - 17368.jpg," *Wikimedia Commons,* accessed 17 April 2023. https://commons.wikimedia.org/w/index.php?title=File:Lochmaben_Castle_-_geograph.org.uk_-_17368.jpg&oldid=716199151

[285] "Torthorwald Castle," Stravaiging Around Scotland, accessed 7 January 2023. http://www.stravaiging.com/history/castle/torthorwald-castle/

[286] Ruth M. Blakely, "The Brus Family in England and Scotland, 1100-c. 1290," 155, 192-193.

[287] PoMS, "No. 8014, person summary," accessed 27 February 2023 https://www.poms.ac.uk/record/person/8014/

[288] PoMS, "No. 2381, person summary," accessed 27 February 2023. https://www.poms.ac.uk/record/person/2381/

*Appendix F: Genealogy of the Border Grahams*

Roughcleuch Burn. This position was strategically important being situated on a main route into south-west Scotland from England with commanding views south and west.[289]

8. **Middlebie Knights Fee.** This knights fee is located on the land that became the Parishes of Middlebie and Tundergarth. The first knight to hold Middlebie may have been Walter de Bois (Bosco).[290] The northern section of this knights fee land had a motte sited at what was later named "Tundergarth." One of the first knights of Middlebie, the Pearsbys, may have been ancestors of the Corries in Tundergarth. David of Pearsby is a witness on a 1260-67 charter by the mother of Robert Avenel regarding a monetary donation to Glasgow Cathedral.[291] This land was subdivided for Carruthers[292] and again subdivided as Dunnabie (later a Graham of Gillesbie farm).[293]

9. **Moffatdale Knights Fee.** This knights fee land became the Parish of Moffat. When the fee was first assigned, building of a motte (timber castle), would have commenced. The Bruce demesne in Moffatdale later moved to Langholm during the reign of Robert I.[294] The knights fee of Erickstane is a surname which evolved from that place.[295] Moffat was later gifted to Sir David Lindsay by Robert I between 1314 and 1329.[296]

10. **Wamphraydale Knights Fee.** This knights fee likely included what became the Parishes of Wamphray and Johnstone, plus the northern tip of Parish Applegarth (Dinwoodie Hill). The original knights fee was controlled by the powerful Levington (Boyville) family,[297] but was later subdivided for the Johnstones[298] and for Adam Dunwoodie.[299] Wamphraydale was subdivided into:

    a. Dinwoodie Hill. Held by the Dunwoodie/Dinwoodie (Wood) family.[300]

---

[289] Alastair Maxwell Irving, "Towers, Hall-houses and Timber Superstructures," *The Castles Studies Group,* Journal no. 31 (2017-2018): 266. http://www.castlestudiesgroup.org.uk/CSGJournal2017-18-rev6-131-340Maxwellp.258-275.pdf

[290] PoMS, "No. 7962, person summary," accessed 27 February 2023. https://www.poms.ac.uk/record/person/7962/

[291] PoMS, "No. 4331," accessed 27 February 2023. https://www.poms.ac.uk/record/source/4331/

[292] PoMS, "No. 10230," accessed 27 February 2023. https://www.poms.ac.uk/record/source/10230/

[293] Historical Manuscripts Commission, *The Manuscripts of His Grace the Duke of Buccleuch and Queensberry,* Fifteenth Report, Appendix, Part VIII (London: Eyre and Spottiswoode, 1897), 26. https://electricscotland.com/webclans/dtog/buccleuchqueens01greauoft.pdf

[294] John and Robert Hyslop, *Langholm As it Was: A History of Langholm and Eskdale from the Earliest Times* (Sunderland: Hills and Company, 1912), 182, 183. https://archive.org/details/langholmasitwashhysl/mode/2up?q=shaw

[295] "Ericstane," Canmore National Record for the Historic Environment, accessed 27 February 2023. https://canmore.org.uk/site/48485/ericstane

[296] PoMS, "No. 10401," accessed 27 February 2023. https://www.poms.ac.uk/record/source/10401/

[297] R.C. Reid "Scott of Wamphray and Their Kinsmen," *Transactions of the Dumfries and Galloway Natural History and Archaelogical Society, (TDGNHAS),* No. 3033 (1956): 18. https://dgnhas.org.uk/sites/default/files/transactions/3033.pdf

[298] William Fraser, *The Annandale Family Book of the Johnstones, Earls and Marquises of Annandale,* Vol. I, xxiii.

[299] William McDowall, *History of the Burgh of Dumfries* (Edinburgh: Adam and Charles Black, 1867), 215. https://www.seibelfamily.net/uploads/1/1/6/5/116501719/history_of_the_burgh_of_dumfries.pdf

[300] Thomas Somerill, "An Attempt at a Brief Family History of the Lairds of Dinwiddie," 1929, Electric Scotland, accessed 27 February 2023.

b. Johnstone Motte. This timber castle was built just north of Lochwood possibly for a knight named Gilbert, son of John in the late twelfth century.³⁰¹ Lochwood Motte was probably part of old Drungree (or Dumgree/Minnygap). It was replaced in the fifteenth century by Lochwood Tower, which is sited on the bailey of the older castle.³⁰² In Temple Applegarth, John (of an unknown surname) was a member of the Bruce household around the year 1200 when the Motte of Annan collapsed, prompting a move to Lochmaben. John's son named Gilbert, also being a Knight of Annan, was given a new estate

*Figure F-17: Lochwood Pele/Peel Tower from the Annandale Family of the Johnstones, Volume 1* ³⁰³

in Lochwood where he built a wooden castle which was later rebuilt with stone. This became the base of the Barony of Johnstone, making Gilbert the son of John, the first Johnstone. A motte further North in Lochwood predates Johnstone but was destroyed before 1200.³⁰³

c. This motte site at Leihenhal in Wamphray is the smallest of the Motte sites. It is located on the Wamphray Water and just north west of St. Cuthbert's church.³⁰⁴ St. Cuthbert and St Serf Dragon cross symbols are prevalent in the area. The proximity to the church indicates a St. Cuthbert patronage of the motte owners reflecting a pre-Norman conquest plantation. Per Appendix D, the church at Wamphray has carvings over its western door that include "Anglian leaf scrolls and early type, but a distinctly Norse, "dragon...dated from A.D. 950 or A.D. 960." ³⁰⁵

In summary, while there is a shortfall of records from the early twelfth century, we were able to make educated guesses for original ten Knights of Annandale and their knights fee lands. Enough evidence has survived to provide circumstantial cases for knights and their families named in Figure F-14. The lands were soon sub-divided for other knights, growing the number of knights fees significantly. In addition, while the lands were hereditary fiefs, they were traded or transferred in marriage, complicating the investigation into the original ten knights fees.

---

³⁰¹ "History of the Clan," Clan Johnstone in America, accessed 15 February 2023. https://clanjohnstone.org/history-of-the-clan/

³⁰² "Lochwood Motte," Stravaiging Around Scotland, accessed 7 January 2023. http://www.stravaiging.com/history/castle/lochwood-motte/

³⁰³ Figure F-17: William Fraser, *The Annandale Family Book of the Johnstones, Earls and Marquises of Annandale*, Vol. I (Edinburgh: 1894), cccxxxii - cccxxxiii. https://archive.org/details/annandalefamilv100fras/page/10/mode/2up

³⁰⁴ "Wamphray Place," Canmore National Record of the Historic Environment, accessed 15 February 2023. https://canmore.org.uk/site/66922/wamphray-place

³⁰⁵ Anne T., "St. Cuthbert's Church (Wamphray)," The Megalithic Portal, 5 April 2019. https://www.megalithic.co.uk/article.php?sid=51598

## Johnstone Land Takeover—The Disenfranchisement of the Grahams Chronology

*Figure F-18: Johnstone Arms: Argent, a Saltire Sable, on a Chief Gules Three Cushions Or, by Kaliforniyka.*[306] *Licensed under CC BY 4.0.*

The progenitors of Clan Johnstone arrived in Annandale with the Norman baron Robert de Brus and for over six hundred years held extensive possessions in the west of the Scottish Marches, where they kept watch against the English.[306] They fought against the English at the Battle of Sark in 1448 and for James II of Scotland in the struggle against the Clan Douglas in 1455. The king rewarded them with the lands of Buittle and Sannoch near "Threave Castle that had previously belonged to the Douglases of Galloway.[307]

The successors of the Black Douglases for control of Annandale, the Maxwells and the Johnstones, continued the land grabbing against other Border clans. The Johnstones also played a role in the previous "Black Douglas Land Grab." It is a Thomas Johnston who acted as attorney for the Douglases when summoning the Border Grahams to provide papers to prove ownership of Hutton lands in 1456.[308] It was a Herbert Johnston that the Duke of Hamilton traded lands with seven years later in 1463, to retrieve the lands of Mosskesswra, Nether Dryfe and Bedokholme (Betok) for William Graham, grandfather of Lang Will and John Graham of Gillesbie.[309] However in 1527, Robert Graham, Laird of Thornik, filed formal complaints against Herbert Johnstone the younger for forcibly occupying "Betok" lands.[310]

The Johnstones had a long feud with the Clan Moffat who were nearly wiped out in 1557.[311] Seventy years later, all of the Moffat lands were passed to the Johnstones due to the Moffats' massive debts. The Johnstones then controlled the regality of Moffat, holding their regality courts in Moffat until heritable jurisdictions were outlawed in 1747.[312] From 1484 to 1516, the Johnstones acquired Corrie Castle and the title of "Laird of Corrie" via marriage and the debt notes of Sir George Corrie.[313]

---

[306] Chief of Clan Johnstone, Lord Annandale, Cecil, Baron Johnson of Kilmaine, and Commissioner to the Chief of Clan Johnstone, "Johnstone Clan History," Scotclans, accessed 7 January 2023. https://www.scotclans.com/blogs/clans-jk/johnstone-clan-history

Figure F-18: Wikimedia Commons contributors, "File:Arms of Johnstone.svg," *Wikimedia Commons*, accessed 17 April 2023. https://commons.wikimedia.org/w/index.php?title=File:Arms_of_Johnstone.svg&oldid=658437123

[307] William Fraser, *The Annandale Family Book of the Johnstones, Earls and Marquises of Annandale*, Vol. I, xix.

[308] R.C. Reid, "The Border Grahams and Their Origins," 89-91.

[309] Historical Manuscripts Commission, *The Manuscripts of the Duke of Hamilton, Knight, Eleventh Report, Appendix, Part VI* (London: Her Majesty's Stationery Office, 1887), 18.

[310] R.C. Reid, "The Border Grahams and Their Origins," *Transactions of the Dumfries and Galloway Natural History and Archaeological Society (TDGNHAS)* No. 3038, (1961): 96.

[311] "Moffat Clan/Family Histories," Rampant Scotland, accessed 7 January 2023. http://www.rampantscotland.com/clans/blclan_moffat.htm

[312] William Fraser, *The Annandale Family Book of the Johnstones, Earls and Marquises of Annandale*, Vol. I, xxiii-xxiv.

[313] J.E. Corrie, *Records of the Corrie Family, 802-1899 A.D.*, 143, 144, 147, 150-152.

At least some of Sir George's lands had been forfeited in 1484 for siding with the Douglases and the Duke of Albany at the Battle of Lochmaben Fair.[314]

From 1492 to 1515, due to a series of court actions filed by the Douglases and Maxwells, and resulting fines and apprisements, the Grahams of Mosskesswra accumulated heavy debt and gradually lost their lands.[315] "Apprisement" in old Scots law refers to the appraisal of lands and goods with the intent of paying a debt—assessing property as collateral. If fines could not be paid, then the property was confiscated.[316] See "Disenfranchisement of the Grahams of Mosskesswra," a section of the historical and documentary chronology at the end of this appendix (p. F-71).

In 1596, Douglas of Torthorwald made a disposition of Mosskesswra to Sir James Johnstone, the chief who was slain in 1608. His son James was retoured heir of the lands of Hutton under the Muir (Nether Hutton), Mosskesswra, Boreland, Cumstoun, Androgillis, Howleyis, Croftend, Cairtartoun, Wolslakkis, Bedokholm and Dryfe, with the advocacy of the churches within the Stewartry of Annandale.

In 1634, Johnstone purchased the superiority of Hutton under the Muir from the earl of Morton, and the long connection of Hutton with Dalkeith came to an end. The Border Grahams were not the only Grahams to be squeezed out of the Annandale Valley.[317]

The second family of Thornik Grahams were descendants of the younger line of William de Graham, being descendants of the Montroses. They settled in Thornik Barony near Moffat in Annandale upon the departure of the first family of Thornik. R.C. Reid gives a detailed account of the gradual loss of the loss of lands by the first (elder line) and second (younger line) Graham families of Thornik and later the Langbeholm Graham lands to the Johnstons.

> "In 1532 all the moveable effects of Robert Graham were escheated by the Crown for the slaughter of a George Kirkpatrick. Escheats were a source of profit and the Crown had granted this one to lord Maxwell who may well have had a watchful eye on the rising sun of the Johnstons... In February 1531, Ninian Graham married Margaret Johnston, daughter, of John Johnston under which contract Robert Graham bound himself to maintain Ninian and his heirs in the lands of Thornik."

James Graham of Gillesbie was a witness and that the contract still has attached two seals, one bearing on a chief, three scallop shells. On Robert's death, the crown gifted to Margaret Johnston, the ward of all the lands of the late Robert Graham of Thornik, while John Johnston was granted the ward and non-entries of the deceased. Ninian predeceased his wife, Margaret Johnston, who then married second husband, Adam Wylkin. "Walter Graham, the transferee of Thornik, is described in Scots Peerage, vi. 225, as a younger son of the first Earl of Montrose's first marriage. When Walter died in 1550, his son, Robert Graham, became known as of Thornik and of Cairnie... In December 1550, John Johnston came to an arrangement with John Graham of Queenshaugh and Walter's widow, Marion

---

[314] C. L. Johnstone, *The History of the Johnstones, 1191-1909* (Edinburgh: W & A.K. Johnston Ltd, 1909), 8-9. https://electricscotland.com/webclans/htol/historyofjohnstons.pdf

[315] R.C. Reid, "The Border Grahams and Their Origins," 91.

[316] John Erskine, James Ivory, *Institute of the Law of Scotland*, Vol. II (Edinburgh: Bell and Bradfute, 1828), 746-750. https://archive.org/details/aninstitutelaws00ivorgoog/page/n4/mode/2up?q=apprisement

[317] Col. William Rogerson, *Hutton Under the Muir*, 30.

Stirling where he traded the lands of Baldoran and Colquhoun in exchange for Marion's life interest in Thornik which in 1566 led to litigation, with Graham trying to eject Johnston from Thornik. Robert Graham vainly persisted in litigation for years afterwards."[318] For details of how Thornik passed to the Johnstons see Percy Adams' *Douglas of Morton,* p. 118.

    The Grahams of Langbedholm were a branch from the first family of Thornik. Once the lands of Thornik had passed to the Johnstones, a few Grahams were permitted to remain. Robert Graham of Langboddam had maintained himself on that small property and his descendants can be traced to about 1750. Early in 1581 Robert was slaughtered by the Johnstons of Newton and Chapel. Robert was followed by James Graham of Langboddam. That December James Graham and his son, Robert, suffered escheat which was granted to Andrew Johnston, son of James Johnston of Beirholm. In 1606, 1607, 1608, the Johnstones filed a Declarator (court order enforcing property rights) against James Graham of Langboddam regarding the lands of Murthat, Myln-toun, Craigielands and others. By 1660, James Graham of Langboddam renounced his rights to Craigielands in favor of James Johnston of Beirholm.[319]

## Battle of Dryfe Sands, 6 December 1593.

    For over half a century, the Maxwells and the Johnstones had feuded and vied for the supremacy of the Scottish West March. On 6 December 1593, the seventh Lord Maxwell, the Earl of Morton, attacked Johnstone territory in Annandale with an army of 2,000 horsemen.

    The Chief of the Johnstones, Sir James Johnstone received intelligence of the approach of the enemy. He called for urgent help and his plea was answered by the Grahams, Scotts, Armstrongs, and others. He mustered barely 1,000 men, however the Johnstones were victorious[320] and by 1608, Sir James Johnstone was appointed Warden of the West Marches, a post previously held by Lord Maxwell.[321]

---

[318] R.C. Reid, "The Border Grahams and Their Origins," 94-98.
[319] R.C. Reid, "The Border Grahams and Their Origins," 98-104.
[320] "The Battle of Dryfe Sands, 6 December 1593," The Border Reivers Website, accessed 7 January 2023. http://www.borderreivers.co.uk/Border%20Battles/Dryfe%20Sands/dryfe%20sands.htm
[321] William Fraser, *The Annandale Family Book of the Johnstones, Earls and Marquises of Annandale,* Vol. I, cxxvi-cxxviii, cxxxviii, cccxxxiv.

## Scottish naming pattern

We can use the Scottish naming pattern (naming children after grandparents and other close relatives[322]) to find connections between families particularly when the naming pattern continually repeats and the names are unique.

- **Alan (Elder and Younger line).** William de Graham's younger son was named Alan, misrecorded in *Peerage* as "John." [323] Also the younger son and heir of Sir John de Graham of Dalkeith, "the Last," descendant of the elder line of William de Graham, was named Alan de Graham, Lord of Morton, in a charter dated 1373.[324] There were Alans using occupational names who were suspected Grahams due to connection to Graham estates such as Alan of Dumfries the Chancellor who turns up in the Grahams/Bruce estates of Succoth Dunbarton[325] and Alan the Constable, of Galloway, who was from the Graham/Bruce memorial lands (St. Patrick, St. Serf, St. Modan lands).[326]

- **Arthur (Elder Line).** The first Celtic person known to have the name Arthur was the oldest son of King Adian McGabrian, Arthuret in Cumberland is named after him.[327, 328] The presence of the name "Arthur" in one's tree usually indicates a connection to the Arthuret Grahams, before and after Lang Will Graham.

- **David (Younger Line)**—the use of the name "David de Graham" is first found in the "younger line" of William de Graham.[329] David Graham of Corbridge, Northumberland was an elder line Graham,[330] but little is known of the Corbridge Grahams. I suspect that his descendants used the name "David" in honor of David I, King of Scots.

- **Helen.** Lang Will's wife was named Helen.[331] Helen was also a common name for Menteith and Montrose women,[332] and certain border clans, like the Armstrongs and Irvines.

- **Henry (elder line).** Use of the name "Henry de Graham," in honor of the son of David I, Earl Henry of Northumberland, is first found in the elder line of William de Graham.[333] Many elder line Graham estates were in Northumberland. Northumberland was under

---

[322] Alex Cox, "A Handy Guide to Traditional Scottish Naming Patterns," FindMyPast, 14 July 2020. https://www.findmypast.com/blog/help/traditional-scottish-naming-patterns

[323] Lloyd D. Graham, *House Graham, From the Antoine Wall to the Temple of Hymen*, 1.

[324] *Registrum Honoris de Morton, Volume II: Ancient Charters*, 88, 115, 117-119.

[325] PoMS, "No. 17483, person summary," accessed 6 January 2023. https://www.poms.ac.uk/record/person/17483/

[326] "Alan of Galloway," Undiscovered Scotland, accessed 17 February 2023. https://www.undiscoveredscotland.co.uk/usbiography/a/alanofgalloway.html

[327] "The Battle of Arfderydd or Arthuret," Carla Nayland, accessed 6 January 2023. http://www.carlanayland.org/essays/battle_arthuret.htm

[328] Peter Bernhard, "The Real "King Arthur" of the Historical Records," *Ancient Templar Knowledge*, accessed 6 January 2023. https://commanderysaintmichael.wordpress.com/2015/01/24/the-real-king-arthur-of-the-historical-record/

[329] Lloyd D. Graham, *House Graham, From the Antoine Wall to the Temple of Hymen*, 2.

[330] PoMS, "No. 4185," accessed 19 January 2023. https://www.poms.ac.uk/record/source/4185/

[331] R. T. Spence, "The Pacification of the Cumberland Borders, 1593-1628," 81-84.

[332] Sir James Balfour Paul, *The Scots Peerage, Founded on Wood's Edition*, Vol. VI (Edinburgh: David Douglas, 1909), 225. https://archive.org/details/scotspeeragefoun06pauluoft/page/148/mode/2up?q=glenny

[333] Lloyd D. Graham, *House Graham, From the Antoine Wall to the Temple of Hymen*, 2.

Scottish control until 1157. Tynedale was under Scottish control until 1296. Grahams retained their estates in Tynedale and Northumberland until 1314. See Figures F-2, F-8 and F-8 notes.

- **Matthew**. The name "Matthew" can be found amongst Border Grahams, likely in honor of Matthew, Earl of Lennox, given his and the Grahams' role in the siege and conquest of Castlemilk fortress in Dumfriesshire.[334] Matthew is also a common name in the Irvines,[335] and the Bell family, another Border clan.[336]

- **Nichol or Nicholas (elder line)**. Sir Nicholas de Graham, heir of the third Sir Henry de Grahame, of the elder line of Grahams and his uncle, Nicholas, are the first Nicholas de Grahams recorded. The name "Nicholas" was a common name in the Avenel and Corrie families that had previously intermarried with the elder line Grahams. There may be a connection to the Nichols Forest near the Scottish-English Border as the elder line Grahams owned large sections of Northumberland, especially in Tynedale, before they forfeited the lands to the English crown circa 1300 A.D.[337] Nicholas Graham of Auchincloich in Stirlingshire, as listed in a property record in 1426, is an elder line Graham, descendant of John Graham of Auchincloich, son of Sir John Graham "the Last" Lord of Dalkeith.[338] John Graham of Auchincloich resigned his rights to Dalkeith in 1370. After Lang Will's final departure from Hutton in Scotland circa 1515, many of his relatives remained behind. Of note is a record from 8 May 1543, of a Nicol Graham of "Meskeswaye" who gave a bond of manrent to "John Johnston of that Ilk." A notary had to sign for him but a portion of his seal is still attached to the document. Significantly it shows a fess between three scallops, two and one.[339] See Appendix E.

- **Ninian (younger line)**. Ninian was a Celtic Culdee saint.[340] See Appendix D. Naming a child after St Ninian indicates a connection to the ancient Celts. The name Ninian can be found amongst the Montrose cadet families, Cairnie Grahams and Inchbrakie Grahams, and Armstrongs.[341]

- **Peter (elder line)** – Peter de Graham, was the eldest son of William de Graham, the first documented Graham in Scotland. He was the Sheriff of Edinburgh.[342] His early

---

[334] "Matthew Stuart: Life Story," *Tudor Times*, 20 May 2018. https://tudortimes.co.uk/people/matthew-stuart-life-story/war

[335] R. T. Spence, "The Pacification of the Cumberland Borders, 1593-1628," 95, 99.

[336] T.F.A., *Memorial of the Clan of the Bells*, (Capetown: Saul Solomon and Co.,1864), 38, 41. https://deriv.nls.uk/dcn23/9495/94952249.23.pdf

[337] *Calendar of Patent Rolls, Edward I:* Vol. 3, 1292-1301, ed. H C Maxwell Lyte (London: 1895), 513, 577. https://babel.hathitrust.org/cgi/pt?id=mdp.39015031081154&view=1up&seq=627&q1=graham

[338] John Reid, "Material for a Place Name Survey of East Stirlingshire," 109. https://spns.org.uk/wp-content/uploads/2019/12/John-Reids-East-Stirlingshire-place-name-data-v2019.pdf

[339] William Fraser, *The manuscripts of J. J. Hope Johnstone, esq. of Annandale* (London: Eyre and Spotswood, 1897), 19. https://archive.org/details/manuscriptsofjjh00grea/page/18/mode/2up?q=nichol

[340] Editors of Encyclopaedia Brittanica, "St. Ninian." *Encyclopedia Britannica*, accessed 10 January 2023. https://www.britannica.com/biography/Saint-Ninian

[341] R.C. Reid," The Border Grahams and Their Origins," 91.

[342] PoMS, "No. 896, person summary," accessed 6 January 2023. https://www.poms.ac.uk/record/person/896/

*Appendix F: Genealogy of the Border Grahams*

descendants include Peter de Graham, Sheriff of Dumfries, and Peter Graham of Brackenwra (who may be the same person).[343] The name "Peter" is not found in the "younger" line, who are descendants of William de Graham's younger son, Alan. See Figure F-1.

- **Richard (elder line)**- The first Richard that is found in the Graham family tree is Richard Graham of Elliston in Roxburghshire.[344] "Richards" can also be found in the Braid family believed to be Graham relatives living on the Dalkeith estate in the early fourteenth century.[345] Theorized descendant of Richard of Elliston is Richard Graham of Netherby, eldest son of Lang Will. Lang Will's great grandfather, and fourth great grandfather were named Richard.[346] Figure F-2. At the time the name "Richard" was common to the Scott family who was resident in Selkirk,[347] which was near Elliston in Roxburghshire (ancestors of Sir Walter Scott, the poet), indicating the mother Richard of Elliston could have been from the Scott clan. The name Richard is also associated with Gilbert Fitz Richer, who passed the lands of Hutton Sub Mora to Christina Fitz Gilbert as a tocher (dowry) upon her marriage to the second Sir Henry de Graham.[348]

- **Thomas (elder line/Armstrongs)**—Thomas Graham of Mosskesswra, uncle of Lang Will Graham, is believed to be the Thomas Graham of Auchencass, who acquired Auchencass by marriage to Janet Kirkpatrick, daughter of Sir Duncan Kirkpatrick.[349] Thomas is also a name common to the Armstrongs of Mangerton. Tradition is that Lang Will married Helen, a sister of Johnnie Armstrong of Gilnockie, a Mangerton Armstrong. He named a son "Thomas."[350]

- **Walter**. The Carnie Grahams (descendants of Walter Graham, the brother of second earl of Montrose) were claimed as ancestors of the second family of Thornik Grahams.[351] Lang Will Graham (1468-1540), chief of the Border Grahams had two grandsons named Walter.[352]

---

[343] PoMS, "No. 10399," accessed 6 January 2023. https://www.poms.ac.uk/record/source/10399/
[344] PoMS, "No. 925," accessed 6 January 2023. https://www.poms.ac.uk/record/source/925/
[345] PoMS, "No. 3945," accessed 6 January 2023. https://www.poms.ac.uk/record/person/3945/
[346] A. W. Cornelius Hallen, "The Grahams of the Border," 162.
[347] "Scott Clan," Scotland in Oils, accessed 6 January 2023. http://www.scotlandinoils.com/clan/Clan-Scott.html
[348] Jane Brankstone Thomas, J.C. B. Sharp, and Michael Anne Guido, "A Cumberland Family with Medieval Roots in Scotland and Northern England: A Study Gilbert Fitz Richer and His Descendants," 359-360.
[349] Sir James Balfour Paul, *The Scots Peerage, Founded on Wood's Edition,* Vol. II (Edinburgh: David Douglas, 1905), 381-382. https://archive.org/details/bub_gb_ELEEAAAAIAAJ/page/381/mode/2up?q=auchincass
[350] T. H. B. Graham, "The Debatable Land, Part II," *Transactions of the Cumberland and Westmoreland Antiquarian and Archaeological Society* (Carlisle: 1913): 149. https://archive.org/details/transactionsofcu14cumb/page/n167/mode/2up?q=lang
[351] Sir James Balfour Paul, *The Scots Peerage, Founded on Wood's Edition,* Vol. VI (Edinburgh: David Douglas, 1909), 225. https://archive.org/details/scotspeeragefoun06pauluoft/page/148/mode/2up?q=glenny
[352] John G. Armstrong, "The Debatable Armstrongs and Their Graham Relations," 3.

## Abbreviated Historical and Documentary Chronology of the Scottish Borderlands

### 1124

- David I invites Norman vassals to settle in Scotland. Grants them estates along the Southern Border with England. William de Graham attends the coronation of David I of Scotland.[353] Granted lands in Dalkeith.[354] Robert de Brus (1070-1141) is declared the first Lord of Annandale.[355]

### 25 March 1183

- By the authority of the pope, the bishop of Glasgow settled a dispute between the canons of Jedburgh and Adam Fitz Gilbert. The Chapel of Hutton would be exempt from the mother church of Sibbaldbie (DMF) and receive the rights of a mother church and have a cemetery.[356]

### 1198

- Sir Henry de Graham (*the first Sir Henry, son of Peter*), Lord of Dalkeith, and Simundburn, Wark in Tynedale, Northumberland. witnesses a charter of King William confirming the grant of the lands of Aberrotwain to Earl Gilbert of Strathearn.[357]

### 1179

- Peter of Corrie issues a charter of the lands of Dalhengun and Bargower in Kyle (Ayrshire) to the Abbey of Melrose and then confirms the transfer via a quitclaim deed in 1205. His seal is a dragon.[358]

### 23 March 1206

- Osbert, clerk of Hutton, confessed the Chapel of Hutton is part of the Church of Dryfesdale, and resigned it into the hands of the judges and to Master Michael, rector of the church of St. Cuthbert. Osbert swore an oath to the Church of Dryfesdale and placed himself under the jurisdiction of Master Michael.[359]

---

[353] Claire Brooks, "Theories on the Origins of the Grahams," *Clan Graham Society Newsletter* (1998). https://clangrahamsociety.org/theories-on-the-origins-of-the-grahams/

[354] Sir Archibald Lawrie, *Early Scottish Charters, Prior to 1153 AD* (Glasgow: James MacLehose and Sons, 1905), 321, 322. https://archive.org/details/earlyscottishcha00lawruoft/page/76/mode/2up

[355] David X. Carpenter, Faculty of History, University of Oxford "Robert de Brus, Tenant in Chief in Yorkshire and Annandale," *Charters of William II and Henry I Project* (8 October 2013), 2. https://actswilliam2henry1.files.wordpress.com/2013/10/h1-robert-de-brus-2013-1.pdf

[356] PoMS, "No. 9117, person summary," accessed 6 January 2023. https://www.poms.ac.uk/record/person/9117/

[357] W. A. Lindsay, J. Dowden and J. M. Thomson, *Charters, Bulls and Other Documents relating to the Abbey of Inchaffray* (Edinburgh: 1908), 4.

[358] PoMS, "No. 5404," accessed 6 January 2023. https://www.poms.ac.uk/record/source/5404/

[359] PoMS, "No. 8361," person summary, accessed 6 January 2023. https://www.poms.ac.uk/record/person/8361/

## 1232

- Sir David Graham of Dundaff, named as a half-brother to "Richard de Faunes," funds a dedication to St. James the Greater in Roxburgh, Scotland.[360]

## Before 1234

- Adam Fitz Gilbert of Kilbucho, Tarbolton and Hutton, royal justiciar (judge), had charter from kinsman, William Comyn, Earl of Buchan the lands of Blith and "Ingolneston."[361] He was the father-in-law of Henry de Graham *(second Sir Henry)*, Lord of Dalkeith.[362]

## Circa 1248

- Dundaff property near Fintry acquired by Sir David Graham, younger line descendant William de Graham.[363]

## Circa 1260

- Patrick of Dundaff acquires Kincardine, Perthshire property via marriage to Annabella, sister of the earl of Strathearn.[364]

## 11 August 1258

- William, Bishop of Glasgow, for canons of Glasgow; gives Church of Hutton (DMF), saving right of Master Ralph del Bois for his lifetime.[365]

## 1271

- Malcolm, the fourth Earl of Lennox, granted Sir Arthur Galbraith the lands of Buchmonyn (Balfunning) and the lands of Gilgirinane near the lands of Cartonewene. The lands named in this Charter are Banchorane, Keangerloch, Fynnard, Kilgerintyn, and Auchincloich.[366]

## 1249 1283

- (Terra Regis Alexander III -TRA3): third Sir Henry de Graham grants a lease to Sir David of Torthorwald for the lands of Superior/Over Dryfe. May have been a tocher (dowry) for his

---

[360] University of Edinburgh, "Dedication DE/EW/6345," Database of Dedications to Saints in Medieval Scotland, 31 December 2022. http://saints.shca.ed.ac.uk/index.cfm?fuseaction=home.adhocform

[361] PoMS, "No. 900, person summary," accessed 6 January 2023. https://www.poms.ac.uk/record/person/900/

[362] Jane Brankstone Thomas, J.C. B. Sharp, and Michael Anne Guido, "A Cumberland Family with Medieval Roots in Scotland and Northern England: A Study Gilbert Fitz Richer and His Descendants," 368.

[363] PoMS, "No.2793," accessed 6 January 2023. https://www.poms.ac.uk/record/source/2793/

[364] Cosmo Innes, *Liber Insule Missarum: Abbacie Canonicorum Regularium B. Virginis Et S. Johannis De Inchaffery Registrum Vetus* (Edinburgh: Ballantyne and Hughes, 1847), xxxiii-xxxiv. https://archive.org/details/liberinsulemissa85inchuoft/page/xxxvi/mode/1up?q=graham

[365] PoMS, "No. 1707," accessed 7 January 2023. https://www.poms.ac.uk/record/source/1707/

[366] PoMS, "No. 7049," accessed 7 January 2023. https://www.poms.ac.uk/record/person/7049/

granddaughter, Christine, daughter of the elder Sir John de Graham and her husband, Sir David. Over (Upper) Dryfe is depicted in Figure F-9. [367]

- Sir David and Christine's only heir is daughter, Isobel. Sir David died circa 1296.[368]
- Isobel marries Humphrey Kirkpatrick circa 1321 bringing lands of Superior/Over Dryfe to the marriage.[369]
- Between 1326 and 1330 Humphrey Kirkpatrick is in the Bruce household in Cardross in Dunbartonshire witnessing charters.[370] King Robert the Bruce died at Cardross on 7 June 1329.[371]
- Humphrey and Isobel's heir was Sir Roger Kirkpatrick (the younger). When Edward Balliol led an invasion into Scotland in 1332, Isobel and Humphrey fled the country. It is possible that before they fled, they left young Roger in the care of Isobel's Graham cousins. If the young Roger and young John Graham ("the Last") were raised together, it would explain their close attachment.[372] In 1357, Humphrey served as a hostage for David II in England.[373]

## 1297

Sir William Wallace ventured to recapture Lochmaben castle from the English but was greatly outnumbered. He retreated to Holehouse (Parish Tinwald). Per author Rev. William Graham: "About 50 men of the Grahams and Kirkpatricks having in the meantime joined him." The Scots were victorious.[374]

## 1298

Sir John Graham of Dundaff, "right hand man of Wallace" dies at Falkirk (15 miles from Dundaff) fighting with Wallace.[375]

---

[367] PoMS, "No. 4859," accessed 7 January 2023. https://www.poms.ac.uk/record/source/4859/
[368] *Kirkpatrick of Closeburn* (London: George Norman, 1858), 4. https://deriv.nls.uk/dcn23/9564/95641358.23.pdf
[369] PoMS, "No.24134," accessed 7 January 2023. https://www.poms.ac.uk/record/person/24134/
[370] John Stuart, and George Burnett, *Rotuli scaccarii regum Scotorum = The Exchequer rolls of Scotland*, Vol. 1 (Edinburgh: His Majesty's General Register House, 1878), 52, 123, 173, 183, 257, 297. https://www.familysearch.org/library/books/viewer/796600/?offset=#page=5&viewer=picture&o=&n=0&q=
[371] "King Robert the Bruce of Scotland," Britroyals.com, accessed 9 March 2023. https://britroyals.com/scots.asp?id=robert1
[372] A.M.T Maxwell-Irving, "Torthorwald Castle," *Cruck Cottage Heritage Association*, 1993. http://cruckcottage.com/torthorwald-castle/
[373] *Kirkpatrick of Closeburn* (London: George Norman, 1858), 12.
[374] Rev. William Graham, *Lochmaben Five Hundred Years Ago* (Edinburgh:Trinity, 1865), 56. https://books.google.com/books/about/Lochmaben_Five_Hundred_Years_Ago_Or_Sele.html?id=qqYHAAAAQAAJ&printsec=frontcover&source=kp_read_button&hl=en&newbks=1&newbks_redir=0#v=onepage&q&f=false
[375] Lloyd D. Graham, *House Graham, From the Antoine Wall to the Temple of Hymen*, (Lulu.com, 2020), 41.

### 7 June 1300

- The king (Edward I) for the good service of Isabella widow of John de Vescy senior, grants to her the lands of Nicholas de Graham a rebel, in Wooler and elsewhere in Northumberland.[376]

### About 1309-1312

- John of Graham, Lord of Dalkeith, has confirmed the donation of the land of Balnebuch (MLO), which Peter of Graham made to the monks of Newbattle.[377] Additionally, grants to Newbattle Abbey general license to quarry the rock called 'sclaytsayn' [slate?] in his quarry of Dalkeith (MLO), <u>either within Braid Wood or outside of it</u>, to take shelter in his house, to have free entrance and exit. Confirms that Braid Wood was a part of Dalkeith.[378]

### 1315-1321

- Robert I, "Robert the Bruce," in his role as Lord of Annandale, grants the lands of Brackenwra in the tenement of Hutton-sub-mora, to Adam Barbour, lands resigned by Peter de Graham.[379]

### October between 1299 and 1311

- John of Graham, knight, son and heir of Sir Nicholas of Graham, Lord of Abercorn and Westerkirk, granted to Melrose Abbey right of patronage of the church of Westerkirk (DMF) of the diocese of Glasgow, with its lands, etc.[380]

### 10 December 1319

- Robert, King of Scots, confirmed the donation made by John Graham the father to William de Soulis all the lands that the said John had in Eskdale in the Barony of Westerker with the advowson (right to appoint clergy, a right that had monetary value and could be sold) of the church of Westerker.[381]

### 1320s

- Sir David Graham of Dundaff/Kincardine had exchanged his property of Cardross in Dunbartonshire, with King Robert for the lands of Old Montrose, Forfarshire.[382]

### 1321

- Robert I, "Robert the Bruce," granted the whole lands and town of Torthorwald, with the three-husbandland of Roucan, in free warren as a reward for services and in part compensation for the

---

[376] *Calendar of Patent Rolls, Edward I: Volume 3, 1292-1301*, ed. 513, 577.
[377] PoMS, "No. 1764, person summary," accessed 5 April 2023. https://www.poms.ac.uk/record/person/1764/
[378] PoMS, "No. 16488, person summary," accessed 7 January 2023. https://www.poms.ac.uk/record/person/16488/
[379] PoMS, "No. 10399," accessed 7 January 2023. https://www.poms.ac.uk/record/source/10399/
[380] PoMS, "No. 16488," person summary, accessed 7 January 2023. https://www.poms.ac.uk/record/person/16488/
[381] PoMS, "No.9859," accessed 7 January 2023. https://www.poms.ac.uk/record/source/9859/
[382] Iain D. Mcintosh, "David Graham of Fintry-30th March 1620," *Book of Emminent Burgesses of Dundee (1513-1885)*, 2020. http://www.fdca.org.uk/1620_David_Graham_of_Fintry.html

destruction of Auchencass, the family's former stronghold. Thereafter Humphrey Kirkpatrick, husband of Isobel of Torthorwald, and his successors were designated 'of Torthorwald' which presumably became their new seat.[383]

## 20 April 1321

- Robert I gave James, Lord of Douglas, knight, half of all the barony of Westerker (DMF) in Eskdale which Sir William de Soulis forfeited, holding in feu and heritage, with homages and services of freeholders, multures, mills, fishing, hawking, and hunting.[384]

## 1325-1327

- King Robert the Bruce granted the lands of Old Montrose in the county of Forfar to David Graham, the elder, in exchange for the lands of Cardross, in the county of Dumbarton, where the king spent the last years of his life.[385]

## 1337

- The elder Sir John de Graham, Lord of Tarbolton, donated to Failford Ministry his right of patronage to the church of Tarbolton. Before 1342, the younger Sir John de Graham "the Last," bestowed it on a cousin, Robert Graham of Weyliston in Tarbolton, who in 1342 transferred it to Melrose Abbey.[386] This meant that both Failford and Melrose had a claim to the revenues of the church in Tarbolton and a dispute ensued.[387]

## Circa 1341

- (The charter is undated, but based on the witnesses, estimated to have been signed in 1341.) John de Graham, Lord of Tarbolton, confirmed to <u>his beloved uncle</u> Henry de Graham and to his heirs and assigns all the lands of Westirbyr with their fees below the barony of Abercorn.[388]

---

[383] Sir James Balfour Paul, *The Scots Peerage, Founded on Wood's Edition,* Vol. II, (Edinburgh: David Douglas, 1905), 381-382. https://archive.org/details/bub_gb_ELEEAAAAIAAJ/page/381/mode/2up?q=auchincass

[384] PoMS, "No. 9878," accessed 7 February 2023. https://www.poms.ac.uk/record/source/9878/

[385] Iain D. Mcintosh, "David Graham of Fintry-30th March 1620," *Book of Emminent Burgesses of Dundee (1513-1885),* 2020. http://www.fdca.org.uk/1620_David_Graham_of_Fintry.html

[386] Sir William Fraser Facsimiles of Scottish Charters and Letters, "Charter by Robert de Graham, Lord of Weyliston, to the Church of St Mary of Melrose, of the patronage of the Church of Torbolton, 11th July 1342," School of History, Classics and Archaeology Teaching Collections, University of Edinburgh, accessed 10 February 2023. http://Col.lections.shca.ed.ac.uk/items/show/92

[387] William J. Dillon, "The Trinitarians at Failford," *Ayrshire Archaeological and Natural History Society Vol 4, (1957):* 76. https://aanhsorg.files.wordpress.com/2018/08/the-trinitarians-of-failford.pdf

[388] Historical Manuscripts Commission, *The Manuscripts of the Duke of Hamilton, Knight, Eleventh Report, Appendix, Part VI,* 219.

*Appendix F: Genealogy of the Border Grahams*

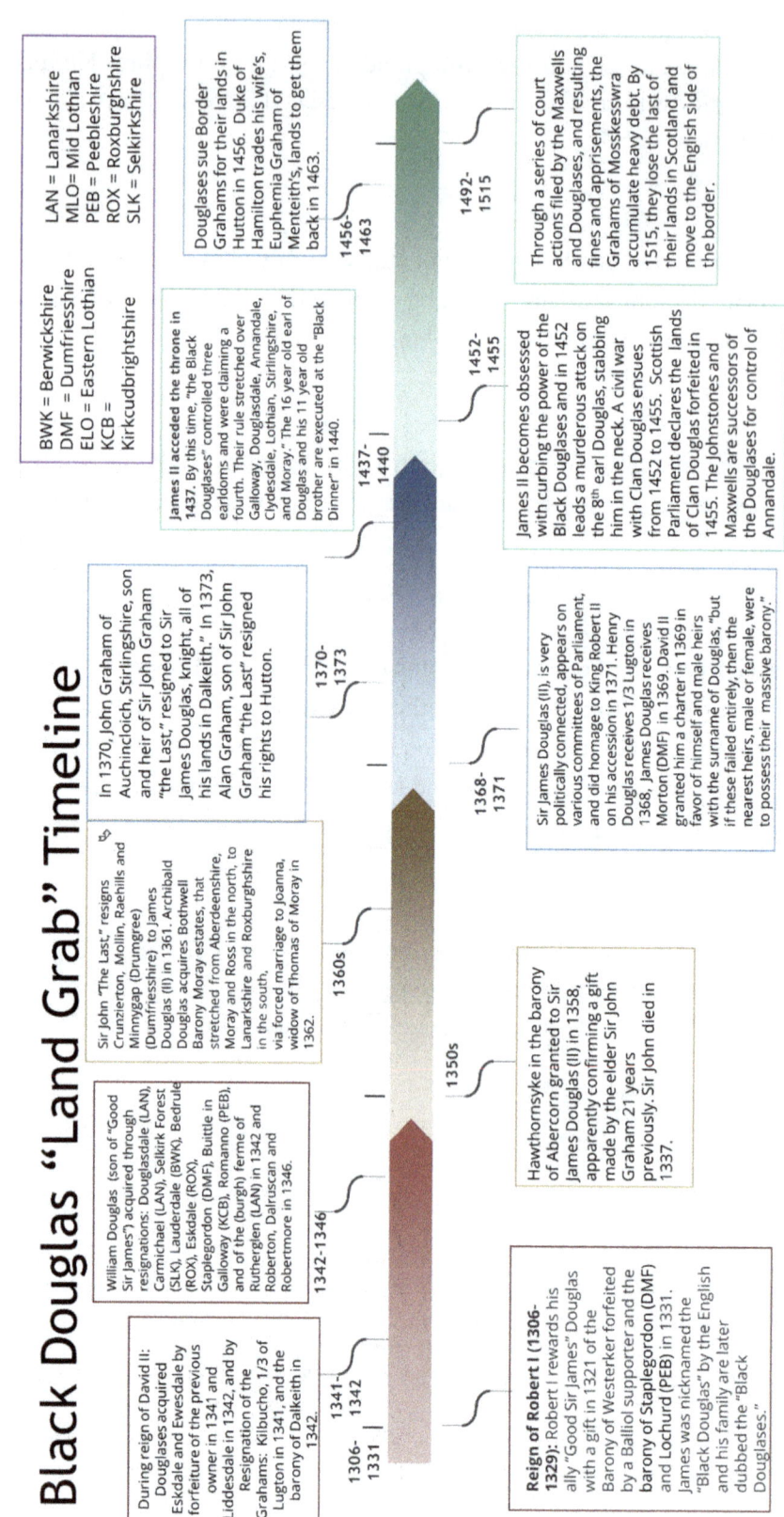

Figure F-19: *Timeline of Scotland's Internal Power Struggle Involving Clan Douglas (1331-1515)* [389]

---

[389] Figure F-19: "County Abbreviations List," People of Medieval Scotland (PoMS), accessed 18 April 2023. https://www.poms.ac.uk/information/county-abbreviations-list/  Remaining sources provided in chronology on pages F-65 to F-71.

## "Black Douglas" Land Grab Begins

### 16 February 1342

- David II gave William of Douglas, knight, all the lands of Liddesdale, which belonged to the late William de Soulis, knight.[390]

### July 1342

- Charter by Robert de Graham, Lord of Weyliston, to the Church of St Mary of Melrose, of the patronage of the Church of Tarbolton, 11th July 1342.[391]

### October 1344

- To the bishop of St. Andrews. Faculty to Avignon, grant dispensation to John de Douglas, knight, and Agnes de Grame (Monfode) to intermarry, they having lived together and had offspring.[392]

### 1347

- John Graham, ninth Earl of Menteith was executed for his part in the Battle of Neville's Cross.[393]

### 1349

- Mary Stirling, widow of Sir John Stewart of Menteith, gave the barony of Roberton to William Douglas.[394]

### 1355-56

- Charter by John de Graham, "the Last," son and heir of Sir John Graham, Laird of Mosskesswra, to Roger de Kirkpatrick, Laird of Torthorwald, setting an annual rent of 40s out of the lands of Over Dryfe.[395]

### 1357

- Sir John Stewart of Darnley received from Robert, seventh High Steward, the fee of the principal tenement of Tarbolton in the barony of Kyle (Ayrshire) upon the resignation of John de Graham.[396]

---

[390] PoMS, "No. 10195," accessed 7 January 2023. https://www.poms.ac.uk/record/source/10195/

[391] William J. Dillon, "The Trinitarians at Failford," 76.

[392] John P. Ravilious, "Agnes De Graham, wife of (1) John de Monfode and (2) John de Douglas," *The Scottish Genealogist*, LXI No. 4, The Scottish Genealogy Society, (December 2014): 129. https://www.academia.edu/34967491/TSG_Agnes_de_Graham_wife_of_John_de_Monfode_and_Sir_John_de_Douglas_TSG_LXI_4_129_133

[393] Michael A. Penman, "The Scots at the Battle of Neville's Cross, 17 October 1346," 167.

[394] Matthew Hammond, "Resignations: David II (1329-71)," The community of the realm in Scotland, 1249-1424: History, law and charters in a recreated kingdom, 21 November 2019. https://cotr.ac.uk/social-network-analysis-political-communities-and-social-networks/forfeitures-resignations-and-escheats/resignations-david-ii-1329-71/

[395] *Registrum Honoris de Morton, Volume II: Ancient Charters*, 2-3.

[396] William J. Dillon, "The Trinitarians at Failford," 91-99.

## 1357

- A gift of lands of Wamphray and Drumcreth (Dumcrieff) in a 16 June 1357 charter to "consanguineo nostro dilecto" or "our beloved cousin" Roger Kirkpatrick by "John of Corry", but the seal is a combination of the Newby Corry and Graham armorials: a Saltire and on chief with three escallops, signed "Sir John Grame, Lord of Mosskesswra." Shortly after, in late June 1357, Roger de Kirkpatrick was assassinated in Caerlaverock Castle by Sir James Lindsey.[397]

## 10 February 1357

- David II gave William Sinclair all the lands of Mertoun and of Merchiston in the sheriffdom of Edinburgh (MLO), which William Bisset resigned.[398]

## 16 February 1358

- David II approved and ratified the donation made by the late John Graham to Agnes of Monfode nee Graham, mother of Sir James Douglas, of the land of Hawthornsyke in the barony of Abercorn.[399]

## 1361-62

- The younger Sir John the Grame of Dalkeith gifted the lands of Elystone or Ellastown to John, son and heir of Richard de Graham. I believe this "Ellastown" was the same as Elliston on the estates of Melrose Abbey. Since the other land gifts made later in life by this Sir John the Grame were to cousins and brothers-in-law, this "giftee" John, son of Richard de Graham, must also be a relative.[400] Figure F-2.

## January 1361

- "John of Corrie" a.k.a.: Sir John "the Last," resigns the lands of Crunzierton, Mollin, Raehills and Minnygap (Drumgree) (Dumfriesshire) to James Douglas, Lord of Dalkeith.[401]

## 6 January 1362

- Confirmation of an earlier resignation of the Barony of Barnbougle (West Lothian) by John Graham, ninth Earl of Menteith to Sir Bartholomew de Leon. This John de Graham was executed by the English in 1347.[402]

---

[397] William Fraser, *The Annandale family book of the Johnstones, Earls and Marquises of Annandale*, Vol. I, 10-11.
[398] PoMS, "No. 23344, person summary," accessed 7 January 2023. https://www.poms.ac.uk/record/person/23344/
[399] PoMS, "No. 23347, person summary," accessed 7 January 2023. https://www.poms.ac.uk/record/person/23347/
[400] T.J. Carlyle, *The Debateable Land*, 10.
[401] PoMS, "No. 23387, person summary," accessed 7 January 2023. https://www.poms.ac.uk/record/person/23387/
[402] Matthew Hammond, "Resignations: David II (1329-71)," The Community of the Realm in Scotland, 1249-1424: History, law and charters in a recreated kingdom, 21 November 2019. https://cotr.ac.uk/social-network-analysis-political-communities-and-social-networks/forfeitures-resignations-and-escheats/resignations-david-ii-1329-71/

## 6 January 1362

- Mary of Menteith, Countess of Menteith, resigns the Barony of Barnbougle (West Lothian) to Phillipa Mowbray.[403]

## 23 July 1362

- Papal dispensation approving the forced marriage of the widow of Thomas de Moray (fifth Lord Bothwell), Joanna of Menteith, to Archibald Douglas. Through this marriage Archibald Douglas became the sixth Lord Bothwell, inheriting the Moray estates that stretched from Aberdeenshire, Moray and Ross in the north, to Lanarkshire and Roxburghshire in the south.[404]

## November 1362

- David II approved and confirmed the donation which William Sinclair made to Alan Graham, of all his demesne land of Mertoun (MLO), except the manor of the same, for the term of his lifetime.[405]

## 10 December 1362

- David II gave John of Carruthers half of all the lands which were the late John of Raffles' within the holding of Mouswald (DMF).[406]

---

[403] Matthew Hammond, "Resignations: David II (1329-71)," The Community of the Realm in Scotland, 1249-1424: History, law and charters in a recreated kingdom, 21 November 2019.

[404] William Fraser, *Douglas Book*, Vol. 1, 352.

[405] PoMS, "No. 23601, person summary," accessed 7 January 2023. https://www.poms.ac.uk/record/person/23601/

[406] PoMS, "No. 23200, person summary," accessed 7 January 2023. https://www.poms.ac.uk/record/person/23200/

Figure F-20: Joan and Cornelius Blaeu and Timothy Pont, *Atlas of Scotland*, Lothian and Linlitquo, Joan et Cornelius Blaeu exc., Amsterdam, Blaeu, 1654. https://maps.nls.uk/view/00000395

# Appendix F: Genealogy of the Border Grahams

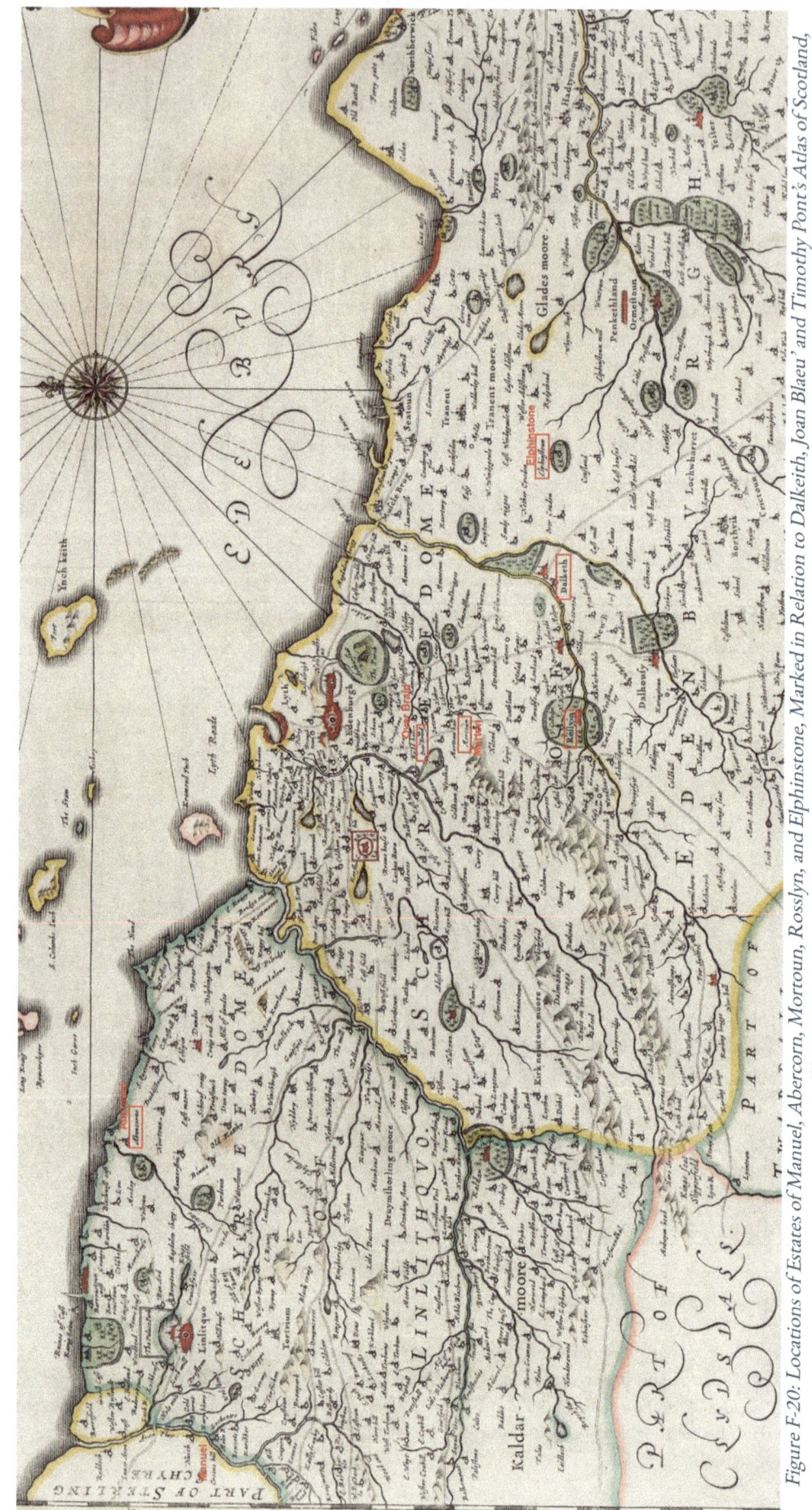

*Figure F-20: Locations of Estates of Manuel, Abercorn, Mortoun, Rosslyn, and Elphinstone, Marked in Relation to Dalkeith, Joan Blaeu' and Timothy Pont's Atlas of Scotland, 1654.*[406] *CC-BY 4.0 Reproduced with the permission of the National Library of Scotland.*

## 23 March 1363

- David II approved that donation which John Graham, son and heir of John Graham of Dalkeith made to John Graham son of Richard Graham, of the lands of Elphinstone (ELO) in the sheriffdom of Edinburgh; holding by Agnes Graham, spouse of Andrew de [?-unknown surname], nearest heir of the said John, as contained in John Graham's letter or charter.[407]

## From 1368 to 1371

- Sir James Douglas, is very politically connected, appears on various committees of Parliament, and did homage to King Robert II on his accession in 1371.[408]

## January 1368

- Sir James Douglas (son of Agnes Graham-Monfode-Douglas and John Douglas, Lord of Aberdour in Perthshire) received permission from David II to repair the Castle of Dalkeith.[409]

## 7 December 1368

- David II gave John [Graham] of Dalkeith a third part of the lands of Lugton in the Sheriffdom of Edinburgh (Midlothian), which belonged to Laurence of Kinpont (Kilpunt). Cousin Henry Douglas, brother of James, also was granted a third part of the lands of Lugton.[410]

## 27 June 1369

- David, King of Scots, has approved, ratified and confirmed that donation which his beloved relative George of Dunbar, Earl of March, made to his beloved and faithful James Douglas, knight, of the lands of Morton (DMF), as contained in the earl's charter; saving the king's service.[411]

## December 1369

- Sir James went through the formality of resigning the barony of Dalkeith so the next day, David II granted him a charter in favor of himself and male heirs with the surname of Douglas, but if these failed entirely, then the nearest heirs, male or female, were to possess the barony.[412]

## 1370

- Sir James Douglas' uncle, Sir William Douglas, who had no surviving children of his own, resigns claims to Dalkeith. Deed is ratified by David II. After this Sir James Douglas, knight, is

---

[407] PoMS, "No. 23643, person summary," accessed 7 January 2023. https://www.poms.ac.uk/record/person/23643/
[408] William Fraser, *Douglas Book*, Vol. 1, 170-172.
[409] PoMS, "No. 23552, person summary," accessed 7 January 2023. https://www.poms.ac.uk/record/person/23552/
[410] PoMS, "No. 10871," accessed 7 January 2023. https://www.poms.ac.uk/record/source/10871/
[411] PoMS, "No. 11008," accessed 7 January 2023. https://www.poms.ac.uk/record/source/11008/
[412] PoMS, "No. 23552," person summary, accessed 7 January 2023. https://www.poms.ac.uk/record/person/23552/

styled in all writs Lord of Dalkeith, his former designation having been Sir James Douglas, knight.[413]

## 1370

- John Graham of Auchincloich, Stirlingshire "On this day at Edinburgh John Graham, described as son and heir of the above, resigned to Sir James Douglas, knight, all of his lands in Dalkeith."[414]

## 1373

- Alan Graham, son and heir of Sir John de Graham, knight, gave up rights to Hutton-Sub-Mora (Hutton Below-the-Moor or Nether Hutton) Kirk to James de Douglas for the payment of £40 sterling. The Douglases were not resident in Hutton but leased or feued the lands of the parish to others.[415]

## 1426

- A deed regarding the possession of a Cambus (storeroom) by Nicholaum le Grahame de Auchincloch (presumed descendant of the John Graham of Auchincloich listed in 1370 record above) in Stirlingshire.[416]

## Prior to 1432

- Thomas Graham of Auchencass, derived his designation from his marriage to Janet Kirkpatrick, daughter of Sir Duncan Kirkpatrick who was the son of the younger Sir Roger Kirkpatrick. Figure F-2. It is entirely possible that this Thomas Graham is the same Thomas Graham of Mosskesswra who was the uncle of Lang Will Graham. Ages, locations, and events match both Thomas Grahams.[417]

## Prior to 1456

- An undated King's letter compelling the Grahams to compear on 12th July and bring with them charters and documents to prove their rights to the lands of Hutton was signed by James II of Scotland. In response, "William, Richard and Henry the Grame" signed a petition to the king, claiming possession of said lands "in feu and heritage"[418] for 100 years or more. The Grames complained of only twelve days' notice.[419] Figure F-21.

---

[413] PoMS, "No. 23552," person summary, accessed 7 January 2023. https://www.poms.ac.uk/record/person/23552/
[414] John Reid, "Material for a Place Name Survey of East Stirlingshire," Scottish Place Name Society, 109. https://spns.org.uk/wp-content/uploads/2019/12/John-Reids-East-Stirlingshire-place-name-data-v2019.pdf
[415] *Registrum Honoris de Morton, Volume II: Ancient Charters*, 88, 115, 117-119.
[416] John Reid, "Material for a Place Name Survey of East Stirlingshire," 109.
[417] Sir James Balfour Paul, *The Scots Peerage, Founded on Wood's Edition*, Vol. II (Edinburgh: David Douglas, 1905), 381-382. https://archive.org/details/bub_gb_ELEEAAAAIAAJ/page/381/mode/2up?q=auchincass
[418] "Feu," *Dictionaries of the Scots Language*, accessed 12 February 2023. https://www.dsl.ac.uk/entry/snd/feu
[419] Figure F-21: Royal Commission on Historical Manuscripts. *Historical Manuscripts Commission, Report on Manuscripts of Sir Archibald Edmonstone of Duntreath, Volumes 5 and 6*, 77.

## 1456

- Sasine from Robert Graham of Fintry to fourth Earl of Angus for lands in Ewesdale (acquired through marriage to Janet Lovel of Ballumbie) witnessed by locals, including "Fergus the Grame." (Probable uncle/great uncle of Lang Will).[420]

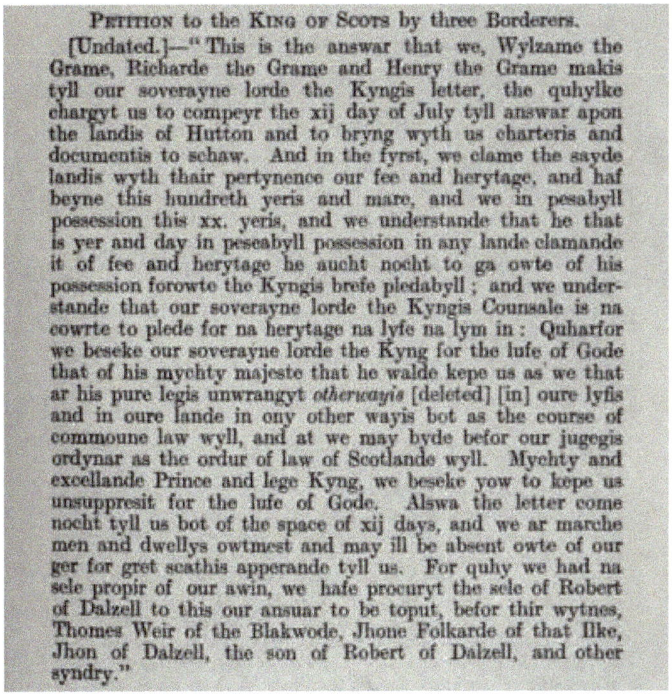
PETITION to the KING OF SCOTS by three Borderers.

[Undated.]—"This is the answar that we, Wylzame the Grame, Richarde the Grame and Henry the Grame makis tyll our soverayne lorde the Kyngis letter, the quhylke chargyt us to compeyr the xij day of July tyll answar apon the landis of Hutton and to bryng wyth us charteris and documentis to schaw. And in the fyrst, we clame the sayde landis wyth thair pertynence our fee and herytage, and haf beyne this hundreth yeris and mare, and we in pesabyll possession this xx. yeris, and we understande that he that is yer and day in peseabyll possession in any lande clamande it of fee and herytage he aucht nocht to ga owte of his possession forowte the Kyngis brefe pledabyll; and we understande that our soverayne lorde the Kyngis Counsale is na cowrte to plede for na herytage na lyfe na lym in: Quharfor we beseke our soverayne lorde the Kyng for the lufe of Gode that of his mychty majeste that he walde kepe us as we that ar his pure legis unwrangyt *otherwayis* [deleted] [in] oure lyfis and in oure lande in ony other wayis bot as the course of commoune law wyll, and at we may byde befor our jugegis ordynar as the ordur of law of Scotlande wyll. Mychty and excellande Prince and lege Kyng, we beseke yow to kepe us unsuppresit for the lufe of Gode. Alswa the letter come nocht tyll us bot of the space of xij days, and we ar marche men and dwellys owtmest and may ill be absent owte of our ger for gret scathis apperande tyll us. For quhy we had na sele propir of our awin, we hafe procuryt the sele of Robert of Dalzell to this our ansuar to be toput, befor thir wytnes, Thomes Weir of the Blakwode, Jhone Folkarde of that Ilke, Jhon of Dalzell, the son of Robert of Dalzell, and other syndry."

*Figure F-21: Petition by Border Grahams to James II Regarding Challenge of Ownership to Lands of Hutton circa 1456, Historical Manuscripts Commission* [419]

## 1456

- From R.C. Reid: "On 30th October 1456 when the third lord (Douglas) of Dalkeith was near death, he resigned the tenement of Hutton in favor of his son and heir, Sir James Douglas. James was given a new title "Earl of Morton," 14 March 1457-8, the sasine given "at the hill of Hutton called the capital messuage" identifiable with the Mote of Hutton. Amongst the witnesses were "Robert de Grame, William de Grame, Richard de Grame and John Grame..." [421]

## 15 May 1463

- After losing the challenge to their rights to Hutton lands in 1456, the Grahams were probably lobbying the court and all their connections to get their lands back. Seven years later, in 1463, the new king on the throne, James III approved[422] a trade between the Duke of Hamilton and his wife Euphemia Graham of Menteith, Countess of Douglas (by her first husband) and Herbert Johnston. The duke resigned his lands of Gledstanys and Auldtown of Machan and his wife resigned the lands of Nether and Upper Brecko and others. In exchange, Herbert granted Mosskesswra, Nether Dryfe, and Bedokholme to "William the Grahame." This William was the grandfather of Lang Will and John Graham of Gillesbie.[423]

## 22 August 1470

- Return of Lands de Brackenwra lying in the tenement of Hutton (near Hutton Sub Mora) to John de Grahame of Gillesbie who purchased "four slags of land" in Brackenwra from James, Earl of Morton. A slag is land where mineral ore waste has been deposited.[424]

---

420 William Fraser, *Douglas Book*, Vol. III (Edinburgh: T. and A. Constable, Edinburgh University Press, 1885),185-186. https://deriv.nls.uk/dcn23/9653/96539705.23.pdf

421 R.C. Reid, "The Border Grahams and Their Origins," 89.

422 Historical Manuscripts Commission, *The Manuscripts of the Duke of Hamilton, Knight, Eleventh Report, Appendix, Part VI* (Her Majesty's Stationery Office, London, 1887), 18. https://archive.org/details/manuscriptsofduk00greauoft/page/18/mode/2up?ref=ol&view=theater&q=moskeswra

423 Historical Manuscripts Commission, *The Manuscripts of the Duke of Hamilton, Knight, Eleventh Report, Appendix, Part VI* (London: Her Majesty's Stationery Office, 1887), 18.

424 *Registrum Honoris de Morton, Volume II: Ancient Charters*, 216-217.

## 1476

- William de Graham (Lang Will's father) and Thomas de Graham served on an assize (jury panel[425]) regarding terce (Church issues/tithes) from Dalduran in Langholm (later known as Westerhall in Parish Westerkirk. Parish Westerkirk was created in 1693.) While the Grahams did not reside in Eskdale at this time, the family, as Dalkeith Graham heirs, retained church advowson rights for Old Langholm which would have required their representation on the assize.[426]

## Disenfranchisement of the Grahams of Mosskesswra

## 1480

- William de Graham (presumed father of Lang Will) filed an action against his superior, James Douglas, the first Earl of Morton, relating to the lands of Croftend of Dryfe.[427]

## 1492

- Earl of Morton retaliates by accusing William de Graham of violent possession of the lands of Cumstoun, Fenton, Bordland (Boreland), Androgilles and Hillies.[428]

## 1493

- Grahams of Mosskesswra and Gillesbie attend the second Earl of Morton's sasine by attorney in Hutton.[429]

## 1507

- Lord Maxwells testimony—he named William Graham of the Knok of Hutton and Pait (Pete) Graham in Huchitoun (Kyle, Ayrshire) as heads of the families of "fugitives" who failed to appear in court. John Carruthers of Holmains, named as surety, had to pay 550 merks in fines for the Grahams' failure to appear, and apprised the Graham lands of Mosskesswra when they failed to pay him back.[430]

## 1510

- Crown charter apprised the five merkland of Meikle Hutton, belonging to William Graham of Mosskesswra. Graham had been fined £70 of which £66 13s 4d was still owing. He had no other moveables, so a portion of the lands were transferred by the Crown to John, Lord Maxwell. This was a likely reason behind the Graham feud with the Maxwells that culminated in the Grahams' role in the Battle of Dryfe Sands in 1593.[431]

---

[425] "Assize," *Dictionaries of the Scots Language*, accessed 13 January 2023. https://dsl.ac.uk/entry/snd/assize
[426] R.C. Reid, "The Border Grahams and Their Origins," 90.
[427] R.C. Reid, "The Border Grahams and Their Origins," 90.
[428] R.C. Reid, "The Border Grahams and Their Origins," 90.
[429] Charles Adrian Kelham, *Bases of Magnatial Power in Later Fifteenth-Century Scotland* (Edinburgh: University of Edinburgh, 1986), 206. https://era.ed.ac.uk/bitstream/1842/6867/1/372968.pdf
[430] R.C. Reid, "The Border Grahams and Their Origins," 90.
[431] R.C. Reid, "The Border Grahams and Their Origins," 91.

## 1515

- John Carruthers, the surety bond holder of William Graham, still owing money to the Crown under the Justiciary Court decree, presumably surrendered some of the Graham lands to the Crown in payment. In November 1515, the Crown granted to Alexander Jardine of Applegarth, the three merkland lands of Mosskesswra that pertained to William Graham.[432]

## 1515

- Mr. Alexander Murray of the Kirk of Hutton levied a complaint against William Graham of Mosskesswra and Robert Graham of Gillesbie for ingathering and detaining the teinds (tithes). Though a procurator defended the Grahams, the Lords of Council found in favor of Mr. Murray. William Graham and cousin John Corry lost their remaining lands in Scotland. William Graham took up residence with his family in the Debatable Land on the English/Scottish Border near "Longtown or "Lang" town, England and was thenceforth known as "Lang Will."[433]

## 1541

- James Graham of Gillesbie and Mosskesswra heads forty retainers at the Wapenshaw at Burnswark, indicating the Gillesbie Grahams remained in Scotland and were prosperous.[434]

## 1543

- On 8 May 1543, Nicol Graham of Mosskesswra (Meskeswaye) gave a bond of manrent to John Johnston. A notary had to sign for him but a portion of his seal is still attached to the document. Significantly it shows a fess between three escallops, two and one.[435]

## 1567

- Heithat and Branriggs were granted by the Regent Earl of Morton to John, son and heir of James Graham of Gillesbie.[436]

## 1593

- Battle of Dryfe Sands. Scottish clan battle between the Clan Maxwell and Clan Johnstone after a hundred years of feuding. The Johnstones won a decisive victory over the Maxwells. The Grahams of the Debatable Lands (formerly of Mosskesswra) fought with the Johnstones against the Maxwells.[437]

---

[432] R.C. Reid, "The Border Grahams and Their Origins," 91.
[433] R.C. Reid, "The Border Grahams and Their Origins," 91.
[434] Col. William Rogerson, *Hutton Under the Muir*, 25.
[435] Sir William Fraser, *The Annandale Family Book of the Johnstones, Earls and Marquises of Annandale*, Vol.I, 111.
[436] Col. William Rogerson, *Hutton Under the Muir*, 31.
[437] The Battle of Dryfe Sands, 6 December 1593," The Border Reivers Website.

## 1596

- Lord Burghley, chief advisor to Elizabeth I, tried to pacify the Western March. The final division of the Debatable land in 1552 allocated a number of Scottish Grahams in the parish of Kirkandrews to England. Burghley found it necessary to prepare a detailed memorandum derived from his Wardens' reports concerning the Grahams living on the Scottish-English border.[438]

## 28 February 1607

- John Grahame, heir of Nicholas Grahame of Cumstoun, father, ~ "5 mereatarum," was confirmed to have the third part of the merited land of Cumstoun old, and a third of the land stretching the aforesaid below dominion and barony of Mosskesswra (Meskesso), parish of Hutton of the stewardship of the Annandale Valley. B. 22s. 2d.[439]

## 17 February 1610

- John Grahame, heir of Nicholas Graham, father, was confirmed in possession of the third part of merited land of Cumpstoun old, stretched out, running to 22 shillings 3 pence, land under the dominion of Mosskesswra, and the earldom of Dalkeith, of the stewardship of the Annandale Valley. E. 22s. 3d.] [440]

## 1608-1610

- Scottish Privy Records. In 1608, Thomas Johnstone of Craigburn issues bonds of 2000 merks and 1000 merks respectively for James Grahame of Langboddam and his brother, Robert Graham of Hoilhouse, to not harm Robert French of Frenchland. In 1609, James Graham of Langboddam is denounced by the Privy Council for failure to appear to answer charges by the Johnstones of appropriating land that they say was theirs.[441]

## October 1611

- The Privy Council acquits "Kirstie Grahme of Millriggis" and "Kirstie Grahme, callit Young Kirstie" of suspected crimes along with many others who answered summons to court in Dumfries.[442]

---

[438] R.C. Reid, "The Border Grahams and Their Origins," 86.

[439] Thomas Thompson, *Inquisitionum ad Capellam Domini Regis Retornatarum, quae in Publicis Srchivis Scotiae adhuc servantur, abbreviation* (London: Great Britain Record Commission, 1811), (28-46), 129. https://books.google.com/books?id=8tQsAQAAMAAJ&printsec=frontcover#v=onepage&q&f=false

[440] Thomas Thompson, *Inquisitionum ad Capellam Domini Regis Retornatarum, quae in Publicis Srchivis Scotiae adhuc servantur, abbreviation* (London: Great Britain Record Commission, 1811), (69-86), 131.

[441] David Masson, *The Register of the Privy Council of Scotland*. First Series (Edinburgh: H.M. General Register House, 1887), Vol. VIII, 647. https://catalog.hathitrust.org/Record/100404514

[442] David Masson, *The Register of the Privy Council of Scotland*. (Edinburgh: H.M. General Register House, 1877), First Series, Vol. 9, 712-713. https://catalog.hathitrust.org/Record/100404514

## 1619

- Complaint from Scottish Privy Council Records by Sir Thomas Hamilton of Bynnie and James Williamson in Mackillgill against James Graham of Langboddam and his son, Robert, for attacking Williamson and his spouse.[443]

## 1624

- Robert Graham of Gillesbie is a cautioner for a bond of 35 pounds for Mr. George Pryde, minister of Hutton.[444]

## 1626

- John (Jok) Graham of Dryfe, a lieutenant in the King's Border Guard, resigned to the earl of Melrose the Temple lands of Shaw and Shawneuk. Then there was a re-grant of said lands to his son John, in which the latter was infeft (officially in possession of heritable land) in 1627. (Annandale Charter Chest.)[445]

## 1635

- James Graham of Gillesbie was a cautioner on 5 December 1635. The last Gillesbie Graham on record for 33 years is this James of Gillesbie in 1635. The tower of Gillesbie was abandoned shortly thereafter.[446]

## 1641

- The Gillesbie Grahams abandoned their tower and left Scotland circa 1641 after a battle between the Graham lairds of Gillesbie and Shaw that left the laird of Shaw dead.[447]

## 1642

- Lord Durie is kidnapped by Col. Will Armstrong and imprisoned for three months in the abandoned "Tower of Grame,"[448] believed to the Tower of Gillesbie.[449] Colonel Armstrong's adult sons left for County Fermanagh, Ireland prior to this time.[450] The timing of the Grahams' of Gillesbie and Armstrongs' of Langholm departure from Scotland roughly coincide, suggesting the two groups departed for Ireland together.

---

[443] R.C. Reid, "The Border Grahams and Their Origins," 99.
[444] R.C. Reid, "The Border Grahams and Their Origins," 93-94.
[445] Col. William Rogerson, *Hutton Under the Muir*, 7.
[446] R.C. Reid, "The Border Grahams and Their Origins," 93-94.
[447] Col. William Rogerson, *Hutton Under the Muir*, 26.
[448] John G. Armstrong, "The Debatable Armstrongs and Their Graham Relations," 3.
[449] Col. William Rogerson, *Hutton Under the Muir*, 26.
[450] James Lewis Armstrong, M.D., *Chronicles of the Armstrongs*, 362.

## 22 Oct 1668

- John Graham of Gillesbie is grantor of bond of his lands, fielded at the Mackenzie's Office.[451]

## 8 Mar 1669

- John Graham of Gillesbie and his wife Margaret Scott are the grantors of a bond and tack with respect to his lands at Mackenzie's Office. Per the 1669 Scotland Register of Deeds. At the restoration of Charles II in May 1660, Scottish property records were divided amongst Durie's, Dalrymple's and Mackenzie's offices.[452]

## 1 Aug 1670

- John Graham of Gillesbie granted a third bond on his lands, suggesting he was heavily in debt.[453]

## 1699

- The Gillesbie estate was under ownership of Robert Scott of Coshogle, brother to Francis Scott of Gilmanschleuch, suggesting the Scotts foreclosed on the debts of the Grahams of Gillesbie.[454]

---

[451] Scottish Record Office, *Index to Register of Deeds, 1668,* Vol. VIII (Edinburgh: His Majesty's Stationery Office, 1924), 181. https://www.google.com/books/edition/Indexes/6ISQFt6Y5ekC?hl=en&gbpv=1&bsq=%20gillesbie

[452] Scottish Record Office, *Index to Register of Deeds, 1669,* Vol. IX (Edinburgh: His Majesty's Stationery Office, 1926), 177.
https://www.google.com/books/edition/Index_to_Register_of_Deeds_Preserved_in/C8wRAAAAIAAJ?hl=en&gbpv=1&bsq=graham

[453] Scottish Record Office, *Index to Register of Deeds, 1670,* Vol. X (Edinburgh: His Majesty's Stationery Office, 1926), 170.
https://www.google.com/books/edition/Index_to_Register_of_Deeds_Preserved_in/vsQRAAAAIAAJ?hl=en&gbpv=1

[454] R.C. Reid, "The Border Grahams and Their Origins," 94.

Appendix F: Genealogy of the Border Grahams

# Table of Figures

Figure F-1: Amended Pedigree of William de Graham (Original Figure provided by Dr. Lloyd D. Graham in "House Graham" ..................................................................................................................F-7

Figure F-2: Pedigree of the Third Sir Henry de Graham and the Proposed Origin of the J1 Border Grahams ..................................................................................................................................................F-8

Figure F-3: Pedigree of Sir Andrew de Murray of Manuel, J1 Graham Patriarch Candidate from The Chiefship of the Clan Murray, Author: "B." The Scottish Antiquary, or, Northern Notes and Queries, Oct., 1900, Vol. 15, No. 58, [38] with modifications in red ......................................................... F-12

Figure F-4: Menteith Coat of Arms [47] Reproduced here under CC BY-SA 4.0. .................................. F-13

Figure F-5: Map of Medieval Scottish Church Dioceses provided by ECNS [Early Church in Northern Scotland] [59]................................................................................................................................... F-15

Figure F-6: Thirteenth and Fourteenth Century Pedigree of the Menteith Earls of Menteith from the "Redbook of Menteith," Volume 1, by William Fraser[66] and the writings of John P. Ravilous [60, 67] CC BY-SA 4.0. ................................................................................................................................................ F-17

Figure F-7: Site of Mosskesso Closs/Close, and the site of the Gillesbie Tower Remains Site of Mosskesso Closs/Close, and the site of the Gillesbie Tower Remains ................................................................ F-27

Figure F-8: Border Liberties (Free Territories) Under Scottish Control Prior to 1286....................... F-30

Figure F-9: Approximate Locations of Graham Estates in Hutton Parish. Upper Dryfe defined as "the marches of Eskdale run, the marches of Wamphray to Dryfehead and thence descending by the marches of Eskdalemuir to Patrickshaw," Lower Dryfe, which includes Nether Hutton (Hutton Sub Mora). The "barony" of Mosskesswra stretches below Cumstoun. The environs of Edinburgh, Haddington, Dunse, Kelso, Jedburgh, Hawick, Selkirk, Peebles, Langholm and Annan, making a complete map of the South East district of Scotland / by John Ainslie. Butterworth junt. script. 1821. [144] CC-BY 4.0 Reproduced with the permission of the National Library of Scotland. ................................................................ F-31

Figure F-10: Medieval Motte and Bailey Castle Design [144] Used here under CC0 1.0 License ........... F-32

Figure F-11: "Charter by King David I to Robert Bruce, of the lands of Annandale and Selkirk in Forest, circa 1125-1129," University of Edinburgh, School of History, Classics and Archaeology Teaching Collections [147] .....................................................................................................................................F-33

Figure F-12: "Charter by William de Bruce to Ivo de Kirkpatrick, of the lands in Pennersax, called Thorbrec, and Williambi and Blacwde, 1194-1214," University of Edinburgh, School of History, Classics and Archaeology Teaching Collections.[240]......................................................................................F-41

Figure F-13: Map of Annandale Churches, Chapels, Priories, Hospitals and Timber Castles which correspond to the estates of the original Knights of Annandale © Crown Copyright: HES https://canmore.org.uk/collection/1917793 ..................................................................................... F-43

Figure F-14: Amended Map of the Original Ten Knights Fees of Annandale. With Author's annotations, and with gratitude to .................................................................................................................. F-44

Figure F-15: Hoddam Castle, View from Repentance Tower. Photo by Scot Hill, 2011. [280]This file is licensed under CC BY-SA 3.0. .............................................................................................................F-48

Figure F-16: Ruins of Lochmaben Castle from the Mid-Fourteenth Century. There was an Earlier Timber Structure on this Site. [284] Photo © Lynne Kirton (CC BY-SA/2.0), 2004. .......................... F-49

Figure F-17: Lochwood Pele/Peel Tower from the Annandale Family of the Johnstones, Vol. 1 [303] ... F-51

Figure F-18: Johnstone Arms: Argent, a Saltire Sable, on a Chief Gules Three Cushions Or, by Kaliforniyka. [306] Licensed under CC BY 4.0. ............................................................................. F-52

Figure F-19: Timeline of Scotland's Internal Power Struggle Involving Clan Douglas (1331-1515) [389] F-63

Figure F-20: Locations of Estates of Manuel, Abercorn, Mortoun, Rosslyn, and Elphinstone, Marked in Relation to Dalkeith, Joan Blaeu' and Timothy Pont's Atlas of Scotland, 1654. [406] CC-BY 4.0 Reproduced with the permission of the National Library of Scotland. ...............................................F-67

Figure F-21: Petition by Border Grahams to James II Regarding Challenge of Ownership to Lands of Hutton circa 1456, Historical Manuscripts Commission [420] ............................................................ F-70

---

[i] Of note, theorized Graham ancestor, Forne Sigulfson was a benefactor to Hexham Priory (Convent).

[ii] The "barony" of Mosskesswra stretches below Cumstoun. Technically, Mosskesswra was not a barony (did not have a tower beside the Motte). Hutton was the name of the barony for that region.

[iii] Ecclesiastical fiefs were granted by churchmen to princes, barons, knights, and others, who thereupon assumed the obligation of protecting the church and domains of the overlord. Fiefs were heritable, passed down to heirs. https://www.newadvent.org/cathen/14512c.htm

[iv] Coincidentally, there is a village named "Boreland" to the south east of Wamphray. Figure 19.

[v] Of note, many of the knights arrived in Annandale without surnames. They acquired surnames from their Scottish estates or an occupation, e.g. "Adam the Barber." https://www.poms.ac.uk/record/person/23013/

[vi] Odard also retained the lands of Gamelsby and Glassanby in Carlisle, a source of continued litigation in the Carlisle family.

[vii] I believe Richard le Fleming is the "Fleming" in the name of Parish Kirkpatrick-Fleming.

[viii] Most of the "Bie" or "By" suffixed estate names (e.g., Lockerbie, Middlebie, Newbie, Piersbie, Sibbaldbie) (Appendix B) were established after the Bruce plantation, meaning they would have been assigned to the lands by the Knights of Annandale, which adds weight to a large part of them being Anglo-Scandanavians who migrated from Cumberland.

[ix] Of interest, the lord of Hutton's knight's fee would have provided at least 40 men at arms for service from the Corrie estates to support "the fourth" Sir Henry de Graham, son of Ralph Corrie, at the Siege of Caerverlock in 1300.
Murray Johnston, "The Size of a Knight's Fee," Watford Knight's Fee, accessed 7 January 2023. https://www.watfordmanors.com/single-post/2018/03/25/The-Size-of-a-Knights-Fee

# Appendix G:  Glossary of Relevant Graham Estates and of Their Kin

*Border Graham "Tribes" and Key Estates (and Their Kin) by Phil Graham and Alicia Graham, in Alphabetical Order*

Ever since the days of William the Lion, there have been Grahams in Hutton Parish. It has been generally accepted that Hutton was part of the Avenel estates and came to the Grahams in 1243 with the heiress of Roger Avenel. But Hutton can never have been Avenel property. It has always been in the great lordship of Annandale and ecclesiastically within that Deanery. The Grahams first acquired Hutton via their Fitz Gilbert and Levington ancestors.[1]

Towards the close of the reign of William the Lion (d. 1214), Henry de Graham, "Lord of Hutton," granted a lease of the pasturage of Upper Dryfe to Sir David de Torthorwald, who paid him 40/- yearly. The bounds are stated to have been "as the marches of Eskdale run, the marches of Wamphray to Dryfsheid (Dryfehead) and thence descending by the marches of Eskdalemuir to Patrickshaw." Figure F-9. Henry de Graham, son of the grantor, was a witness. Later the lands were transferred to the Kirkpatricks and then to the Grahams of Auchencass via marriage.[2]

**Abercorn.** The bishopric of Abercorn, established by the Angles in 681 A.D., was the oldest bishopric in Scotland. In 684 A.D., the Picts regained control of lands from the Scots and Angles "north of the Firth of Forth," what is now northeastern Scotland. Shortly thereafter, Bishop Trumwine, who had been commissioned as Bishop to the Picts, retreated south. As a precaution, he evacuated the monastery at Abercorn, which was on the border of the lands controlled by the Scots and lands controlled by the English.[3] The English must have returned because we find that just before the arrival of David I and his Norman land barons in 1124, Abercorn and Edinburgh were subject to the bishopric of Lindisfarne in Northumbria (Holy Island, base of St. Cuthbert).[4] The barony of Abercorn, including church lands, transferred to the Norman Avenel family soon after 1124. Abercorn passed to the elder line Grahams of Dalkeith with the marriage of the third Sir Henry de Graham to the heiress of Roger Avenel circa 1248. Control of the barony passed to the More/Mure/Muir family via Sybilla Graham and her husband, Sir William More/Muir prior to 1363. However, portions of Abercorn had previously been granted to Graham cousins (e.g., Grahams of Westirbyr or "West Binns," Henry of Braids).

---

[1] John P. Ravilious, "Grahams of Dalkeith: Their Comyn Ancestry," Narkive-Newsgroup Archive, 9 June 2007. https://soc.genealogy.medieval.narkive.com/nIG6OfnE/graham-of-dalkeith-their-comyn-ancestry

[2] *Registrum Honoris de Morton, Volume II: Ancient Charters* (Edinburgh: The Bannatyne Club, 1858), 2-3. https://archive.org/details/registrumhonoris02bann/page/2/mode/2up?ref=ol&view=theater&q=grah

[3] Robert Craig MacLagen, *The Perth Incident of 1396* (Edinburgh and London: William Blackwood and Sons, 1905), 31. https://www.forgottenbooks.com/en/readbook/ThePerthIncidentof1396_10016162#0

[4] Neil McGuigan, "Neither Scotland nor England: Middle Britain, c. 850-1150" (PhD Thesis, University of St. Andrews, 2015), 154. https://research-repository.st-andrews.ac.uk/bitstream/handle/10023/7829/NeilMcGuiganPhDThesis.pdf.txt;jsessionid=CF828DB2AB4E15189D9BDC94939C4671?sequence=7

**Airth Grahams.** The first earl of Airth was William Graham, seventh Earl of Menteith. The title of "Earl of Airth" was created on 21 January 1633 by Charles I. The title became extinct two generations later with the death of his grandson in 1694. Earl William was at one point very influential and had enjoyed the support of Charles I. However, when he requested the return of the earldom of Strathearn that had once belonged to the Grahams, a request in which he highlighted his own royal pedigree, he was seen as a threat and therefore lost favor in court. He was given the much smaller earldom of Airth instead.[5]

**Arthuret.** Also known as Motte of Liddel and Nichol Forest. Arthuret is named for Prince Arthur, son of King Adian McGabrian.[6,7] Arthuret is the site of the Battle of Arthuret between the kingdoms of Strathclyde and York in 573. A thousand years later, in 1515, when Lang Will Graham and his family first arrived in England after losing their lands in Scotland, they settled in the area near Arthuret called Netherby, where they had relatives. In 1628, Charles I confirmed the lands of Netherby called "Nicholsforest" to Sir Richard Graham of Plomp, who had purchased the estate from the previous title-holder, Francis Clifford.[8]

The king's forest was a buffer zone between the Celts and the Anglians (Anglo-Saxons). It became Nichol Forest in Northumberland, which is on the English side of the Scottish/English border between Bewcastle and Kershopefoot in the map in Figure G-3, just west of Netherby and Moat.[9]

**Auchencass Grahams.** Grahams in northwest Kirkpatrick-Juxta Moffatt, a.k.a. Saint Patrick's Kirk. Thomas Graham of Auchencass derived his designation from his marriage to Janet Kirkpatrick, from the family of Roger Kirkpatrick of Torthorwald, prior to 1432.[10] Roger's son, Sir Duncan Kirkpatrick, was granted the barony of Torthorwald in 1398. Leaving no male issue, his estates devolved upon his three daughters, the eldest of whom, Elizabeth Kirkpatrick, inherited Torthorwald, while the next daughter, Janet, received part of the lands of Kirkpatrick with Auchencass. Janet married Thomas Graham of Auchencass. Janet's sister, Elizabeth, married William Carlyle, son and heir of Sir John Carlyle. Sir Duncan died before June 1425, after which time William was designated "of Torthorwald." In 1436 Carlyle agreed to exchange Auchencass lands with Thomas Graham for half the

---

[5] William Fraser, *The Red Book of Menteith*, Vol. I (Edinburgh: 1880), 331-379. https://digital.nls.uk/histories-of-scottish-families/archive/96774276#?c=0&m=0&s=0&cv=217&xywh=-282%2C-337%2C5611%2C4159

[6] "The Battle of Arfderydd or Arthuret," Carla Nayland, accessed 6 January 2023. http://www.carlanayland.org/essays/battle_arthuret.htm

[7] Peter Bernhard, "The Real "King Arthur" of the Historical Records," Ancient Templar Knowledge, accessed 6 January 2023. https://commanderysaintmichael.wordpress.com/2015/01/24/the-real-king-arthur-of-the-historical-record/

[8] "Not All Grahams Were Treated Badly, One was Honored," Reivers.Info, 22 March 2019. http://reivers.info/pacification-graham-banished/

[9] Charles Smith, *Smith's New Map of England and Wales with Part of Scotland*, Map (London: C. Smith, 1827), Vision of Britain Through Time, accessed 8 February 2023. https://www.visionofbritain.org.uk/maps/sheet/smith_1806/smith4_1806

[10] Sir James Balfour Paul, *The Scots Peerage, Founded on Wood's Edition*, Vol. II (Edinburgh: David Douglas, 1905), 381-382. https://archive.org/details/bub_gb_ELEEAAAAIAAJ/page/381/mode/2up?q=auchincass

lands of Roucan, in the barony of Torthorwald.[11] Thomas Graham first appears on record as lord of Rowcan on 28 June 1432.[12]

Thomas' descendants claimed descent from Montrose; however, it is likely that Thomas Graham of Auchencass and Thomas Graham of Mosskesswra (uncle to Lang Will Graham and his brother John of Gillespie and Brackenwra) were one and the same. There are few documented Thomas Grahams in the "younger" line of William de Graham. This Thomas is the right age and in the right place to be Thomas Graham of Mosskesswra, uncle of Lang Will Graham. See Figure 41.

### Armstrongs of Mangerton.
The first laird of Mangerton was Alexander Armstrong (born about 1262). He acquired the lands of Mangerton on the Hermitage Water in Liddesdale later in the thirteenth century. His son, also named Alexander, was the second laird who was famously murdered by anti-Bruce conspirator William de Soulis in Hermitage Castle in 1320.[13] Alexander's descendants remained until the last laird, Archibald Armstrong, was, according to one account, "denounced rebel to Scotland and put to the horn," and in another account, "executed" in 1610.[14] With the Union of the Crowns in 1612, Mangerton Castle was destroyed by the forces of James VI/I, resulting in most of the clan leaving for Ireland.[15] The only parts of Mangerton Castle that survive are portions of the tower and the west and south walls of the fortalice (small fortress).[16]

### Armstrongs of Terwinney, Macguiresbridge, Ireland.
A branch of the Mangerton Armstrongs. Alexander, John, Colonel Thomas, and Captain Edward Armstrong, sons of Colonel William Armstrong, son of Christopher Armstrong of Barnegleish, the elder (Figure 21), arrived in Ireland about 1641.[17] Edward and his family settled in Macguiresbridge in southeastern County Fermanagh. Later Captain Armstrong earned a military land grant in Terwinney in Parish Magheraculmoney in northern County Fermanagh. His brother John settled in Longfield in County Leitrim, and his brother Alexander settled in Kilmore in County Leitrim. Thomas may be the same

---

[11] R.C. Reid, "The Border Grahams and Their Origins," *Transactions of the Dumfries and Galloway Natural History and Archaeological Society (TDGNHAS)* No. 3038, (1961): 94-95.

[12] A.M.T. Maxwell-Irving, "Torthorwald Castle," Cruck Cottage Heritage, accessed 8 February 2023. http://cruckcottage.com/torthorwald-castle/

[13] Derek James Stewart, *The Armstrongs, The History of a Riding Family (1040-1650)* (Salt Lake City: American Academic Press, 2017), 159-60. https://books.google.com/books?id=an0uDwAAQBAJ&pg=PA160&lpg=PA160&dq=murder+of+alexander+armstrong+soules&source=bl&ots=X6VfmxHDuJ&sig=ACfU3U0RahIJwmYVvu1L30S4ZoNV3eWSlQ&hl=en&sa=X&ved=2ahUKEwjkvLTSk_X8AhUFEFkFHUPdA-MQ6AF6BAgpEAM#v=onepage&q=murder%20of%20alexander%20armstrong%20soules&f=false

[14] Thomas Elmer Armstrong, *History of the Armstrong Family from 980 to 1939 A.D, and Genealogy of David Armstrong and Sarah Harris Armstrong (1746-1939)* (Sharon, Pennsylvania: I.O. Moyer, 1939), 10. https://archive.org/details/historyofarmstro00arms/mode/2up?q=mangerton

[15] "Mangerton Tower," The Castles of Scotland, accessed 8 February 2023. https://www.thecastlesofscotland.co.uk/the-best-castles/scenic-castles/mangerton-tower/

[16] Thomas Elmer Armstrong, *History of the Armstrong Family from 980 to 1939 A.D, and Genealogy of David Armstrong and Sarah Harris Armstrong (1746-1939)* (Sharon, Pennsylvania: I.O. Moyer, 1939), 10. https://archive.org/details/historyofarmstro00arms/mode/2up?q=mangerton

[17] James Lewis Armstrong, M.D., *Chronicles of the Armstrongs* (Queensborough, N.Y: The Marion Press in Jamaica, 1902), 19, 35. https://archive.org/details/chroniclesofarms00arms/mode/2up?ref=ol&view=theater&q=terwinney

Thomas Armstrong who moved to Dublin. A number of Irish Armstrongs migrated to America circa 1721.[18]

**Blaatwood Grahams.** William Graham of Carlisle acquired Blaatwood in the aftermath of the 1542 Battle of Solway Moss. John Carruthers of Holmendis granted on 3 August 1544 the land of Blaatwood with the fishings of Skarris and Loupis (Coupis) to William Graham of Carlisle. To this was added on 6 November 1550, the nearby coastal land of Torduff by Michael, Lord Carlisle, and Esota Carlisle, his spouse. William left Blaatwood to his son Arthur. Arthur of Blaatwood had one daughter and sons named: William, Fergus, David, Arche, Alexander, Johne, and Arthur (II). [19]

**Braid/Braids of Midlothian.** Descendants of the Grahams of Dalkeith via a Graham daughter. The first and second "Henry of Braid" were the first and second Sir Henry de Graham. The third Henry of Braid was a nephew to the third Sir Henry de Graham. See Figure 38. In 1305, at the inquest of the death of the third Henry of Braid, his mother testified the Braids lands of Bavelaw and Groittehill (Groathill) were her dowry, which then passed to her son and heir, the 16-year Henry of Braid and his betrothed, a daughter of William Sinclair.[20] The elder Sir John Graham of Dalkeith later confirmed in a charter to Newbattle Abbey, in the 1320s or 1330s, made previously by Peter Graham,[i] that the Braid Wood lands and quarry are Graham lands.[21] Therefore, the mother of the third Henry of Braid must have been a Graham, likely a daughter of the second Sir Henry de Graham and Christina Fitz Gilbert. She may have been an heir to the uncle who died without issue, Radulpho (Ralph) de Graham, grantee of the heritable lands of Cousland, Pentland, and Gogar by William the Lion about 1170.[22] The Pentlands Forest region was a part of the estate of Henry of Braid in the late thirteenth century.[23]

**Brackenwra Grahams.** The Brackenwra associated with the Grahams of Mosskesswra is located in Annandale.[ii] Regarding the etymology, "wrae" can be used for "an enclosed stretch of water," such as a harbor.[24] Between 1315 and 1321, King Robert the Bruce (as Lord of Annandale) granted to Adam Barbour (Barbitonsor) the lands of Brackenwra in the tenement of Hutton-sub-mora, resigned by Peter de Graham. On 22 August 1470, John de Grahame of Gillesbie purchased "four slags of land" — in Brackenwra, in the tenement of Hutton where mineral ore waste had been deposited,[25] — from James, Earl of Morton. On 12 August 1474, John the Graham of Gillesbie granted a reversion to James Douglas, Earl of Morton, that when the earl repaid him the sum of four score merks on the high altar of Hutton Church on 40 days' notice, Graham would resign to the earl the lands of "Brakinwra in the

---

[18] Ibid.

[19] William Fraser, *The Annandale Family Book of the Johnstones, Earls and Marquises of Annandale,* Vol. I, 124.

[20] PoMS, "No. 9004," accessed 25 January 2023. https://www.poms.ac.uk/record/source/9004/

[21] PoMS, "No. 7444," accessed 25 January 2023. https://www.poms.ac.uk/record/source/7444/

[22] PoMS, "No.5942, factoid," accessed 13 February 2023. https://www.poms.ac.uk/record/factoid/5942/

[23] PoMS, "No. 4388," accessed 8 February 2023. https://www.poms.ac.uk/record/source/4388/

[24] "Ree, Rie, Rea, Rae, Wrae," *Dictionaries of the Scots Language,* accessed 3 January 2023. https://www.dsl.ac.uk/entry/snd/ree_n1_v1

[25] *Registrum Honoris de Morton, Volume II: Ancient Charters,* 216-217.

tenement of Hutton." John Graham of Gillesbie and Brackenwra was brother to Lang Will Graham.[26] See Figure 41.

**Canonbie Grahams.** Descendants of Prior John Graham of Canobie are referenced in Scottish Privy Council records in 1561,[27] 1569,[28] and 1571[29] where they were accused of participating in a raid with other outlaws and "broken men" on the estate of Applegarth.[30] Phil Graham suspects that prior was a hereditary post as Prior John's sons, John and George, were called to answer to the Privy Council regarding teinds of Canobie Priory in 1561.[31] Staplegordon (Old Royal Demesne) apparently passed to Prior John. Their connection to the Border Grahams is unclear.

**Claverhouse Grahams.** A branch of the Grahams of Fintry. The first Graham of Claverhouse was John Graham of Claverhouse, the elder son of Robert Graham of Strathcarron and Fintry, and Matilda Scrymgeour, who acquired the lands of Claverhouse in the early sixteenth century.[32] The most famous Claverhouse Graham was Colonel William Graham, the seventh Laird of Claverhouse, posthumously dubbed "Bonnie Dundee" in a poem of the same name by Sir Walter Scott. Colonel Graham was the elder son of Sir William Graham and Lady Madeline Carnegie and was educated at the University of St Andrews in the 1660s. His military career began in the French army of Louis XIV. Dundee distinguished himself at the Battle of Seneff in Belgium in 1674, where he is said to have saved the life of the Prince of Orange.[33, 34]

**Cumstoun (Cumston) Grahams.** The first documented Graham of Cumstoun is Nicholas Graham. John Grahame was his son and heir, and his possession of a third of Cumstoun "below dominion and barony of Mosskesswra, parish of Hutton of the stewardship of the Annandale

> **Phil's note:** Henry of Gillenbie may have been a Corrie or Graham younger son. His estate in 1296 is called: *Cumston juxta Stobohill* (also spelled "Stuble") in the Corrie Barony.

---

[26] Charles Adrian Kelham, "Bases of Magnatial Power in Later Fifteenth-Century Scotland" (PhD Thesis, University of Edinburgh, 1986), 195. https://www.era.lib.ed.ac.uk/bitstream/1842/6867/1/372968.pdf

[27] John Hill Burton, *The Register of the Privy Council of Scotland*, 1545-1569 (Edinburgh: H.M. General Register House, 1877), Vol. I, 165. https://books.google.com/books/about/The_Register_of_the_Privy_Council_of_Sco.html?id=r6InAQAAMAAJ

[28] John Hill Burton, *The Register of the Privy Council of Scotland*, 1569-1578 (Edinburgh: H.M. General Register House, 1878), Vol. II, 45-46. https://books.google.com/books/about/The_Register_of_the_Privy_Council_of_Sco.html?id=AbkOwgEACAAJ

[29] John Hill Burton, *The Register*, 1569-1578, 95-96.

[30] John Hill Burton, *The Register*, 1569-1578, 45-46.

[31] John Hill Burton, *The Register*, 1545-1569, 165.

[32] Charles Sandford Terry, *John Graham of Claverhouse, Viscount of Dundee, 1648-1689* (London: Archibald Constable and Company, 1905), 2-4. https://www.forgottenbooks.com/fr/download/JohnGrahamofClaverhouse_10188273.pdf

[33] Charles Sanford Terry, "The Homes of the Claverhouse Grahams," *The Scottish Historical Review* 2, no. 5 (1904): 72–76. http://www.jstor.org/stable/25517552

[34] "John Graham 1st Viscount Dundee," Undiscovered Scotland, accessed 9 February 2023. https://www.undiscoveredscotland.co.uk/usbiography/g/johngrahamdundee.html

Valley" was renewed in 1607[35] and 1610.[36] Cumstoun/Cumstone may have come into the Grahams' possession through marriage with the Corrie family. Cumstoun was initially a part of the ancient barony of Tynham in Cumberland that was divided among the Levington heiresses, one of whom married Walter de Corry.[37]

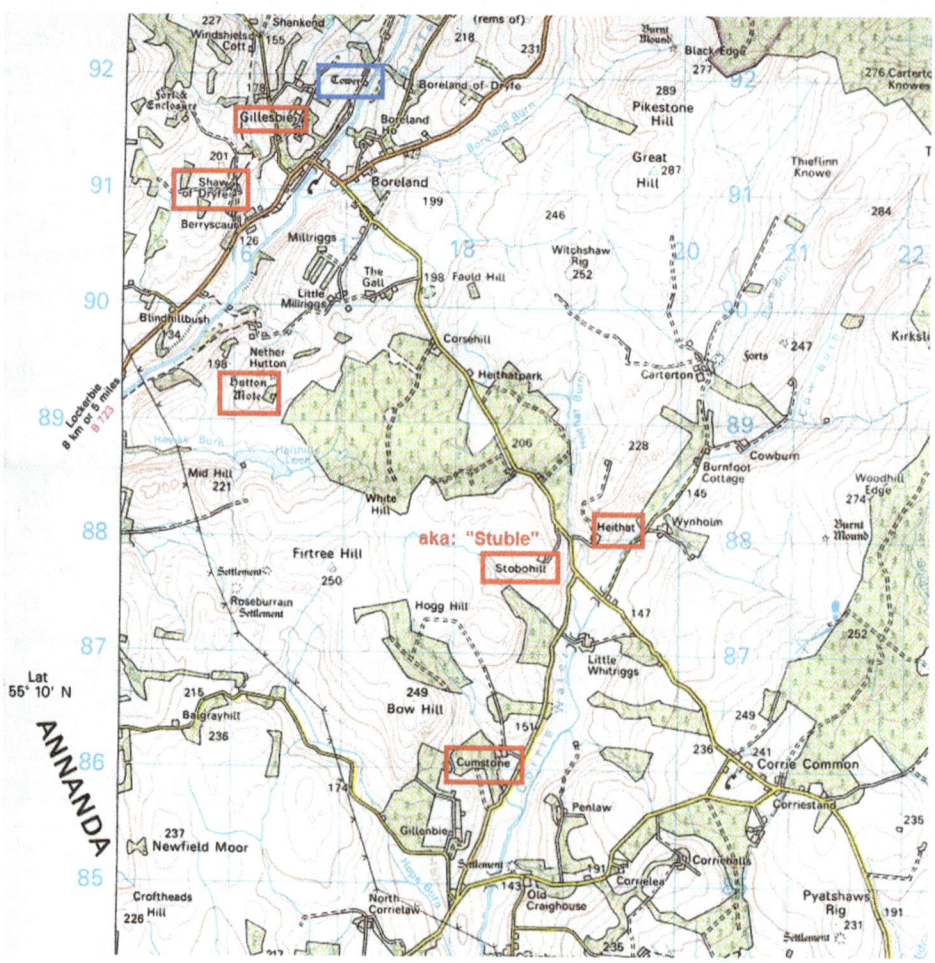

*Figure G-1: Map of the Dryfe Valley, Hutton and Corry Parish, in NW Dumfriesshire, Scotland; Ordnance Survey (map GB.) Landranger Series SCALE OF 1; 50 000, SHEET NO 79 HAWICK & ESKDALE (LANGHOLM) Ordnance Survey license number 100066333. All rights reserved. © Copyright and database right 2022.*

**Dalkeith Grahams.** The first Graham of Dalkeith was also the first documented Graham in Scotland, a knight named "William de Graham," who arrived with David I in 1124. William's elder son

---

[35] R.C. Reid, "The Border Grahams and Their Origins," *Transactions of the Dumfries and Galloway Natural History and Archaeological Society (TDGNHAS)* No. 3038 (1961): 86.

[36] Thomas Thompson, *Inquisitionum ad Capellam Domini Regis Retornatarum, quae in Publicis Srchivis Scotiae adhuc servantur, abbreviation* (London: Great Britain Record Commission, 1811), (46) and (75). https://books.google.com/books?id=8tQsAQAAMAAJ&printsec=frontcover#v=onepage&q&f=false

[37] R.C. Reid, "Cumstoun Castle," *Transactions of the Dumfries and Galloway Natural History and Archaeological Society (TDGNHAS)* No. 3018 (1934): 410-411.

Peter and Peter's descendants inherited Dalkeith.[38] This estate on the Esk is the boundary between East and West Lothians.[39]

**Dryfedale/Dryfesdale Grahams.** Includes Grahams from Upper Dryfe (Gillesbie, Brackenwra, Mosskesswra) and Lower/Nether Dryfe (Hutton). See Figure F-9. One family used the name Drysdale. Another family used the name Gillespie[40] and possibly some of the local Shaws were Grahams of Shaw.

**Drynie Grahams.** Branch of the Inchbrakie Grahams. Robert Graham, Archdeacon of Ross, the youngest son of Patrick Graeme of Inchbrakie and grandson of William, Earl of Montrose, is the founder of the Grahams of Drynie.[41]

**Edmond Castle Grahams.** The Grahams of Edmond Castle in Cumberland are first mentioned in 1603 in the household accounts of Lord William Howard, who paid a small sum to "Andrew Graham of Edmond Castle."[42] According to tradition, the castle was named after its builder, called "Edmond Graham" of the Grahams in nearby Hayton. By the standards of the time, the Grahams of Edmond Castle and Hayton were a wealthy landed gentry family.[43] Burke's *History of Landed Gentry* registered the first Graham of Edmond Castle as a Thomas Graham, born about 1640, and speculated these Grahams descended from a branch of the Grahams of Esk; however, there is no proof.[44] If they were already in place prior to the arrival of Lang Will Graham in 1515, it is possible they descended from the Tynedale Grahams, some of whom remained on the English side of the border after the Wars of Scottish Independence. Another possibility is a connection to the family of Lord William Howard, the youngest son of the fourth Duke of Howard. He was from the same family that are lords of Greystoke today, theorized ancestors of the Grahams in Scotland. Lord William Howard was buried at Greystoke Church in 1640.[45] Also, the name "Edmund" is connected with the original lords of Greystoke,

---

[38] Claire Brooks, "Theories on the Origins of the Grahams," *Clan Graham Society Newsletter* (1998). https://clangrahamsociety.org/theories-on-the-origins-of-the-grahams/

[39] "Dalkeith, Midlothian," Gazeteer for Scotland, accessed 29 April 2023. https://www.scottish-places.info/towns/townfirst251.html

[40] K. M. Brown, *The Records of the Parliaments of Scotland to 1707* (St. Andrews: 2007-2023), accessed 10 February 2023. https://www.rps.ac.uk/search.php?action=print&id=10520&filename=jamesvi_trans&type=trans

[41] Hew Scott, *Fasti ecclesiae scoticanae; the succession of ministers in the Church of Scotland from the reformation*, Vol. VII (Edinburgh: Oliver and Scott, 1928), 10. https://archive.org/details/fastiecclesiaesc07scot/page/n7/mode/2up?q=drynie

[42] Surtees Society, *Selections from the Household Accounts of Lord William Howard of Naworth Castle* (Durham: Andrews & Co., Edinburgh: Blackwood & Sons, 1878), 247. https://books.google.com/books?id=macwAAAAYAAJ&q=edmond#v=snippet&q=edmond&f=false

[43] James Sneyd, *Rich Man, Poor Man, Beggar Man, Thief* (Auckland, 2009), 105, 106, 110, 117. http://www.burningviolin.org/family/book/book.html

[44] Sir John Bernard Burke, *Burke's Genealogical and Heraldic History of the Landed Gentry: including American families with British Ancestry*, Vol. I (London: Burke's Peerage, 1939), 972. (Requires account.) https://www.familysearch.org/library/books/viewer/469709/?offset=0#page=968&viewer=picture&o=search&n=0&q=garvock

[45] British Newspaper Archives, "Exhumation of the Reliques of Lord William Howard, in the Chancel of Greystoke Church," Cumbria Family History Society, accessed 9 February 2023. https://cumbriafhs.com/smfmsgbrd/index.php?topic=5818.0

specifically a son of Forn Sigulfson, the first Lord of Greystoke. "Edmund, son of Forn," moved to Scotland in the twelfth century.[46]

### Eskdale Grahams (1). Upper Eskdale Grahams.
This region includes: Liddesdale, Langholm, Westerker, Ewesdale, Upper Esk above Langholm (St. Brides at Wauchope), Watcarick Kirk, Byken Kirk, and Westerker Kirk. The Grahams barony of Upper Eskdale became the barony of Watcarick, given as memorial gifts for deceased Avenels, Grahams, and Corries at Melrose Abbey.[47]

### Eskdale Grahams (2). Mid Eskdale Grahams.
This region covers Langholm, south to Canonbie, and north to the Grahams' Bentpath Mill. It also includes descendants of Prior John Graham of Canonbie.[48]

### Eskdale Graham (3). Lower Eskdale Grahams.
Lower Eskdale includes: the Mote of Liddel, Arthuret, and Plomp lands of Solway Moss. *Note*: several other Grahams estates are called "of Esk": Lovat Graham of Esk, Morphie Graham of Esk, and the Dalkeith Grahams, who acquired Eskdale via marriage to the Avenel heiress.[49]

### Fintry Grahams.
Sir William Graeme of Kincardine and his second wife had five sons. The eldest was Robert of Strathcarron, first great baron of Fintry in Stirlingshire.[50] The Fintries were staunch Jacobites and Royalists,[51] as well as suspected members and supporters of the knightly orders. Most notable was David Graham of Fintry, who was executed in 1592 for his part in the Roman Catholic conspiracy known as the "Spanish Blanks Plot."[52]

---

[46] Michael Gervers, *Documents of Early England Data Set (DEEDS) database*, University of Toronto, 1975-present, Charter Number: 05130214, accessed 18 October 2022. https://deeds.library.utoronto.ca/charters/05130214/Forn

[47] Monsignor Seton, *An Old Family or The Setons of Scotland and America*, (New York: Bretano's, 1899), 8-9. https://deriv.nls.uk/dcn23/9572/95729930.23.pdf

[48] *The Topographical, Statistical and Historical Gazetteer of Scotland*, Vol. 1 (Glasgow: A. Fullarton and Co, 1842), 505-506. https://play.google.com/store/books/details?id=T3P-6fnN47sC&rdid=book-T3P-6fnN47sC&rdot=1

[49] J. H. S. "The Grahams: The First Line of the Grahams (Continued)," *The Scottish Antiquary, or, Northern Notes and Queries* 17, no. 68 (1903), 178. http://www.jstor.org/stable/25517111

[50] Louisa Grace Graeme, *Or and Sable: a Book of Graemes and Grahams* (Edinburgh: William Brown, 1903), 540-546. https://archive.org/details/orsablebookofgra00grae/page/n23/mode/2up?q=drynie

[51] John Burke, *A Genealogical and Heraldic History of the Commoners of Great Britain and Ireland Enjoying Territorial Possessions Or High Official Rank: But Uninvested with Heritable Honours*, Vol. 3 (London: Henry Colburn, 1838), 121. https://books.google.com/books?id=yshsAAAAMAAJ&pg=PA121

[52] Iain D. Mcintosh, "David Graham of Fintry-30th March 1620," *Book of Emminent Burgesses of Dundee (1513-1885)*, 2020. http://www.fdca.org.uk/1620_David_Graham_of_Fintry.html

*Appendix G: Index on Relevant Graham Estates and of Their Kin*

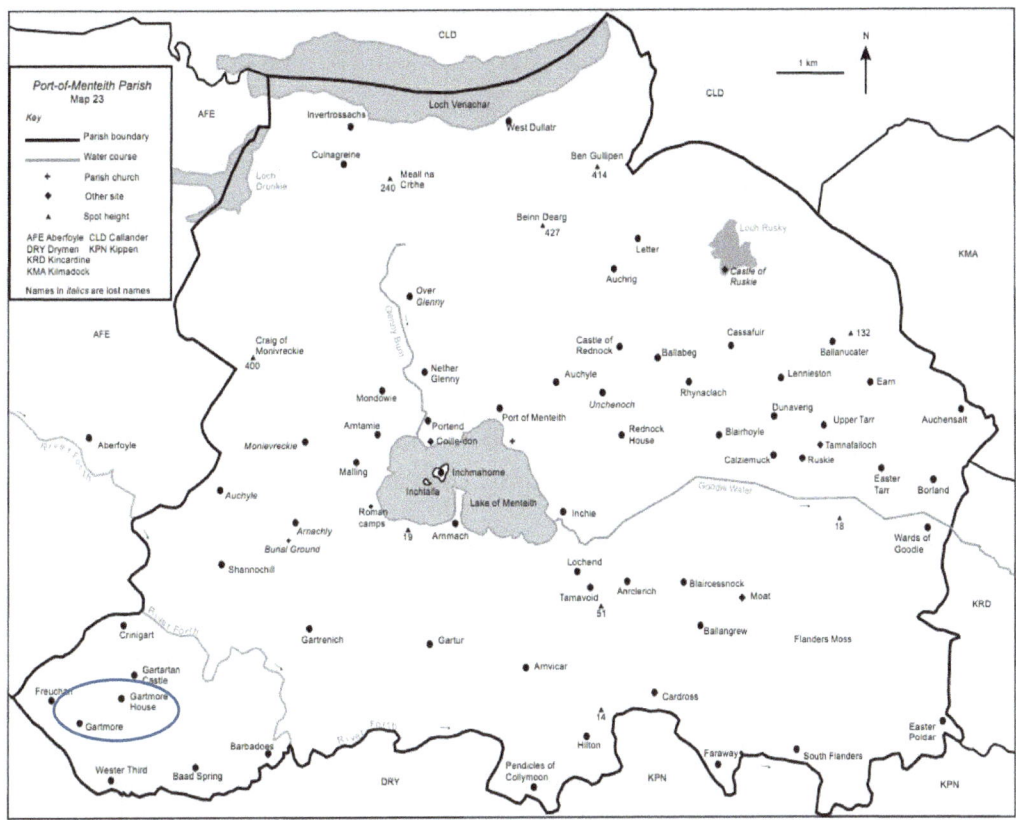

*Figure G-2: Parish of Port-of-Menteith Map. Copyright © 2011 Peter McNiven* [53]

**Gartmore Grahams.** Branch of the Menteith Grahams connected to the village of Gartmore (see Figure G-2) since 1554.[53] The first Graham of Gartmore was Robert Graham, youngest son of William Graham, third Earl of Menteith, who acquired the lands of Gartmore from Alexander Macawley of Erngabill. Robert's heir was his nephew, William Graham.[54] William was a supporter of Charles II and took the place of the Earl of Airth, leading his men in the Third Civil War. George Crawford wrote in 1716: "And his Majesty King Charles II placed so great Confidence in Gartmore's Loyalty, and Affection to his Service, that on the 12th of July, 1651, he gave him a Commission to guard the Passes on the River of Forth."[55]

**Garvock Grahams.** From Volume I of Burke's *History of Landed Gentry*: William Graeme, third son of Sir William Graeme of Kincardine and Princess Mary Stewart, was the first earl of Garvock.[56]

---

[53] Figure G-2: Peter Edward McNiven, "Gaelic Place-names and the Social History of Gaelic Speakers in Medieval Menteith" (Ph D Thesis, University of Glasgow, 2011), 486. https://theses.gla.ac.uk/2685/1/2011mcnivenphd.pdf

[54] William Fraser, *The Red Book of Menteith*, Vol. I (Edinburgh: 1880), 311-315. https://digital.nls.uk/histories-of-scottish-families/archive/96774276#?c=0&m=0&s=0&cv=217&xywh=-282%2C-337%2C5611%2C4159

[55] George Crawford, *The peerage of Scotland: containing an historical and genealogical account of the nobility of that Kingdom* (Edinburgh: George Stewart, 1716), 331.
https://quod.lib.umich.edu/cgi/t/text/pageviewer-idx?cc=ecco;c=ecco;idno=004896390.0001.000;seq=341;page=root;view=text

[56] "Graeme of Garvock," House of Graemes, accessed 9 February 2023. https://inchbrakie.tripod.com/abookofthegraemes/id58.html

William was a soldier and was granted Garvock barony for faithful services to his uncle, King James I of Scotland. Garvock was confirmed to him in a charter in 1473. In 1502, he was succeeded by his son, "Mathew le Grame," second earl of Garvock.[57]

**Gillesbie Grahams.** The first Graham of Gillesbie and Brackenwra was John Graham of Gillesbie (b. abt 1450- d. after 1515), brother of Lang Will Graham, chief of the Border Grahams.[58] When Lang Will and his family resettled in England in 1515, the Gillesbies remained in Scotland. For the next 125 years, they enjoyed relative prosperity and expanded their territory. In 1567, a descendant, also named John Graham of Gillesbie, was granted additional lands called Heithat (Figure G-1) and Branriggs. It all changed by 1641 after an unfortunate fight between the laird and his kinsman, the laird of Shaw, that left the latter dead. This resulted in the subsequent departure of the laird of Gillesbie and the majority of the clan for Ireland.[59] The few Gillesbie Grahams that remained fell into debt[60] and lost their heavily mortgaged lands to their creditors, who happened to also be their Scott in-laws, by 1699.[61]

**Gilsland Grahams.** In 1597, there were two bailiffs surnamed Graham in Gilsland Barony, which straddles the boundary of Cumbria and Northumberland: Robert Graham, the bailiff of Croglin Manor, and Richard Graham of Brackenhill, the bailiff of Askerton Manor. Richard Graham of Brackenhill was a son of Fergus Graham of Mote and grandson of Lang Will Graham. There were twelve bailiffs subordinate to the land sergeant of Gilsland Barony. Of note, Lancelot Carleton (later from County Fermanagh, Ireland) was the bailiff of Brampton Manor, and Christopher Blennerhasset was the bailiff of Irthington Manor. In 1598, Thomas Musgrave was appointed land sergeant of Gilsland Barony and was granted Askerton Castle; however, it was forcibly retained by Thomas Carelton. The Grahams and Carleton, had been engaged in a deadly feud with the Musgraves in retaliation after Thomas Musgrave murdered a grandson of Lang Will prior to 1583. It was a strained situation until 1601 when Lord William Howard the elder paid Elizabeth I an exorbitant fee for Gilsland and retained the tenants.[62]

**Inchbrakie Grahams (Graemes).** The first Graeme of Inchbrakie, a cadet branch of the Montrose Grahams, was Patrick, Baron of Inchbrakie (1513-1538),[63] son of William, first Earl of

---

[57] Sir John Bernard Burke, *Burke's Genealogical and Heraldic History of the Landed Gentry: Including American families with British Ancestry*, Vol. I (London: Burke's Peerage, 1939), 938.

[58] Charles Adrian Kelham, "Bases of Magnatial Power in Later Fifteenth-Century Scotland," (Phd Thesis: University of Edinburgh, 1986), 195. https://era.ed.ac.uk/bitstream/1842/6867/1/372968.pdf

[59] Col. William Rogerson, *Hutton Under the Muir* (Dumfries, Scotland: Dumfries and Galloway Courier and Herald, 1908), 7, 25, 26, 31.
https://www.google.com/books/edition/Hutton_under_the_muir_notes_on_the_past/BiwVAAAAQAAJ?hl=en&gbpv=1

[60] Scottish Record Office, *Index to Register of Deeds, 1670*, Vol. X (Edinburgh: His Majesty's Stationery Office, 1926), 170.
https://www.google.com/books/edition/Index_to_Register_of_Deeds_Preserved_in/vsQRAAAAIAAJ?hl=en&gbpv=1

[61] R.C. Reid, "The Border Grahams and Their Origins," 94.

[62] T.H.B. Graham, *The Barony of Gilsland* (Kendal: Thomas Wilson & Son, 1934), viii-ix.
https://www.forgottenbooks.com/pt/download/TheBaronyofGilsland_10898634.pdf

[63] Louisa Grace Graeme, *Or and Sable: A Book of Graemes and Grahams* (Edinburgh: William Brown, 1903), Sketch 1, 1-2. https://archive.org/details/orsablebookofgra00grae/page/642/mode/2up?q=netherby

Montrose, and his second wife, Christian Wavane.[64] The Inchbrakies were known for their battle prowess and support of the Marquis of Montrose in the English Civil War 1642-1644.[65]

**Kilbucho Grahams.** The estate of Kilbucho (as well as Hutton and Tarbolton) passed to the Dalkeith Grahams (elder line) from Adam Fitz Gilbert and his wife, Ideona Comyn of Northumberland, upon the marriage of their daughter Christiana/Christina to the second Sir Henry de Graham of Dalkeith, the Sheriff of Edinburgh. (See Figure 38). [66, 67] Kilbucho transferred from the Grahams to Sir William Douglas in 1341, presumably as a dowry when he married Elizabeth Graham of Dalkeith (elder line).[68]

**Kincardine Grahams.** Sir David Graham of Dundaff and Kincardine (younger line) was the first Graham of Kincardine and ancestor to the Grahams of Montrose.[69] He served as deputy justiciar (judge) of Lothian in 1248 and was Sheriff of Berwick by 1264.[70] See Figure F-1. This David Graham is the same David that we suspect of being involved in the finances of the Knights Templar.

**Kirkpatricks (Kilpatricks).** The first recorded Kirkpatricks were knights named Roger and Ivo who served the Bruces, lords of Annandale circa 1194-1214.[71] Ivo married Euphemia Bruce, a daughter of Robert de Brus. Between 1194 and 1212, Ivo's sons, Roger de Kirkpatrick and a Robert de Kirkpatrick, are witnesses to a charter of William de Brus granting the monks at Holm Cultram Abbey in Allerdale fishing and hunting rights at "Torduff" [72] and Sark.[73] A descendant also named Sir Roger de Kirkpatrick, called by Buchanan "Roger de Cella Patricii," was famously one of those who attended King Robert I in Dumfries when Sir Robert Comyn was killed in the Greyfriars Monastery Chapel in Dumfries in 1306.[74] Sir Roger's eldest son, Sir Humphrey, married Isabel, the daughter of Christine Graham and Sir David of Torthorwald, circa 1321.[75] Figure F-2.

---

[64] Lloyd D. Graham, *House Graham, From the Antoine Wall to the Temple of Hymen* (Lulu.com, 2020), 6. https://clangrahamsociety.org/wp-content/uploads/2020/09/House-GRAHAM-eBook.pdf

[65] James Fargo, "Clan Donnachaidh History," Clan Donnachaidh Society of the Mid-Atlantic, accessed 8 February 2023. https://www.robertson.org/G_history-general.html

[66] Jane Brankstone Thomas, J.C. B. Sharp, and Michael Anne Guido, "A Cumberland Family with Medieval Roots in Scotland and Northern England: A Study Gilbert Fitz Richer and His Descendants," Foundation for Medieval Genealogy, *Foundations* (2008): 360. https://fmg.ac/phocadownload/userupload/foundations2/JN-02-05/358Richer.pdf

[67] PoMS, "no. 5972-Tarbolton," accessed 18 October 2022. https://www.poms.ac.uk/record/source/5972/; PoMS, "No. 4425-Kilbucho," accessed 18 October 2022. https://www.poms.ac.uk/record/source/4425/; PoMS, no. 11964-Hutton, accessed 18 October 2022. https://www.poms.ac.uk/record/person/11964/

[68] Sir James Balfour Paul, *The Scots Peerage, Founded on Wood's Edition*, Vol. VI, 196-197.

[69] Lloyd D. Graham, *House Graham, From the Antoine Wall to the Temple of Hymen* (Lulu.com, 2020), 3-7. https://clangrahamsociety.org/wp-content/uploads/2020/09/House-GRAHAM-eBook.pdf

[70] PoMS, "No. 2005, person summary," accessed 18 October 2022. https://www.poms.ac.uk/record/person/2005/

[71] Ruth M. Blakely, "The Brus Family in England and Scotland, 1100-c 1290" (PhD Thesis, University of Durham, 2000), 34-36. http://etheses.dur.ac.uk/1594/

[72] Figure G-3: Joan and Cornelius Blaeu and Timothy Pont, *Atlas of Scotland,* Annandiae praefectura, Vulgo, Joan et Cornelius Blaeu exc., Amsterdam, Blaeu, 1654. https://maps.nls.uk/view/00000402

[73] PoMS, "No. 40943, factoid," accessed 10 February 2023. https://www.poms.ac.uk/record/factoid/40943/

[74] *Kirkpatrick of Closeburn* (London: George Norman, 1858), 1, 6, 7. https://archive.org/details/kirkpatrickofclo00kirk/page/nundefined/mode/1up?ref=ol&view=theater

[75] A.M.T. Maxwell-Irving, "Torthorwald Castle," Cruck Cottage Heritage, accessed 8 February 2023. http://cruckcottage.com/torthorwald-castle/

**Knockdolian Grahams.** Sir William Graham of Mugdock was a son of Patrick Graham of Dundaff and Kincardine.[76] His youngest son by his second wife, Princess Mary Stewart, was Sir Walter Graham, ancestor of the Knockdolian Grahams of Ayrshire.[77]

*Figure G-3: Blaeu's Atlas of Scotland, 1654, Based on surveys by Timothy Pont, showing Tornduff, Blaatwood, Renpatrick, and Ryid Kirk Lands.* [72] CC-BY 4.0 *Reproduced with the permission of the National Library of Scotland.*

**Langboddam (Langbedholm) Grahams.** This branch of the Graham clan, from Langboddam in the parish of Kirkpatrick Juxta,[78] is from the first family of Thornik. From R.C. Reid, "Once the 80 merkland of Thornik had passed to the Johnstons, few of the Graham clan could have remained on the lands; only one branch is known to have survived. Robert Graham of Langboddam had maintained himself on that small property and his descendants can be traced to about 1750. His exact position in the Thornik pedigree is not clear." The earliest record of this Robert is from 1579 in the *Register of*

---

[76] Lloyd D. Graham, *House Graham, From the Antoine Wall to the Temple of Hymen* (Lulu.com, 2020), 6.

[77] Sir James Balfour Paul, *The Scots Peerage, Founded on Wood's Edition,* Vol. VI (Edinburgh: David Douglas, 1909), 219. https://archive.org/details/scotspeeragefoun06pauluoft/page/n5/mode/2up?q=graham

[78] Francis James Grant, *The Commissariot Record of Dumfries : Register of Testaments, 1624-1800* (Dumfries, 1863), 32. https://www.familysearch.org/library/books/records/item/25260-the-commissariot-record-of-dumfries-register-of-testaments-1624-1800?offset=2971 (Requires account.)

*the Privy Council.*[79] The Langboddam Grahams and Johnstones engaged in a bloody feud over the Graham lands that lasted several generations into the late seventeenth century. They raided each other's cattle. Assaults and slaughter occurred on both sides.[80]

**Menteith Grahams.** The Menteith lands changed hands a number of times in Scottish history. Menteith was an estate initially belonging to the Gaelic earls or Mormaers of Menteith for centuries, and transferred to Walter Comyn on his marriage to the Menteith heiress, Isabella, circa 1229. Then transferred from the Comyns to the Stewarts, then to the Grahams with the marriage of Sir John Graham (likely of Abercorn) to Countess Mary of Menteith circa 1332, then back to the Stewarts when Countess Margaret Graham of Menteith married Sir Robert Stewart, later Duke of Albany in 1361. See Figure F-6. The Stewarts continued to serve as earls of Menteith until 1425. In 1427, Malise Graham, son of Sir Patrick Graham and Euphemia Stewart, was awarded that title by James I in exchange for taking Malise's Strathearn estates.[81]

**Moffat (Bedokholme/Beattock) Grahams.** A branch of the first family of Thornik Grahams. In May 1463, Euphemia Graham, sister of Malise Graham, Earl of Menteith, resigned some of her estates to trade Herbert Johnstone the elder for the lands of Mosskesswra, Nether (Lower) Dryfe, and Bedokholme in Hutton so they could be granted to "William the Grahame" (grandfather of Lang Will), presumably to return them.[82] In 1527, Robert Graham, Laird of Thornik, filed formal complaints against Herbert Johnstone the younger for forcibly occupying "Betok" lands.[83] Phil Graham notes there is a connection between the Grahams of Bedokholme (Betok/Beattock) in west Moffat and the family who took the surname "Moffat" of east Moffat who were granted lands in Westerker Barony by Robert I after Bannockburn in 1314.[84] Many Grahams who remained in Moffat/Beattock became tradesmen (merchants, tailors, weavers, masons, wheelwrights, etc.) in the seventeenth and eighteenth centuries.[85, 86]

---

[79] David Masson, *The Register of the Privy Council of Scotland*. Edinburgh, First Series (Edinburgh: H.M. General Register House, 1880), Vol. III, 386.
https://www.google.com/books/edition/The_Register_of_the_Privy_Council_of_Sco/i7nUcH-JxsUC?hl=en&gbpv=1&bsq=graham

[80] R.C. Reid, "The Border Grahams and Their Origins," 98-104.

[81] William Fraser, *The Red Book of Menteith*, Vol. I (Edinburgh: 1880), vi-xi. https://digital.nls.uk/histories-of-scottish-families/archive/96774276#?c=0&m=0&s=0&cv=217&xywh=-282%2C-337%2C5611%2C4159

[82] Historical Manuscripts Commission, *The Manuscripts of the Duke of Hamilton, Knight, Eleventh Report, Appendix, Part VI* (London: Her Majesty's Stationery Office, 1887), 18.
https://archive.org/details/manuscriptsofduk00greauoft/page/18/mode/2up?ref=ol&view=theater&q=moskeswra

[83] R.C. Reid, "The Border Grahams and Their Origins," *Transactions of the Dumfries and Galloway Natural History and Archaeological Society (TDGNHAS)* No. 3038, (1961): 96.

[84] John and Robert Hylsop, *Langholm As it Was: A History of Langholm and Eskdale from the Earliest Times* (Sunderland: Hills and Company, 1912), 182, 183. https://archive.org/details/langholmasitwashhysl/mode/2up?q=shaw

[85] Francis James Grant, *The Commissariot Record of Dumfries : Register of Testaments, 1624-1800* (Dumfries, 1863), 32. https://www.familysearch.org/library/books/records/item/25260-the-commissariot-record-of-dumfries-register-of-testaments-1624-1800?offset=2971 (Requires account.)

[86] Ancestry.com, "UK, Register of Duties Paid for Apprentices' Indentures, 1710-1811."
https://www.ancestry.com/search/collections/1851/#:~:text=About%20UK%2C%20Register%20of%20Duties,trade%20to%20have%20an%20apprentice (Requires account.)

**Montrose Grahams.** The "noble" or younger line of Montrose descends from the first Earl of Montrose, David de Graham, son of Patrick de Graham of Dundaff and Kincardine and Annabella of Strathearn. See Figure F-1. Sir David Graham had exchanged his property of Cardross in Dunbartonshire (Figure G-2), in March 1325 with King Robert I, "Robert the Bruce," for the lands of Old Montrose in Forfarshire.[87, 88] The most famous Montrose descendant is the first Marquess of Montrose, James de Graham (1612-1650), who was a Scottish army general known for his tactical genius on the battlefield during the English Civil War against Cromwell's Parliament forces. He was later executed for this role in 1650 and was buried in St. Giles Cathedral in an elaborate funeral in 1661.[89] The current Duke of Montrose, James Graham, the eighth Duke of Montrose, is also the Graham clan chief.[90]

Figure G-4: Arms for Sir Robert Graham of Morphie Illustrated by Dr. Lloyd Graham[97]

**Morphie Grahams.** Per *Burke's Genealogical and Heraldric History of Landed Gentry*, the first Graham of Morphie was a Gilbert le Graham who received the lands of Morphie in a 1398 charter from Robert III. His son/heir was Henry Graham of Morphie. Henry's heir was his daughter Helen Graham, who in 1407 married Alexander de Barclay, third of Mathers. Helen and Alexander's children took their mother's surname.[91] Coincidentally, after her first husband Hugh de Ross died at the Battle of Haldidon Hill in 1333, Margaret Graham of Abercorn/Strathearn (elder line) married John de Barclay, tenth of Gartley, brother of Alexander de Barclay, first of Mathers. See Figure 41. Alexander, first of Mathers, was the grandfather of the previously mentioned Alexander, third of Mathers.[92] Taking into account he named his son "Henry," and also his granddaughter Helen's and great-aunt Margaret's marriages into the Barclay of Mathers family, Gilbert, the first Graham of Morphie, was likely an elder line Graham and a younger son of John Graham, of Auchencloich, son of Sir John "the Last" of Dalkeith (elder line) as claimed in *Peerage*[93] and heraldry sources.[94]

---

[87] Sir James Balfour Paul, *The Scots Peerage, Founded on Wood's Edition,* Vol. VI (Edinburgh: David Douglas, 1909), 209. https://archive.org/details/scotspeeragefoun06pauluoft/page/n5/mode/2up?q=graham

[88] Rev William Graham, *Lochmaben Five Hundred Years Ago* (Edinburgh: Trinity, 1865), 168. https://www.google.com/books/edition/Lochmaben_five_hundred_years_ago_or_sele/XlpZAAAAcAAJ?hl=en&kptab=editions&gbpv=1

[89] Sir James Balfour Paul, *The Scots Peerage, Founded on Wood's Edition,* Vol. VI (Edinburgh: David Douglas, 1909), 242-254. https://archive.org/details/scotspeeragefoun06pauluoft/page/n5/mode/2up?q=graham

[90] "Chief of Clan Graham, James Graham, 8th Duke of Montrose," Clan Graham Society, accessed 8 February 2023. https://clangrahamsociety.org/about/

[91] Sir John Bernard Burke, *Burke's Genealogical and Heraldic History of the Landed Gentry: including American families with British Ancestry*, Vol. I (London: Burke's Peerage, 1939), 949-950.

[92] John P. Ravilious, "Queen Euphemia and Her Ancestry," *The Scottish Genealogist*, The Scottish Genealogy Society (June 2017): 49-50. https://www.academia.edu/35370666/Queen_Euphemia_and_her_ancestry_TSG_LXIV_2_49_52

[93] Sir James Balfour Paul, *The Scots Peerage, Founded on Wood's Edition,* Vol. VI (Edinburgh: David Douglas, 1909), 213.

[94] "House Graham of Tamrawer," WappenWiki, accessed 9 February 2023. https://wappenwiki.org/index.php?title=House_Graham_of_Tamrawer

In the late sixteenth century, Sir Robert Graham of Morphie was knighted by his chief, John, Earl of Montrose, chancellor and viceroy of Scotland under James VI.[95] His arms are described by *Nisbet's Heraldry* as "sable a chevron argent, between three escallops or."[96] See Figure G-4.[97] The single chevron in the Morphie coat of arms is associated with the Barclay/Berkeley family.[98] By 1743, when the Grahams of Morphie were without male heirs again, a Graham cousin, William of Barclay, accepted the Morphie lands, title, and Graham surname.[99]

**Murrays of Atholl, Tullabardine.** According to *Peerage*, the progenitor of the Murrays of Atholl and Tullabardine was Sir Malcolm de Moray, who was Sheriff of Perth in 1276.[100] Malcolm's father was John de Moray, Sheriff of Perth and third great-grandson of Freskin, the patriarch of the Moray/Murray family in Scotland.[101] See Figure G-6.

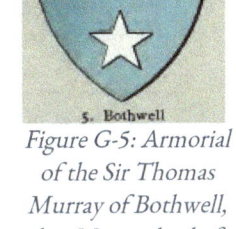

*Figure G-5: Armorial of the Sir Thomas Murray of Bothwell, last Murray lord of Bothwell, from "The Heraldry of the Murrays"* [100]

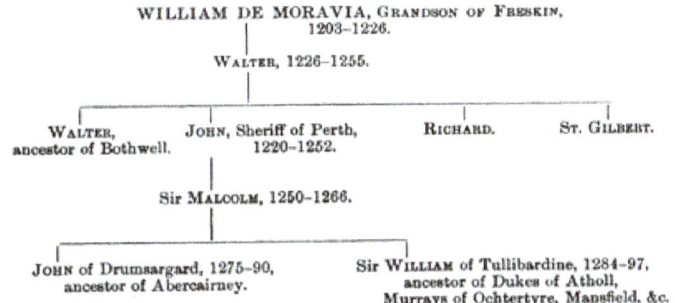

*Figure G-6: Primary Murray Line and the Branches of Bothwell, Abercairney, Tullibardine, Atholl, Ochtertyre and Mansfield from "The Chiefship of Clan Murray"* [101]

**Murrays of Bothwell.** The first earl of Moray/Moravia was a knight named Freskin who accompanied King David I to suppress an insurrection in Northern Scotland in 1130 and, as a result, was granted the lands of Moray. From him descend: Sir Andrew Murray, Regent (Guardian) of

---

[95] Alexander Nisbet, *A System of Heraldry*, Vol. I (Edinburgh: William Blackwood, 1816), 79-80. https://www.ibydeit.org/books/ASystemOfHeraldry.pdf

[96] "Nisbet's A System of Heraldry," The Heraldry Society of Scotland, accessed 8 February 2023. http://www.heraldry-scotland.co.uk/nisbets.html

[97] Figure G-4: Lloyd D. Graham, *House Graham, From the Antoine Wall to the Temple of Hymen* (Lulu.com, 2020), Fig. 1.9b. https://clangrahamsociety.org/wp-content/uploads/2020/09/House-GRAHAM-eBook.pdf

[98] "British Armorial Bindings," University of Toronto Libraries, accessed 8 February 2023. https://armorial.library.utoronto.ca/stamps/IBER014_s1

[99] Sir John Bernard Burke, *Burke's Genealogical and Heraldic History of the Landed Gentry: including American families with British Ancestry*, Vol. I (London: Burke's Peerage, 1939), 949-950.

[100] Figure G-5: G. Harvey Johnston, *The Heraldry of the Murrays* (Edinburgh and London: W & A.K. Johnston Ltd, 1910), 17. https://archive.org/details/heraldryofmurray00john

[101] Figure G-6: Author: "B," "The Chiefship of the Clan Murray," *The Scottish Antiquary, or, Northern Notes and Queries*, Vol. 15, No. 58 (Edinburgh University Press, October 1900): 74. https://www.jstor.org/stable/25516988

Scotland during the minority of David II until his death in 1338, the Murrays of Bothwell, Duffus, and the earls of Sutherland.[102]

## Murrays of Cockpool.
The Murrays of Cockpool in Dumfriesshire descend from the Murrays of Ryvale (Ruthwell).[103] The Murrays of Cockpool were the ancestors of the Murray family who became lords of Annandale beginning in March 1624 when John Murray of Cockpool, Lord Murray of Lochmaben, was created the first Earl of Annandale and Lord Murray of Tynningham.[104]

*Figure G-7: "Double Tressure Round the Stars" Armorial of the Murrays of Cockpool* [104]

## Murrays of Manuel, Touchadam, Polmaise.
This family descends from Sir Andrew Murray of Manuel, who was made Sheriff of Stirlingshire in 1368 and died in 1392. While he was an heir to Sir Andrew Murray the Regent and was named a cousin to David Bruce (David II),[105] his specific relation to the Regent is unclear. He was more likely a grandson of the Regent and his second wife, Christian Bruce, via a daughter. The identity of Sir Andrew's father is a mystery.

> **The Father of Sir Andrew Murray of Manuel**
>
> *Burke's Landed Gentry* speculated that the father of Sir Andrew Murray of Manuel was the Sir William de Moravia, of Sandford, who was taken prisoner by the English in 1306 and released in 1314. However, Sir William was rather old to be Sir Andrew's father. If he was 18 years old when he was captured in 1306, that equates to a birth year of 1288. Given Sir Andrew (who died in 1392) was likely born in the 1340s, the youngest William could have been at Andrew's birth would have been 52 years old when the average lifespan was 48.

His second wife, Janet Kirkhalche (Kirkintilloch), can be confirmed; however, the identity of Sir Andrew's first wife is unknown.[106] Sir Andrew of Manuel's first wife may have been the suspected matriarch of the Border Grahams, Agnes de Graham, daughter and heir of John de Graham, giftee of Elliston in Roxburghshire in 1361, Elphinstone in Lothian in 1363 (Figure F-3), and, likely lands in Hutton about the same time.[107]

Robert, a younger son of Andrew Murray of Manuel, was named as a cousin to Sir Thomas Murray of Ryvale in a 1411

---

[102] G. Harvey Johnston, *The Heraldry of the Murrays* (Edinburgh and London: W & A.K. Johnston Ltd, 1910), 2-53.

[103] Author: "B," "The Chiefship of the Clan Murray," *The Scottish Antiquary, or, Northern Notes and Queries*, Vol. 15, No. 58 (Edinburgh University Press, October 1900): 72. https://www.jstor.org/stable/25516988

[104] Figure G-7: G. Harvey Johnston, *The Heraldry of the Murrays* (Edinburgh and London: W & A.K. Johnston Ltd, 1910), 99.

[105] R.C. Reid, "The Border Grahams and Their Origins," *Transactions of the Dumfries and Galloway Natural History and Archaeological Society (TDGNHAS)* No. 3038 (1961): 67, 72.

[Father of Sir Andrew Murray of Manuel blurb] Sir John Bernard Burke, *Burke's Genealogical and Heraldic History of the Landed Gentry: including American families with British Ancestry*, Vol. I (London: Burke's Peerage, 1939),1655.

Neil Cummins, "Lifespans of the European Elite, 800-1800," Cambridge University Press, 12 June 2017. https://www.cambridge.org/core/journals/journal-of-economic-history/article/lifespans-of-the-european-elite-8001800/BE252C4B25C4AAC29ED62D591A1675AC

[106] Author: "B," "The Chiefship of the Clan Murray," *The Scottish Antiquary, or, Northern Notes and Queries*, Vol. 15, No. 58 (Edinburgh University Press, October 1900): 72. https://www.jstor.org/stable/25516988

[107] PoMS, no. 10636-Elphinstone in East Lothian confirmation to "Agnes de Grame, wife of Andrew de ?," accessed 19 October 2022. https://www.poms.ac.uk/record/source/10636/

charter.[108] How the Murrays of Ryvale/Cockpool and the Murrays of Manuel are related to each other and to the Murrays of Bothwell is unknown. It is possible the relationship is on the distaff (female) side. The families did adopt similar armorials. The Murrays of Touchadam and Polmaise adopted the "double tressure round the stars" arms as early as 1463 while the Murrays of Cockpool adopted "double tressure round the stars" (Figure G-7) as early as 1477.[109] Interestingly, the Murrays of Cockpool from Dumfriesshire were also connected to the Border Grahams. For example, the Grahams of Blaatwood owned the adjoining property to the Murrays of Cockpool, and the two families engaged in litigation from 1621 to 1649.[110]

**Pentlands.** Area eight miles south of Edinburgh. Radulpho (Ralph) de Graham, suspected kin of Henry of Braid, sheriff of Edinburgh, (Figure 38) was granted the heritable lands of Cousland, Pentland, and Gogar by William the Lion about 1170.[111] Bavelaw, Groathill,[112] and the Pentlands Forest region were a part of the estate of the same Henry of Braid in the late thirteenth century, part of his mother's dowry.[113] Phil Graham believes that prior to 1165, Pentlands was a free forest to the Braids and Dalkeith Grahams (elder line) as a buffer zone.[114]

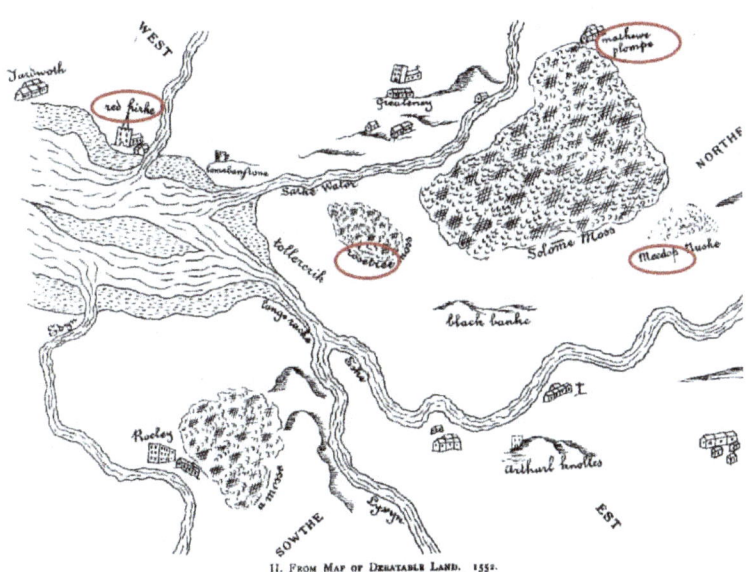

*Figure G-8: Map of Debatable Land, Glasgow Archaeological Society, November 1896* [115]

---

[108] Author: "B," "The Chiefship of the Clan Murray," *The Scottish Antiquary, or, Northern Notes and Queries*, Vol. 15, No. 58 (Edinburgh University Press, October 1900): 69-70.

[109] G. Harvey Johnston, *The Heraldry of the Murrays*, vi, 55-56.

[110] R.C. Reid, "The Border Grahams and Their Origins," *Transactions of the Dumfries and Galloway Natural History and Archaeological Society (TDGNHAS)* No. 3038 (1961): 111-112.

[111] PoMS, "No. 5942, factoid," accessed 13 February 2023. https://www.poms.ac.uk/record/factoid/5942/

[112] PoMS, "No. 961, person summary for Henry of Braids," accessed 13 February 2023. https://www.poms.ac.uk/record/person/961/

[113] PoMS, "No. 4388," accessed 8 February 2023. https://www.poms.ac.uk/record/source/4388/

[114] PoMS, "No. 4388," accessed 8 February 2023.

**Plomp Grahams.** The earliest known Graham of Plomp was Matthew of Springhill (near Gretna, Scotland), father of Fergus Graham of Plomp who was born abt. 1590. Their specific relation to the first Grahams of Netherby is unclear. However, Matthew's lands are sandwiched[115] amidst the sons of Lang Will Graham in 1552, Figure G-8, indicating a familial relationship to the Border Grahams.[116] Sir Richard Graham of Plomp, later Viscount of Preston, re-purchased the old Graham Lordship of Arthuret from the earl of Cumberland in 1629, founding the "new" Grahams of Netherby, ancestors of the Grahams of Norton-Conyers in Yorkshire.[117]

**Scotts.** The Scott family rose to power for their role in the fall of the Douglases at the Battle of Arkinholm in 1455. Sir Walter Scott and his son David were rewarded for their valor by James III with territories in Hawick in Roxburghshire in 1455. The first Lord Scott of Buccleuch, Sir Walter Scott (1565-1611), great-grandson of the Sir Walter from the Battle of Arkinholm, was elevated to the title by James VI in 1606. Notable Scotts include Sir Michael Scott, second Lord of Rankilburn and Murthockston (1320-1346), who also had lands in Selkirk in Roxburghshire. Like the Grahams and Kirkpatricks,[118] Sir Michael was a supporter of Robert the Bruce and was actively engaged in the Wars of Scottish Independence, falling at the ill-fated battle of Neville's Cross on 17 October 1346.[119] The famous nineteenth-century poet Sir Walter Scott, who wrote of the exploits of the border clans, was from a junior branch, the Scotts of Harden.[120] It is possible that a Scott from this family was the mother of Richard Graham of Elliston in Roxburghshire (Figure F-2). Given the close proximity of Elliston to Selkirk and the close relationship of the Scotts to the Border Grahams, perhaps the first name "Richard" entered the Graham elder line with a marriage to a member of the Scott clan. Richard was a name common amongst the Scott family. The Scotts also intermarried with the remnants of the Grahams of Gillesbie and eventually assumed ownership of the Gillesbie lands.[121]

**Shaw Grahams.** The Grahams of Shaw descend from "Jok of Dryfe," John Graham, brother to James Graham, Laird of Gillesbie, in 1582. "Jok" was a lieutenant in the King's Border Guard, a mounted constabulary led by Sir John Murray of Lochmaben.[122] He was granted the Temple lands of Shaw and Shawneuk in 1626, thereby becoming the progenitor of the Grahams of Shaw in Upper Dryfe.[123] See map in Figure F-9.

**Sinclairs.** William Sinclair of Roslin (carved from the Kettle of Braids in 1290) took ward of the deceased Sir Henry of Braids son, also named Henry, age sixteen, in 1304. Presumably, he wanted to

---

[115] Figure G-8: George Neilson, "Annals of the Solway Until A.D. 1307" (Glasgow: Glasgow Archeological Society, 1899), Figure II "From Map of Debatable Land, 1552." http://www.stevebulman.f9.co.uk/cumbria/solway_f.html

[116] Edward Aglionby, "The Aglionby Platt of the Opposite Border of Scotland to Ye West Marches," Dec 1590, Gatehouse Gazeteer, accessed 27 December 2022. http://www.gatehouse-gazetteer.info/APHome.html

[117] A. W. Cornelius Hallen. "The Grahams of the Border," 161.

[118] Rev William Graham, *Lochmaben Five Hundred Years Ago* (Edinburgh: Trinity, 1865), 56.

[119] William Fraser, *The Scotts of Buccleuch*, Vol. I (Edinburgh: 1878), 11-15, 38, 162, 163. https://archive.org/details/scottsofbuccleuc11fras/page/n3/mode/2up

[120] Rev William Graham, *Lochmaben Five Hundred Years Ago* (Edinburgh: Trinity, 1865), 123, 131, 145.

[121] R.C. Reid, "The Border Grahams and Their Origins," 94.

[122] David Masson, *The Register of the Privy Council of Scotland*. Edinburgh, First Series (Edinburgh: H.M. General Register House, 1895), Vol. XII, 657-659. https://catalog.hathitrust.org/Record/100404514

[123] Col William Rogerson, *Hutton Under the Muir* (Dumfries, Scotland: Dumfries and Galloway Courier and Herald, 1908), 26.

ensure the young Henry would be able to fulfill his late father's pledge for him to marry William Sinclair's daughter and, in the process, ensure that the Sinclairs would get the Braids estates in Bavelaw, in the Graham's Barony of Dalkeith, pledged in the agreement.[124]

William Sinclair of Roslin also shared Lovat-Bissets estates in Inverness and Rossshire with David Graham of Lovat. Sinclairs are later found as the guardian of the heirs of Bisset, acquiring the lands of Bruce Clackmannan Forest,[125] Midlothian,[126] and parts of Dunipace in Stirlingshire in the process.[127] Curiously, John Graham of Auchencloich, son of Sir John "the Last" Lord of Dalkeith, David Graham of Lovat, and David Graham of Dundaff, are found locked in a power struggle over Dunipace lands late in the fourteenth century.[128] The quarrel seems to stem from private gifts to the Temple being reclaimed by descendants, similar to the Dalkeith Graham disputes with Melrose Abbey which required Bruce the King to mediate a solution.[129] Cambuskenneth Abbey near Stirling held lands in Dunipace and required papal protections for its valuable lands as early as 1195.[130]

**Tamrawer Grahams.** Tamrawer and Auchencloich in the Parish of Kilsyth in Stirlingshire were one land until 1614 when Robert Graham of Auchencloich subdivided the lands of Tamrawer from the Auchencloich estate and granted Tamrawer to his kinsman, William Graham.[131] This Auchencloich is the same associated with John, son of Sir John "the Last" of Dalkeith in *Peerage*,[132] and the Tamrawer Grahams may have well been his descendants.[133] The village of Auchinclech connected with Walter Graham of Wallacetown is near Hiltoun in Aberdeenshire.[134] This Auchinclech should not be confused with the Auchencloich in Stirlingshire[135] or the one in Dunbartonshire.[136]

**Thornik Grahams.** There were two families named "Grahams of Thornik." The first family was a branch of the Grahams of Auchencass, and the second family was from the Grahams of Montrose and Cairnie. The old barony of Thornik was a substantial area of valuable land amounting to an 80 merkland (approximately 2,800 acres), including part of Wamphray extending up to the upper waters

---

[124] PoMS, "No. 9004," accessed 8 February 2023. https://www.poms.ac.uk/record/source/9004/
[125] PoMS, "No. 9808," accessed 10 February 2023. https://www.poms.ac.uk/record/source/9808/
[126] PoMS, "No. 10342," accessed 10 February 2023. https://www.poms.ac.uk/record/source/10342/
[127] John Anderson, *Historical Account of the Family of Frisel or Fraser, Particularly Fraser of Lovat* (Edinburgh and London: William Blackwood and T. Cadell, 1825), 18, 27, 30, 31. https://deriv.nls.uk/dcn23/9494/94945677.23.pdf
[128] Marquess of Bute, *Registrum of Monasterii of S. Marie de Cambuskenneth A.D. 1147-1535* (Edinburgh: 1872), 112-122. https://ia800302.us.archive.org/26/items/registrummonaste00cambuoft/registrummonaste00cambuoft.pdf
[129] Nicholas Graham of Auchencloich, a Dalkeith Graham descendant, may be "Nicholas, Keeper of Holy Cross," and if so, he would expect to be able to collect Dunipace revenue on behalf of his Office.
[130] PoMS, "No.3469, Cambuskenneth Abbey," accessed 30 March 2023. https://www.poms.ac.uk/record/source/3469/
[131] James Edward Graham, *The Grahams of Tamrawer* (Edinburgh: Edinburgh Press, 1895), 10-12. https://archive.org/details/grahamsoftamrawe00grah
[132] Sir James Balfour Paul, *The Scots Peerage, Founded on Wood's Edition,* Vol. VI (Edinburgh: David Douglas, 1909), 213.
[133] John Reid, "Material for a Place Name Survey of East Stirlingshire," 109. https://spns.org.uk/wp-content/uploads/2019/12/John-Reids-East-Stirlingshire-place-name-data-v2019.pdf
[134] James Edward Graham, *The Grahams of Tamrawer* (Edinburgh: Edinburgh Press, 1895), 5.
[135] John Reid, "Material for a Place Name Survey of East Stirlingshire," 109.
[136] James Edward Graham, *The Grahams of Tamrawer* (Edinburgh: Edinburgh Press, 1895), 4-5.

of the Dryfe. The lands once belonged to the Kirkpatricks, seneschals of Annandale in the thirteenth century, seated at Auchencass but later at Torthorwald.[137] See Figure F-9.

The first Thornik Graham was Robert Graham of Auchencass and Thornik, heir of Thomas Graham of Auchencass. R.C. Reid writes: "The object of the Johnstons was to enmesh, absorb, oust and finally to replace the Grahams with younger landless men of the Johnston clan."[138] The 1587 Privy Council records detail further attempts by the Johnstones regarding Thornik lands.[139] About that time, the Thornik Grahams named a younger son of the earl of Montrose as heir of most of their Dryfe Valley properties (Murthwait, Mylntoun, Mosslands, Craigielands, Brumelands, Baithok/Beattock) by way of a gift to prevent the Johnstones from "stealing" them from the Dryfe children. The Thornik Grahams did retain the small estate of Langboddam (Langbedholm).

Regarding the second family called "Grahams of Thornik": per *Scots Peerage,* Walter Graham, a younger son of the first earl of Montrose's first marriage, "who in 1541-1542 received a nineteen year tack of Little Cairnie from the abbot of Inchaffray, appears to have been the ancestor of the second family of Graham of Thornik who received the referenced gift from the first family of Thornik."[140] The new Grahams of Thornik battled the Johnstons through litigation for decades until 1607, when the Johnstons successfully acquired Thornik.[141]

**Tynedale Grahams (and Swinburnes).** The Tynedale Grahams were from an earlier generation of the Grahams of Dalkeith (elder line). Four of the five sons of the third Sir Henry de Graham and the Avenel heiress had estates in or some connection to Tynedale or Northumberland. See Figure F-8. Their daughter Idonea married Adam Swinburne, Sheriff of Northumberland, and obtained the Tynedale lands of Simondburn from her brother Henry upon their marriage. Only Peter, Sheriff of Dumfries (sheriff or justiciar/judge being a Graham family profession), did not own lands in England.[142] See Figure F-2.

Sir Nicholas de Graham, the eldest Dalkeith son, married a Muschamps co-heiress, thereby obtaining the baronies of Strathearn and Wooler.[143] A younger son, David Graham of Corbridge,[144] likely operated a mint there for Alexander III. The other Northumberland mint at Bamburgh was under the

---

[137] R.C. Reid, "The Border Grahams and Their Origins," *Transactions of the Dumfries and Galloway Natural History and Archaeological Society (TDGNHAS)* No. 3038 (1961): 87.

[138] R.C. Reid, "The Border Grahams and Their Origins," *Transactions of the Dumfries and Galloway Natural History and Archaeological Society (TDGNHAS)* No. 3038 (1961): 94-100.

[139] John Hill Burton, David Masson, *The Register of the Privy Council of Scotland*, Edinburgh, First Series, Vol. IV (Edinburgh: H.M. General Register House, 1881), 197. https://catalog.hathitrust.org/Record/100404514

[140] Sir James Balfour Paul, *The Scots Peerage, Founded on Wood's Edition*, Vol. VI (Edinburgh: David Douglas, 1909), 225.

[141] R.C. Reid, "The Border Grahams and Their Origins," *Transactions of the Dumfries and Galloway Natural History and Archaeological Society (TDGNHAS)* No. 3038 (1961): 98.

[142] Sir James Balfour Paul, *The Scots Peerage, Founded on Wood's Edition*, Vol. VI (Edinburgh: David Douglas, 1909), 193-197.

[143] Robert Bartlett, "England Under the Norman and Angevin Kings, 1075-1225" (Oxford: Oxford University Press, 2000), 543. https://archive.org/details/englandundernorm00bart_0/page/426/mode/2up?q=muschamps

[144] PoMS, "No. 944, person summary," accessed 10 February 2023. https://www.poms.ac.uk/record/person/944/

control of the lords of Bamburgh,[145] the Muschamp family. The Tynedales (Tindals) later appeared in Scotland after the 1318 Siege of Wark Castle. Presumably, they were expelled from Wark when the castle was assaulted and demolished.[146] The town of New Wark in Dumfries may have been named for their former home base of Wark in Northumberland. It is possible that the David Graham of Netherby, who married a daughter of Lang Will Graham before the family arrived in England in 1515, was a Tynedale Graham, connected to David Graham of Corbridge.

**Wamphray Grahams.** Assumed to be a branch of the Auchencass Grahams who gained the lands of Wamphray through marriage to Janet Kirkpatrick, co-heiress of Sir Duncan Kirkpatrick.[147] Wamphray was firstly Avenel territory, acquired by the elder line Grahams upon marriage to the Avenel heiress.[148] Sir Duncan's father, Sir Roger Kirkpatrick, "dear cousin" to Sir John "the Last" Graham Lord of Dalkeith, received the lands of Wamphray from Sir John in 1357.[149] The Grahams reacquired it when Thomas Graham of Auchencass married Janet Kirkpatrick in 1432.[150] See Figure F-2.

**Westerkirk Grahams.** Westerker Barony was part of the Avenel-Graham Eskdale lands, half of which was given to Melrose Abbey in 1320.[151] The other half of the Westerker Barony included the Hermitage portion given to Nicholas de Soulis circa 1242.[152] By 1321, Sir James Douglas acquired both portions of the Westerker barony.[153] Despite the Douglas' acquisition of Westerker Barony, they seemingly did not acquire advowson rights[iii] to the kirk of Westerker (Westerkirk), for in 1476, William and Thomas Graham served on an assize (jury panel[154]) regarding terce (Church issues/tithes) from Dalduran in Langholm.[iv] While the Grahams did not reside in Eskdale at this time, the family retained church advowson rights for Old Langholm, which would have required their representation on the assize.[155] It is unclear from which branch of Grahams the Westerkirk Grahams descend. Phil Graham notes that the children of Agnes Graham Monfode Douglas carried elder line Graham Christian names

---

[145] British Hammered and Milled Coins," SPINK: Where History is Valued, accessed 10 February 2023. https://www.spink.com/lot/21006000064

[146] William Hutchison, *A View of Northumberland with an Excursion to the Abbey of Mailross in Scotland* (Newcastle: T. Saint, 1778), 6. http://name.umdl.umich.edu/004863774.0001.002

[147] Sir James Balfour Paul, *The Scots Peerage, Founded on Wood's Edition*, Vol. II (Edinburgh: David Douglas, 1905), 381-382.

[148] John Patterson, *Wamphray: Pages from the History and Traditions of a Famous Parish in Upper Annandale* (Lockerbie: James Halliday, 1906), 11. (Requires account.) https://www.familysearch.org/library/books/viewer/796621/?offset=&return=1#page=1&viewer=picture&o=&n=0&q=

[149] William Fraser, *The Annandale Family Book of the Johnstones, Earls and Marquises of Annandale*, Vol. I (Edinburgh: 1894), 10-11. https://archive.org/details/annandalefamilv100fras/page/10/mode/2up

[150] Sir James Balfour Paul, *The Scots Peerage, Founded on Wood's Edition*, Vol. II (Edinburgh: David Douglas, 1905), 381-382.

[151] Robert Bruce Armstrong, *The History of Liddesdale, Eskdale, Ewesdake, Wauchopedale and the debateable land, Part 1* (Edinburgh: David Douglas, 1883), 150. https://www.familysearch.org/library/books/viewer/425315/?offset=153266#page=177&viewer=picture&o=&n=0&q=

[152] "Hermitage Castle," The Sons of Scotland, accessed 8 February 2023. http://www.thesonsofscotland.co.uk/hermitagecastle.htm

[153] Robert Bruce Armstrong, *The History of Liddesdale, Eskdale, Ewesdake, Wauchopedale and the debateable land, Part 1* (Edinburgh: David Douglas, 1883), 150-151.

[154] "Assize," *Dictionaries of the Scots Language*, accessed 13 January 2023. https://dsl.ac.uk/entry/snd/assize

[155] R.C. Reid, "The Border Grahams and Their Origins," 90.

(e.g., Henry, Nicholas, John, William). See Figure F-2. It is a possibility that one or more of her sons reverted to using their mother's Graham surname to retain her lands. Y-DNA ties the Grayville, Illinois Grahams to Grahams in Westerkirk and Langholm in the eighteenth century. I believe the latter were descendants of the remnants of the Gillesbie Grahams who remained in Scotland when the rest of the clan left for Ireland circa 1641[156] and lost their lands to creditors by 1699.[157]

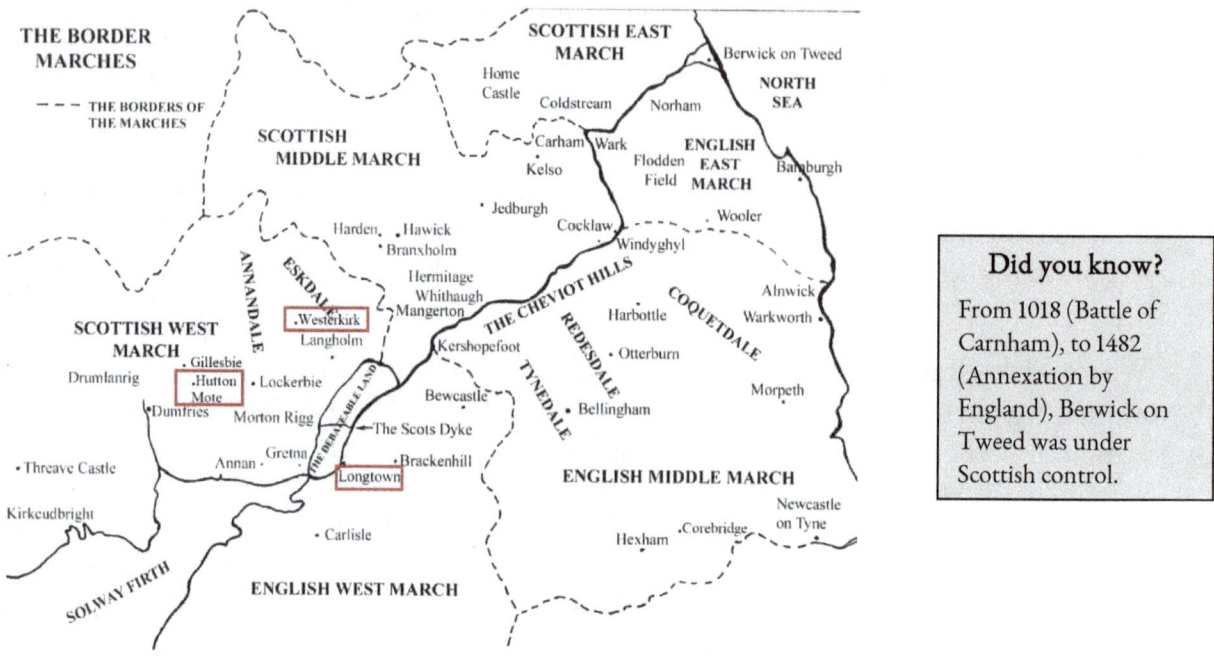

*Figure G-9: Map of the Scottish-English Border showing the divisions into Marches, by Tom Moss. Reproduced here under* CC BY 4.0. *With Additions.* [158]

**Did you know?**

From 1018 (Battle of Carnham), to 1482 (Annexation by England), Berwick on Tweed was under Scottish control.

**Wooler Grahams.** Branch of the Tynedale Grahams. Author Joseph Bain gave evidence that Sir Nicholas Graham married a Muschamp heiress (Figure F-2), acquiring Wooler Barony on the East March of England,[158] Figure G-9, and his descendants in Tynedale may well have been the forerunners of the Grahams of Nicol Forest on the English side of the Esk.[159] During David I's reign, beginning in 1136, Northumbria and Cumberland (Carlisle) were under Scottish control. David's son, Henry, was titled "Earl of Northumbria and Huntingdon." It wasn't until 1237 that the territories reverted to

---

[156] Col William Rogerson, *Hutton Under the Muir* (Dumfries, Scotland: Dumfries and Galloway Courier and Herald, 1908), 26.

[157] R.C. Reid, "The Border Grahams and Their Origins," 94.

[158] Figure G-9: Tom Moss, "Border-Reivers-March-Wardens-of-the-English-Scottish-Border," *Border Reivers from the 13th to the 17th Centuries*, 26 September 2010. https://wwwborderreiverstories-neblessclem.blogspot.com/2013/01/border-reivers-march-wardens-of-english.html

[159] J. Bain, *The Border Papers: Calendar of letters and papers relating to the affairs of the borders of England and Scotland preserved in Her Majesty's Public Record Office*, Vol. I, 1560-1594, Vol. II 1595-1603 (London, Edinburgh: H.M. General Register House, 1894), 123, 124, 135, 176, 177, 270, 751, 778, 779, 807. https://archive.org/details/borderpaperscale02grea/mode/2up?q=burghley

[Blurb on Berwick on Tweed] Jim McLaughlin, "The Border Reivers," Calgary Burns Club, September 2019. https://www.calgaryburnsclub.com/uploads/1/0/6/3/106351037/the_border_reivers_website_copy.pdf

England when Scotland renounced claims to Cumberland and Northumberland in the Treaty of York.[160]

## Table of Figures

Figure G-1: Map of the Dryfe Valley, Hutton and Corry Parish, in NW Dumfriesshire, Scotland; Ordnance Survey (map GB.) Landranger Series SCALE OF 1; 50 000, SHEET NO 79 HAWICK & ESKDALE (LANGHOLM) Ordnance Survey license number 100066333. All rights reserved. © Copyright and database right 2022. ...................................................................................................... G-6

Figure G-2: Parish of Port-of-Menteith Map. Copyright © 2011 Peter McNiven [53] ........................... G-9

Figure G-3: Blaeu's Atlas of Scotland, 1654, Based on surveys by Timothy Pont, showing Torndudff, Blaatwood, Renpatrick, and Ryid Kirk Lands. [72] CC-BY 4.0 Reproduced with the permission of the National Library of Scotland. ...................................................................................................... G-12

Figure G-4: Arms for Sir Robert Graham of Morphie Illustrated by Dr. Lloyd Graham[97] ............. G-14

Figure G-5: Armorial of the Sir Thomas Murray of Bothwell, last Murray lord of Bothwell, from "The Heraldry of the Murrays" [100] ...................................................................................................... G-15

Figure G-6: Primary Murray Line and the Branches of Bothwell, Abercairney, Tullibardine, Atholl, Ochtertyre and Mansfield from "The Chiefship of Clan Murray" [101] ............................................ G-15

Figure G-7: "Double Tressure Round the Stars" Armorial of the Murrays of Cockpool [104] ............ G-16

Figure G-8: Map of Debatable Land, Glasgow Archaeological Society, November 1896 [115] .......... G-17

Figure G-9: Map of the Scottish-English Border showing the divisions into Marches, by Tom Moss. Reproduced here under CC BY 4.0. With Additions. [158] .................................................................. G-22

## Endnotes

[i] This Peter Graham was likely the uncle of the elder Sir John de Graham. He was also the Sheriff of Dumfries. Peter stepped to manage the estate of his brother, Sir Nicholas de Graham, after his death in 1307, since Nicholas' son John was a minor.

[ii] Brackenwra in Annandale should not to be confused with Brackenwra in Langholm.

[iii] Advowson rights were rights to appoint clergy, a right that had monetary value and could be sold.

[iv] Daldurran in Langholm Parish became Westerhall by 1476. Westerhall was located in what became Parish Westerkirk, a parish that was created in 1693.

---

[160] "Treaty of York-1237," Scotland's History, BBC, accessed 8 February 2023. https://www.bbc.co.uk/scotland/history/scotland_united/treaty_of_york/

# Bibliography

## A

ActiveMe. "Queen Scotia's Grave Walk, Scotia's Glen, Tralee, Kerry, Ireland." Active Me Irelands Travel Guide, Accessed 15 December 2022. https://www.activeme.ie/guides/queen-scotias-grave-walk-scotias-glen-kerry/

Elizabeth Adams-Osborn, Heather. "The Story of Princess Scota, Atlantis, Egypt, and Ireland: The Story of Princess Scota." Ancient Mysteries, ARE, February 2007. https://www.researchgate.net/publication/277713025_'Atlantis_Egypt_and_Ireland_The_Story_of_Princess_Scota'_Ancient_Mysteries_ARE_Feb_2007

Addison, Charles G. The History of the Knights Templar, the Temple Church and the Temple. London: Longman, Brown, Green, Longmans, 1842. https://archive.org/details/historyofknights00addiuoft

Aglionby, Edward. "The Aglionby Platt of the Opposite Border of Scotland to Ye West Marches," map, December 1590. Gatehouse Gazetteer, Accessed 27 December 2022. http://www.gatehouse-gazetteer.info/APHome.html

AlphaDictionary.com. "Hamlet." Accessed 28 December 2022. https://www.alphadictionary.com/goodword/word/hamlet#:~:text=This%20ham%20was%20borrowed%20from,borrowed%20back%20as%20English%20haunt

Abu-Amero, Khaled K., Ali Hellani, Ana M. González, et al. Saudi Arabian Y-Chromosome diversity and its relationship with nearby regions. BMC Genet **10**, 59 (2009). https://doi.org/10.1186/1471-2156-10-59

Amoako, Henry Kwadwo. "Did Queen Scotia Really Exist in The Days of The Biblical Moses?" African Research Consult, 22 March 2022. http://african-research.com/research/did-queen-scotia-really-exist-in-the-days-of-the-biblical-moses/

Ancestry.com. Ireland, Indexes to Wills, 1384-1858. Provo, UT: USA: Ancestry.com Operations, Inc., 2014. https://www.ancestry.com/search/collections/9144/

Ancient and Scheduled Monuments, History on the Ground. "Hutton Mote/Motte." Accessed 12 February 2023. https://ancientmonuments.uk/120722-hutton-mote-motte-annandale-north-ward#.Y7eqLxXMKU1

Ancient Monuments. "Gillesbie Tower in Annandale North and Dumfries and Galloway," Source ID: SM10433. Accessed 4 January 2023. https://ancientmonuments.uk/123372-gillesbie-tower-annandale-north-ward#.Y0dVzXbMJPa

Anderson, John. Historical Account of the Family of Frisel or Fraser, Particularly Fraser of Lovat. Edinburgh and London: William Blackwood and T. Cadell, 1825. https://deriv.nls.uk/dcn23/9494/94945677.23.pdf

Anderson, Marjorie Ogilvie. Chronicle of Holyrood. Edinburgh: University Press, 1938. https://deriv.nls.uk/dcn23/1266/1376/126613769.23.pdf

AnnanTheHistoryTown.org. "Motte and Bailey." Accessed 10 March 2023. https://www.annanthehistorytown.org/defensive-annan-2/motte-bailey/

Antoninewall.org. The Antonine Wall, "The Romans in Scotland." Accessed 15 December 2022. https://www.antoninewall.org/about-the-wall/the-romans-in-scotland

Armstrong Clan Association. "Armstrong Clan History: Armstrong Origins." Accessed 20 December 2022. https://www.armstrongclan.info/clan-history.html .

Armstrong, James Lewis M.D. Chronicles of the Armstrongs. Jamaica, Queensborough, N.Y: The Marion Press, 1902.
https://archive.org/details/chroniclesofarms00arms/mode/2up?ref=ol&view=theater

Armstrong, John G. "The Debatable Armstrongs and Their Graham Relations." Armstrong Clan Association News (2009), 1-3. https://clangrahamsociety.org/wp-content/uploads/2020/01/TheDebatable-ArmstrongsandtheirGrahamRelations-JohnGArmstrong.pdf

AskAboutIreland. "Griffith Evaluation." Accessed 31 December 2022.
https://www.askaboutireland.ie/griffith-valuation/

# B

Author: "B." "The Chiefship of the Clan Murray." The Scottish Antiquary, or, Northern Notes and Queries, Vol. 15, No. 58. Edinburgh University Press, October 1900): 56.
https://www.jstor.org/stable/25516988

Bailey, Geoff. "History of Kinneil Kirk." Kinneil.org, 9 September 2019.
https://kinneil.org/2019/09/09/history-of-kinneil-kirk-by-geoff-bailey/

Bain, Joseph. The Border Papers: Calendar of letters and papers relating to the affairs of the borders of England and Scotland preserved in Her Majesty's Public Record Office, Volume I, 1560-1594,Volume II 1595-1603. London, Edinburgh: H.M. General Register House, 1894.
https://archive.org/details/borderpaperscale02grea/mode/2up?q=burghley

Bain, Joseph. The Border Papers: Calendar of letters and papers relating to the affairs of the borders of England and Scotland preserved in Her Majesty's Public Record Office, Volume II. London, Edinburgh: H.M. General Register House, 1881.
https://archive.org/details/calendarofdocume02grea/page/134/mode/1up?q=graham

Bain, Joseph. Calendar of Documents Relating to Scotland preserved in Her Majesty's Public Record Office, Volume III (1307-1357). London, Edinburgh: H.M. General Register House, 1887.
https://archive.org/details/calendarofdocume03edin

Bain, Joseph. Calendar of Documents Relating to Scotland, Volume IV, 1357 A.D. – 1509. Edinburgh: H.M. General Register House, 1888.
https://www.electricscotland.com/history/records/bain/calendarofdocuments04.pdf

Bain, Joseph. Calendar of Documents Relating to Scotland preserved in Her Majesty's Public Record Office, Volume I, (1108-1272). London, Edinburgh: H.M. General Register House, 1881.
https://www.electricscotland.com/history/records/bain/calendarofdocuments01.pdf

Bartlett, Robert. "England Under the Norman and Angevin Kings, 1075-1225." Oxford: Oxford University Press, 2000.
https://archive.org/details/englandundernorm00bart_0/page/426/mode/2up?q=muschamps

Beam, Amanda, John Bradley, Dauvit Broun, John Reuben Davies, Matthew Hammond, Neil Jakeman, Michele Pasin and Alice Taylor (with others). People of Medieval Scotland (PoMS) 1093-1371. Glasgow and London: 2019, Accessed 29 December 2022. https://www.poms.ac.uk/

Belanger, Ann. "Cadets and Septs of the Grahams." Clan Graham Society Website, Accessed 18 October 2022. https://clangrahamsociety.org/about/#septs

Bellow, Sir George."The Fleur de Lys." Coat of Arms, no. 6 (1951). https://www.theheraldrysociety.com/articles/the-fleur-de-lys/

Bernhard, Peter. "The Real "King Arthur" of the Historical Records." Ancient Templar Knowledge, Accessed 6 January 2023. https://commanderysaintmichael.wordpress.com/2015/01/24/the-real-king-arthur-of-the-historical-record/

Black, George Fraser and Mary Elder. The Surnames of Scotland: Their Origin, Meaning, and History. New York: New York Public Library, 1946. https://babel.hathitrust.org/cgi/pt?id=mdp.39015011274175&view=1up&seq=415&q1=graham

Blaeu, Joan, and Pont, Timothy. Annandiae praefectura, Vulgo, The Stewartrie of Annandail, Atlas of Scotland, 1654, map, National Library of Scotland. https://maps.nls.uk/view/00000402#zoom=5&lat=3489&lon=4316&layers=BT

Blaeu, Joan, and Pont, Timothy. Provinciae Edinburgenae description, Atlas of Scotland, 1654, National Library of Scotland. https://maps.nls.uk/view/00001284

Blair, D. O. Hunter. "Holyrood Abbey." Mary Foundation, Accessed 14 February 2023. https://www.catholicity.com/encyclopedia/h/holyrood_abbey.html

Blakely, Ruth M. "The Brus Family in England and Scotland, 1100-c. 1290." PhD Thesis, University of Durham, 2000. http://etheses.dur.ac.uk/1594/

Boles, Dr David B. "A Partly Hypothetical Pedigree of the Early Boyle Family of Kelburn, Ayrshire, Scotland." The Genealogist's Craft, 9 April 2020. https://bolesbooksblog.wordpress.com/tag/boyville/

Borland, Craig. "Eye on Millig: Remembering St. Kessog of Luss." Helensburgh Advertiser, 14 March 2017. https://www.helensburghadvertiser.co.uk/news/15156671.eye-on-millig-remembering-st-kessog-of-luss/

Boston College, The Boise Center Papers on Religion in the United States. "Introduction to Christian Theology." Accessed 19 January 2023. https://www.bc.edu/content/dam/files/centers/boisi/pdf/bc_papers/BCP-Christianity.pdf

Bosworth, C.E. "'ARAB i. Arabs and Iran in the pre-Islamic period."Encyclopaedia Iranica, II/2, 201-203, Accessed 30 December 2012. http://www.iranicaonline.org/articles/arab-i

Bovey, Alixe. "The Medieval Church: From Dedication to Dissent."British Library, 30 April 2015. https://www.bl.uk/the-middle-ages/articles/church-in-the-middle-ages-from-dedication-to-dissent

Brain, Jessica. "The Lindisfarne Gospels." HistoricUK.com, 8 March 2021. https://www.historic-uk.com/HistoryUK/HistoryofEngland/Lindisfarne-Gospels/#:~:text=A%20famous%20illuminated%20manuscript%20created,beauty%2C%20ornate%20detail%20and%20design

Brankstone, Jane Thomas, J.C. B. Sharp, and Michael Anne Guido. "A Cumberland Family with Medieval Roots in Scotland and Northern England: A Study Gilbert Fitz Richer and His Descendants." Foundation for Medieval Genealogy, Foundations (2008): 360. https://fmg.ac/phocadownload/userupload/foundations2/JN-02-05/358Richer.pdf

Brankstone, Jane Thomas, J.C. B. Sharp, and Michael Anne Guido. "Further Addendum to the Five Odards: Eva de Hodelholm and her Step Children." Foundation for Medieval Genealogy,

Foundations (2008): 360-362. https://fmg.ac/phocadownload/userupload/foundations3/JN-03-03/267Eva.pdf

Brauner, Jesse. "Boar." Accessed 4 December 2022. https://www.symbols.com/symbol/boar

Gairdner, James, editor. Letters and Papers, Foreign and Domestic, Henry VIII, Volume 12 Part 1, January-May 1537. London: Her Majesty's Stationery Office, 1890, British History Online, Accessed 28 December 2022. http://www.british-history.ac.uk/letters-papers-hen8/vol12/no1

Brewer, Ebeneezer Cobham. Historic Note Book. Philadelphia: Lippincott, 1892. https://www.google.com/books/edition/Historic_Note_book/YmwUAAAAYAAJ?hl=en&gbpv=1&dq=order+of+mathurin+first+established+in+scotland&pg=PA575&printsec=frontcover

Britroyals.com. "King Robert the Bruce of Scotland." Accessed 9 March 2023. https://britroyals.com/scots.asp?id=robert1

Brooks, Claire. "Theories on the Origins of the Grahams." Clan Graham Society Newsletter (1998). https://clangrahamsociety.org/theories-on-the-origins-of-the-grahams/

Brown, Ryk. "Duncan Graham of Nether Glenny (1708-1759)." Brown's Genealogy Database and Stewarts of Balquhidder, 16 November 2022. https://rykbrown.net/TNG/getperson.php?personID=I7082&tree=BROWN

Bruce, William P. "The Bowmen of Saint Sebastian." Family of Bruce International, February 2017. https://familyofbruceinternational.org/the-bowmen-of-saint-sebastian/

Bullen, Damian Beeson. "Nefrubity and Princess Scota." Academia.edu, Accessed 28 December 2022. https://www.academia.edu/45466704/NEFERUBITY_and_PRINCESS_SCOTA

Burnes, James. Sketch of the History of the Knights Templar, Second Edition. Edinburgh: William Blackwood and Sons, London: Payne & Foss, Dublin: John Cumming, 1840. https://ia600200.us.archive.org/18/items/sketchofhistoryo00burn/sketchofhistoryo00burn.pdf

Burton, John Hill. The Register of the Privy Council of Scotland. Edinburgh, First Series, Volume I. Edinburgh: H.M. General Register House, 1878. https://catalog.hathitrust.org/Record/100404514

Bute, John, Marquess of, J.R.N. Macphail, and H.W. Lonsdale. The Arms of the Royal and Parliamentary Burghs of Scotland. Edinburgh: William Blackwood & Sons, 1897. https://play.google.com/store/books/details?id=7VA4AQAAMAAJ&rdid=book-7VA4AQAAMAAJ&rdot=1

Bute, Marquess of. Registrum of Monasterii of S. Marie de Cambuskenneth A.D. 1147-1535. Edinburgh: 1872. https://ia800302.us.archive.org/26/items/registrummonaste00cambuoft/registrummonaste00cambuoft.pdf

Butler, Rev. Alban. The Lives of the Fathers, Martyrs, and Other Principal Saints, Volume III. Dublin: James Duffy, 1866; Bartleby.com, 2010. https://www.bartleby.com/210/3/043.html

Butler, Dugald and Herbert Story, Scottish Cathedrals and Abbeys. London: A&C Black, Edinburgh: R&R Clark Ltd, 1901. https://www.gutenberg.org/files/21688/21688-h/21688-h.htm

## C

CalcMaps. "Map Area calculator." Accessed 17 November 2022. https://www.calcmaps.com/map-area/

Canmore-National Record of the Historic Environment. "Abernethy "Culdee Monastery." Accessed 16 January 2023. https://canmore.org.uk/site/27936/abernethy-culdees-monastery

Canmore-National Record of the Historic Environment. "Applegarth Motte." Accessed 7 January 2023. https://canmore.org.uk/site/66813/applegarth-motte

Canmore-National Record of the Historic Environment. "Closeburn Old Church." Accessed 20 December 2022. https://canmore.org.uk/site/319020/closeburn-old-church. https://canmore.org.uk/site/search/result?NUMLINK=66755&view=map

Canmore-National Record of the Historic Environment. "Coats Hill." Accessed 27 February 2023. https://canmore.org.uk/site/48372/coats-hill

Canmore-National Record of the Historic Environment. "Dumbarton, St. Mary's Collegiate Church." Accessed 6 March 2023. https://canmore.org.uk/site/42351/dumbarton-st-marys-collegiate-church

Canmore-National Record of the Historic Environment. "Dryfe, Old Parish Church and Churchyard," Archaeology Notes. Accessed 9 January 2023. https://canmore.org.uk/site/67816/bentpath-westerkirk-old-parish-church?fbclid=IwAR3A0F74PCA1gcl775XfpT0dVw-xzwvBj7wJImEQhQ-w0EcP4eHfsacrcfQ

Canmore-National Record of the Historic Environment. "Ericstane." Accessed 27 February 2023. https://canmore.org.uk/site/48485/ericstane

Canmore-National Record of the Historic Environment. Gretna Old Church and Parish Church." Accessed 9 January 2023. https://canmore.org.uk/collection/382638

Canmore-National Record of the Historic Environment. "Isle of May, St. Adrian's Chapel." Accessed 17 February 2023. https://canmore.org.uk/site/57873/isle-of-may-st-adrians-chapelv

Canmore-National Record of the Historic Environment. "Wamphray Church," Archaeology Notes. Accessed 9 January 2023. https://canmore.org.uk/site/66905/wamphray-church

Carpenter, David X., Faculty of History, University of Oxford. "Robert de Brus, Tenant in Chief in Yorkshire and Annandale." Charters of William II and Henry I Project, 8 October 2013. https://actswilliam2henry1.files.wordpress.com/2013/10/h1-robert-de-brus-2013-1.pdf

Carlyle, T.J. The Debateable Land. Dumfries, W.R. McDarmid and Co., 1868. https://ia600206.us.archive.org/0/items/debateablelandr00carlgoog/debateablelandr00carlgoog.pdf

Carla Nayland. "The Battle of Arfderydd or Arthuret." Accessed 6 January 2023. http://www.carlanayland.org/essays/battle_arthuret.htm

Clan Carruthers Society International. "Clan Carruthers: The Secret Seat of the Templar." 10 August 2019. https://clancarrutherssociety.org/2019/08/10/clan-carruthers-the-secret-seat-of-the-templar/

Clan Carruthers Society. "Clan Carruthers: The Carruthers Chiefs and the Templar Link." 12 September 2020. https://clancarrutherssociety.org/2020/09/12/clan-carruthers-the-carruthers-chiefs-and-the-templar-link/

Clan Carruthers—Warriors. "The Templars in Annandale-Carruthersland." 13 January 2007. https://clancarruthers228187931.wordpress.com/tag/ruthwell/

Clan Douglas Society of North America. "Carruthers." Accessed 2 January 2023. http://clandouglassociety.org/carruthers/

Castelow, Ellen. "Surnames." HistoricUK, Accessed 1 January 2023. https://www.historic-uk.com/CultureUK/Surnames/

CatholicIreland.net. St. Cuthbert of Lindisfarne (634-687)." Accessed 14 February 2023. https://www.catholicireland.net/saintoftheday/st-cuthbert-of-lindisfarne-634-687/

Catholic News Agency. "St. John Ogilvie." Accessed 6 March 2023. https://www.catholicnewsagency.com/saint/st-john-ogilvie-173

Catholic.net. "Saint Waltheof of Melrose." Accessed 16 January 2023. https://catholic.net/op/articles/3008/cat/1205/st-waltheof-of-melrose.html

Catholic.net. "Saint Columba of Iona." Accessed 17 January 2023. https://www.catholicnewsagency.com/saint/st-columba-of-iona-722

Catholic News World. "St. Margaret of Scotland, Queen of Scotland." Last updated 13 November 2015. http://www.catholicnewsworld.com/2015/11/saint-november-16-st-margaret-of.html

Catholic Online. "Saint Catherine of Alexandria." Accessed 3 January 2023. https://www.catholic.org/saints/saint.php?saint_id=341

Catholic Online. "Saint Catherine of Siena." Accessed 19 January 2023. https://www.catholic.org/saints/saint.php?saint_id=9

Catholic Online. "Saint David I of Scotland." Accessed 5 March 2023. https://www.catholic.org/saints/saint.php?saint_id=5790

Catholic Online. "St. Malachy." Accessed 5 March 2023. https://www.catholic.org/encyclopedia/view.php?id=7429

Catholic Online. "St. Peter." Accessed 16 January 2023. https://www.catholic.org/saints/saint.php?saint_id=5358

Catholic Online. "Saint Sebastian." Accessed 16 January 2023. https://www.catholic.org/saints/saint.php?saint_id=103

Catholic.org. "St. Malachi." Catholic.org. Accessed 20 January 2023. https://www.catholic.org/saints/saint.php?saint_id=4431

Catholic.org. "Mary, the Blessed Virgin." Accessed 20 January 2023. https://www.catholic.org/saints/saint.php?saint_id=4967

Celtic Christianity. "Celtic Saints Alphabetic References." Accessed 16 January 2023. http://www.celticchristianity.infinitesoulutions.com/saints_alpha.html

Census of Ireland. *General Alphabetical Index to the Townlands and Towns, parishes and Baronies of Ireland*. Dublin: Alexander Thom, 1861. https://archive.org/details/op1248631-1001

Chalmers, George. *Caledonia or an Historical and Topographical Account of North Britain, Volume VI*. Paisley: Alexander Gardner, 1890. https://www.electricscotland.com/books/pdf/caledoniaorhisto06chal.pdf

Clan Arthur. "Saint Kentigern-Patron Saint of Glasgow, Nephew of King Arthur." Accessed 6 March 2023. http://clanarthur.org/history/arthur-the-chieftain/st-kentigern-patron-saint-of-glasgow-nephew-of-king-arthur/

Clan Johnstone in America. "History of the Clan." Accessed 15 February 2023. https://clanjohnstone.org/history-of-the-clan/

Clan Mac Farlane and Associated Clans Genealogy. "Andrew de Campbell (1319-after 1367)." Accessed 2 January 2023. https://www.clanmacfarlanegenealogy.info/genealogy/TNGWebsite/getperson.php?personID=I2295&tree=CC

Clan Mac Farlane and Associated Clans Genealogy. "Andrew de Cunningham of Drumquhassil." Accessed 2 January 2023.
https://www.clanmacfarlanegenealogy.info/genealogy/TNGWebsite/getperson.php?personID=I38279&tree=CC

Clausen, Daniel J. "Origins of Masonic Templarism in the French Ordre du Temple." Academia, Accessed 13 March 2023.
https://www.academia.edu/53226567/Origins_of_Masonic_Templarism_in_the_French_Ordre_du_Temple

Co-Curate. "Pele Tower." Accessed 17 February 2023. https://co-curate.ncl.ac.uk/pele-tower/

College of St Kessog. "About St Kessog." Accessed 3 January 2023.
http://kessog.lochac.sca.org/about.htm

Collingwood, W.G. Northumbrian Cross of the Pre-Norman Age. London: Faber & Gwyer, 1927.
https://iiif.wellcomecollection.org/pdf/b31350987

Compostela, Joining Heaven and Earth. "History of Charlemagne and Roland, Compostela and the Legend of the Milky Way." Accessed 7 March 2023.
https://compostela.co.uk/mythology/charlemagne-and-the-legend-of-the-milky-way/

Cormack, W. F. "Fergus Graham of Mossknow, and the Murder at Kirkpatrick." Transactions of the Dumfries and Galloway Natural History and Archaeological Society (TDGNHAS) No. 3064, Vol 64 (1989): 94-97.

Corrie, J. E. Records of the Corrie Family, 802-1899 A.D. London: Mitchell and Hughes, 1899.
https://archive.org/details/recordsofcorrief01corr

Coutts, Rev. Alfred. The Knights Templar in Scotland. Scottish Church History Society, 1941.
https://archive.org/details/rschsv07p2coutts/page/126/mode/2up

Cohen, Jennie. "History of the Knights Templar." History.com, 3 September 2018.
https://www.history.com/news/who-were-the-knights-templar-2

Coursol, Bruno. "The endless fights between Sun god Ra and the Great Serpent god Apep (Apophis) in the Underworld are representations of the grand gallery impactor operating cycle of the Great Pyramid of Khufu." 1001 Tasses, 24 September 2021.
https://www.milleetunetasses.com/amp/blog/the-great-pyramid-of-khufu/sun-god-ra-and-the-great-serpent-god-apep-apophis-fights-in-the-underworld.html

Cowan, Ian B. P.H.R. Mackay and Alan Macquarrie. Knights of St. John of Jerusalem in Scotland, Volume 19. Edinburgh, Clark Constable, 1983. https://digital.nls.uk/126638043

Cowan, Ian Borthwick. Medieval Religious Houses, Scotland: with an appendix on the Houses on the Isle of Man, second edition. London and New York: Longman Group Limited, 1976.
https://archive.org/details/medievalreligiou0000cowa/page/174/mode/2up

Cousens, Roger. "Griffith's Valuation: Fermanagh Town Maps and Ordnance Survey Maps." Fermanagh Gold, Accessed 31 December 2022. https://fermanagh-gold.com/_media/roger_cousens/town_maps_and_proni.pdf

Cox, Alex. "A Handy Guide to Traditional Scottish Naming Patterns." FindMyPast, 14 July 2020.
https://www.findmypast.com/blog/help/traditional-scottish-naming-patterns

Cramp, Rosemary. "Sequence of Ornament." Northumbrian Crosses of the Pre-Norman Age, Vol. 1. London: Faber & Gwyer Limited, 1927 via the University of Durham, Accessed 16 December

*Bibliography*

 2022. https://iiif.wellcomecollection.org/pdf/b31350987 or https://corpus.awh.durham.ac.uk/1chap4.php

Crampton, William G. "This Sceptered Isle." The Guardian, Accessed 16 December 2022. https://www.theguardian.com/notesandqueries/query/0,1574,00.html.

Crosslé, Francis and Phillip. *Crosslé Genealogical Abstracts, 1620-1850*, "Beatty notebooks, v. 6-12." FindmyPast.com. Accessed 27 December 2022. (Requires Account.) https://search.findmypast.com/record?id=S2%2FIRE%2FNAI%2F007634818%2F00600&parentid=IRE%2FNAI%2FGENABS%2F00602219%2F1 Also available in non-indexed form at: https://www.familysearch.org/search/catalog/234637?availability=Family%20History%20Library

Crumplin, Sally. "Rewriting History in the Cult of St. Cuthbert, from the Ninth to the Twelfth Centuries, St. Andrews Research Repository." Phd Thesis, University of St. Andrews, 2004. https://core.ac.uk/download/pdf/1154335.pdf

Cumming, James E. "Saint Moluag of Mortlach." June 1966. https://dufftown.info/2022/05/28/saint-moluag-of-mortlach-1966/

Curtis, Rebekah. "Contemplaiting." First Things, 27 June 2017. https://www.firstthings.com/web-exclusives/2017/06/contemplaiting

Cushie Enterprises. "Map of the Medieval Scottish Dioceses." The Early Church in Northern Scotland, Accessed 14 February 2023. https://www.cushnieent.com/medievalchurch/map_scotland.htm

Cushie Enterprises. "The Medieval Church in Alba." The Early Church in Northern Scotland, 14 December 2022. https://www.cushnieent.com/medievalchurch/medieval_portal.htm

## D

Dalton, Paul. "Feudal Politics in Yorkshire, 1066 x 1054." PhD Thesis, University of Sheffield, 1990. https://etheses.whiterose.ac.uk/1870/

Dalrymple, David. Annals of Scotland from The Accession of Robert I, Surnamed Bruce, to The Accession of the House of Stewart. Edinburgh: Balfour and Smellie, 1879. https://www.google.com/books/edition/Annals_of_Scotland_From_the_Accession_of/POMUSyU9KfoC?hl=en&gbpv=1&dq=thomas+moray+died+1361&pg=PA249&printsec=frontcover

Davies, Arthur Charles Fox. A Complete Guide to Heraldry. London: T.C and E.C. Jack, 1909. https://www.gutenberg.org/files/41617/41617-h/41617-h.htm#page290.

Davies, Arthur Charles Fox. "Trees, Leaves, Fruits, and Flowers." in A Complete Guide to Heraldry Edinburgh, UK: T.C. & E.C. Jack, 1909. Accessed December 17, 2022 via Wikisource. https://en.wikisource.org/w/index.php?title=A_Complete_Guide_to_Heraldry/Chapter_18&oldid=6647208

Davis, Rachel Meredith. "Commentary on No. 21 Robert Bruce, sixth lord of Annandale." Modified 27 June 2022. Accessed 20 December 2022. https://scalar.missouri.edu/vm/vol3-plates26-30-scottish-seals-plate28

DBPedia.org. "About Patrick Graham (bishop)." Accessed 9 January 2023. http://live.dbpedia.org/page/Patrick_Graham_(bishop)

Debrett's Peerage, Baronetage, Knightage, and Companionage. London: Dean & Son, Limited, 1903. https://archive.org/details/b24883797/page/n427/mode/2up?ref=ol&q=grimthorpe

Documents of Early England Data Set (DEEDS). By Michael Gervers. Accessed 6 March 2023. https://deeds.library.utoronto.ca/charters/05130072

Definitions.net. "Definitions for Manrent." Accessed 3 January 2023. https://www.definitions.net/definition/manrent

Delahunt, Gail. "Everything You Need to Know About the Apostle St. James the Greater." Follow the Camino, 27 December 2019. https://followthecamino.com/en/blog/history-of-the-apostle-saint-james/

Department of Ancient Near-Eastern Art."The Phoenicians 1500-300 B.C." The Metropolitan Museum of Art, October 2004. https://www.metmuseum.org/toah/hd/phoe/hd_phoe.html

Dictionaries of the Scots Language. "Advocatioun." Accessed 13 January 2023. https://dsl.ac.uk/entry/dost/advocatioun

Dictionaries of the Scots Language. "Assize," Accessed 13 January 2023. https://dsl.ac.uk/entry/snd/assize

Dictionaries of the Scots Language. "Feu." Accessed 12 February 2023. https://www.dsl.ac.uk/entry/snd/feu

Dictionaries of the Scots Language. "Fiar." Accessed 4 January 2023. https://www.dsl.ac.uk/entry/snd/fiar_n1

Dictionaries of the Scots Language. "Lin, Linn." Accessed 3 January 2023. https://www.dsl.ac.uk/entry/dost/lin_n

Dictionaries of the Scots Language. "Ree, Rie, Rea, Rae, Wrae." Accessed 3 January 2023. https://www.dsl.ac.uk/entry/snd/ree_n1_v1

Dictionaries of the Scots Language. "Tenement." University of Glasgow, Accessed 17 November 2022. https://www.dsl.ac.uk/entry/snd/tenement

Dictionaries of the Scots Language. "Tocher, Tochir." Accessed 4 January 2023. https://www.dsl.ac.uk/entry/dost/tocher_n

Dictionary.com. "Prebend." Accessed 13 January 2023. https://www.dictionary.com/browse/prebend

Dictionary of National Biography. "1885-1900/Cuthbert (d.687)." Wikisource, Accessed 10 January 2023. https://en.wikisource.org/wiki/Dictionary_of_National_Biography,_1885-1900/Cuthbert_(d.687)

Dictionary of the National Biography. "Graham, Patrick (d. 1478)." Accessed 20 January 2023. https://en.wikisource.org/wiki/Dictionary_of_National_Biography,_1885-1900/Graham,_Patrick

Dillon, William J. "The Trinitarians at Failford" Ayrshire Archaeological and Natural History Society Vol 4 (1957): 76, 91-93. https://aanhsorg.files.wordpress.com/2018/08/the-trinitarians-of-failford.pdf

Dixon, M.C. "The Knightly Families of Northumberland: A Crisis in the Fourteenth Century." Masters Thesis, Durham University, 2000. http://etheses.dur.ac.uk/4373/1/4373_1893.pdf

Dobson, David. Directory of Scots Banished to the American Plantations, 1650-1775. Baltimore: Genealogical Publishing Co., 1984. https://www.google.com/books/edition/Directory_of_Scots_Banished_to_the_Ameri/QZDSAQ9CRGQC?hl=en&gbpv=1&bsq=graham

Dowden, Rev. John. The Bishops of Scotland. Glasgow: John Maclehose and Sons, 1912. https://archive.org/details/bishopsofscotlan00dowdrich/page/194/mode/2up?q=turpin

Dray, Danielle. "The Melrose Casket and Robert the Bruce." Historic Environment Scotland, 24 June 2018. https://blog.historicenvironment.scot/2018/06/melrose-casket-robert-bruce/

Dugdale, William. Monasticon Anglicanum: A History of the Abbies and Other Monasteries, Hospitals, Frieries, and Cathedral and Collegiate Churches, with Their Dependencies, in England and Wales; Also of All Such Scotch, Irish, and French Monasteries, as Were in Any Manner Connected with Religious Houses in England, Volume 3. London: Longman, Hurst, Rees, Orme and Brown, 1821. https://quod.lib.umich.edu/e/eebo/A36798.0001.001?view=toc

Dumbarton and Vale of Leven Reporter. "The Funeral Procession of King Robert the Bruce," 12 March 2013. https://www.dumbartonreporter.co.uk/opinion/13957969.the-funeral-procession-of-king-robert-the-bruce/

Durrani, Nadia. "Mass burials in England attest to a turbulent time, and perhaps a notorious medieval massacre." ARCHAEOLOGY magazine (online), November/December 2013. https://www.archaeology.org/issues/109-1311/features/1421-viking-england-st-brices-day

Duchess of Cleveland. The Battle Abbey Roll, Volume I. London: John Murray, 1889. https://books.google.com/books/about/The_Battle_Abbey_Roll.html?id=yV8JAAAAIAAJ

Dumfriesshire Ordnance Survey. "Dragon's Well." Name Books 1848-1858, Volume 27, Parish of Hutton & Corrie -- Plan 43/12 Trace 5, 219. https://scotlandsplaces.gov.uk/digital-volumes/ordnance-survey-name-books/dumfriesshire-os-name-books-1848-1858/dumfriesshire-volume-27/219

Durham World Heritage Site. Accessed "William of St. Calais." Accessed 13 January 2023. https://www.durhamworldheritagesite.com/learn/history/prince-bishops/early-bishops/william-calais

Durham World Heritage Site. Accessed "Cuthbert's Move to Durham: Two Stories." 16 January 2023. https://www.durhamworldheritagesite.com/learn/history/st-cuthbert/body/durham

# E

Edgar, Robert. An Introduction to the History of Dumfries, Volume I. Dumfries: J. Maxwell and Sons, 1915. https://archive.org/details/cu31924028091233/page/n173/mode/2up?q=crosbie

EditorBee. "The St Brice's Day Massacre." The Armchair Anglophile, 13 November 2011. http://www.armchairanglophile.com/st-brices-day-massacre/

Educalingo.com. "Dictionary, Watchtower." Accessed 17 February 2023. https://educalingo.com/en/dic-en/watchtower

Ekins, Jayne. "Y-DNA Haplogroup: E1b1b and E1b1a." Your DNA Guide (blog), Accessed 14 December 2022. https://www.yourdnaguide.com/ydgblog/ydna-haplogroup-e

Electric Scotland. "Graham." Accessed 30 December 2022. https://electricscotland.com/webclans/dtog/graham.html

Electric Scotland. "The Scottish Nation, Cunningham." Accessed 13 February 2023. https://electricscotland.com/history/nation/cunningham.htm

Encyclopedia Britannica. Editors of Encyclopaedia Brittanica, "St. Ninian." Accessed 10 January 2023. https://www.britannica.com/biography/Saint-Ninian

England, Gerald England. "Old Gretna Parish Church." Geograph.org, Accessed 9 January 2023. https://www.geograph.org.uk/photo/5511143

Engliscan Gesiðas (The English Companions). "Death of Bishop Trumwine, 2nd December 704," Accessed 16 January 2023. https://www.tha-engliscan-gesithas.org.uk/events-in-anglo-saxon-times/on-this-day/on-this-day-in-december/

English Heritage. "Our Guide to Heraldry," Accessed 16 December 2022. https://www.english-heritage.org.uk/easter/preparing-for-easter-adventure-quests/our-guide-to-heraldry/

English Monarchs. "King David I, Dunfermline Abbey." Accessed 6 March 2023. https://www.englishmonarchs.co.uk/dunfermline_abbey.html

Esparza, Daniel. "Was Saint Peter Really Crucified Upside Down?" Aleteia, 26 August 2021. https://aleteia.org/2021/08/26/was-saint-peter-really-crucified-upside-down/

Erskine, John, and James Ivory. Institute of the Law of Scotland, Volume II. Edinburgh: Bell and Bradfute, 1828. https://archive.org/details/aninstitutelaws00ivorgoog/page/n4/mode/2up?q=apprisement

Estes, Roberta. 442 Ancient Viking Skeletons Hold DNA Surprises – Does Your Y or Mitochondrial DNA Match?" DNAeXplained-Genetic Genealogy (blog), 18 September 2020. https://dna-explained.com/2020/09/18/442-ancient-viking-skeletons-hold-dna-surprises-does-your-y-or-mitochondrial-dna-match-daily-updates-here/comment-page-1/

Estes, Roberta. "You Might Be a Pict If …" DNAeXplained-Genetic Genealogy (blog), 24 August 2013. https://dna-explained.com/2013/08/24/you-might-be-a-pict-if/

Estes, Roberta. "Concepts—Genetic Distance." DNAeXplained Genetic Genealogy, Accessed 20 October 2022. https://dna-explained.com/2016/06/29/concepts-genetic-distance/

Etymology Online Dictionary. "pray (v)," Accessed 19 January 2023. https://www.etymonline.com/word/pray

Evans, Lorraine. Kingdom of the Ark: The Startling Story of how the Ancient British Race is Descended from the Pharaohs. London: Simon & Schuster, 2000.

Exeter, Walter of. Franciscan Friar and Witness to the Siege. The Siege of Carlaverock, 1300, Accessed 18 October 2022. https://www.deremilitari.org/RESOURCES/SOURCES/carlaverock.htm

# F

FamilySearch. "Scotland Births and Baptisms, 1564-1950," "Hugh Graham, 1788."FamilySearch.org, Accessed 11 February 2020. https://familysearch.org/ark:/61903/1:1:X14T-6XS

Familysearch.org. "Hugh Graham (28 July 1788-20 July 1880)." Accessed 30 December 2022 (restricted). https://www.familysearch.org/tree/person/sources/97RX-DKK

Family Search Wiki. "Ireland Church Registers (National Institute)." Accessed 31 December 2022. https://www.familysearch.org/en/wiki/Ireland_Church_Registers_(National_Institute)

FamilySearch Wiki contributors. "Ireland Maps."FamilySearch Wiki, Accessed 8 December 2022. https://www.familysearch.org/en/wiki/index.php?title=Ireland_Maps&oldid=5063315

FamilySearch Wiki contributors. "Researching Ancestors with Patronymic Surnames (National Institute)." FamilySearch Wiki, Accessed November 17, 2022. https://www.familysearch.org/en/wiki/index.php?title=Researching_Ancestors_with_Patronymic_Surnames_(National_Institute)&oldid=1853326

FamilySearch Wiki contributors."Westerkirk, Dumfriesshire, Scotland Genealogy." FamilySearch Wiki, Accessed 9 January 2023.

https://www.familysearch.org/en/wiki/index.php?title=Westerkirk,_Dumfriesshire,_Scotland_Genealogy&oldid=5140745

FamilyTreeDNA. "Iberian Askenaz Y-DNA Project, Accessed 10 March 2023.
https://www.familytreedna.com/groups/iberian-surnamesof-ashkenaz/about/background

FamilyTreeDNA. "Calhoun/Colquhoun Y-DNA Surname Project Results." FamilyTreeDNA.com, Accessed 30 December 2022.
https://www.familytreedna.com/public/calhoun/default.aspx?section=ycolorized

FamilyTreeDNA. "Corey/Cory Y-DNA Surname Project Results." FamilyTreeDNA.com, Accessed 30 December 2022. https://www.familytreedna.com/public/CoryorCorey?iframe=ycolorized

FamilyTreeDNA. "Cunningham Y Chromosome DNA Surname Project Results." FamilyTreeDNA.com, Accessed 30 December 2022.
https://www.familytreedna.com/public/cunningham?iframe=ycolorized

FamilyTreeDNA. "Dalton America DNA Surname Project Results." FamilyTreeDNA.com, Accessed 30 December 2022. https://www.familytreedna.com/public/dalton?iframe=ycolorized

FamilyTreeDNA. "Gillespie Y-DNA Surname Project Results." FamilyTreeDNA.com, Accessed 30 December 2022.
https://www.familytreedna.com/public/GillespieDNAProject?iframe=ycolorized

FamilyTreeDNA. "Jordan Family Surname DNA Project Results." FamilyTreeDNA.com, Accessed 30 December 2022. https://www.familytreedna.com/public/Jordan-Surname-Project?iframe=ycolorized

FamilyTreeDNA. " Kirk(Kil)patrick/Kilpatrick Results." FamilyTreeDNA.com, Accessed 27 December 2022. https://www.familytreedna.com/public/kirkpatrick?iframe=ycolorized

FamilyTreeDNA. "Graham DNA Surname Project News." FamilyTreeDNA.com, Accessed 29 December 2022. https://www.familytreedna.com/groups/graham/about/news

FamilyTreeDNA. "Graham DNA Surname Project Background." FamilyTreeDNA.com, Accessed 29 December 2022. https://www.familytreedna.com/groups/graham/about/background

Family Tree DNA. "Lyons Surname Y-DNA Project Results." FamilyTreeDNA.com, Accessed 15 December 2022. https://www.familytreedna.com/public/lyon?iframe=ycolorized

Family Tree DNA. "Murray Clan DNA Research Project." FamilyTreeDNA.com, Accessed 28 December 2022. https://www.familytreedna.com/groups/murray/about/background

FamilyTreeDNA. "Scientific Details Haplogroup J-BY65," Country Frequency. Gene by Gene, Ltd., Accessed 8 November 2022. https://discover.familytreedna.com/y-dna/J-BY65/frequency?view=table

FamilyTreeDNA. "Scientific Details Haplogroup J-FGC58460." Gene by Gene, Ltd., Accessed 8 November 2022. https://discover.familytreedna.com/y-dna/J-FGC58460/story

FamilyTreeDNA. "Scientific Details Haplogroup J-BY89." Gene by Gene, Ltd., Accessed 8 November 2022. https://discover.familytreedna.com/y-dna/J-BY89/story

FamilyTreeDNA. "Scottish Y-DNA Project Results." FamilyTreeDNA.com, Accessed 30 December 2022. https://www.familytreedna.com/public/Scottishdna?iframe=ycolorized

FamilyTreeDNA. "JL1253 News." FamilyTreeDNA.com, Accessed 30 December 2022.
https://www.familytreedna.com/groups/j-1c-3d-with-snp-l1253/about/news

FamilyTreeDNA. "Scientific Details Haplogroup J-ZS1559." Gene by Gene, Ltd., Accessed 30 December 2022. https://discover.familytreedna.com/y-dna/J-ZS1559/story

FamilyTreeDNA. "Haplogroup Story J-L1253." FamilyTreeDNA.com, Accessed 8 February 2023. https://discover.familytreedna.com/y-dna/J-L1253/story

FamilyTreeDNA. "Scientific Details Haplogroup J-FTC68260." Gene by Gene, Ltd., Accessed 8 November 2022. https://discover.familytreedna.com/y-dna/J-FTC68260/story

FamilyTreeDNA. "R-BY3265, R-BY3266 Subclade & Brittany > Matignon > Grouazel and other families Y-DNA Classic Chart." FamilyTreeDNA.com, Accessed 30 December 2022 https://www.familytreedna.com/public/Grouazel_Pays_de_Matignon/default.aspx?section=yresults

FamilyTreeDNA. Big Y-DNA Barry Scott Graham." FamilyTreeDNA.com, Accessed 30 December 2022. https://www.familytreedna.com/my/ydna/matches/detail-view (restricted access)

Family Tree DNA. Y-DNA Matches for Barry Scott Graham. FamilyTreeDNA.com, Accessed 20 October 2022. https://www.familytreedna.com/my/ydna/matches/detail-view (restricted access)

FamilyTreeDNA. "Normandy Y-DNA Project Results." FamilyTreeDNA.com, Accessed 15 December 2022. https://www.familytreedna.com/public/Normandy?iframe=ycolorized

FamilyTreeDNA. "Moffat-Rutherford DNA Surname Project Results." FamilyTreeDNA.com, Accessed 30 December 2022. https://www.familytreedna.com/groups/moffittmoffett/about/results

FamilyTreeDNA. "Stewart Stuart (royal) Y-DNA Project Results." FamilyTreeDNA.com, Accessed 30 December 2022. https://www.familytreedna.com/public/Stuart?iframe=ycolorized

FamilyTreeDNA. "St Clair Sinclair Y-DNA Study Results." FamilyTreeDNA.com, Accessed 30 December 2022. https://www.familytreedna.com/public/Sinclair?iframe=ycolorized

Family Tree DNA Learning Center. "Subclade." FamilyTreeDNA.com, Accessed 29 December 2022. https://learn.familytreedna.com/faq-items/subclade/

FamilyTreeDNA. "My FamilyTree DNA Project Website, "Corey/Cory Surname - Y-DNA Colorized Chart." Accessed 20 December 2022. https://www.familytreedna.com/public/CoryorCorey?iframe=ycolorized.

Farmer, Jim. "Syrian Scots on the Borderlands." Academia.edu, 9 June 2009. https://www.academia.edu/36354861/Syrian_Scots_on_the_Borderlands_No_Pics

Farrer, William, Hon. D. Litt., Editor. Early Yorkshire Charters, Volume II. Edinburgh: Ballantyne, Hanson & Co., 1915-1916. https://archive.org/details/earlyyorkshirech02farruoft/page/126/mode/2up?q=bertram

Findlater, Alex Maxwell. "Hoddam, A Medieval Estate in Annandale." Transactions of the Dumfries and Galloway Natural History and Archaeology Society, (TDGNHAS) No. 3082 (2008): 80.

Foljambe, Anthony. "Chaptre the 17th, The Scallop Shells Crusades." 1615-1669: An English Normand in America, Anthony Foljambe Blog. https://anthonyfoljambe.blogspot.com/2017/01/chaptre-17th-scallop-shells-crusades.html

Fontaine, John & Alexander and Edward Porter. The journal of John Fontaine; an Irish Huguenot son in Spain and Virginia, 1710-1719. Williamsburg, Virginia: Colonial Williamsburg Foundation, 1972; distributed by the University Press of Virginia.

Fraser, Iain. "The Dragon of Corriehills." Transactions of the Dumfries and Galloway Natural History and Archaeology Society (TDGNHAS) No. 3074 (2000): 107-111. https://draft.dgnhas.org.uk/sites/default/files/transactions/3074.pdf#page=112

Fraser, William. The Annandale Family Book of the Johnstones, Earls and Marquises of Annandale, Volume I. Edinburgh: 1894.
  https://archive.org/details/annandalefamilv100fras/page/10/mode/2up

Fraser, William. The Book of Carlaverock, Volume I: Memoirs of the Maxwells, Earls of Nithsdale, Lords Maxwell & Herries. Edinburgh, 1873.
  https://electricscotland.com/webclans/m/bookofcarlaverv100fras.pdf

Fraser, William. Douglas Book, Volume I. Edinburgh: T. and A. Constable, Edinburgh University Press, 1885. https://digital.nls.uk/histories-of-scottish-families/archive/96806202?mode=transcription

Fraser, William. Douglas Book, Volume III. Edinburgh: T. and A. Constable, Edinburgh University Press, 1885. https://deriv.nls.uk/dcn23/9653/96539705.23.pdf

Fraser, William. The Melvilles and the Leslies, the Earls of Melville and the Earls of Leven, Volume I. Edinburgh: 1900. https://deriv.nls.uk/dcn23/9666/96660715.23.pdf

Fraser, William. The Red Book of Menteith, Volume I. Edinburgh: 1880.
  https://digital.nls.uk/histories-of-scottish-families/archive/96774276#?c=0&m=0&s=0&cv=217&xywh=-282%2C-337%2C5611%2C4159

Fraser, William. The Red Book of Menteith, Volume II. Edinburgh: 1880.
  https://digital.nls.uk/histories-of-scottish-families/archive/97146821

Fraser, William. The Manuscripts of J. J. Hope Johnstone, Esq. of Annandale. London: Eyre and Spotswood, 1897.
  https://archive.org/details/manuscriptsofjjh00grea/page/18/mode/2up?q=nichol

French, Morvern. "The Barony of Kervale and its Links with some Key Moray Families." University of St. Andrews, 20 March 2015. https://flemish.wp.st-andrews.ac.uk/2015/03/20/the-barony-of-kerdale-and-its-links-with-some-key-moray-families/

## G

Gadalla, Moustafa. "Matrilineal/Matriarchial Society." Egyptian Wisdom Center, Accessed 8 November 2022. https://egyptianwisdomcenter.org/matrilineal-matriarchal-society/

Gairdner, James, editor. Letters and Papers, Foreign and Domestic, Henry VIII, Volume 12 Part 1, January-May 1537. London: Her Majesty's Stationery Office, 1890, British History Online, Accessed December 28, 2022. http://www.british-history.ac.uk/letters-papers-hen8/vol12/no1

Gazetteer for Scotland, The Editors of The. "St. Michael's Parish Church." Gazetteer for Scotland, Accessed 9 January 2023. https://www.scottish-places.info/features/featurefirst1011.html

Gazeteer for Scotland. "St. Blane, St. Blaan," Accessed 17 February 2023. https://www.scottish-places.info/people/famousfirst1606.html

Galles, Duane L.C.M. "Pilgrims and Heraldry." Coat of Arms no. 45 (Spring 1989).
  https://www.theheraldrysociety.com/articles/pilgrims-and-heraldry/

Garlinghouse, Tom. "Who were the Picts, the Early Inhabitants of Scotland?" Live Science, Last updated August 2022. https://www.livescience.com/who-were-picts-scotland

GeneticHomeland.com. "DNA Marker Pedigree Display for: I-A17650, I-A6227, I-BY172227, R-A6703, R-A6704, R-CTS3104, R-DF105, R-L165, R-L21, R-L47, R-M167, R-M222, R-P25, R-S21809, R-U106, R-Y10968, R-Y37962, R-Z255, R-Z9, and Y48464 on Chromosome: Y." Accessed 30 December 2022. https://www.genetichomeland.com/welcome/

Genealogy for the United Kingdom and Ireland (GENUKI). "GENUKI Gazetteer-Find Places." Accessed 31 December 2022. https://www.genuki.org.uk/gazetteer#results

GENUKI. "Ireland." Accessed 31 December 2022. https://www.genuki.org.uk/big/irl

GENUKI. "Scotland." Accessed 31 December 2022. https://www.genuki.org.uk/big/sct

GENUKI. "GENUKI Gazetteer-Refine Your Selection." Accessed 31 December 2022. https://www.genuki.org.uk/gazetteer#refine

GENUKI. "St. Mungo (or Castlemilk) Parish in Annandale." Accessed 9 January 2023. https://www.genuki.org.uk/big/sct/DFS/St.Mungo

GENUKI. "Kirkpatrick-Fleming." Accessed 9 January 2023. https://www.genuki.org.uk/big/sct/DFS/KirkpatrickFleming

Ghidrai, George. "Motte and Bailey Castles-The Original Castle Design." The World of Castles, Accessed 5 January 2023. https://www.castlesworld.com/tools/motte-and-bailey-castles.php

Gervers, Michael. Documents of Early England Data Set (DEEDS). Accessed 6 March 2023. https://deeds.library.utoronto.ca/content/about-deeds

Gibraltar Timeline. "A Brief History of Gibraltar." Accessed 8 November 2022. http://gibraltartimeline.com/brief-history-of-gibraltar/

Gilbert, Rosalie. "Medieval Hairstyles." Rosalie's Medieval Woman, Accessed 3 January 2023. https://rosaliegilbert.com/hairstyles.html

Gilchrist, Roberta. "Monastic Archaeology and National Identity: The Scottish Monastic Experience." Cambridge University Press (20 December 2019): 52. https://www.cambridge.org/core/books/sacred-heritage/monastic-archaeology-and-national-identity-the-scottish-monastic-experience/6BD6F88E5222E126AFF581466E3D9F75

Gillies, H. Cameron, M.D. The Place-Names of Argyll. London: David Nutt, 1906. https://www.electricscotland.com/books/placenames/placenamesofargy00gill.pdf

Gould, S. Baring and John Fisher. The Lives of British Saints, Volume II. London: Charles J. Clark, 1908. https://archive.org/details/livesofbritishsa02bariuoft/page/240/mode/2up?view=theater&q=kentigern

GPSMyCity. "Cathedral Close Tour (Self Guided), Salisbury." Accessed 31 December 2022. https://www.gpsmycity.com/tours/cathedral-close-tour-5144.html

Graeme, Louisa Grace. Or and Sable : a Book of Graemes and Grahams . Edinburgh: William Brown, 1903. https://archive.org/details/orsablebookofgra00grae/page/642/mode/2up?q=archdeacon

Graham, Alicia. "Fergus Graham of Mossknowe, aka: Fergus the Rascal." Clan Graham Society Newsletter, November 2022.

Graham, John. Condition of the Border at the Union: Destruction of the Graham Clan. London: George Routledge and Sons Ltd, 1907. https://archive.org/details/conditionofborde00grahuoft/page/n10/mode/1up?ref=ol&view=theater&q=hutchin

Graham, Lloyd D., PhD, House Graham, From the Antoine Wall to the Temple of Hymen. Lulu.com, 2020. https://clangrahamsociety.org/wp-content/uploads/2020/09/House-GRAHAM-eBook.pdf

Graham, T.H.B. "Nunnery." Transactions of the Cumberland and Westmoreland Antiquarian and Archaeological Society (23 April 1915): 5-7.
https://archive.org/details/transactionsofcu17cumb/page/6/mode/2up?q=fergus+graham

Graham, T.H.B. "The de Levingtons of Kirklinton." Transactions of the Cumberland and Westmoreland Antiquarian and Archaeological Society (Carlisle: 1911): 63, 67-69.
https://archive.org/details/transactionsofcu12cumb/page/60/mode/2up?q=graham

Graham, T.H.B. "The Debatable Land, Part II." Transactions of the Cumberland and Westmoreland Antiquarian and Archaeological Society (Carlisle: 1913): 149.
https://archive.org/details/transactionsofcu14cumb/page/n167/mode/2up?q=lang

Graham, Rev. William. Lochmaben Five Hundred Years Ago. Edinburgh: Trinity, 1865.
https://books.google.com/books/about/Lochmaben_Five_Hundred_Years_Ago_Or_Sele.html?id=qqYHAAAAQAAJ&printsec=frontcover&source=kp_read_button&hl=en&newbks=1&newbks_redir=0#v=onepage&q&f=false

Grand Priory of the Knights Templar in the United Kingdom. "Military Commandery of St. James the Greater." Accessed 6 March 2023. https://www.osmthgpuk.org/military

Gray, Iain. "Masonic Parable and the Legend of the Pillar." The Herald, 4 October 1989.
https://www.heraldscotland.com/news/11929072.masonic-parable-and-legend-of-the-pillar/

Great Britain Ordnance Survey. 6-inch to 1 mile, Dumfriesshire, Sheet XXXIV, map, Survey date: 1857, Publication date: 1861. https://maps.nls.uk/view/228777274

Great Britain, Parliament, House of Commons. Report of the House of Commons Select Committee on Ecclesiastical Titles and Roman Catholic Relief Acts, Vol. VIII. London: House of Commons, 2 August 1867.
https://books.google.com/books?id=RylcAAAAQAAJ&pg=PA89#v=onepage&q&f=false

Great Britain, Record Commission. State papers, published under the authority of His Majesty's Commission. King Henry the Eighth, Volume 5. London: G. Eyre and A. Strahan, printers to the King's Most Excellent Majesty, 1836.
https://archive.org/details/statepaperspubli05grea/page/194/mode/2up?q=bishop+stewart

Green, Cynthia Whiddon, University of Houston. "Saint Kentigern, Apostle to Strathclyde: A Critical Analysis of a Northern Saint." Fordham University, December 1998.
https://sourcebooks.fordham.edu/basis/cynthiawhiddengreen-saintkentigern1998.asp

Grenham, John. "Catholic Parishes in Ireland." JohnGrenham.com, Accessed 30 December 2022.
https://www.johngrenham.com/places/rcmap_index.php

Grenham, John. "Irish Placenames-search window." JohnGrenham.com, Accessed 30 December 2022.
https://www.johngrenham.com/places/

Grenham, John. "Irish Placenames-Details," JohnGrenham.com, Accessed 31 December 2022.
https://www.johngrenham.com/browse/retrieve_text.php?text_contentid=64#Property

Grenham, John. "Poor Law Unions (1851)." JohnGrenham.com, Accessed 31 December 2022.
https://www.johngrenham.com/places/plu_index.php

Griffith, Richard. "Griffith Evaluation." AskAboutIreland, Accessed 31 December 2022.
https://www.askaboutireland.ie/griffith-valuation/

Groam House Museum, "Pictish People," Accessed 16 December 2022.
https://openvirtualworlds.org/omeka/exhibits/show/groam-house-museum/pictish-people

Groome, Francis H. Ordnance Gazetteer of Scotland, Volume V. Edinburgh: Thomas C. Jack, Grange Publishing Works, 1884. https://digital.nls.uk/gazetteers-of-scotland-1803-1901/archive/97385114?mode=transcription

Guild of One-Name Studies. "Laidman Family History, Robert, Lord of Curry Mallet in Somerset." 7 June 2022. https://laidman.one-name.net/getperson.php?personID=I32627&tree=Laidman

# H

Halsall, Paul. "Internet Medieval Sourcebook, Saints' Lives." Fordham University, Accessed 10 January 2023. https://sourcebooks.fordham.edu/sbook3.asp

Hall, Hubert, F.S.A., editor. "The Red Book of the Exchequer, Volume I." London: Printed for Her Majesty's Stationery Office by Eyre and Spottiswoode, 1896. https://archive.org/details/redbookofexchequ9911grea/page/342/mode/2up?ref=ol&view=theater&q=muschamp

Hallbarns-Simonburn. "The Great Parish of Simonburn, from Hadrian's Wall to Carter's Bar." Accessed 19 January 2023. http://www.hallbarns-simonburn.co.uk/simonburn.htm

Hallen, A. W. Cornelius. "The Grahams of the Border." The Scottish Antiquary or Northern Notes and Queries 9, no. 36 (1895): 162. https://www.google.com/books/edition/The_Scottish_Antiquary/Zdyk2WG8ILQC?hl=en&gbpv=1&bsq=netherby

Halpin, David. "Thoth's Storm: New Evidence for Ancient Egyptians in Ireland?" Ancient Origins, 19 June 2021. https://www.ancient-origins.net/opinion-guest-authors/thoth-s-storm-new-evidence-ancient-egyptians-ireland-005187

Hay, Maciamo. "Genetic History of the Italians." Eupedia.com, Last updated December 2017. https://www.eupedia.com/genetics/italian_dna.shtml

Hay, Maciamo. "Haplogroup J1 (Y-DNA)." Eupedia.com. https://www.eupedia.com/europe/Haplogroup_J1_Y-DNA.shtml

Hay, Maciamo. "Haplogroup R1b (Y-DNA)." Eupedia.com, Last updated October 2021. https://www.eupedia.com/europe/Haplogroup_R1b_Y-DNA.shtml

Hammond, Matthew, PhD. "Resignations: David II (1329-71), The community of the realm in Scotland, 1249-1424: History, law and charters in a recreated kingdom." 21 November 2019. https://cotr.ac.uk/social-network-analysis-political-communities-and-social-networks/forfeitures-resignations-and-escheats/resignations-david-ii-1329-71/

Henderson, Ebeneezer. The Annals of Dunfermline and Vicinity. Glasgow: John Tweed, 1879. https://archive.org/details/cu31924091208359/page/n9/mode/2up?q=four+burghs

HeraldryandCrests.com. "Symbolism of Heraldry A-K." Accessed 16 December 2022. https://www.heraldryandcrests.com/pages/symbolism-of-heraldry

John Herkless and Robert Kerr Hannay, The Archbishops of St. Andrews, Volume I (Edinburgh and London: William Blackwood and Son, 1907), 12, 13, 62-65, 75-77, 82. https://www.familysearch.org/library/books/viewer/197574/?offset=&return=1#page=5&viewer=picture&o=&n=0&q=

Herkless, Sir John. The Archbishops of St. Andrews, 1855-1920. Edinburgh: W. Blackwood, 1907. https://archive.org/details/thearchbishopsof05herkuoft

Hershenzon, Daniel. "Ransom: Between Economic, Political, and Salvific Interests."The Captive Sea: Slavery, Communication, and Commerce in Early Modern Spain and the Mediterranean. Philadelphia: University of Pennsylvania Press, 2019. https://doi.org/10.9783/9780812295368-004

Hewison, James King. The Isle of Bute in the Olden Time: With Illustrations, Maps, and Plans, Volume 2. Edinburgh and London: W. Blackwood and sons, 1895.
https://archive.org/details/isleofbuteinolde02hewiuoft/page/290/mode/2up?q=graham

Highland Historic Environment Record. "Monastic Settlement, Rosemarkie, Church Place." Accessed 14 February 2023. https://her.highland.gov.uk/monument/MHG25214

Hill, Ninian. The Story of the Scottish Church From Earliest Times. Glasgow: James Maclehose and Sons, 1919.
https://www.forgottenbooks.com/en/download/TheStoryoftheScottishChurch_10216219.pdf

Hills, Dr. Catherine. "The Anglo-Saxon invasion and the beginnings of the 'English.'" Ourmigrationstory.org.uk, Accessed 15 December 2022.
https://www.ourmigrationstory.org.uk/oms/anglo-saxon-migrations

H.M. General Register House. The Register of the Privy Council of Scotland, First Series, Volume 9. Edinburgh, 1877. https://catalog.hathitrust.org/Record/100404514

His Majesty's Stationery Office. Calendar of the Patent Rolls: Edward VI. United Kingdom: H.M. Stationery Office, 1926.
https://www.google.com/books/edition/_/Olg4AQAAMAAJ?hl=en&sa=X&ved=2ahUKEwjvtsLhpYP8AhWYlmoFHYdPAwIQ7_IDegQIDRAE

Historical Manuscripts Commission. The Manuscripts of the Duke of Hamilton, Knight, Eleventh Report, Appendix, Part VI. London: Her Majesty's Stationery Office, 1887.
https://archive.org/details/manuscriptsofduk00greauoft/page/18/mode/2up?ref=ol&view=theater&q=moskeswra

Historical Manuscripts Commission. The Manuscripts of His Grace the Duke of Buccleuch and Queensberry, Fifteenth Report, Appendix, Part VIII. London: Eyre and Spottiswoode, 1897.
https://electricscotland.com/webclans/dtog/buccleuchqueens01greauoft.pdf

Historic Environment Scotland. "William the Lion penny." Accessed 16 January 2023.
https://www.historicenvironment.scot/archives-and-research/archives-and-collections/properties-in-care-collections/object/william-the-lion-penny-1165-1214-medieval-arbroath-abbey-1254

Historic Environment Scotland. "Hutton Mote-motte." Accessed 6 January 2023.
http://portal.historicenvironment.scot/designation/SM1

History Ireland. "An Eye on the Survey." Summer 2001. https://www.historyireland.com/an-eye-on-the-survey/

Holden, Edward S. A Primer of Heraldry for Americans. New York: The Century Co, 1898.
https://upload.wikimedia.org/wikipedia/commons/8/89/A_primer_of_heraldry_for_Americans_%28IA_primerofheraldry00holdrich%29.pdf

Hope, Robert Charles. The Legendary Lore of the Holy Wells of England. London: Elliott Stock, 1894.
https://insearchofholywellsandhealingsprings.files.wordpress.com/2014/03/legendaryloreofholywellshope.pdf

House of Names. "Maxwell History, Family Crest and Coat of Arms," Accessed 20 February 2023.
https://www.houseofnames.com/maxwell-family-crest

Hudson, Benjamin. The Picts. New York: John Wiley & Sons, 2014.

Hylsop, John and Robert. Langholm As it Was: A History of Langholm and Eskdale from the Earliest Times. Sunderland: Hills and Company, 1912.
https://archive.org/details/langholmasitwashhysl/mode/2up?q=shaw

# I

Idle Speculations. "The Saint with Two Names: St. Kentigern/St. Mungo." 25 December 2006.
http://idlespeculations-terryprest.blogspot.com/2006/12/saint-with-two-names-st-kentigernst.html

Innes, Cosmo. Liber Insule Missarum: Abbacie Canonicorum Regularium B. Virginis Et S. Johannis De Inchaffery Registrum Vetus. Edinburgh: Ballantyne and Hughes, 1847.
https://archive.org/details/liberinsulemissa85inchuoft/page/xxxvi/mode/1up?q=graham

InternationalHeraldry.com. "International Heraldry and Heralds." Accessed 16 December 2022.
https://www.internationalheraldry.com/

Irish Central Staff. "The Symbolic Meaning of the Celtic Cross." IrishCentral.com, 27 May 2017.
https://www.irishcentral.com/roots/history/celtic-cross-meaning

Irish Open Street Map Community. "Irish Townlands," Accessed 31 December 2022.
https://www.townlands.ie/

Irving, Alastair Maxwell. "Towers, Hall-houses and Timber Superstructures." The Castles Studies Group, Journal no. 31 (2017-2018): 266. http://www.castlestudiesgroup.org.uk/CSGJournal2017-18-rev6-131-340Maxwellp.258-275.pdf

Irving, J. Bell Esq. "List of Armorial Bearings Noted in Dumfriesshire and Neighboring Counties." Transactions of the Dumfries and Galloway Natural History and Archaeological Society (TDGNHAS), Third Series, Volume 1 (1912-1913): 130-131.
https://archive.org/details/transactionsjour31191213dumf/mode/2up?q=escallop

Irving, Joseph. The Book of Dumbartonshire, Volume II, Parishes. Edinburgh and London: W. and A. K. Johnston, 1879. https://deriv.nls.uk/dcn23/9539/95398878.23.pdf

Irvine, James M. and Kevin Irvin. "Interpreting yDNA Test Results." Clan Irwin Surname DNA Study, Accessed 29 December 2022. https://www.clanirwin-dna.org/interpreting-ydna-test-results

# J

J. H. S. "The Grahams: The First Line of the Grahams (Continued)." The Scottish Antiquary, or, Northern Notes and Queries 17, no. 68 (1903), 178. http://www.jstor.org/stable/25517111

Jamieson, John. An Historical Account of the Ancient Culdees of Iona. Edinburgh: John Ballantyne and Company, 1811.
https://archive.org/details/historicalaccoun00jami/page/n6/mode/1up?ref=ol&view=theater

Johnson, Charles and H.A. Cronne. Regesta Regum Anglo-Normannorum, Volume II, 1100-1135. Oxford: Clarendon Press, 1956. https://deeds.library.utoronto.ca/cartularies/0378

Johnston, Christopher, PhD. "The Early History of the Corries of Annandale." Transactions of the Dumfries and Galloway Natural History and Archaeological Society (TDGNHAS) No. 3001 (1913): 86-87.

Johnstone, C.L. The Historical Families of Dumfriesshire and the Border Wars, CHAPTER XII, Ancient Provosts of Annan. Dumfries: Anderson & Son, 1889.
https://archive.org/details/historicalfamili00grah

Johnstone, C. L. The History of the Johnstones, 1191-1909. Edinburgh: W & A.K. Johnston Ltd, 1909.
https://electricscotland.com/webclans/htol/historyofjohnstons.pdf

## K

Kelham, Charles Adrian. Bases of Magnatial Power in Later Fifteenth-Century Scotland. Edinburgh: University of Edinburgh, 1986. https://era.ed.ac.uk/bitstream/1842/6867/1/372968.pdf

Kennett, Debbie. "Haplogroup." International Society for Genetic Genealogy (ISOGG) Wiki, 27 June 2022. https://isogg.org/wiki/Haplogroup

Kennett, Debbie. "Y-DNA Project Help." International Society for Genetic Genealogy (ISOGG) Wiki, 28 October 2022. https://isogg.org/wiki/Y-DNA_project_help

Kentigern Way. "The St. Kentigern Way, Following the Saint's Journey from Hoddom to Glasgow." Accessed 9 January 2023. http://kentigernway.com/page22.html

Khalf, Salim George. "Phoenician Canaanite History Timeline." Phoenicia.org, Accessed 8 November 2022. https://phoenicia.org/phoeniciatimeline.html

Kiddle. "List of Former Cathedrals in Great Britain." Accessed 13 January 2023.
https://kids.kiddle.co/List_of_former_cathedrals_in_Great_Britain

King, Andy. "War, Politics, and Landed Society in Northumberland, c. 1296-c. 1408." PhD Thesis, Durham University, 2001. http://etheses.dur.ac.uk/1729/

King, Edwin James. The Knights Hospitallers in the Holy Land. London: Methuen & Co. Ltd., 1931.

King, Jeffrey. "Scotichronicon." World History Encyclopedia, 15 January 2019.
https://www.worldhistory.org/Scotichronicon/

King, Laura. "The Book of Kells." Color Theory Virginia Commonwealth University, Accessed 22 December 2022. http://www.people.vcu.edu/~djbromle/color-theory/color04/laura/bookofkells.htm

Kirkcudbright History Society. "St. Mungo and His Galloway Connections," 13 January 2021.
https://www.kirkcudbrighthistorysociety.org.uk/wp-content/uploads/2021/02/St-Mungo-talk.pdf

Klimczak, Natalia. "Exploring the Little Known History of Celtic Warrior in Egypt." Ancient Origins, 4 January 2016. https://www.ancient-origins.net/history/exploring-little-known-history-celtic-warriors-egypt-005100

## L

Laing, Henry. Impressions from Ancient Scottish Seals. Edinburgh: Bannatyne and Maitland Clubs, 1850.
https://ia902606.us.archive.org/22/items/descriptivecatal00bann/descriptivecatal00bann.pdf

L'Anson, William A. "The Lass of Richmond Hill." Notes and Queries, Oxford Journals 6, Vol. 2 (July-December 1880), 112.
https://www.google.com/books/edition/Notes_and_Queries/nhf4FlLFM3wC?hl=en&gbpv=1&dq=fergus+greyme+coat+of+arms+1553&pg=PA112&printsec=frontcover

Lapa, Dmitry. "Saint Aebba of Coldingham." The Postil Magazine, 1 July 2021. https://www.thepostil.com/saint-aebba-of-coldingham/

Lapa, Dmitry. "St. Bega, The Anchoress of Cumbria." Pravoslavie, Accessed 17 February 2023. https://pravoslavie.ru/82258.html

Lapa, Dmitry. "A Family of Saints: Sts. Kentigerna, Fillian and Comgan of Scotland." Orthodox Christianity, Accessed 10 January 2023. https://orthochristian.com/76644.html

Larsen, Mille. "How Old is the Arabic Language, and Where Did it Come From, A Look at Three Historical Arabic Languages." Autolingual, Accessed 16 December 2022. https://autolingual.com/arabic-how-old/

Lawrie, Sir Archibald. Early Scottish Charters, Prior to 1153 AD. Glasgow: James MacLehose and Sons, 1905. https://archive.org/details/earlyscottishcha00lawruoft/page/76/mode/2up

Lazaro, Tim. "Dragons, Celts and Druids." Dragon Dreaming Blog, Accessed 16 December 2022. https://dragondreaming.wordpress.com/dragons-celts-druids/

Le Fevre, Arnaud. "On the genetic trace of the Vikings in Normandy: the DNA of Coténtin speaks." Hag'dik Historical Society, 28 January 2018. http://hagdik.fr/sur-la-trace-des-vikings-ladn-cotentinois-parle/?fbclid=IwAR0zB8hVlfAD_POHtnxMcjcXE2_gk0i24DPxPvfw-S2WoFNxXcKOp8F8UHs

Lehman, John. "The Aikman Coat of Arms— Its elements, history, and geographical distribution." Modified 12 August 2017, Accessed 20 December 2022. https://victorianweb.org/history/heraldry/aikman.html

Lessman, Rev. Mary. "Walking the Camino de Santiago: A Saint Michael Pilgrimage." Saint Michael and All Angels Episcopal, Accessed 23 January 2023. https://www.saintmichael.org/blog/walking-the-camino-de-santiago-a-saint-michael-pilgrimage/

Lewis, C. P. "Companions of the Conqueror (act. 1066–1071)." Oxford Dictionary of National Biography, 24 May 2007. https://doi.org/10.1093/ref:odnb/95594

Lewis, Stephen M. Université de Caen Normandie. Forne Sigulfson-"The 'First' Lord of Greystoke in Cumbria." The Wild Peak Blog, 2013. https://thewildpeak.wordpress.com/2013/03/30/forne-sigulfson-the-first-lord-of-greystoke-in-cumbria/

Lewis, Stephen M. Lewis. Université de Caen Normandie." A Likely Story- Eleanor Grisdale and the King of Mardale." Wild Peak Blog, August 2014. https://grisdalefamily.wordpress.com/tag/william-the-conqueror/

Lindsay, W. A., J. Dowden and J. M. Thomson. Charters, Bulls and Other Documents relating to the Abbey of Inchaffray. Edinburgh: 1908.

Linton, S. "Mount Heredom and the Holy Grail." 16, Academia.edu, November 2010. https://www.academia.edu/25560426/Mount_Heredom_And_the_Holy_Grail

Lyte, H. C. Maxwell, editor. Calendar of Patent Rolls, Edward I: Volume 3, 1292-1301. London: 1895. https://babel.hathitrust.org/cgi/pt?id=mdp.39015031081154&view=1up&seq=627&q1=graham

Lythgoe, Darrin. "Graemes of Inchbrakie." Clan MacFarlane and Associated Clans Genealogy, Accessed 29 December 2022. https://www.clanmacfarlanegenealogy.info/genealogy/TNGWebsite/getperson.php?personID=I23489&tree=CC

M

Macalister, Robert Alexander Stewart. Lebor gabála Érenn: The book of the taking of Ireland, Part IV. Dublin: Educational Company of Ireland, Ltd.,1941. https://archive.org/details/leborgablare04macauoft

Macdonald, William Rae. Scottish Armorial Seals. Edinburgh, UK: William Green and Sons, 1904. https://www.electricscotland.com/books/pdf/scottisharmorial00macd.pdf.

Macgibbon, David and Thomas Ross. The ecclesiastical architecture of Scotland from the earliest Christian times to the seventeenth century, Volume 3. Edinburgh: George Waterson and Sons, 1897, digitized/produced by Chuck Greif, Project Gutenberg. https://www.gutenberg.org/files/65014/65014-h/65014-h.htm#page_423

Macleay, Kenneth. Highlanders of Scotland. Portraits illustrative of the principal clans and followings, and the retainers of the royal household at Balmoral, in the reign of her majesty Queen Victoria, Volume II. London: Mr. Mitchell, 1870, "Hugh Grahame," Plate 24. https://www.splrarebooks.com/collection/view/highlanders-of-scotland.-portraits-illustrative-of-the-principal-clans-and-

MacKinlay, James Murray. Influence of the Pre-Reformation Church on Scottish Placenames. Edinburgh and London: Blackwood and Sons, 1904. https://archive.org/details/cu31924028080566/page/n159/mode/2up?q=closeburn

MacKinlay, James Murray. Ancient Church Dedications in Scotland. Edinburgh: David Douglas, 1914. https://archive.org/stream/cu31924092331242/cu31924092331242_djvu.txt

MacKinlay, James Murray. "St. Kessog and His Cultus in Scotland."Transactions of the Glasgow Archaeological Society 3, no. 2 (1899): 347. http://www.jstor.org/stable/24680608

MacLellan, Rory PhD. "Templars and Hospitallers: the military-religious Orders in Scotland, 1128-1564." Pressreader, Accessed 13 March 2023. https://www.pressreader.com/uk/history-scotland/20210101/282136409152361

Mansom, Colin. "Saint Patrick Saltire History."  My Secret Northern Ireland, 23 October 2018. https://my-secret-northern-ireland.com/saint-patrick-saltire-html/

MacPherson, Hamish."The History of Scotland's First Patron Saint, Saint Kessog." The National, 8 March 2020.  https://www.thenational.scot/news/18288418.history-scotlands-first-patron-saint-saint-kessog/

MacQueen, Douglas. "Marjorie, Countess of Carrick and Mother of Scottish King Robert the Bruce." Transceltic, 27 June 2017. https://www.transceltic.com/blog/marjorie-countess-of-carrick-and-mother-of-scottish-king-robert-bruce

Marsden, Cathy. "An Unfortunate End, The Rebellious David Graham's Album Amicorum." Lyon and Turnbull, Accessed 9 January 2023. https://www.lyonandturnbull.com/news/article/an-unfortunate-end/

Masson, David. The Register of the Privy Council of Scotland. Edinburgh, First Series, Volume III. Edinburgh: H.M. General Register House, 1880. https://www.google.com/books/edition/The_Register_of_the_Privy_Council_of_Sco/i7nUcH-JxsUC?hl=en&gbpv=1&bsq=graham

Masson, David. The Register of the Privy Council of Scotland. First Series, Volume VIII. Edinburgh: H.M. General Register House, 1887. https://catalog.hathitrust.org/Record/100404514

Masson, David. The Register of the Privy Council of Scotland, First Series, Volume IX.  Edinburgh: H.M. General Register House, 1877. https://catalog.hathitrust.org/Record/100404514

Matthiesen, Diana Gale. Lyon(s) Families Association. "Results of Y-DNA Testing for Surname LYON and Its Variations, Haplogroup R1b Links Hub." Diana, Goddess of the Hunt—For Ancestors! Accessed 30 December 2022. http://dgmweb.net/DNA/Lyon/LyonDNA-results-R1b-Hub.html

Maxwell-Irving, A.M.T "Torthorwald Castle." Cruck Cottage Heritage Association, 1993. http://cruckcottage.com/torthorwald-castle/

McAndrew, Bruce A. "The Sigillography of the Ragman Roll." Proceedings of the Society of Antiquaries of Scotland, (2000); 684. http://journals.socantscot.org/index.php/psas/article/view/10060

McClintock and Strong Bible Clopedia. "Culdees." Accessed 9 January 2023. https://www.biblicalcyclopedia.com/C/culdees.html

McDowall, William. History of the Burgh of Dumfries. Edinburgh: Adam & Charles Black, 1874. https://books.google.com/books/about/History_of_the_Burgh_of_Dumfries.html?id=MD0PAAAAYAAJ

McIntosh, Iain D. "Scottish Freemasonry and England 1700- 1750." Grand Lodge of Scotland, Accessed 6 March 2023. http://www.pglforfarshire.org/Scottish_Freemasonry_and_England_Part02.html

Mcintosh Iain D. "David Graham of Fintry-30th March 1620." Book of Eminent Burgesses of Dundee (1513-1885), 2020. http://www.fdca.org.uk/1620_David_Graham_of_Fintry.html

McLeary, Erik. "Saint Patrick." The Dumbarton Castle Society, Accessed 6 March 2023. https://www.dumbartoncastle.co.uk/saint-patrick

McNiven, Peter Edward. "Gaelic place-names and the social history of Gaelic speakers in medieval Menteith." PhD thesis, University of Glasgow, 2011. https://theses.gla.ac.uk/2685/

McQuiston, Jim. "Templars." ILoveScotland.net, Accessed 1 March 2023. http://www.ilovescotland.net/templars.html

MedievalWarfare.info. "The Templars and other Monastic Military Orders." Accessed 10 January 2023. https://www.medievalwarfare.info/templars.htm

Medieval Bruce Heritage Trust. Accessed "Overview." 16 January 2023. http://www.brucetrust.co.uk/places-events.html

Mingren, Wu. "Niall of the Nine Hostages, One of the Most Fruitful Kings in History." Ancient Origins. Accessed 22 April 2023. https://www.ancient-origins.net/history-famous-people/niall-nine-hostages-0011410

Moeller, Charles."Order of Saint James of Compostela." The Catholic Encyclopedia, Volume 13. New York: Robert Appleton Company, 1912. http://www.newadvent.org/cathen/13353a.htm.

Molina, Hector. "What Does an Upside Down Cross Mean?" Catholic Answers, 17 July 2014. https://www.catholic.com/magazine/online-edition/the-upside-down-cross-satanic-or-symbolic

Moors Knowledge. "Guisborough Priory." Accessed 19 February 2023. http://www.yorkshiremoors.co.uk/gazetteer/guisborough_priory.html

Mudie, Sir Francis and David M. Walker. "Mains Castle and the Grahams of Fintry." Abertay Historical Society No. 9 (1964): 1-36. https://abertay.org.uk/wp-content/uploads/2017/08/MainsCastle&Grahams.pdf

My Family Silver. "Grimthorpe Family Crests." Accessed 8 November 2022. https://www.myfamilysilver.com/crestfinder-search/grimthorpe-family-crest

## N

National Archives of Ireland. "Valuation Office Records." Accessed 31 December 2022. https://www.nationalarchives.ie/article/valuation-office-records/

National Records of Scotland. "The Declaration of Arbroath." Accessed 8 November 2022. https://www.nrscotland.gov.uk/Declaration

National Records of Scotland. Graham of Mossknowe Papers (GD1/403/25). See also GD1/403/45.

National Records of Scotland. "Records of Abercorn / Abercorn North Kirk Session." Accessed 9 January 2023. https://catalogue.nrscotland.gov.uk/nrsonlinecatalogue/browseDetails.aspx?reference=CH2/835&

National Records of Scotland. "Saint Andrew." Accessed 16 December 2022. https://www.nrscotland.gov.uk/research/image-gallery/hall-of-fame/saint-andrew.

National Records of Scotland. Acts of the Lords of Council (Acta Dominorum Concilii) 4 Oct. 1478 to 15 May 1532. https://www.nrscotland.gov.uk/research/research-guides/research-guides-a-z/court-of-session-records

National Records of Scotland. Acts and Decreets of the Lords of Council and Session, 26 June 1542 to 26 February 1659. https://digital.nls.uk/histories-of-scottish-families/archive/95649035?mode=transcription

Neilson, George. "Annals of the Solway Until A.D. 1307." Glasgow: Glasgow Archeological Society, 1899. http://www.stevebulman.f9.co.uk/cumbria/solway_f.html

Newbattle Abbey. "History, Tours and Filming." Accessed 14 January 2023. https://newbattleabbey.com/filming-historical-tours-scotland/

Nicolas, Nicholas Harris. The Siege of Caerverlock, with the Earls, Barons and Knights Who Were Present for the Occasion. London: J.B. Nichols, 1878. https://archive.org/details/siegecarlaveroc00waltgoog/page/n370/mode/2up?ref=ol&view=theater&q=graham

Nisbet, Alexander. A System of Heraldry. Edinburgh: Printed for W. Blackwood, 1722. http://www.heraldry-scotland.co.uk/nisbets.html

Nisbet, R.W. BRO. C.C. "Historical Sketch." The Provincial Grand Lodge U.S.A. Accessed 8 March 2023. https://roosusa.org/about-us/ https://roosusa.org/about-us/

Norman, George, publisher. Kirkpatrick of Closeburn. London: George Norman, 1858. https://deriv.nls.uk/dcn23/9564/95641358.23.pdf

## O

O'Connor, Kathleen. "Early and Iron Age Celtic Society." Women in Ancient Celtic Society, Accessed 8 November 2022. https://ancientcelticwomen.weebly.com/society.html

O'Hart, John. Irish Pedigrees Volume II. Dublin: James Duffy and Co Limited, 1892. https://ia600202.us.archive.org/12/items/irishpedigreesor01ohar/irishpedigreesor01ohar.pdf

Order of the Blessed Virgin Mary of Mercy, Mercedarian Friars USA. "Our History." Accessed 16 January 2023. https://www.orderofmercy.org/our-history

Omnium Sanctorum Hiberniae. "Saint Kessog of Lennox. March 10," 10 March 2014. http://www.omniumsanctorumhiberniae.com/2014/03/saint-kessog-of-lennox-march-

10.html#:~:text=St.,%2C%20Patron%20of%20Lennox%2C%20Scotland.&text=This%20holy%20bishop%20is%20venerated,living%20for%20ever%20in%20heaven

# P

Paul, Sir James Balfour. The Scots Peerage, Founded on Wood's Edition, Volume II. Edinburgh: David Douglas, 1905.
https://archive.org/details/bub_gb_ELEEAAAAIAAJ/page/381/mode/2up?q=auchincass

Paul, Sir James Balfour. The Scots Peerage, Founded on Wood's Edition, Volume VI. Edinburgh: David Douglas, 1909.
https://archive.org/details/scotspeeragefoun06pauluoft/page/n5/mode/2up?q=graham

Penman, Michael. "'Sacred Food for the Soul': In Search of the Devotions to Saints of Robert Bruce, King of Scotland, 1306-1329."Speculum 88, no. 4 (2013): 1041. http://www.jstor.org/stable/43576866

Penman, Michael. "Robert the Bruce, the Piety of the of the Victor of Bannockburn." History Scotland, 18 June 2014. https://www.historyscotland.com/history/robert-the-bruce-the-piety-of-the-victor-of-bannockburn/

Penman, Michael. University of Stirling, "The Scots at the Battle of Neville's Cross, 17 October 1346." The Scottish Historical Review, volume 80, no. 210 (October 2001): 167.
https://core.ac.uk/download/pdf/9048861.pdf

Pitcaithly, Marcus."The Dragon Slaying Bishop of Caithness." Home Page of Author Marcus Pitcaithly, Accessed 17 February 2023. https://www.marcus-pitcaithly.com/single-post/2018/03/16/st-gilbert-and-the-dragon

Porteous, Alexander. The Town Council Seals of Scotland. Edinburgh and London: W & A.K. Johnston, Ltd, 1906. https://electricscotland.com/council/wamphray3.pdf

Public Record Office of Northern Ireland (PRONI). "PRONI Historical Maps Viewer." NIDirect Government Services, Accessed 8 December 2022. https://www.nidirect.gov.uk/services/search-proni-historical-maps-viewer

Public Record Office of Northern Ireland (PRONI) Historical Maps. "Ordnance Survey of Northern Ireland® (OSNI)." NIDirect Government Services, Accessed 8 December 2022.
https://apps.spatialni.gov.uk/PRONIApplication/

Public Record Office of Northern Ireland (PRONI). "About PRONI Historical Maps Viewer." NIDirect Government Services, Accessed 31 December 2022.
https://www.nidirect.gov.uk/articles/about-proni-historical-maps-viewer

Public Record Office of Northern Ireland (PRONI). "Search eCatalogue. " Accessed 22 February 2023. https://apps.proni.gov.uk/eCatNI_IE/BrowseSearchPage.aspx

Profilpelajar.com. "Diocese of Ireland." Accessed 31 December 2022.
https://profilpelajar.com/article/Dioceses_of_Ireland

Provyn, Hunter. "What Do All These Codes Mean?" PhyloGeographer.com, 25 April 2020.
https://phylogeographer.com/what-do-all-these-codes-mean/

# Q

Queally, Jackie. The Culdees: An Ancient Religious Enigma in Scotland. United Kingdom: Celtic Trails, 2007. http://www.earthwise.me/wp-content/uploads/culdeebook.pdf

Queen's University Belfast. "Discover the Origin of our Local Placenames." Placenamesni.org-Northern Ireland Place-Name Project, Accessed 30 December 2022.
https://experience.arcgis.com/experience/9b31e0501b744154b4584b1dce1f859b

Queen's University Belfast. "Ecclesiastical Administrative Divisions." Placenamesni.org-Northern Ireland Place-Name Project, Accessed 30 December 2022.
https://experience.arcgis.com/experience/9b31e0501b744154b4584b1dce1f859b/page/Useful-Information/?views=Ecclesiastical-Administrative-Divisions

Queen's University Belfast. "Land Units." Placenamesni.org-Northern Ireland Place-Name Project, Accessed 30 December 2022.
https://experience.arcgis.com/experience/9b31e0501b744154b4584b1dce1f859b/page/Land-Units/

Queen's University Belfast. "Languages." Placenamesni.org-Northern Ireland Place-Name Project, Accessed 31 December 2022.
https://experience.arcgis.com/experience/9b31e0501b744154b4584b1dce1f859b/page/Useful-Information/?views=Languages

Queen's University Belfast. "Secular Administrative Divisions, Land Units." Placenamesni.org-Northern Ireland Place-Name Project, Accessed 30 December 2022.
https://experience.arcgis.com/experience/9b31e0501b744154b4584b1dce1f859b/page/Useful-Information/?views=Secular-Administrative-Divisions

Quiles, Carlos, Jari Kinnunen, and Jean Manco. "Ancient Y-DNA and mtDNA." Indo-European.eu, Accessed 30 December 2022. https://indo-european.eu/ancient-dna/

Quiles, Carlos, Jari Kinnunen, and Jean Manco. "Ancient DNA: https://ancientdna.info, Map based on public dataset on www.haplogroup.info (www.indo-european.eu), I-DF29." Haplotree Information Project, Accessed 30 December 2022.
https://haplotree.info/maps/ancient_dna/slideshow_samples.php?searchcolumn=Y_Haplotree_Variant&searchfor=I-DF29&ybp=500000,0

Quiles, Carlos, Jari Kinnunen, and Jean Manco. "Ancient DNA: https://ancientdna.info, Map based on public dataset on www.haplogroup.info (www.indo-european.eu) I-Y4738." Haplotree Information Project, Accessed 30 December 2022.
https://haplotree.info/maps/ancient_dna/slideshow_samples.php?searchcolumn=Y_Haplotree_Variant&searchfor=I-Y4738&ybp=500000,0

Quiles, Carlos, Jari Kinnunen, and Jean Manco. "Ancient DNA: https://ancientdna.info. Map based on public dataset on www.haplogroup.info. (www.indo-european.eu) I-BY463." Haplotree Information Project, Accessed 30 December 2022.
https://haplotree.info/maps/ancient_dna/slideshow_samples.php?searchcolumn=Y_Haplotree_Variant&searchfor=I-BY463*&ybp=500000,0

Quiles, Carlos, Jari Kinnunen, and Jean Manco. "Ancient DNA: https://ancientdna.info. Map based on public dataset on www.haplogroup.info (www.indo-european.eu), I-P109." Haplotree Information Project, Accessed 30 December 2022.
https://haplotree.info/maps/ancient_dna/slideshow_samples.php?searchcolumn=Y_Haplotree_Variant&searchfor=I-P109&ybp=500000,0

Quiles, Carlos, Jari Kinnunen, and Jean Manco. "Ancient DNA: https://ancientdna.info. Map based on public dataset on www.haplogroup.info (www.indo-european.eu), J-FGC8224/J-FGC8223." Haplotree Information Project, Accessed 30 December 2022.

https://haplotree.info/maps/ancient_dna/slideshow_samples.php?searchcolumn=Y_Haplotree_Variant&searchfor=J-FGC8224&ybp=500000,0

# R

Raine, James. The Priory of Hexham, Its Chroniclers, Endowments and Annals, Volume I. Durham: The Surtees Society, Andrews and Co, 1864. https://archive.org/details/prioryofhexham01rain

Radford, C.A. Ralegh. "Two Reliquaries Connected with South-West Scotland." Transactions of the Dumfries and Galloway Natural History and Archaeological Society (TDGNHAS) No. 3032 (1955): 116.

Rafferty, J. "The Kirk and Parish of St. Mungo." Transactions of the Dumfries and Galloway Natural History and Archaeological Society, (TDGNHAS), No. 3033 (1956):170.

Rampant Scotland. "Moffat Clan/Family Histories." Accessed 7 January 2023. http://www.rampantscotland.com/clans/blclan_moffat.htm

Ranker.com. "Sorry William Wallace, In Real Life, Robert The Bruce Was The True Violent Hero Called Braveheart." https://factsandhistory.com/sorry-william-wallace-in-real-life-robert-the-bruce-was-the-true-violent-hero-called-braveheart/

Rankin, Rev. James. "Celtic Saints and Ancient Churches of Strathearn." Chronicles of Strathearn (Crieff: David Philips, 1896). https://www.gutenberg.org/files/26342/26342-h/26342-h.htm

Rankin, Rev. James. A Handbook of the Church of Scotland. Edinburgh and London: Blackwood and Sons, 1888. https://ia600703.us.archive.org/22/items/handbookofchurch188800rank/handbookofchurch188800rank.pdf

Ravilious, John P. "Agnes De Graham, wife of (1) John de Monfode and (2) John de Douglas." The Scottish Genealogist, LXI No. 4, The Scottish Genealogy Society, (December 2014): 129. https://www.academia.edu/34967491/TSG_Agnes_de_Graham_wife_of_John_de_Monfode_and_Sir_John_de_Douglas_TSG_LXI_4_129_133

Ravilious, John P. "Queen Euphemia and Her Ancestry." The Scottish Genealogist, The Scottish Genealogy Society (June 2017): 50. https://www.academia.edu/35370666/Queen_Euphemia_and_her_ancestry_TSG_LXIV_2_49_52

Ray, Angus J. Associates Inc."The Grahams: These are Your People." Clan Graham Society, Accessed 23 January 2023. https://clangrahamsociety.org/the-grahams-these-are-your-people/

Reames, Sherry L. "Katherine of Alexandria-Introduction." University of Rochester-Teams Middle English Text Series, 2003. https://d.lib.rochester.edu/teams/text/reames-middle-english-legends-of-women-saints-katherine-of-alexandria-introduction

Reeves, William. Life of St. Columba, written by Adamnan. Edinburgh: Edmonston and Douglas, 1874. https://archive.org/details/lifeofsaintcolum00adamuoft/page/n11/mode/2up .

Reid, John. "Material for a Place Name Survey of East Stirlingshire." Scottish Place Name Society, 109. https://spns.org.uk/wp-content/uploads/2019/12/John-Reids-East-Stirlingshire-place-name-data-v2019.pdf

Reid, R.C. "The Border Grahams and Their Origins." Transactions of the Dumfries and Galloway Natural History and Archaeological Society (TDGNHAS) No. 3038 (1961): 91.

Reid, R.C. and W.F. Cormack ,"Two Medieval Crosses at Kirkpatrick Fleming." TDGNHAS, Vol 62, 3038, (1987): 17-20.

Reid, R.C. "The Monastery at Applegarth." Transactions of the Dumfries and Galloway Natural History and Archaeological Society, (TDGNHAS), No. 3035 (1961): 158.

Reid, R.C. "The Early History of the Corries of Annandale." Transactions of the Dumfries and Galloway Natural History and Archaeological Society (TDGNHAS) No. 3004 (1916): 34.

Reid, R.C. "The Scottish Avenels." Transactions of the Dumfries and Galloway Natural History and Archaeological Society (TDGNHAS) No. 3037 (1960): 76-77.

Reid, R.C. "Scott of Wamphray and Their Kinsmen." Transactions of the Dumfries and Galloway Natural History and Archaelogical Society, (TDGNHAS), No. 3033 (1956): 18.

Rest, Friedrich. Our Christian Symbols. Cleveland: The Pilgrim Press, 1954.
https://archive.org/details/ourchristiansymb00fred/mode/2up?q=peter

Rhys, Dani. "Popular Celtic Symbols-A-List (with images)." SymbolSage, Accessed 16 December 2022.
https://symbolsage.com/popular-celtic-symbols-a-list/

Rich, Tracey R. "Ashkenazic and Sephardic Jews." Judaism 101, Accessed 16 December 2022.
https://www.jewfaq.org/ashkenazic_and_sephardic

Rixson, D. "Killearn Table-Eschend." Land Assessment Scotland, Accessed 2 January 2023.
http://las.denisrixson.com/2016/11/killearn-table/

Robinson, John. The Attwood Family. Sunderland: 1903.
https://www.forgottenbooks.com/en/download/TheAttwoodFamily_10485733.pdf

Rogerson, Col William. Hutton Under the Muir. Dumfries, Scotland: Dumfries and Galloway Courier and Herald, 1908.
https://www.google.com/books/edition/Hutton_under_the_muir_notes_on_the_past/BiwVAAAAQAAJ?hl=en&gbpv=1

Rohling, Dr. Geraldine. "St. Michael the Archangel: Warrior and Protector." The Basilica of the National Shrine of the Immaculate Conception, 9 November 2021.
https://www.nationalshrine.org/blog/st-michael-the-archangel-warrior-and-protector/

Roman Catholic Saints. "Marian Apparition to Saint Catherine," Accessed 10 January 2023.
https://www.roman-catholic-saints.com/apparition-to-saint-catherine.html

Ross, Andrew and Francis Grant. Alexander Nisbet's Heraldic Plates Originally Intended for His System of Heraldry. Edinburgh: George Waterson & Sons, 1892.
https://www.familysearch.org/library/books/viewer/448766/?offset=0#page=1&viewer=picture&o=&n=0&q=

Royal Commission on Historical Manuscripts. Historical Manuscripts Commission, Report on Manuscripts of Sir Archibald Edmonstone of Duntreath, Volumes 5 and 6. Hereford: Anthony Brothers Limited, 1909.
https://archive.org/details/variousmanuscripts05greauoft/page/n83/mode/2up

Royal Commission on the Ancient and Historical Monuments and Constructions of Scotland. Seventh Report with Inventory of Monuments and Constructions in the County of Dumfries. Edinburgh:1920. https://scotlandsplaces.gov.uk/digital-volumes/rcahms-archives/inventories/dumfries-1920

Russell, Mark. "Why is Saint Michael so Important to Airborne Troops?" The Veterans Site, Accessed 20 January 2023. https://blog.theveteranssite.greatergood.com/saint-michael/

Ryan, Gregg. "Church of Ireland Synod: Merger of two dioceses approved." Church Times, 28 May 2019. https://www.churchtimes.co.uk/articles/2019/24-may/news/uk/church-of-ireland-synod-merger-of-two-dioceses-approved

# S

Sahakyan, H., A. Margaryan, L.Saag, et al. "Origin and diffusion of human Y chromosome haplogroup J1-M267." Scientific Reports 11, 6659 (2021). https://doi.org/10.1038/s41598-021-85883-2

Saints in Scottish Place-Names. "St. Michael's Church Mauchline." Accessed 16 January 2023. https://saintsplaces.gla.ac.uk/place.php?id=1325863152

St. Kentigern Way. "Route Heritage," Accessed 10 January 2023. http://kentigernway.com/page22.html

Saint Thomas Church, New York City. "Thomas Becket, Archbishop of Canterbury, Martyr, b. 1118, died December 29, 1170." Accessed 16 January 2023. https://www.saintthomaschurch.org/liturgical_date/thomas-becket/

Scott, Archibald B. The Pictish Nation, Its People and Its Church. Edinburgh and London: T.N. Foulis, 1918. https://archive.org/details/pictishnationits00scotrich

Seraphim, Abba. "On the Trail of the Seven Coptic Monks in Ireland." The British Orthodox Church, Accessed 9 January 2023. https://britishorthodox.org/miscellaneous/on-the-trail-of-seven-coptic-monks-in-ireland/

St. Clair Research. "Sinclair Groupings, our Caithness, Shetland, and Orkey Families." Accessed 30 December 2022. http://www.stclairresearch.com/content/groupingsCaithness.html

Snell, Melissa."The Avignon Papacy-When the Popes Resided in France." ThoughtCo, 24 June 2020. https://www.thoughtco.com/the-avignon-papacy-1789454

St. George Orthodox Ministry. "Coptic Influence in the Early British Church." 30 January 2018. http://www.stgeorgeministry.com/coptic-influence-early-british-church/

St. James Cathedral, Seattle. "The Legends of Saint James." Accessed 6 March 2023. https://www.stjames-cathedral.org/prayer/jameslegend.aspx

Steuart, A. Francis. "Scotland and the Papacy during the Great Schism." The Scottish Historical Review 4, no. 14 (1907): 144–58. http://www.jstor.org/stable/25517825

Schleeter, Ryan. "First Rulers of the Mediterranean." National Geographic Resource Library, updated 20 May 2022. https://education.nationalgeographic.org/resource/first-rulers-mediterranean

Seton, Monsignor. An Old Family or The Setons of Scotland and America. New York: Bretano's, 1899. https://deriv.nls.uk/dcn23/9572/95729930.23.pdf

School of History, Classics and Archaeology Teaching Collections, University of Edinburgh. "Sir William Fraser Facsimiles of Scottish Charters and Letters." Accessed 19 January 2023. http://collections.shca.ed.ac.uk/collections/show/1

School of History, Classics and Archaeology Teaching Collections, University of Edinburgh. Sir William Fraser Facsimiles of Scottish Charters and Letters, "Charter by Robert de Brus to Roger Crispin of the lands of Cuoculeran c. 1218." Accessed 27 February 2023. http://collections.shca.ed.ac.uk/items/show/36

School of History, Classics and Archaeology Teaching Collections, University of Edinburgh. Sir William Fraser Facsimiles of Scottish Charters and Letters, "Charter by Robert de Graham, Lord of

Weyliston, to the Church of St Mary of Melrose, of the patronage of the Church of Torbolton, 11th July 1342." Accessed 10 February 2023. http://collections.shca.ed.ac.uk/items/show/92

Scotclans. Johnstone Clan History." Accessed 7 January 2023.
https://www.scotclans.com/blogs/clans-jk/johnstone-clan-history

Scotclans. "David I (1124-1153)." Accessed 5 March 2023. https://www.scotclans.com/pages/david-i-1124-1153

Scott, Hew. Fasti Ecclesiae Scoticanae, Volume II. Edinburgh: Oliver and Boyd, 1917.
https://play.google.com/store/books/details?id=l3_ZAAAAMAAJ&rdid=book-l3_ZAAAAMAAJ&rdot=1

Scotland in Oils. "Scott Clan." Accessed 6 January 2023. http://www.scotlandinoils.com/clan/Clan-Scott.html

Scotlands Places. Midlothian Ordnance Survey Name Books, 1852-1853, Midlothian Volume 52, OS1/11/52/15. Accessed 14 March 2023. https://scotlandsplaces.gov.uk/digital-volumes/ordnance-survey-name-books/midlothian-os-name-books-1852-1853/midlothian-volume-52/15

Scottish Archive Network. "Teinds." Accessed 16 January 2023.
https://www.scan.org.uk/researchrtools/glossary_t.htm

Scottish Archive Network. Burghs of Regality and Barony." Accessed 14 February 2023.
https://www.scan.org.uk/knowledgebase/topics/burgh.htm#:~:text=These%20were%20burghs%20granted%20by,in%20criminal%20and%20civil%20law

Scottish American Society. "Clan Jardine." Accessed 29 December 2022.
http://www.scottishamericansociety.org/id23.html

Scottish Record Office. Index to Register of Deeds, 1668, Volume VIII. Edinburgh: His Majesty's Stationery Office, 1924.
https://www.google.com/books/edition/Indexes/6ISQFt6Y5ekC?hl=en&gbpv=1&bsq=%20gillesbie

Scottish Record Office. Index to Register of Deeds, 1669, Volume IX. Edinburgh: His Majesty's Stationery Office, 1926.
https://www.google.com/books/edition/Index_to_Register_of_Deeds_Preserved_in/C8wRAAAAIAAJ?hl=en&gbpv=1&bsq=graham

Scottish Record Office. Index to Register of Deeds, 1670, Volume X. Edinburgh: His Majesty's Stationery Office, 1926.
https://www.google.com/books/edition/Index_to_Register_of_Deeds_Preserved_in/vsQRAAAAIAAJ?hl=en&gbpv=1

Shirley, G.W. "Notes of the Arms of the Royal Burgh of Dumfries." Transactions of the Dumfries and Galloway Natural History and Archaeological Society (TDGNHAS) No. 3011 (1925): 162-165.

Surname Coats of Arms UK. "Graham Coat of Arms." Accessed 20 December 2022.
https://surnamecoatsofarms.uk/shop/product/graham-ireland-coat-of-arms-family-crest-instant-download/

Simpson, David. "Kingdom of Northumbria 450 AD to 866AD, Edwin's Conversion." England's Northeast, Accessed 16 January 2023. https://englandsnortheast.co.uk/kingdom-northumbria/

Simpson, Grant G. and James D. Galbraith, The Border Papers: Calendar of letters and papers relating to the affairs of the borders of England and Scotland preserved in Her Majesty's Public Record

Office, Volume V (1108-1516). London, Edinburgh: H.M. General Register House, 1881. https://archive.org/details/calendarofdocume05grea/page/10/mode/2up

Solé-Morata, Neus, Patricia Villaescusa, Carla García-Fernández, et al. "Analysis of the R1b-DF27 haplogroup shows that a large fraction of Iberian Y-chromosome lineages originated recently in situ." Scientific Reports (4 August 2017): 1. https://www.nature.com/articles/s41598-017-07710-x

Somerill, Thomas. "An Attempt at a Brief Family History of the Lairds of Dinwiddie." 1929, Electric Scotland, Accessed 27 February 2023. https://electricscotland.com/webclans/dtog/dinwiddie4.html

Spence, Richard T. "The Pacification of the Cumberland Borders, 1593-1628." Northern History, 13:1 (1977): 122.

Spencer, Robin PhD. "The Extinction of Lines." Tracking Back-A Website for Genetic Genealogy Tools, Experimentation and Discussion, Scaled Innovation, 31 March 2020. http://scaledinnovation.com/gg/extinctionDemo.html

Spencer, Robin PhD. "SNP Tracker," Timelines Tab for SNP: L1253. Tracking Back-A Website for Genetic Genealogy Tools, Experimentation and Discussion, Scaled Innovation, Accessed 28 December 2022. http://scaledinnovation.com/gg/snpTracker.html

Spencer, Robin PhD. "Comments on determining age of the J1-L1253 Haplogroup." England Great Britain Groups EIJ, E I J G R T England Scotland Wales Ireland Norman & Diverse Others, Activity Feed, FTDNA Surname Project, Accessed 20 October 2002. https://www.familytreedna.com/groups/england-gbgroups-eij/activity-feed

Spencer, Robin PhD. "Extending Time Horizons with DNA," (video lecture). FamilySearch, 8 March 2022. 1:00:45. https://www.youtube.com/watch?v=wppXD1Zz2sQ

Squaducation. "The First Union Flag." Accessed 20 March 2023. https://www.squaducation.com/blog/first-union-flag

Starmans, Barbara J. "Royal Mail History." The Social Historian, Accessed 3 January 2023. https://www.thesocialhistorian.com/royal-mail-history/

Stevenson, J.H. Heraldry in Scotland, Volume I. Glasgow: James Maclehose and Sons, 1914. https://ia800300.us.archive.org/14/items/heraldryinscotla01stev/heraldryinscotla01stev.pdf

Stodart, Robert Riddle. Scottish Arms, Being a Collection of Armorial Bearings A.D. 1370 – 1678, Volume I. Edinburgh: William Patterson, 1881. https://archive.org/details/ScottishArmsV1/page/n205/mode/2up?q=79A

Story, Joanna. "The Viking Raid on Lindisfarne." English Heritage, Accessed 15 December 2022. https://www.english-heritage.org.uk/visit/places/lindisfarne-priory/History/viking-raid/

St. Peter and St. Paul Coptic Orthodox Church, Santa Monica CA. "The Coptic Church." Accessed 9 January 2023. https://stpeterandstpaul.org/coptic-church/
https://draft.dgnhas.org.uk/sites/default/files/transactions/2021.pdf#page=138

Stravaiging Around Scotland. "Auchen Castle." Accessed 7 January 2023. http://www.stravaiging.com/history/castle/auchen-castl

Stravaiging Around Scotland. "Elliston Castle." Accessed 9 January 2023. http://www.stravaiging.com/history/castle/elliston-castle/

Stravaiging Around Scotland. "Lochwood Motte." Accessed 7 January 2023. http://www.stravaiging.com/history/castle/lochwood-motte/

Stravaiging Around Scotland. "Torthorwald Castle." Accessed 7 January 2023.
  http://www.stravaiging.com/history/castle/torthorwald-castle/

Stuart, John and George Burnett. Rotuli Scaccarii Regum Scotorum, The Exchequer Rolls of Scotland Volume I. Edinburgh: H.M. Register House, 1878.
  https://www.familysearch.org/search/catalog/192327?availability=Family%20History%20Library

Study.com. "The English Reformation." Accessed 15 March 2023.
  https://study.com/learn/lesson/english-reformation-timeline-summary.html

SurnameDB. "Last name: Jordan." SurnameDB.com, Accessed 29 December 2022.
  https://www.surnamedb.com/Surname/Jordan

SurnameCoatofArms.uk. "Graham (Ireland) Coat of Arms." Accessed 23 January 2023.
  https://surnamecoatsofarms.uk/shop/?s=drumgoon

Sutter, Janine Honey. "Assets to the Country: Countesses in 14th Century England." MA Thesis, Clemson University, 2017.
  https://tigerprints.clemson.edu/cgi/viewcontent.cgi?article=3683&context=all_theses

# T

T., Anne. "St Cuthbert's Church (Wamphray)." The Megalithic Portal, 5 April 2019.
  https://www.megalithic.co.uk/article.php?sid=51598

Taggart, Katherine and Erin Devine. "Exploring Meaning—The Lindisfarne Gospels." Longwood University-Incite, Accessed 17 February 2023.
  https://blogs.longwood.edu/incite/2011/09/08/exploring-meaning-%E2%80%93-the-lindisfarne-gospels/

Tate, George. History of the Borough, Castle and Barony of Alnwick. Alnwick: Henry Blair, 1866.
  https://books.google.com/books?id=CgkNAAAAYAAJ&pg=PA397&lpg=PA397&dq=v..#v=onepage&q=v..&f=false

Taylor, James. The Pictorial History of Scotland Volume I. London: James S. Virture, 1859.
  https://www.electricscotland.com/books/pdf/pictorialhistory01tayluoft.pdf

Taylor, James. The Great Historic Families of Scotland, Volume II. London: J.S. Virtue & Co. Ltd, 1889. https://play.google.com/store/books/details?id=-0xHAQAAMAAJ&rdid=book--0xHAQAAMAAJ&rdot=1

Taylor, T.L. "Hutton Mote." Transactions of the Dumfries and Galloway Natural History and Archaeological Society (TDGNHAS) No. 3018 (1934): 384.

The Bannatyne Club. Registrum Honoris de Morton, Volume II: Ancient Charters. Edinburgh: The Bannatyne Club, 1858.
  https://archive.org/details/registrumhonoris02bann/page/n3/mode/2up?ref=ol&view=theater

The Bannatyne Club, Registrum de Dunfermelyn (Edinburgh: 1842), 236-237.
  https://ia600901.us.archive.org/31/items/registrumdedunfe00bann/registrumdedunfe00bann.pdf

The Border Reivers. "The Battle of Dryfe Sands, 6 December 1593." Accessed 7 January 2023.
  http://www.borderreivers.co.uk/Border%20Battles/Dryfe%20Sands/dryfe%20sands.htm

The Border Reivers. "The Jardine Clan." Accessed 28 December 2022.
  http://www.borderreivers.co.uk/Border%20Families/Surnames/Jardine%201.htm

Annan, The History Town. "Motte & Bailey." Accessed 6 January 2023. https://www.annanthehistorytown.org/history/

The Merlin Trail. "Moffat History Trail." Accessed 9 January 2023. http://merlintrail.com/the-moffat-history-trail/

The Order of the Fleur de Lis. "John Graham of Claverhouse." Accessed 30 November 2021. https://www.orderofthefleurdelys.org.uk/order-history/john-graham-of-claverhouse/

TheKnightsTemplar.org. "The Order of the Temple in Scotland." Accessed 10 January 2023. http://www.theknightstemplar.org/scottish-templars/

The Scotsman. "Was the "Bruce's 'Blessed Kessog' our Patron Saint before Andrew?" 9 March 2008. https://www.scotsman.com/news/was-bruces-blessed-kessog-our-patron-saint-andrew-2480540

The British Pilgrimage Trust. "Whithorn Way." Accessed 9 January 2023. https://britishpilgrimage.org/portfolio/whithorn-way/

The Catalogue of Good Deeds. "How Apostle Andrew Became the Patron Saint of Scotland." 13 December 2017. https://catalogueofstelisabethconvent.blogspot.com/2017/12/how-apostle-andrew-became-patron-of.html

The House of Kirkpatrick. "Events The Shaped The Kirkpatrick Family: 1300-1499." Accessed 29 December 2022. https://pppat.tripod.com/index.html

The Church of England. "Ancient Wisdom, Modern Mission-Saint Andrew Complete Resource Guide." Accessed 20 January 2023. https://www.churchofengland.org/sites/default/files/2020-10/ST%20ANDREW%20COMPLETE%20RESOURCE%20PDF.pdf

The Great, Parliamentary, or Bannerets' Roll, c. 1312. The British Museum's manuscript collection: MS. Cotton, Caligula A. XVIII, ff. 3-21b. Accessed 13 November 2022. http://www.aspilogia.com/N-Parliamentary_Roll/N-0592-0701.html

Thompson, Thomas. Inquisitionum ad Capellam Domini Regis Retornatarum, quae in Publicis Srchivis Scotiae adhuc servantur, abbreviation. London: Great Britain Record Commission, 1811. https://books.google.com/books?id=8tQsAQAAMAAJ&printsec=frontcover#v=onepage&q&f=false

Thomson, John. "Dumfriesshire." Atlas of Scotland, 1832. National Library of Scotland, Accessed 27 December 2022. https://maps.nls.uk/view/74400175

Thomson, John Maitland. Register of the Great Seal of Scotland, A.D. 1306-1424. Edinburgh: H.M. General Register House, 1912. https://www.google.com/books/edition/The_Register_of_the_Great_Seal_of_Scotla/ZbI3AQAAMAAJ?hl=en

Tomkins, Sir Thomas Edlyne. The Law Dictionary Explaining the Rise, Progress and Present State of British Law, Volume I. London: J and W.T. Clarke, 1835. https://www.google.com/books/edition/The_Law_dictionary_Explaining_the_Rise_P/Q0pKAAAAcAAJ?hl=en&gbpv=1&bsq=demesne

Toorians, Lauren. "Flemish Settlements in Twelfth-Century Scotland." Revue belge de philologie et d'histoire, Tome 74 fasc. 3-4, (1996): 667, 684, 689. https://www.academia.edu/33460121/Lauran_Toorians_Flemish_Settlements_in_Twelfth_Century_Scotland

Tornabene, Hugh. "Jacobite Rebellion Ships." Immigrant Ships Transcribers Guild, 1 August 2007. https://immigrantships.net/jacobite/indexjacobite.html

Travels in a Campervan. "Visiting Some of the Knights Templar Sites." 22 September 2018.
https://www.vanvoyage.co.uk/2018/09/visiting-some-of-knights-templar-sites.html

TempleVillage.org.uk. "Temple History-Brief," Accessed 9 January 2023.
http://www.templevillage.org.uk/temple-village/temple-village-history/

Truly Edinburgh. "Holyrood Abbey: Edinburgh Old Town." Accessed 17 January 2023.
https://trulyedinburgh.com/things-to-do-in-edinburgh/holyrood-abbey/

Tudor Times. "Matthew Stuart: Life Story." 20 May 2018.
https://tudortimes.co.uk/people/matthew-stuart-life-story/war

Turgot, Bishop of Saint Andrews. The Life of St. Margaret, Queen of Scotland. Translated by William Forbes-Leith. Edinburgh: William Patterson, 1884.
https://archive.org/details/lifeofstmargaret00turguoft/page/n9/mode/2up

Turnbull, Michael T.R.B. "A History of St. Andrew." Scotland.org, 20 November 2016.
https://www.scotland.org/features/a-history-of-st-andrew

Turpie, Thomas J. M. "Scottish Saints Cults and Pilgrimage from the Black Death to the Reformation, c. 1349-1560." PhD thesis, University of Edinburgh, 2011.
https://era.ed.ac.uk/bitstream/handle/1842/5983/Turpie2011.pdf?sequence=2

## U

Undiscovered Scotland. "Abernethy." Accessed 16 January 2023.
https://www.undiscoveredscotland.co.uk/abernethy/abernethy/index.html

Undiscovered Scotland. "Alan of Galloway." Accessed 17 February 2023.
https://www.undiscoveredscotland.co.uk/usbiography/a/alanofgalloway.html

Undiscovered Scotland. "Saint Kessog." Accessed 10 January 2023.
https://www.undiscoveredscotland.co.uk/usbiography/k/stkessog.html

Undiscovered Scotland. "King Kenneth I. "Accessed 21 January 2023.
https://www.undiscoveredscotland.co.uk/usbiography/monarchs/kennethi.html

Undiscovered Scotland. "Melrose Abbey." Accessed 9 January 2023.
https://www.undiscoveredscotland.co.uk/melrose/melroseabbey/index.html

Undiscovered Scotland. "St. Serf." Accessed 10 January 2023.
https://www.undiscoveredscotland.co.uk/usbiography/s/stserf.html

Unique Travel Photo. "Visit Dunfermline, Scotland's Ancient Capital." 5 June 2021.
https://www.uniquetravelphoto.com/visit-dunfermline-scotlands-ancient-capital/

University of Edinburgh, School of History, Classics and Archaeology. Database of Dedications to Saints in Medieval Scotland, Survey of Dedications to Saints in Medieval Scotland. 31 December 2022. http://saints.shca.ed.ac.uk/index.cfm?fuseaction=home.adhocform

Unknown author. Monastic Annandale Caledonia, Volume III, Chapter 2. Dumfriesshire.

Unofficial Royalty. The Laird O'Thistle, "Royal Saints of the British Crown." 26 October 2008.
https://www.unofficialroyalty.com/columnists/the-laird-othistle/royal-saints-of-the-british-crown/

## V

Vatican News. "St. Patrick, Bishop, Apostle of Ireland." Accessed 16 January 2023.

Vela de Jerusalen. "St. John the Baptist." Accessed 6 March 2023. https://santosepulcro.co.il/en/saints/st-john-the-baptist/

Vexilo. "Wessex." British County Flags, 20 September 2013. https://britishcountyflags.com/2013/09/20/wessex-flag/

VisitScotland. "About St Andrew and the Saltire." Accessed 16 December 2022. https://www.visitscotland.com/about/uniquely-scottish/st-andrews-the-saltire/

VisitScotland. "Churchyard of St. Kentigern." Accessed 9 January 2023. https://www.visitscotland.com/info/see-do/churchyard-of-st-kentigern-p254441

# W

Waddell, Lawrence Austine. The Phoenician Origins of Britons, Scots and Anglo-Saxons, Chapter 2. London: Williams and Norgate, 1924. https://www.jrbooksonline.com/pob/pob_toc.html

Wade, James A. History of St. Mary's Abbey, Melrose and the Monastery of Old Melrose. Edinburgh: Thomas C. Jack, 1861. https://books.google.mu/books?id=-BEFAAAAYAAJ&printsec=frontcover#v=onepage&q&f=false

Walcott, Mackenzie E.C. Scoti Monasticon-The Ancient Church of Scotland. London: Virtue, Spalding and Daldy, 1874. https://ia600309.us.archive.org/22/items/scotimonasticona00walc/scotimonasticona00walc.pdf

Walker, John. "The Patronage of the Templars and the Order of St. Lazarus in England in the Twelfth and Thirteenth Centuries." PhD Thesis, University of St. Andrews, 1990. https://core.ac.uk/download/pdf/9045114.pdf

Walsh, Bruce, University of Arizona. "Most Recent Common Ancestor Calculator." Genetics Society of America, June 2001. http://www.moseswalker.com/mrca/calculator.asp?q=1

Webster, James Moir. Notes on the Burgh of Dunfermline. Dunfermline: Pitcairn Publications, 1949. http://www.royaldunfermline.com/Resources/notes_on_dunfermline_burgh.pdf

Welsh, T.C. "The Renfrewshire Templelands." Renfrewshire Local History Forum (RLHF) Journal Volume 3 (1991/2,): 3. https://rlhf.info/wp-content/uploads/3.1-Templelands-Welsh.pdf

Whitby Abbey, North Yorkshire, UK. Synod of Whitby." Accessed 16 January 2023. https://www.whitbyabbey.co.uk/whitby-abbey/synod-whitby/

Wikipedia contributors. "List of former cathedrals in Great Britain." Wikipedia, The Free Encyclopedia, Accessed 9 January 2023. https://en.wikipedia.org/w/index.php?title=List_of_former_cathedrals_in_Great_Britain&oldid=1127504741

Wikipedia contributors. "Order of St. Michael and St. George." Wikipedia, The Free Encyclopedia, Accessed 10 January 2023. https://en.wikipedia.org/w/index.php?title=Order_of_St._Michael_and_St._George&oldid=1131968343

Wikipedia contributors. "Lion (heraldry)." Wikipedia, Modified 9 November 2022. Accessed 17 December 2022. https://en.wikipedia.org/w/index.php?title=Lion_(heraldry)&oldid=1120931771

Wikipedia contributors. "Saint George's Cross." Wikipedia, Modified 22 October 2022. Accessed 17 December 2022. https://en.wikipedia.org/w/index.php?title=Saint_George%27s_Cross&oldid=1117555278.

Wikipedia contributors. "Ruthwell Cross." Wikipedia, Modified 9 June 2022. Accessed 17 December 2022. https://en.wikipedia.org/w/index.php?title=Ruthwell_Cross&oldid=1092344422

Wiktionary. "Gris." Accessed 4 November 2022.
https://en.wiktionary.org/w/index.php?title=gris&oldid=69567367.

Wiktionary. "Stoc." Accessed 5 December 2022.
https://en.wiktionary.org/w/index.php?title=stoc&oldid=68776363.

Wiktionary contributors. "Pendragon." Wiktionary, The Free Dictionary, Accessed 23 January 2023.
https://en.wiktionary.org/w/index.php?title=pendragon&oldid=70936150

Williams, Edison. "Did you see that Family Tree DNA has made public the world's largest yDNA Haplotree?" WikiTree.com, 28 September 2018. https://www.wikitree.com/g2g/691651/that-family-tree-made-public-worlds-largest-ydna-haplotree

Wikiwand. "List of Monastic Houses in Scotland. Accessed 9 January 2023.
https://www.wikiwand.com/en/List_of_monastic_houses_in_Scotland

Wilson, Rev. John Marius. Imperial Gazetteer of Scotland Volume 2. London and Edinburgh: A. Fullarton and Co., 1868. https://digital.nls.uk/gazetteers-of-scotland-1803-1901/archive/97473162

Wilson, Rev. James. "Some Extinct Cumberland Families." The Ancestor Quarterly Review, No. 3, (Oct 1902):80.
https://archive.org/details/ancestorquarterl03unse/page/n5/mode/2up?q=levington

Wikisource contributors. "Catholic Encyclopedia (1913)/Devotion to the Blessed Virgin Mary." Wikisource , Accessed 6 March 2023.
https://en.wikisource.org/w/index.php?title=Catholic_Encyclopedia_(1913)/Devotion_to_the_Blessed_Virgin_Mary&oldid=10729898

Wikisource contributors. "The Folk-Lore Journal/Volume 6/Folk-Lore of Sutherlandshire (September)." Wikisource, Accessed 19 January 2023.
https://en.wikisource.org/w/index.php?title=The_Folk-Lore_Journal/Volume_6/Folk-Lore_of_Sutherlandshire_(September)&oldid=10058354

Winchester, Angus J. L. "The Distribution and Significance of 'Bordland' in Medieval Britain." The Agricultural History Review 34, no. 2 (1986): 129–139. http://www.jstor.org/stable/40274465

Wood, Anthony. Appendix to the History and antiquities of the colleges and halls in the University of Oxford (Oxford, Clarendon Press, 1790), 13. https://archive.org/details/appendixtohistor00wood

WordHippo.com. "How to say 'my' in Scots Gaelic." Accessed 3 January 2023.
https://www.wordhippo.com/what-is/the/scots-gaelic-word-for-3ece1471f44f63177cbc35ba0b904e0c096b6783.html

World History Encyclopedia. "Crusades Timeline. Accessed 16 January 2023.
https://www.worldhistory.org/timeline/Crusades/

Wylie, Rev. J.A. The History of the Scottish Nation, Volume 3. London: Hamilton, Adams and Co., 1886.
https://www.originofnations.org/books,%20papers/history%20of%20the%20scots/scothistvol3.pdf

WyrdLight.com. "The Medieval Castle: Four Different Types." History on the Net, Accessed 17 February 2023. https://www.historyonthenet.com/medieval-castle

## Y

Yfull. "Yfull Tree for J-FGC11." YFull.com, Accessed 30 December 2022. https://www.yfull.com/tree/J-FGC11/

YFull. "YTree v10.07.00 Classic Chart for the J1/Y3441/L1253 Haplogroup." YFull.com, 16 November 2022. https://www.yfull.com/chart/tree/J-Y3441/

Your DNA Guide. "Y-DNA Test, Which Y-DNA Test is Best?" Accessed 29 December 2022. https://www.yourdnaguide.com/ydna#:~:text=YDNA%20is%20the%20DNA%20inherited,back%20than%20autosomal%20DNA%20tests

*Triple Gate at the Southern Wall of the Temple Mount (built during the time of Herod the Great (before 4 B.C.).*

Photo by Barry S. Graham

www.ingramcontent.com/pod-product-compliance
Lightning Source LLC
Chambersburg PA
CBHW060302010526
44108CB00042B/2611